AF901356

dreamlands

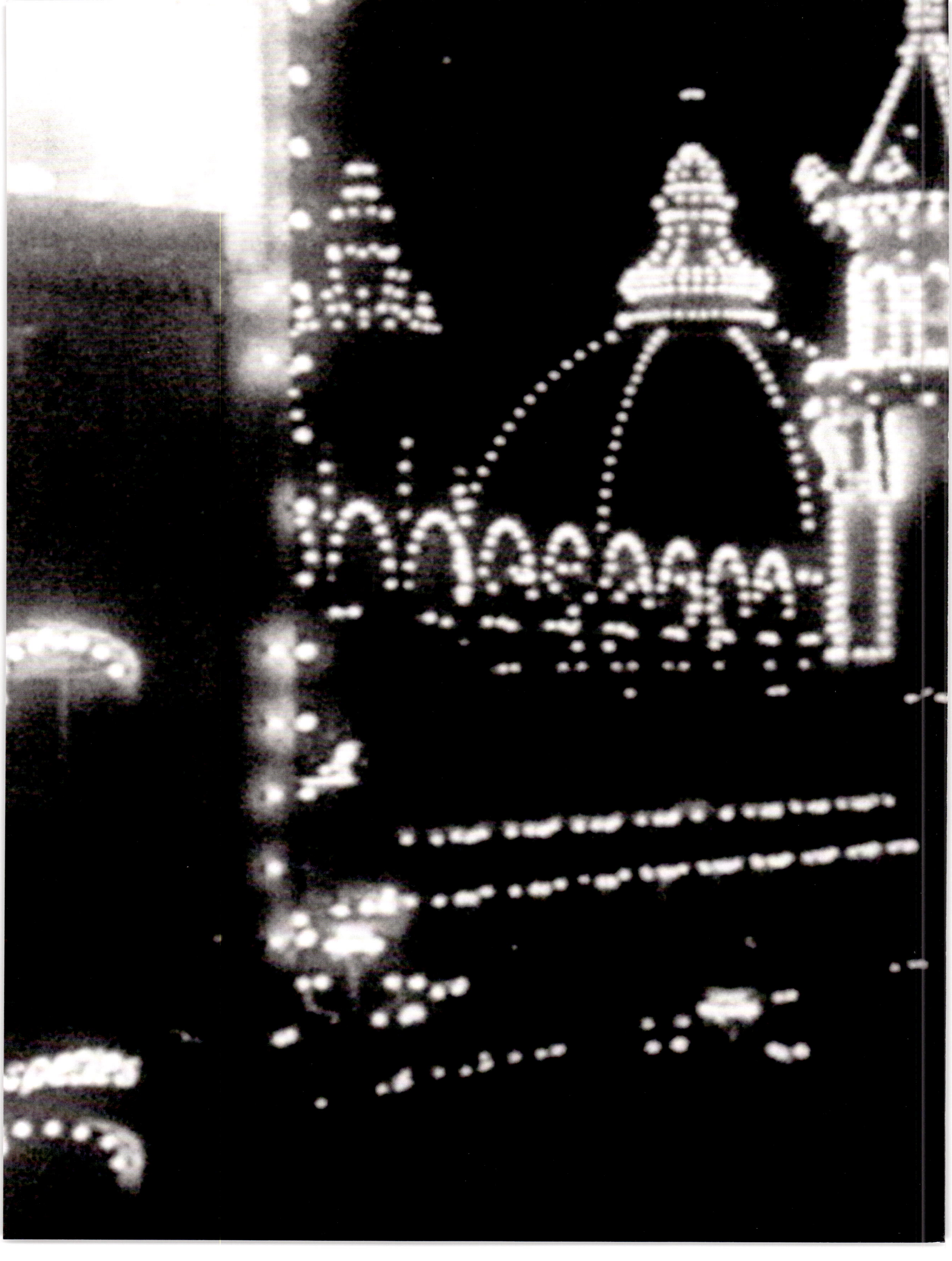

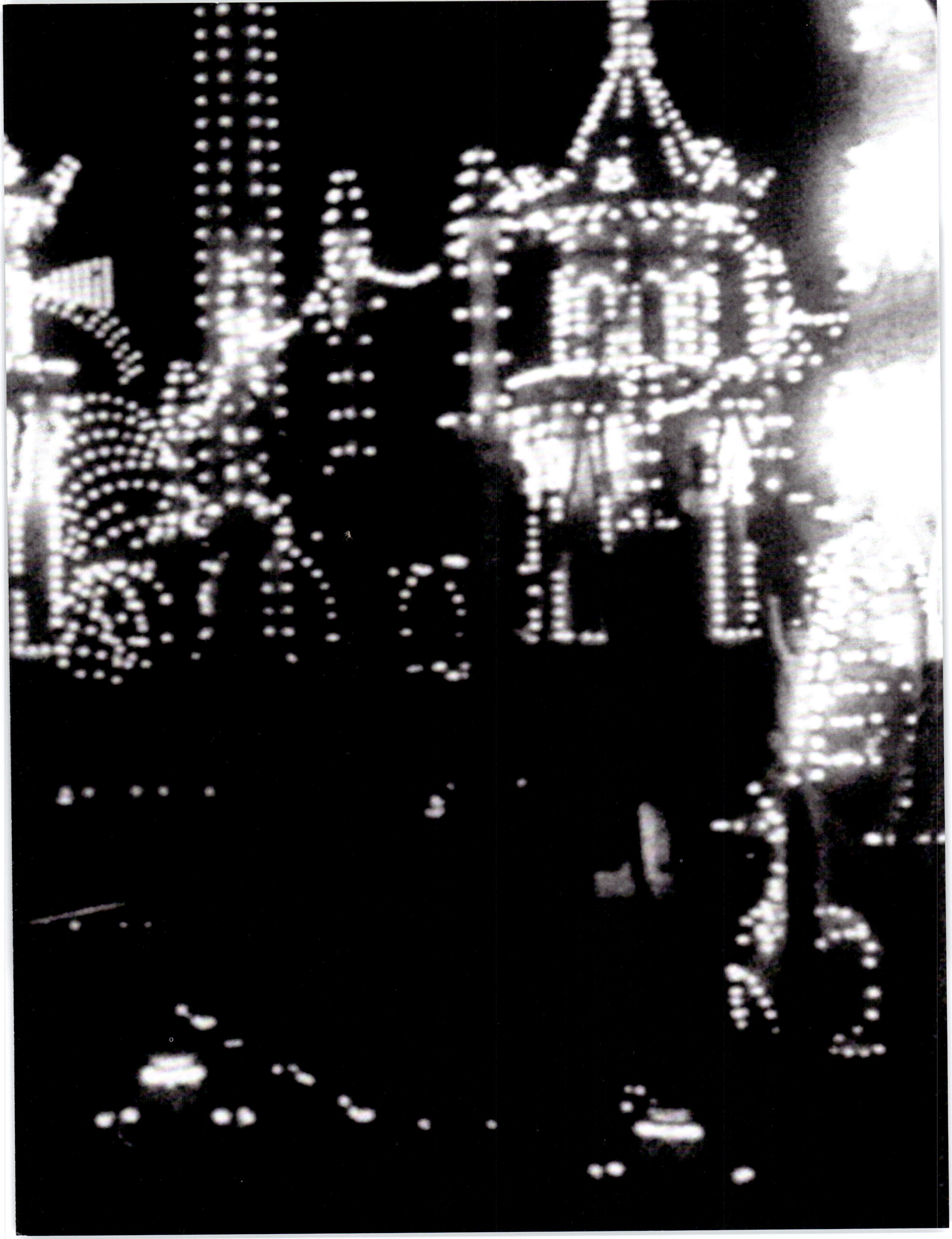

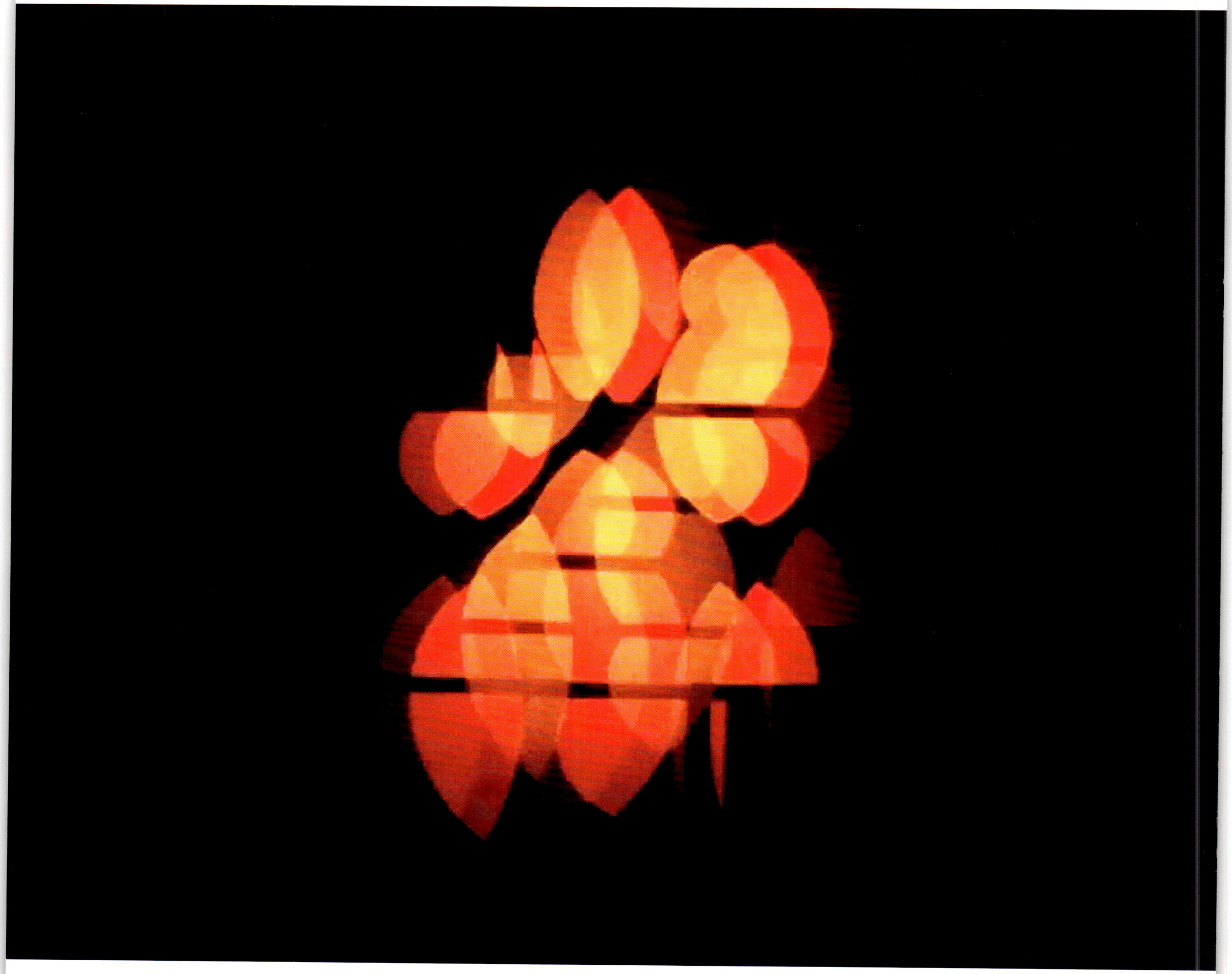

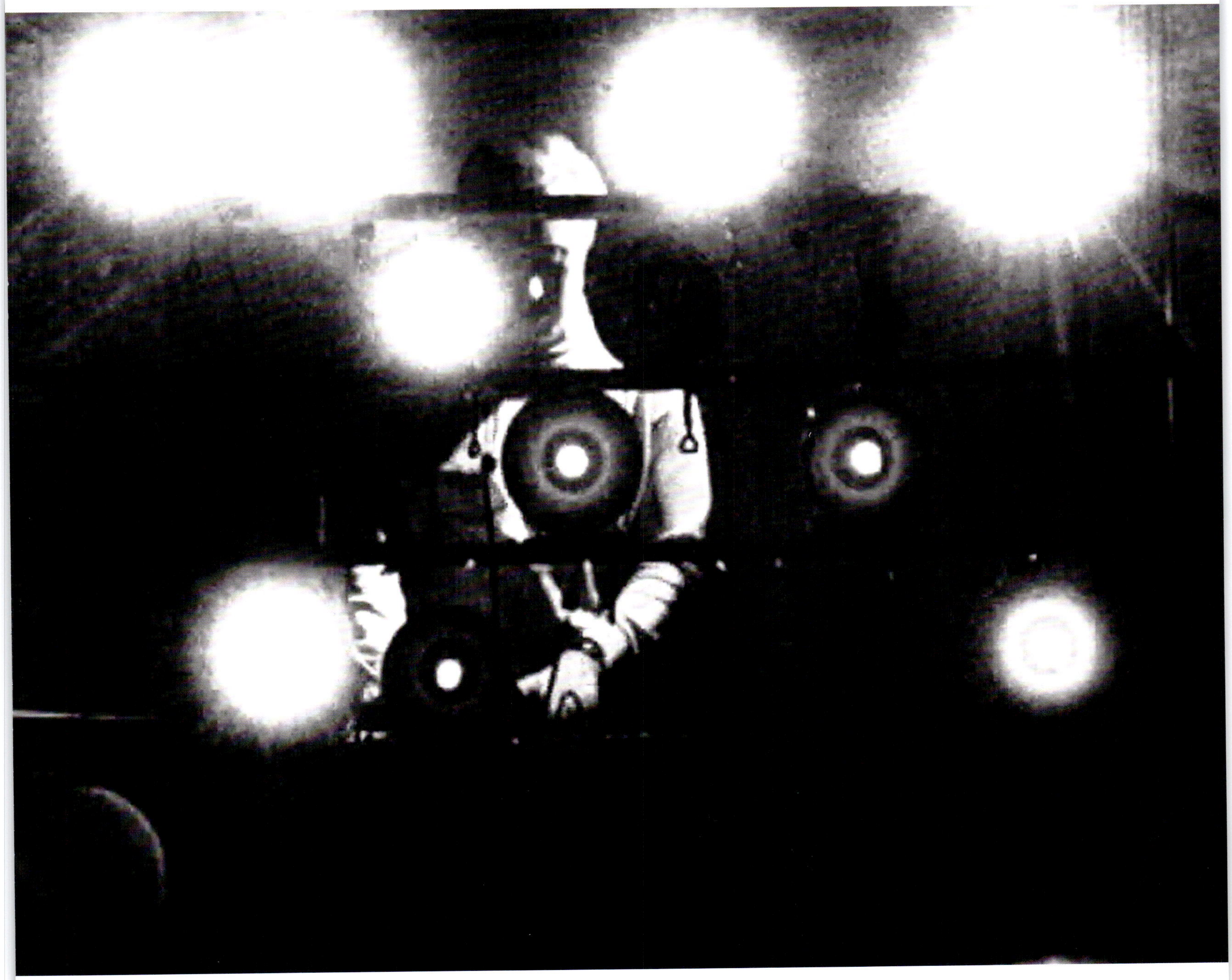

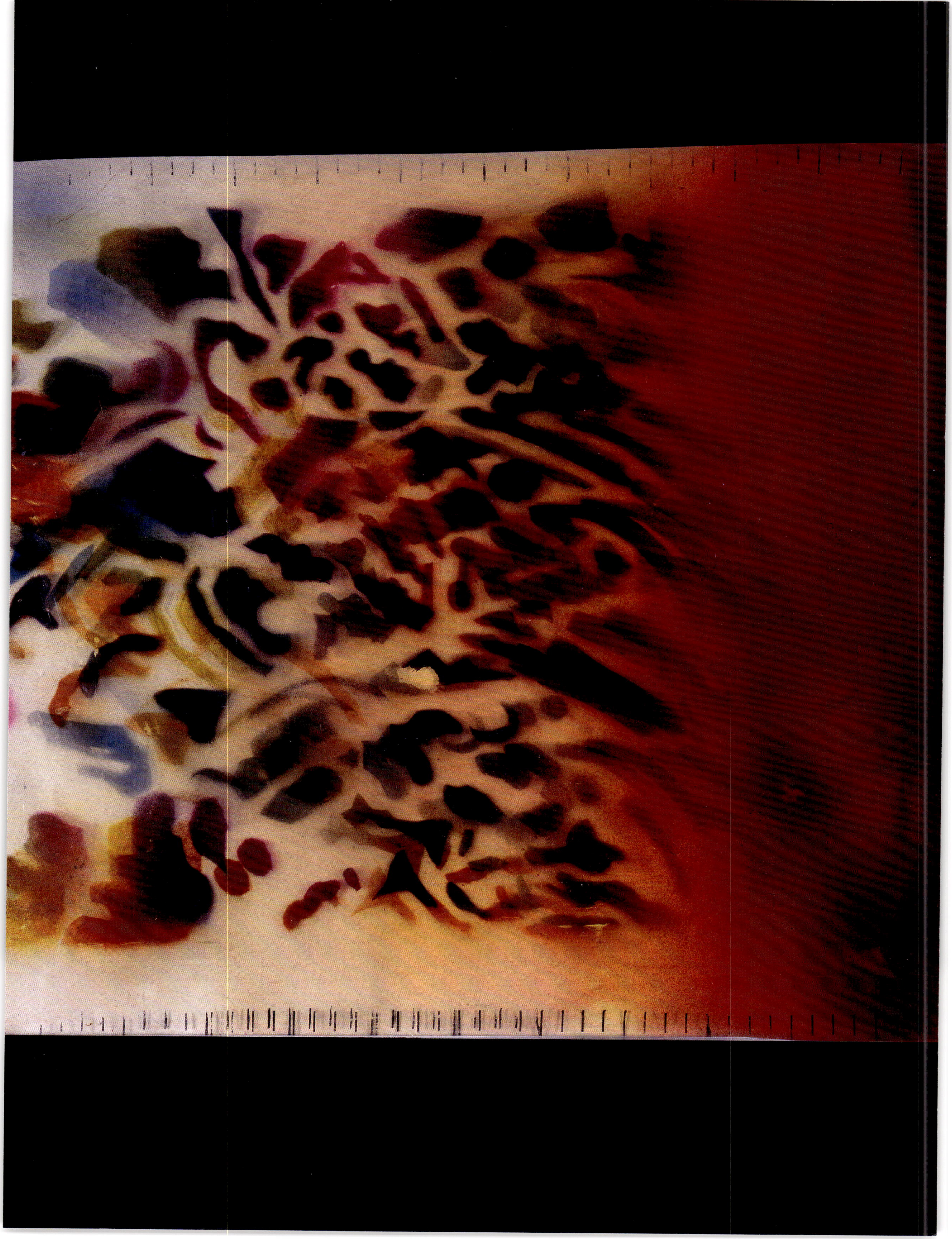

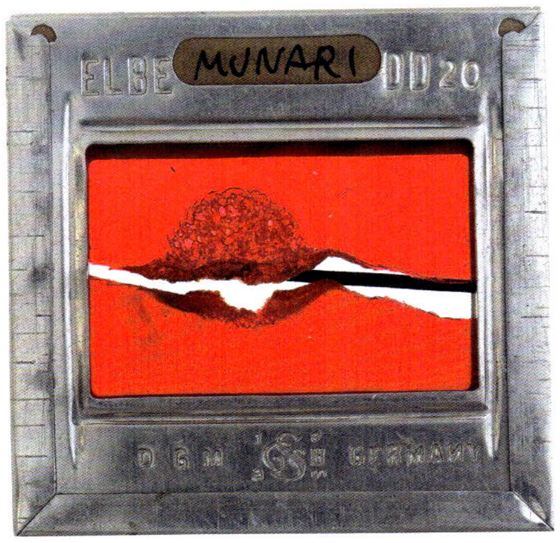
MUNARI

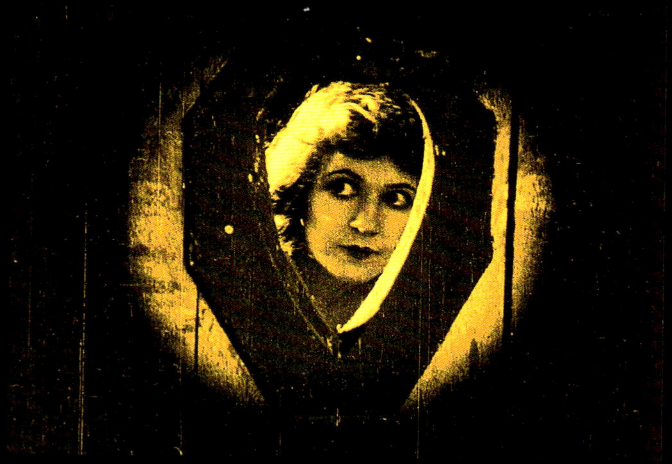

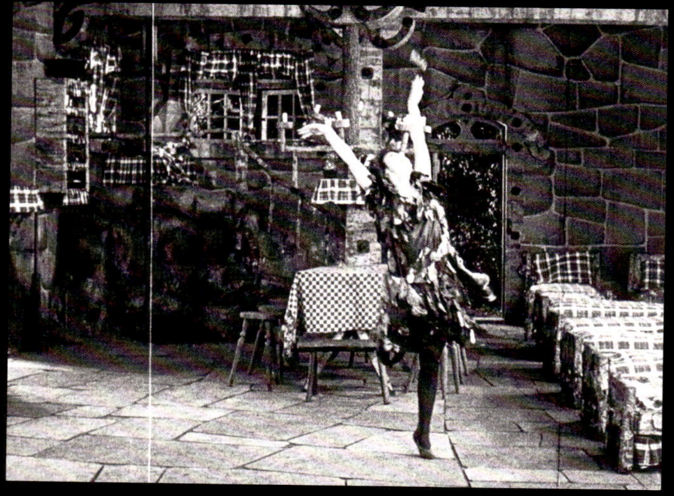

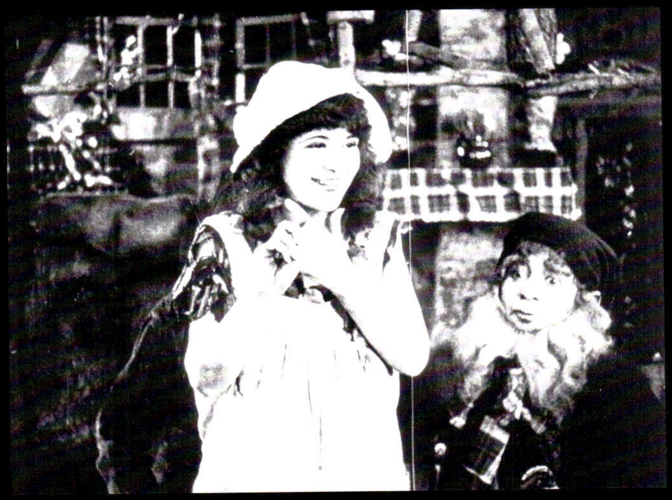

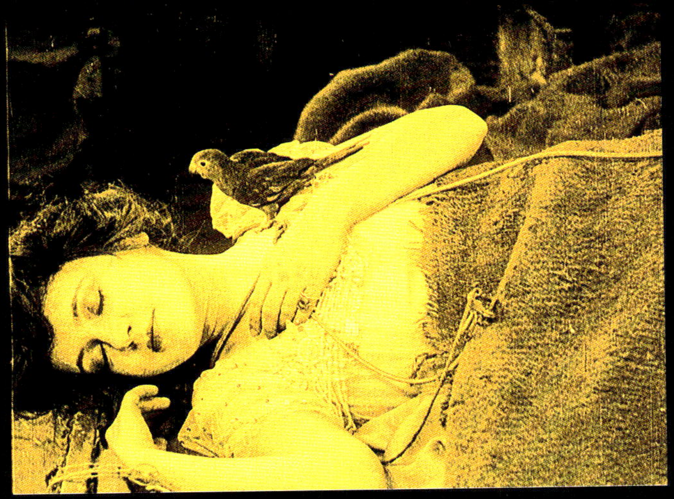

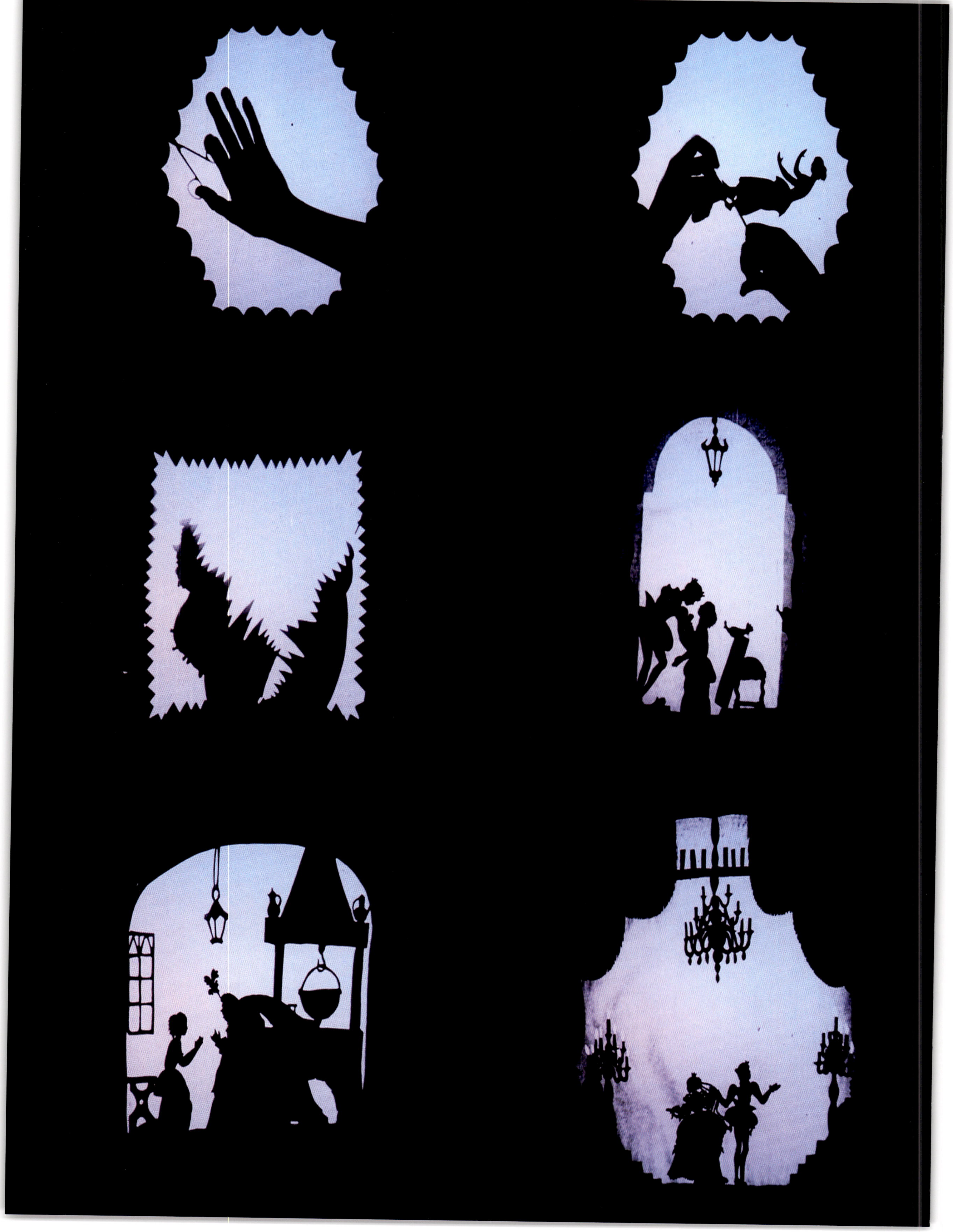

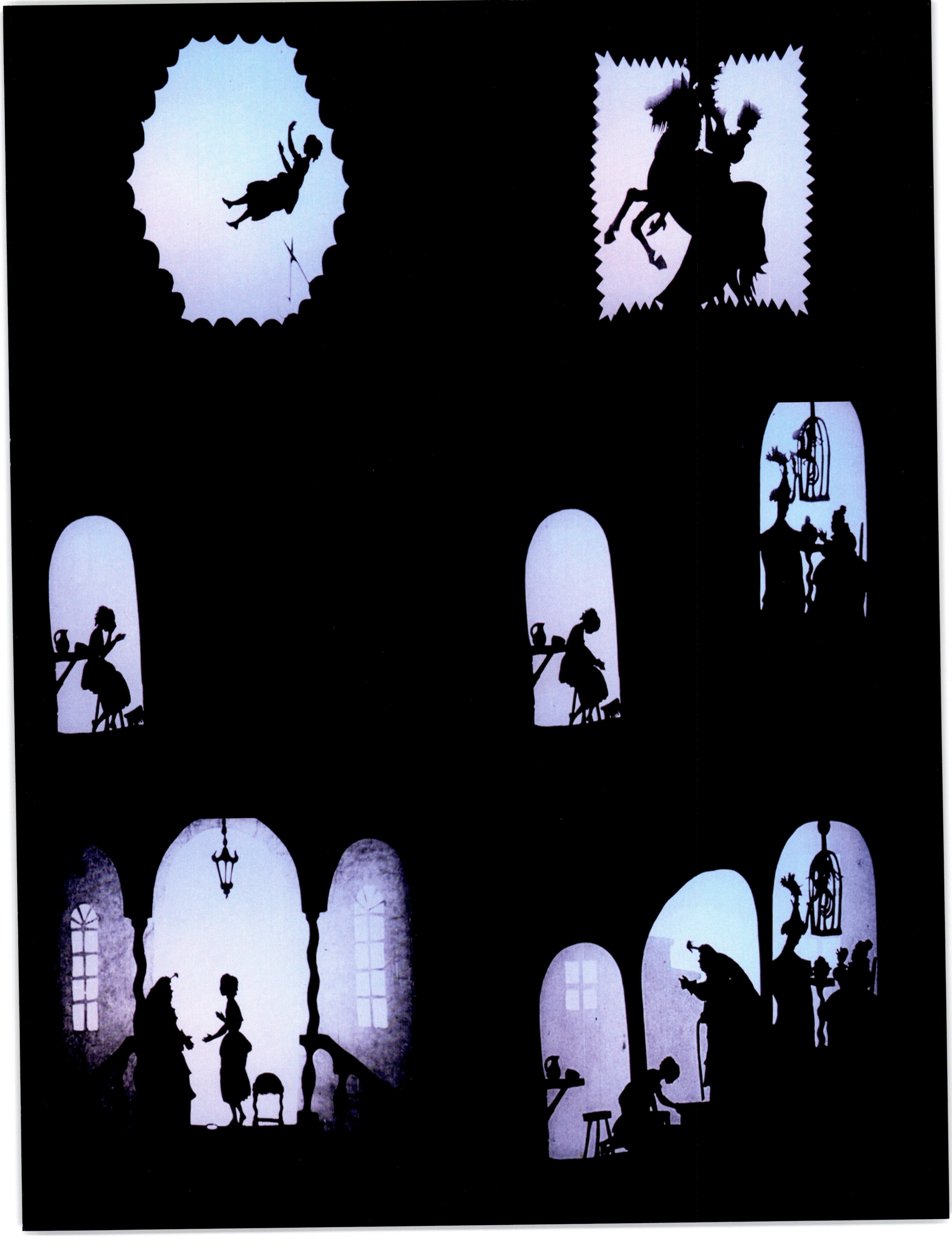

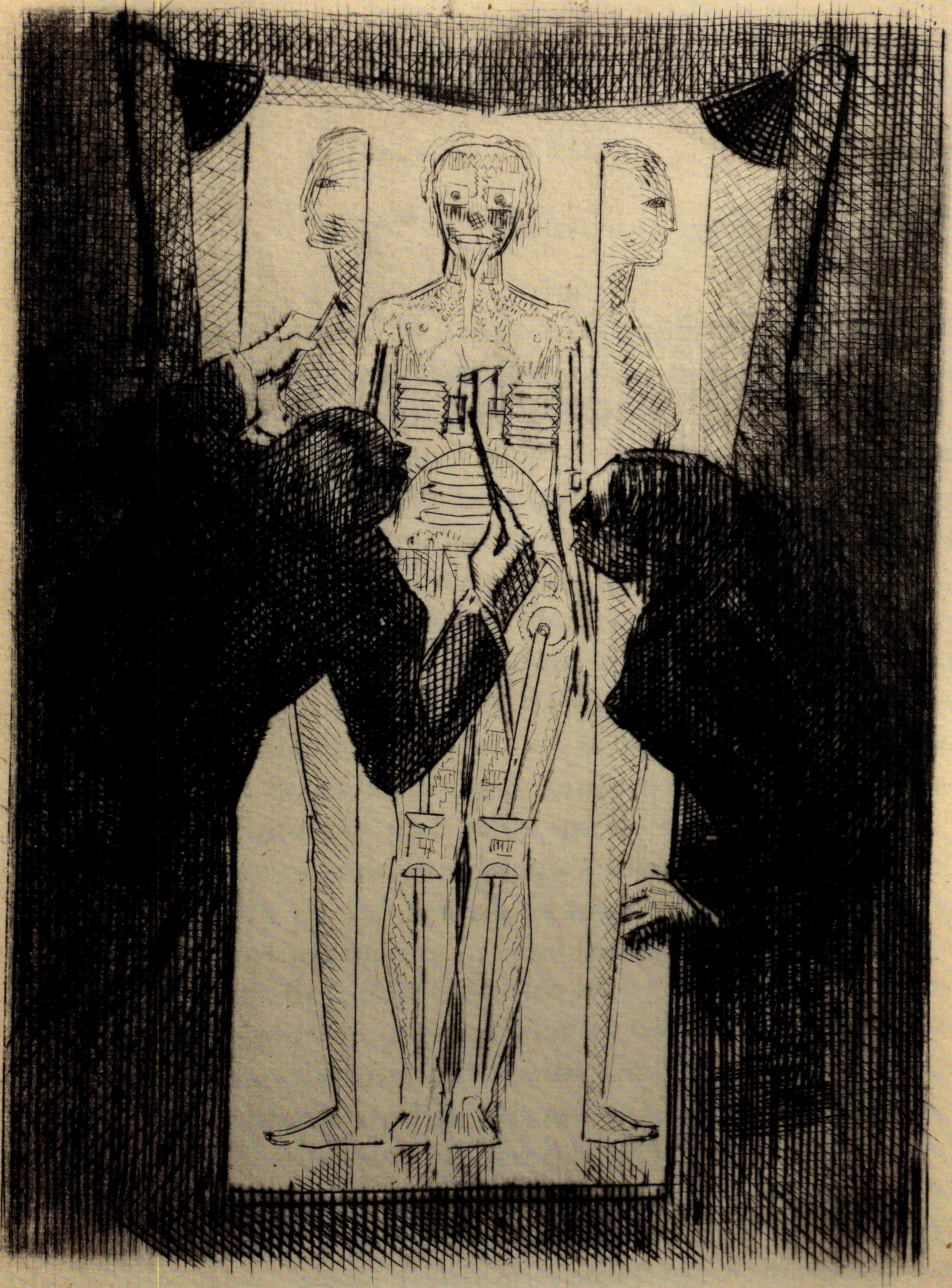

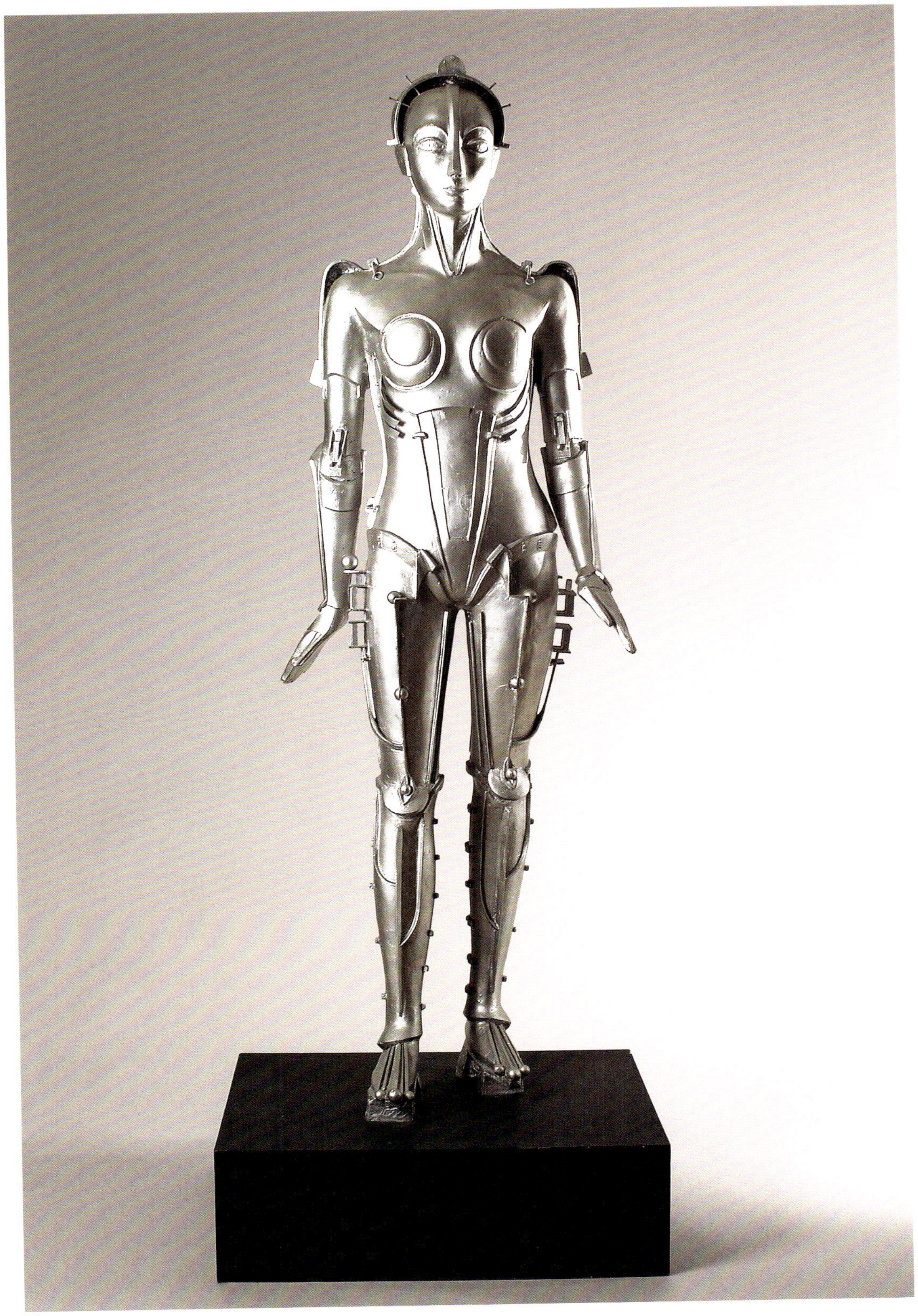

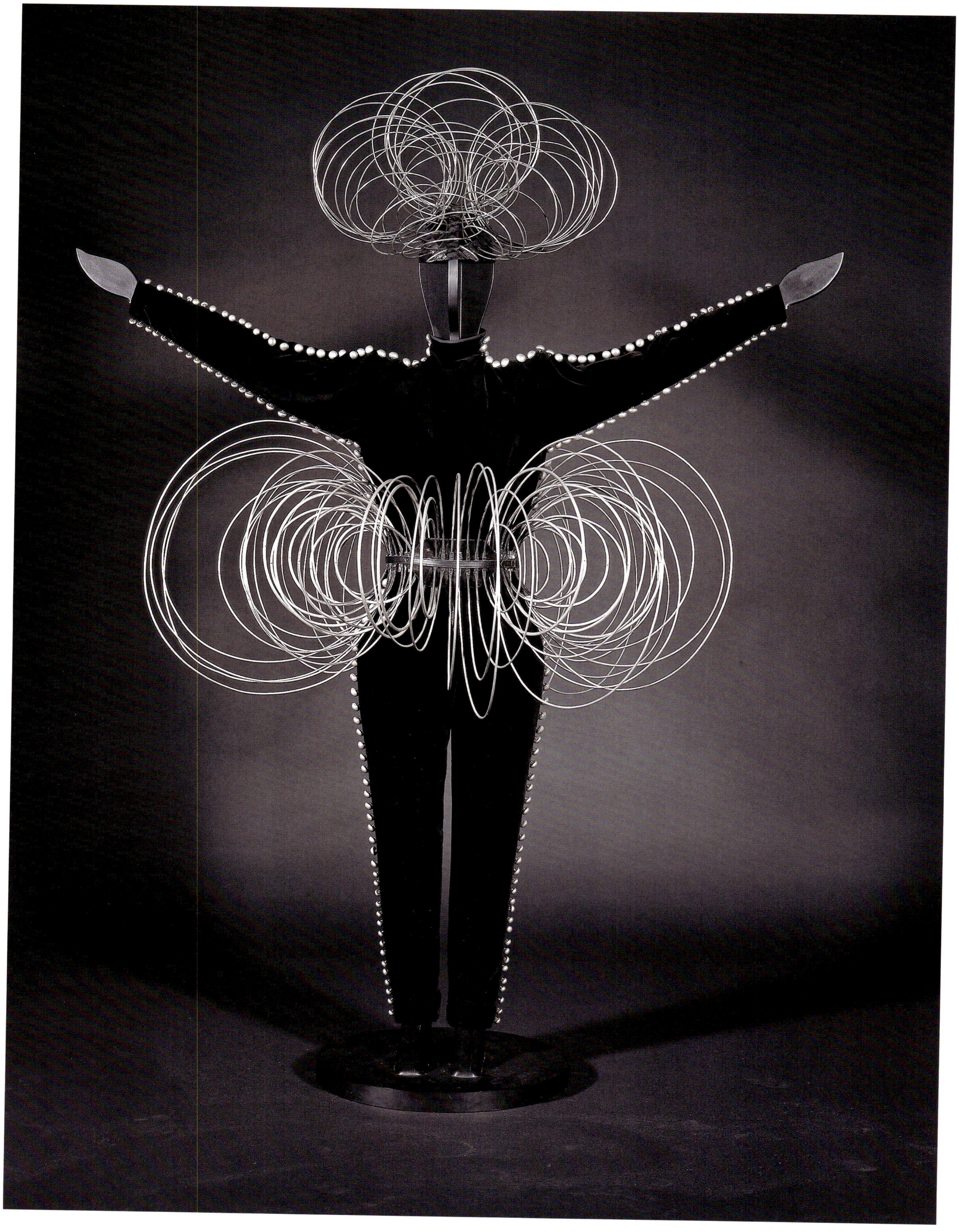

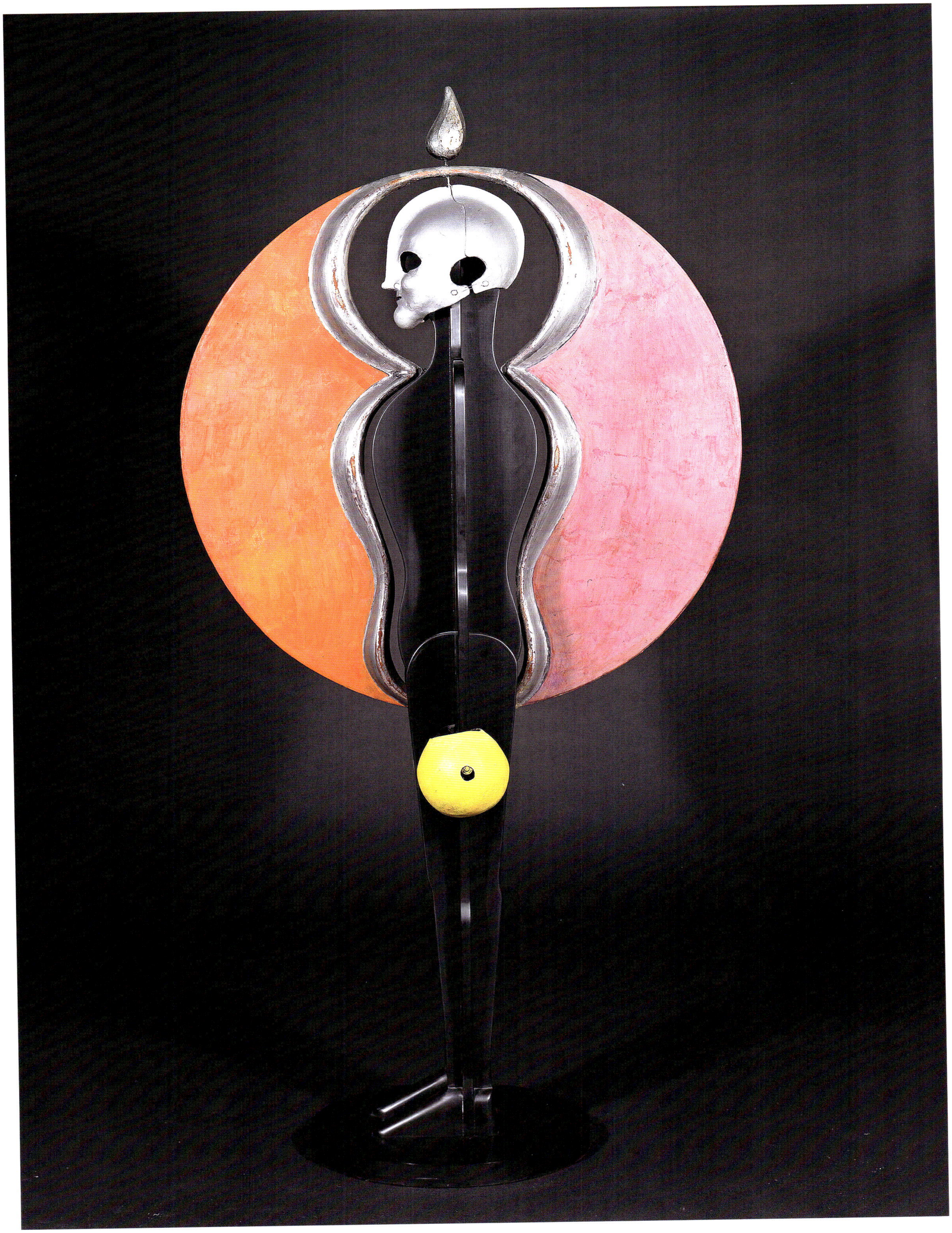

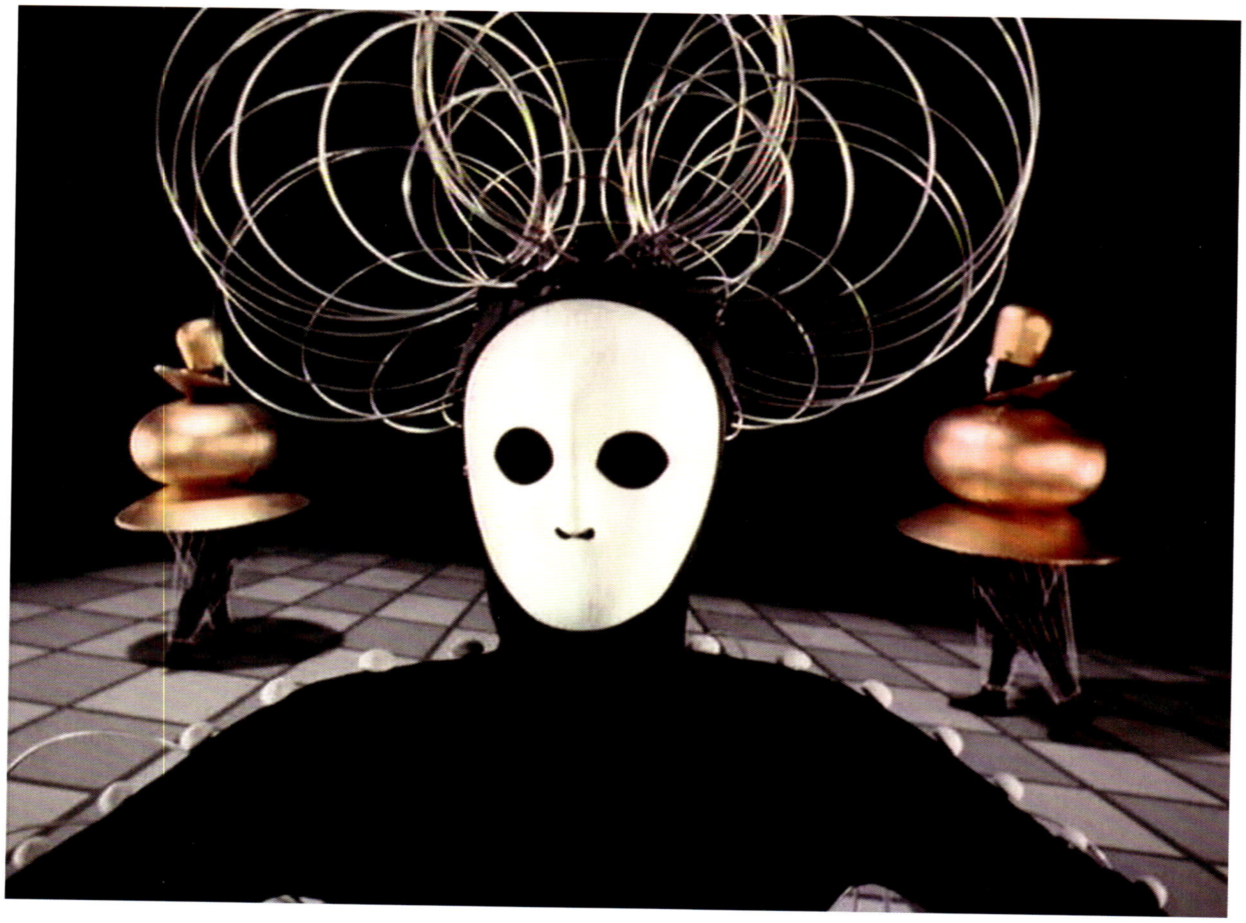

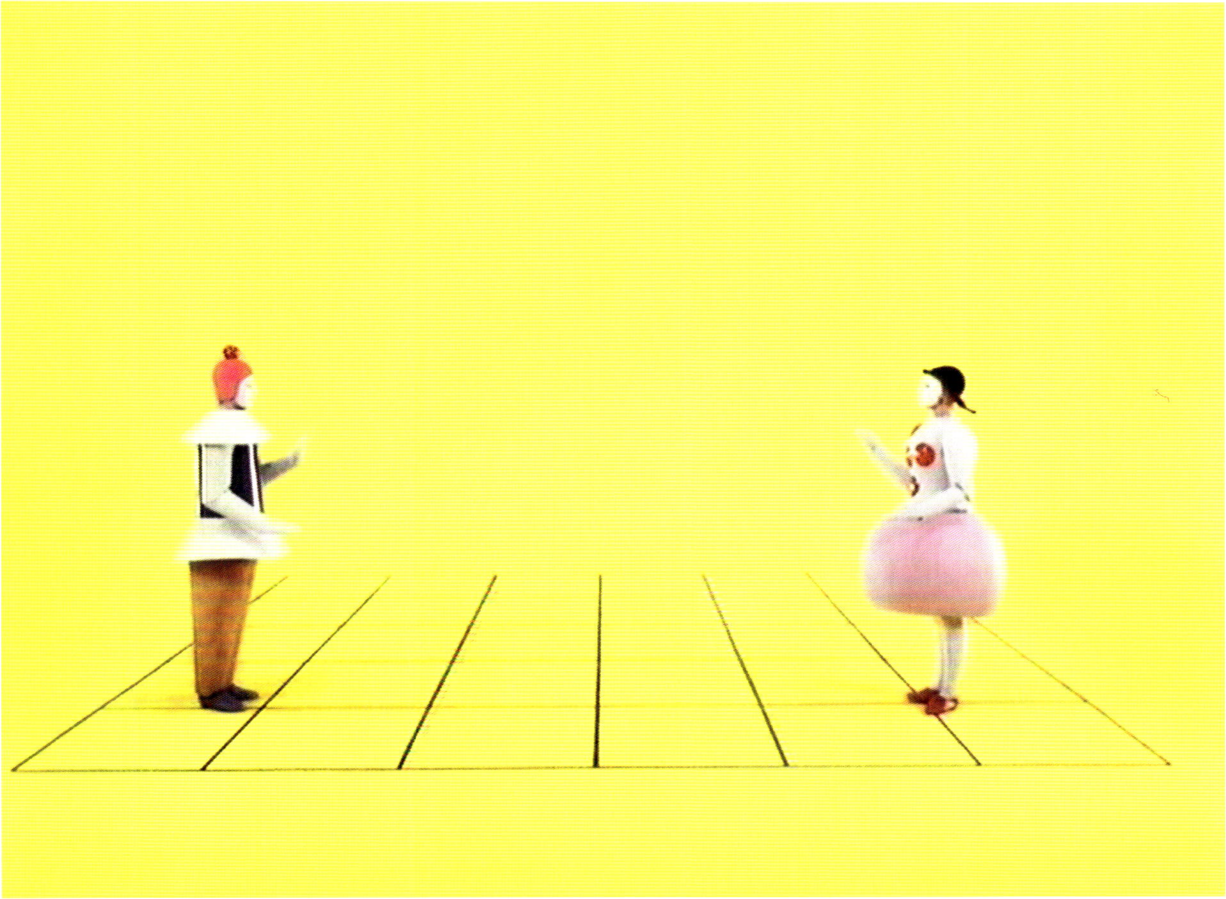

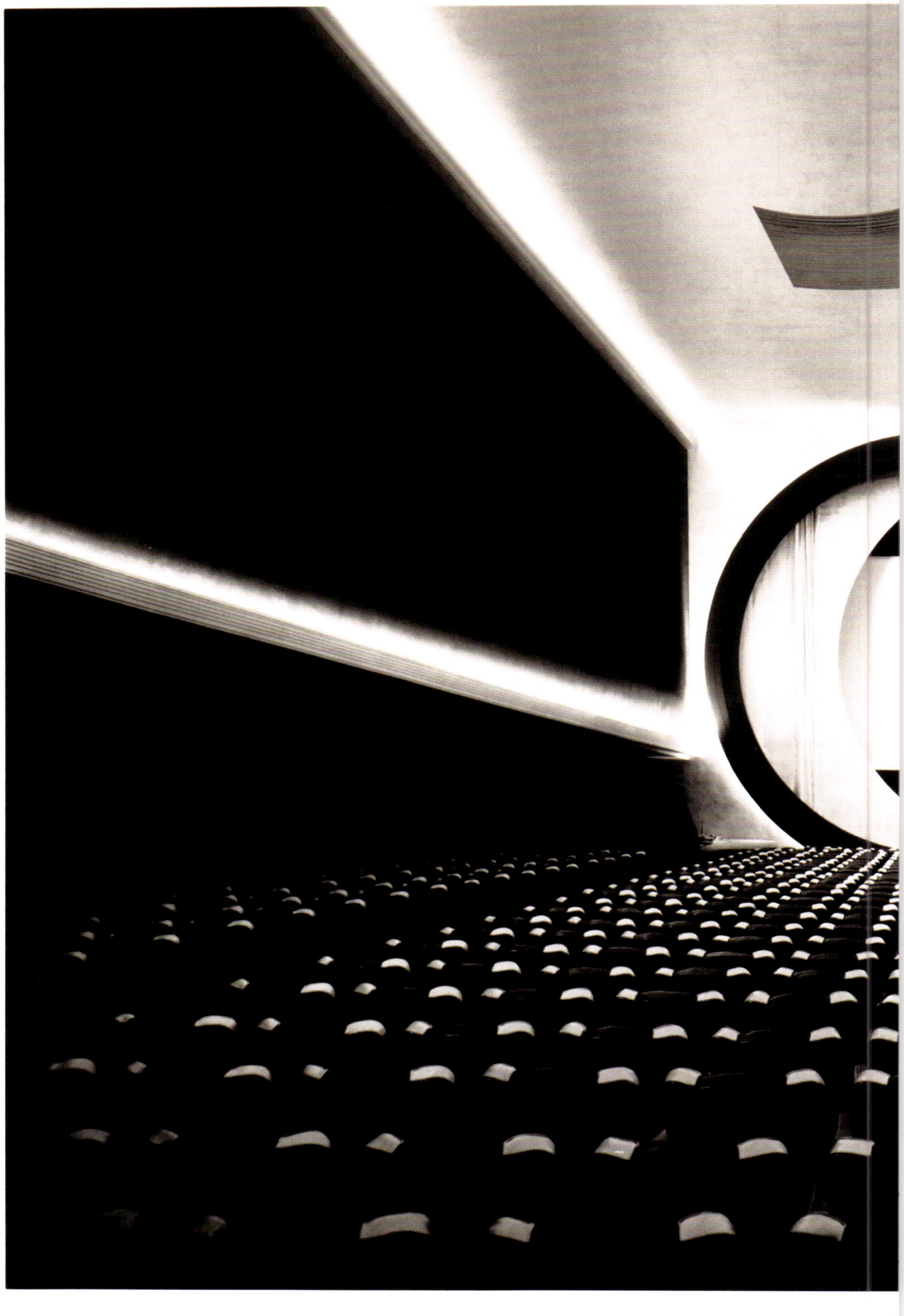

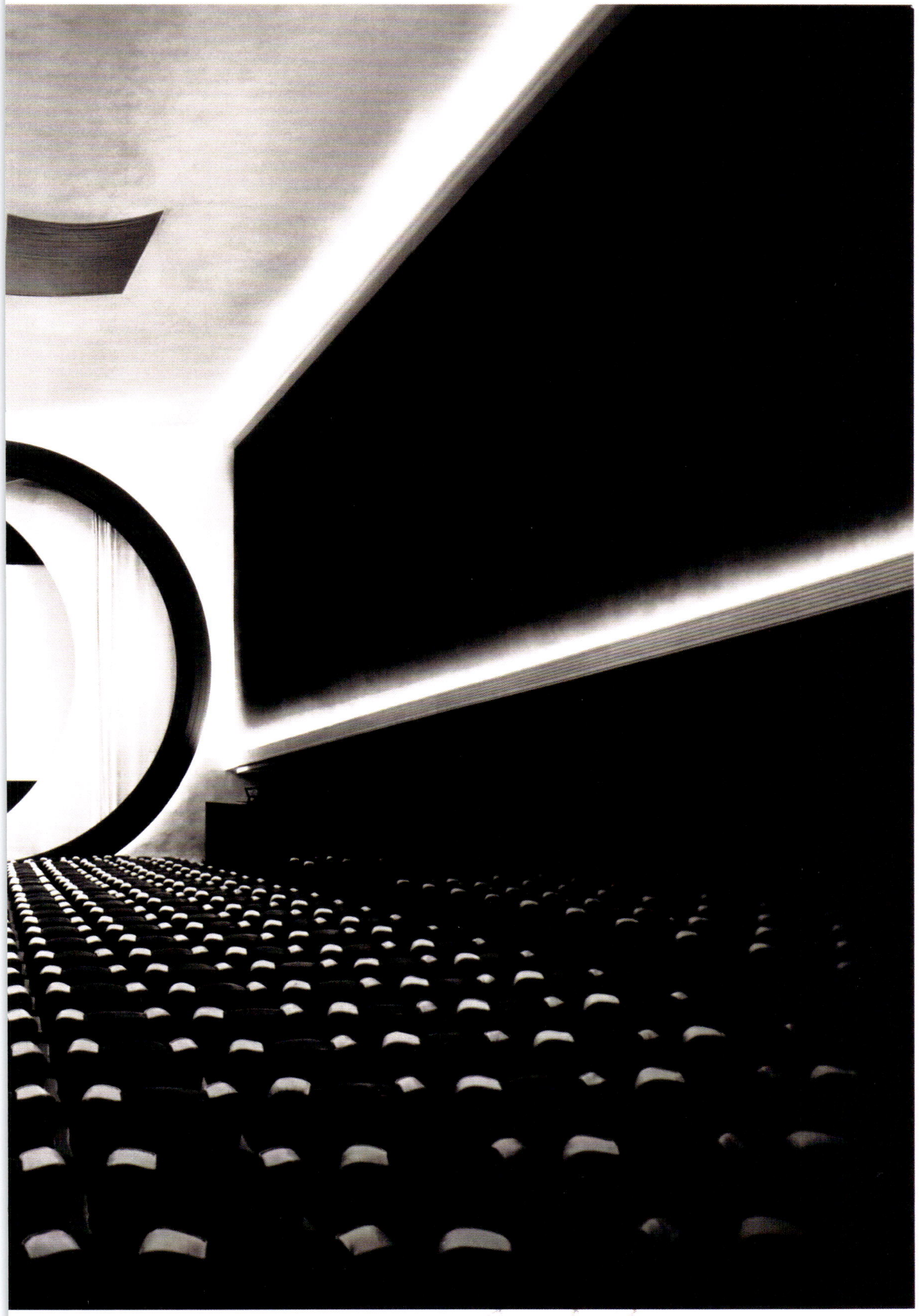

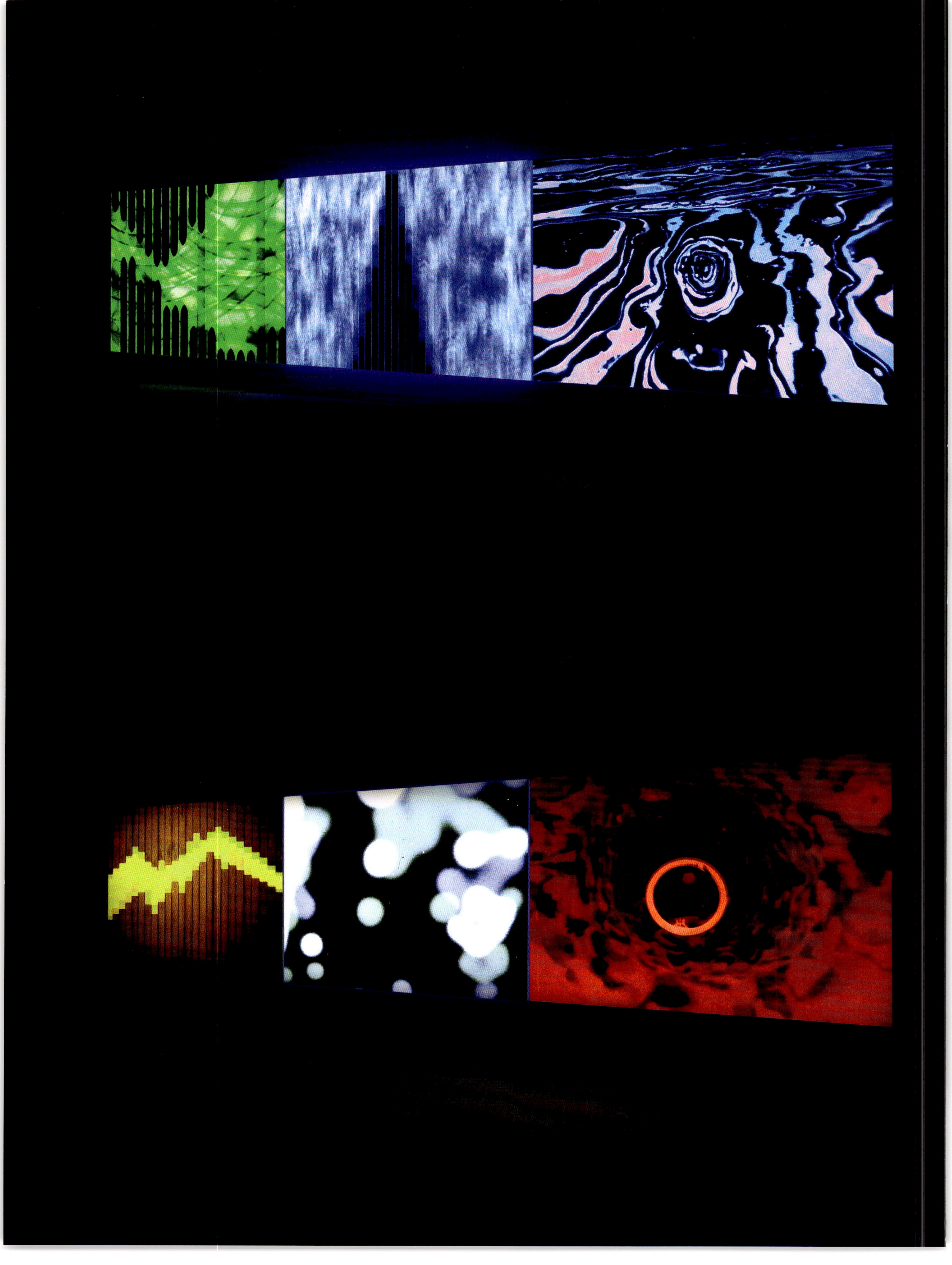

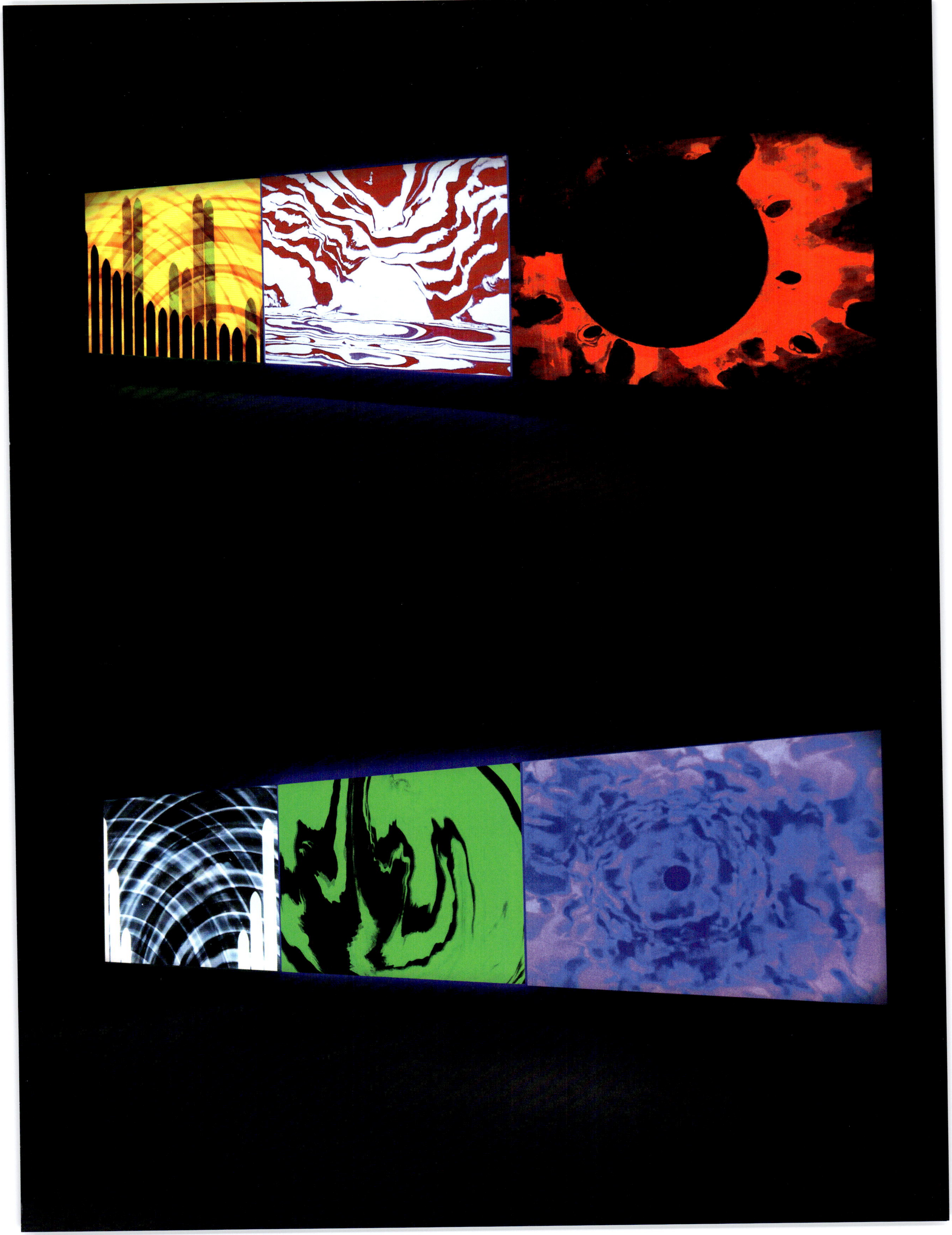

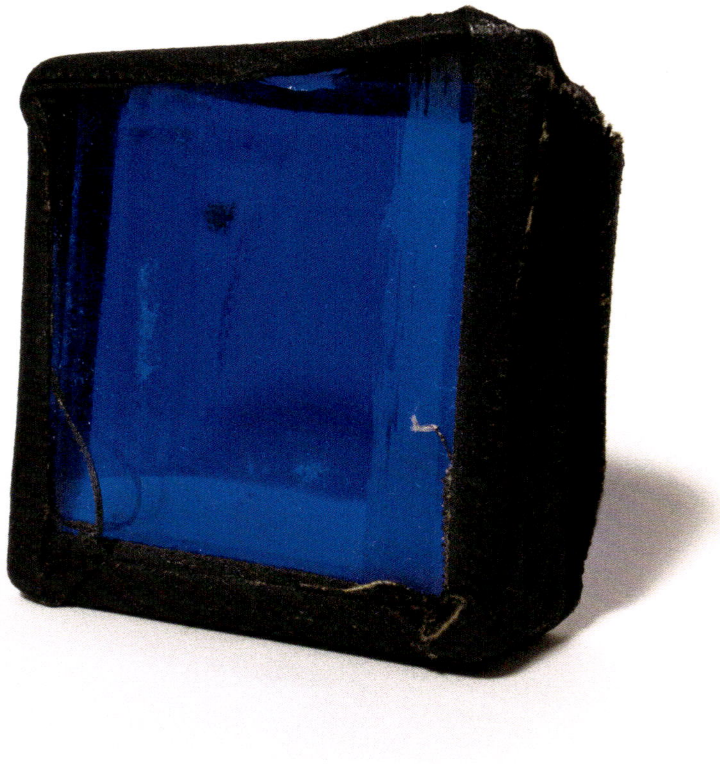

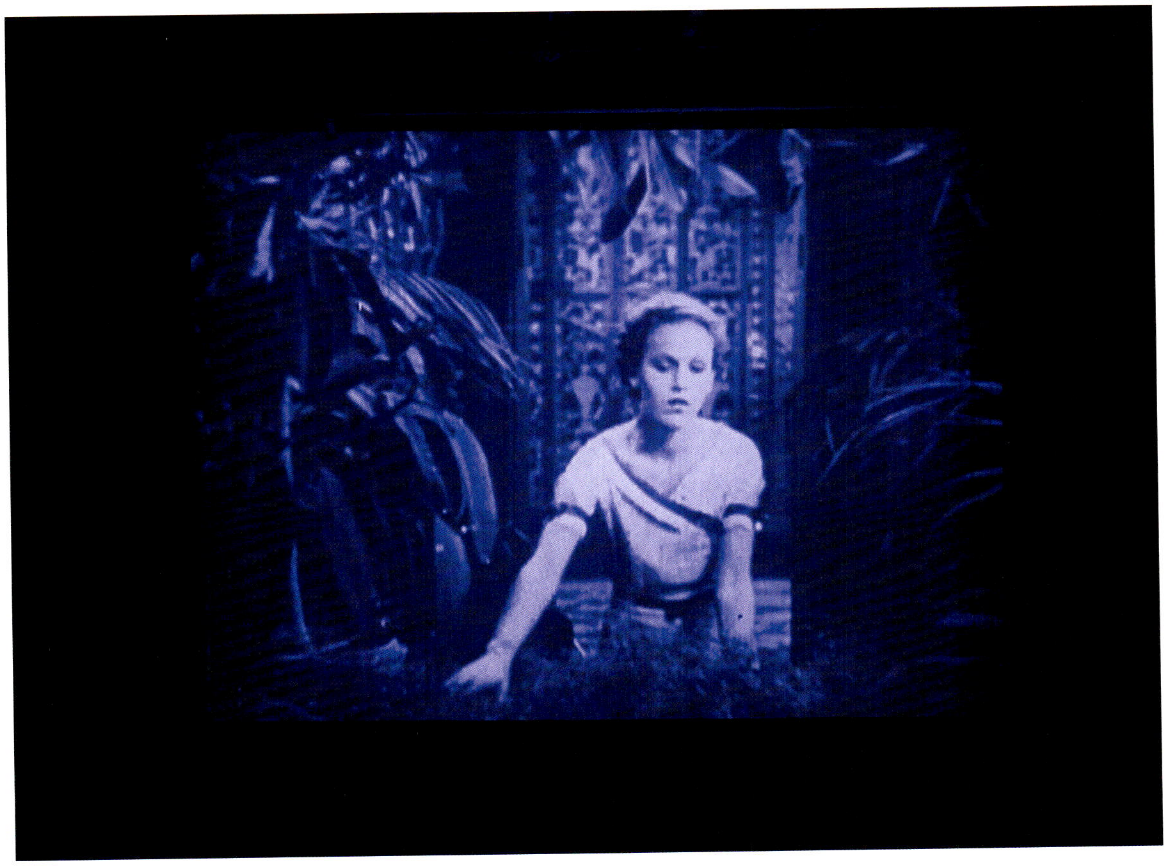

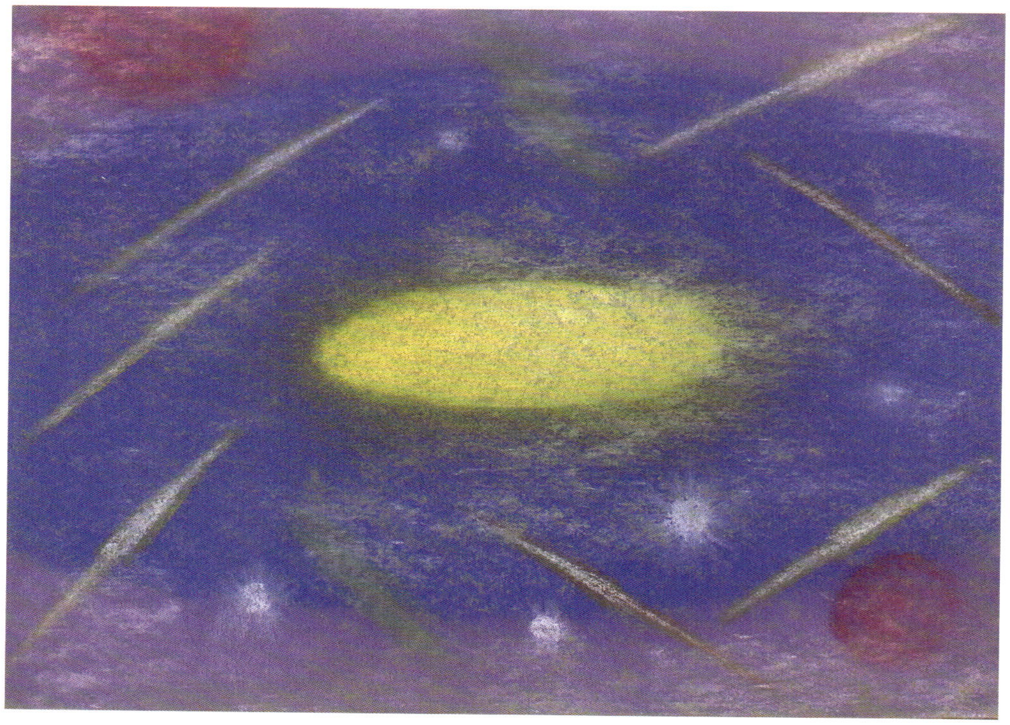

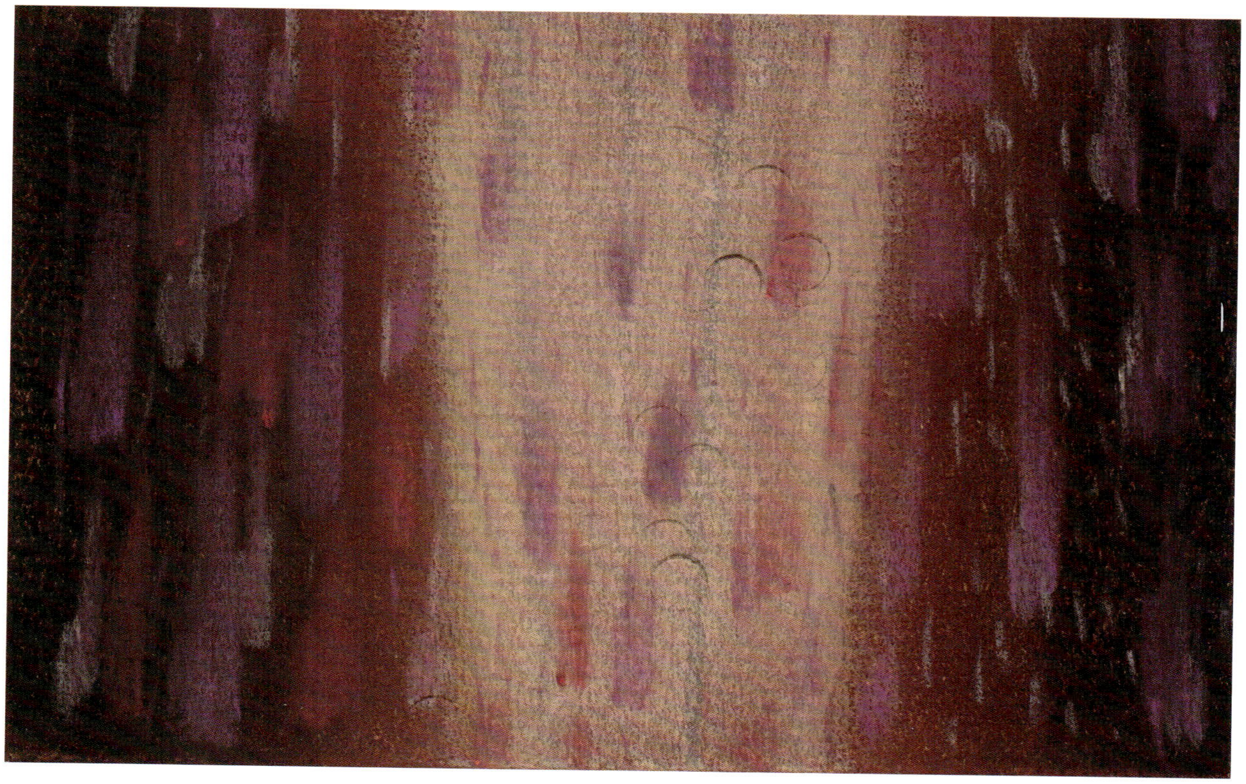

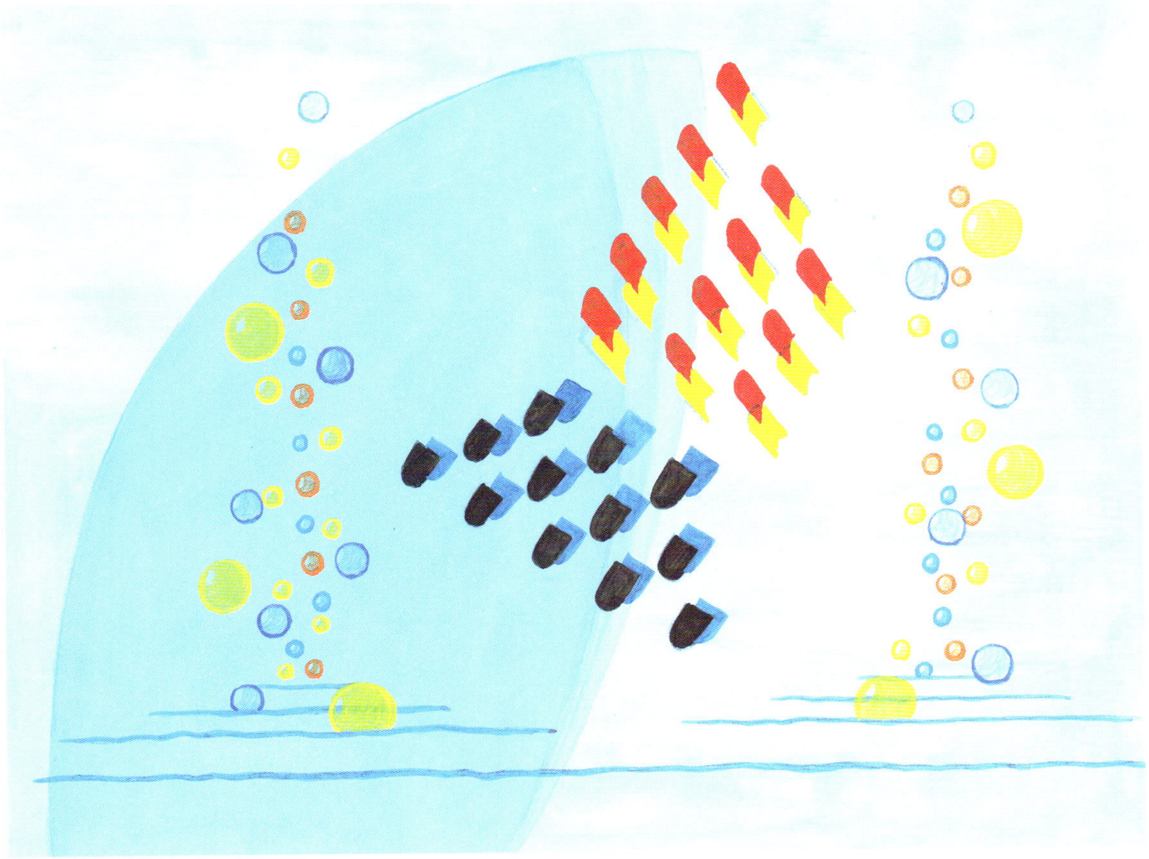

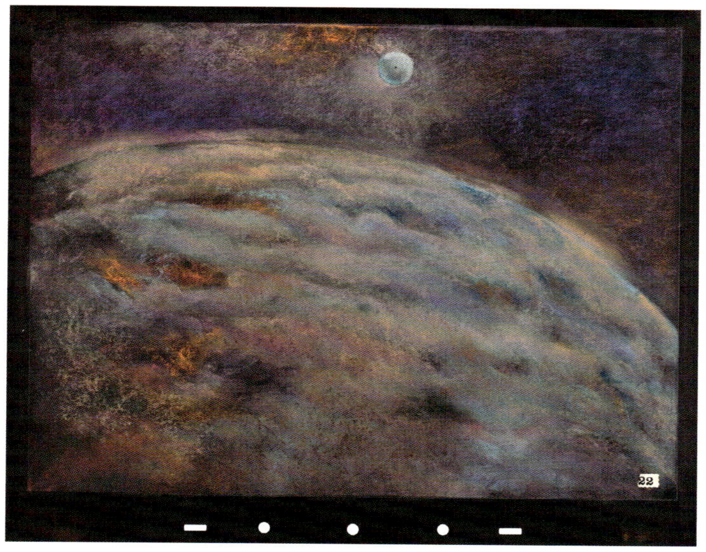
22

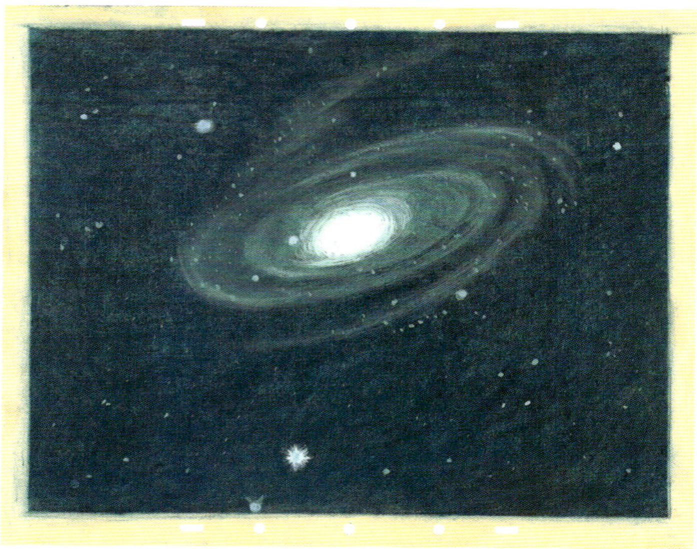

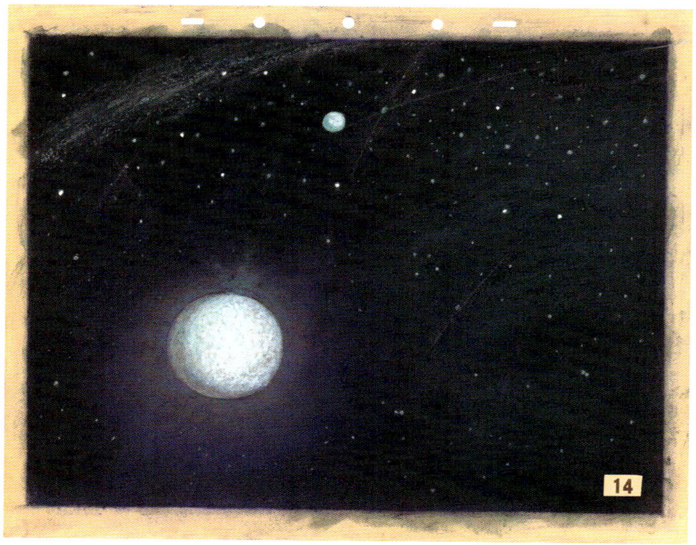
14

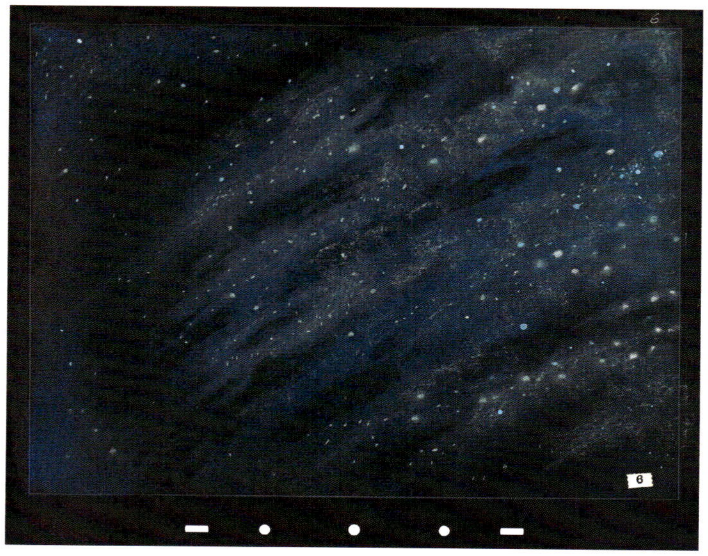
6

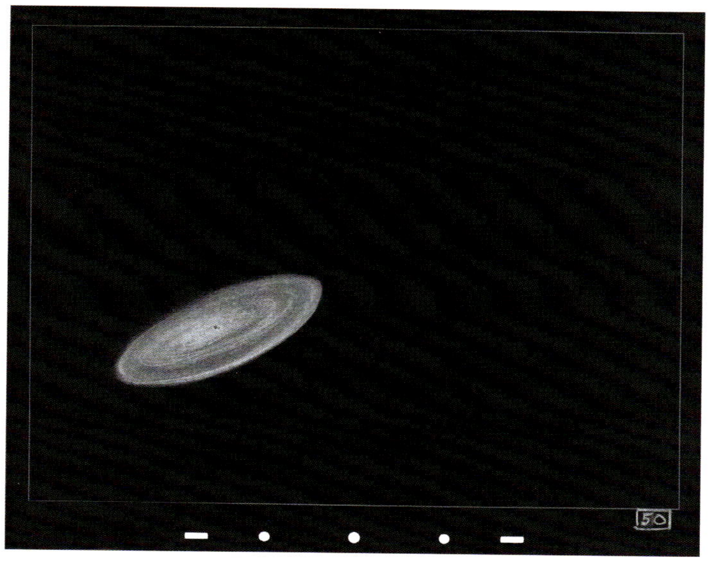
50

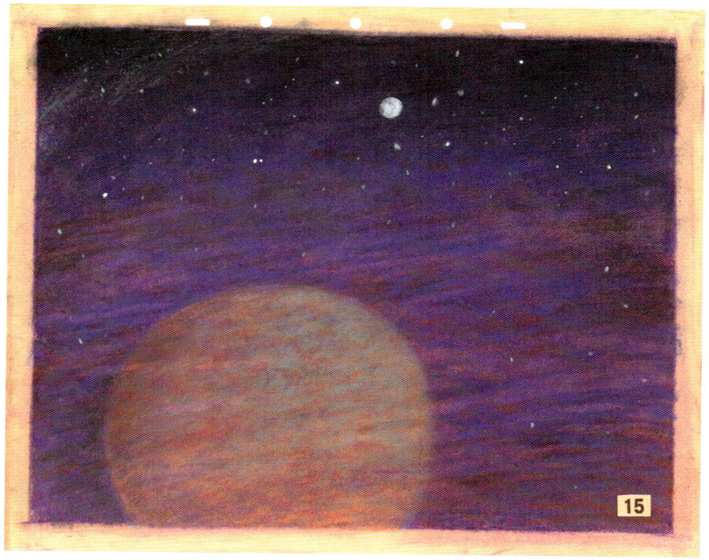
15

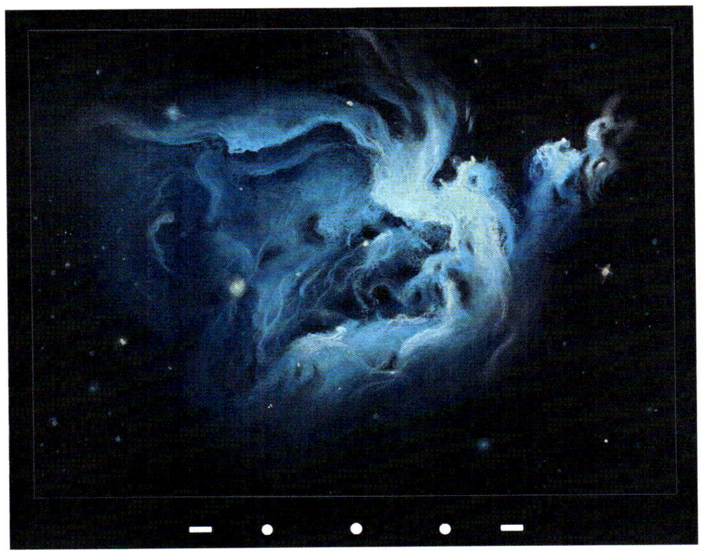

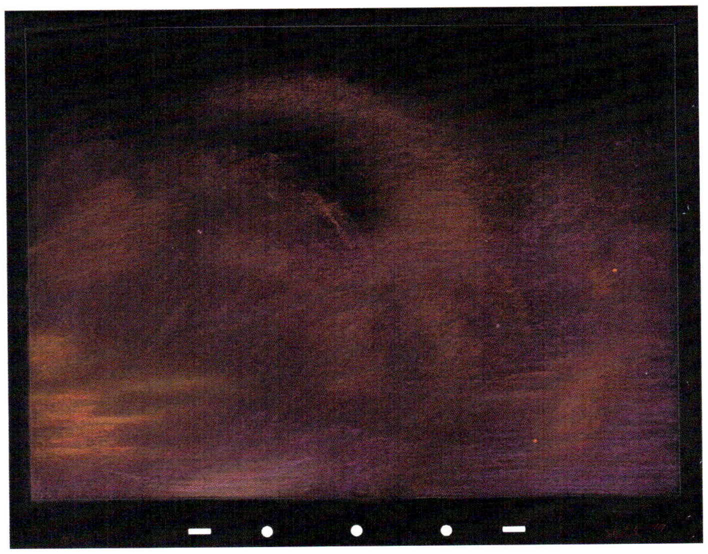

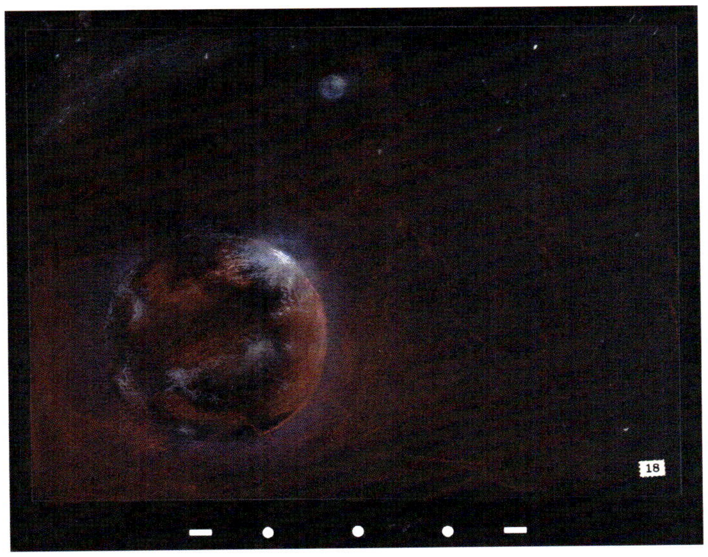
18

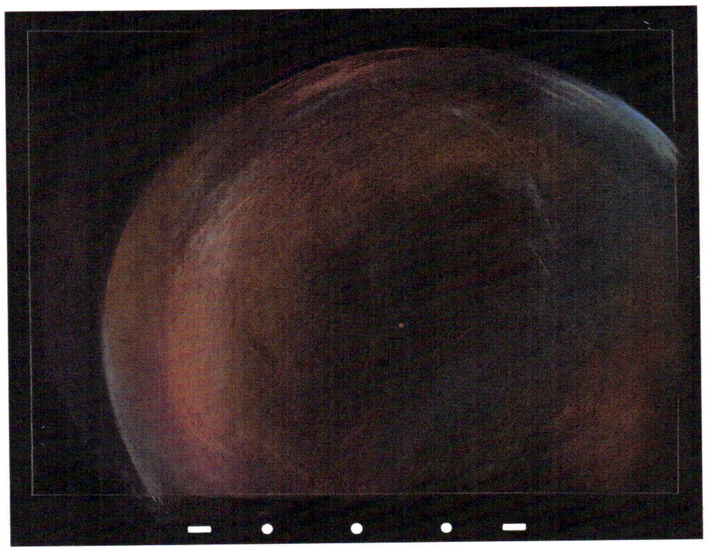

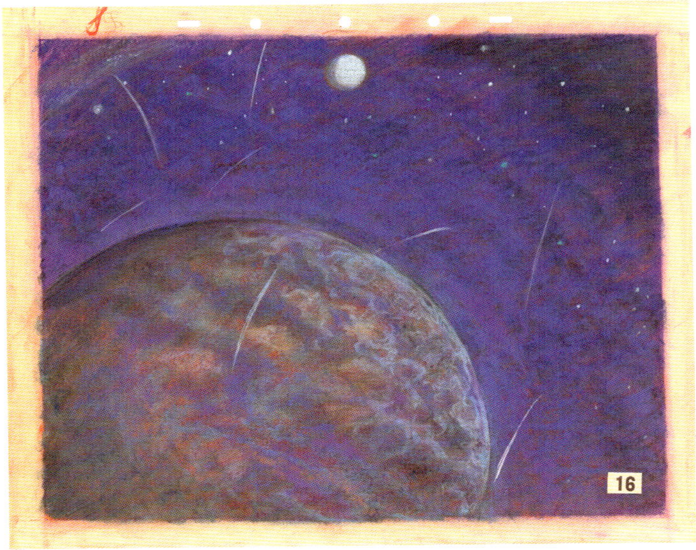
16

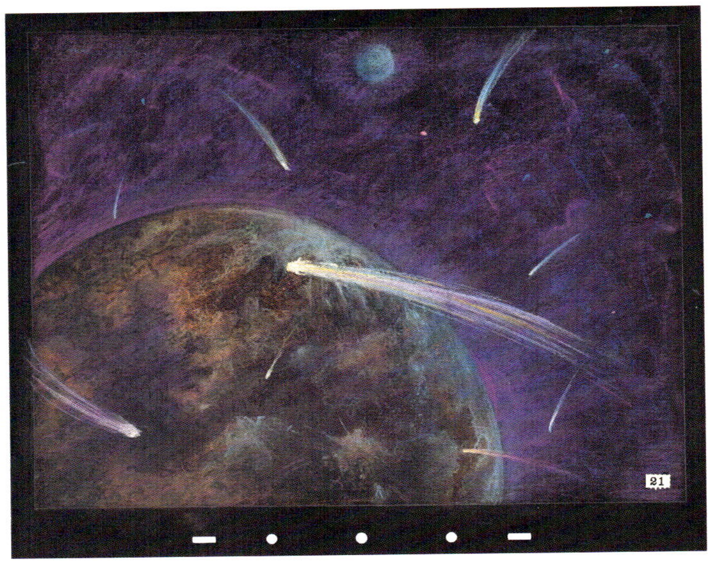
21

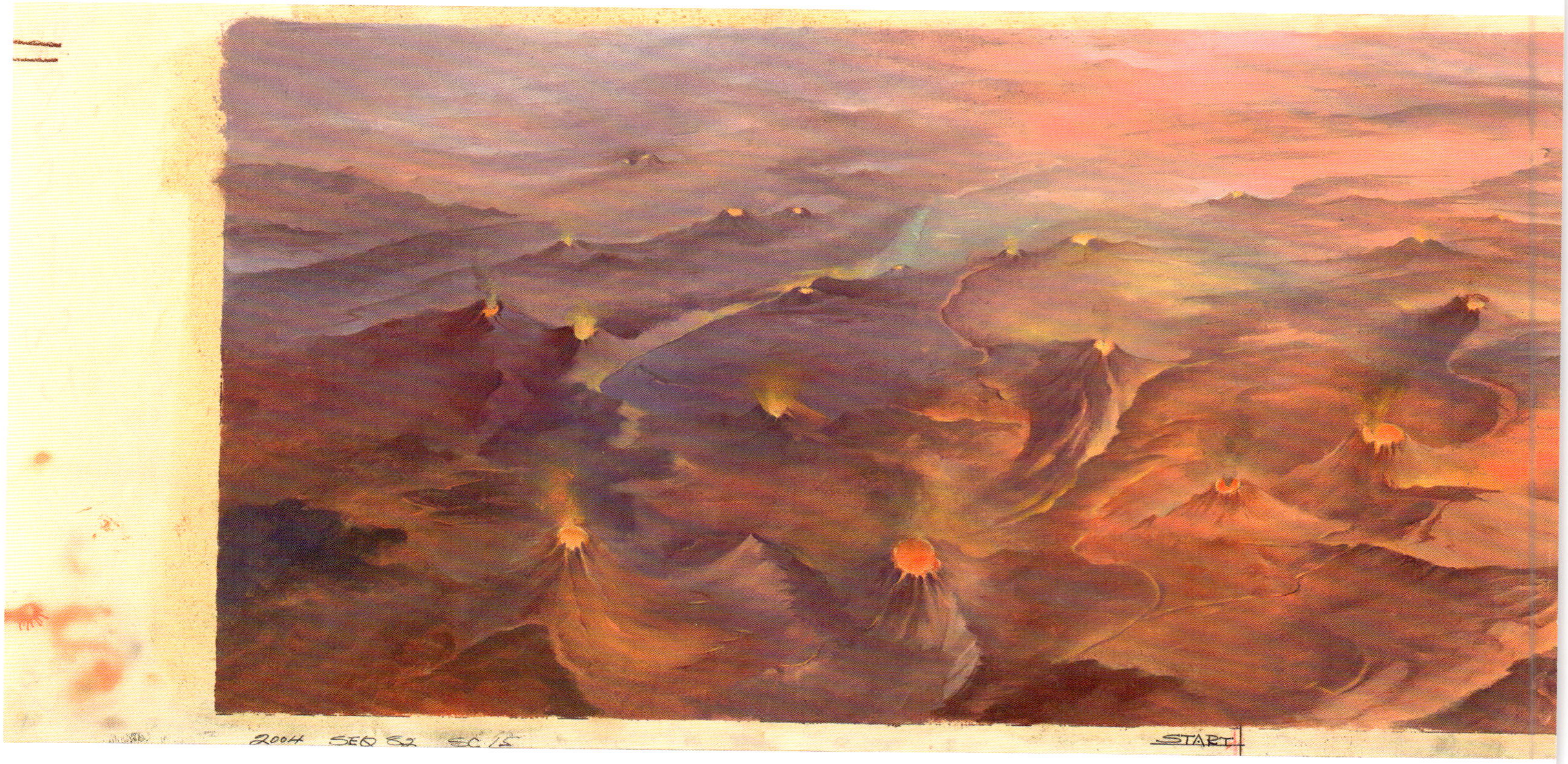
2004 SEQ 82 SC 15
START

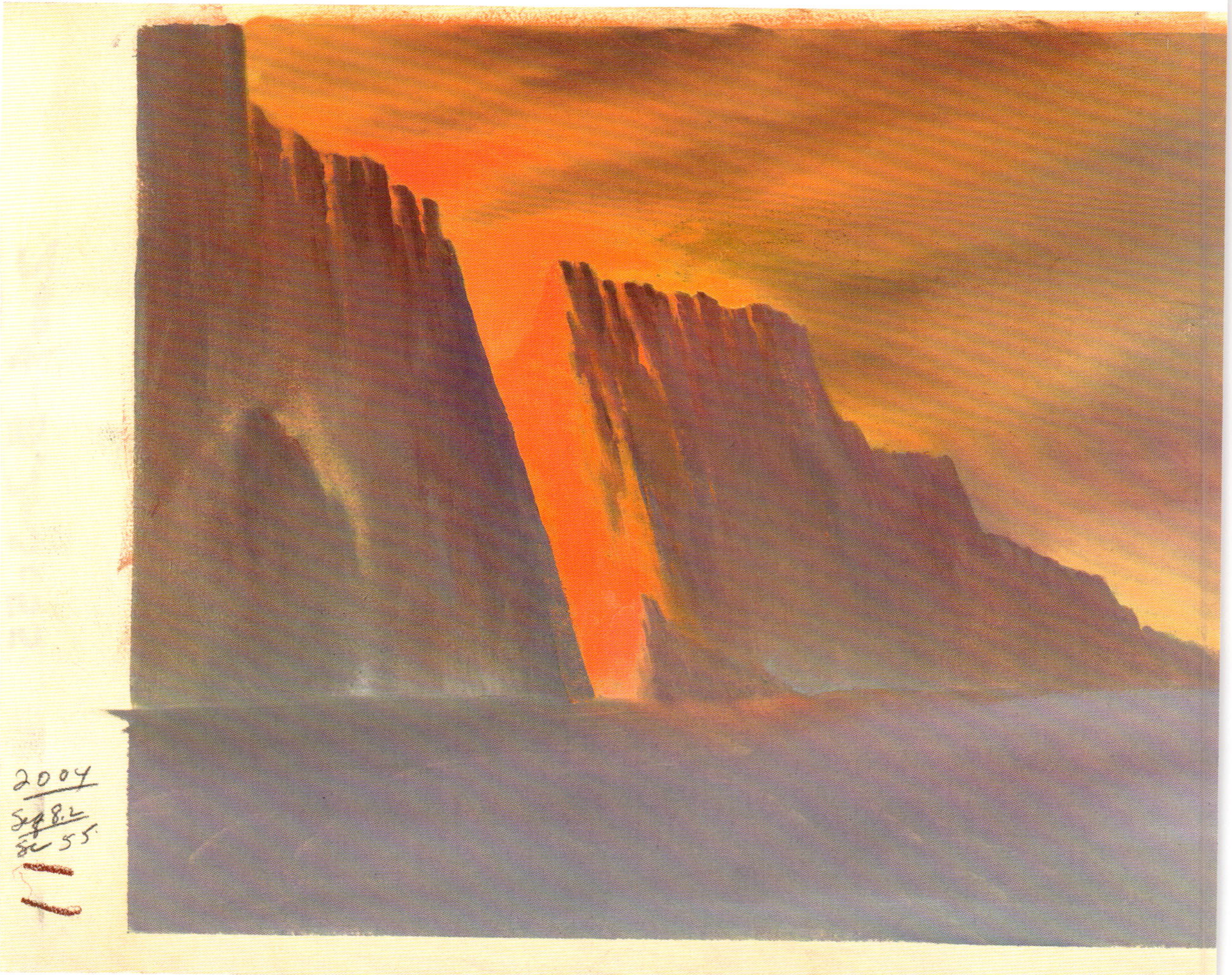
2004
Seq 8.2
Sc 55.

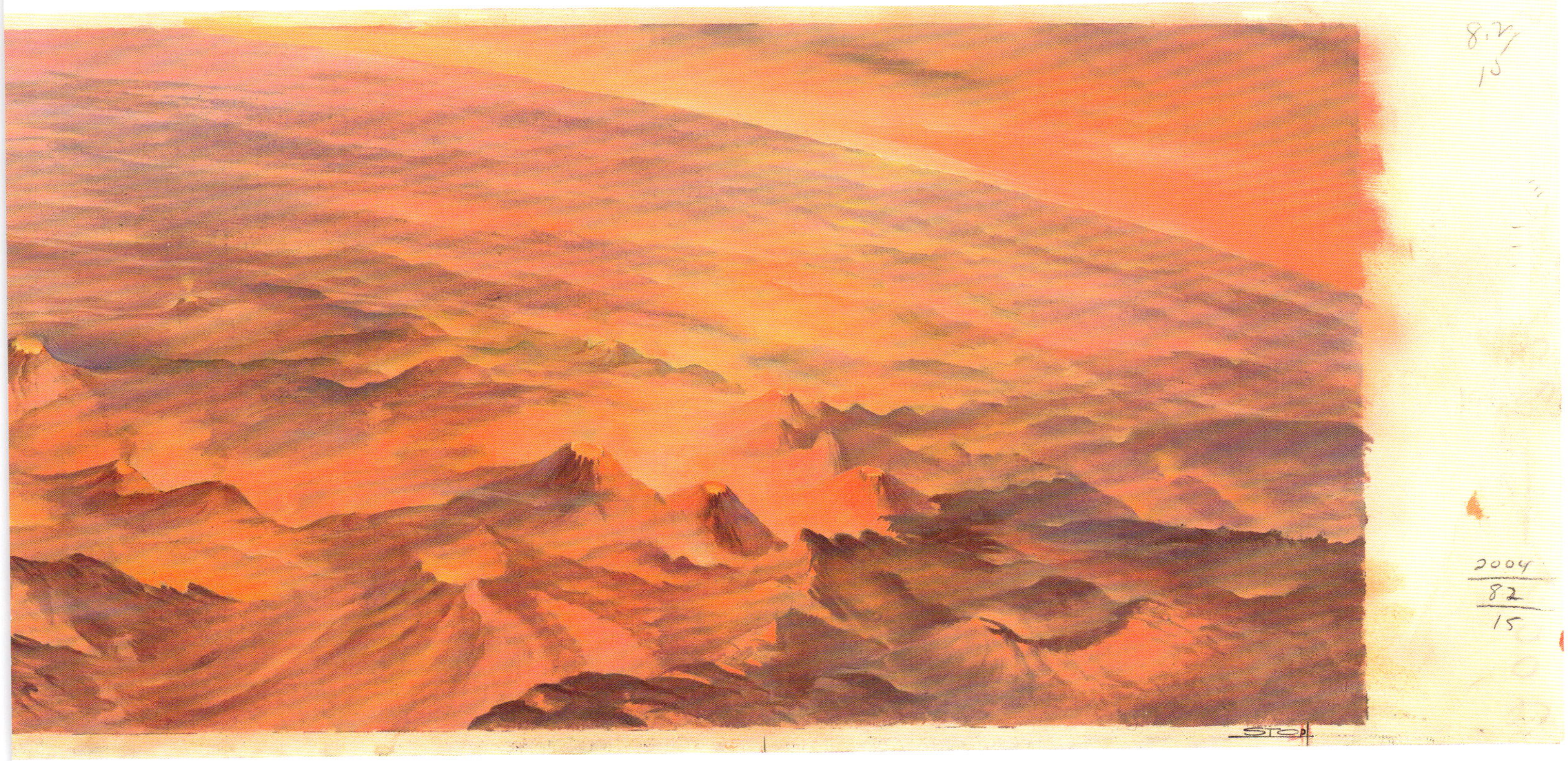
2004
82
15

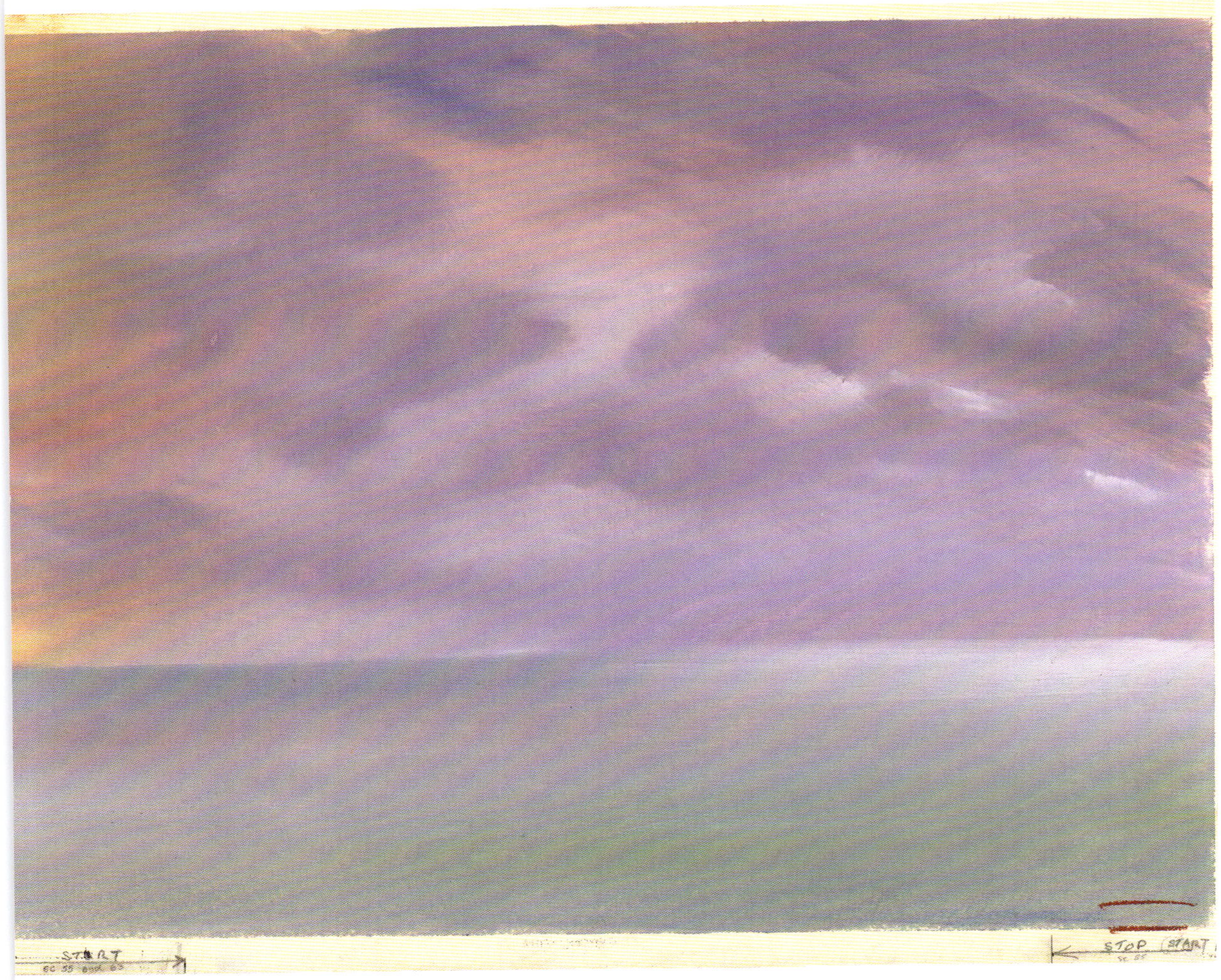
START
STOP (START

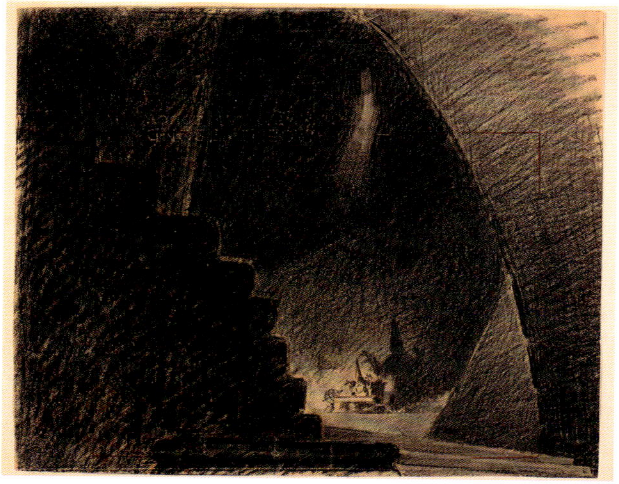
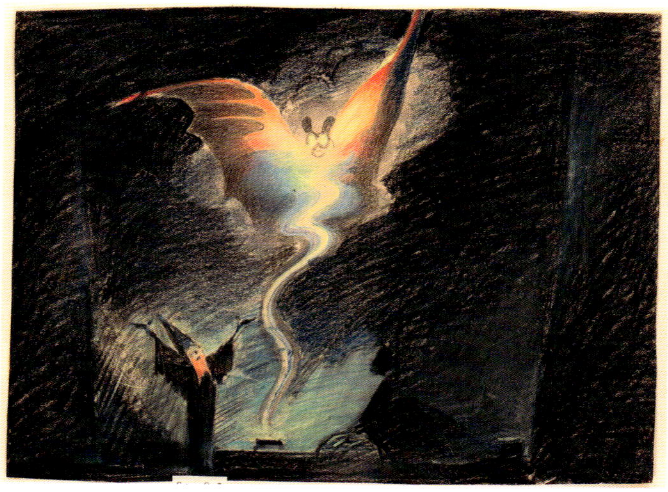
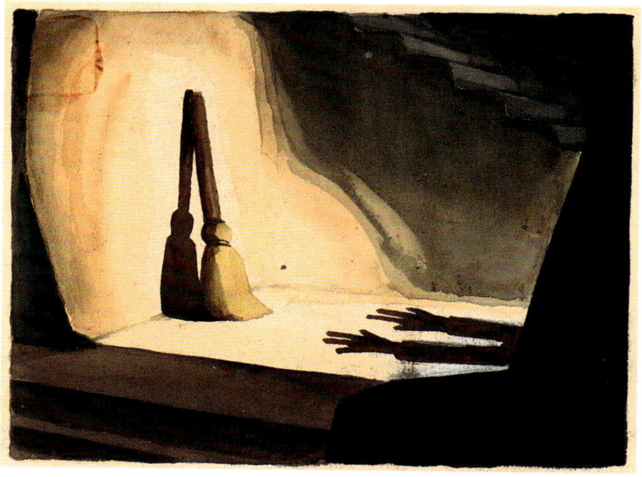
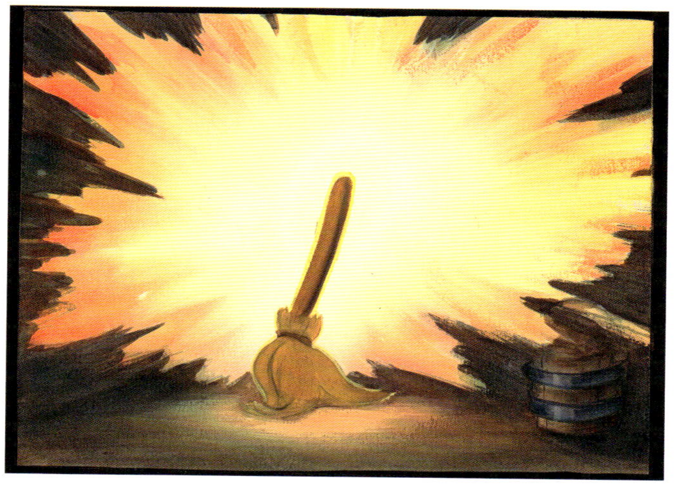
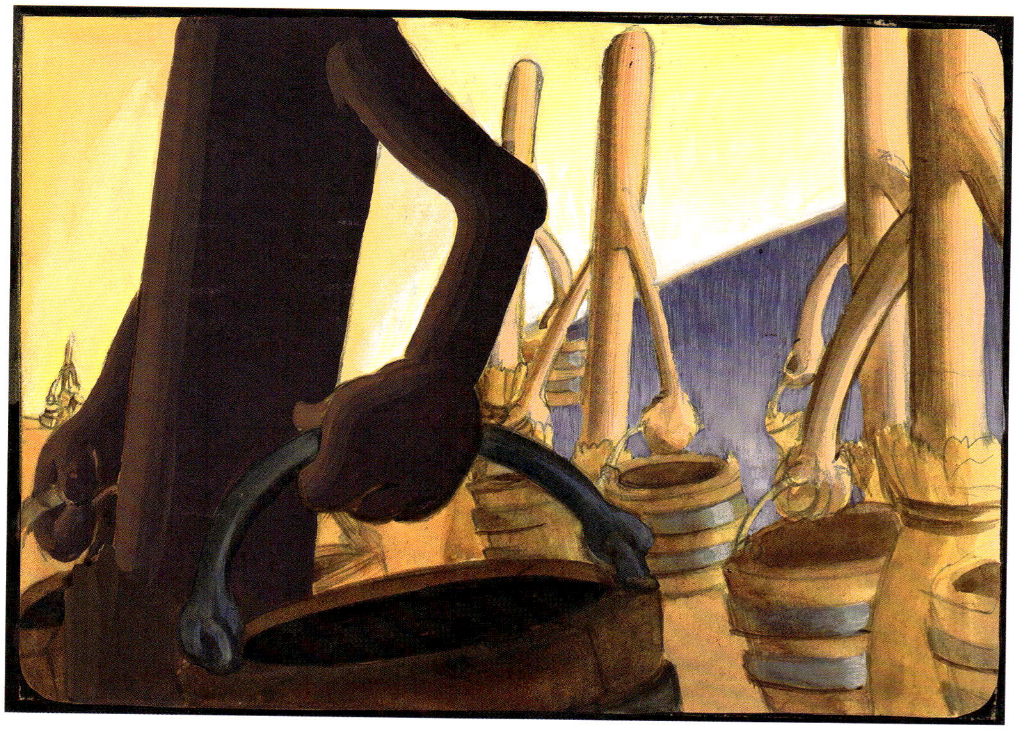

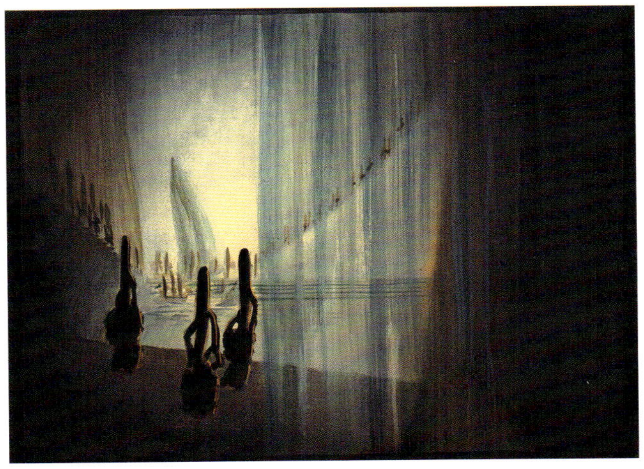

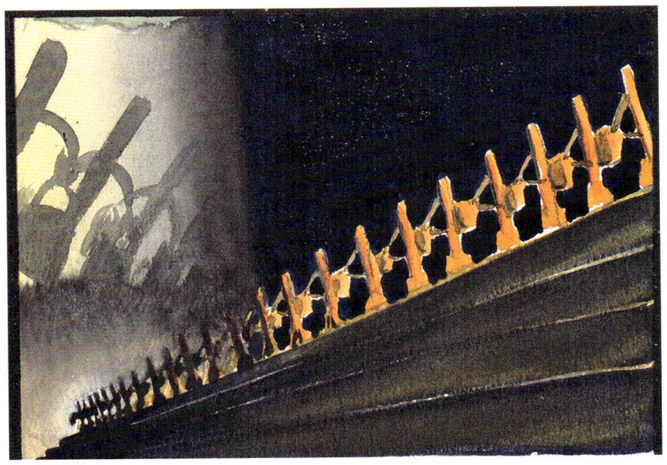

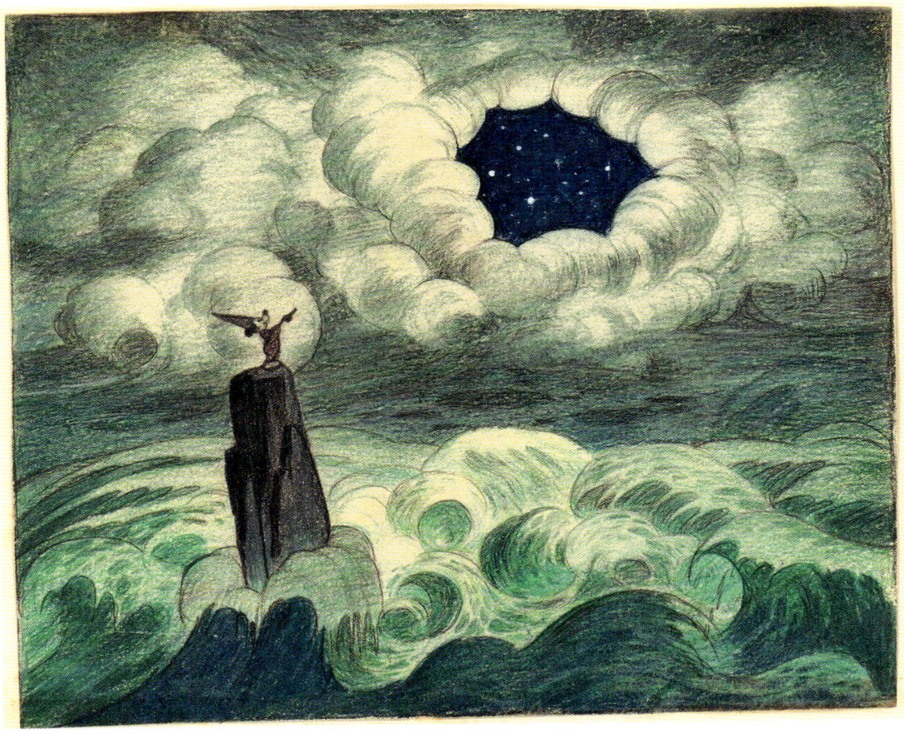

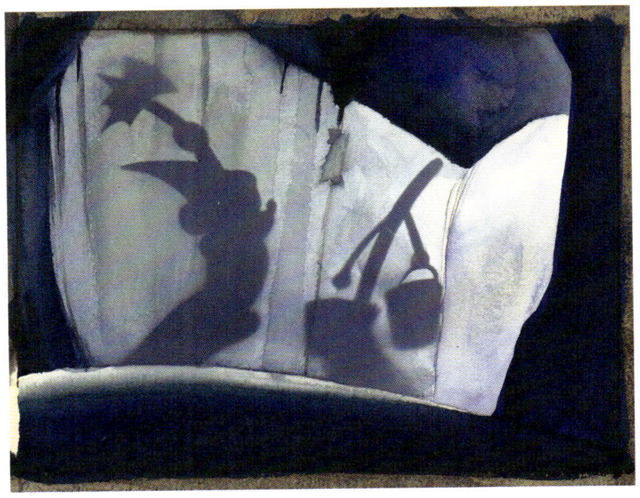

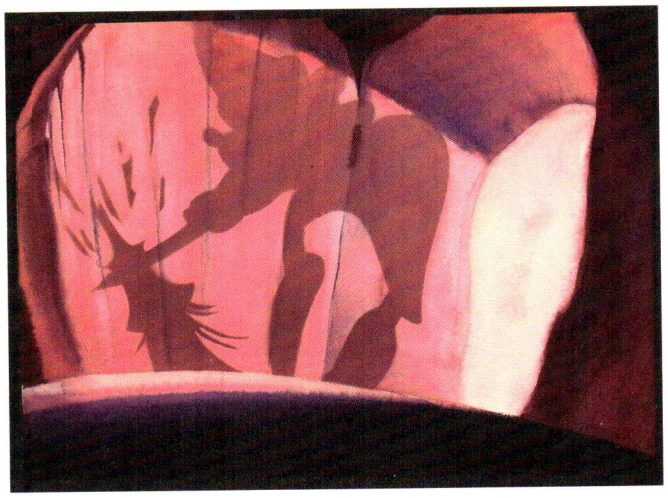

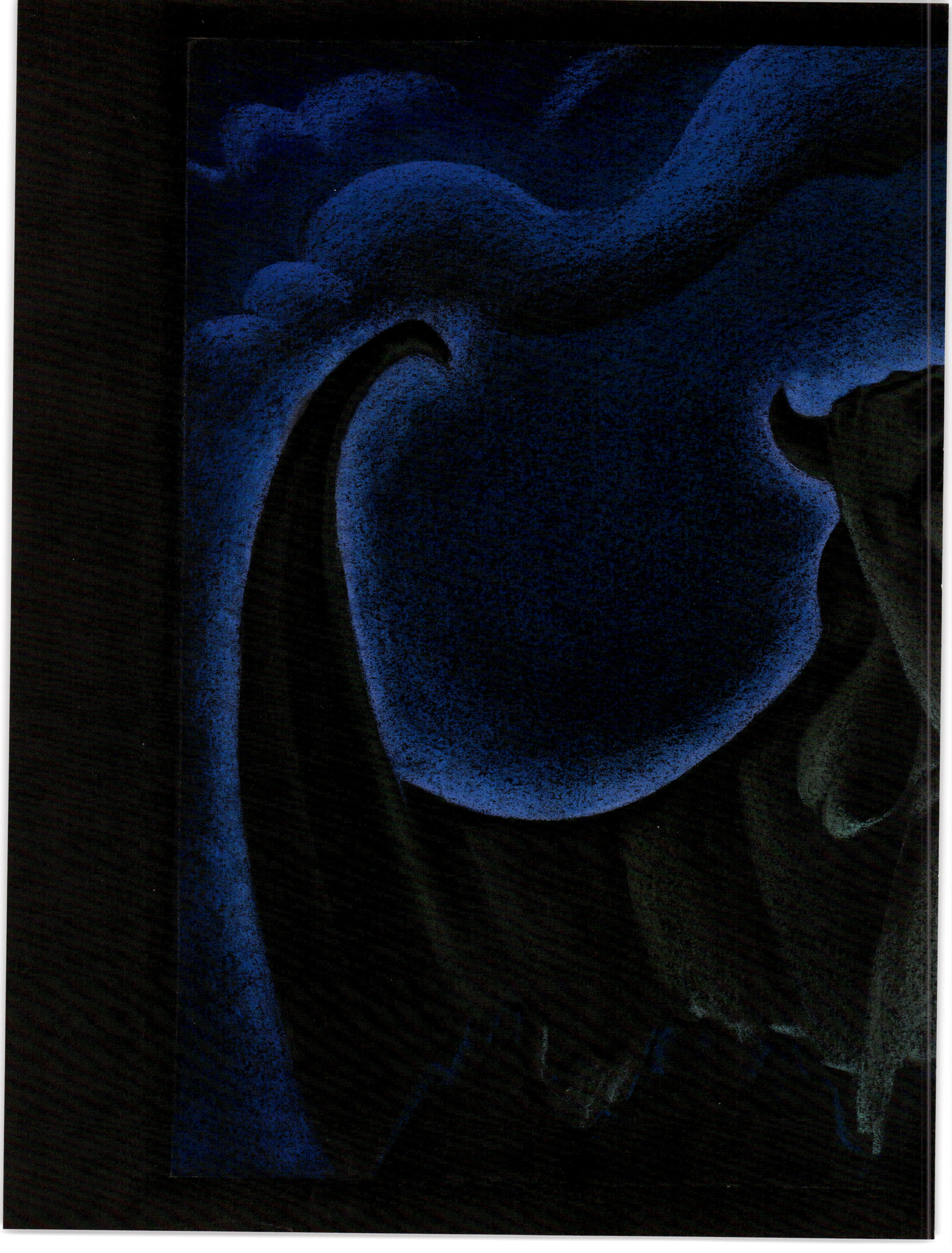

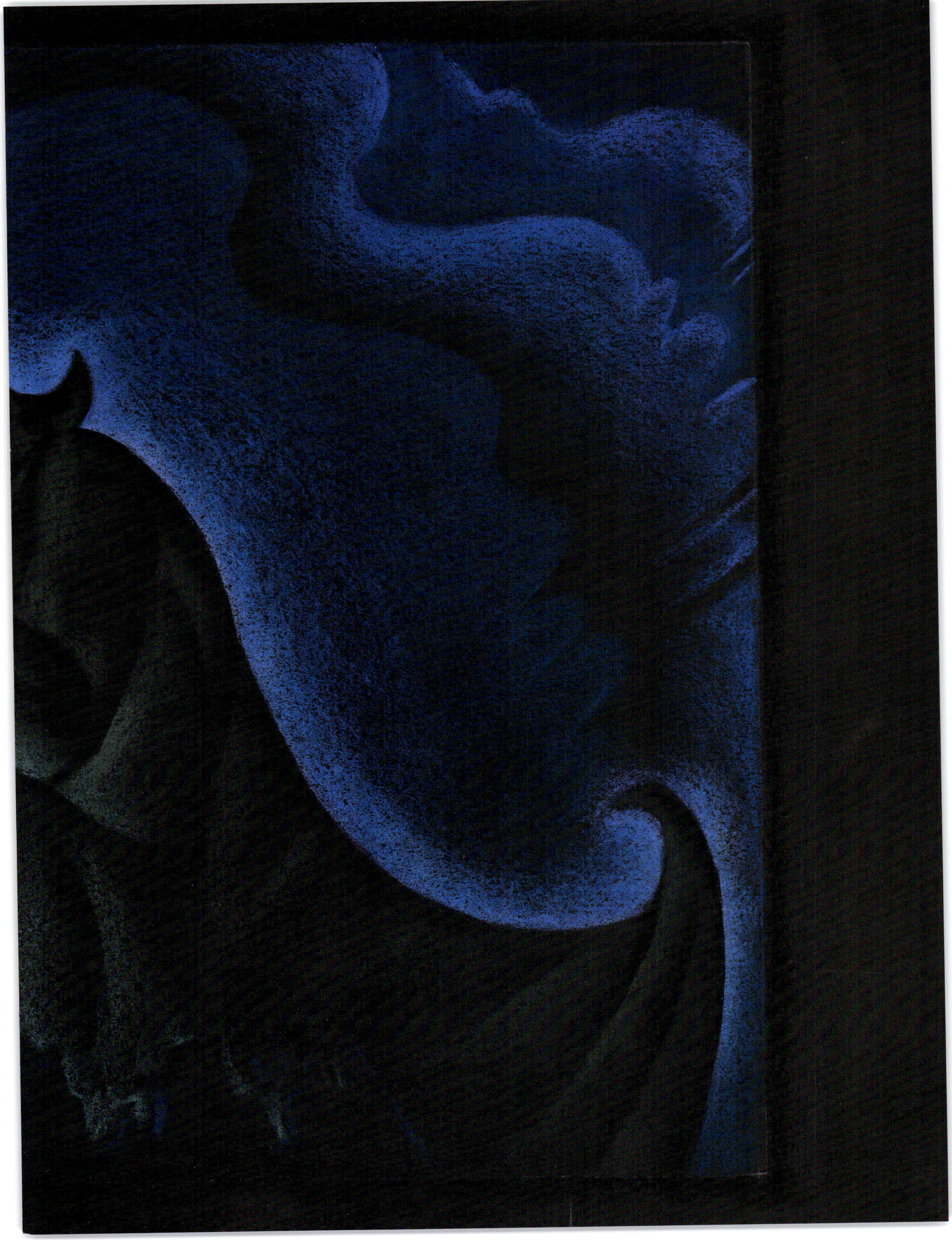

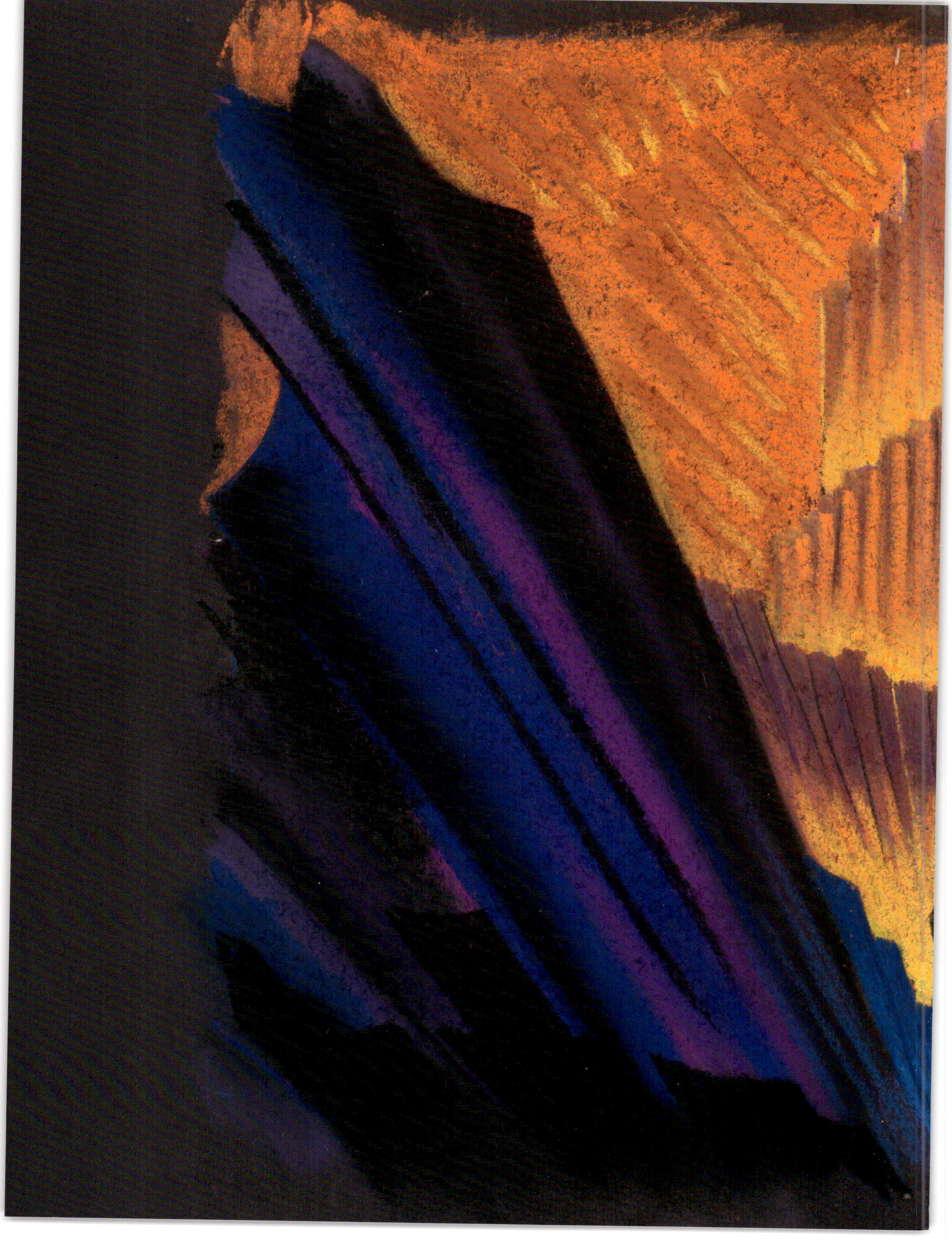

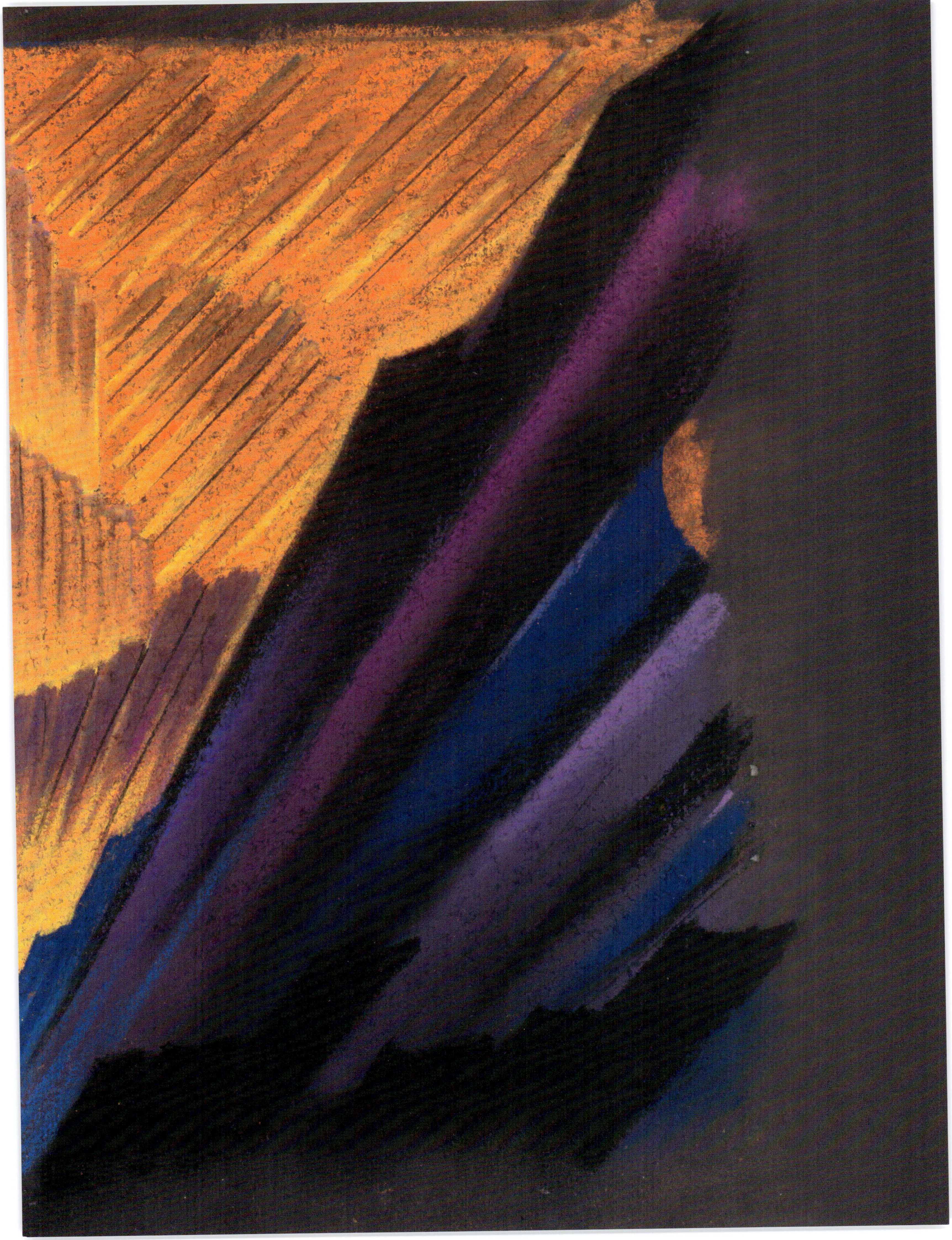

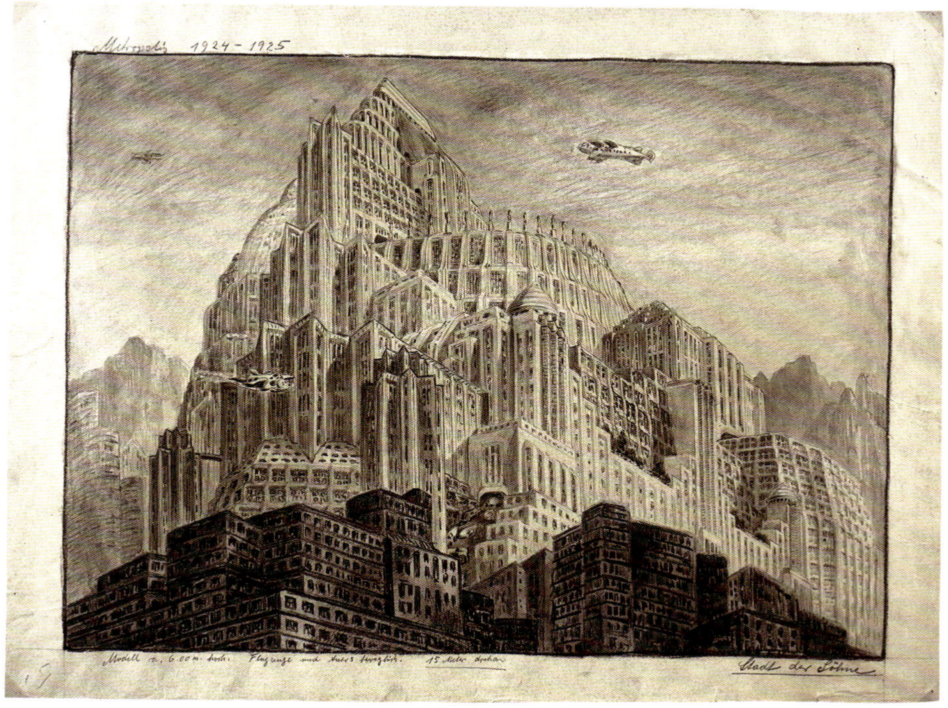

Metropolis 1924 - 1925
Stadt der Söhne


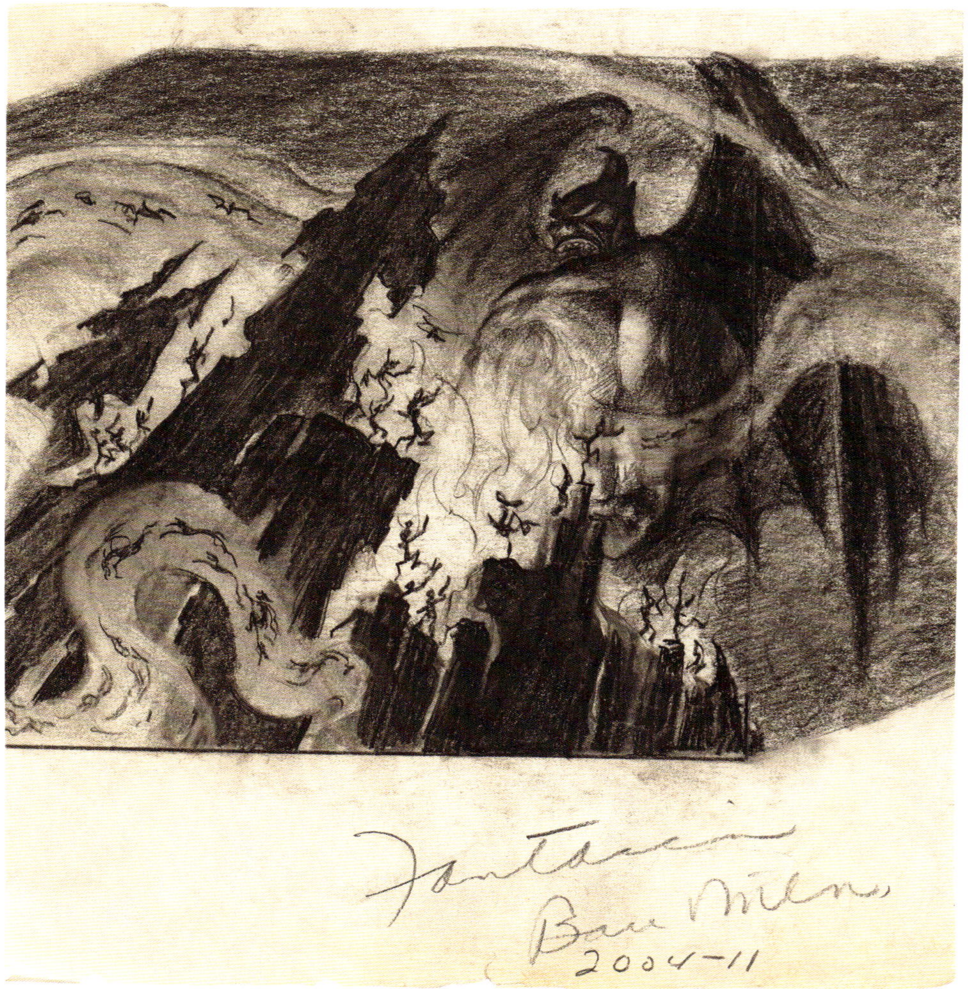

Fantasia
2004-11

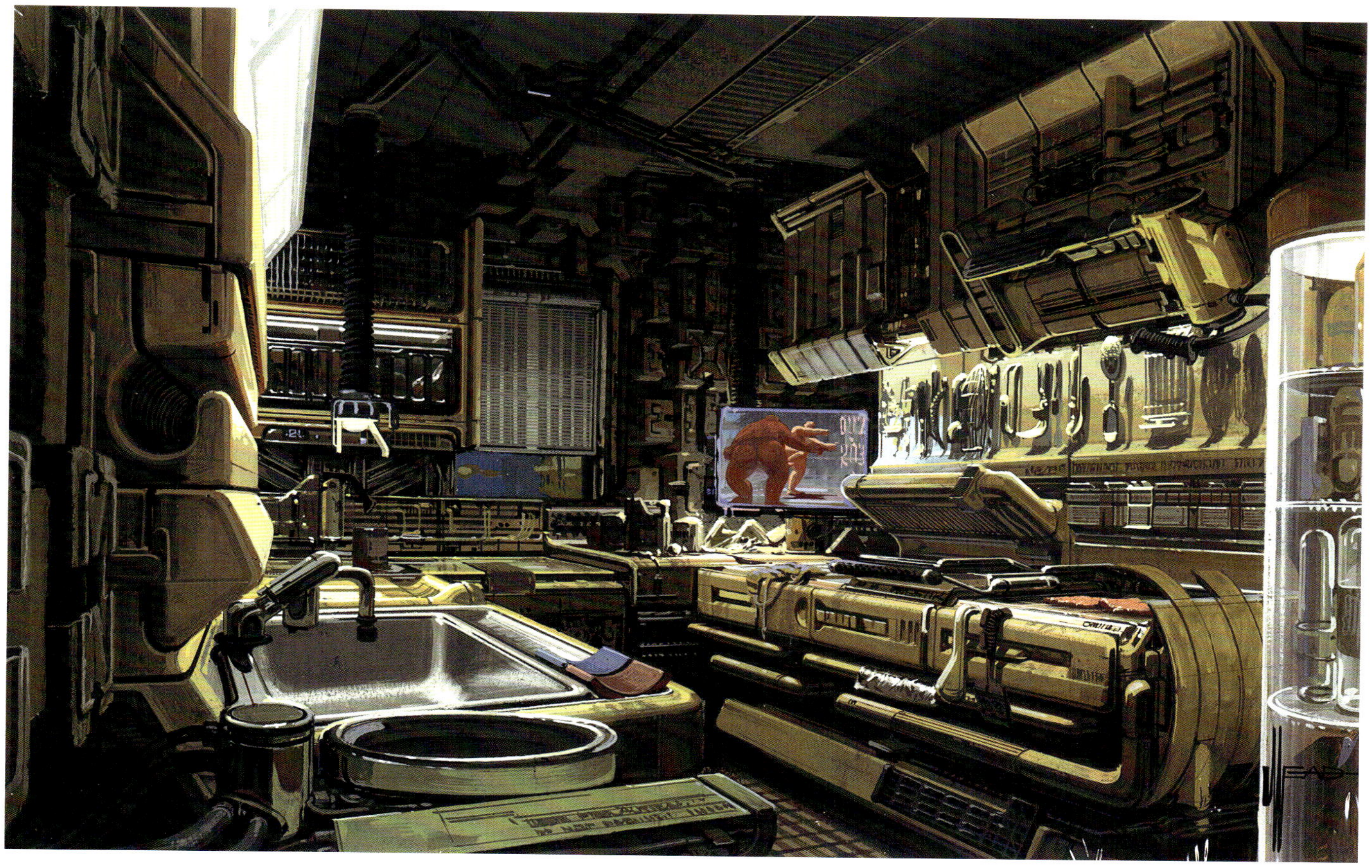

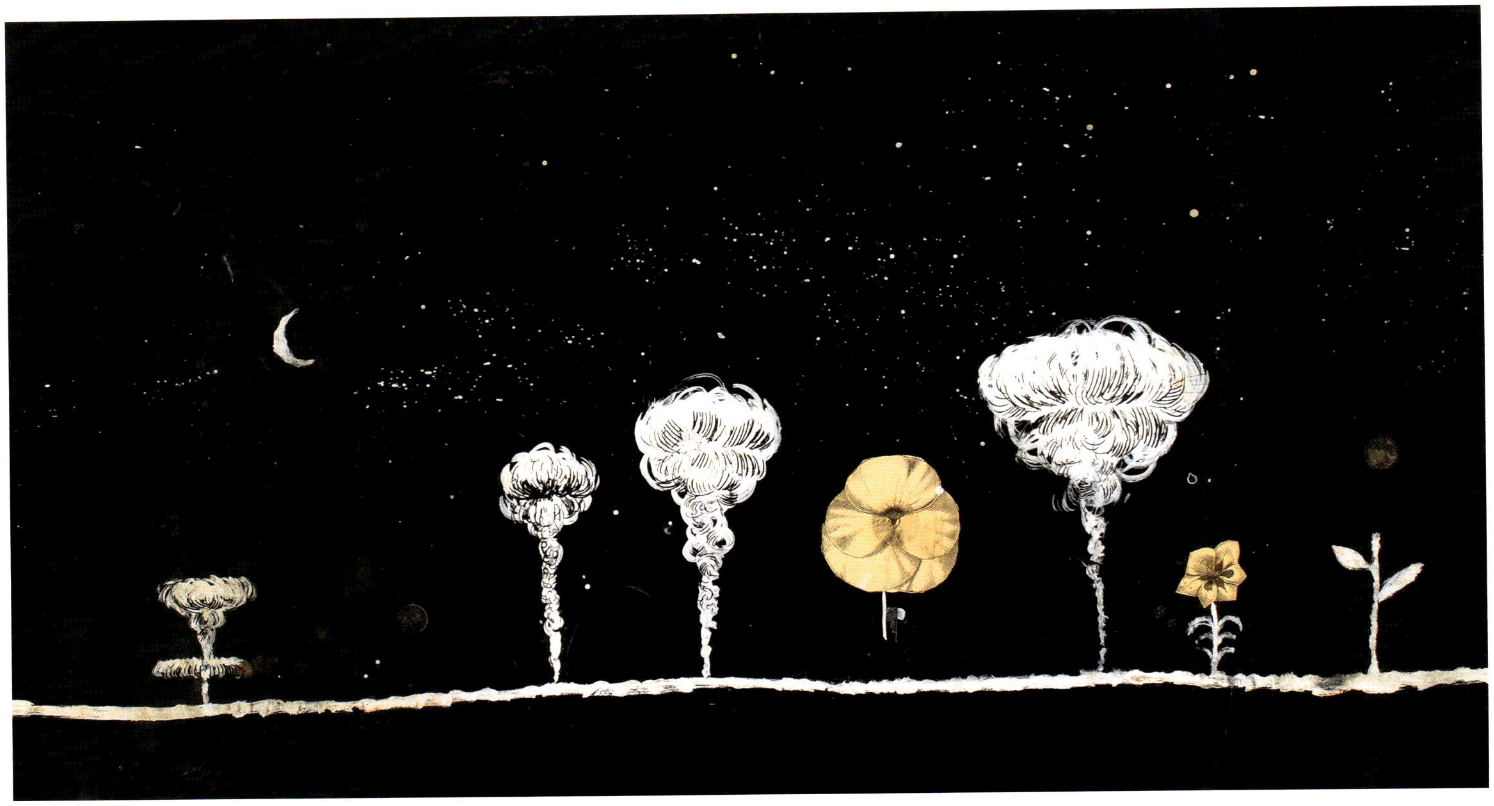

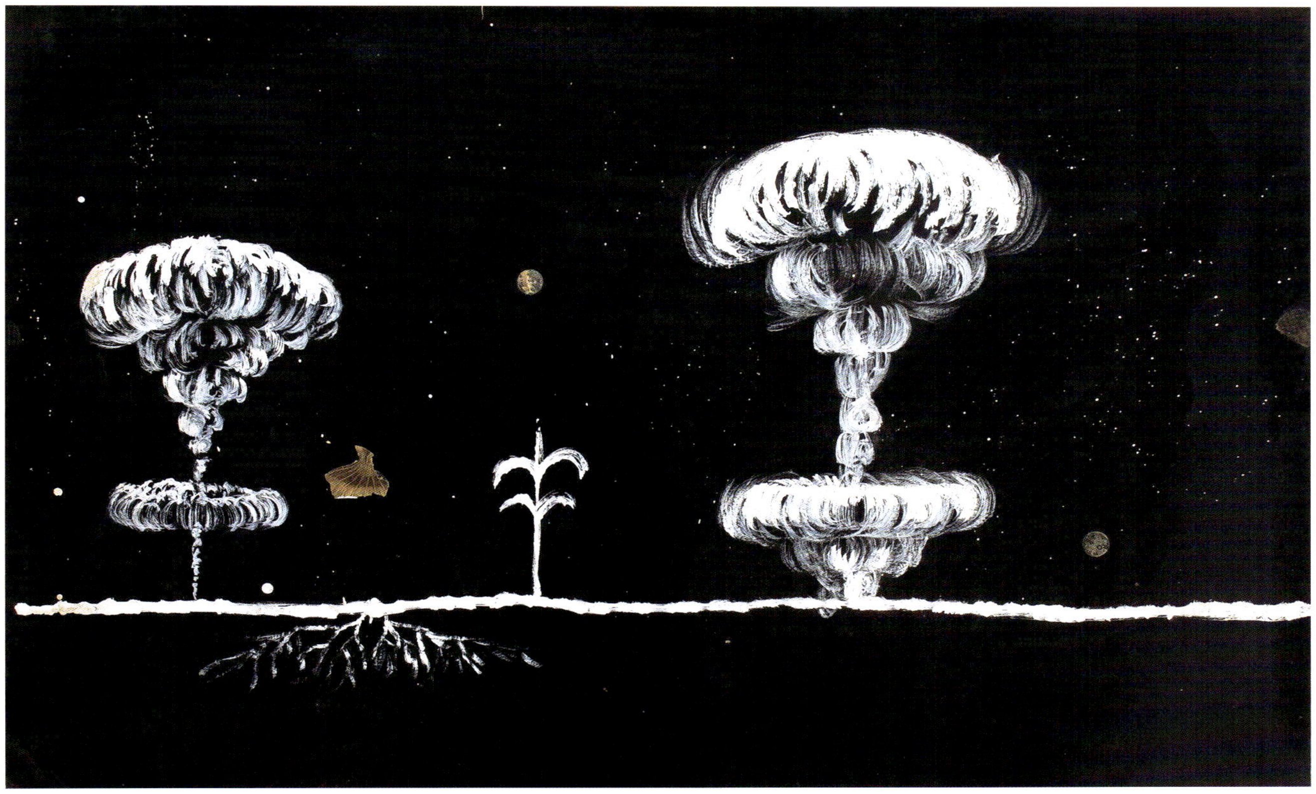

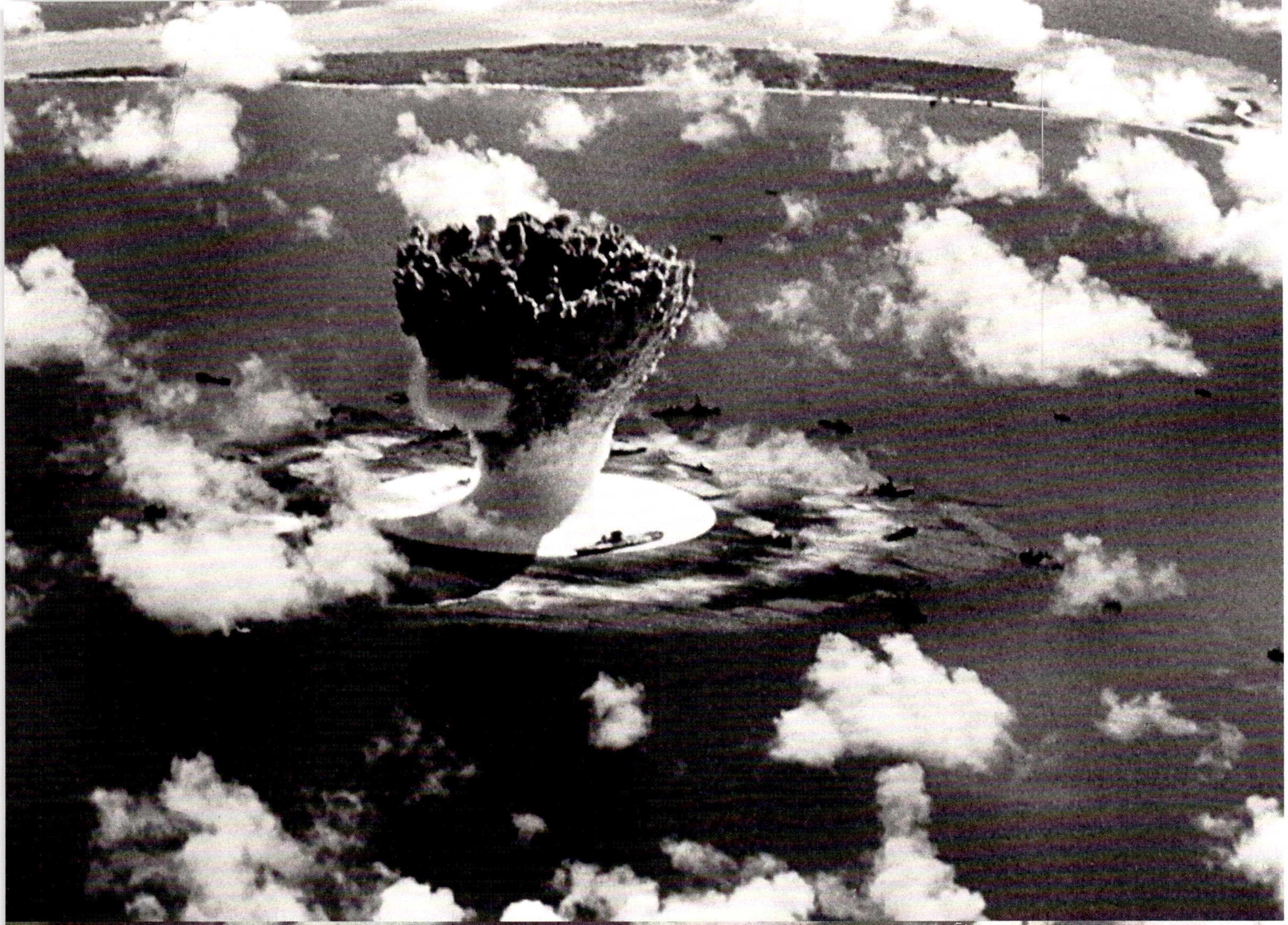

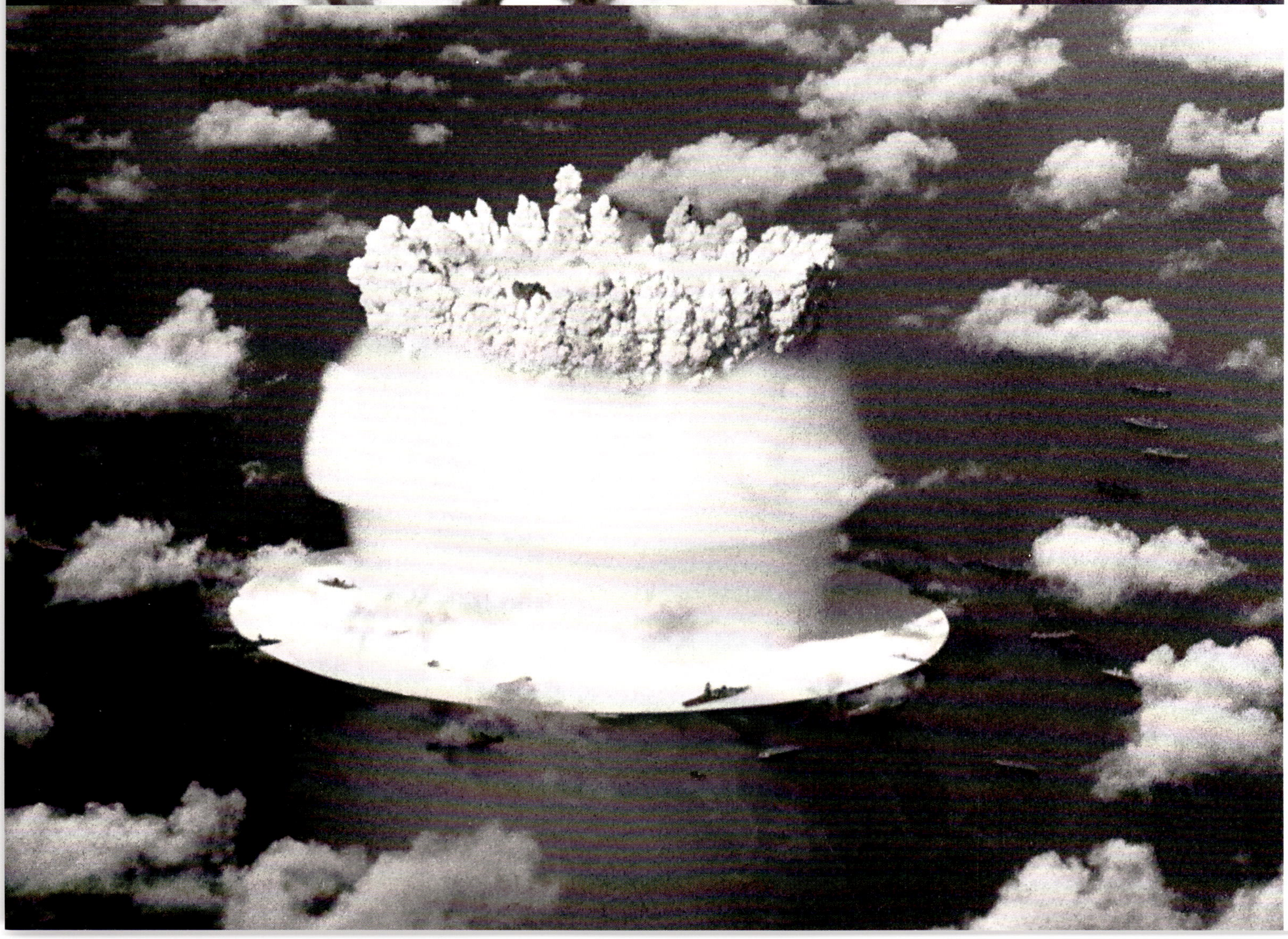

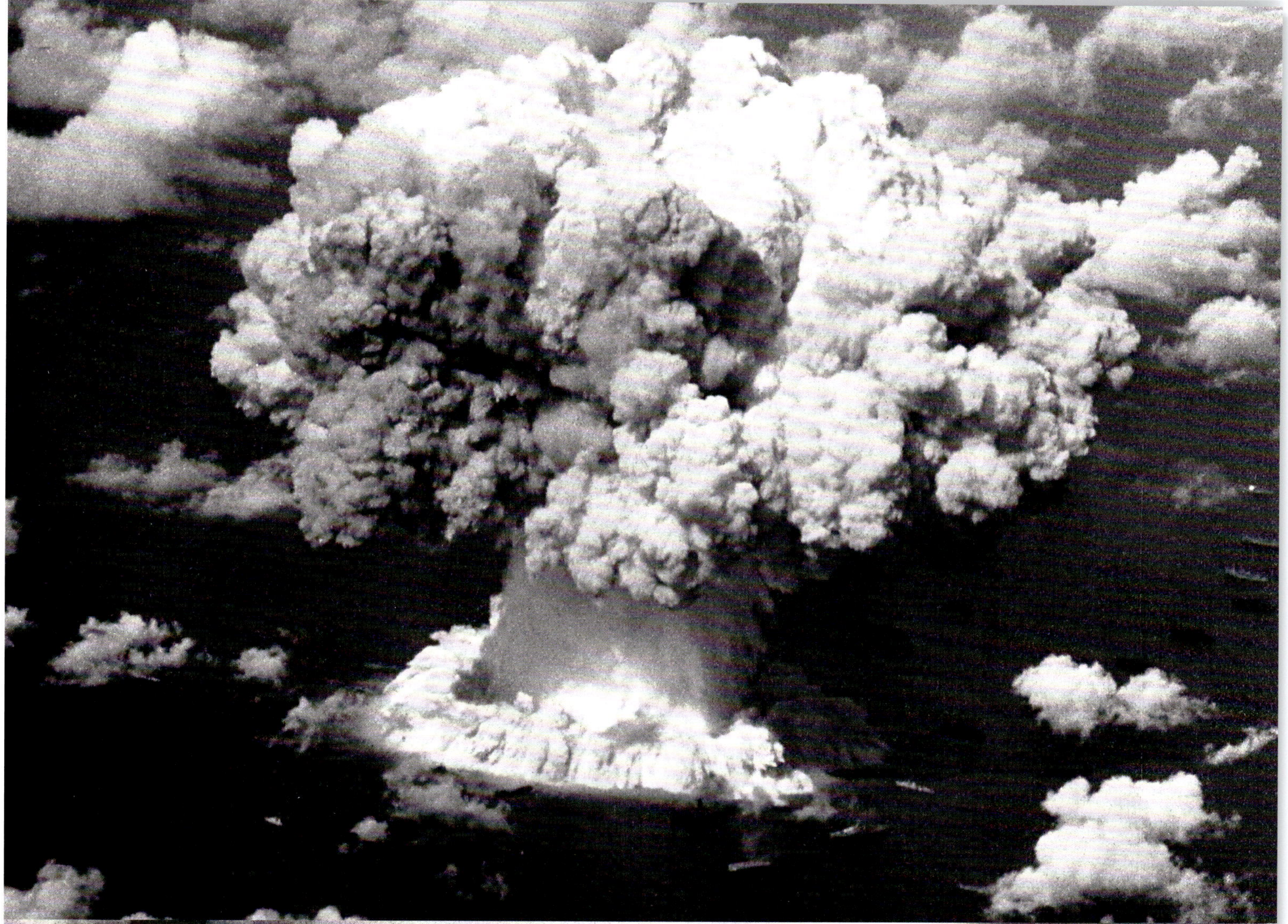

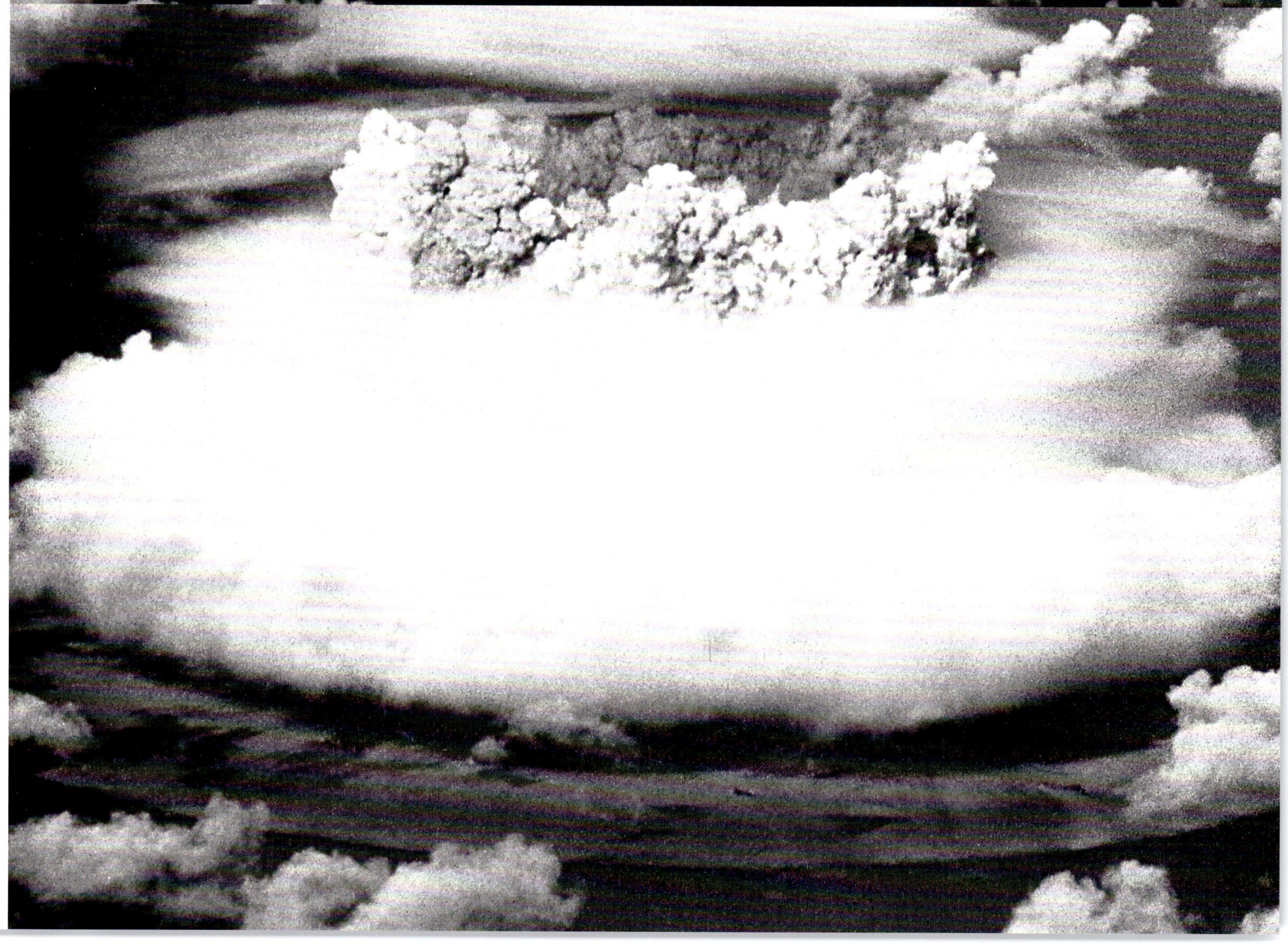

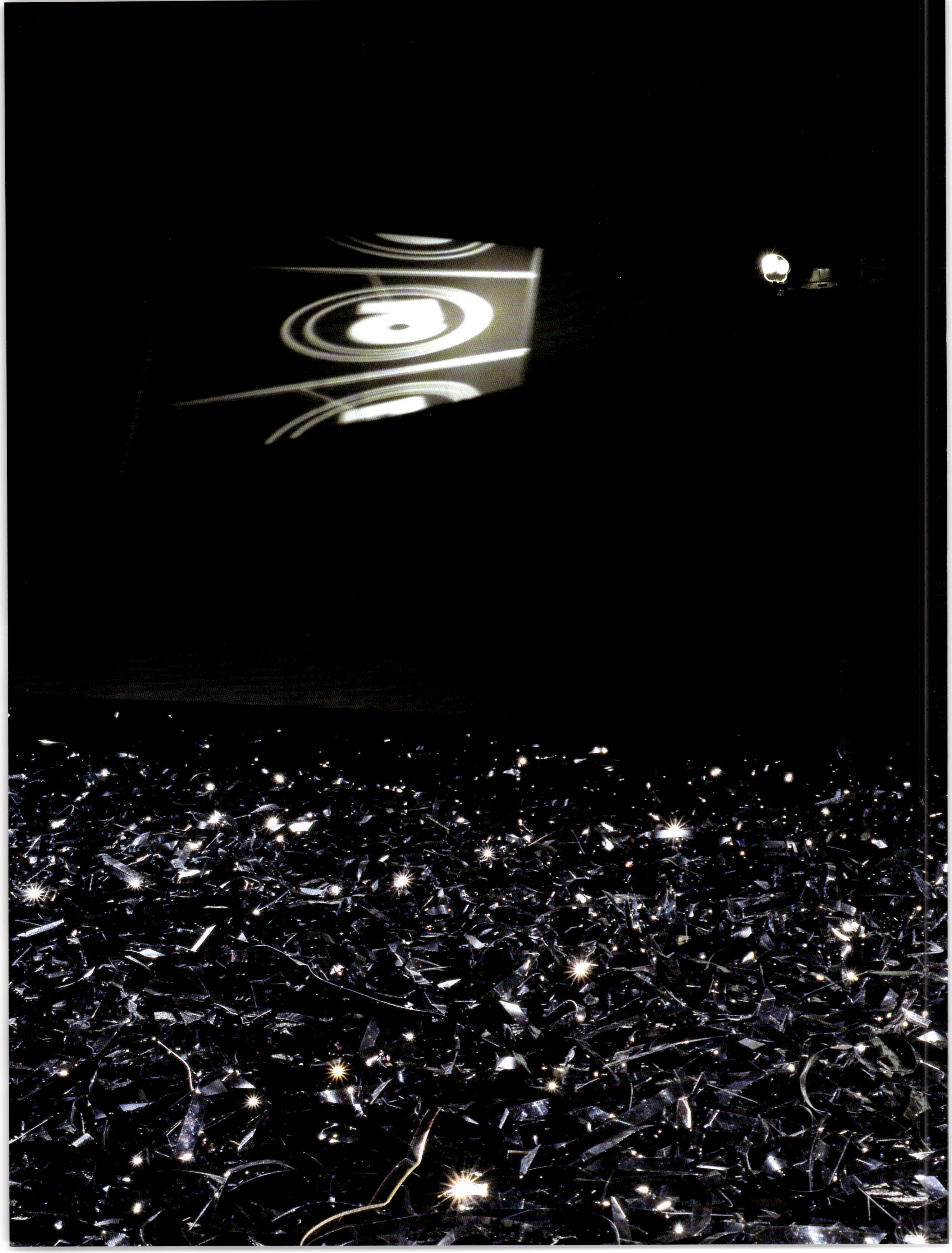

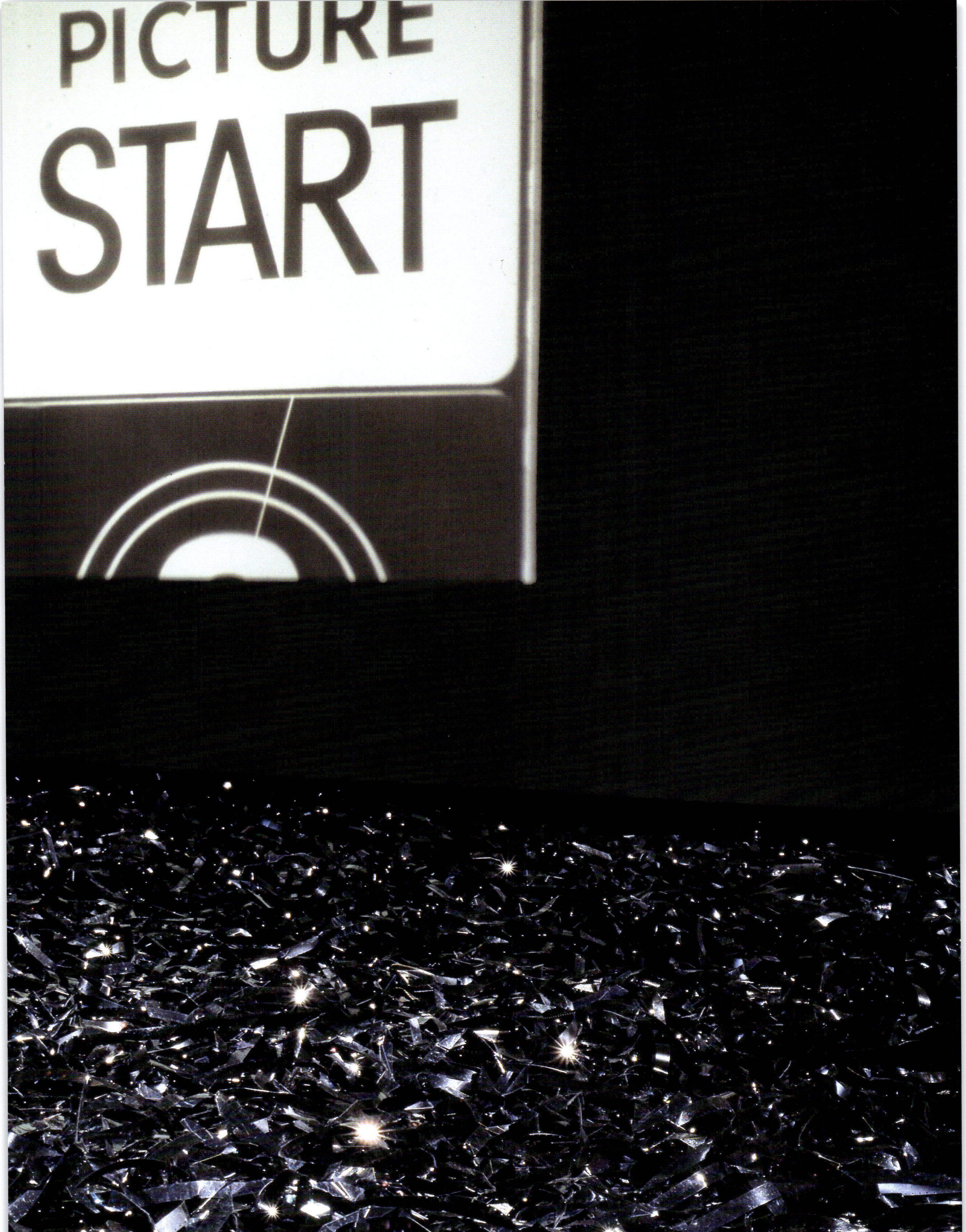
PICTURE
START

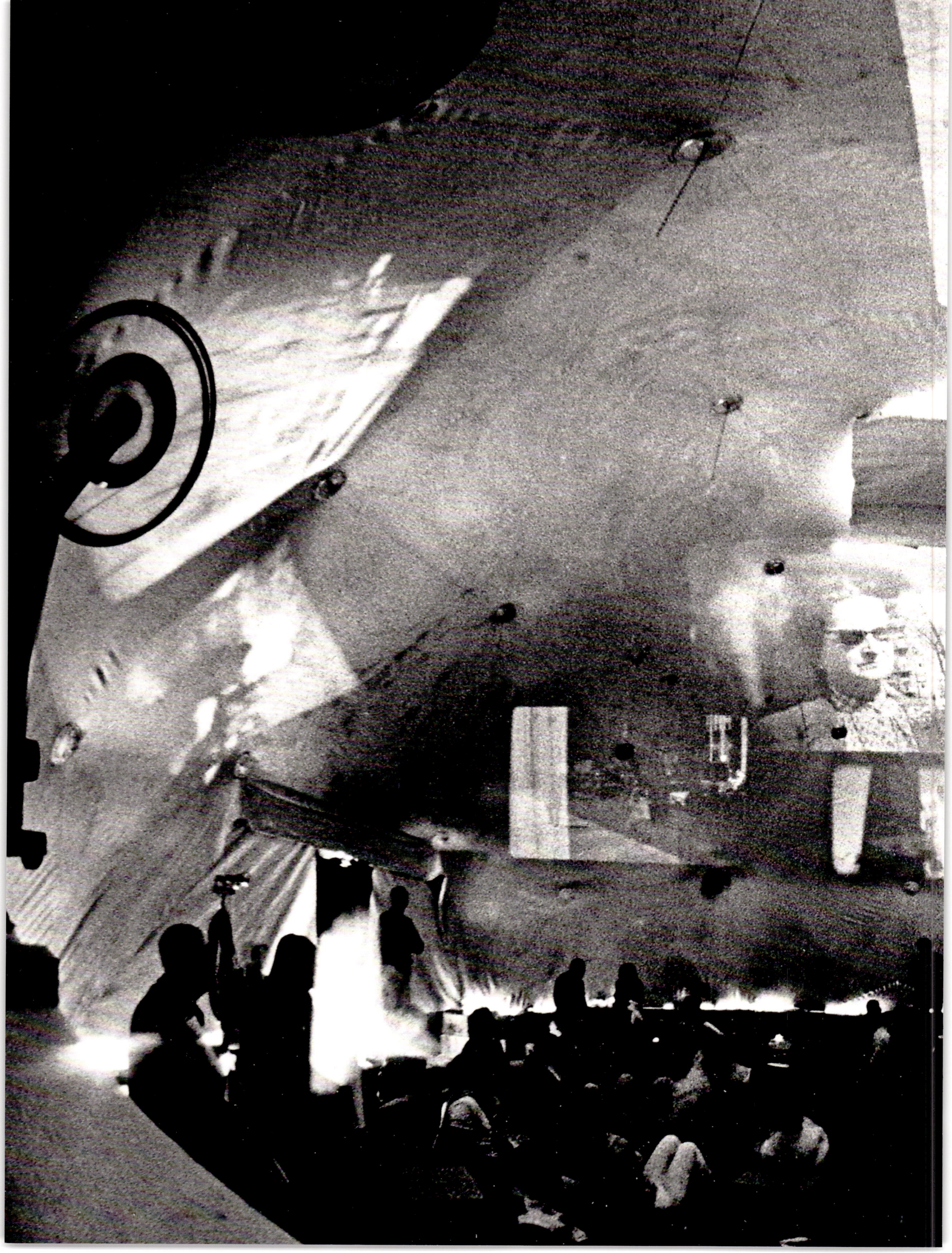

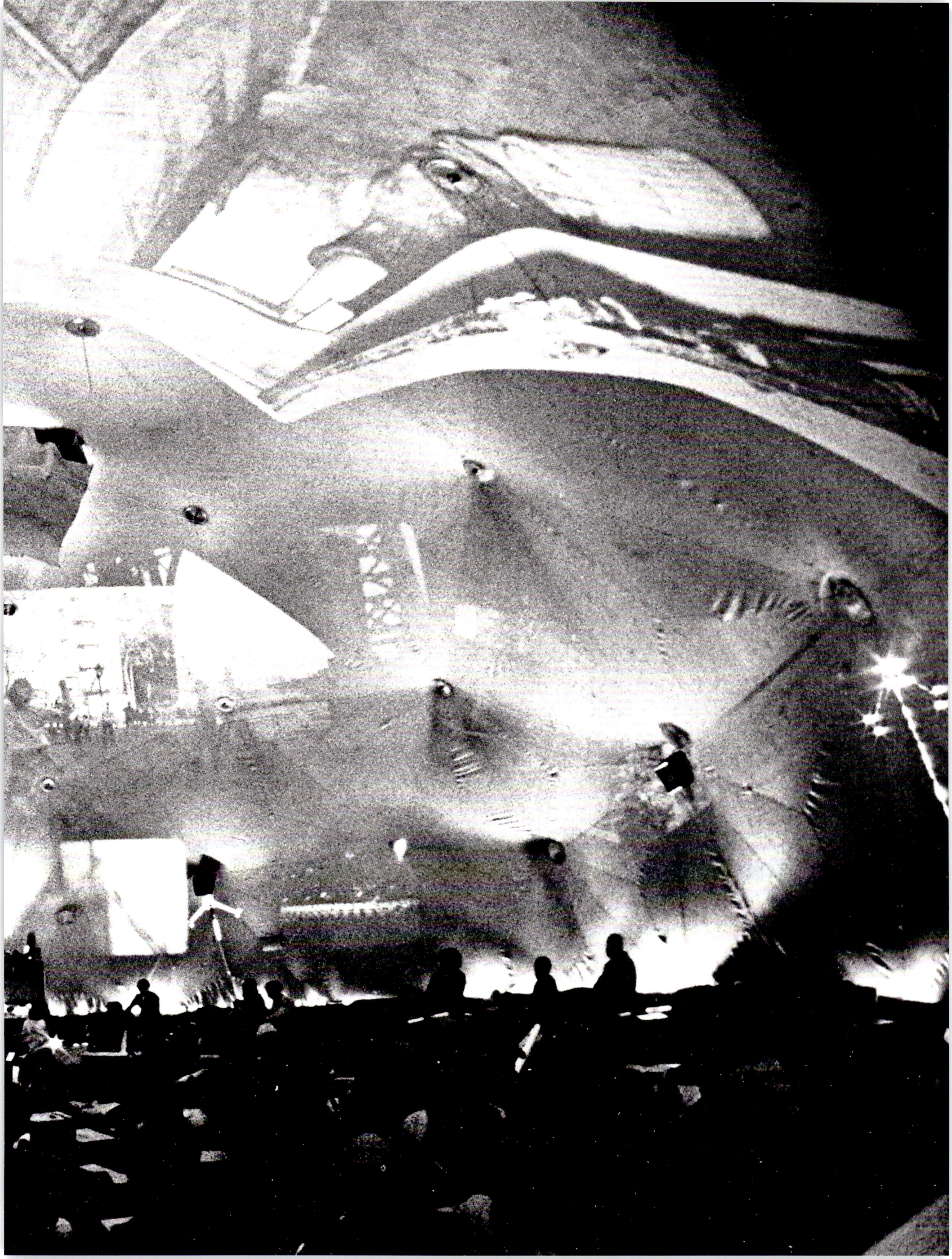

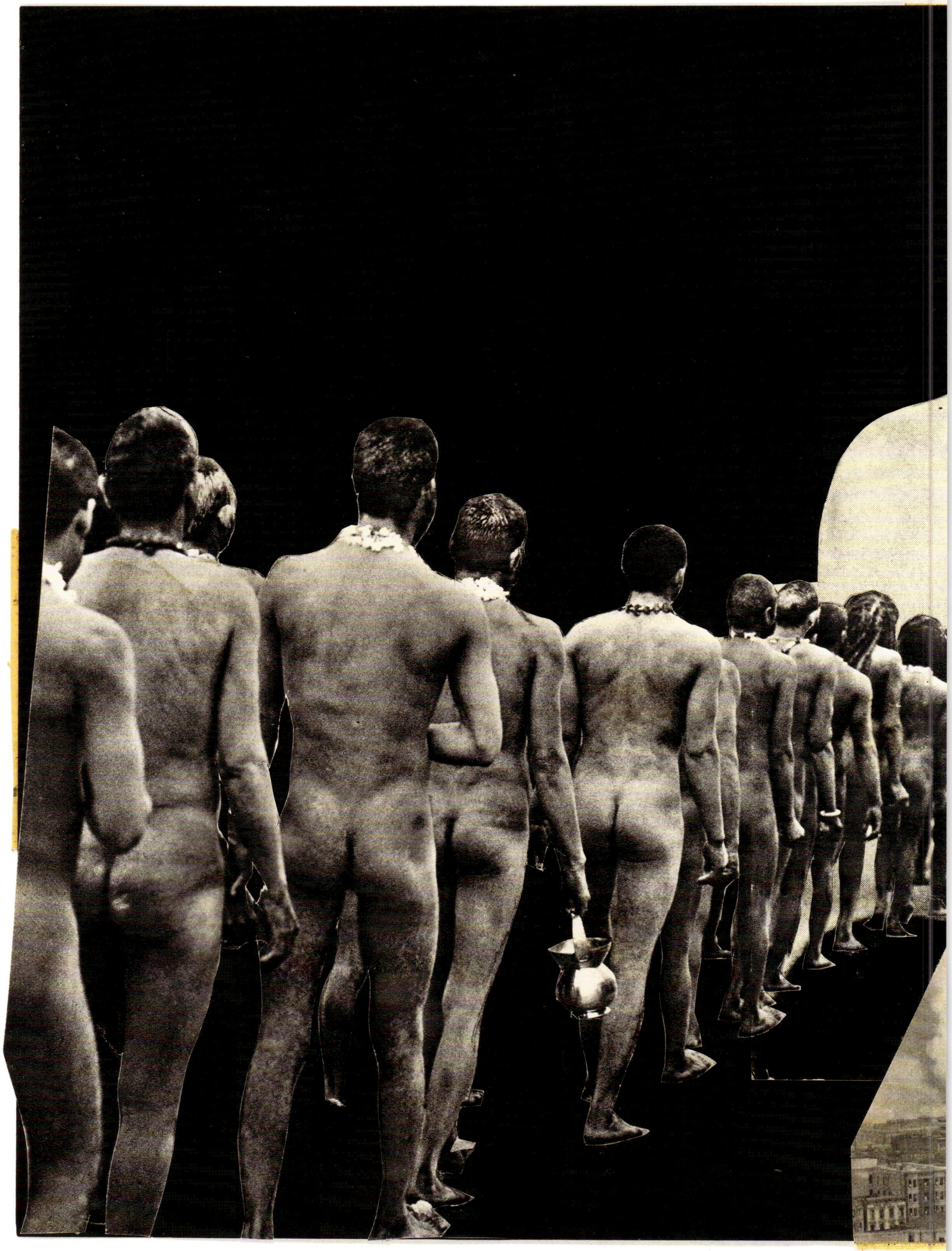

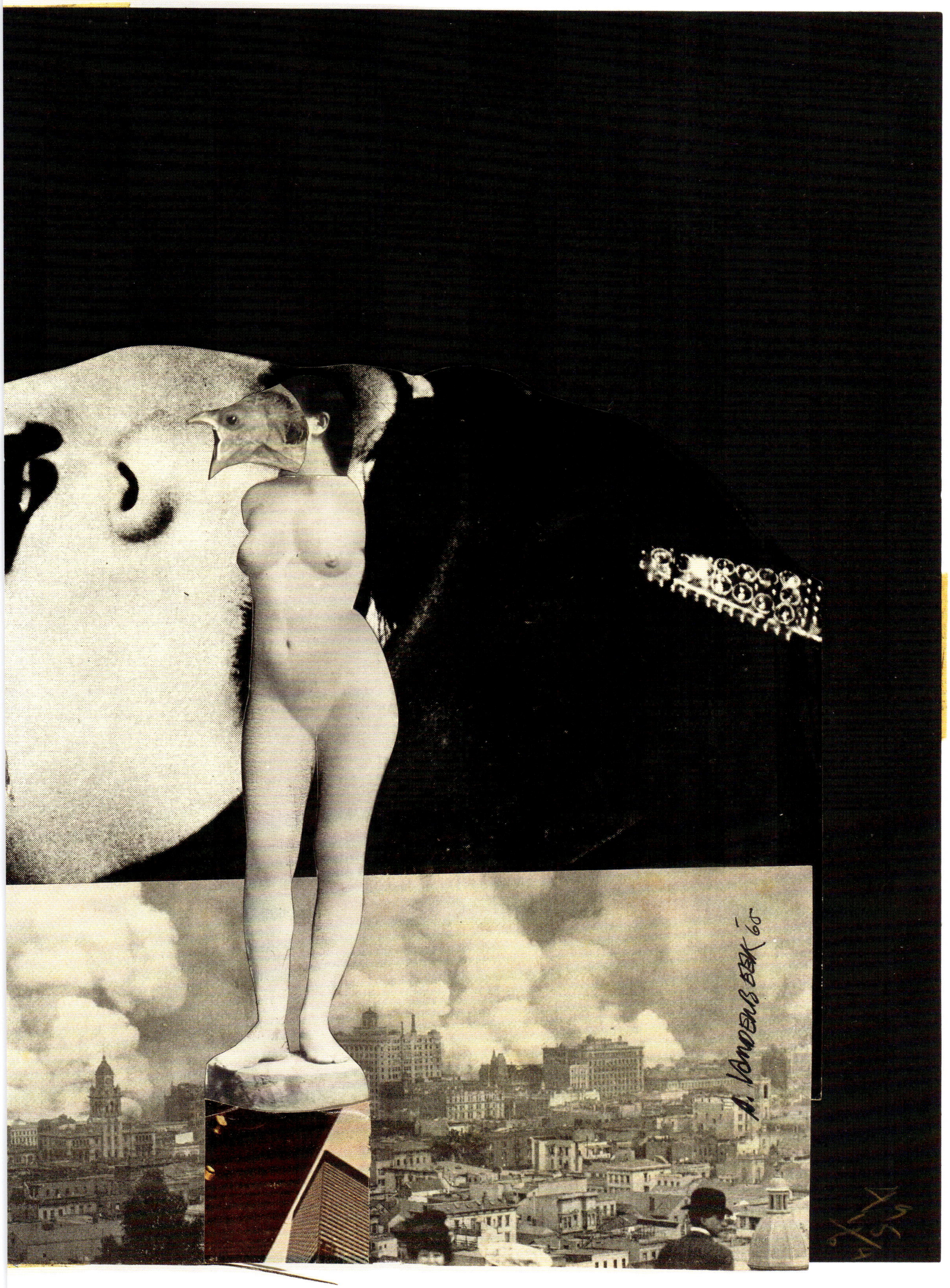
A. VANDERBEEK '65

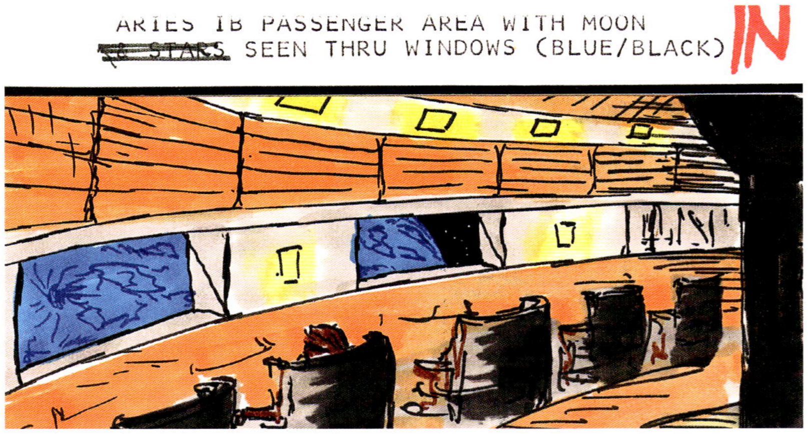
ARIES IB PASSENGER AREA WITH MOON
& STARS SEEN THRU WINDOWS (BLUE/BLACK)
IN

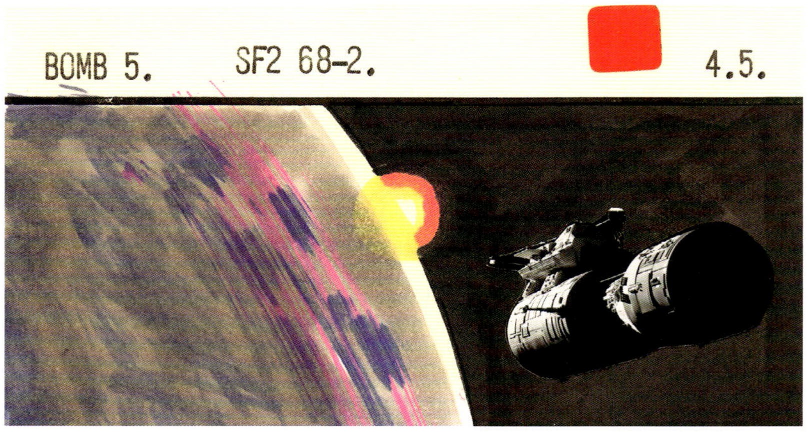
BOMB 5.
SF2 68-2.
4.5.

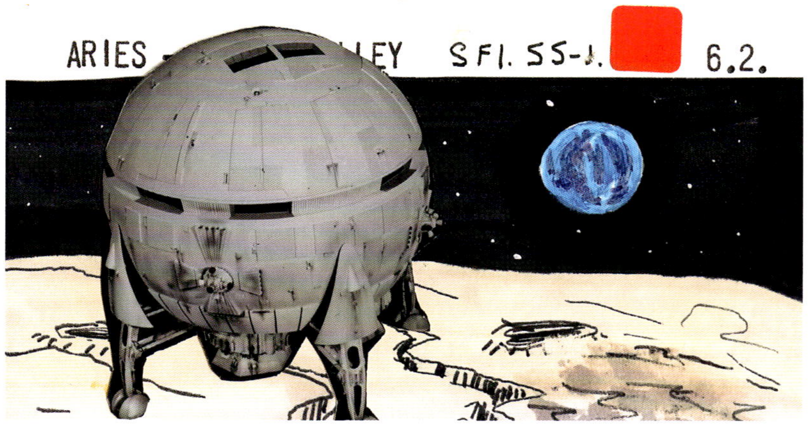
ARIES
SF1. 55-1.
6.2.

.G. = SL 84-6.
RIES COCKPIT POV – CLAVIUS BASE. 6.4A.

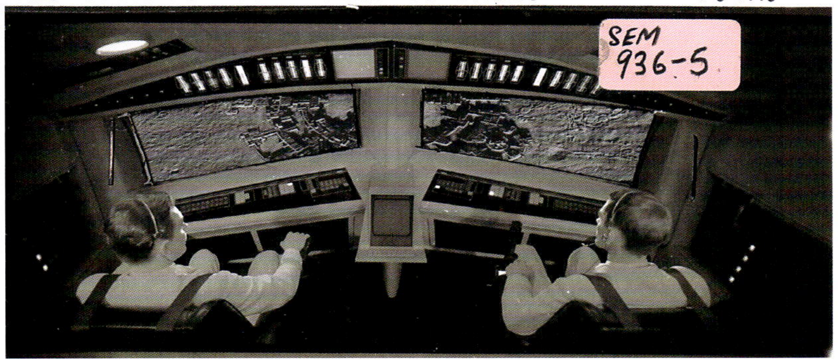


BOMB 1. SF2 67-3. 4.1.

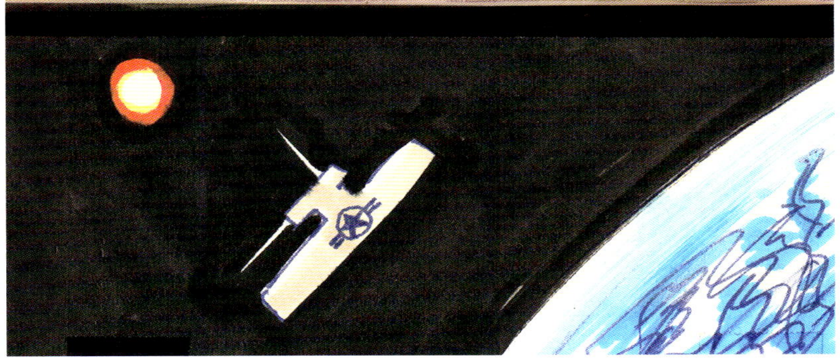

EARTH = AS 819.
ORION FLY BY NO 2. SF2 255-1. 4.6A.

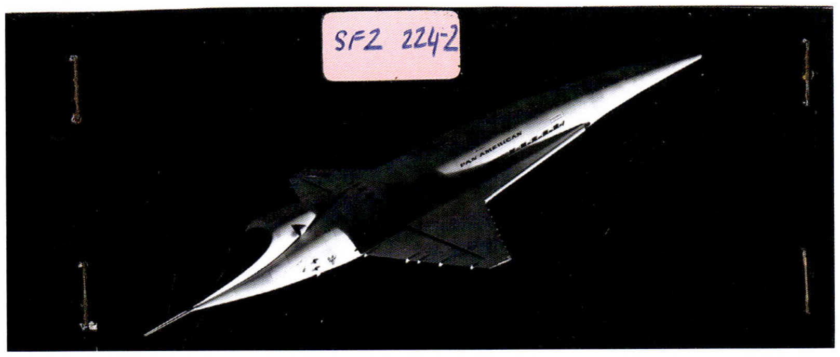

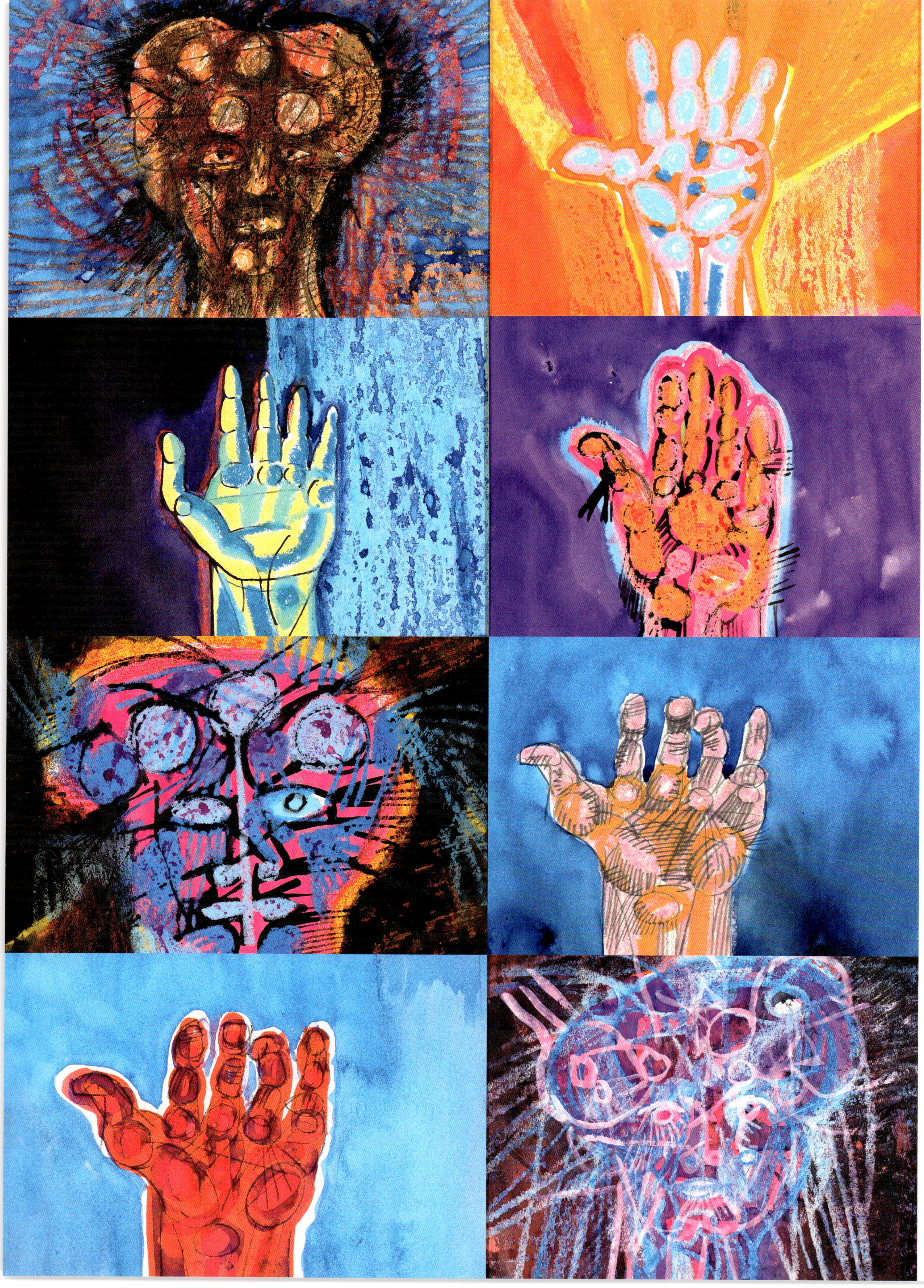

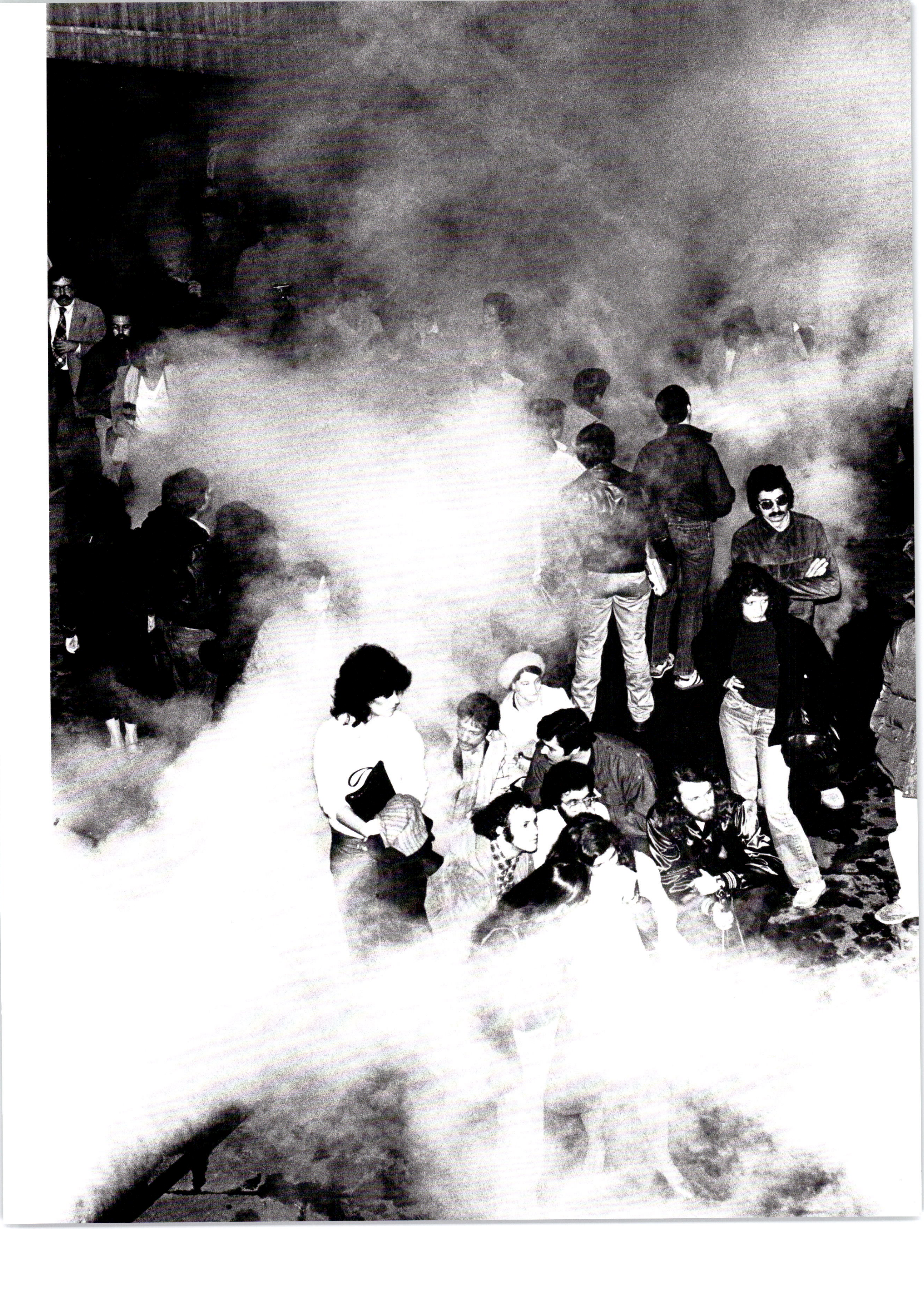

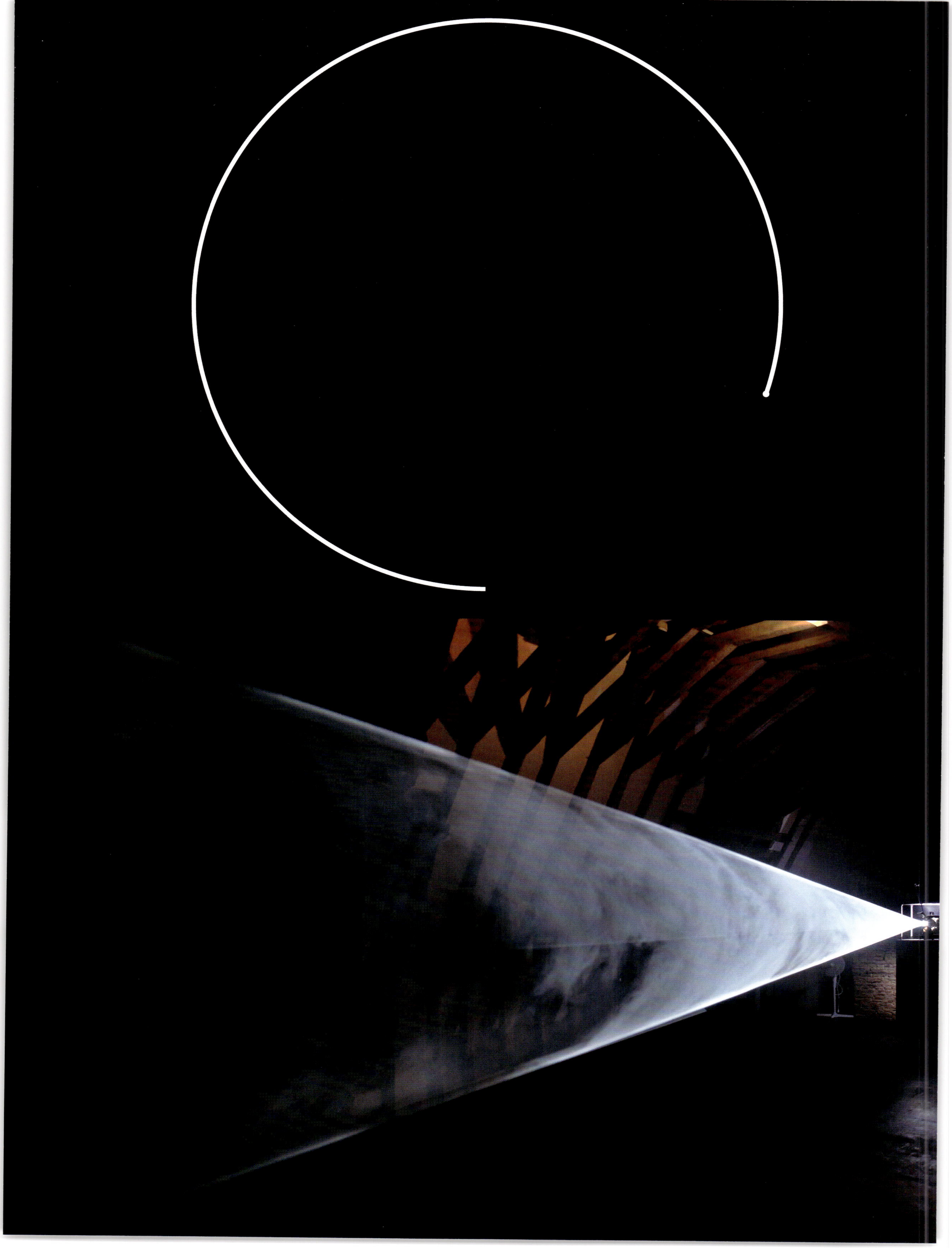

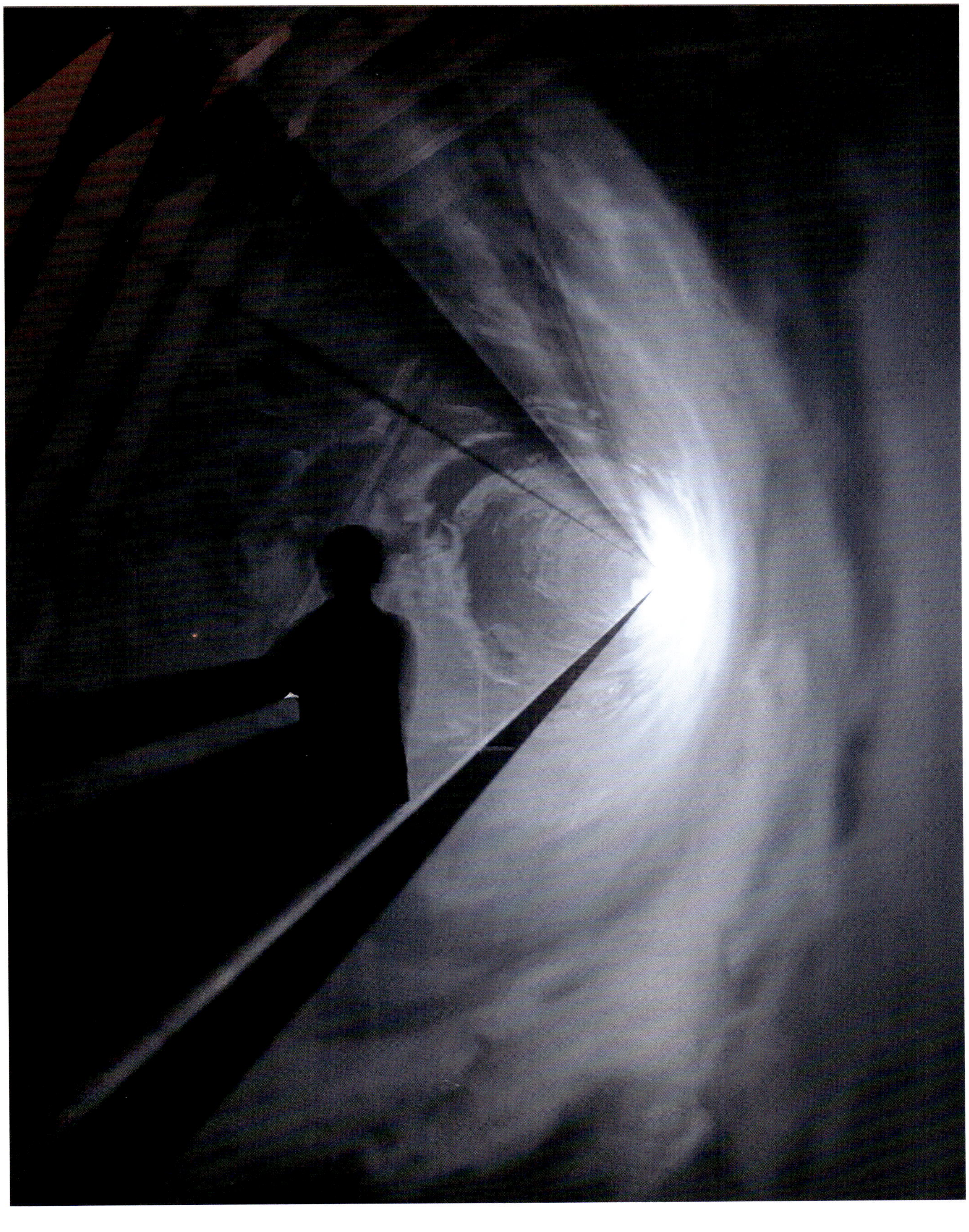

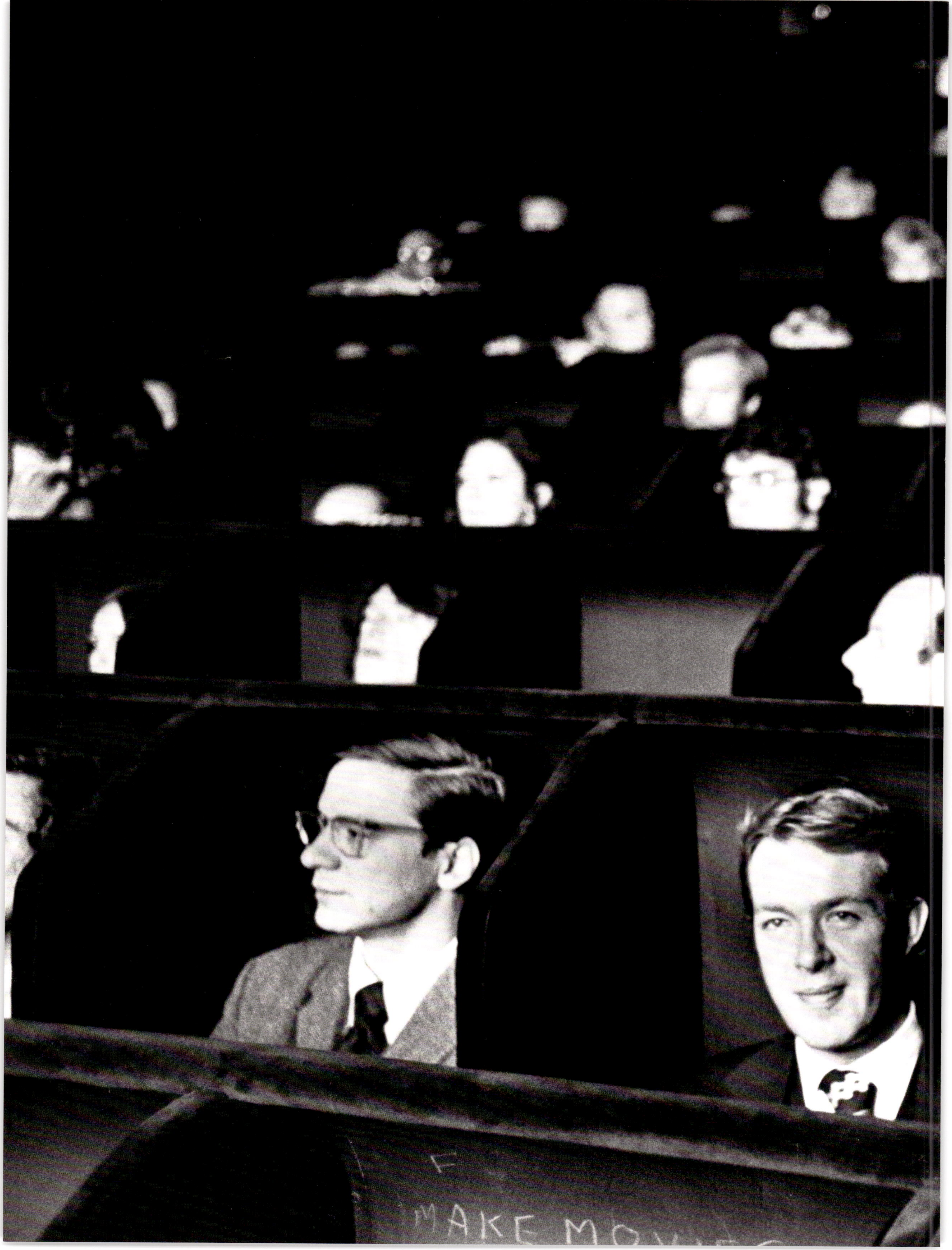
MAKE MOV

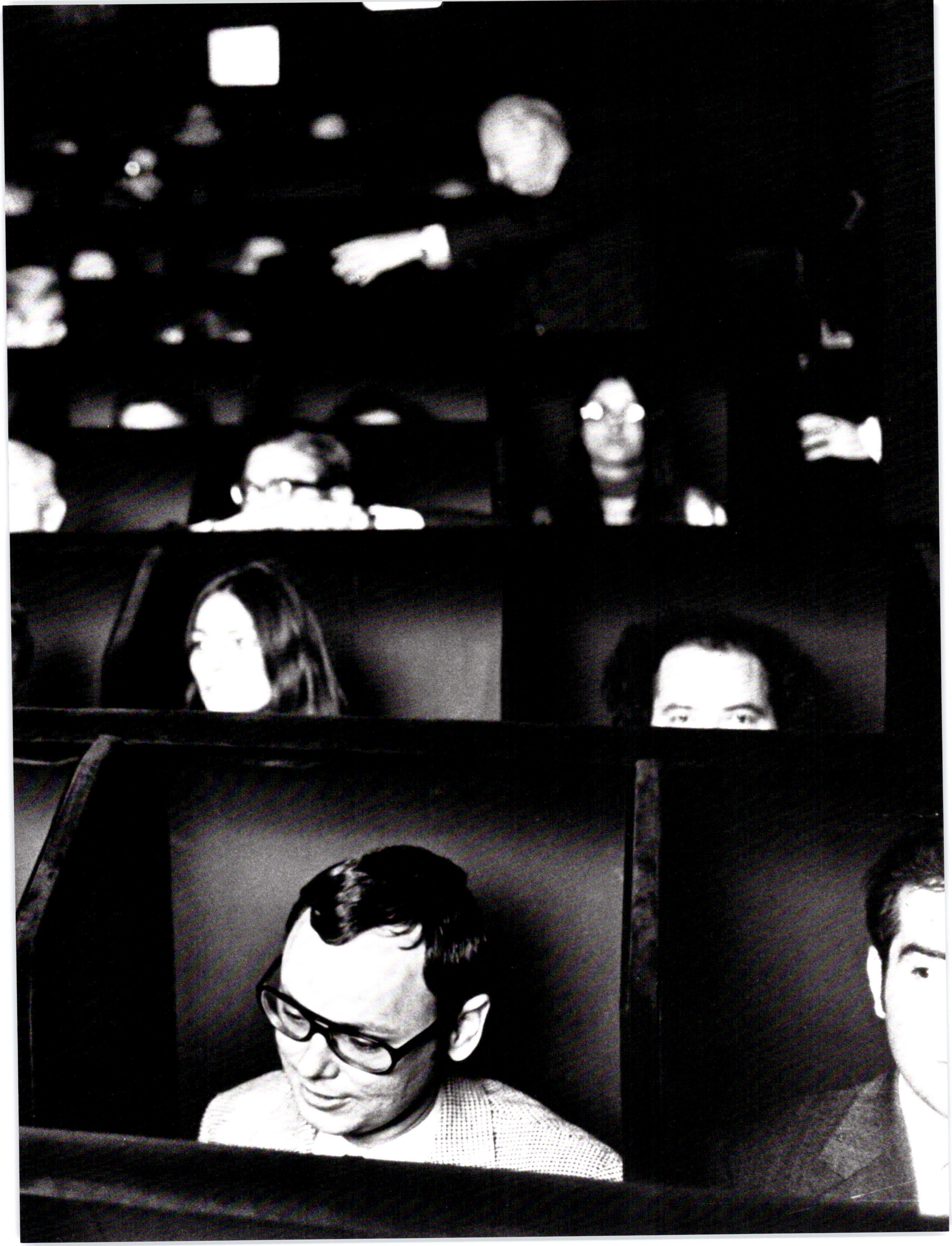

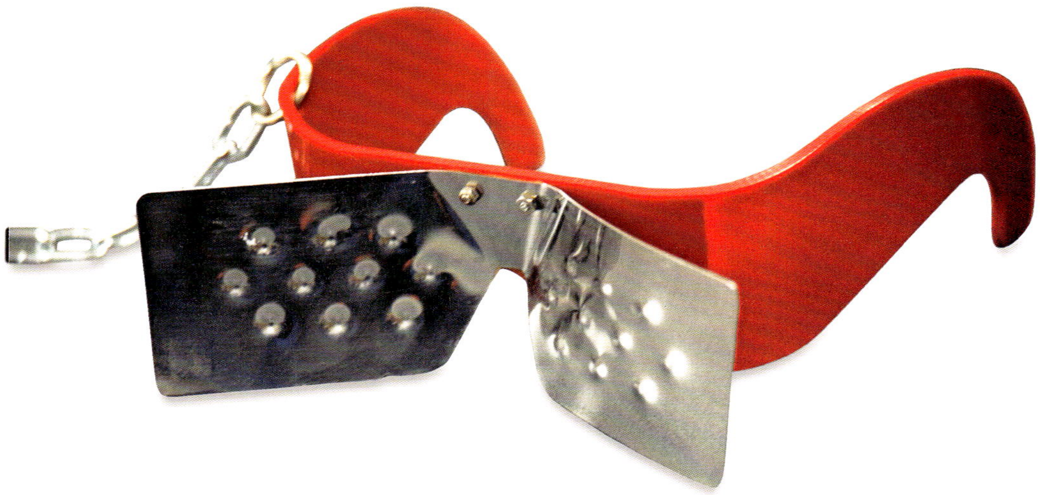

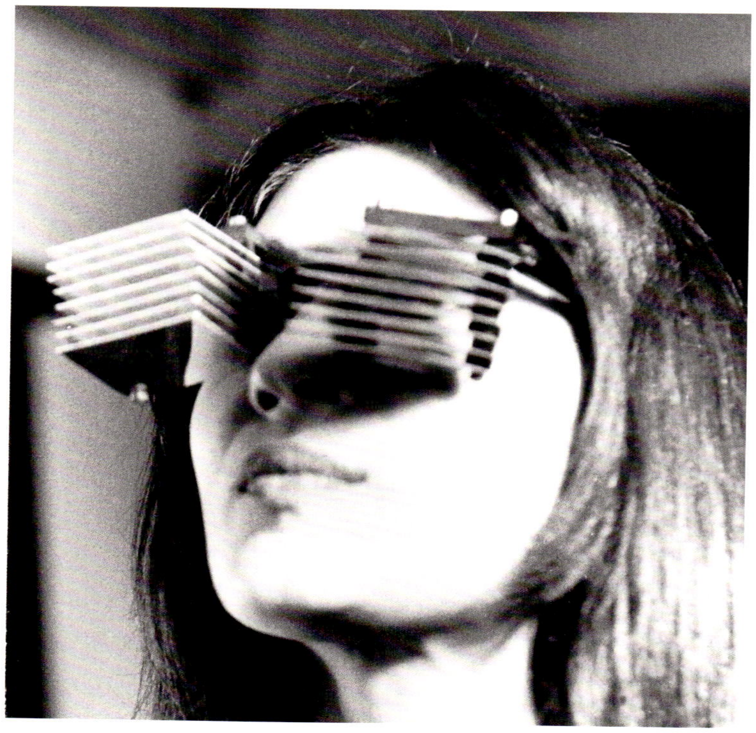

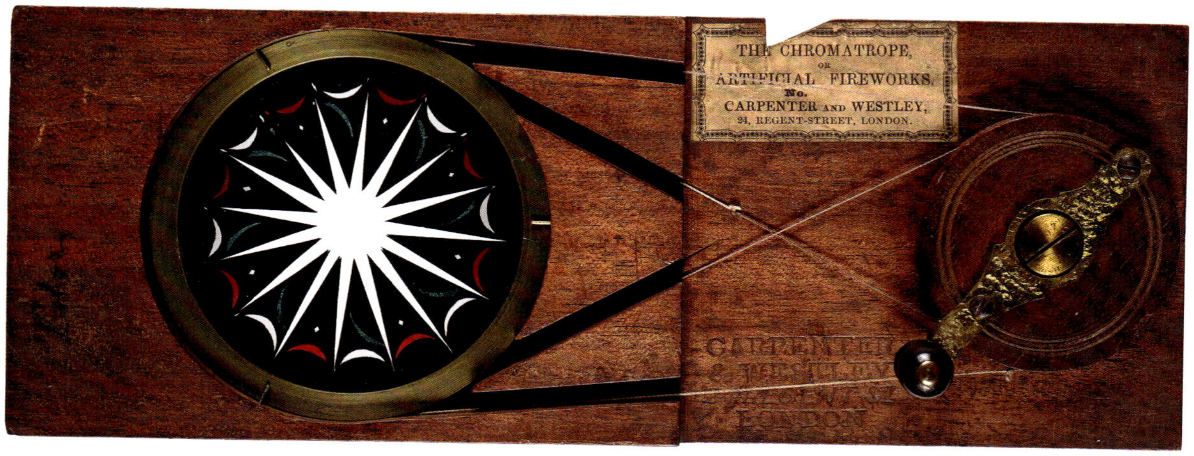
THE CHROMATROPE,
OR
ARTIFICIAL FIREWORKS.
No.
CARPENTER AND WESTLEY,
24, REGENT-STREET, LONDON.

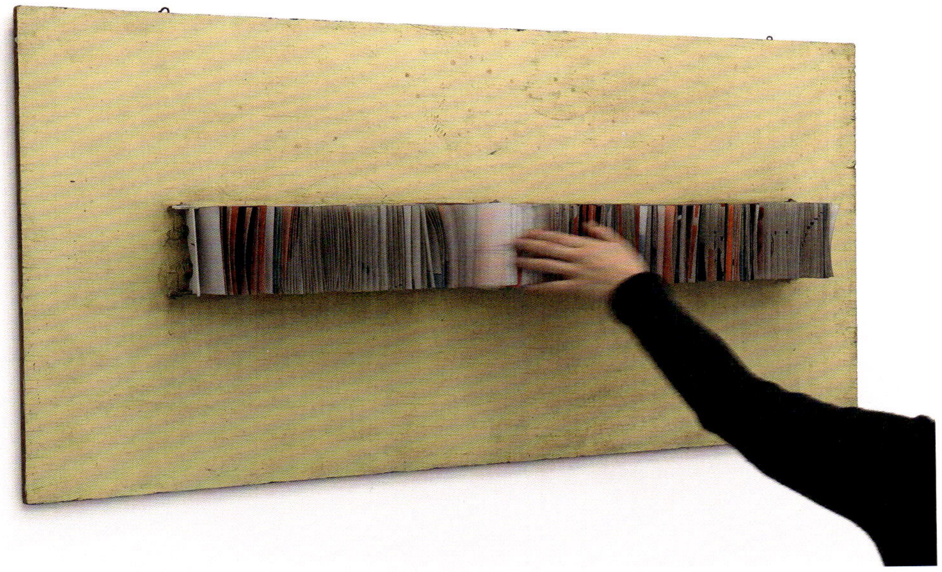

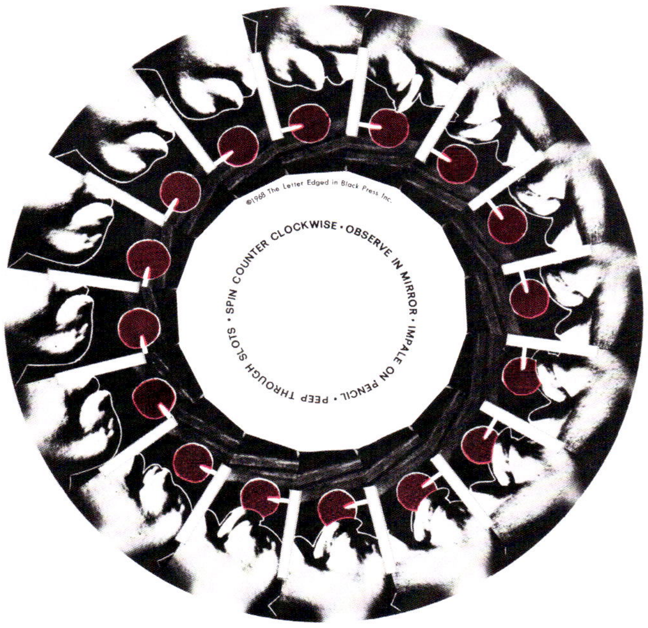
©1968 The Letter Edged in Black Press Inc.
SPIN COUNTER CLOCKWISE • OBSERVE IN MIRROR • IMPALE ON PENCIL • PEEP THROUGH SLOTS •

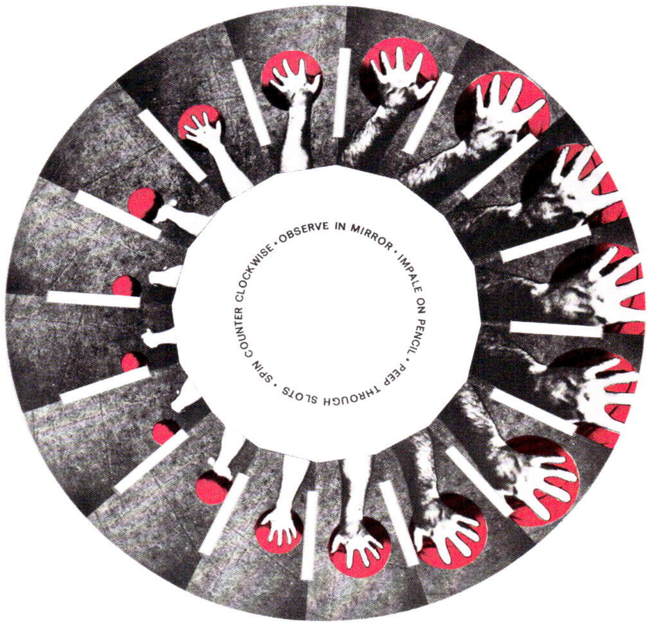
SPIN COUNTER CLOCKWISE • OBSERVE IN MIRROR • IMPALE ON PENCIL • PEEP THROUGH SLOTS •

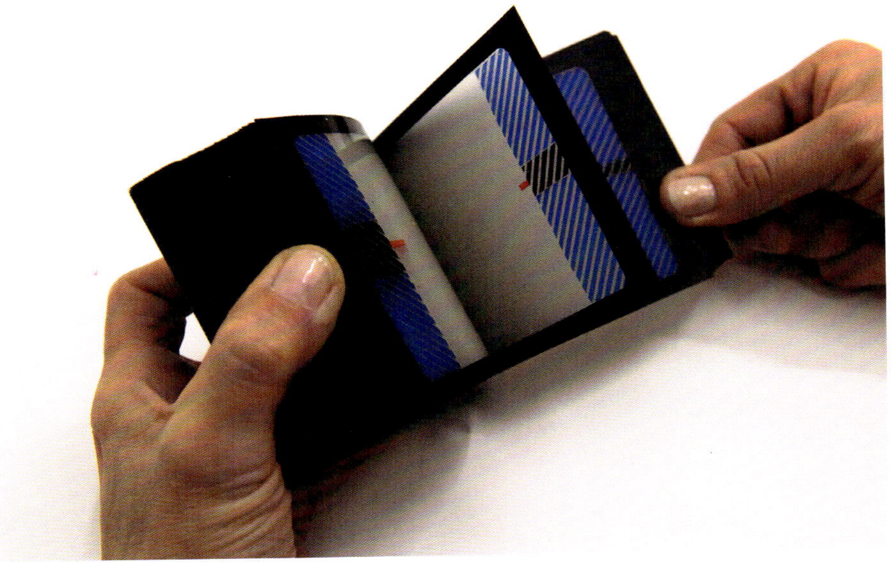

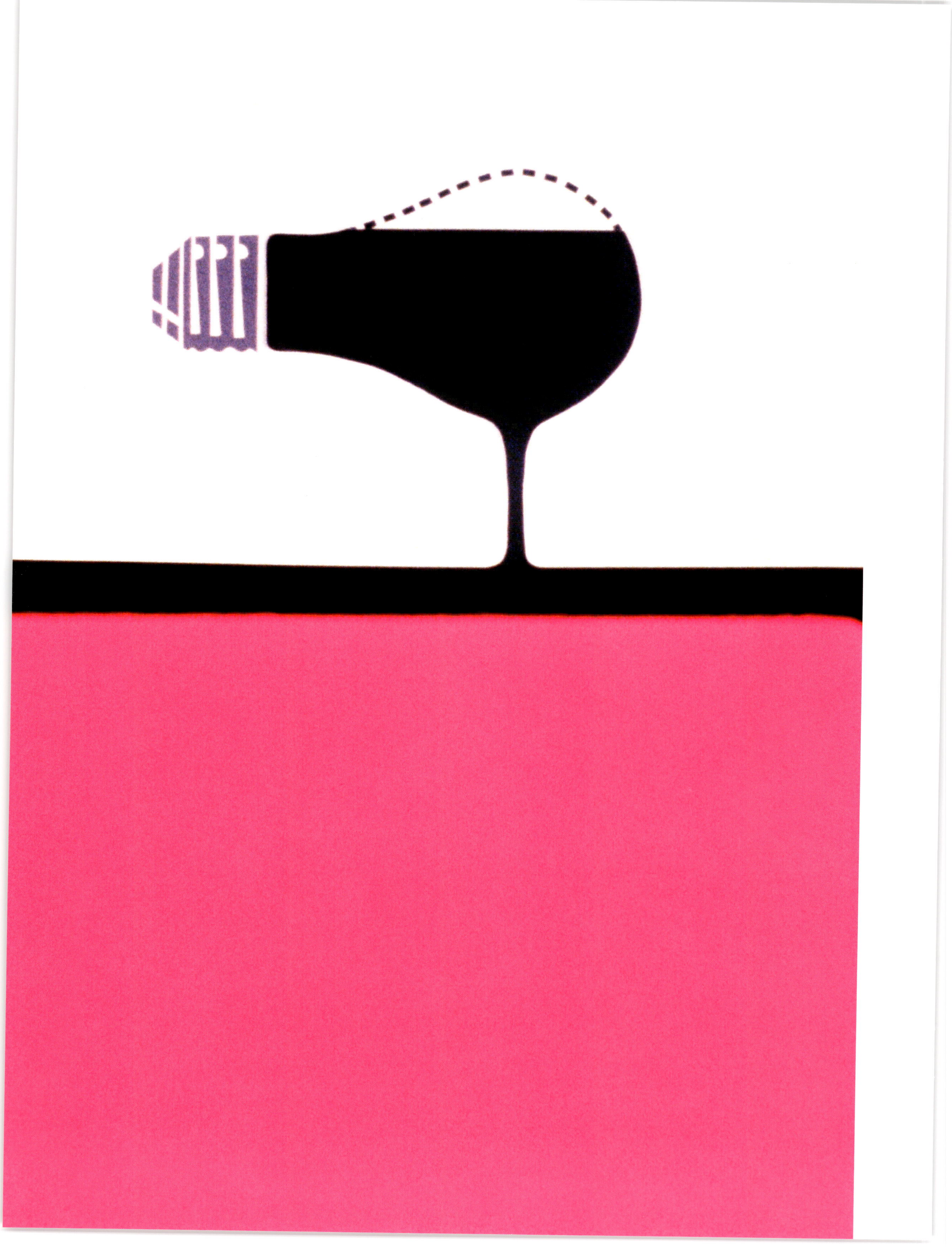

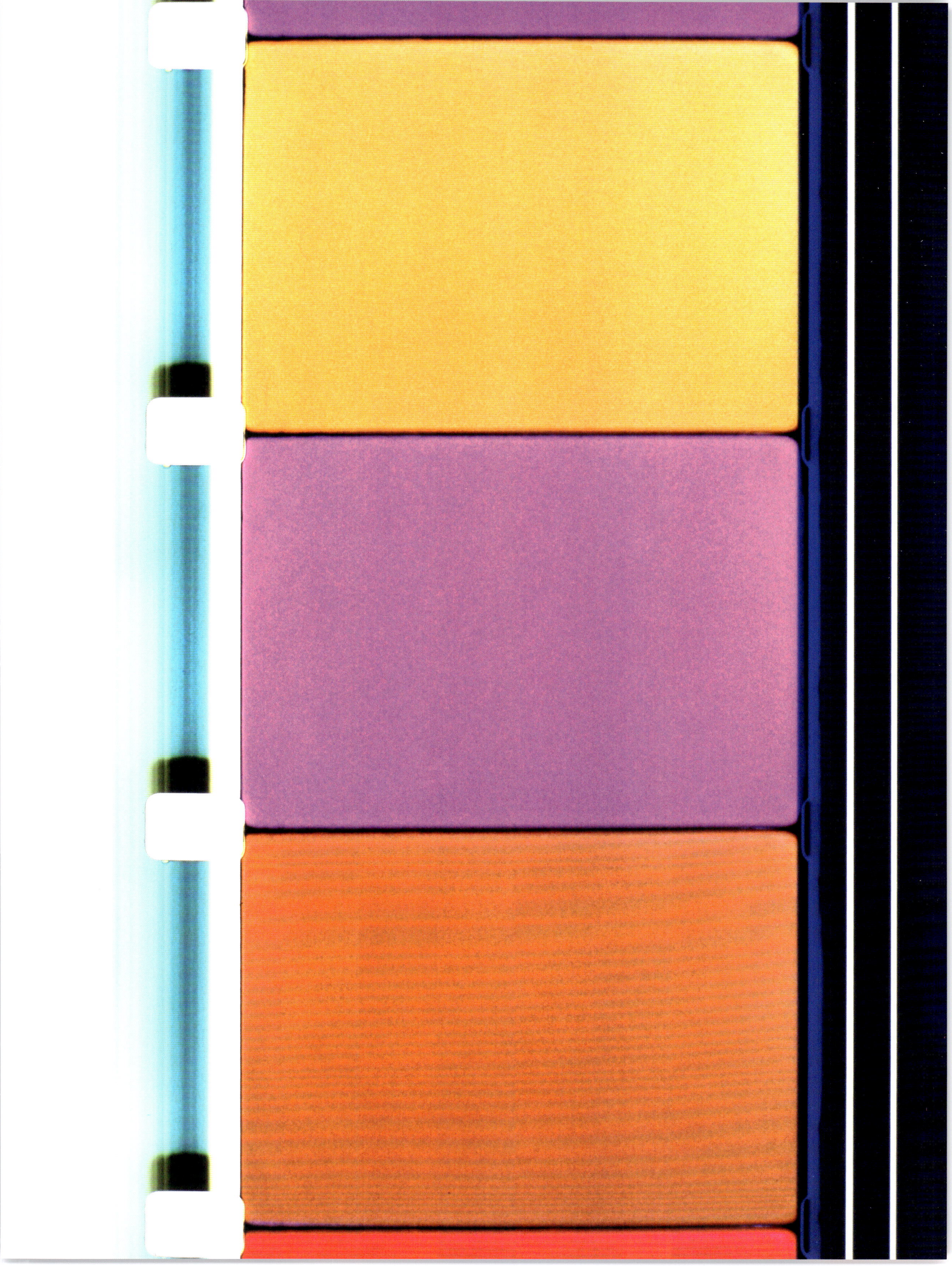

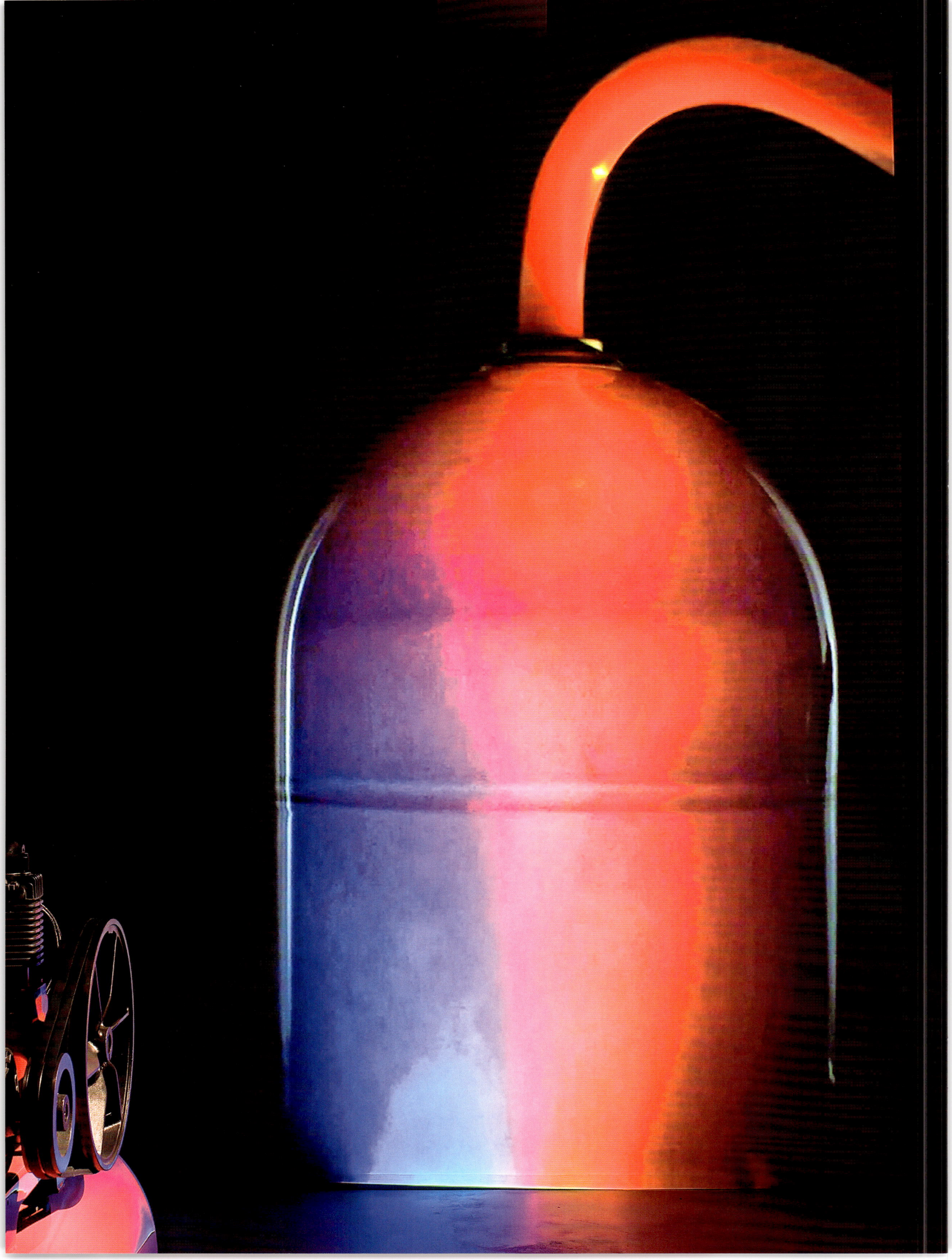

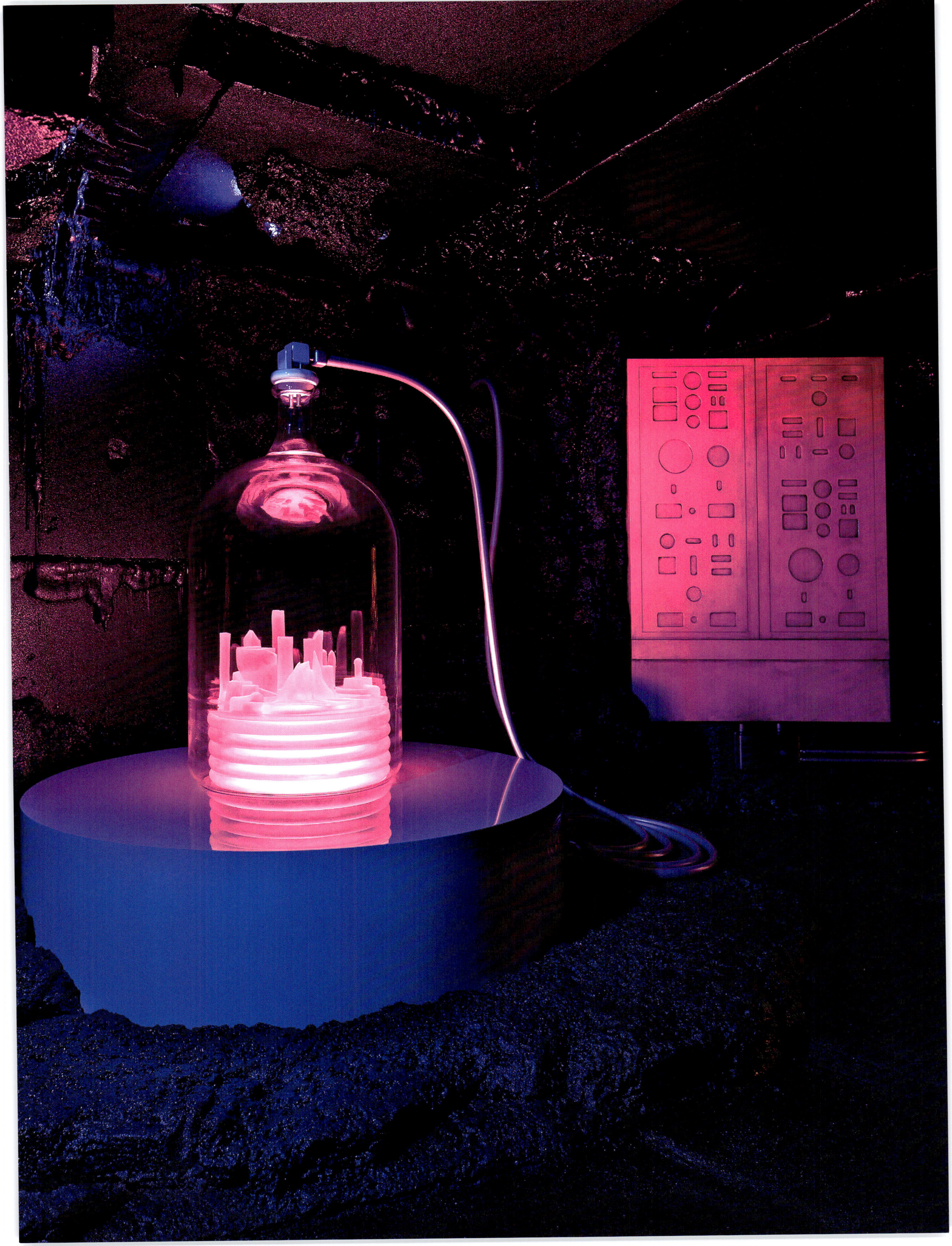

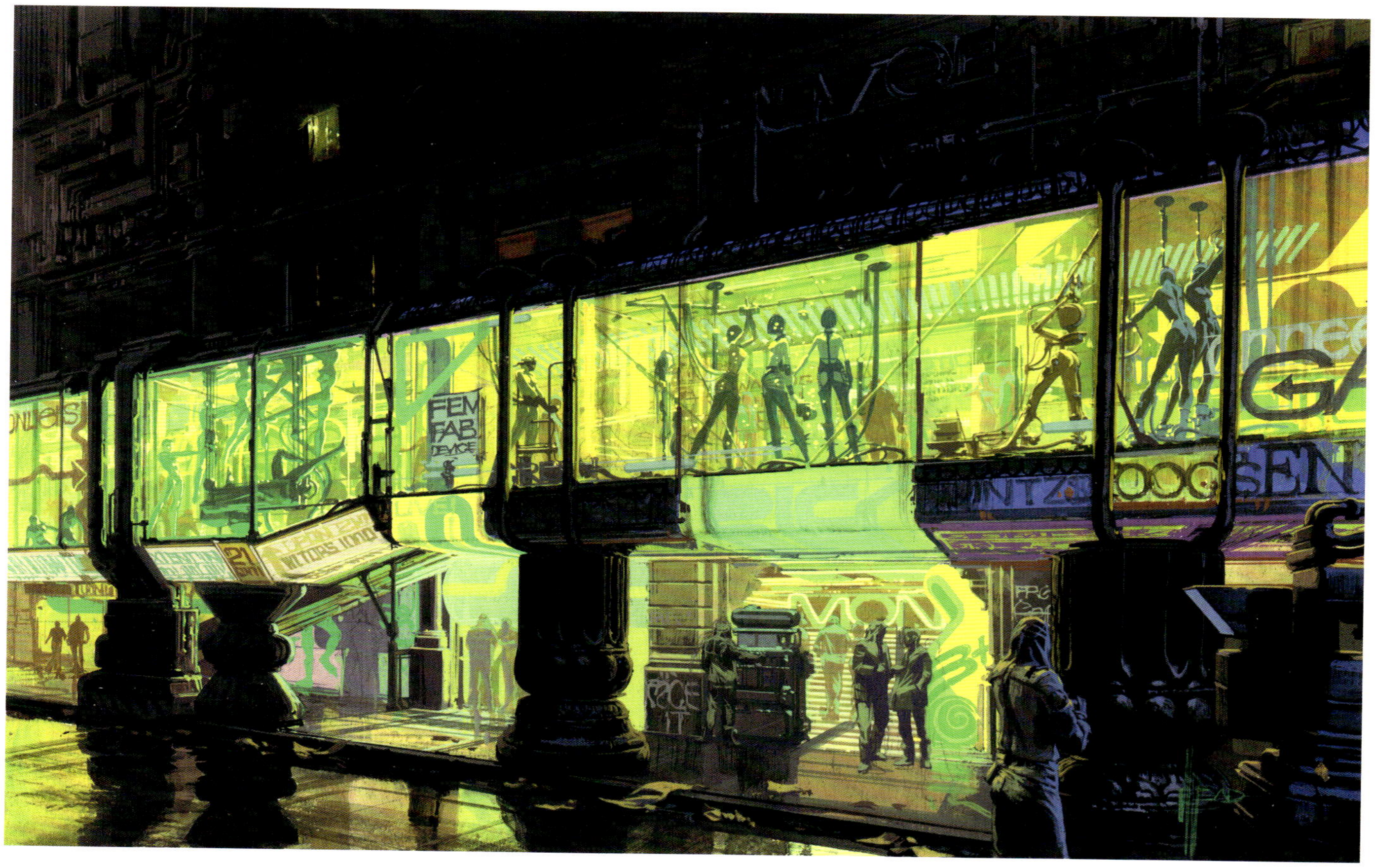
FEM
FAB
DEVICE
RAGE
IT

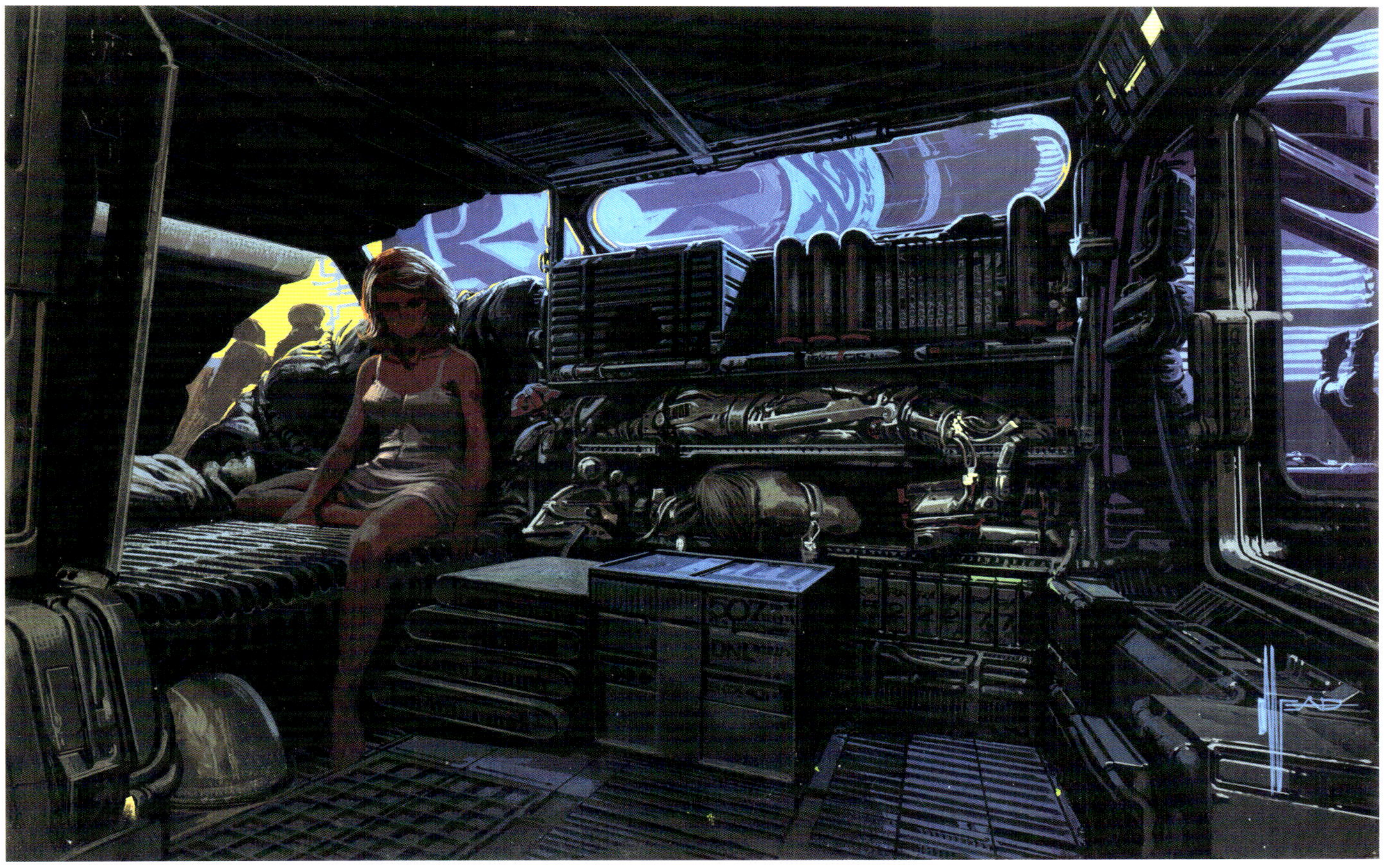

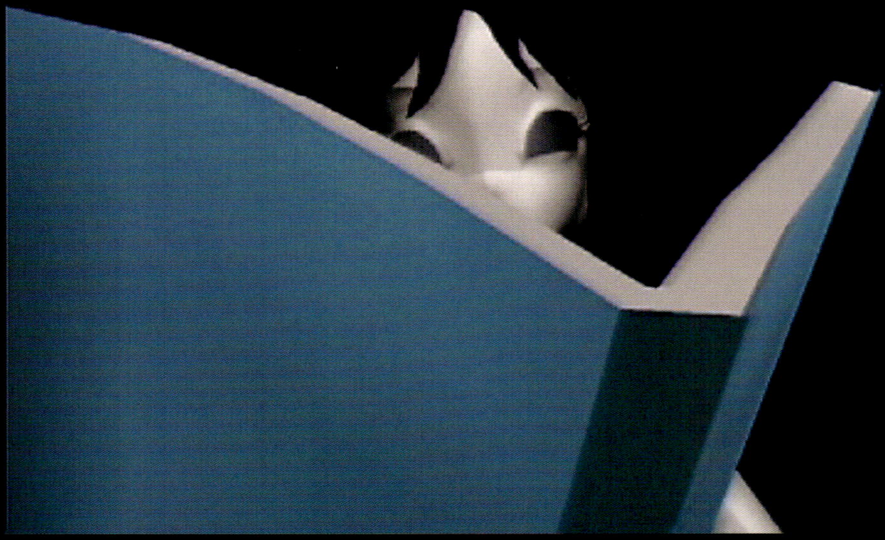

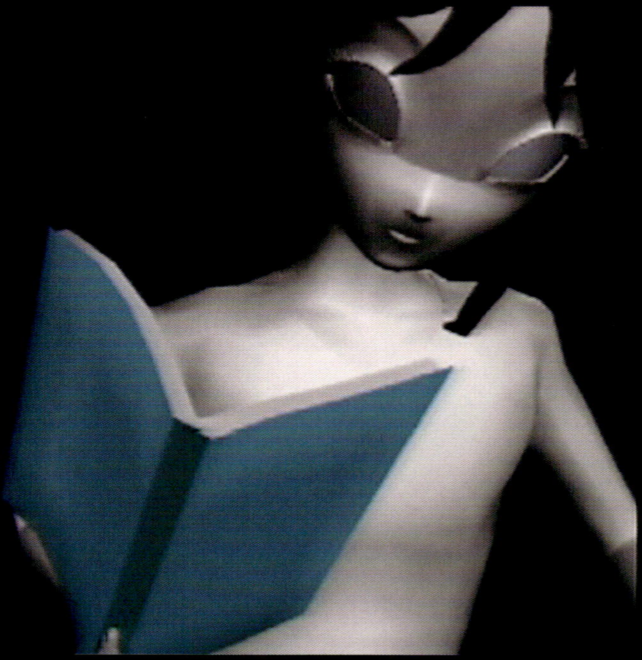

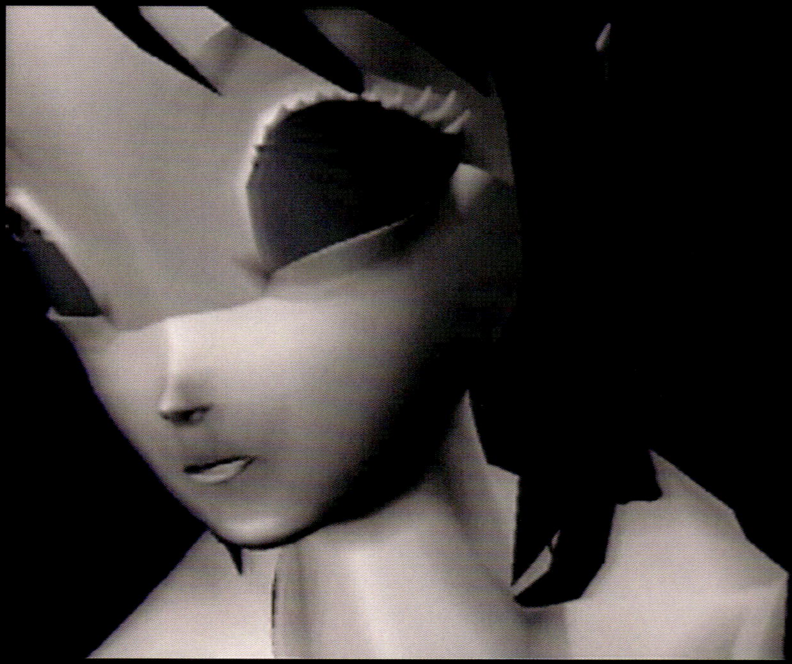

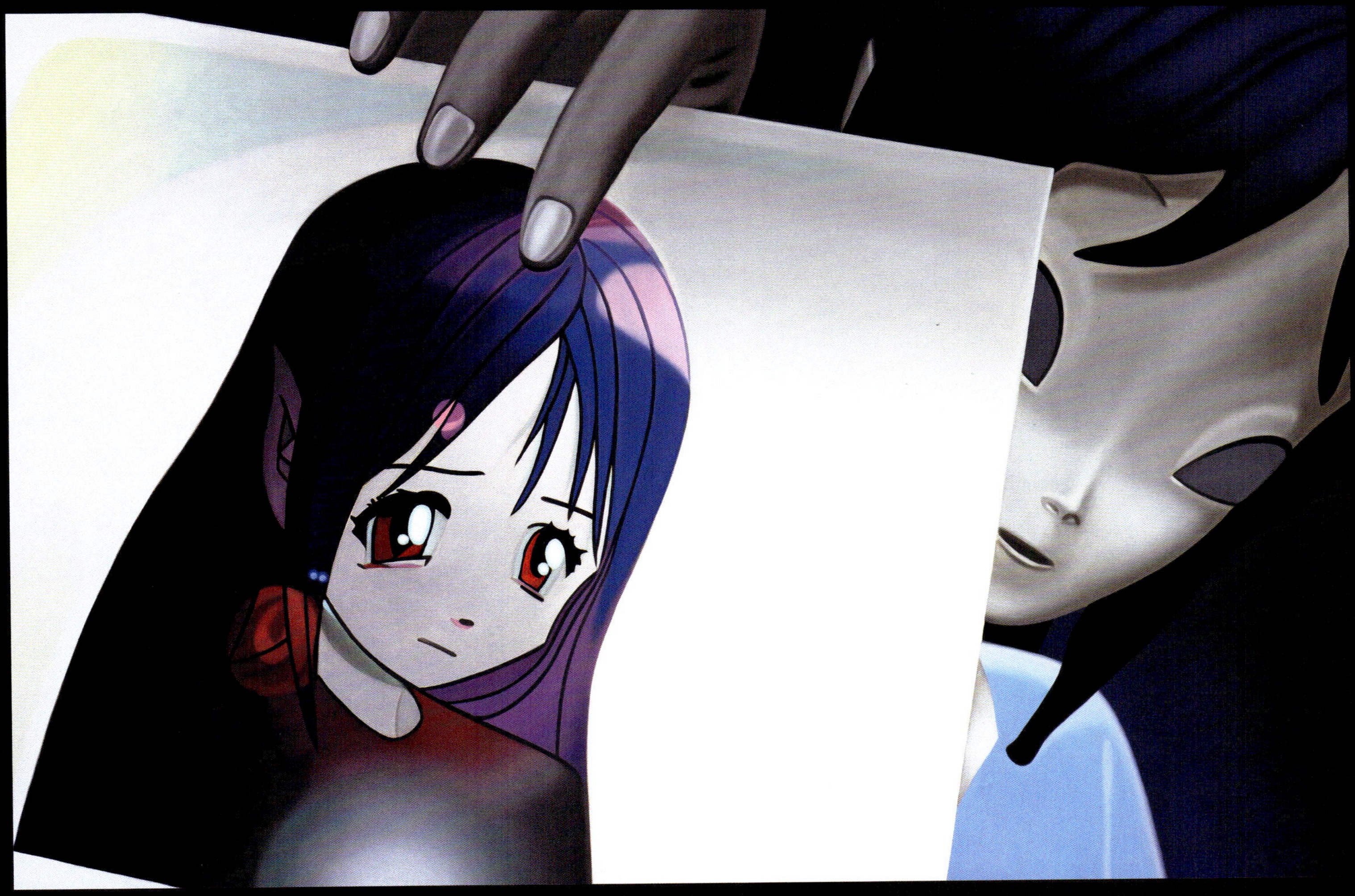

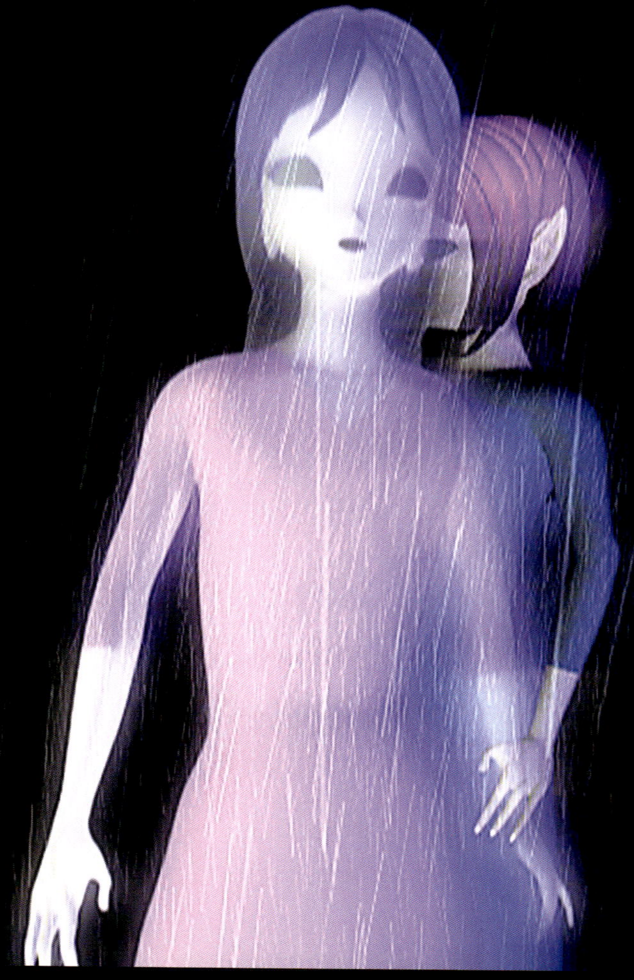

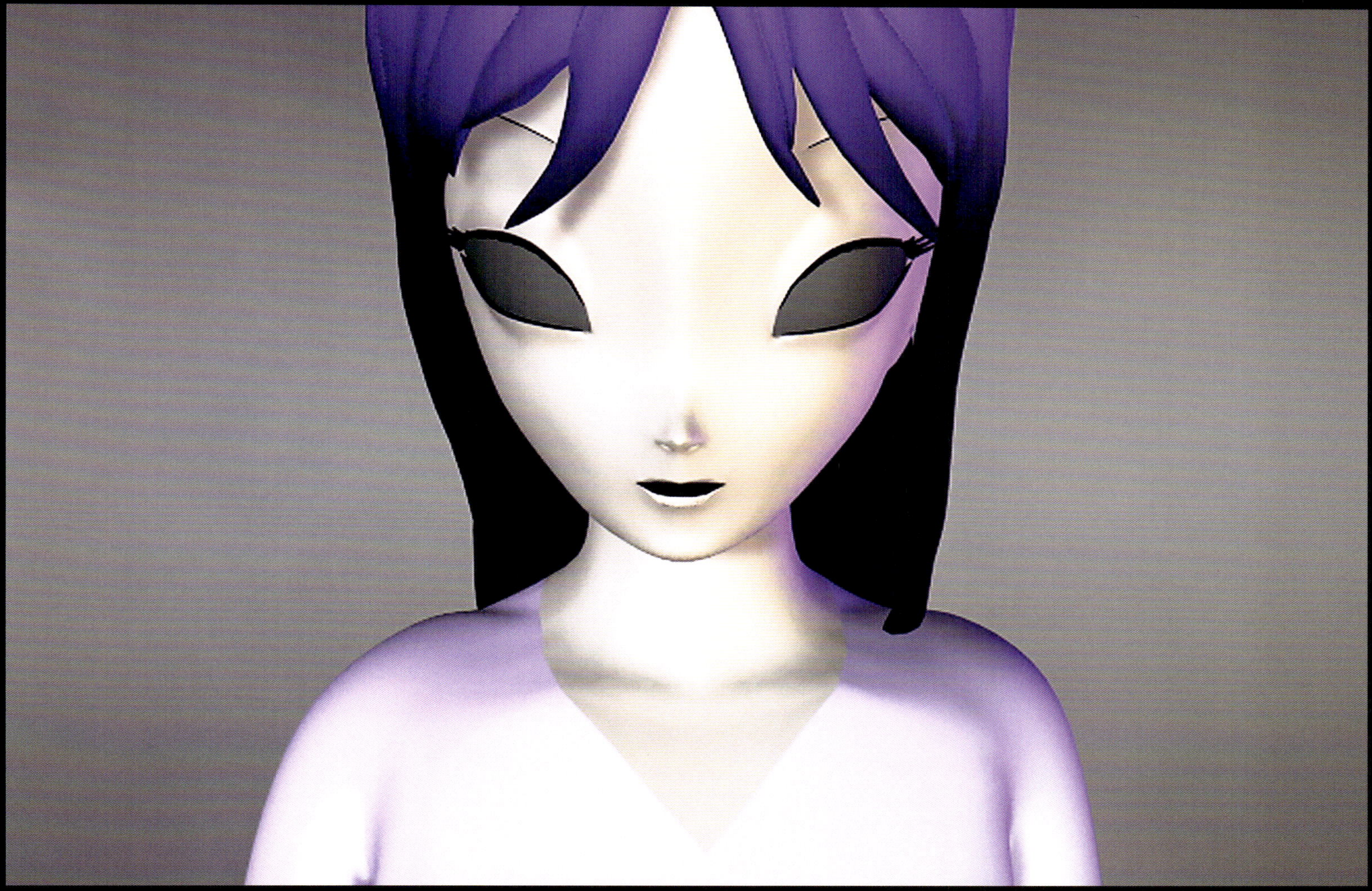

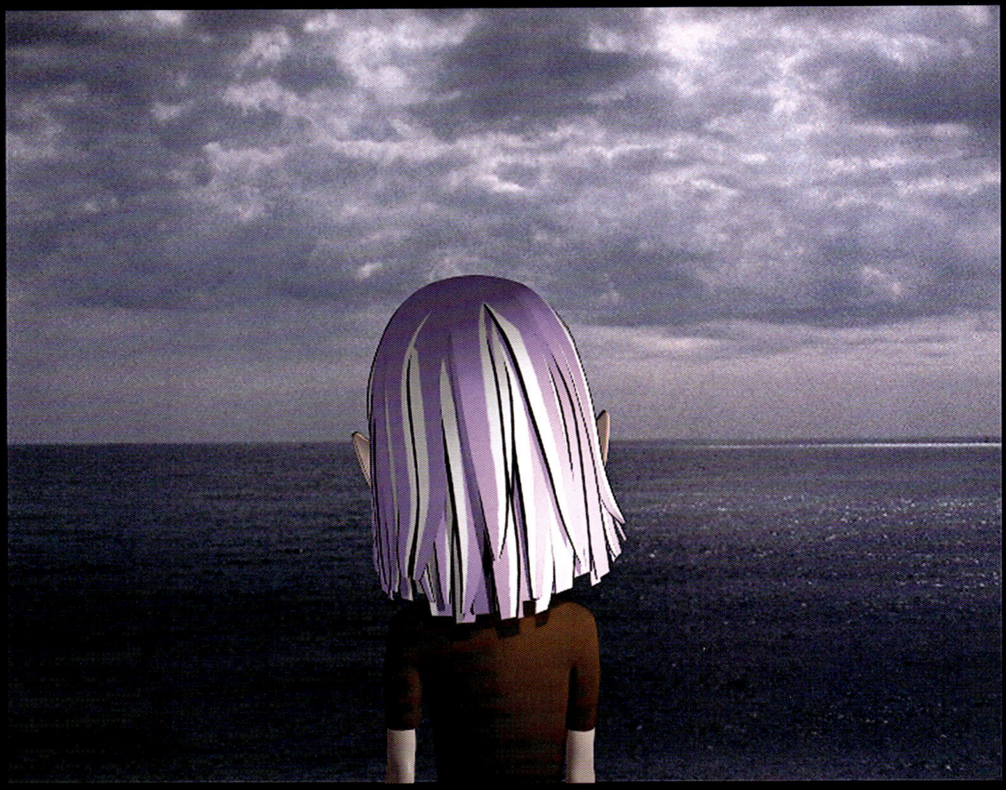

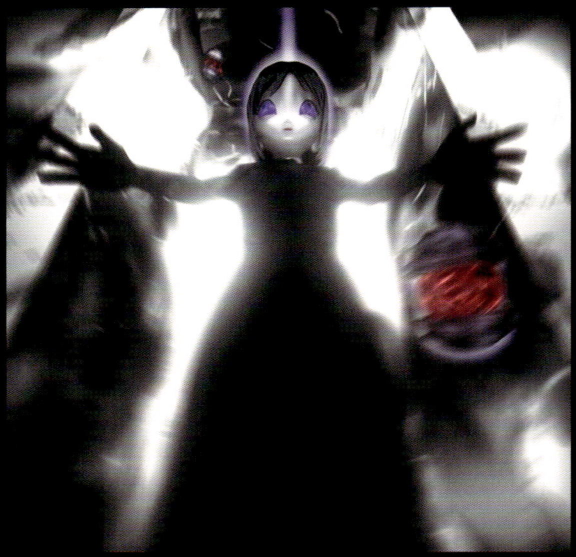

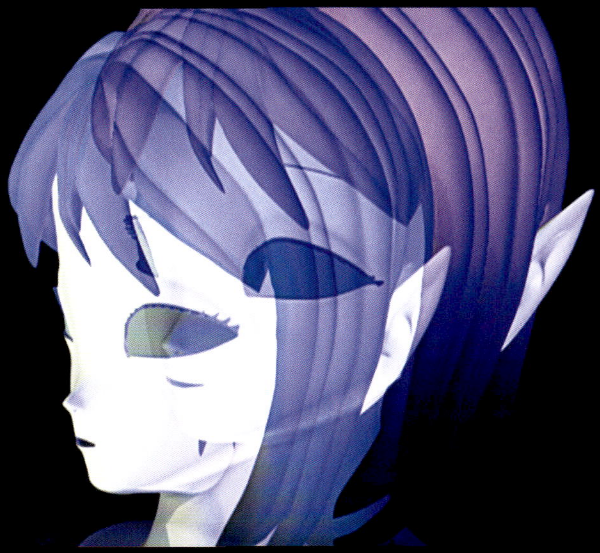

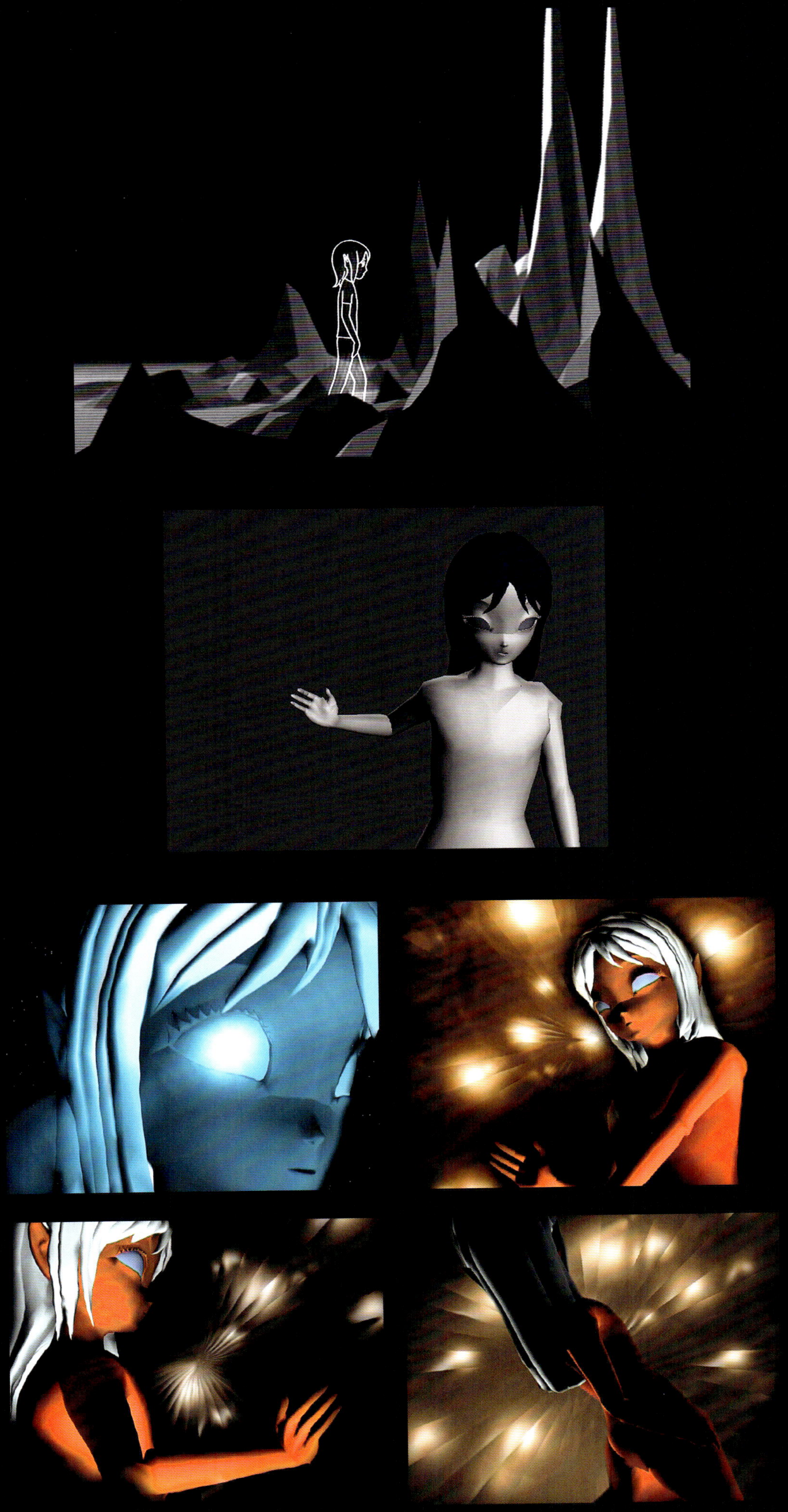

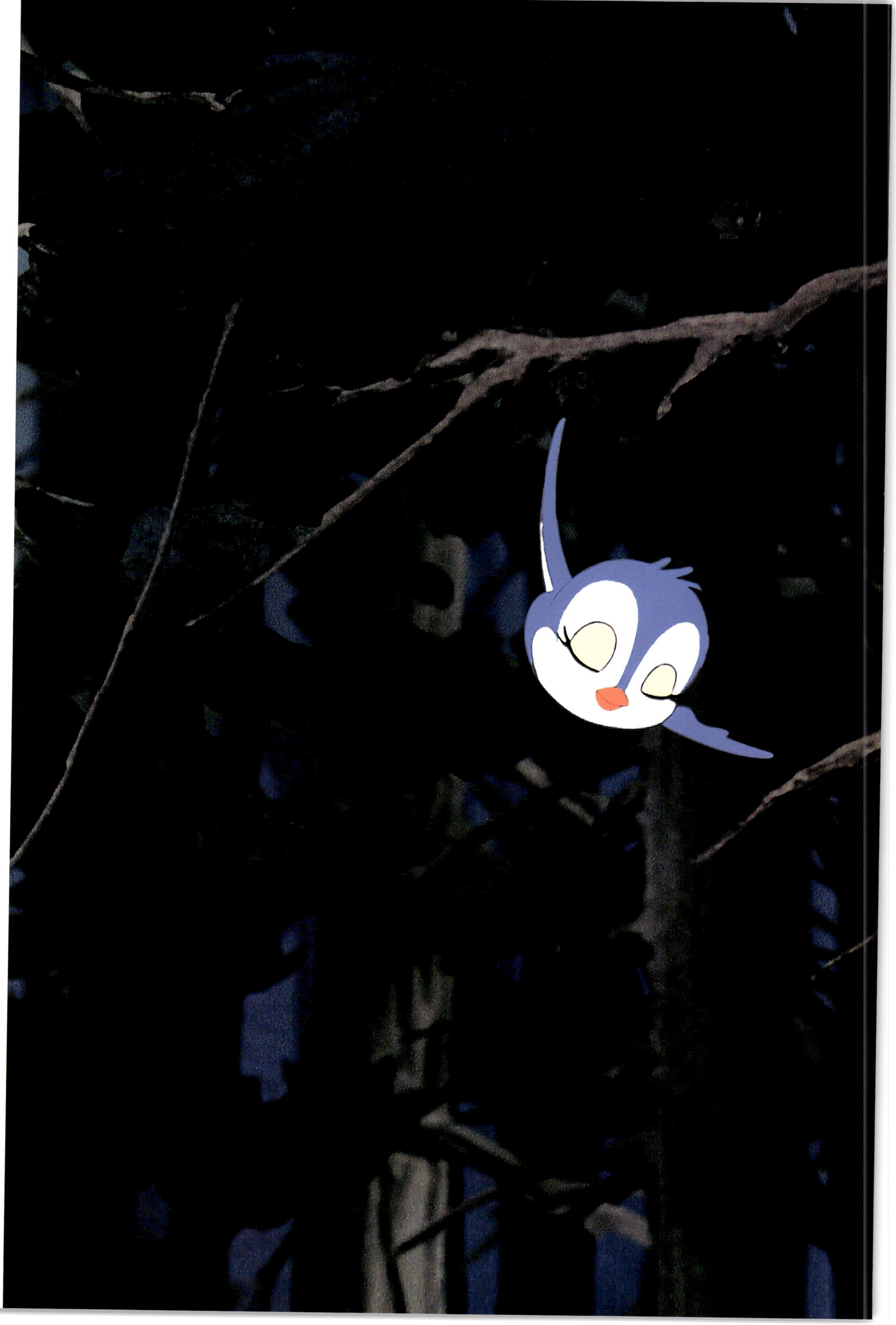

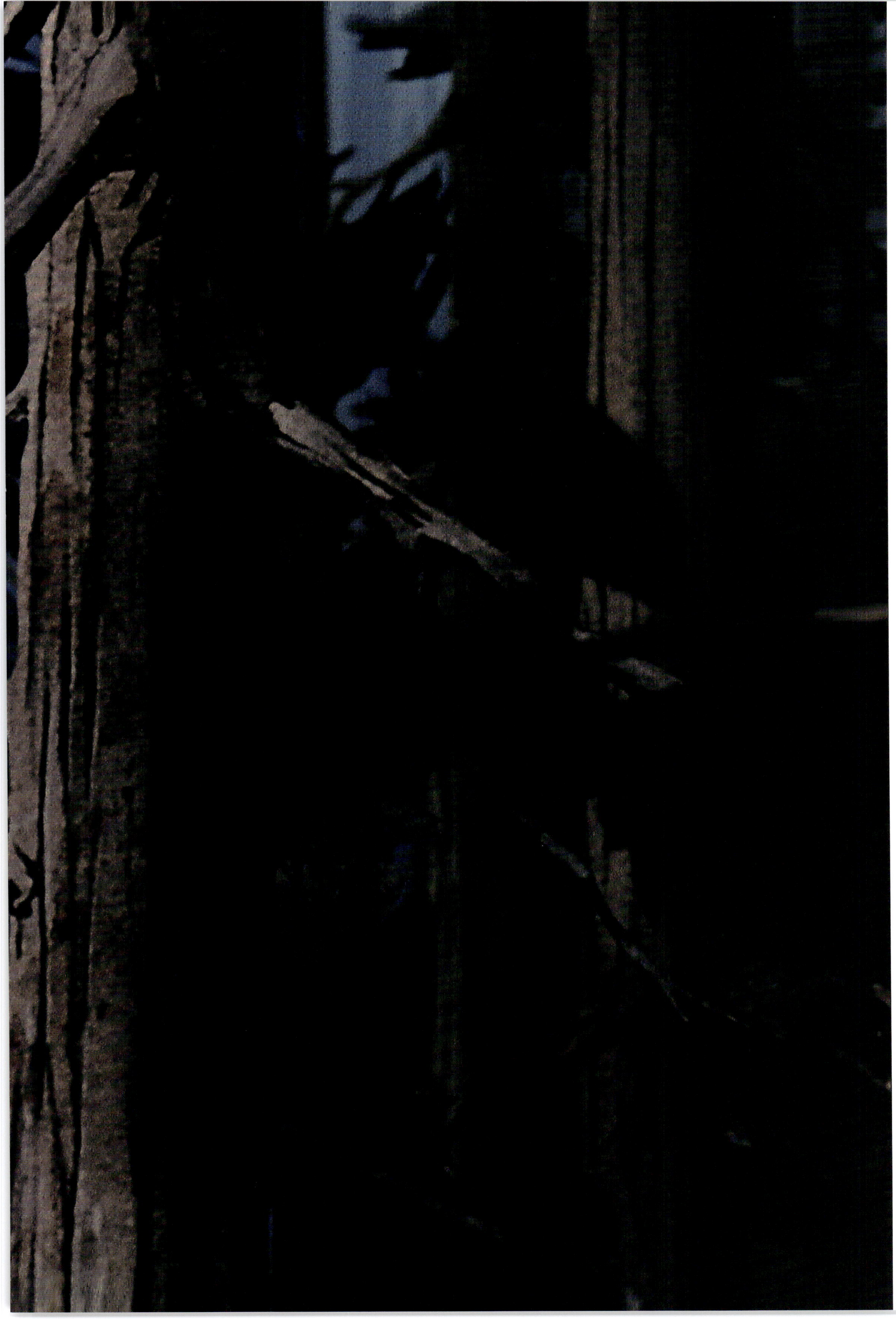

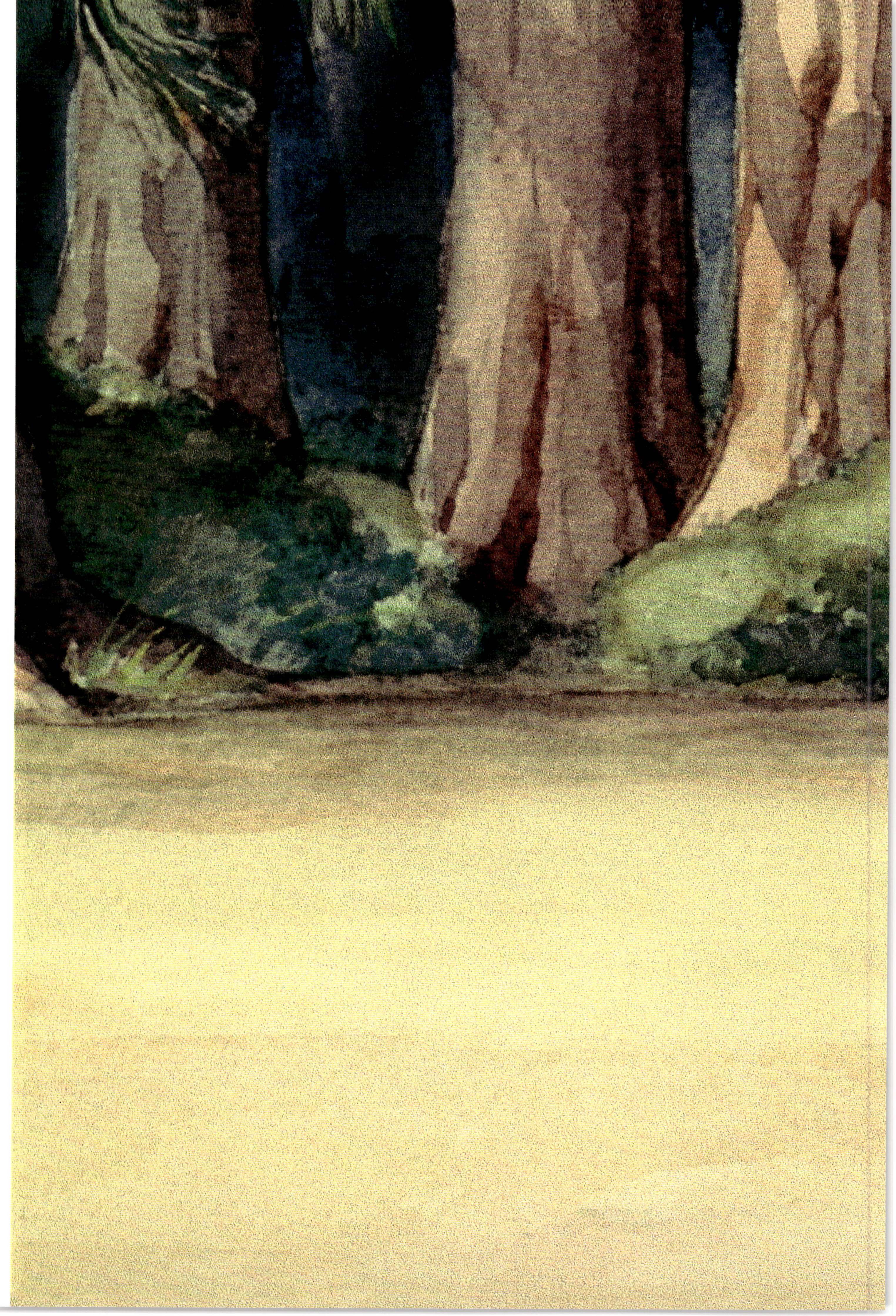

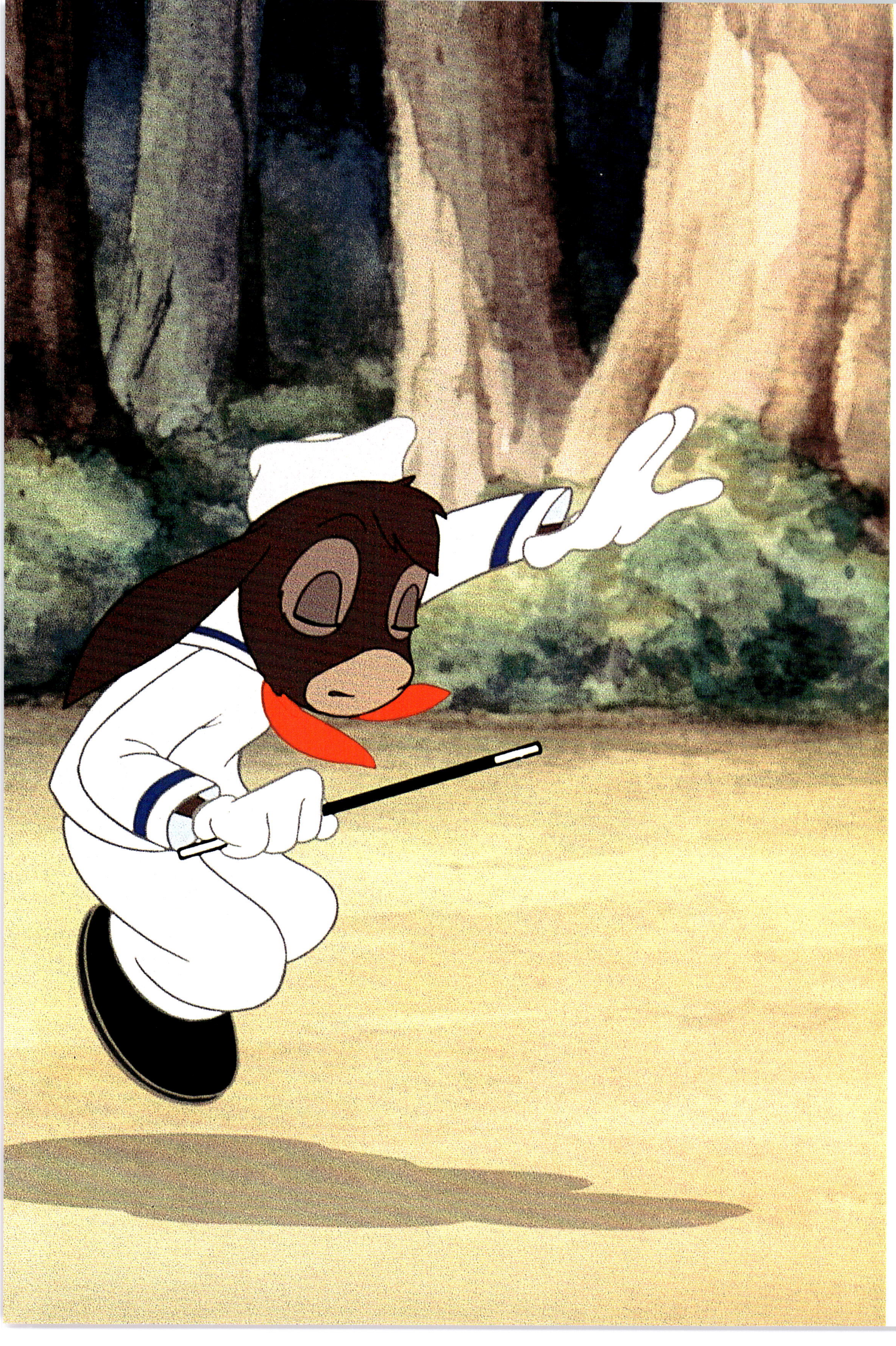

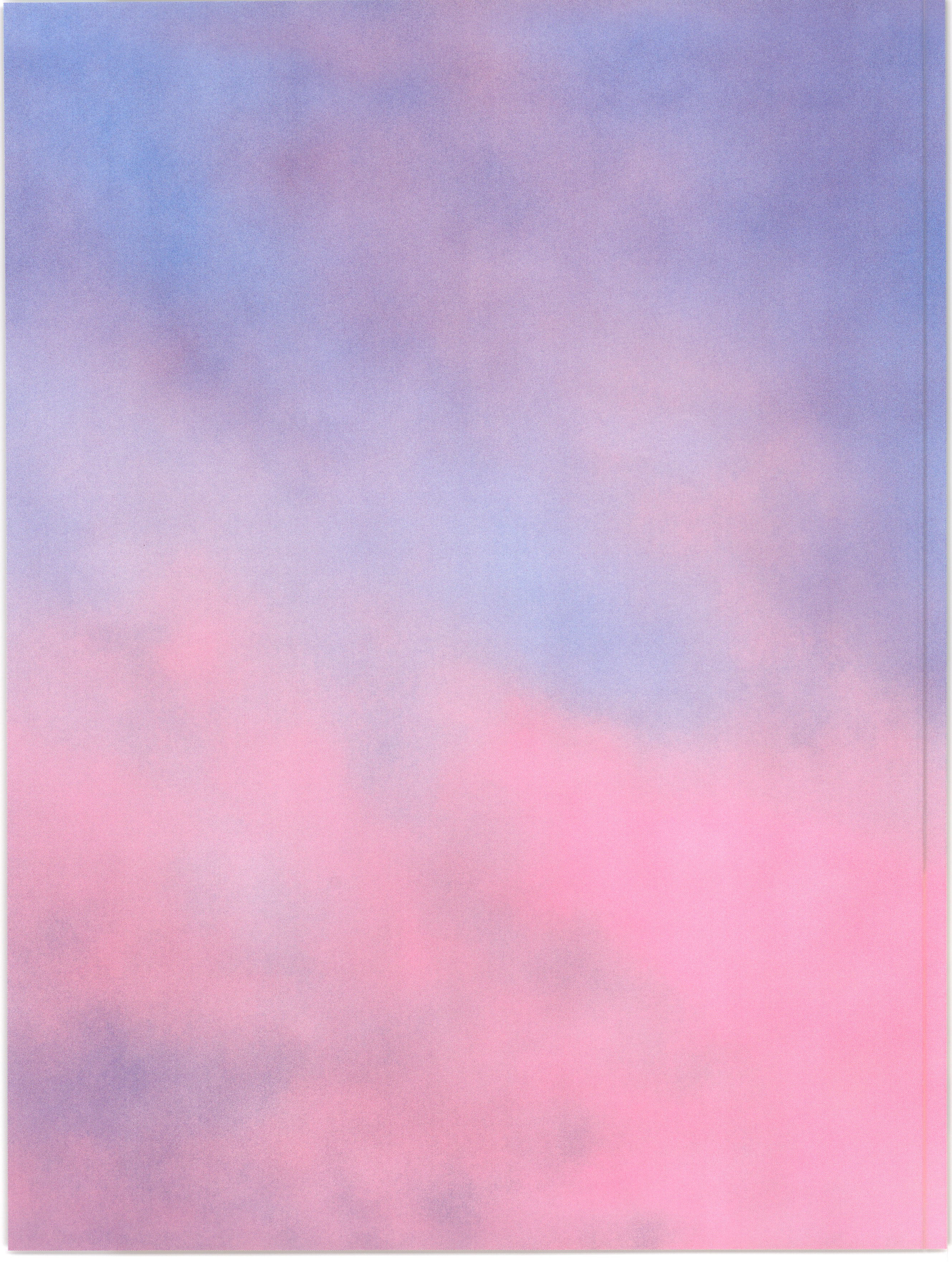

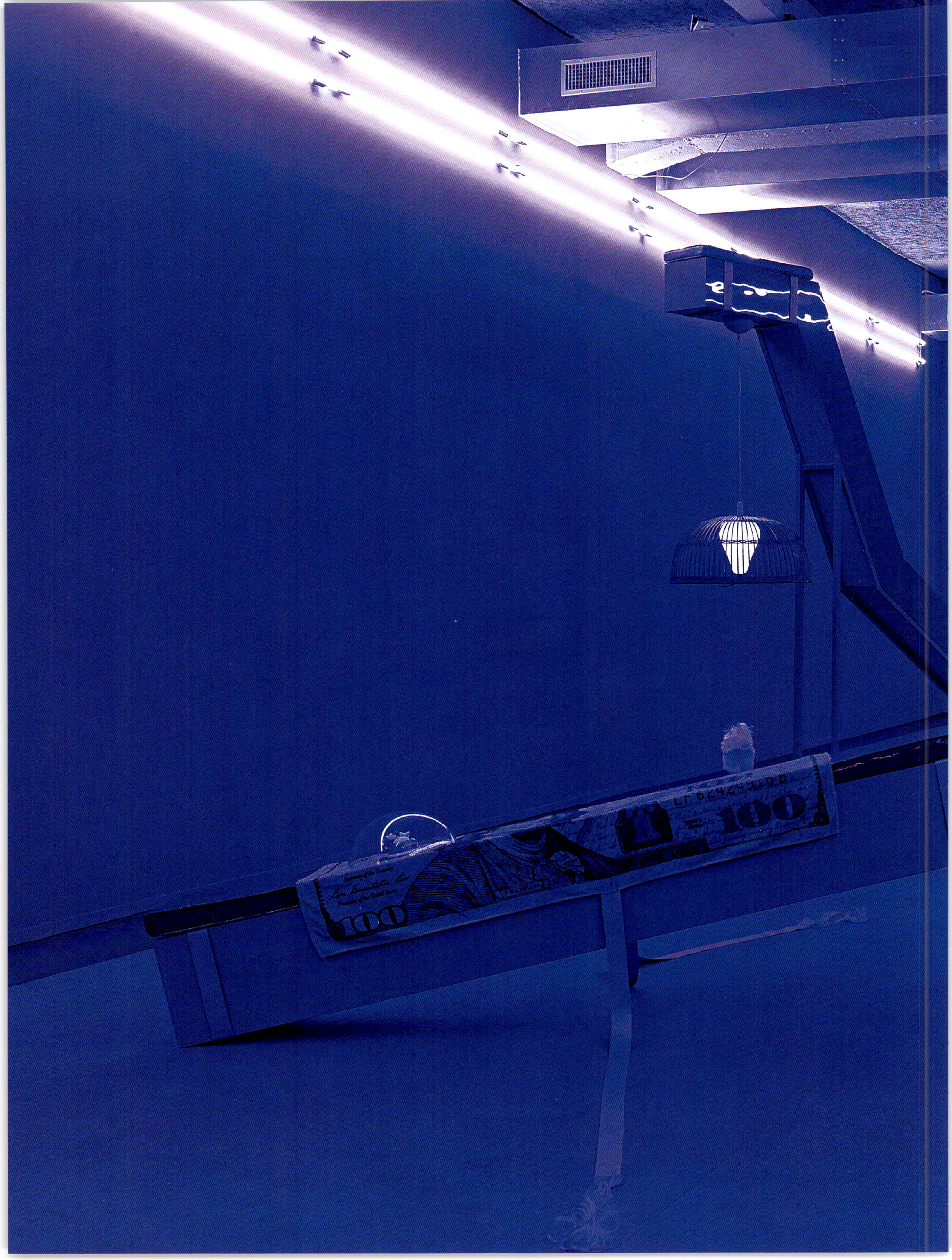

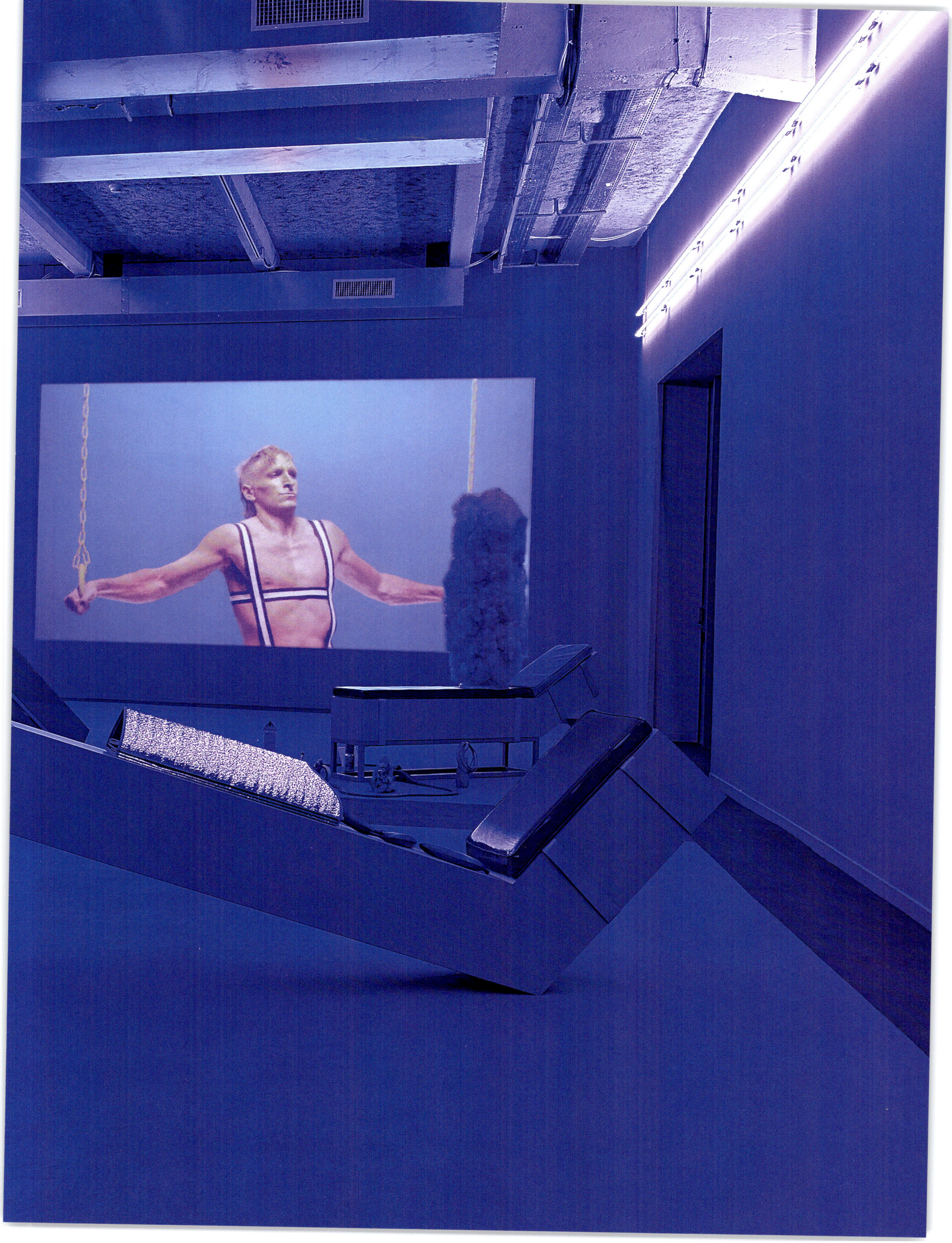

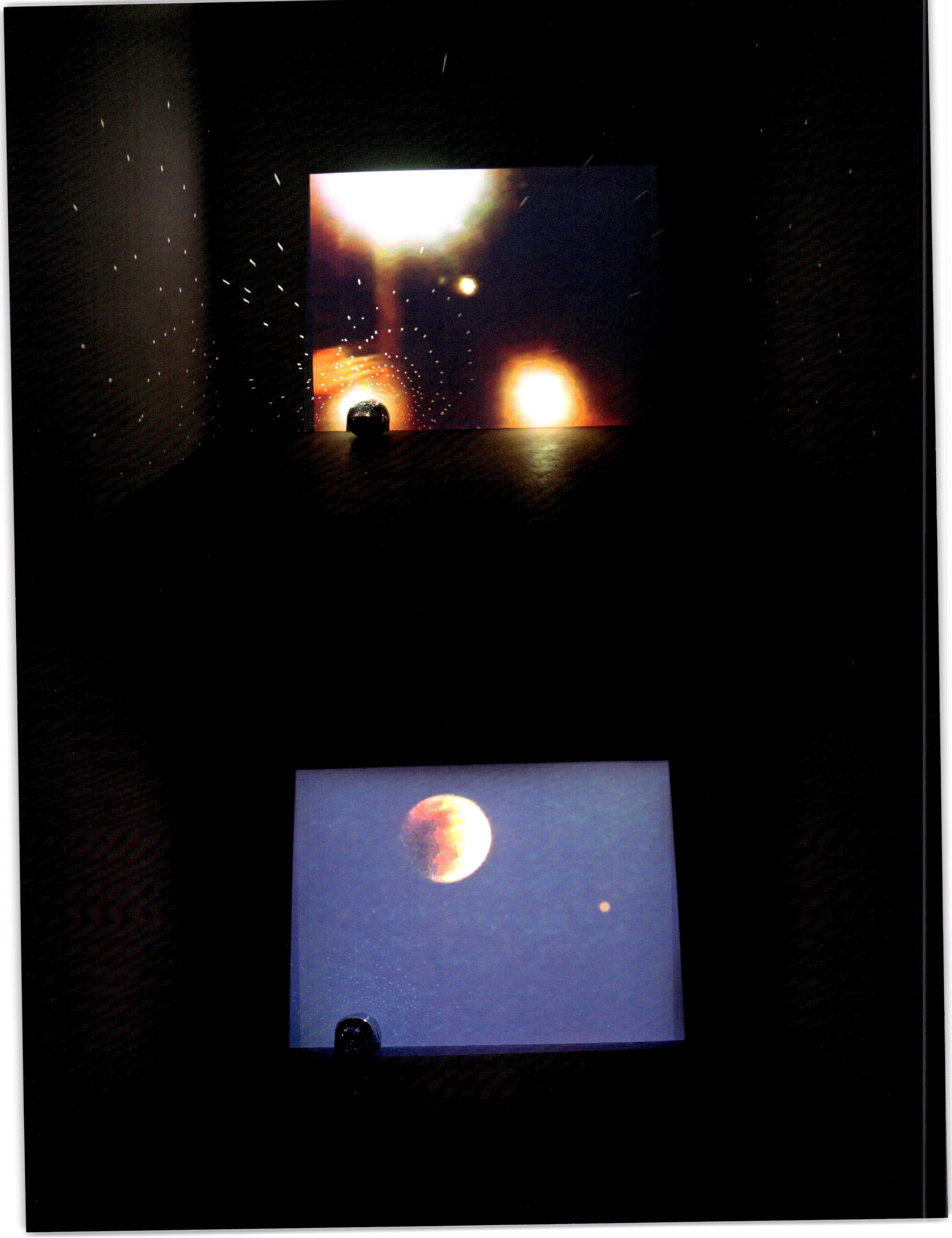

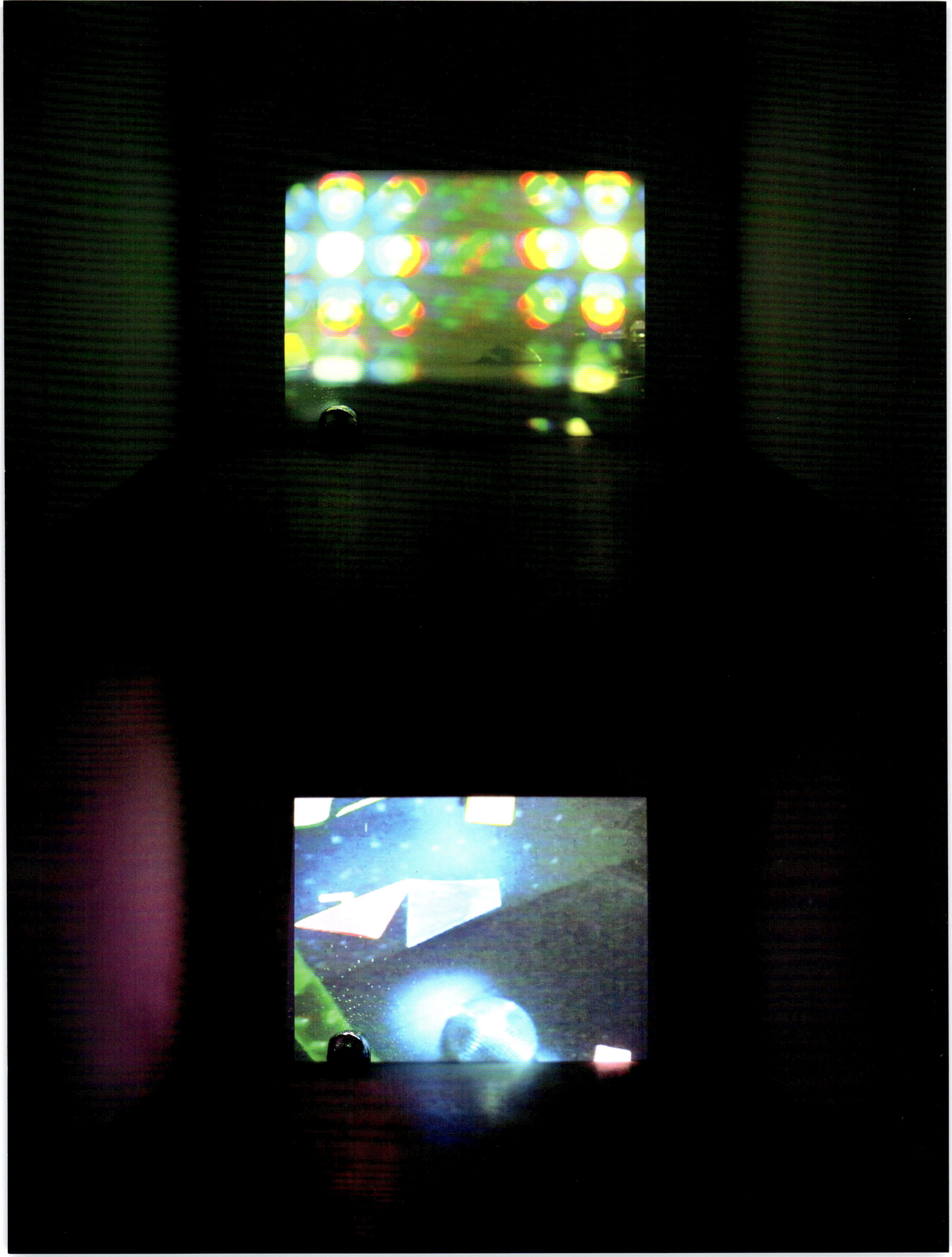

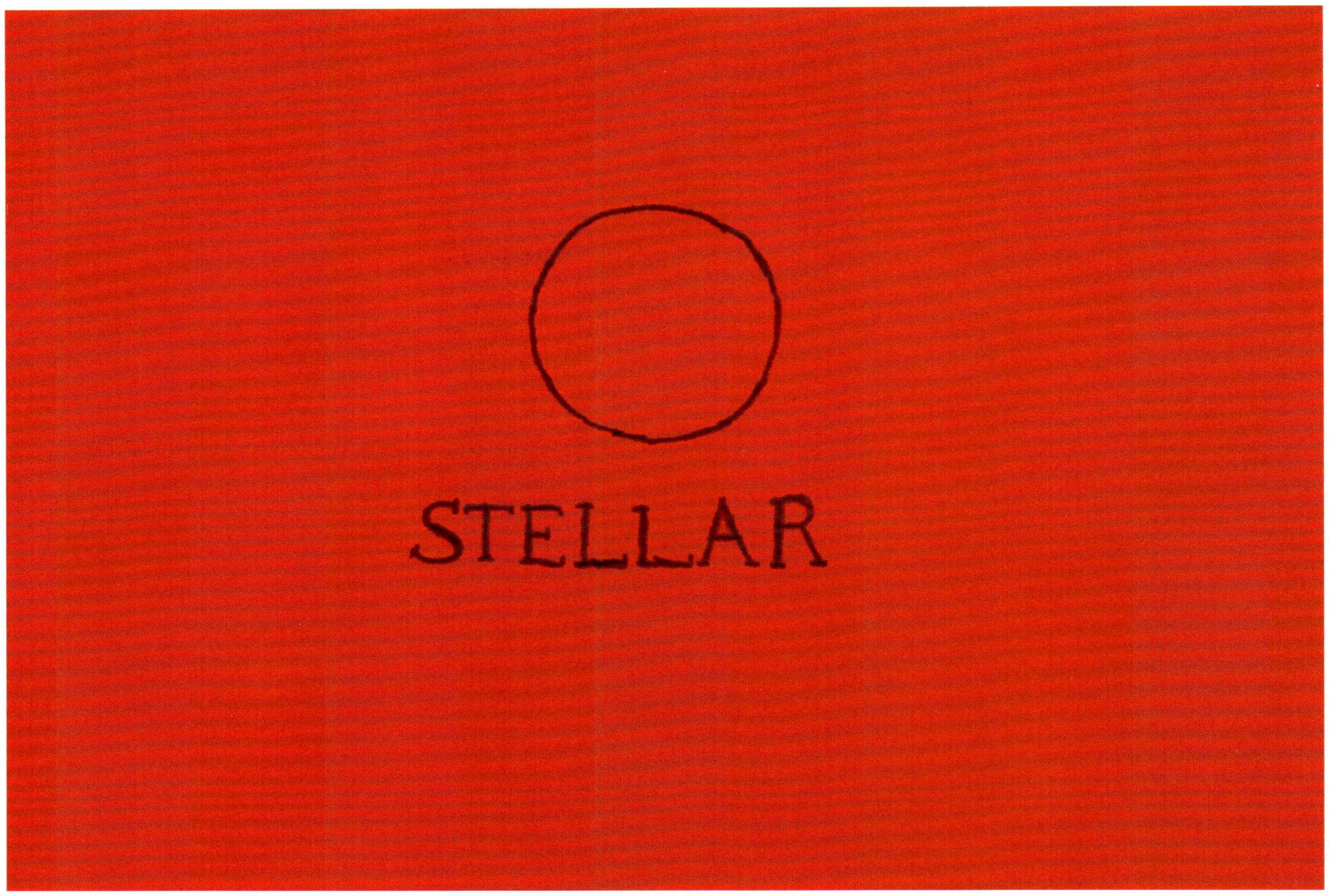
STELLAR

STARLIGHT

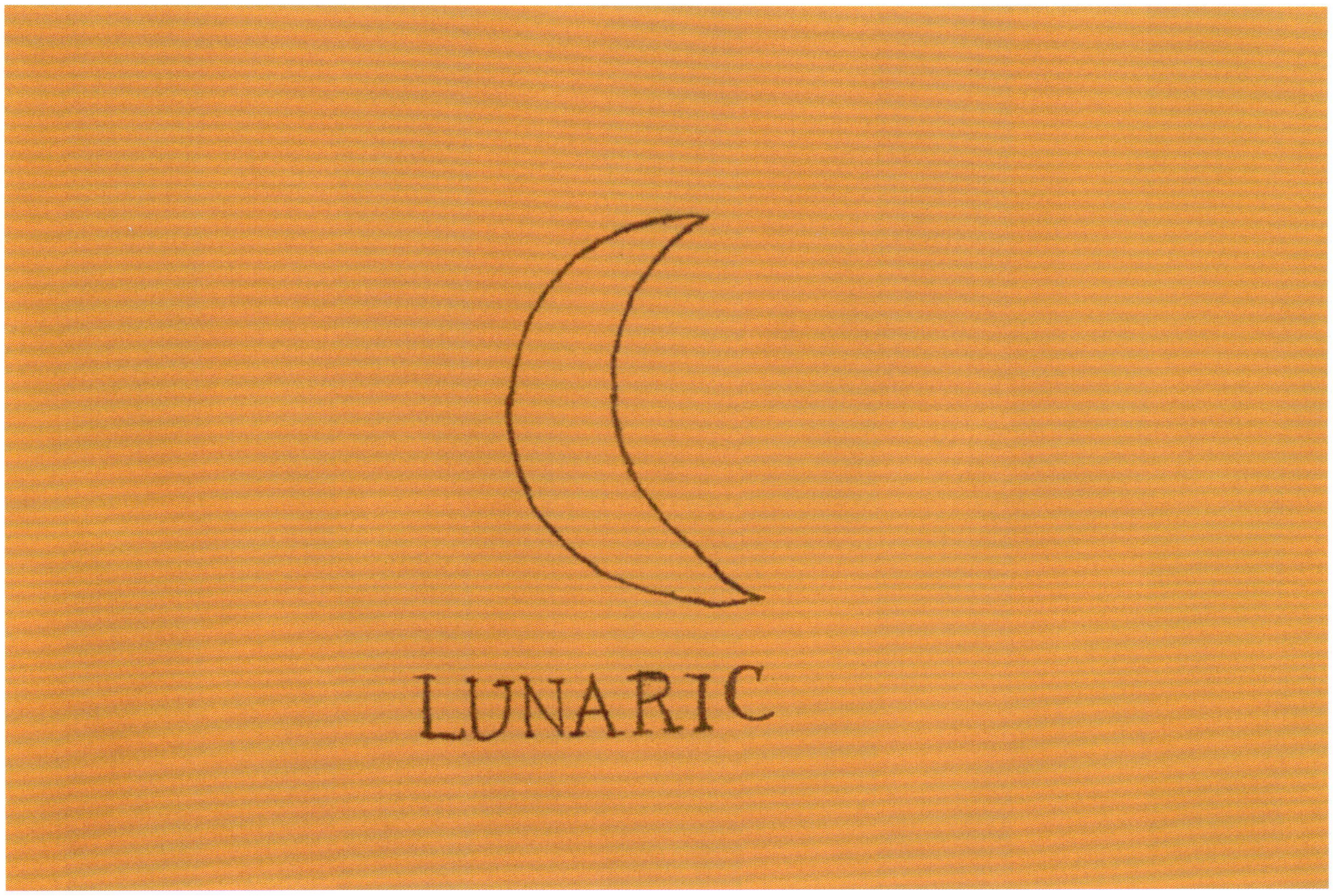
LUNARIC

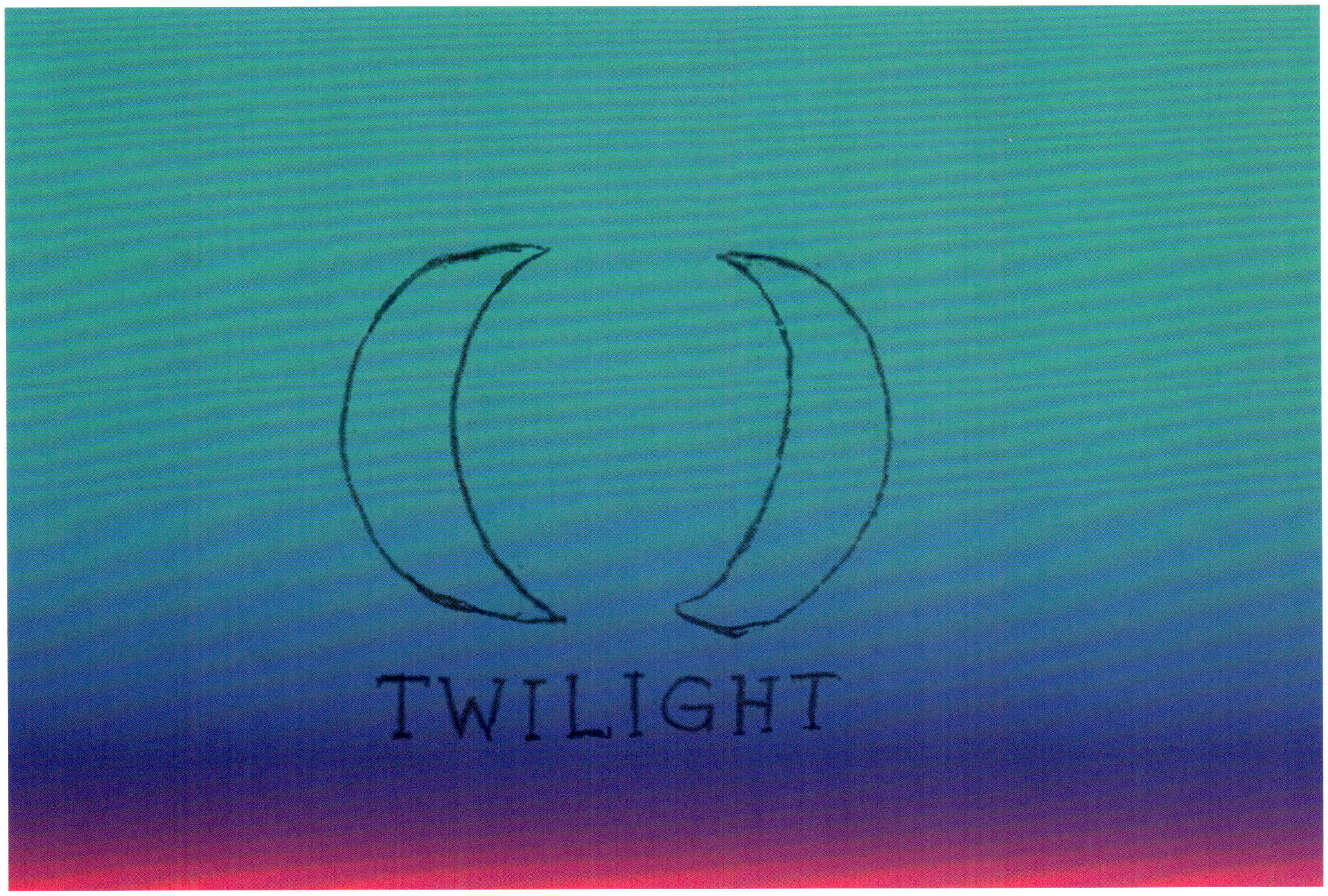
TWILIGHT

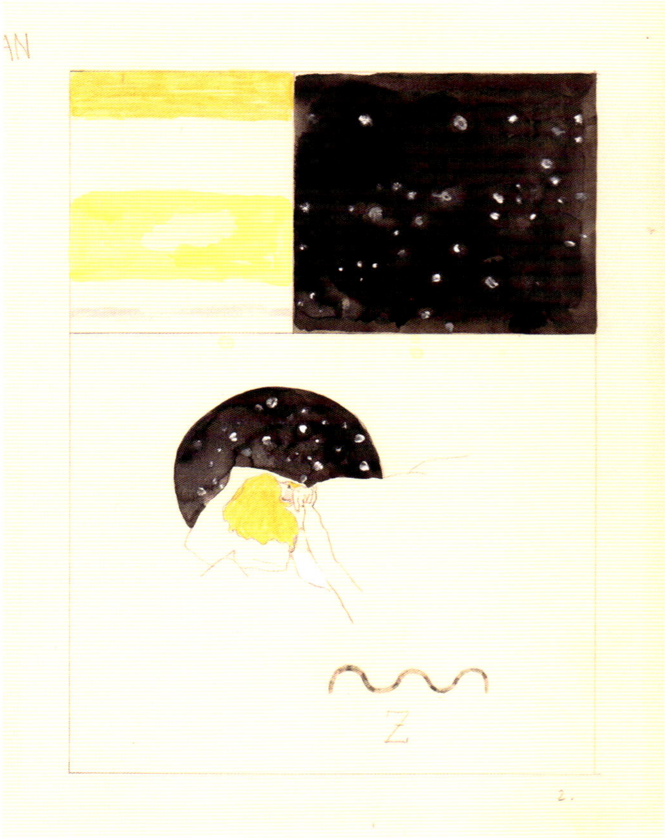
Z

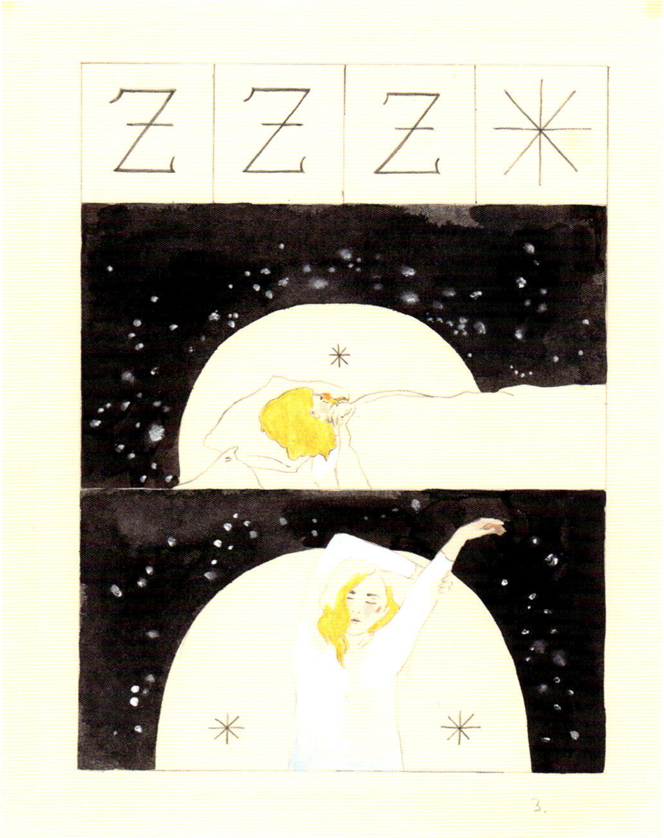
Z Z Z

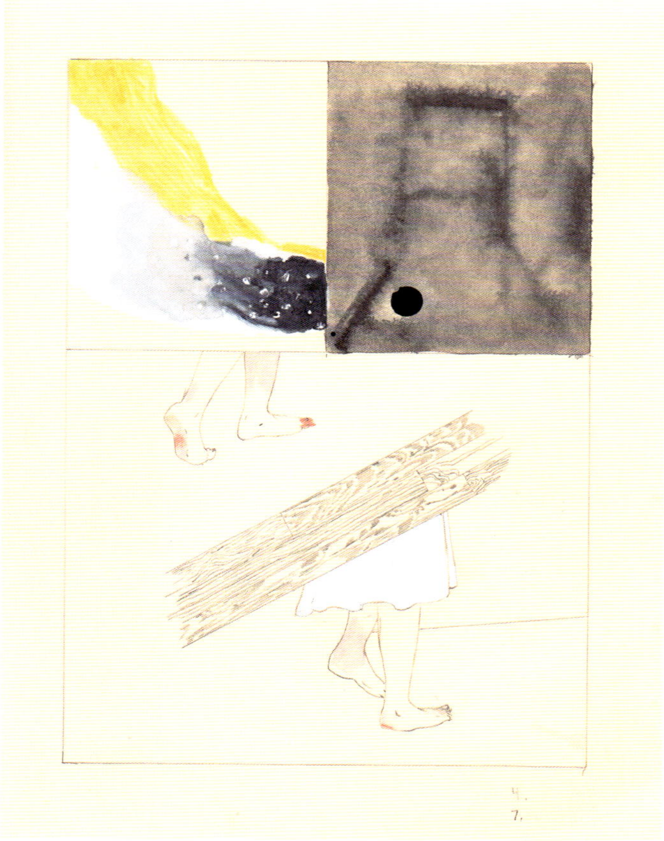

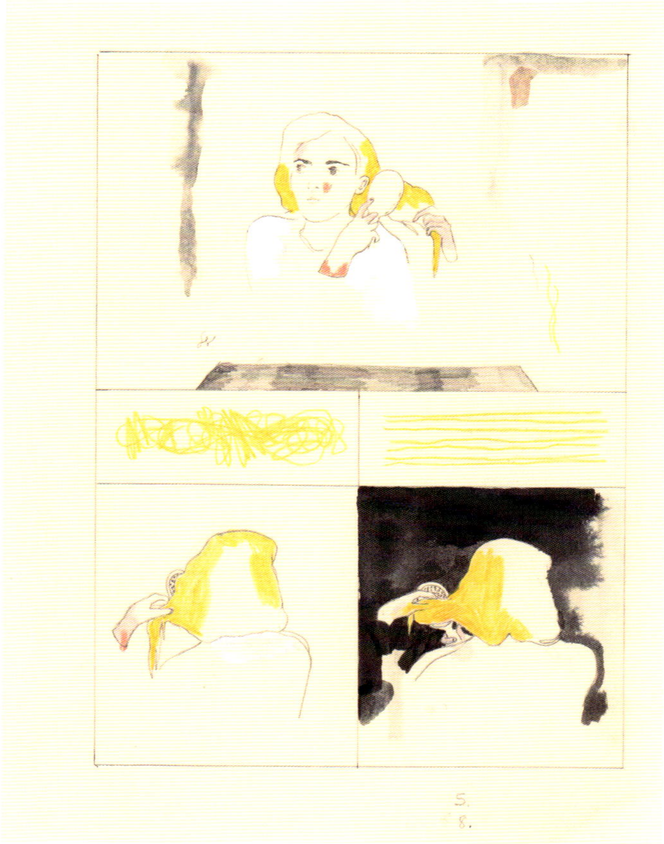

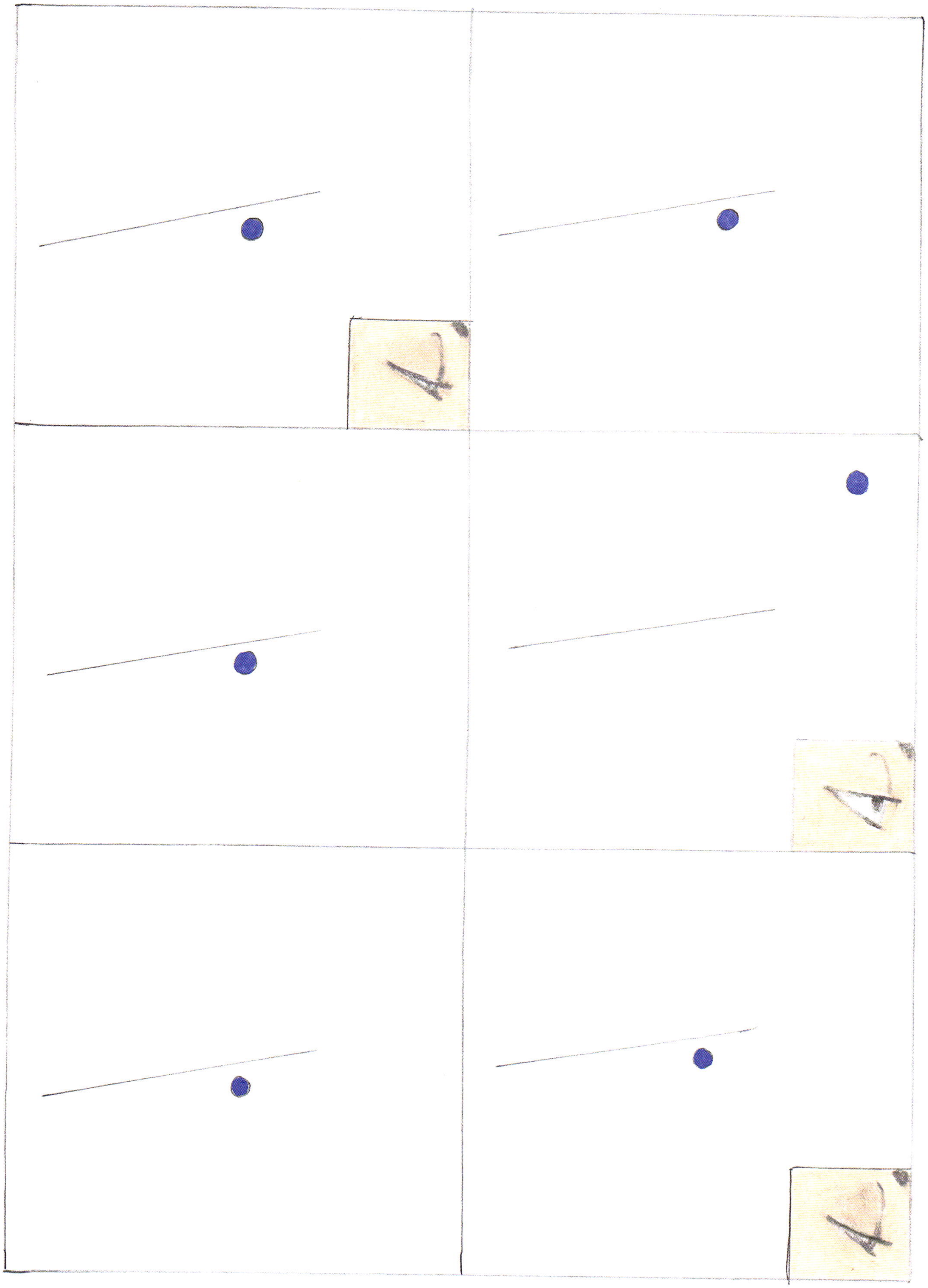

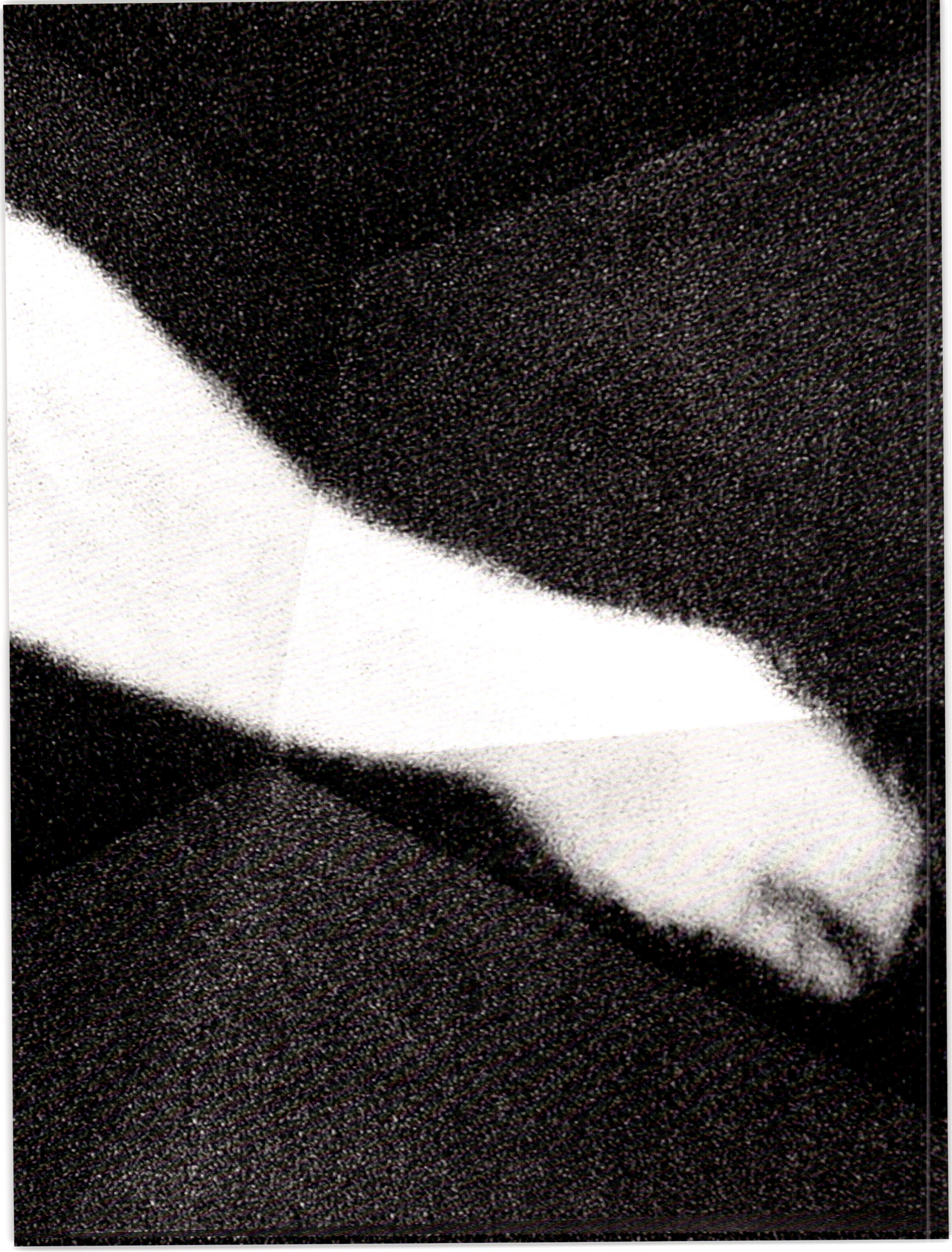

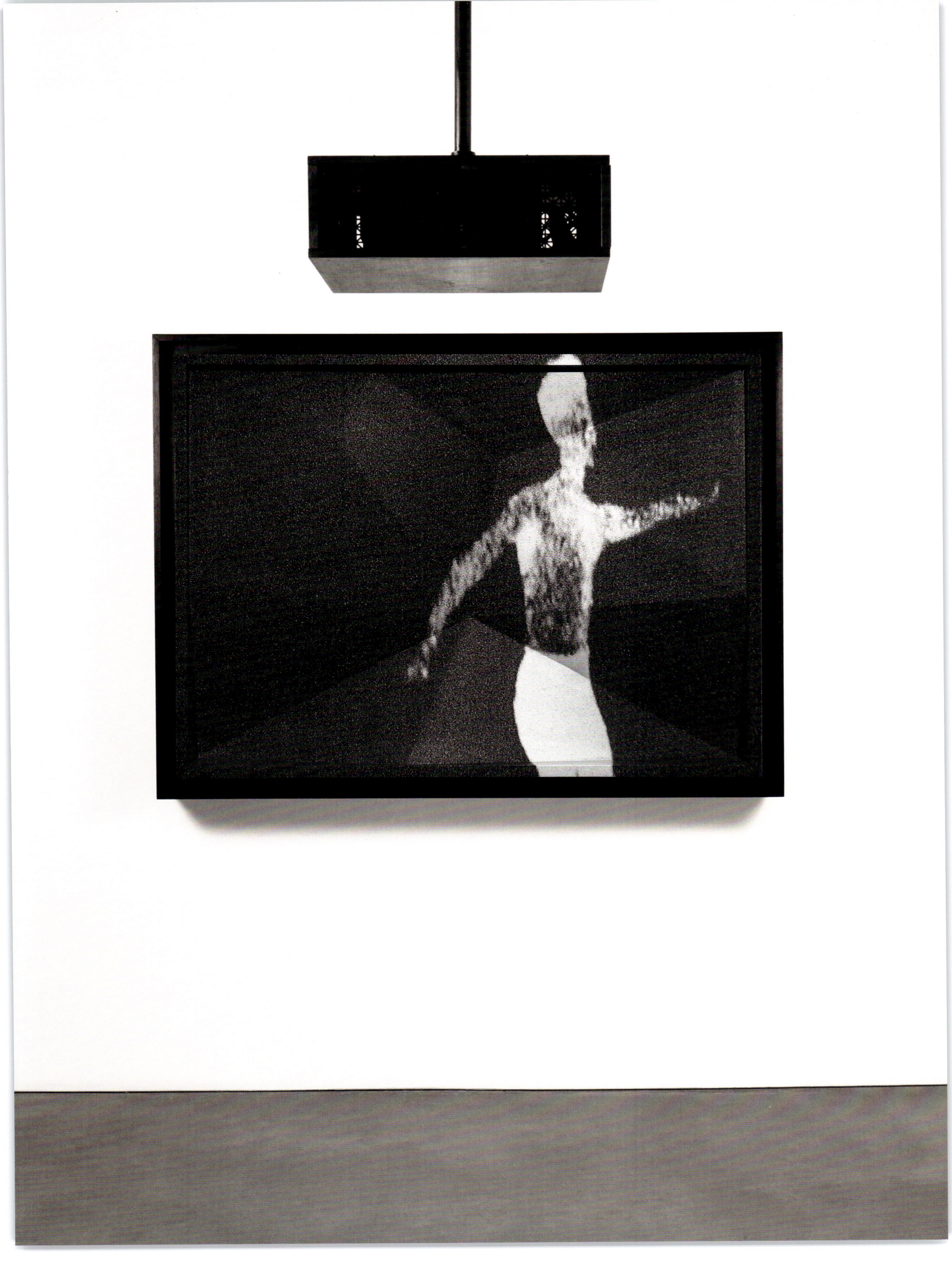

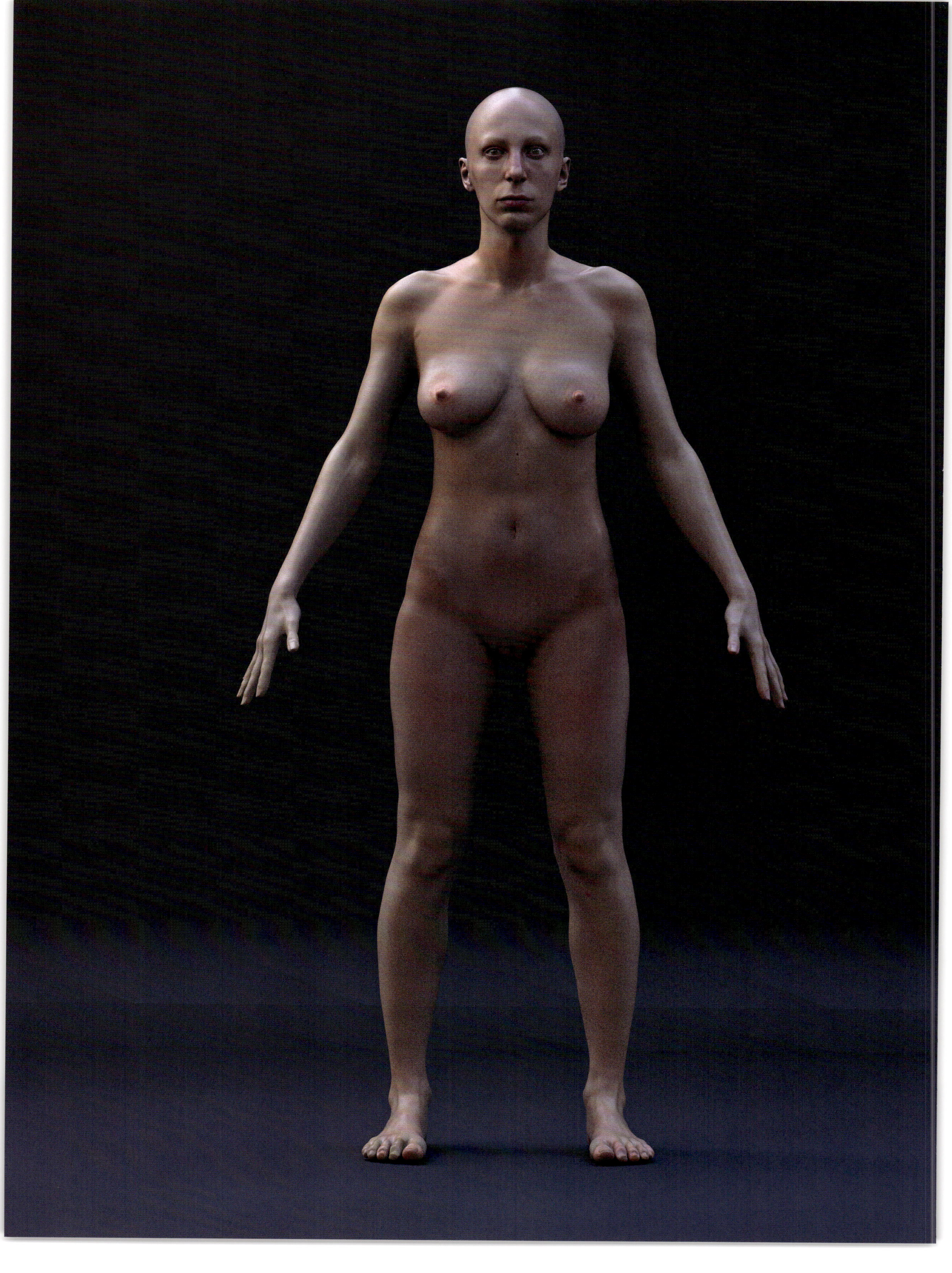

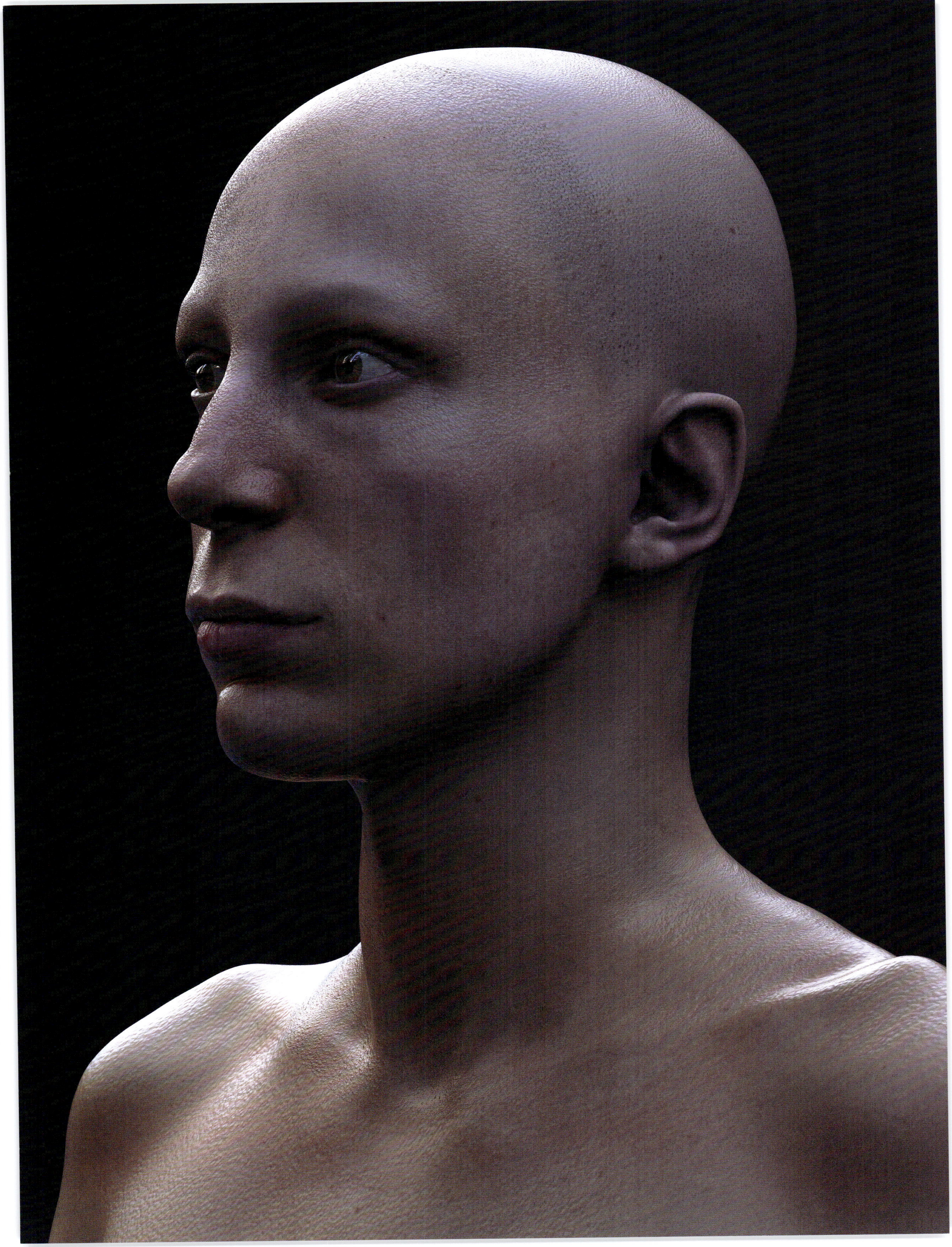

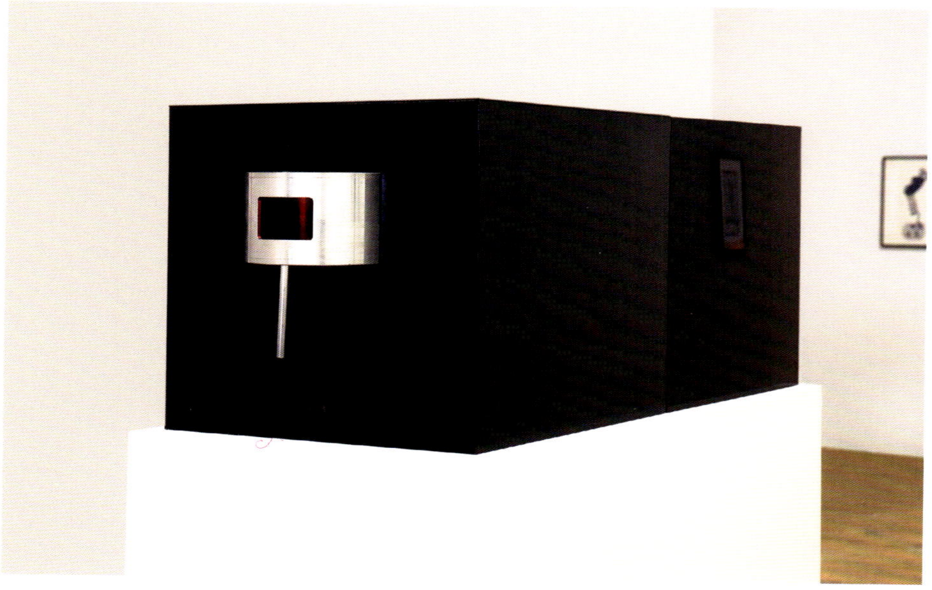

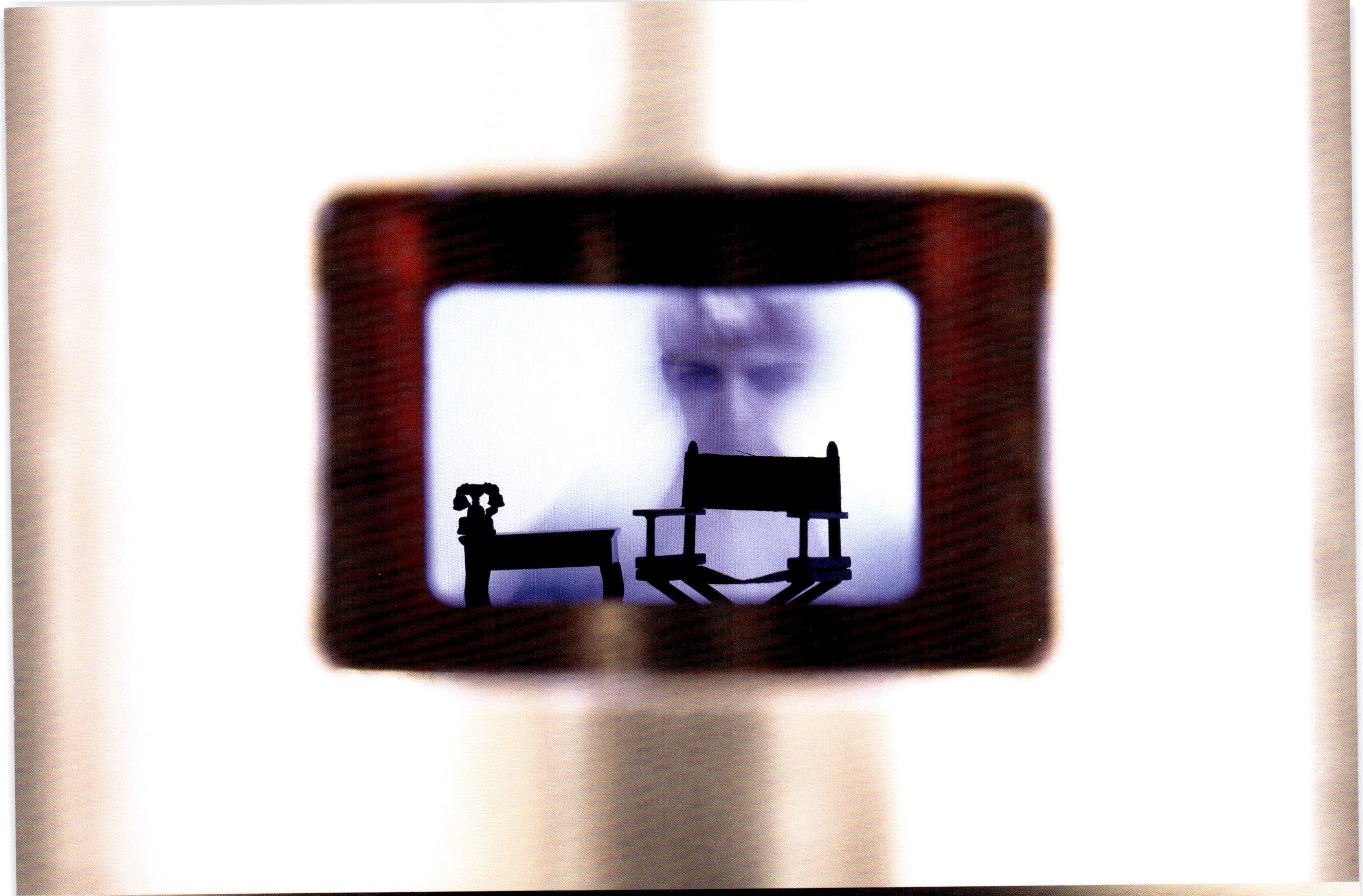

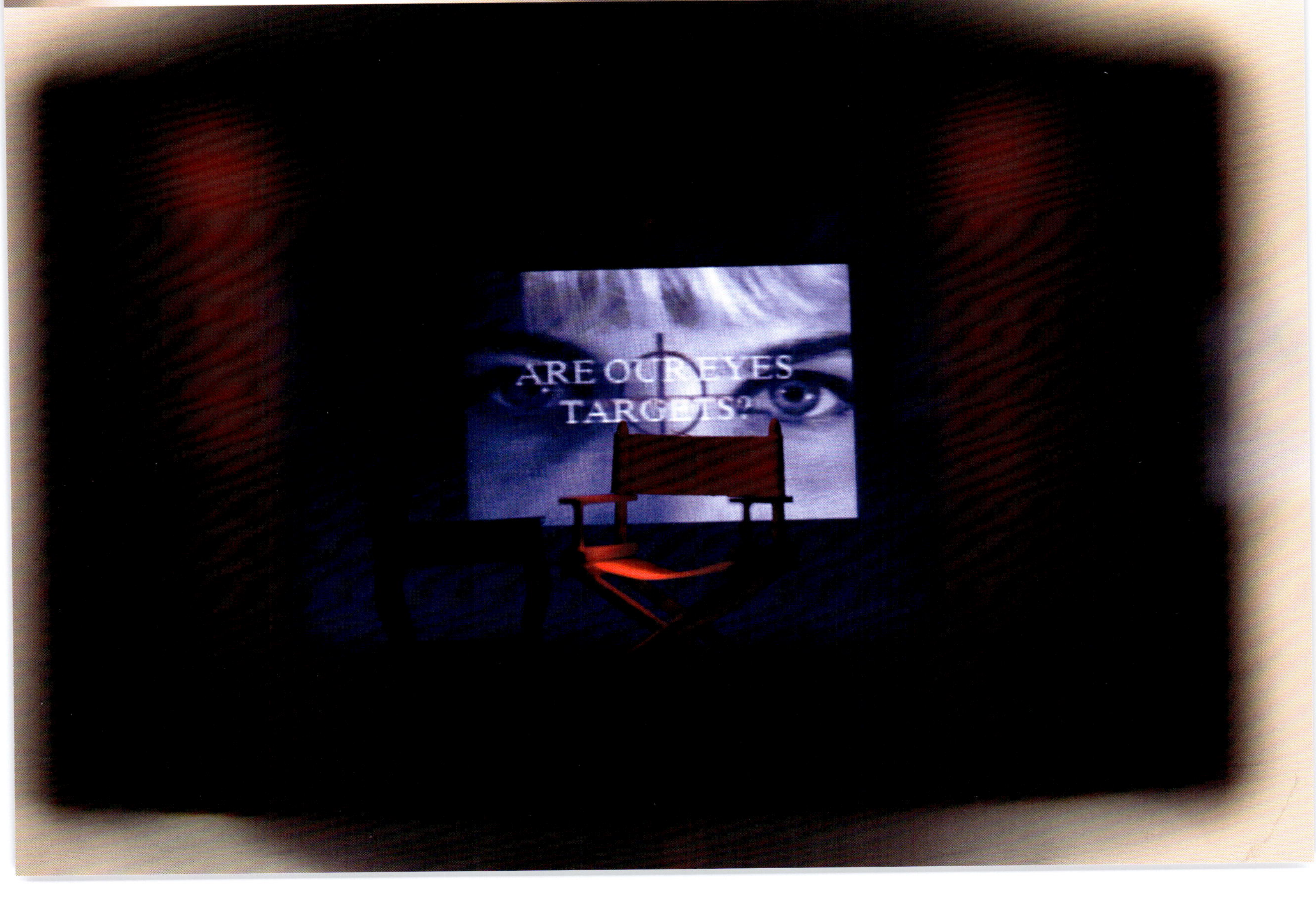
ARE OUR EYES
TARGETS?

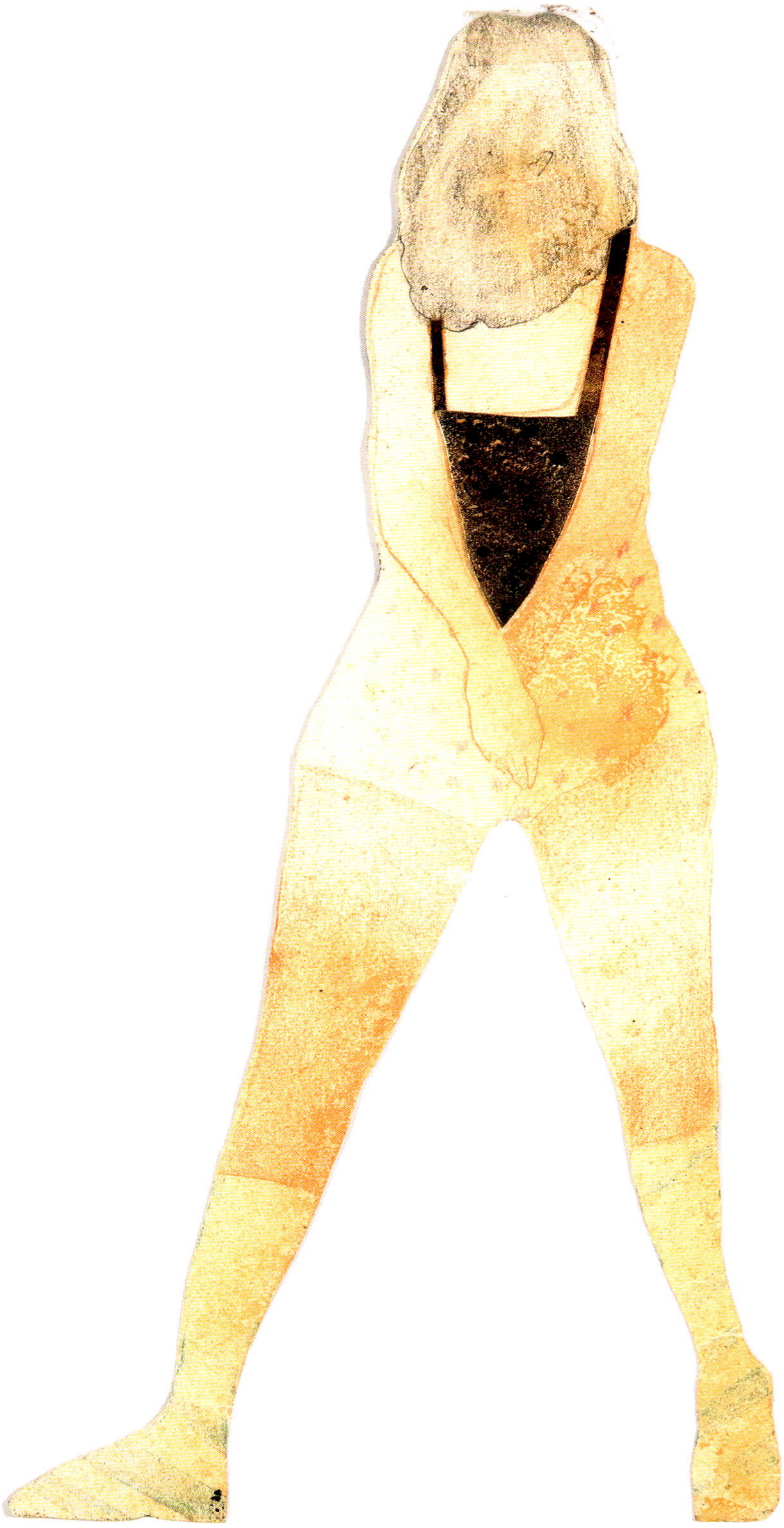

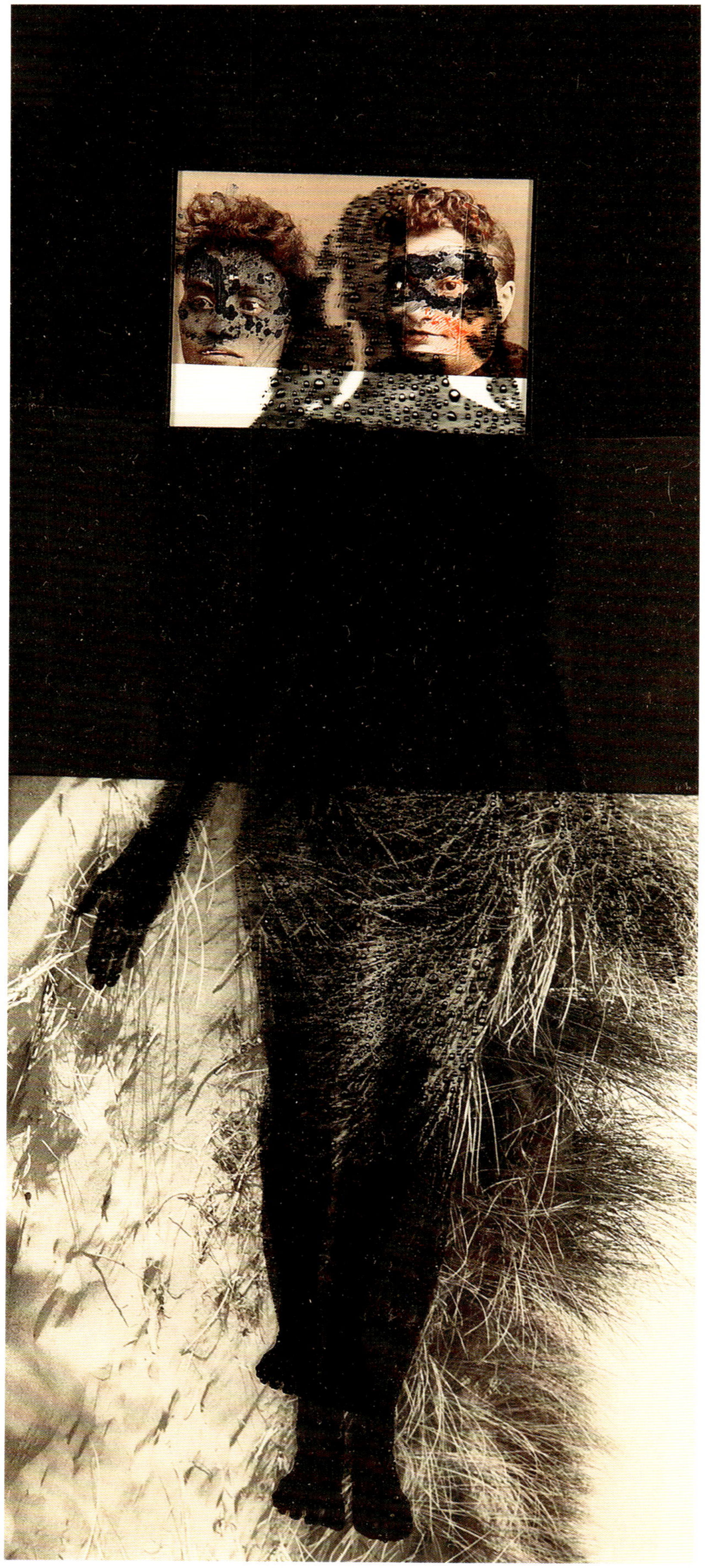

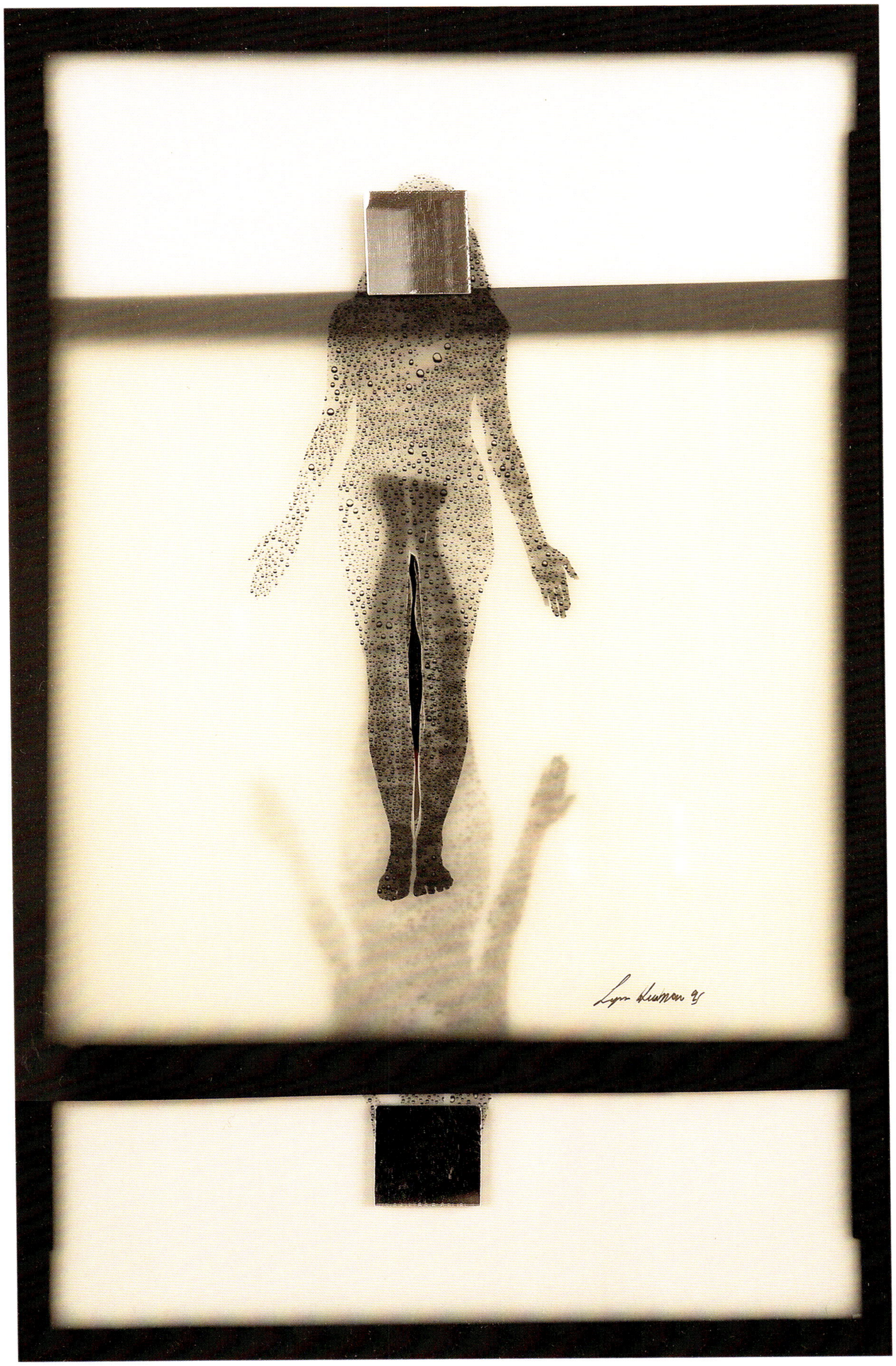

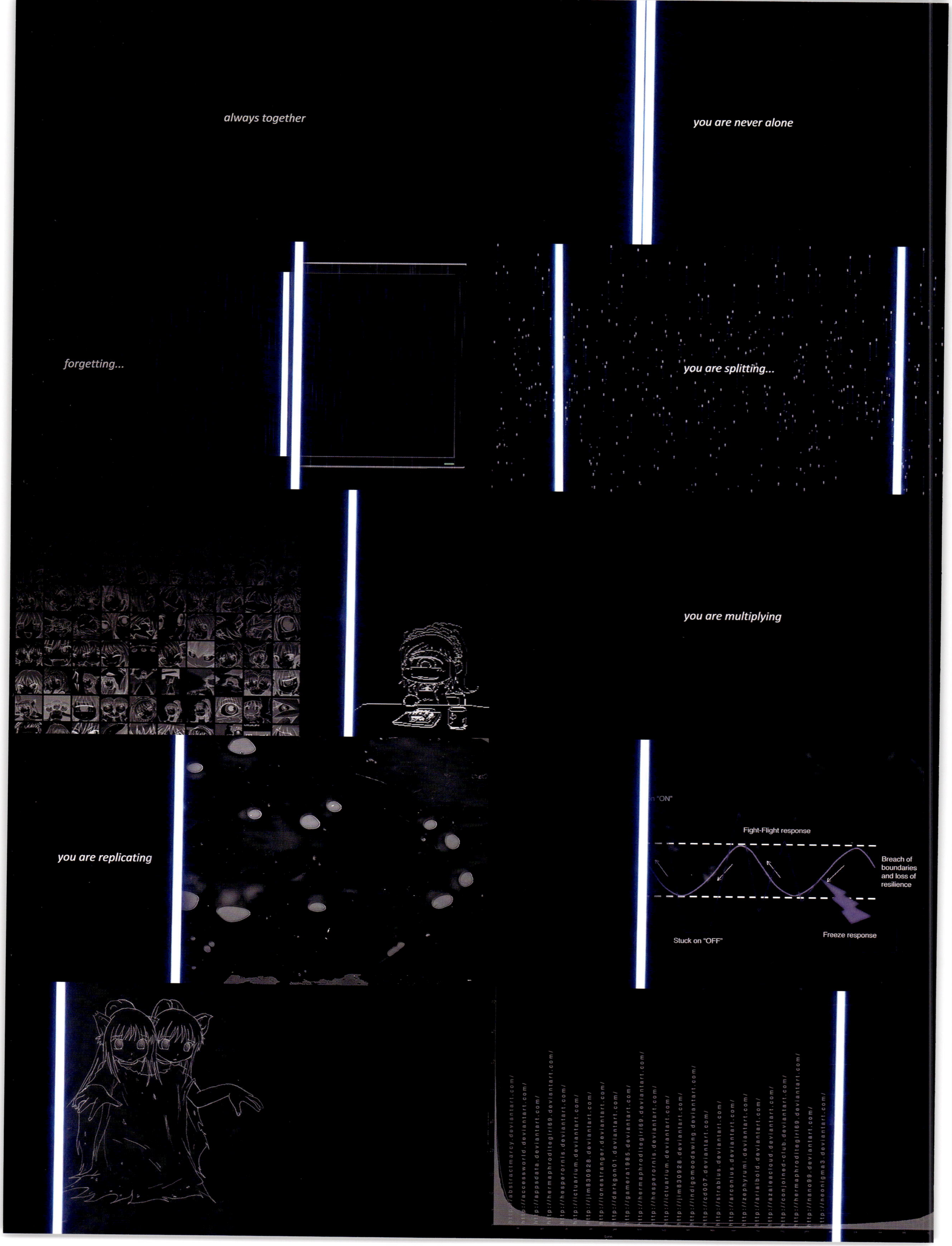

always together
you are never alone
forgetting...
you are splitting...
you are multiplying
you are replicating
"ON"
Fight-Flight response
Breach of boundaries and loss of resilience
Stuck on "OFF"
Freeze response
http://abstractmarcy.deviantart.com/
http://accessworld.deviantart.com/
http://appsdata.deviantart.com/
http://hermaphroditegirl69.deviantart.com/
http://hesperornis.deviantart.com/
http://ictuarium.deviantart.com/
http://jim830928.deviantart.com/
http://lonestranger.deviantart.com/
http://darkgon01.deviantart.com/
http://gamera1985.deviantart.com/
http://hermaphroditegirl69.deviantart.com/
http://hesperornis.deviantart.com/
http://ictuarium.deviantart.com/
http://jim830928.deviantart.com/
http://indigomoodswing.deviantart.com/
http://cd007.deviantart.com/
http://strabius.deviantart.com/
http://arconius.deviantart.com/
http://zephyrumi.deviantart.com/
http://arialbold.deviantart.com/
http://azaleacloud.deviantart.com/
http://conjoined-club.deviantart.com/
http://hermaphroditegirl69.deviantart.com/
http://nano99.deviantart.com/
http://neonigma3.deviantart.com/

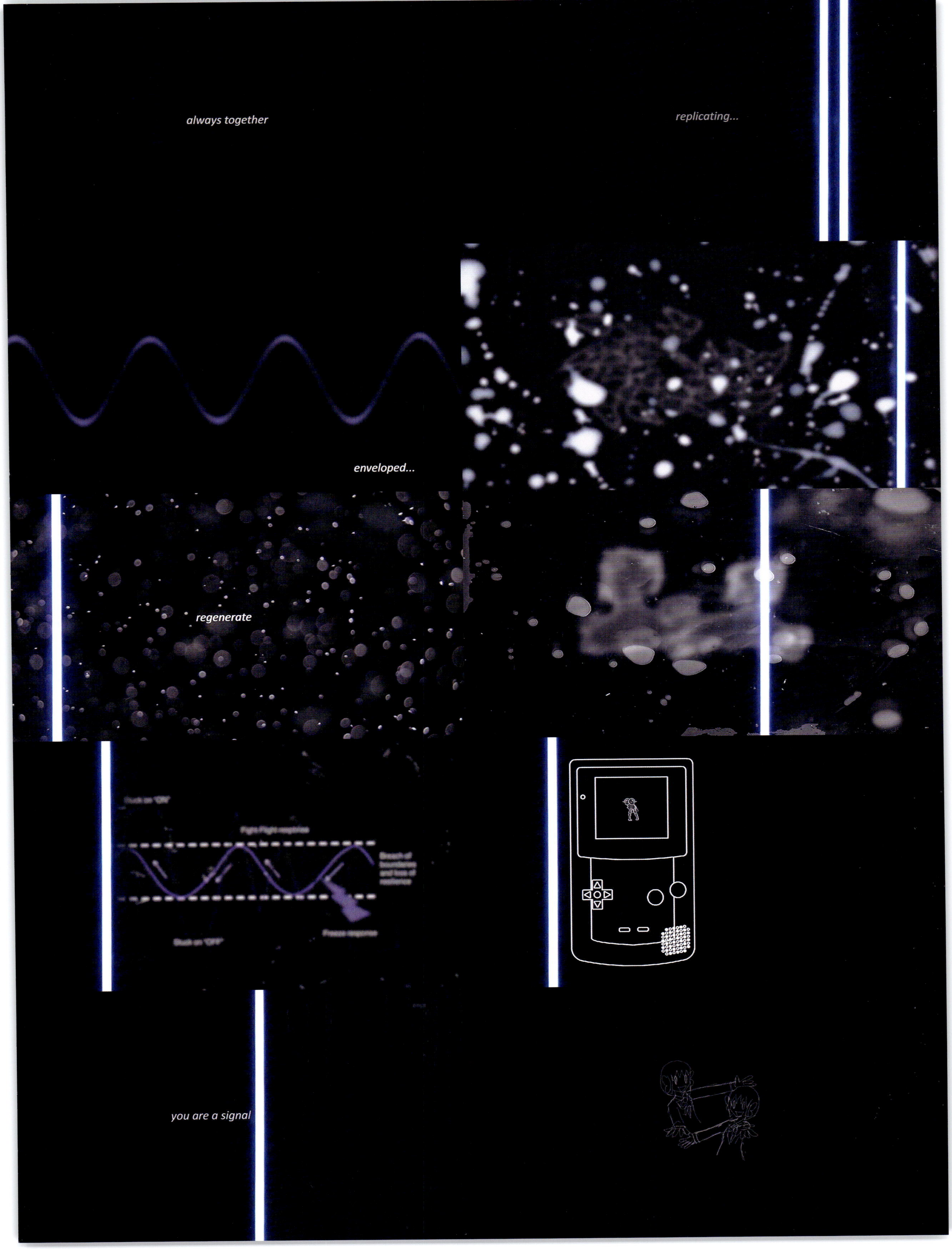
always together
replicating...
enveloped...
regenerate
you are a signal

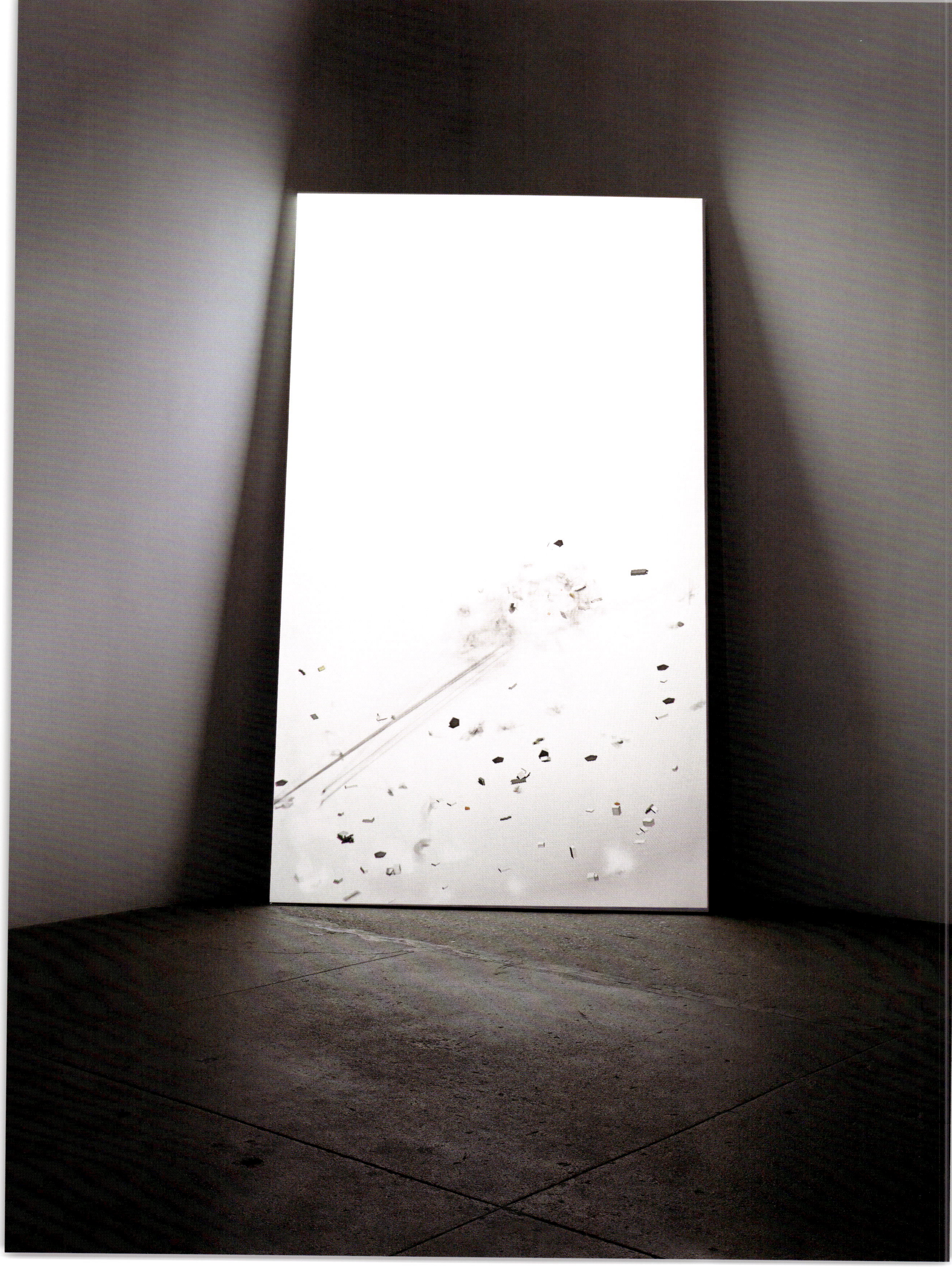

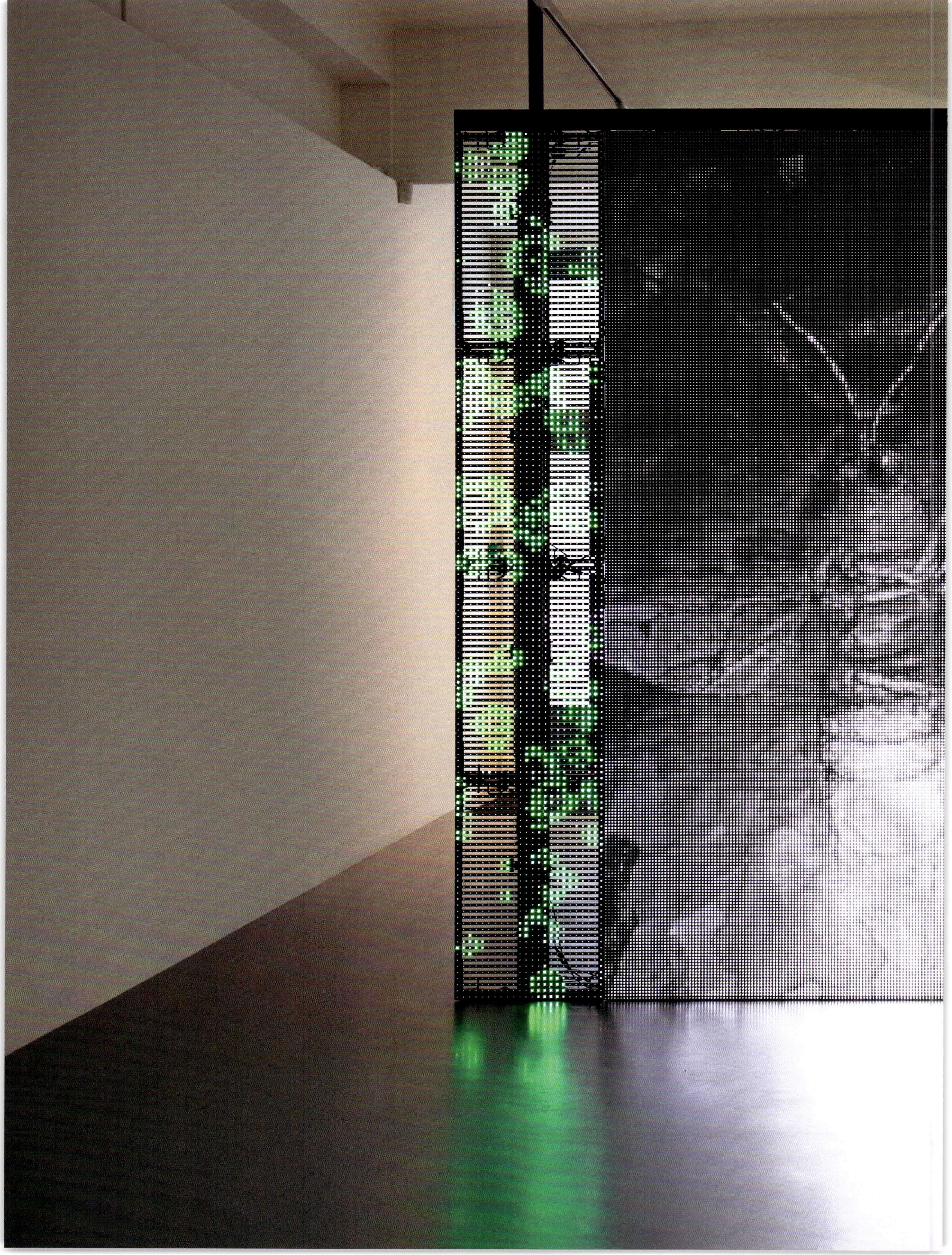

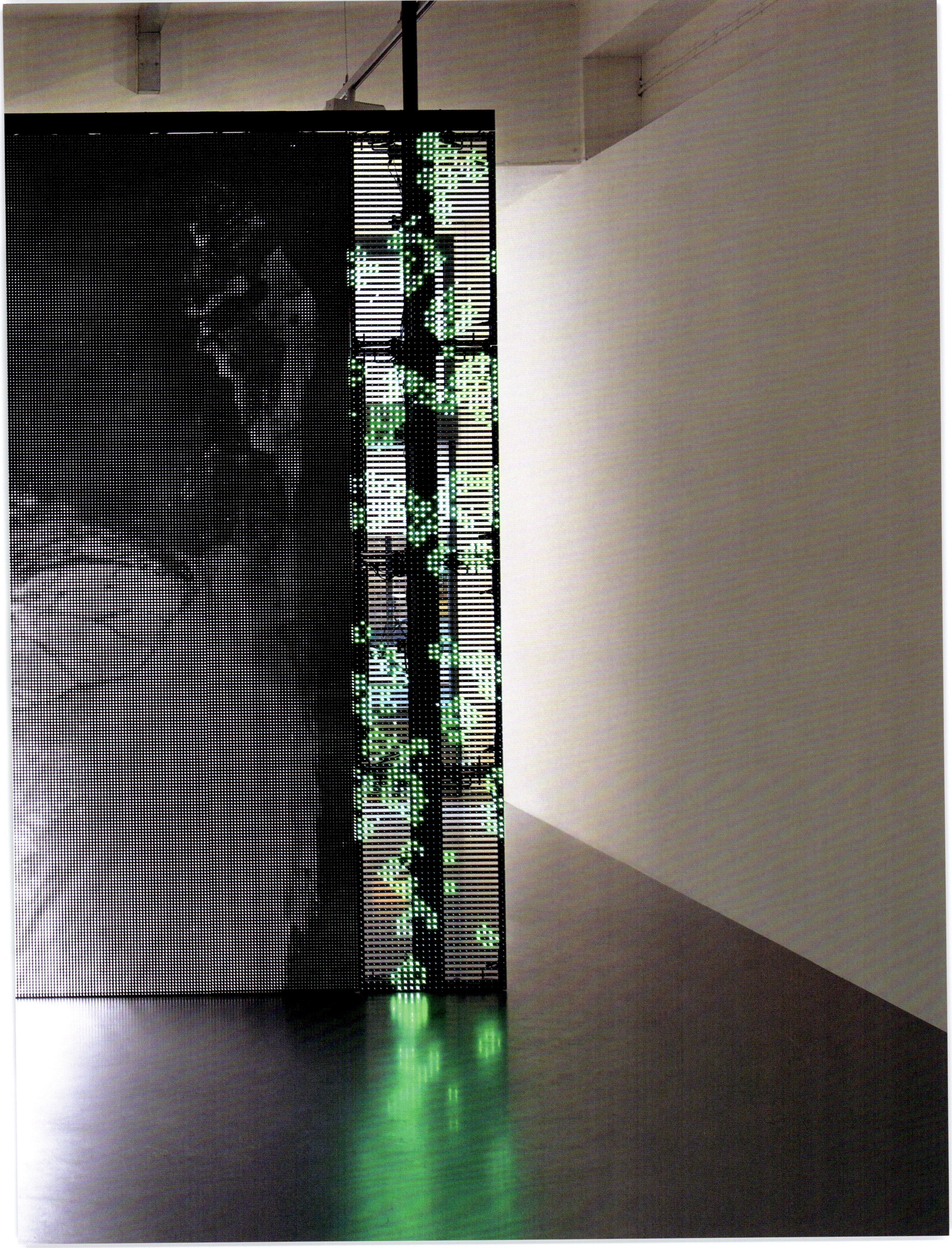

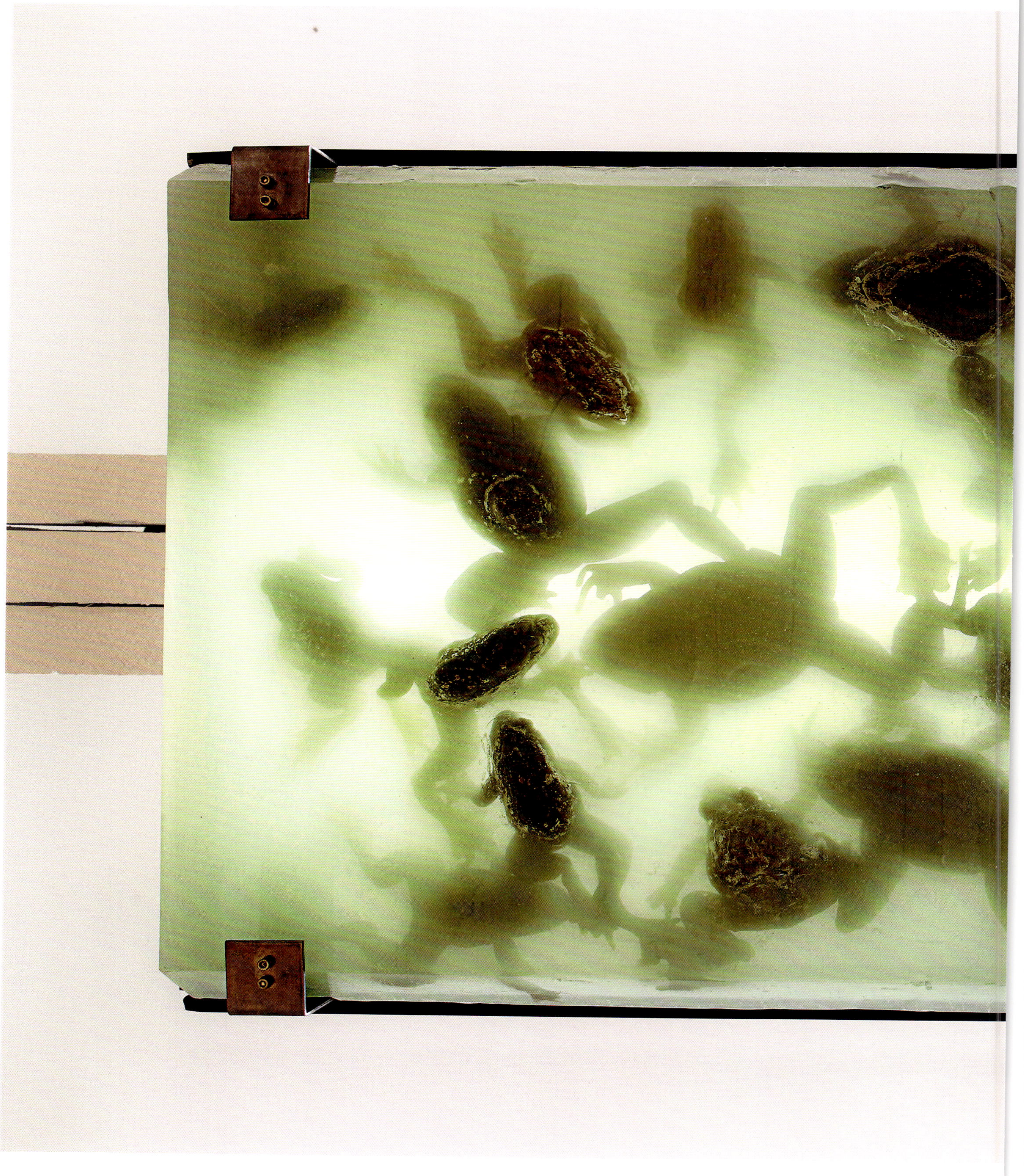

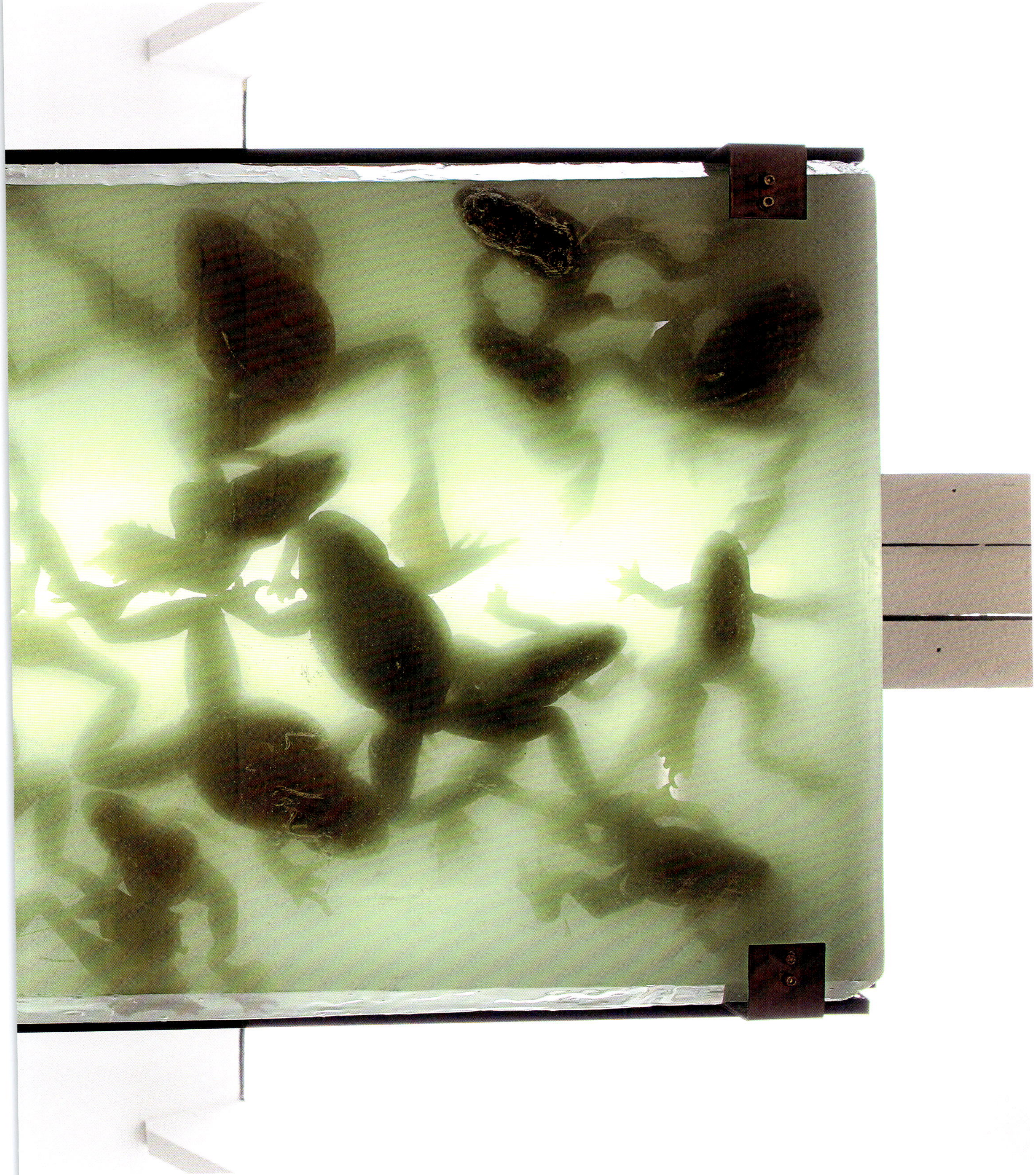

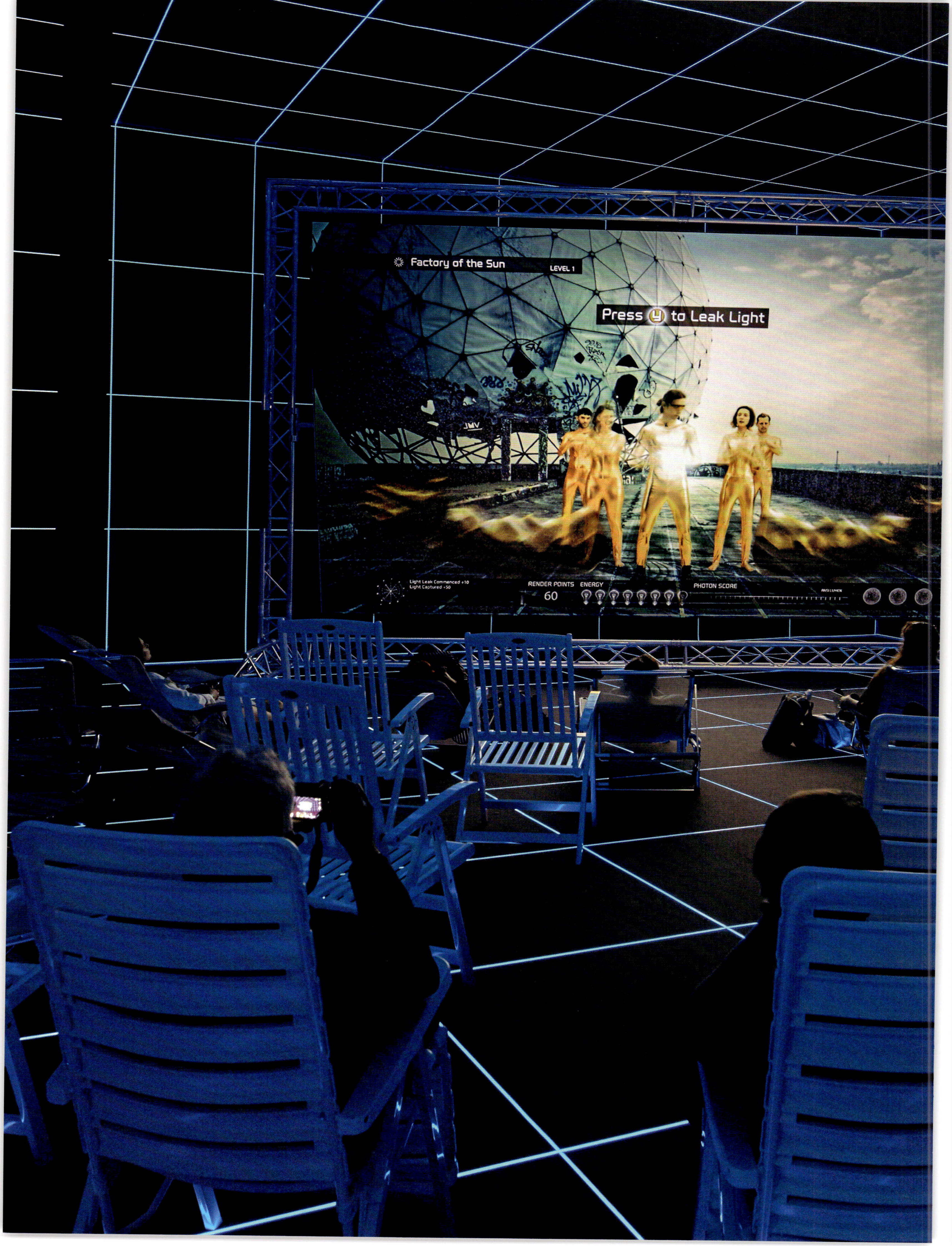
Factory of the Sun
LEVEL 1
Press Y to Leak Light
RENDER POINTS
60
ENERGY
PHOTON SCORE

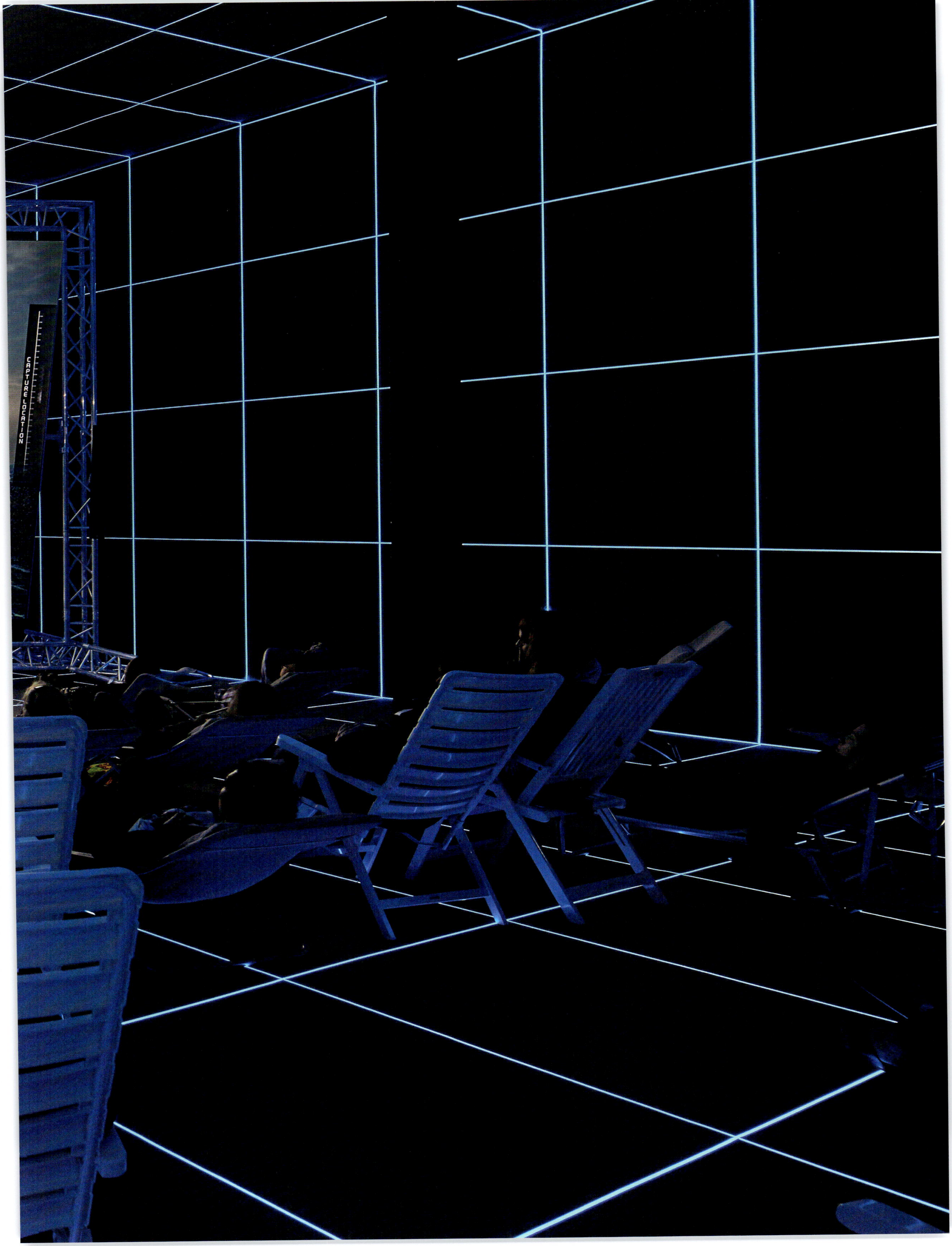
CAPTURE LOCATION

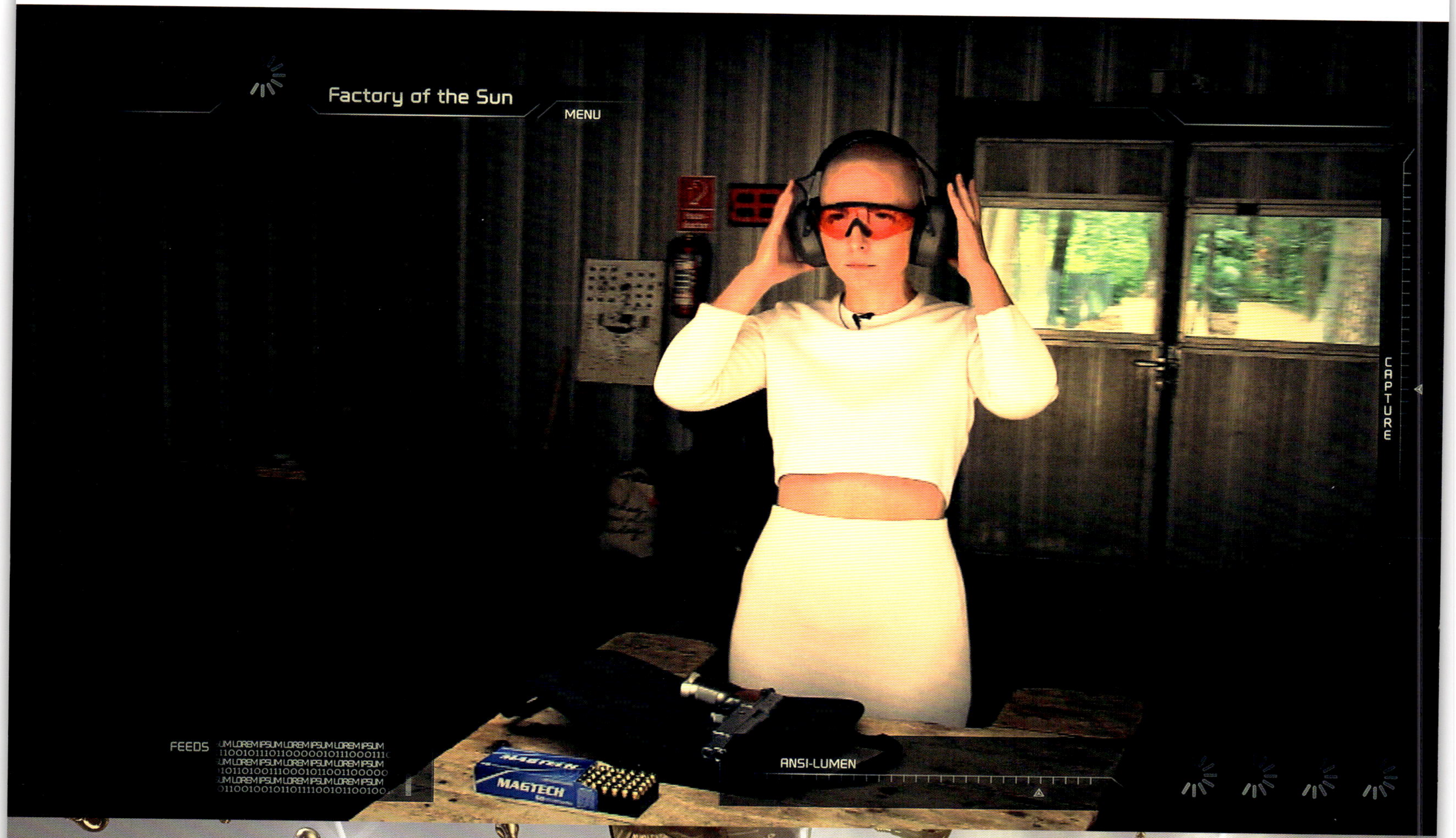
Factory of the Sun
MENU
CAPTURE
FEEDS
MAGTECH
ANSI-LUMEN

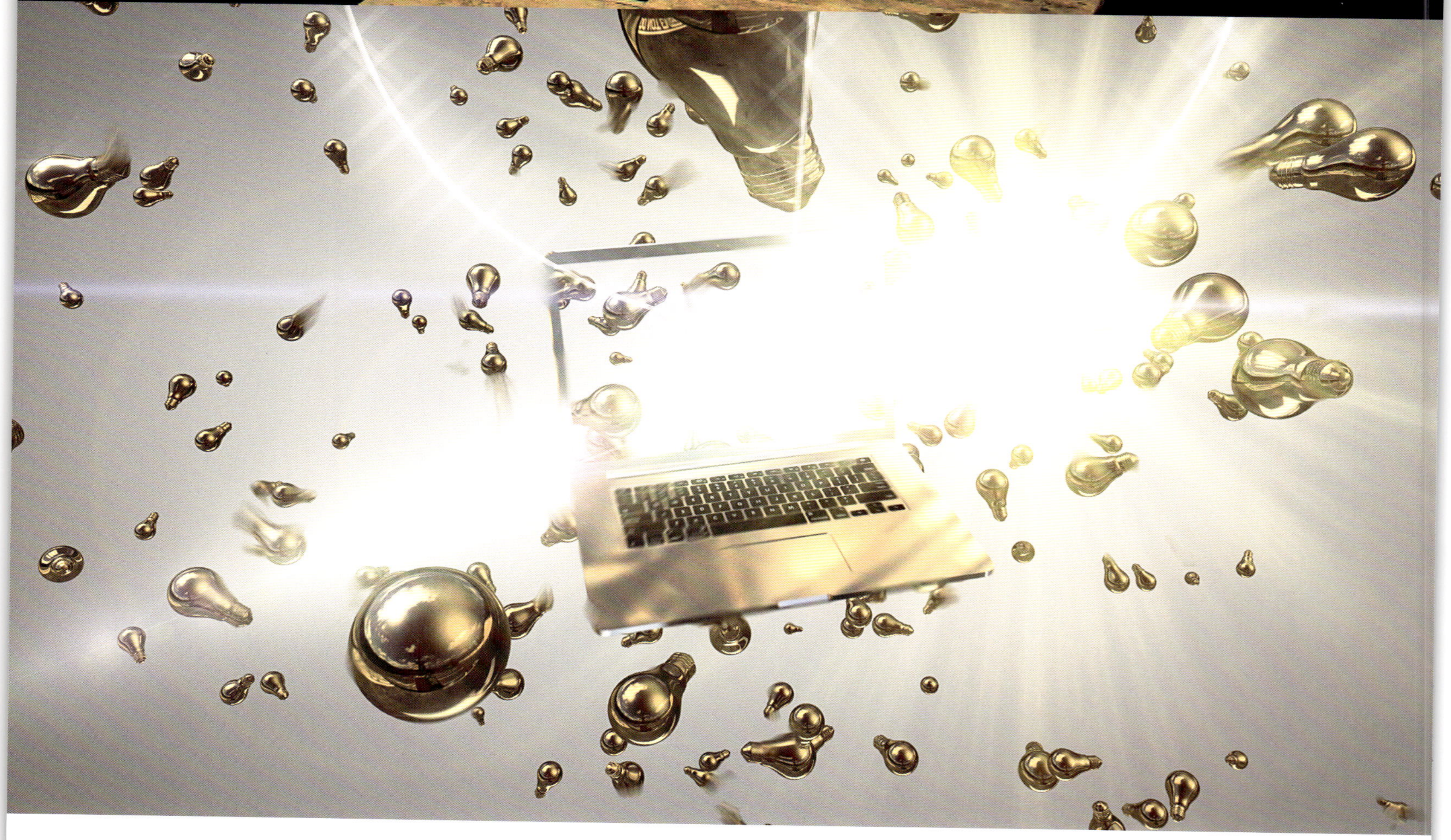

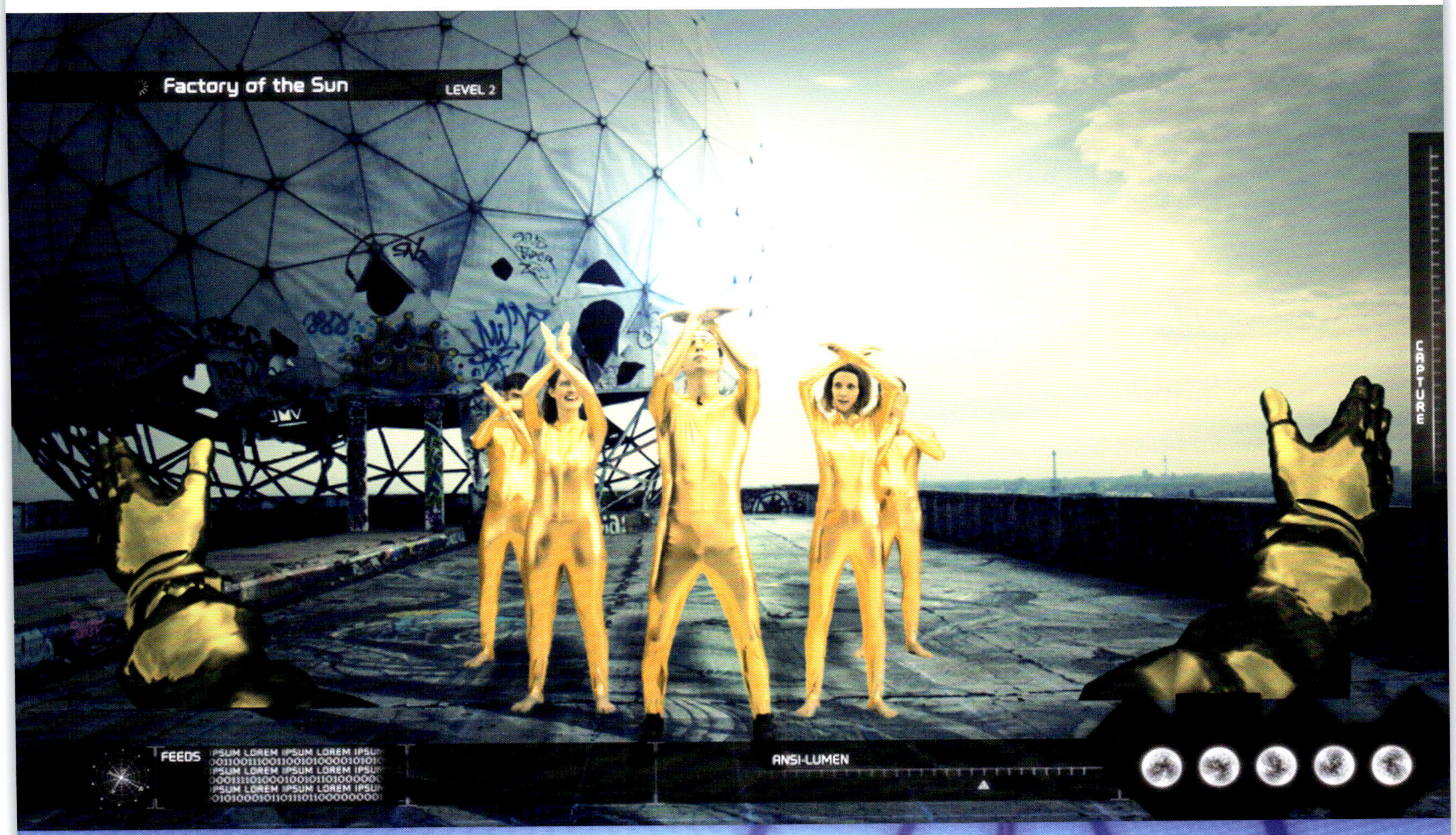
Factory of the Sun
LEVEL 2
CAPTURE
FEEDS
ANSI-LUMEN

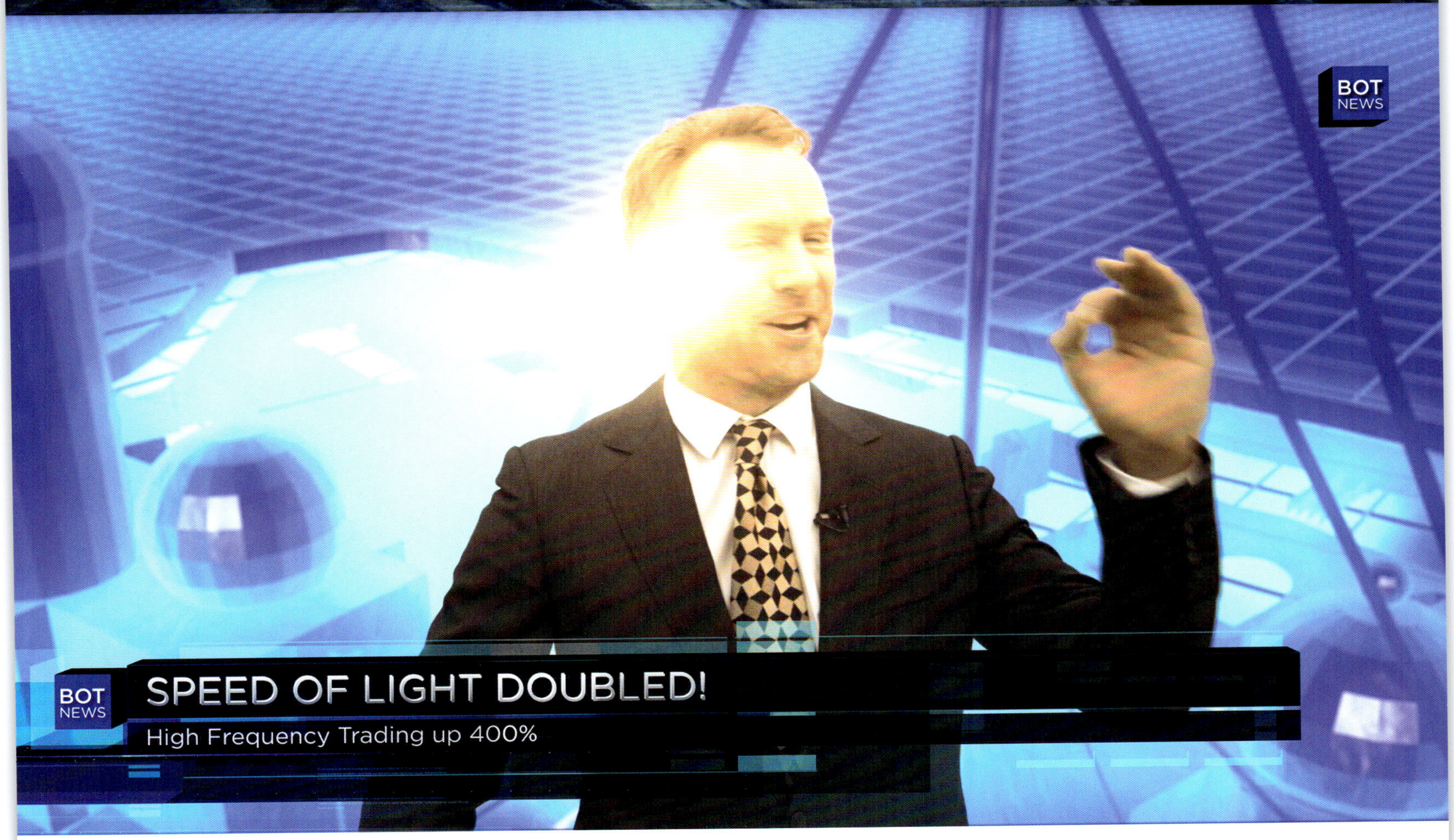
BOT
NEWS
BOT
NEWS
SPEED OF LIGHT DOUBLED!
High Frequency Trading up 400%

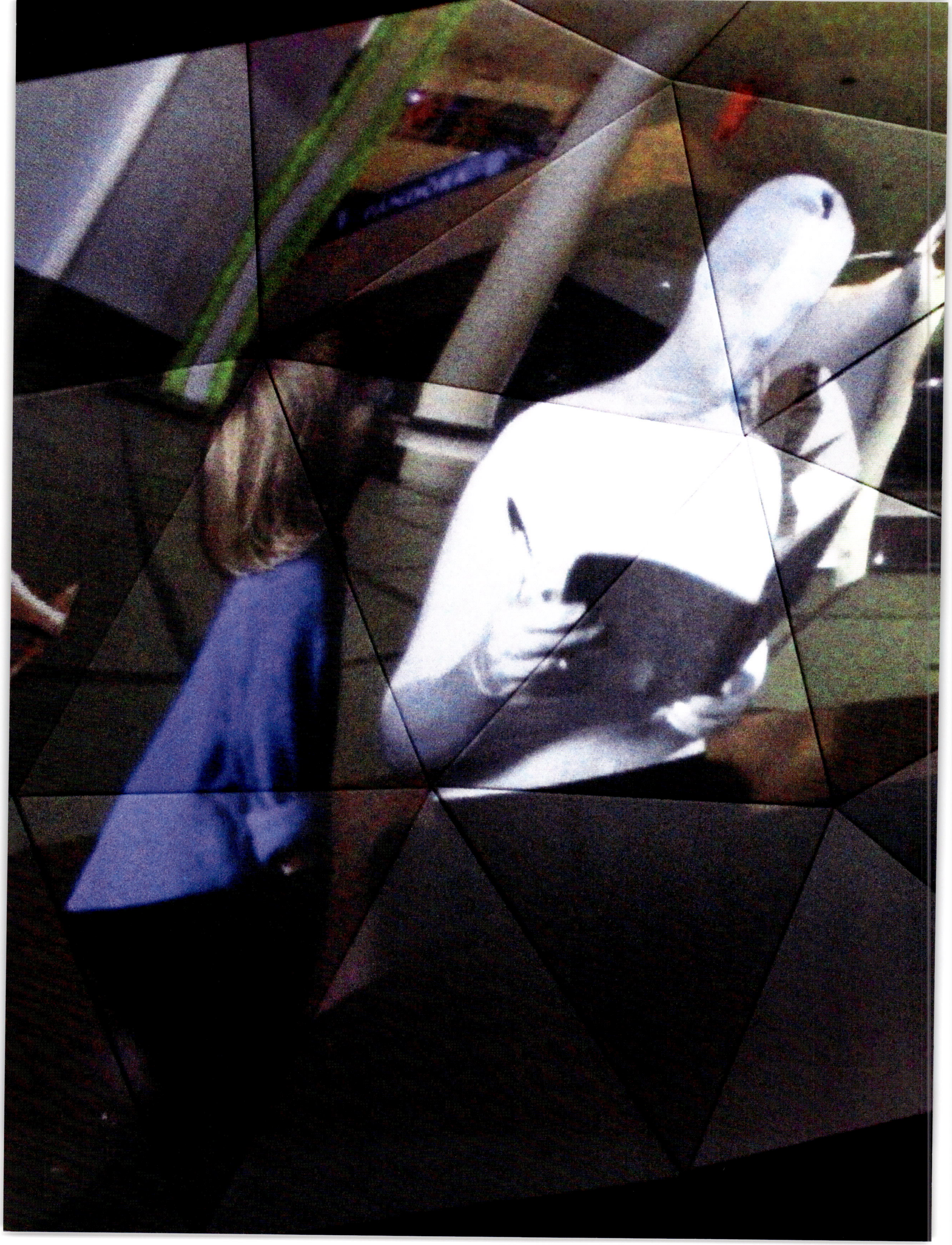

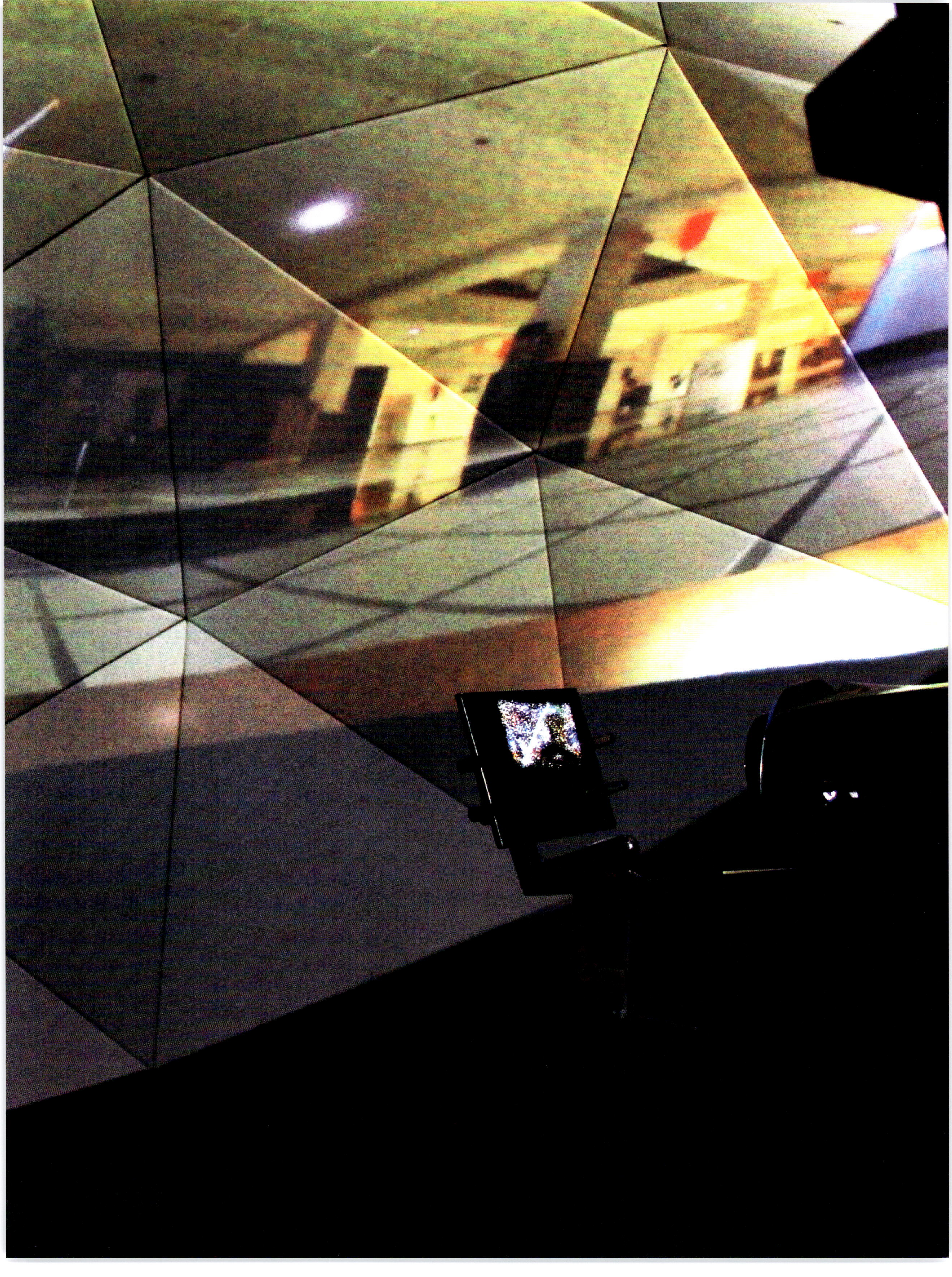

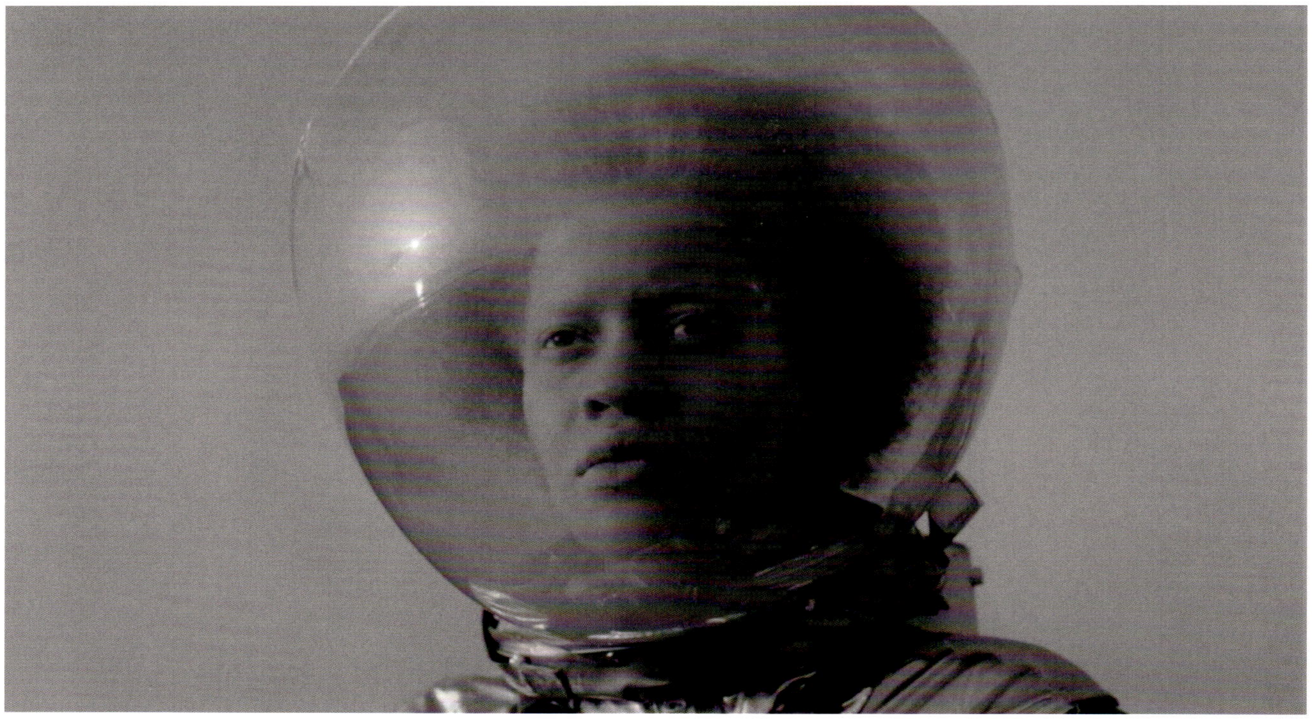

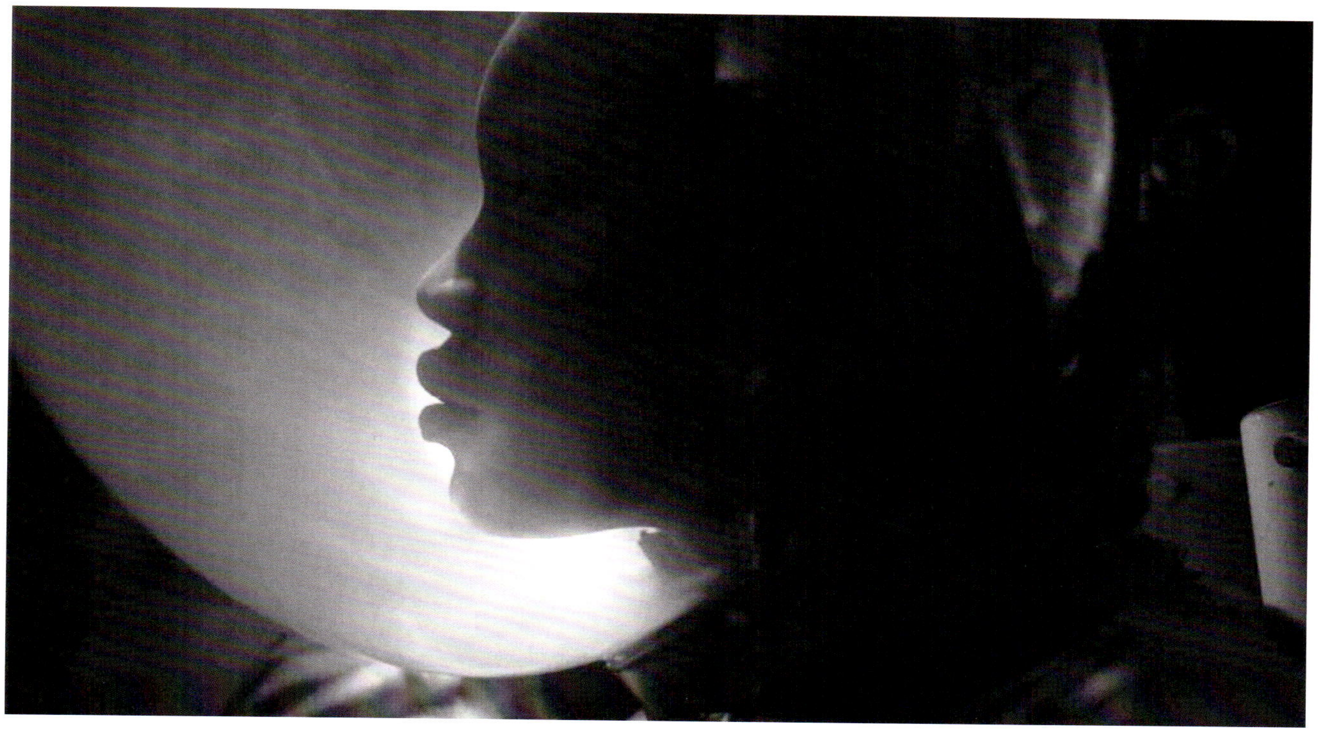

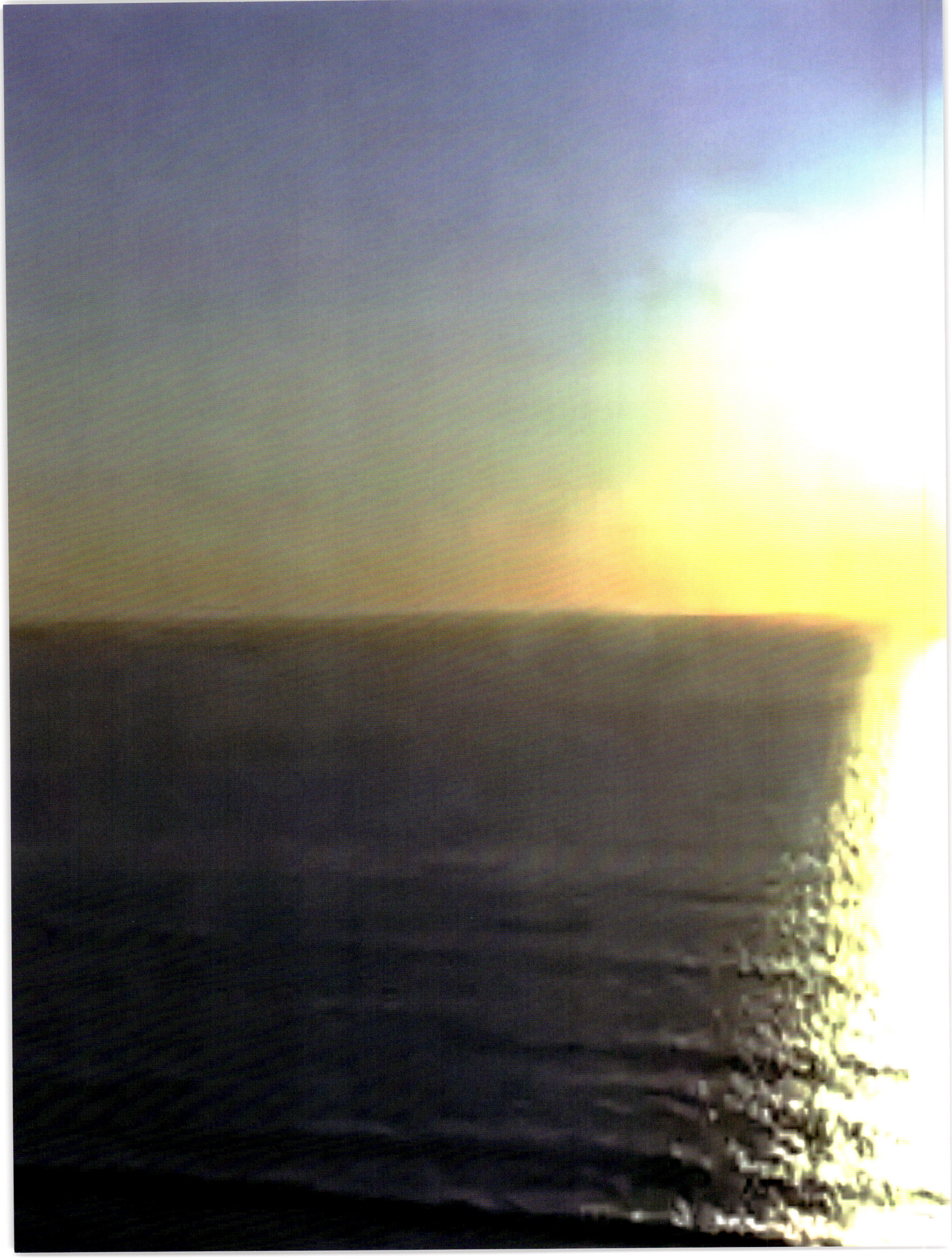

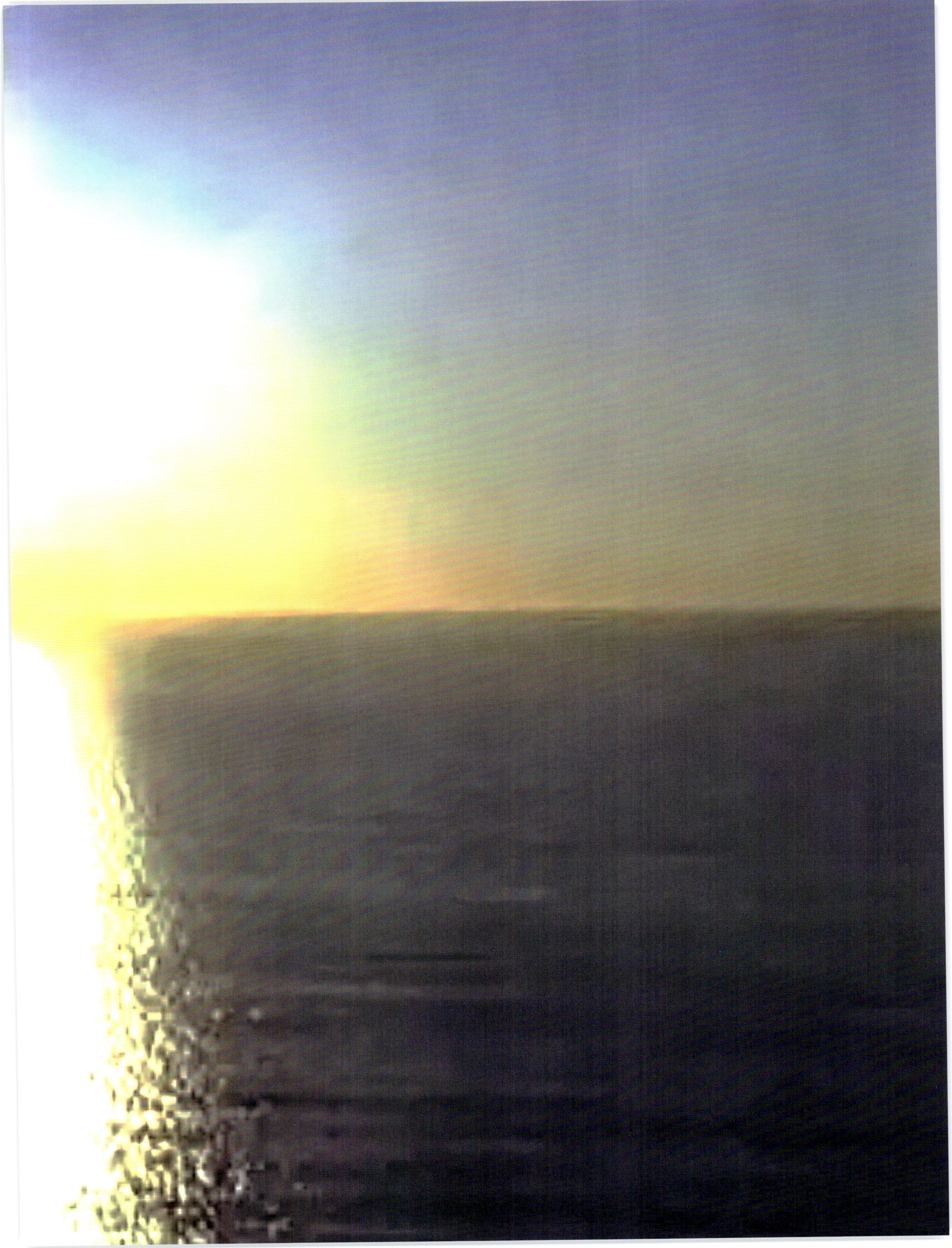

# **Dreamlands**: **Immersive Cinema and Art, 1905–2016**

Chrissie Iles

Whitney Museum of American Art, New York
Distributed by Yale University Press, New Haven and London

Contents

Foreword

In 1913 the thirty-six-year-old Italian immigrant artist Joseph Stella began a revolutionary group of literally spectacular paintings based on his encounter with Coney Island's amusement parks at night. Hypnotized by the sheer voltage of electric lights, and under the thrall of dynamic, Italian Futurist painting, which he had seen recently in Paris, these kaleidoscopic, almost hallucinatory, works were as revolutionary for him personally as they were for art in America. The Whitney Museum is fortunate to possess the intimate, jewel-like canvas *Luna Park* (c. 1913), one of several in a series that culminates in the large-scale *Battle of Lights, Coney Island, Mardi Gras* (1913–14; Yale University Art Gallery, New Haven). These paintings collectively captured not only the vivid light and brilliant color of the amusement parks on Brooklyn's Atlantic coast but also the vertiginous motion of the rides and the frenetic energy of the bustling crowds. In the Whitney's small, dense, and intense oil, Stella captured the feeling and psychological impression of Coney Island more than simply recording its look. The invention of photography freed him, as it had so many artists, from mimesis—imitating the look of the real world—enabling him to experiment with the fundamentals of color, form, and materiality in order to create a synesthetic experience. As Barbara Haskell wrote about *Battle of Lights* in her monograph on Stella, although it applies equally to the Whitney's *Luna Park*: "With the most densely painted areas concentrated in the center, the painting fulfilled the Futurist's admonition to 'put the spectator in the center of the picture.'"[1]

This catalogue and exhibition, *Dreamlands: Immersive Cinema and Art, 1905–2016*, organized by Chrissie Iles, in part takes its title from the larger competitor of Luna Park: Dreamland (1904–11), a fifteen-acre park that boasted about its one million electric light bulbs (four times as many as neighboring Luna Park).[2] But what does Stella's painting of Coney Island have to do with cinema? In her insightful essay in this volume, Iles argues that the dominance of a photographically based narrative cinema (that is, cinema as storytelling) has, until very recently, obscured the importance of what she terms the "haptic spatial experience" of cinema—the sensory, immersive model (the visceral experience). The earliest work she presents as an example, and the film that opens the exhibition, is Edwin S. Porter's *Coney Island at Night* (1905)—a two-minute nearly continuous pan, with occasional zooms, of the glowing, luminescent, phantasmagoric "landscape" of Dreamland and the other amusement parks of Coney Island. The film is not a document of place but rather a semi-abstract experience of light and energy itself; it is an experience like that of the Stella painting, positioning viewers at the center of all they see.

As Iles points out, much of this viewer-centric, spatialized cinema had its origins in the German experimental and animated films of the 1920s (not to mention Bauhaus performance) by directors from Fritz Lang to Oskar Fischinger. Fischinger's *Raumlichtkunst* [Space Light Art] (1926), also part of the exhibition, is a multiprojector work, radically conceived more as a performance event or an environmental installation than as a film. The poet and critic Herman G. Scheffauer, writing in 1920, commented that in its nascency film had been "the lively daughter of dead photography. . . . It mimicked the photograph, the theatrical stage, the painted picture, the formal tableau."[3] He went on to say that film was now in revolution: "The sixth sense of man, his feeling for space or room—his *Raumgefühl* [the conception of defined space]—has been awakened and given a new incentive. Space has been given a voice. It has become a presence. It moves and operates by its distances and by its masses, static yet instinct with the expression of motion; it speaks with forms and with color-values."[4] As *Dreamlands* reveals, instances of immersive cinema can be found throughout the twentieth century, although they have proliferated in recent years with artists taking advantage of new cinematic technologies as well as the physical space of architecture itself to create environmental experiences. Such projects range from Mathias Poledna's hyperillusionistic, Disney-style animation *Imitation of Life* (2013),

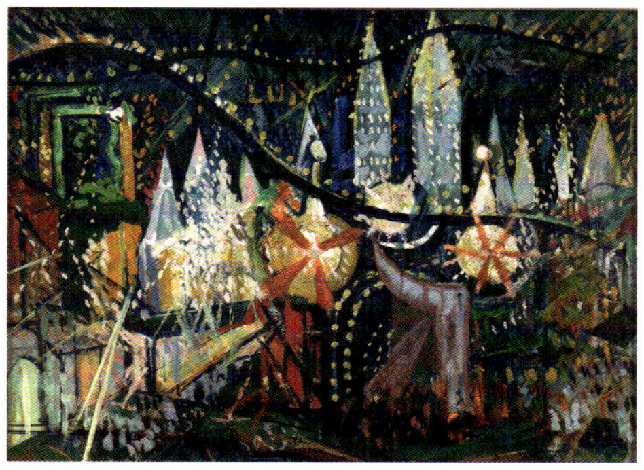

Joseph Stella (1877–1946), *Luna Park*, c. 1913. Oil on composition board, 17 ½ x 23 ½ in. (44.5 x 59.7 cm). Whitney Museum of American Art, New York; gift of Mrs. Charles A. Goldberg 72.147

which was made from over five thousand handmade drawings, to Trisha Baga's *Flatlands* (2010), a low-tech full-room installation work complete with disco ball; and from Hito Steyerl's *Factory of the Sun* (2015), a digital video that viewers watch from within a three-dimensional mock-up of the grid that generated it, to Ian Cheng's *Baby feat. Ikaria* (2013), a large vertical screen featuring swirling animated fragments and chatbots (fueled by artificial intelligence) talking to one another.

Throughout this exhibition and catalogue, Iles also proposes that there is a critical and direct relationship between the cinema and the body. Tom Gunning, in his foundational essay for this volume, traces this idea to the turn-of-the-twentieth-century dancer Loïe Fuller, who, to his mind, "could be considered an inventor of cinema, since she devised a spectacle of highly focused electric light, color, and movement based in a transforming series of images and forms that premiered in Paris in 1893, just two years before the Lumières offered the first public exhibitions of the Cinématographe." In this view, the performative—as with the Stella painting—shares a role in the instigation and creation of immersive cinema. In so many of the works in this exhibition, the viewer in effect serves as a stand-in for the performer.

*Dreamlands* builds on Iles's acclaimed 2001 Whitney Museum exhibition *Into the Light: The Projected Image in American Art 1964–1977*, which also, with a narrower focus, examined the idea of an expanded cinema. It is also the latest example in a long and robust history of Whitney exhibitions and installations that reconsider the space of film, art, and performance within the context of the museum. In particular, I refer to the New American Filmmakers series[5] (1970–98), which featured intermedia film-based installations by pioneering artists such as Joan Jonas, Meredith Monk, Yvonne Rainer, and Paul Sharits; as well as to *Re-Vision: Projects and Proposals in Film and Video*, organized by John G. Hanhardt in 1979, which was the first large museum exhibition devoted to film and video as installation forms in New York.

I am especially grateful to those whose support enabled us to realize this ambitious exhibition and catalogue. Audi generously sponsored *Dreamlands: Immersive Cinema and Art, 1905–2016*, while the Dalio Foundation, the Horace W. Goldsmith Foundation, the Robert Rosenkranz Foundation, and the National Committee of the Whitney Museum of American Art provided essential support as well. The exhibition also benefitted from important contributions by Susan and Matthew Blank, Alexandre and Lori Chemla, Colby Jordan, George and Mariana Kaufman, the Orentreich Family Foundation, Melissa Schiff Soros, and the New York City Department of Cultural Affairs in partnership with the City Council. My great thanks to Scott Rothkopf, deputy director for programs and the Nancy and Steve Crown Family Chief Curator, for his guidance on all aspects of this highly complex endeavor, as well as to Donna De Salvo, deputy director for international initiatives and senior curator, who championed this exhibition from the start in her former role as deputy director for programs and chief curator and emboldened us to present it early on at the new downtown Whitney.

Finally, I would like to congratulate Chrissie Iles, who for many years has wrestled with this complex subject and who understands that immersive cinema has become central to our experience of art and life and is likely to continue to be for many years to come. Thematic exhibitions are among the toughest to conceive and execute but, as in the case with *Dreamlands*, offer great rewards. The Whitney is extremely proud to present this remarkable exhibition, which explores how artists working in film and video have always embraced emerging technology to construct, create, and refine an immersive cinematic space that reframes our perception of reality. One can only imagine the possibilities that tomorrow's technology will bring or how tomorrow's artists will interpret the world through it.

—Adam D. Weinberg, Alice Pratt Brown Director

NOTES

1. Barbara Haskell, *Joseph Stella* (New York: Whitney Museum of American Art, 1994), p. 44.

2. Mario Puzo, "Meet Me Tonight in Dreamland," *New York*, September 3, 1979, p. 30.

3. Herman G. Scheffauer, "The Vivifying of Space," *The Freeman* 2, no. 37 (November 24, 1920); reprinted in Francis Neilson and Albert Jay Nock, eds., *The Freeman, Volume 2* (New York: The Freeman, Inc., 1921), p. 248.

4. Ibid., pp. 248–49.

5. Founded in 1970 as the New American Filmmakers Series, the exhibition series changed its name in 1988 with the forty-fifth program to the New American Film and Video Series; the final program in the series, the eighty-fifth, was held in October–November 1998.

# The Cyborg and the Sensorium

Chrissie Iles

We are living in a moment that the science-fiction writer William Gibson predictively described as a "consensual hallucination,"[1] in which the world has been more radically transformed by technology than at any other moment in history. Our environment has become an all-surrounding, all-surveilled sensorium in which cyberspace determines the contours of everything, from military strategy and economics to politics, architecture, social and intimate relationships, entertainment, the body, and visual perception.

In this new reality, different, pluralistic models of visuality have dismantled the fiction of linear perspective, profoundly altering the ways in which space is constructed, controlled, and experienced. As Hito Steyerl has argued, the global redistribution of perspective onto a vertical, aerial axis of surveillance and control has created a "disembodied . . . post-humanized gaze, outsourced to machines and other objects,"[2] whose vertiginous destabilizing of space is presenting new possibilities for artists and filmmakers, as predominant forms of image making transition from physiological to virtual optics. *Dreamlands: Immersive Cinema and Art, 1905–2016* brings together a group of artists and filmmakers whose work articulates this profound shift, through a broad engagement with cinematic space. This is not a show about cinema. Rather, it takes cinema's role as a discursive site of visual perception as a point of entry, to explore the impact of the transition from the spatial to what Jens Schröter has termed the transplanar image.[3]

Schröter's term, referring specifically to 3D, describes the shift of the image from a two-dimensional plane depicting space (in cinema, the rectangle of the screen) to a multi-planar surface that opens up the optical border between two- and three-dimensional space, intensifying our perception of both, and replacing perspectival looking with a kind of beholding. Extending Schröter's term from the 3D image into physical space, the interplanar cinematic environment becomes a portal into new readings of space, surface, time, materiality, identity, and corporeal presence. The dominance of a photographically based narrative cinema has, until recently, obscured the importance of this haptic model in mapping successive new conceptualizations of human subjectivity. Now, as the camera's efficacy has receded, rendered marginal by CGI, artificial intelligence, and virtual reality, the immersive cinematic space has become perhaps the most potent spatial visualization of the multiple new identities, perspectives, and imaginative realms through which new technology is rendering the visual future.

This haptic model is as fluid and prismatic as the experiences to which it gives form. It operates by prioritizing the senses, the eye, immersive space, the body, and the all-surrounding image, using surprise, shock, touch, light, darkness, synesthesia, and spectacle. It erases the horizon line, flattens space through animation and abstraction, or heightens the illusion of three-dimensionality through 3D, color, interplanar structures, physical objects, and special effects. It dismantles the elements by which cinema is conventionally constituted—projection, apparatus, film, the frontal rectangular screen, darkness, immobility, cinematography, linear narrative—and reassembles them in new forms that are in many cases barely recognizable as having any relationship to cinema at all. It asserts kaleidoscopic vision as a liberating device. It recalibrates our experience of visual surface as tactile materiality, and reframes our perception of reality by revealing it to be one side of a Möbius strip whose reverse is artifice.

In the midst of this cinematic sensorium, the figure of the cyborg continually reappears, a chimeric figure in the form of a body, often female, assembled from a combination of organic and technological elements, that both absorbs and reflects a collective anxiety and ambivalence toward technology's saturation of our personal and social identities. The cyborg populates science, medicine, sex, and war.[4] In the cinematic space, its presence similarly addresses production, reproduction, and the erasure of binaries,

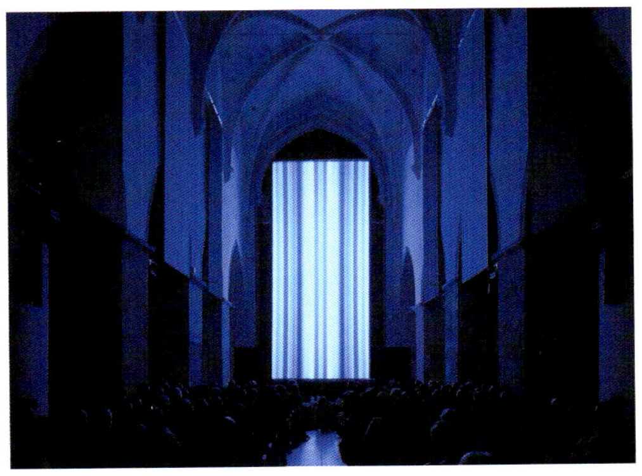

View of Vertical Cinema, a project organized by Sonic Arts featuring ten commissioned vertical 35mm Cinemascope films made by experimental filmmakers and audiovisual artists, at the Klangraum Krems Minoritenkirche, Austria, October 2013

through haptic encounters with the boundary of what constitutes the biological and the technological, the fictive and the real.

*Dreamlands* explores the arc of this model of the cinematic as a haptic spatial experience, from early twentieth-century projective experiments to contemporary works in film, installation, drawing, 3D environments, expanded cinema events, sculpture, performance, artificial intelligence, and online space. Its title references the science-fiction writer H. P. Lovecraft's "Dreamlands," an alternate dimension whose underworld terrain of cities, forests, and mountains can be visited only through dreams. In our current 24/7 environment, perpetuated by a society in which we are all disposable units—deprived, as Jonathan Crary argues,[5] of the full withdrawal through sleep that allows pause, and perhaps dissent, from consumerism and surveillance—the spaces in *Dreamlands* unfold like a map of interior dimensional dreaming.

The structure of this immersive map produces a matrix of interconnections between different historical moments. The fear of technology's destructive power articulated in Fritz Lang's *Metropolis* (1927) and Walt Disney's *Fantasia* (1940) is confirmed in the terrible sublime of atomic explosion in Bruce Conner's CROSSROADS (1976), and echoed in the noir concept artwork by illustrator Syd Mead for Ridley Scott's *Blade Runner* (1982), whose narrative source is the postapocalyptic wasteland of Philip K. Dick's novel *Do Androids Dream of Electric Sheep?*. The cyborg that appears as Maria in *Metropolis* reappears as Rose Hobart in Joseph Cornell's 1936 collage film of the same name, as an army of brooms in *Fantasia*, and as humanoid replicants in *Blade Runner*. It is sometimes located in the audience itself, as it moves through the ethereal surface of the projector beam in Anthony McCall's *Line Describing a Cone* (1973); or as different versions of itself, as in the various personae given to Pierre Huyghe and Philippe Parreno's anime figure Annlee. Sometimes it appears symbolically, as in Mathias Poledna's animated donkey in *Imitation of Life* (2013); as a collaged body, in Lynn Hershman Leeson's cyborg drawings; or as a mythical body to be propelled into outer space in Frances Bodomo's film *Afronauts* (2014). In Dora Budor's immersive installation, we step into the interior architecture of a cyborgian body and re-animate it through our movements. And in Hito Steyerl's *Factory of the Sun* (2015), Yulia, a female cyborg, narrates the film as it switches between different levels of reality.

Throughout the exhibition, we are made aware of how the location of the screen and the image in space mirrors the continual redefinition of the boundaries of social space by urban culture and technology and how the frontality traditionally associated with cinematic viewing is as much a modernist construct as the white cube of the gallery. In 1917, several thousand children gathered in Kansas City's Convention Hall to watch J. Searle Dawley's silent film *Snow White* (1916) back-projected onto four large screens arranged in a square and suspended in the center of the room. The wide horizontal image of Abel Gance's triple-screen film *Napoléon* (1927) could arguably be read as a flattening out and narrowing of these earlier spatialized moving images, just as CinemaScope's widening of the image in commercial cinema in the 1950s predicted not a new experience of cinematic space, but the return to an earlier model. Roland Barthes' observation in 1954 that with CinemaScope, "I am no longer under the image but in front of it, in the middle of it"[6] marks him as a modernist observer, suspended between two models of immersion: an earlier projective panorama and a future distracted environment of the atomized digital image.

The current all-surrounding social space has blurred the boundaries between the real and the virtual, producing what Paul Virilio described as an "image" energy or "information" energy that "eliminates the 'line' of the visible horizon in favor of the linelessness of a deep and imaginary horizon." In this new reality, "touch and tactile telepresence" muddy the distinction between the real and the virtual, casting doubt on our presence here and now.[7] Virilio's description of tactility as a condition of a horizonless temporal space underlines the presence of the body in the haptic cinematic model as cyborgian, occupying space as a fusion of organic form and technological immateriality. This fusion took form in the 1920s not only metaphorically, in films such as *Metropolis*, but also as direct corporeal experience, in immersive film and light organ experiments. Antonin Artaud, writing about cinema, declared that "the human skin of things, the epidermis of reality[,] . . .

is the primary raw material of cinema."[8] The cyborgian figures that populate the spaces of this exhibition articulate Artaud's desire for a cinema that could "produce a shock to thought, rearranging our experience of our own body." The broken bodies of Oskar Schlemmer's mechanical figures in *Das Triadische Ballett* [Triadic Ballet] (1922) become, in the ethereal screen of Parreno's *With a Rhythmic Instinction to be Able to Travel Beyond Existing Forces of Life* (2014), fleeting cellular fragments that briefly form into fireflies, then disappear.

The cyborgian body also appears in the exhibition as an object of desire trapped inside the machine of the commercial film industry, as in the chimeric figure of Rose Hobart in Joseph Cornell's 1936 film named for the actress, in which the artist cut up a print of the "schlock horror"[9] Hollywood film *East of Borneo* (1931) and reassembled it using only the parts in which Hobart appeared. The actress, now exquisite corpse, was projected through blue glass and in slow motion, transforming her into a cyborgian montage of the human and the technological, trapped mutely between the deathly surfaces of celluloid and blue light, like a specimen (see pp. 22–23).

The immersion of both the film and the viewer in color and sound occurs spectacularly in *Fantasia* (1940), Walt Disney's most experimental work, for which he created a synesthetic screening environment that engaged the senses, and which included an early version of surround sound. Its prioritizing of the haptic, sensory experience over conventional narrative situates it both as part of the end of the prewar utopian cinematic experiments of the 1920s and 1930s, and as a precursor to the all-surrounding media environment that emerged following the end of World War II. The cyborg and the sensorium are brought together in The Sorcerer's Apprentice section of the film, in which Mickey Mouse, cast as the Sorcerer's Apprentice, brings a cyborg to life in the form of a broom leaning against the wall in the workshop (see pp. 30–31). An uncontrollable technological force is unleashed as the cyborg sprouts hands, then rapidly clones itself, producing an unending procession of copies that march robotically back and forth carrying buckets of water, drowning the workshop and everything in it, until order is finally restored by the Sorcerer. The scene takes its title from Goethe's cautionary poem of the same name, written in 1797, immediately after the shock of the French Revolution, when all the talk was of science fiction and automatons. That historical iteration of cyborgian anxiety is transformed by Disney and his team into a portentous immersive fusion of music, color, and sound, in which the cyborg and the sensorium threaten to engulf reality, just at the moment when the world had become engulfed by war.

In the new technological environment that emerged following the end of World War II, as the haptic became increasingly predominate, the cinematic cyborg split into two. One form continued to develop within the science-fiction context that had given birth to the android in literary form during the first phase of the Industrial Revolution in the eighteenth century, in mainstream films such as Stanley Kubrick's *2001: A Space Odyssey* (1968, as HAL 9000), *Alien* (1979, as the alien creature), or *Blade Runner* (1982, as the replicant). The other transferred the cyborg from the screen to the audience, as part of a growing detachment of the screen from its fixed position within the darkness of the theater and its dispersion into expanded cinema and performative cinematic installations, in which viewers' bodies became fused with the technological presence of the filmic apparatus in physical space.

The most phantasmagoric example of this new, dispersed, mobile cyborgian presence occurs in Anthony McCall's *Line Describing a Cone* (1973), a thirty-minute film showing a large white circle gradually appearing on a black background, projected against the wall of a darkened space. The light emanating from the projector is made more visible by a fine mist introduced into the space (originally cigarette smoke, now generated by a

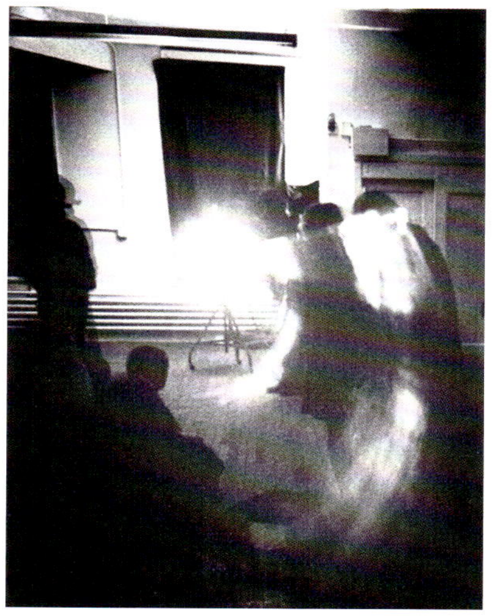

Peter Moore (1932–1993), Installation view of Anthony McCall's *Line Describing a Cone* (1973), Artists Space, New York, 1974

haze machine), as the beam changes from a thin line into a curved plane, and finally a large hollow cone, extending the circle into its projective volumetric equivalent. Created by McCall on an animation stand using hundreds of carefully mapped-out drawings, the slow formation of the circle allows the viewer time to encounter the cone in stages—to first gaze upon, then touch, then enter, and finally move around inside it, inhabiting it collectively, like architecture.

In drawing viewers inside the film's physical center, we become both part of the film and part of the screen onto which it is projected. Each new viewer becomes yet another "screen," fracturing the cone across as many different surfaces as there are bodies interacting with it. Enclosed by the beam, each viewer can watch the penetration of its interior by the disembodied hands, faces, torsos, and legs of other viewers as they play with the beam's porous surface. *Line Describing a Cone* predicts the contemporary digital touchscreen but takes its tactility further, since, unlike the touchscreen, it can be penetrated by the entire body. Through this performative penetration, viewers become temporary cyborgs, transformed into hybrid cinematic bodies for the duration of their merging with the technology of the filmic space that they momentarily inhabit.

McCall's hybrid of the phantasmagoric and the cybernetic signals the shift away from image to surface that had begun in the first half of the twentieth century. In 1936 in Paris, Kandinsky, Duchamp, Picabia, Arp, Sirato, and others had signed the *Dimensionist Manifesto*, declaring that "a completely new art form will develop. . . . The human being, rather than regarding the art object from the exterior, becomes the center and five-sensed subject of the artwork."[10] The advent of television accelerated this transition. While the movies, as Marshall McLuhan argued, extended "one single sense, in high definition,"[11] television was "low definition," like a cartoon, and demanded a more instant, participatory viewing experience that extended all the senses in a "total field of awareness" that signaled the cinematic's migration into a new, cybernetic environment.

One of the hallmarks of this new environment was the increasing visibility of the private, the subliminal, and the hidden, as the boundary between the interior physical and psychic self and the exterior world became increasingly porous. Synthesizing experiences through all the body's senses rendered it conceptually transparent. Lynn Hershman Leeson articulated the impact of this cyborgian transparency on identity in a series of cyborg drawings, begun in 1963, in which the female body, traced out like a cross between a paper doll and an anatomical drawing, floats in an indeterminate space, its skin traversed with diagrammatic lines and its inner organs visible, as though captured in x-ray, layered with parts of a machine. In the first cyborg drawing, made in 1963, two hearts—one large, the other small—sit below her lungs, and her left arm, barely visible, disappears like an amputated limb. In a clear dialogue with the cyborg bodies of Weimar Dada collage—in particular, the political images of Hannah Höch—Leeson's cyborgs evoke Giuliana Bruno's analogy of cinematic looking at the female body with dissection. Bruno compares the cinema screen with the anatomical dissecting table in an anatomy lesson, the viewing of which was traditionally, like cinema, an intimate public spectacle.[12]

The phantasmagoric mechanics of cinema have often been likened to a raising of the dead, in which the apparatus breathes life into the body through electricity and light, like Frankenstein or the Sorcerer. Leeson's cyborgs bring to mind science fiction in its fusion of this historical, corporeal model of the cinematic with the futuristic, humanistic cyborg "made of soft human tissue on the outside [and] hi-tech circuitry and computer chips on the inside."[13] As Mary Ann Doane argues, the fears of the female body and of technology are united in the female cyborg, whose mechanical interior suggests, to the male, the attractive possibility of being brought under control. In the 1866 science-fiction

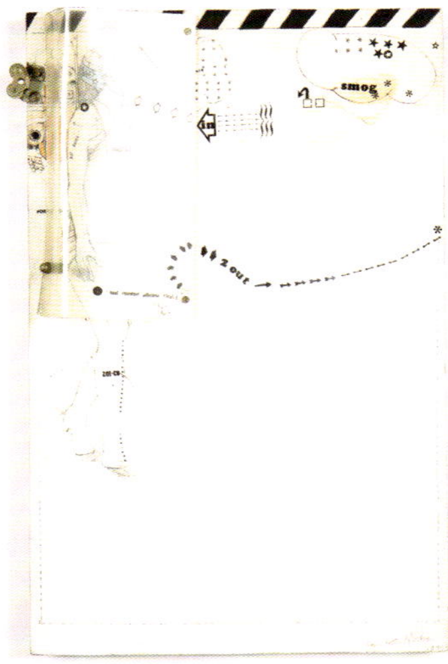

Lynn Hershman Leeson (b. 1941), *Untitled (Cyborg)*, 1970. Acrylic, ink, plastic, and metal on board, 18 x 12 in. (45.7 x 30.5 cm). Private collection

novel *L'Ève future* [Tomorrow's Eve] by Auguste Villiers de L'Isle-Adam, a female android named Hadaly[14] is invented by a fictionalized Thomas Edison (who at the time was, in actuality, producing some of the first experiments in film). In the novel, Edison creates the android to provide his friend Lord Ewald with a more satisfactory version of his physically desirable but intellectually lacking fiancée, Miss Alicia Clary, who is unwittingly cloned into Hadaly and given life through the spirit of Edison's dead assistant, Sowana (see p. 12).

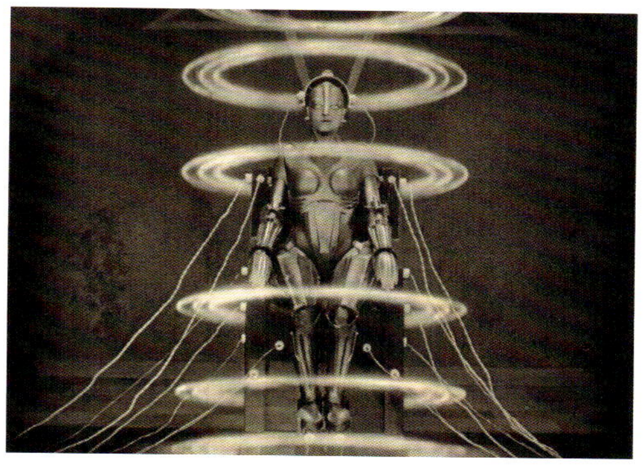

Fritz Lang (1890–1976), still from *Metropolis*, c. 1927. 35mm film, black-and-white, silent; 150 min.

Doane describes the interior of the android that Edison shows Lord Ewald in order to prove to him that it is a machine and not a living woman: "Hadaly's interior is a maze of electrical wizardry including coded metal discs that diffuse warmth, motion and energy throughout the body; wires that imitate nerves, arteries and veins; a basic electro-magnetic motor, the Cylinder, on which are recorded the 'gestures, the bearing, the facial expressions and the attitudes of the adored being'; and two golden phonographs that replay Hadaly's only discourse, words 'invented by the greatest poets, the most subtle metaphysicians, the most profound novelists of this century.' Hadaly has no past, no memories except those embodied in the words of 'great men.'"[15]

The necessity Edison feels to reassure his friend that his invented android is not real points to the uncanny underpinnings of the tension between artifice and reality that has defined the cinematic from its earliest beginnings, as well as the potency of the female body as a screen onto which fear of both women and technology could be projected, and merged. Science fiction became the framework within which this tension would be played out in cinematic terms. The weightlessness of Leeson's figures, suspended in space, or, in her later Water Woman collages (see pp. 92–93), water (a conductor of electricity, and symbolic of the unconscious) evokes the futuristic cyborgs of science-fiction cinema. Yet unlike Villiers's Hadaly, Leeson's personae, created and controlled by the artist's hand, are born not out of a perceived lack, but out of a desire to expand the possibilities of self through the exploration of alternative identities. In her text "Romancing the Anti-Body," Leeson identifies the Internet as a potent location for this expanded construction of identity, in which, by shedding the body altogether and adopting electronic disguises, "one could simultaneously be one or several other people."[16] The artificial body, atomized in cyberspace, becomes "an imaginary screen, onto which psychic energies [can be] projected."[17]

As Matthew Biro observed of the cybernetic environment that emerged in the 1960s: "The more machines automated human functions, the more interrelated humans became, making it progressively harder to distinguish where the 'self' ended and the 'other' began. . . . To view human beings as cybernetic systems was thus to recognize their collaborative nature." A cyborg, he continued, is "a creature of information . . . subject to constant dispersal, transformation and exchange."[18] Philippe Parreno and Pierre Huyghe's collaborative project *No Ghost Just a Shell* (1999–2002; pp. 64–69) disperses a female cyborg across a cinematic plane that includes eight films, animations, and videos, as well as sculpture, painting, sound, installation, prints, posters, and performance. The artists bought the rights to an anime of a fictional eleven-year-old girl named Annlee from an agency supplying figures for the Japanese anime industry. The Annlee character had been underdeveloped, rendering her of little commercial value in the industrial marketplace, but a perfect screen onto which Parreno,

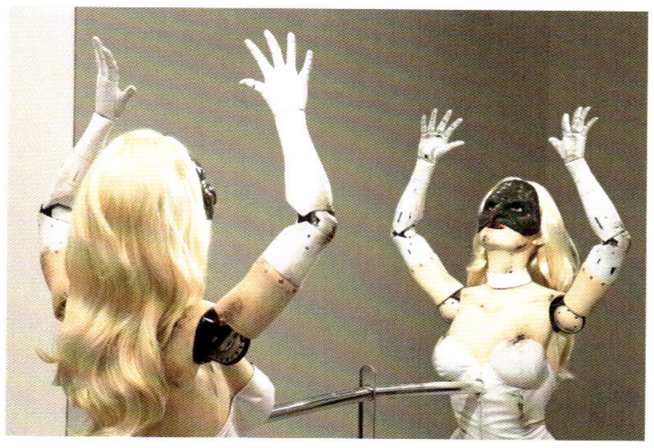

Jordan Wolfson (b. 1980), *(Female figure)*, 2014. Mixed media, 90 ½ x 72 x 29 in. (229.9 x 182.9 x 73.7 cm). Jordan Wolfson's animatronic woman engages the viewer with her eyes as she dances to a soundtrack of narrative and music, in an uncanny echo of Villiers's Hadaly

Huyghe, and eleven other artists they invited to participate[19] could each project their interpretations of her identity.

The industry from which Annlee came is, like the anime medium itself, cyborgian, producing generic figures for manga cartoons, video games, animated films, television, and advertising, each context of which shapes the stories for, and destiny of, the anime, whose character must be robust and complex enough to survive them and move on to the next. The anime form—graphic, smooth, empty, flat—is, as Rayna Denison has argued, designed "so that no one element is more important than any other,"[20] creating the perfect empty container, or "shell." Annlee, appealing to look at with her large, blank, almond-shaped eyes and childlike face, but lacking any character or personality, is given form through the ideas of an international group of artists, most of whom choose to place her within apocalyptic science-fiction movie narratives, not so much removing her from commercial popular culture as repositioning her within it. In Dominique Gonzalez-Foerster's *Ann Lee in Anzen Zone* (2000), she warns of a forthcoming invasion. In Rirkrit Tiravanija's *(Ghost Reader C.H.)* (2002), she reads aloud the complete text of Philip K. Dick's *Do Androids Dream of Electric Sheep?*, the science-fiction novel that inspired the film *Blade Runner* (1982), whose bio-robotic replicants, roaming a devastated post-atomic landscape, are indistinguishable from humans and animals. Liam Gillick's *Annlee You Proposes* (2001), made in collaboration with computer animation director Lars Magnus Holmgren (aka Dr. Frankenskippy), brings Annlee to life as a sorceress with magical powers in the Japanese city of Kitakyushu, which narrowly escaped the American atomic bomb at the end of World War II by a fluke of the weather. Yet again, the sorcerer presides over the dangerous power of technology, here in female form, in a video whose brevity operates as a trailer for an implied longer movie that never materializes.

A sense of the unfinished pervades Annlee's character. In Huyghe's animation *One Million Kingdoms* (2001), she is barely visible, a glowing green outline traversing a dark, craggy lunar landscape like an extraterrestrial visitor, at one point speaking the words of Neil Armstrong, the first astronaut to walk on the moon, and quoting from Jules Verne's science-fiction novel *Journey to the Center of the Earth* (1864). As Heather Warren Crow argues, "If women are supposed to be finished paintings, girls are sketches. . . . The goal of the performance of girlhood in the media is to extend, infinitely and forever, the cartoon in time and space."[21] Malleability and mutability, fundamental principles of the digital image, render Annlee perpetually unfinished. She is a "girled image" that "needs to be bought, rescued, possessed, exported, passed around, and transformed . . . [by] a group project(ion). Annlee never just is; she becomes, through collective labor. She is a body under construction."[22] The implications of Parreno and Huyghe's Annlee project echo those of the cyborgian persona of *L'Ève future*'s Alicia, whose empty robotic double is filled by Edison, like a radio, with the recorded words of great cultural figures of the time, who speak through, and for, her. Like Maria—whose android double, brought to life by the inventor Rotwang in *Metropolis*, unleashes a dangerous (female) technological energy that must be brought back under control—Alicia and Annlee stand in for the empty subject produced by the numbing effects of mechanical work and a ubiquitous, technologized mass consumer culture. The female cyborg performs the function of a screen onto which the shifting contours of the cinematic are mapped, from the womanly figure of the robot to the faintly drawn outline of a prepubescent girl.

In the cinematic, the cyborg is always connected to the sensorium, a space that was first defined, at the beginning of modernity, by the new metropolis of the city. Janet Ward argues that the "society of the spectacle" described by the French theorist Guy Debord originated in the Berlin of the 1920s, an environment of "multifarious complexities of light, space, plane, form, motion, sound."[23] A Berliner at the time wrote: "Chains and streams of light accompany [the bystander]. Light-architecture rises up, light shards appear from the fronts of palaces, disappear, appear, sparkling towers grow tall, collapse, grow tall. Flaming wheels thunder, words manifest themselves letter by letter and are obliterated by Balthazzar's wall, suns burn from mirrored portals."[24] This hyperbolic description of the city, whose electrifying spectacle Smith describes as a flirtation "with immersion in pure simulacrum,"[25] evokes the short film shot by Edwin S. Porter in

1905, showing two Coney Island amusement parks, Dreamland and Luna Park, lit up at night (see pp. 2–3). Luna Park, opened in 1903, was designed with an oriental theme that included more than a thousand red-and-white painted domes, minarets, and spires, lit with 250,000 lights. The centerpiece was the Kaleidoscope Tower, lit with 20,000 incandescent lights and surrounded by fountains. Dreamland, the even larger amusement park that opened next to Luna Park a year later, had four times as many lights as its competitor. It boasted the 350-foot-tall Beacon Tower, lit by 100,000 lights, as well as the largest dome in the world, a replica of Switzerland, a circus, and three theaters. The short, silent black-and-white film of this nocturnal spectacle that Edison commissioned from Porter expresses everything that defines what Tom Gunning has famously termed a "cinema of attractions": "Non-illusionistic, non-deceptive, non-voyeuristic. It aims to astonish rather than deceive."[26] The film's title, *Coney Island at Night*, writes itself in capital letters in lights, in the same style as the billboard names of the parks themselves, reproducing experience by mimesis rather than narrative, and collapsing the boundary between reality and artifice.

Positioned at a considerable height, the camera pans rapidly from right to left across the illuminated city. In the second of only three edits in the entire film, the camera zooms in on the pinnacle of the tower, outlined like a drawing in lights. The camera pans slowly down the tower and then reverses, continuing beyond the globe at the top and into the darkness above. In the second half of the film, the camera pans from left to right across a glittering spectacle of arcades, spires, turrets, arches, and domes looming out of the night. The city is abstracted twice: once by the artifice of its reproduction as an amusement park, and again by its flattening into a luminous animation whose nonnarrative visual spectacle repeats, in cinematic terms, the mesmerizing sensory effect of an optical toy, activated by the camera—a prosthetic extension of the viewer's hand.

The horizontal expanse of Porter's film evokes the immersive panoramic spectacles such as the one shown at the 1900 Paris *Exposition universelle*, in which viewers would be transported to cities across the world in a collage of films projected onto an enormous circular screen. In *Coney Island at Night*, that circularity is interrupted by the single vertical panning shot up and down Luna Park's enormous tower, flattening the curved interior space of the panorama and rupturing its horizontality in order to assert a larger, nonillusory, brief experience of space as attraction—as cinematic, rather than cinema, viewed inside the architecture of the theater, or sensorium.

The paradoxical combination of immersion and distraction in *Coney Island at Night* predicts the complex experience of contemporary digital space. Both belong to major transitional periods in the experience of the cinematic across several models—moving images projected onto a large screen inside a darkened theater or gallery, or experienced on a small screen inside an object, in an open, lit space. The earliest cinematic viewings in the 1890s fused both experiences, as Edison installed a group of Kinetoscopes—small boxes into which individuals peered to view a silent film—in a theater. Immersion was a solitary event, with the viewer disembodied yet still present in a lit room and visible to others, much like the contemporary experience of Oculus Rift virtual reality in galleries and museums.

This paradoxical viewing condition continued within the theater environment into which the attraction film soon migrated. Siegfried Kracauer, writing in Berlin during the 1920s, observed that even in the dark, the theater has things that "rivet the viewer's attention to the peripheral, so that they will not sink into the abyss. The stimulations of the senses succeed one another with such rapidity that there is no room left between them for even the slightest contemplation. Like life buoys, the refractions of the spotlights and the musical accompaniment keeps the spectator above water."[27] For Kracauer, the sense of unreality that this cinematic dislocation produced was positive—indeed, political. As Miriam Hansen argues, Kracauer felt that the world is already distorted, and that "the point is not to mirror the world that is literally going to pieces, but to advance that process" and evoke "the threatening and liberating possibility of liquefying fixed structures of social, cultural and intellectual gendered identity."[28]

The cinematic, in other words, held a radical potential that narrative cinema could not approach—something that Sergei Eisenstein understood, in his argument that the viewer should be subjected

Tacita Dean (b. 1965), *FILM*, 2011. 35mm film, black-and-white and color, anamorphic film with hand tinted sequences, silent; 11 min., looped. Installation view, Tate Modern, London, 2011. Tacita Dean's 42-foot-tall silent film was made using analog techniques, including masking, glass matte painting, and hand painting. To make this sequence, different areas of the Tate Modern's Turbine Hall were lit up by a different colored light, filmed separately, and put together to make a composite image. This fusion of architecture, color, and light evokes Taut's Glass Pavilion

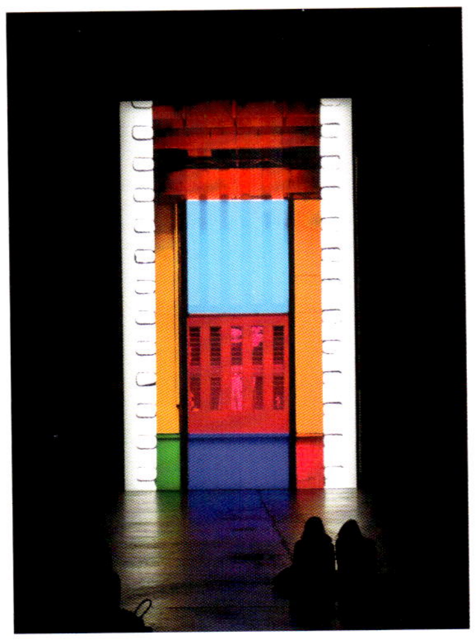

to "a sensual or psychological impact . . . to produce in him certain emotional shocks"[29] that would jolt them out of their conventional habits of perception.

One of the key elements of the cinematic's agitation of the visual field is color. Its earliest appearance in film involved the hand-coloring, tinting, and toning of the bodies of female dancers and apparitions conjured by sorcerers in puffs of smoke, in garish hues that intensified a sense of vivid artifice. Color was read as a primitive form of special effects, designed not to depict the naturalistic, but rather as a visceral tool to stimulate the viewer's emotions, conjuring the erotic, the magical, and the uncanny. As Joshua Yumibe observes, Kodak described a particular tinted Sonochrome film stock, designed to evoke a synesthetic response in viewers by combining sound and color, thus: "Rose Doree: a rose pink that quickens the respiration. The tint of passionate love, excitement, abandon, fete days, carnivals, heavily sensuous surroundings."[30] It is perhaps not a coincidence that Cornell, revisiting his film *Rose Hobart* in the late 1960s and considering a permanent tint, chose rose pink.

The origins of cinematic affect in mass culture were clearly evident to those witnessing artists' experimentation with color's abstract potential. Observing the painter Leopold Survage's *Colored Rhythm: Study for the Film* (1913), whose animation cels (never translated to film, for practical and financial reasons) produced an abstract color composition, Guillaume Apollinaire noted that Survage's experiment "draws its origins from fireworks, fountains, electric signs, and those fairy tale palaces which at every amusement park accustom the eyes to enjoy kaleidoscopic changes of hue."[31] To that list we could add optical toys, and in particular the kaleidoscope, whose intimate spectacle of color, activated by the viewer's hand, produces, in miniature, a sense of "delirium, kinesis and immersion . . . disintegrat[ing] any fixed perspective."[32]

Once the manual location of moving images shifted into the architectural sensorium of the theater, their cinematic references became those of the modern metropolis, the prism through which abstract moving images came into being. The Berlin architect Bruno Taut went further, imagining the possibility of "the architectural object itself [acting] as a light-shaping, light-producing apparatus . . . a crystalline screening space . . . as a highly calculated spectacle that organizes the subject's passage from mobile visitor to stunned spectator."[33] His Glass Pavilion (1914) included a glass screen onto which kaleidoscopic images were back-projected. Kracauer's description of the street as "fragmentary"—"the kaleidoscopic sights mingle with unidentified shapes . . . life is eternally dissolving the patterns which it is about to form"[34]—specifically addressed the city of Berlin, where Oskar Fischinger had set himself up as a filmmaker and producer of special effects for the bourgeoning movie industry, including Fritz Lang's 1929 science-fiction film *Frau im Mond* [Woman in the Moon].

Fischinger had begun to produce a body of abstract films in Frankfurt in the early 1920s, experimenting with colored liquids, wax, and clay, using his skills with special effects to invent a wax-slicing machine to cut vertical slices of modeled wax forms that could be tinted and animated into swirling shapes. His cinematic language fused color, music, and dynamic abstract forms to create what was then called "Absolute Film"—a term similar to the Bauhaus's "Total Theater," and indicative of the radical experimental thinking of the time regarding the fusion of different mediums within a unified space. Fischinger's thinking during this period resonates with that of Kazimir Malevich, who wrote seven essays on film between 1925 and 1929. After Malevich's 1927 visits to the Bauhaus and Berlin, where he met Hans Richter and saw his abstract film *Rhythmus 25* (c. 1925), the Russian artist conceived an abstract film whose immersive space would evoke the sensation of pure feeling outlined in his suprematist manifesto.

In 1926, Fischinger collaborated with the Hungarian composer Alexander László on a series of *Farblichtmusik* (color-light music) concerts at venues such as the Munich State Theater. The Munich performance in March 1926 marked the first presentation of its kind, opening up the cinematic model of attractions into a new, multidimensional articulation of extended spatial and temporal spectacle. Fischinger's films were screened on a projector, in combination with a color-light piano invented by László, colored spotlights, and slide projectors, all set to compositions by László and other modernist composers, including Alexander Scriabin. Fischinger quickly moved on to create his own multiple-projector performances, including *Raumlichtkunst* [Space Light Art] (1928), in which three 35mm reels of abstract, tinted and black-and-white nitrate films were projected simultaneously, accompanied by live percussive music. In these performances, Fischinger combined a number of his experiments with abstract form, including moiré patterns made from wax and tinted liquid color, vertical geometrical shapes, and hypnotic spirals, occasionally intercut with special-effects images evoking his commercial work, such as a composite black-and-white image of a galaxy of planets, a beer-bottle label, and an apocalyptic color-tinted photograph of flames (see pp. 20–21).

In this immersive projective environment Fischinger realized his desire to create "an intoxication of light from a thousand sources. . . . A happening of the soul, of the eyes, of the eye's waves, wave streams, Sun flowing, a level vanishing, a sudden eruption, an awakening, ceremonial, sunrising, effervescent, Star rhythms, star lustre, a singing, surf breaking over chasms, a world of illusions, of movements, of lights, sound, and song tamed."[35] *Raumlichtkunst* echoes Kracauer's dynamic, kaleidoscopic metropolis, creating a hypnotic state of heightened emotion in which the viewer is transported—by color, spectacle, light, dynamic abstract form, and intense affect—into another world, or even galaxy, in which the screens "produced a sense of motion in the static spectator, and thence a mobilization of space itself."

Fischinger's description recalls Walter Benjamin's arguments regarding the ability of what he termed "unconscious optics"[36] to deepen psychic perception. *Raumlichtkunst*'s immersive cinematic state, conjured from a fusion of organic visual and aural forms with technological mechanics, reflects the wider cultural condition of Weimar Germany, the most advanced industrialized country in Europe at the time, and the one most engaged with American models of industrial production and mechanization, including that of cinema. In 1936 Fischinger moved from Berlin to Los Angeles. Soon after, Walt Disney hired him to work on *Fantasia*, whose synesthetic sense of immersion in color, music, and dynamic form resonated strongly with Fischinger's own ideas. (Although his work was not included in the film in the end, three of his preliminary sketches can be seen on pp. 24–25 of this volume.)

The Bauhaus's utopian call for a Total Theater was, as Matthew Smith argues, aimed at redeeming the evils of technology (keenly felt in Germany in the decade following World War I) by embracing technological forms of creativity, including commercial production, and fusing the organic (the body) with the mechanical. Oskar Schlemmer's 1922 Triadic Ballet, though not a work of film, nevertheless embodies the cinematic, in its widest form, by bringing together the cyborg and the sensorium on an abstracted architectural "screen." Schlemmer's own statements regarding space, form, light, and the body read like a description of a cinema of attraction: "We can therefore take pleasure in the purely optical; we can manipulate forms and discover surprising effects in mechanical motion from concealed sources; we can convert and transfigure space through form, color and light."[37] The body takes its place as part of the space, rather than dominating it. "Out of plane geometry, out of the pursuit of the straight line, the diagonal, the circle and the curve, a stereometry of space evolves, almost of itself, by the moving line of the figure."[38]

Each segment of this three-act ballet unfolds against a single plane of color—yellow, pink, and black, respectively—marked with a flat geometric grid, across which three dancers wearing eighteen different costumes move. The dancers and their costumes are constructed with the same artifice, built from layers of flatness, color, and exaggerated form. Each body is grotesque, broken, missing limbs, extended by prosthetics, or restricted in its stylized movements by the costume design. Schlemmer uses the affect of cinematic attraction—artifice, color, spectacle, shock, flattened space, presentation—to re-form bodies (and, by implication, psyches) broken by the technology of war into new, hybrid human forms and identities, revealing both to be constructions: vulnerable, mutable cyborgs.

Throughout the first half of the twentieth century, the cinematic was dispersed between two opposing models of the sensorium: the conventional dark space of the cinema and the kind of environment epitomized by the Bauhaus Total Theater. The latter, as described by László Moholy-Nagy in 1924, aimed to create a "great dynamic-rhythmic process, which can compress the greatest clashing masses or accumulations of media."[39] In this open-ended process, various technologies could be employed, including "film, automobile, elevator, airplane, and other machinery, as well as optical instruments, reflecting equipment and so on,"[40] allowing the audience to fuse with the action onstage. This contrasted with what Noam M. Elcott has called the "artificial darkness"[41] of the cinema, in which the body becomes immersed in order to disappear. This model evokes the Black Maria film workshop that Edison designed in 1893, which doubled as a film set and a private screening room for the Kinetoscope filmstrips that Edison produced there. The building was, as Philippe-Alain Michaud describes, "an eccentric, irregular oblong shape[,] . . . [its interior] covered with black panels to prevent any refraction of light emanating from the screen. . . . [It was] a non-illusionist, unspecified space, dedicated not to the imitation of appearances, but to the restoration of presence."[42] Single figures performing simple actions (a dance, a sneeze, a fight) loomed out of the darkness as though phantasmagorically emerging out of the screen. Edison's Black Maria became the default environment for cinema after the cinema of attractions became absorbed into the larger hegemonic structure of narrative film that came to dominate cinema.

By the 1950s, the expanded model of distraction threatened to engulf Edison's classical cinema space, as the emergence of a television-based media culture, as well as the international space race, had a profound impact on the cinematic. In his 1951 *Technical Manifesto of Spatialism*, the Italian artist Lucio Fontana wrote: "Man's true conquest of space is his detachment from the earth, from the horizon line. . . . A new aesthetic is being formed, luminous forms crossing in space."[43] The shock and spectacle of the cinematic was catapulted out of the cinema and dispersed into the global sensorium of media culture, less as an image/event and more as information. The disappearance of the horizon line first into darkness, artifice, and abstraction, then into cybernetics, and now into digital cyberspace, took on, in the 1950s, a cosmic dimension that realized Fischinger's "intoxication by light from a thousand sources" as an experience now defined by the infinity of outer space, in which the cinematic became reborn as science fiction.

The apocalyptic spectacle of the atomic bombing of Hiroshima and Nagasaki, approaching science fiction in its unimaginability, was televised for the first time in 1952, seven years after it occurred, as a domestic event to be experienced at home, in low resolution, on a TV set whose design evoked Edison's Kinetoscope, but stripped of the focused physical intimacy of viewing. Twenty-four years later, Bruce Conner reasserted the power of the cinematic as image/event in the dark space of the theater—by then a viewing environment under siege—in CROSSROADS (1976; pp. 40, 41), a thirty-six-minute collage of declassified military footage filmed by more than five hundred cameras at the scene of Operation Crossroads, the U.S. government's underwater test explosion of an atomic bomb in the Bikini Atoll on July 25, 1946. The awe-inspiring explosion, which produced a mushroom cloud two miles wide and a wall of vaporized seawater two thousand feet high, is restored to its full, terrible "nuclear sublime"[44] as an image, through montage, repetition, extreme slow motion, and an enveloping soundtrack composed by Patrick Gleeson and Terry Riley. Conner's film translates the hypnotic power of that single unimaginable moment, in which, according to contemporary eyewitnesses "time stood still. . . . Space contracted to a pinpoint." into the most spectacular cinematic attraction in history.

If the terrible sublime of Conner's atomic phantasmagoric spectacle presented the ultimate realization, in cinematic terms, of the technological dangers that the female cyborg appeared to represent, other cinematic projects explored the positive implications of a vision that could extend beyond Earth's horizon line. These projective environments erased not merely the single projected image, or even the screen and the rectangular frame of the projected film, but also the rectangular box of the theater and gallery altogether. The immersive darkness of the theater, which produced a haptic sense that both the viewer and the projected image were floating weightlessly, had obvious allusions to outer space that were continually paralleled by depictions of outer space in commercial science-fiction films.

One of the first post-World War II experiments with projective environments took place at the Morrison Planetarium in San Francisco, where, from 1957 to 1960, Jordan Belson, in collaboration with the composer Henry Jacobs, staged more than a hundred "Vortex Concerts." Using seventy projectors, including the planetarium's own powerful, thirteen-foot-long star projector, Jacobs screened abstract films made by himself, John and James Whitney, and others in an immersive 360-degree environment, while experimental music emanated from fifty speakers placed around the circular space. As Belson observed of his experiments projecting film with no frame lines, "not only was the image free of the frame, but free of space somehow. . . . I used films . . . plus strobes, star projectors, rotational sky projectors, kaleidoscopic projectors, and four special dome projectors. We were able to project images over the entire dome, so that things would come pouring down from the center, sliding along the walls."[45] The Vortex Concerts inhabited a space that was neither cinema, nor museum, nor commercial amusement park, yet fused elements of all three in an architectural pastiche of outer space, re-imagining it as a cinema of attractions of the abstract sublime.

Stan VanDerBeek's *Movie-Drome*, conceived in the late 1950s and realized in 1963 in a field in Stony Point, New York, shifted the cosmic experience of the Vortex Concerts into a smaller, more self-contained projective environment, filled with newsreels, found film footage, glass slides, and VanDerBeek's own experimental films, beamed from thirty projectors in all directions onto the makeshift domed interior (see pp. 44–45). VanDerBeek's sensorium, occupied by a small audience sitting on cushions on the floor, belongs to cyberspace rather than outer space. Its design, as a prototype for a globally networked communications system that he hoped might connect audiences around the world, anticipates the ubiquitous intimacy and distance of digital space, and was extended into a portable form in *Movie Mural* (1968) two years later. Yet its unveiling during the New York Film Festival in 1966 demonstrates its complex location within a cinematic tradition in crisis—on the verge of giving way to what was eventually to become the immaterial, yet haptic, touchscreen environment of cyberspace.

At this very moment of crisis, the Austrian filmmaker Peter Kubelka introduced the idea of "Invisible Cinema," a pitch-black theater with raked seating and hood-like blinders between every seat to prevent communication with, and distraction from, other patrons. The stated aim of Kubelka's invention was to preserve the concentrated experience of watching film in a cybernetic age; as such, it was merely asserting the conventions of classical cinema. Kubelka and Jonas Mekas built the Invisible Cinema inside the Joseph Papp Theater on Lafayette Street in New York, and showed a mixture of classic films and avant-garde and structural films by Stan Brakhage, Paul Sharits, and others (see pp. 54–55).

As Noam M. Elcott argues, the Invisible Cinema contained a paradox. The exaggerated immersive viewing conditions of its pitch-black environment and bright screen evoke the immersive experience of Edison's Kinetoscope rather than the shared social space of classical cinema.[46] Yet most of the programmed films belonged to the conventional narrative tradition that had enveloped, and rendered invisible, the prenarrative cinema of attractions. As Elcott asserts, it was through the tactile materiality of films by Sharits and Brakhage that the cinema-of-attraction model was reasserted—paradoxically locating the avant-garde within the frame of affect, shock, and spectacle.[47]

Jud Yalkut's *Destruct Film* (1967; pp. 42–43) marks an important moment in the transition between these paradoxical forms of the cinematic and the digital future. Inside a darkened space in the Judson Memorial Church on New York's Washington Square, viewers waded through reams of 16mm film strewn across the floor, surrounded by a disorientating kaleidoscope of film stills projected from 35mm slide projectors and spun around the room by beam splitters. In interacting with the unspooled film on the floor, the viewer's engagement with film, and the image that it carries, is immediately shifted from the visual to the haptic. To be given permission to touch the film, trample over it, immerse ourselves in it, pick it up, look through it, wind it round our bodies, put our fingermarks on its translucent surface, returns us to the experience of the optical toy, expanded into the cinema space to which it originally gave birth. The only thing we cannot do is make the image move.

As Michaud observes, at the first moment of its invention, film was described by Eastman House as "as thin, light and flexible as paper, and as transparent as glass."[48] *Destruct Film* asserts the vulnerability of film's organic, material reality by allowing us to do to the image all the things that the cold, hard, flat-screen surface does not allow us to do. But no amount of swiping, pinching, or tapping will spark the images into life; only the apparatus can do that, as demonstrated by a film projected against the back wall of the space, almost as an afterthought. The stable screen provides the only evidence of what once might have been a coherent cinema space, but refuses any possibility of narrative absorption by repeatedly showing the countdown leader to a film that never begins. By staging the death of cinema, *Destruct Film* dismantles the old model of the sensorium in order to make way for new ones.

The most recent works in *Dreamlands*—by artists including Trisha Baga, Frances Bodomo, Dora Budor, Ian Cheng, Ben Coonley, Andrea Crespo, Alex Da Corte, Alex Israel, Aidan Koch, Jenny Perlin, and Artie Vierkant—articulate the breadth and complexity of these new models. In the current digital environment, the haptic has become a central element in the recalibration of the relationship between the body and technology, through a continual online exchange and transformation of images, visual styles, avatars, anime, and identities. The infinite manipulability of the digital image, now dominated by the graphic, animated form, special effects, and virtual reality, has produced a new visual ecosystem in which, as Cheng remarks, "art is like . . . a hack on our cognition . . . an interface, a stimulus or irritant, for rehearsing new neural activation patterns."[49]

Cheng's description evokes the flattened space of Alex Da Corte and Jayson Musson's synesthetic video environment *Easternsports* (2014), a multilingual tableau in the round, projected onto four freestanding screens, whose spatial coordinates are diffused through changing tonalities of color, pattern, and light, and with the scent of oranges strewn across a carpet whose pattern echoes the walls in the projection, as well as a haunting soundtrack by the synesthetic composer Devonté Hynes, creating a complex narrative sensorium that echoes Schlemmer's Triadic Ballet, including its handmade sets and costumes, invoking the depthless sensation of digital space through color, sensation, light, and sound.

A similar dialogue between two- and three-dimensional (analog and digital) space occurs in works by Trisha Baga, Ben Coonley, and Jenny Perlin, to different perceptual ends. Like Da Corte and Musson's *Easternsports*, Perlin's film-loop installation *Twilight Arc* (2016) explores the synesthetic possibilities of color, light, and sound in the construction of space. Perlin's installation investigates the history of the color organ through a hand-drawn animated 16mm film whose tinting Perlin allowed film laboratory technicians to determine, rendering the film a score performed in colors whose hues radiate from the screen into the gallery. Its collaborative synthetic structure evokes the final scene of Steven Spielberg's *Close Encounters of the Third Kind* (1977), in which a scientist communicates with a spaceship that has landed on Earth by applying a hand-sign learning system for deaf children to a large color organ, to which the artificial intelligence inside the spaceship responds in kind.

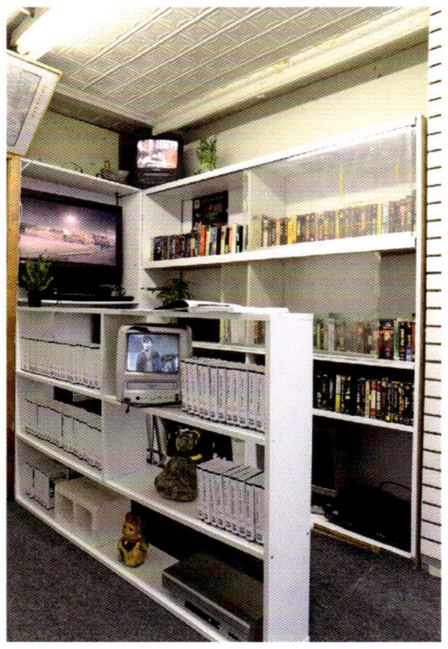

Installation view, *New Release*, curated by Erin Goldberger, at New Release, 60 Mulberry Street, New York, 2015. The current interest in analog formats and processes is reflected in this exhibition of videos by twenty-five artists. The artists' videos were transferred onto VHS tapes and displayed alongside tapes of Hollywood films like *Rambo* and *9 ½ Weeks* for visitors to select and either take home or else watch in the abandoned video store in Chinatown where the exhibition was held

In an optical paradox, Baga renders three-dimensional space two-dimensional in order to create an interplanar spatial experience in her video installation *Flatlands* (2010; pp. 78–79). A mirrored disco ball is inserted into the space between the viewer (wearing 3D glasses) and a 3D projected image. The ball reflects pinpoints of light onto the gallery walls, introducing a second projective layer and creating a larger spatial image, which, when seen through 3D glasses, includes the mirrored ball, the 3D objects inside the video projection, and the physical space of the gallery.

Coonley's *Trading Futures* (2016; pp. 106–107), by contrast, tilts the axis upward, projecting a 3D video shot with a 360-degree camera onto the interior of a large cardboard geodesic dome, whose sections are held together with file clips. The simple DIY aesthetic of Buckminster Fuller's cardboard dome, first introduced in 1954, during the golden era of 3D Hollywood cinema, sits in stark contrast, and yet in perfect sync, with the high-tech virtual reality space of Coonley's video, whose complex transitions between 2D and 3D, at one point unsyncing the 3D so that the left and right eye read the image separately, push the new technology to its limit. In the video, Coonley delivers a lecture on trading futures and the technical properties of 3D, adopting different avatars as he moves through a series of interior and exterior spaces, floating, dancing, and spinning, released from gravity by the optics of technology and digital space. The 360-degree camera, the first of its kind, enables the entire room or space to be filmed at once, rather than recorded in panning shots, demonstrating in clear technical terms the vertiginous loss of a stable horizon that characterizes our contemporary visual environment. The additional possibility of viewing Coonley's video, just outside the dome, on Oculus Rift devices, introduces another level of immersion that replaces reality with its virtual simulation, abstracted through 3D animation, doubling the spatial, optical, and perceptual artifice, and reducing its corporeal experience to the eyes. In the virtual sensorium, the body takes on the heaviness of the dreamer, tethered to its terrestrial moorings, as the eye and the mind travel through space.

A different sense of disorientation occurs in Aidan Koch's watercolors for the book *Little Angels* (2016), in which a sequence of empty panels becomes progressively overwhelmed by a dark wash of color until the viewer's eyes enter an indeterminate space whose claustrophobic darkness leaves little room to breathe. Koch, working with comics, graphic books, and animation, collapses the space between image and text, replacing conventional narrative with an ambiguous immersive sensation somewhere between looking and reading.

A key historical cinematic exploration of the body's weightless movement through an indeterminate space lies in Maya Deren's short film *The Very Eye of Night* (1958), in which a group of dancers move across a night sky through a constellation of stars, rising, falling, floating and tumbling, sometimes upside down or on their sides, their bodies abstracted like cyborgs by white light. Josiah McElheny's *Projection Painting II* (2015) takes footage from Deren's film, reworked to further abstract its ghostly imagery, and projects it onto a rectangular construction of dark, undulating, painted planes, superimposing the dark sky onto an abstracted planar surface that reads, simultaneously, as both painting and sculpture. McElheny's composite space indicates the possibility of a fourth dimension, its physical contours evoking the system of colored cubes invented by the nineteenth-century mathematician and science-fiction writer Charles Howard Hinton to visualize what four-dimensional space might look like.[50]

As Norman Klein has argued,[51] the shifting parameters of what constitutes the real that characterize our contemporary virtual space have been in flux since the Renaissance, played out in painting through its staging of reality as artifice within three-dimensional space. In *Ways of Something*, a collaborative video essay in four episodes, Lorna Mills invited 113 new media, digital, and web artists to respond to *Ways of Seeing*, a four-part BBC television series from 1972 in which the British art historian John Berger critiques the conventions of Western art-historical analysis, drawing on the ideas of Walter Benjamin. *Ways of Something* retains the audio soundtrack of the original television program, but replaces Berger's visual analysis with digital artworks responding to, and critiquing, his now-dated thesis. A critical analysis of linear perspective, the body, and painting that seemed radical in 1972 triggers a new rethinking when juxtaposed with virtual, digital imagery and webcam videos that turn art-historical conventions of the visual image inside out.

Mathias Poledna's *Imitation of Life* (2013; pp. 70–73) presents the viewer with a similar paradox in a short 35mm animation film, drawn by veteran animators who once worked for The Walt Disney Studios, that looks exactly like a Disney film. The soundtrack—"I've Got a Feelin' You're Foolin'," from the classic 1935 musical *Broadway Melody of 1936*, rerecorded with a full orchestra—doubles the artifice, placing the viewer in the position of the donkey who sings: "I've got a feelin' you're foolin' / I've got a notion it's make believe / I think you're laughin' right up your sleeve / Foolin' with me." Appearing at the height of interest in the virtual image in visual culture, Poledna's reanimation of a once all-powerful and now outmoded industrial film technique draws attention to the boundary between the animate and inanimate in the production of culture.

Alex Israel's sky paintings also question art-historical convention through techniques associated with film. Israel hires Hollywood backdrop painters to make paintings of skies normally rendered for movies, using an analog technique that has now been replaced by digital photography. Stripping away the camera, lighting, and special effects that make the sky appear real in a film, Israel presents these paintings on canvas as artworks in their own right. By shifting the artifice of backdrop into real space, these works reveal the skill of the painter in creating a sky that appears simultaneously natural and artificial.

This paradox is also evident in Artie Vierkant's video *Exposure Adjustment on a Sunset* (2009; pp. 110–11), in which the sky remains brightly lit as the sun sets. This persistent, unnatural glow lends to nature the uncanniness of science fiction, evoking a sense of the technological apocalyptic and recalling the moment in *2001: A Space Odyssey* when the camera tilts first toward Jupiter and then toward where the sun should be, only to find the Star Gate in its place. The unchanging light of Vierkant's sunset folds the estrangement of the natural inside the artifice of commercial photographic kitsch, restaging this "first-ever movie" as an image of erased darkness.

During the same period that *2001: A Space Odyssey* was released, in the middle of the space race, Edward Makuka Nkoloso, a schoolteacher and founder of the Zambia National Academy of Science, Space Research and Philosophy, established a space program in his newly independent country, with the aim of sending a seventeen-year-old girl and two cats to the moon. His weightlessness training consisted of rolling the trainees down a hill inside oil drums, and the rocket that was to propel the female astronaut, Matha Mwabwa, into space was a ten-by-six-foot cylinder. Nkoloso's project never left the ground, but forty-seven years later filmmaker Frances Bodomo's *Afronauts* (2014; pp. 108, 109), titled after Nkoloso's name for his team, explores the story from Matha's point of view. Inspired by the ambitious yet improbable attempt to beat the Americans into space, Bodomo addresses its failure as part of a wider black diasporic attempt to move beyond the sense of exclusion created by a white, Western technological vision of the future and the alien "other" of science fiction. Mwabwa's contemplation of her fate as she prepares to be launched into space reflects on the importance of mythmaking in the projection of possible alternative futures for black people.

The accessibility of digital tools and like-minded online communities has opened up multiple possibilities for radical shifts in self-representation in ways that are challenging the norms of technological power and control. In Andrea Crespo's work, this shift is expressed through the presentation of identity as a complex state of being formed by "a multiple system, a composite of selves which do not come from a discrete psychic interiority, but from the informational neuro-ecologies that comprise the digital present."[52] Just as Hannah Höch's Weimar cyborgs suggested the possibility of new approaches to gender and sensory experience by making visible the impact of technology on normative perceptions of the body, Crespo's digital video *parabiosis: neurolibidinal induction complex 2.2*

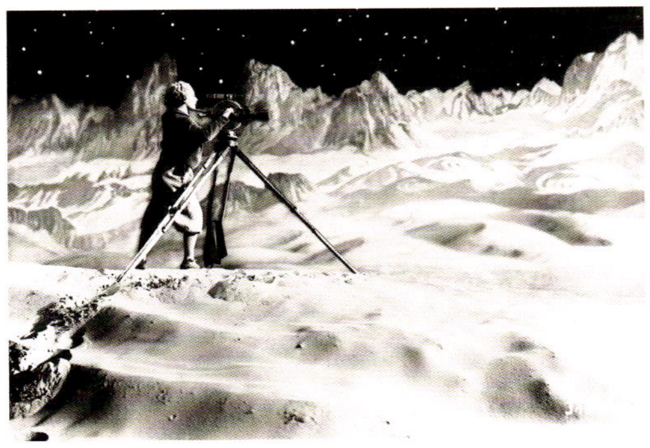

Fritz Lang (1890–1976), still from *Frau Im Mond [Woman in the Moon]*, 1929. 35mm film, black-and-white, silent; 108 min. Special effects by Oskar Fischinger

(2015; pp. 94, 95) rewrites our relationship to the screen, shifting our reading of it not as a surface to be physically or psychically projected onto, but as a sensual, tactile interface on which "beings and their projections are constantly splitting and rejoining, doubling and reducing, disappearing and reappearing."[53]

Crespo's figures appear against a visceral dark-blue background whose painterly texture creates a warmth that holds the figures, text, and intense white light of the vertical scanner moving slowly back and forth across it, in a fine cyborgian balance between the organic and the technological. Redrawn Japanese anime figures of various sizes—three young girls with wide eyes and large ears composited into a single body; tiny figures drawn in a cluster, kickboxing, or in a row moving across the screen, then sliding into the tiny screen of a large, line-drawn Gameboy—are revealed one after the other. Each is punctuated by words and phrases describing internal states—"you are ghosting" . . . "invisible" . . . "splitting" . . . "iatrogenize"—as the scanner wipes away the previous image or text from the dark-blue background, as though turning pages in a book.

The back-and-forth horizontal movement of the scanner, one of the basic elements of digital printing, is in direct counterpoint to the apparatus of the celluloid film projector, in which successive images, printed onto the film vertically, are animated in one direction, linearly, from top to bottom. The scanner's movement engages the viewer's entire sensory perceptive field by appearing to sweep not only the internal space of the screen but also the body of the viewer standing in front of it, revealing light, sound, text, and image as each appears within an indeterminate, abstract space, regulated by the calming movement of the scanner's hypnotic light, which mirrors our own vertical orientation as perceiving viewers in a way that almost incorporates us into the image.

Crespo's somasthetic[54] engagement of the viewer articulates a new kind of visual field made possible by digital technology. In Ian Cheng's work, digital space is visualized not as a place, but as a site for a narrative in a perpetual state of evolution. In *Baby feat. Ikaria* (2013; pp. 96, 97), the surface of a large vertical screen leaning against a wall teems with animated chatbots talking to each other or themselves. This endlessly morphing activity acts out what Cheng describes as live simulations: "a virtual space with a huge accumulation of mini-behaviors and laws that act and react to each other with no master design."[55] Created from a cannibalized gaming engine, the chatbots are artificial intelligences with statements of their own, and their randomly generated conversation, aimed to engage potential virtual consumers or sexual partners but here turned in on itself, bears no connection to human logic, yet tells us much about how the self is constituted. Unlike Lynn Hershman Leeson's artificial-intelligence bot *DiNA* (2000–6) whose head, given the human form of the actress Tilda Swinton, appears on a mirrored screen, ready to converse with the viewer via an attached microphone, Cheng's bots talk only to each other, in random parallel monologues. In this virtual domain, immersion is a cognitive occurrence between simulations, and the detachment of these cyborgian presences from the human viewer underlines both the growing presence of artificial intelligence as a reality and the potential alienation that might result from its increasing integration into human life.

The technological uncanniness of Cheng's vertical screen evokes the monolith around which the apes gather at the beginning of *2001: A Space Odyssey*, touching its blank surface as if hoping that it will come alive and communicate. As many have argued, the monolith appears as the representation of an intelligent alien presence contacting the human race to offer guidance, and Stanley Kubrick experimented with projecting images onto it, rendering the first potential cinematic depiction of a touchscreen science fiction. The appearance of a strange new entity capable of transforming the existing order is one of the key tropes of science fiction. In Kubrick's scenario, the blank coldness of an artificial intelligence is set against, and, by implication, superior to, the corporeal warmth of the mammalian body.

Dora Budor's work articulates a new, posthuman, transspecies condition, in which real, imagined, biological and technological entities have become interdependent contact zones. Her recent work in *Dreamlands*, a large immersive environment, fuses the body with architecture, technology, and light to create a symbiogenetic biological structure. The interior walls pulse with electrical light traveling across cast-resin panels from the ground to the ceiling when triggered by human movement in the space, as though activating the synapses of a brain. The ascending flickering light directs the viewer's gaze upward to a ceiling teeming with thousands of frogs—special-effects props used in the amphibian rain scene of the Hollywood film *Magnolia* (1999). The ambiguity of the resin panels—readable as either the ceiling or as the bottom of another, unseen space—recalls the author Charles Fort's repeated references to "showers of frogs" raining down from the sky in *Book of the Damned* (1919), the book that inspired *Magnolia*'s apocalyptic scene: "Bottoms of ponds dripping out—very interesting ponds, having no earth at bottom—vast drops of water afloat in what is called space."[56]

As *Magnolia* director Paul Thomas Anderson remarked, "The frogs are a barometer for who we are as a people. We're polluting ourselves, we're killing ourselves, and the frogs are telling us so."[57] The disturbing inertness of the mass of frogs above our heads defines Budor's environment as a site of anxiety and portent, evoking the unknown threats built into a maze of luminous rooms from which protagonists try desperately to escape in the science-fiction horror movie *Cube* (1997). The sculpture's uncanny glowing interior also evokes the electrochemical signaling of the body's nervous system. Its translation of movement into light causes the room to become a conductor, echoing the way impulses are conducted through synaptic connections between neurons in the brain. Budor's immersive environment draws us in so that our presence can bring it to life and reanimate the image on its ceiling, creating another kind of monolith that speaks to the humans around it, this time of a future in which bodies might merge with both the architectural environment and artificial intelligence to become a single living organism.

The interconnectedness of the cyborgian body to a larger technological and spatial field evokes McLuhan's predictive description of what he termed an "acoustic" media space "that has no center or margins . . . [and is] organic and integral, perceived through the simultaneous interplay of all the senses."[58] Hito Steyerl's immersive installation *Factory of the Sun* (2015; pp. 102–105) folds digital space inside a three-dimensional mock-up of the grid that generated it, situating the audience inside a virtual cinematic space whose coordinates are flattened by a luminous grid laid across the floor, walls, and ceiling. White lounge chairs scattered across the grid appear to float in space, in front of a large screen on which a scripted video game is being created inside a space that is described as a factory of the sun. In a clear reference to *Metropolis*—in which the female cyborg Maria brings a group of factory workers disgruntled by the inhuman conditions of their mechanized environment back into harmony—the chief protagonist in the video game, Yulia, programs the movements of a group of dancers dressed in futuristic gold body suits as they dance across the motion-capture studio, transforming from bodies into light impulses: immaterial digital fragments that proceed to do battle with each other, like biological cells in combat.

Steyerl's dystopic futuristic environment sets the natural power of sunlight against the ambivalent utopian possibilities of digital technology, in whose "deadly transparency . . . we have become data-objects to be mined."[59] Combining sensation, color, music, and the rhythm of dance with the mechanized rhythm of digital technology, Steyerl references Weimar Berlin and Schlemmer's radical flattening of space within which the organic living body fuses with the cold surface of technology, held together by the device of special effects. The ambivalent yet transformative possibilities of Steyerl's factory of the sun evoke Pier Paolo Pasolini's idea of cinema as another kind of factory, in a metaphor that could embrace all the works in the exhibition and the exhibition itself: a structure in motion, a text in progress, a dynamic form striving to be another form, in a continual state of transformation, regeneration, and renewal.

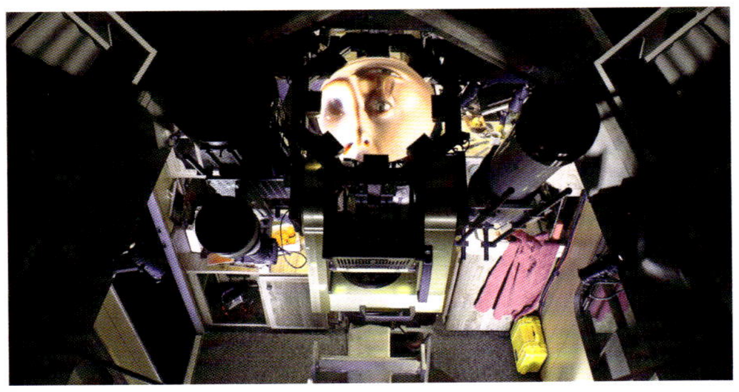

Douglas Trumbull (b. 1942), still from *UFOTOG*, 2014– . 35mm film transferred to 3D 4K video, color, sound; 10 min., projected at 120 fps. 3D glasses, subwoofer speakers. This short science-fiction film demonstrates Douglas Trumbull's pioneering MAGI process, in which 3D video is projected at 120 frames per second, five times the standard speed. The movie is viewed from within a small pod-shaped theater he also designed, with raked seating, a curved widescreen, and subwoofer speakers that immerse the viewer in a 3D cinematic environment

NOTES

1. William Gibson, *Neuromancer* (New York: Ace Books, 1984), p. 69, quoted by Omar Kholeif in "Electronic Superhighway: Towards a Possible Future for Art and the Internet," in *Electronic Superhighway: From Experiments in Art and Technology to Art after the Internet*, exh. cat. (London: Whitechapel Gallery, 2016), p. 25.
2. Hito Steyerl, "In Free Fall: A Thought Experiment on Vertical Perspective," *e-flux*, no. 24 (2011), http://www.e-flux.com/journal/in-free-fall-a-thought-experiment-on-vertical-perspective/.
3. Jens Schröter, *3D: History, Theory and Aesthetics of the Transplane Image* (London: Bloomsbury Academic, 2014).
4. See Donna Haraway, "A Cyborg Manifesto: Science, Technology and Socialist-Feminism in the Late Twentieth Century," in *Simians, Cyborgs, and Women: The Reinvention of Nature* (New York: Routledge, 1991), pp. 149–81.
5. Jonathan Crary, *24/7: Terminal Capitalism and the Ends of Sleep* (London: Verso, 2013), p. 127.
6. Roland Barthes, "On CinemaScope" (1954), trans. Jonathan Rosenbaum, http://english.chass.ncsu.edu/jouvert/v3i3/barth.htm.
7. Paul Virilio, *Open Sky* (London: Verso, 1997), p. 45.
8. Antonin Artaud, quoted in Jennifer M. Barker, *The Tactile Eye: Touch and the Cinematic Experience* (Berkeley: University of California Press, 2009), p. 26.
9. Myrna Oliver, "Rose Hobart: SAG Official; Blacklisted Actor," *Los Angeles Times*, August 31, 2000. Hobart recalled the experience of shooting on the film: "For two solid weeks, I was working with alligators, jaguars and pythons out on the back lot. I thought, 'This is acting?'" Ibid.
10. Charles Sirato, *The Dimensionist Manifesto* (1936), trans. Oliver Botar, http://www.artpool.hu/TamkoSirato/manifest.html.
11. Marshall McLuhan, *Understanding Media: The Extensions of Man* (Cambridge, MA: MIT Press, 1994), p. 36.
12. Giuliana Bruno, "Spectatorial Embodiments: Anatomies of the Visible and the Female Bodyscape," *Camera Obscura* 28 (January 1992), pp. 239–62.
13. Sean Redmond, "Liquid Metal: The Cyborg in Science Fiction," in *Liquid Metal: The Science Fiction Film Reader*, ed. Sean Redmond (New York: Wallflower Press, 2007), p. 156.
14. According to the novel, Hadaly's name means "ideal" in Persian.
15. Villiers de L'Isle-Adam, *Tomorrow's Eve* (Urbana: University of Illinois Press, 1982), p. 13, quoted in Mary Ann Doane, "Technophilia: Technology, Representation and the Feminine," in Redmond, *Liquid Metal*, p. 183.
16. Lynn Hershman, "Romancing the Anti-body: Lust and Longing in (Cyber)space," http://www.lynnhershman.com/wp-content/uploads/2015/03/Romancing-the-Anti-body-Lust-and-Longing-in-Cyberspace.pdf.
17. Gabriele Schwab, "Cyborgs: Postmodern Phantasms of Body and Mind," *Discourse* 9 (1987), p. 68.
18. Matthew Biro, *The Dada Cyborg: Visions of the New Human in Weimar Berlin* (Minneapolis: University of Minnesota Press, 2009), p. 3.
19. The other artists were Liam Gillick, Dominique Gonzalez-Foerster, Rirkrit Tiravanija, Pierre Joseph, François Curlet, Melik Ohanian, Joe Scanlan, M/M, Anna Lena Vaney, Richard Phillips, and Mehdi Belhaj Kacem.
20. Rayna Denison, *Anime: A Critical Introduction* (New York: Bloomsbury Academic, 2015), p. 8.
21. Heather Warren Crow, *Girlhood and the Plastic Image* (Lebanon, NH: Dartmouth College Press, 2014), p. 60.
22. Ibid., p. 56.
23. Janet Ward, quoted in Matthew W. Smith, "Schlemmer, Moholy Nagy, and the Search for an Absolute Stage," *Theater* 32, no.3 (Fall 2002), p. 97.
24. Ibid.
25. Ibid. p. 98.
26. Tom Gunning, quoted in Warren Buckland, "A Rational Reconstruction of the Cinema of Attractions," in *The Cinema of Attractions Reloaded*, ed. Wanda Strauven (Amsterdam: Amsterdam University Press, 2006), p. 50.
27. Siegfried Kracauer, quoted in Giuliana Bruno, "Motion and Emotion: Film and the Urban Fabric," in *Cities in Transition: The Moving Image and the Modern Metropolis*, ed. Andrew Webber and Emma Wilson (London: Wallflower Press, 2008), p. 17.
28. Miriam Bratu Hansen, *Cinema and Experience: Siegfried Kracauer, Walter Benjamin, and Theodor W. Adorno* (Berkeley: University of California Press, 2012), p. 12.
29. Jenny Sager, *The Aesthetics of Spectacle in Early Modern Drama and Modern Cinema: Robert Greene's Theater of Attractions* (Houndmills, UK: Palgrave Macmillan, 2013), p. 8.
30. Joshua Yumibe, *Moving Color: Early Film, Mass Culture, Modernism* (New Brunswick, NJ: Rutgers University Press, 2012), p. 144.
31. Ibid. p. 18.
32. Scott Bukatman, *Matters of Gravity: Special Effects and Supermen in the Twentieth Century* (Durham, NC: Duke University Press, 2003), p. 114.
33. Lutz Roberts, "Modern Architecture in the Age of Cinema: Mies van der Rohe and the Moving Image" (PhD dissertation, School of Architecture, Princeton University, January 2012), pp. 9–10.
34. Siegfried Kracauer, "Once Again the Street," quoted in Anthony Vidler, *Warped Space: Art, Architecture, and Anxiety in Modern Culture* (Cambridge, MA: MIT Press, 2002, p. 110.

35. Cindy Keefer, "Space Light Art—Early Abstract Cinema and Multimedia, 1900–1959," http://www.centerforvisualmusic.org/CKSLAexc.htm.
36. Allen Meek, *Trauma and Media: Theories, Histories, and Images* (New York: Routledge, 2011), p. 48.
37. Oskar Schlemmer, "Theater at the Bauhaus," lecture delivered at the Bauhaus, March 16, 1927, https://thecharnelhouse.org/2013/07/20/theater-buhne/.
38. Susanne Lahusen, "Oskar Schlemmer: Mechanical Ballets?" *Dance Research: The Journal of the Society for Dance Research* 4, no. 2 (Autumn 1986), p. 71.
39. Matthew Wilson Smith, *The Total Work of Art: From Bayreuth to Cyberspace* (New York: Routledge, 2007), p. 60.
40. Richard Kostelanetz, *Moholy-Nagy: An Anthology* (New York: Praeger, 1970; reprint, New York: Da Capo, 1991), p. 14.
41. Noam M. Elcott, *Artificial Darkness: An Obscure History of Modern Art and Media* (Chicago: University of Chicago Press, 2016).
42. Philippe-Alain Michaud, *Aby Warburg and the Image in Motion*, trans. Sophie Hawkes (Brooklyn, NY: Zone Books, 2007), p. 50.
43. Mansoor, "Fontana's Atomic Age Abstraction," p. 151.
44. William C. Wees, "Representing the Unrepresentable: Bruce Conner's *Crossroads* and the Nuclear Sublime," *Incite!*, no. 2 (Spring–Fall 2010), http://www.incite-online.net/wees2.html.
45. Gene Youngblood, *Expanded Cinema* (New York: E. P. Dutton, 1970), p. 157.
46. Noam M. Elcott, "Darkened Rooms: A Geneology of Avant-Garde Filmstrips from Man Ray to the London Film-Makers' Co-op and Back Again," *Grey Room* 30, Winter 2008, pp. 6–37.
47. Ibid.
48. Michaud, *Aby Warburg*, p. 47.
49. Ian Cheng, quoted in "In Conversation with Ian Cheng," in Elodie Evers et al., *Ian Cheng: Live Simulations*, exh. cat. (Dusseldorf: Kunsthalle Dusseldorf, 2015), p. 114.
50. Charles Howard Hinton, "What Is the Fourth Dimension?" quoted in Ana Teixeira Pinto, "Enantiomorphs in Hyperspace: Living and Dying in the Fourth Dimension," *E-flux Journal*, no. 72 (April 2016), http://www.e-flux.com/journal/enantiomorphs-in-hyperspace-living-and-dying-on-the-fourth-dimension/.
51. Norman M. Klein, *The Vatican to Vegas: A History of Special Effects* (New York: New Press, 2004).
52. Jack Kahn, "Parabiosis: Neurolibidinal Induction Complex," *DIS*, http://dismagazine.com/dystopia/72978/andrea-crespo-sis-parabiosis/.
53. Joe Bucciero, "We Contain Multitudes: The Hybrid Identities of Andrea Crespo," *Artslant.com*, http://www.artslant.com/9/articles/show/43506.
54. The term *somesthetic* has been defined as relating to, or concerned with bodily sensations: "a somesthetic image of the body created by the brain from sensory inputs of touch, pressure, cold, heat, and pain"; *Merriam-Webster Medical Dictionary*, http://www.merriam-webster.com/medical/somesthetic.
55. Cheng, in "In Conversation with Ian Cheng," p. 111.
56. Charles Fort, *Book of the Damned* (New York: Boni and Liveright, 1919), p. 87.
57. Paul Thomas Anderson, quoted in Dora Budor's proposal for this exhibition, November 2015.
58. "The Playboy Interview: Marshall McLuhan," *Playboy Magazine*, March 1969, p. 6.
59. Giuliana Bruno, "The Body of Pasolini's Semiotics," in *Pier Paolo Pasolini: Contemporary Perspectives*, ed. Patrick Allen Rumble and Bart Testa (Toronto: University of Toronto Press, 1994), p. 95.

# What Is Cinema?: The Challenge of the Moving Image Past and Future

Tom Gunning

## I. So What Is It?

> *Cinema* is a Greek word for movies.
> —Hollis Frampton[1]

When a multivolume collection of essays by André Bazin, perhaps the greatest of all film theorists, was published posthumously in the late 1950s and early 1960s, it was given the title *What Is Cinema?* All film theory and much of film practice has been engaged by this question. Cinema is not something easily defined, but rather poses an ongoing question that can only be answered by engaging with the medium, through either speculation or actual filmmaking. It takes on even greater urgency today when a transformation of media seems to some to have abolished cinema and replaced it with . . . well, what? This hanging question indicates that—far from simply being a historical issue—the enigma posed by cinema will continue to haunt us. Some film critics have claimed that, with the end of the filmstrip and the movie projector, with the multiplication of platforms on which movies are viewed, cinema is no more.

But perhaps it is not *cinema* that no longer exists, but merely *film*, the flexible, semitransparent strip that registered images that could be projected onto a screen. This artifact is disappearing or becoming a museum piece. But the images that film projected, however transformed, continue to appear on various sorts of screens and to generate fantasies, artistic visions, and monetary profits. Cinema still *is*—but what is it? Some have suggested we drop the term "cinema" and substitute "motion pictures," and certainly that term says and includes much (though the role of sound seems muffled by it). I myself think we should stick with "cinema," not only because it refers to the effect, the motion we see on whatever type of screen, but also because it has a long history, including various genres, styles, and major technical transformations (silent to sound, the various color systems, and digital and analog processes). The fascination of cinema is rooted in *kinesis*, and, although transformed technically by new processes, it retains this basic perceptual amazement of seeing images move.

## II. It Moves through Me

> The task I am trying to achieve is above all to make you see.
> —D.W. Griffith[2]

Cinema, before it is anything else—before it is a story, a canvas for special effects, a display of the beauty and grace of stars, before it weaves a tissue of ideology or makes us laugh and cry—presents images that move. This is why it was invented, what separates it from the previous arts of depiction, and also what it shares with the torrent of emerging technological media. But this is also what we take for granted in watching movies and other moving-image media. The movement of imagery invites our imagination, drives our narratives, evokes gasps of astonishment, provokes moments of tender recognition. It is also, I would claim, what we have to a large degree forgotten, not with complete oblivion, but with that taken-for-granted lack of attention—the form of forgetfulness that habit induces. The automatism of perception leads us to ignore the things we see most often; overfamiliarity, as the great theorist of Formalism Victor Shklovsky said nearly a century ago, "eats away at things, at clothes, at furniture, at our wives and our fear of war."[3] Art exists, Shklovsky argued, in order to renew our perception of these things, to vividly restore our awareness of them. Cinema was

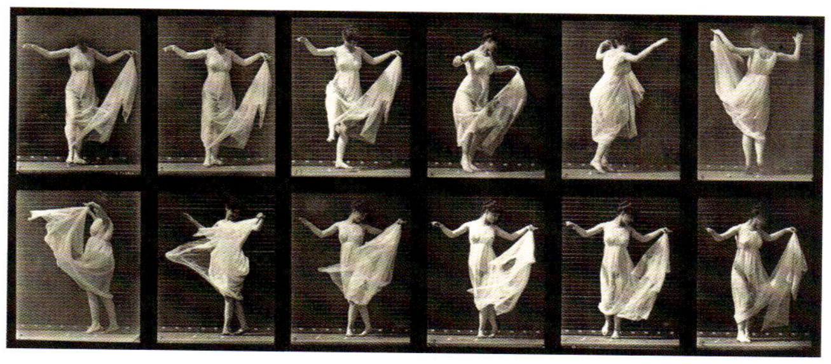

Fig. 1. Eadweard Muybridge (1830–1904), *Woman Dancing (Fancy)*: Plate 187 from *Animal Locomotion* (1887), 1884–86. Collotype, 7 ¼ x 16 ¾ in. (18.4 x 42.5 cm). The Museum of Modern Art, New York; gift of Mrs. Jane K. Murray

invented so we could see motion in all its vividness, whether to study it with scientific precision, as in the early chronophotography of Eadweard Muybridge and Étienne-Jules Marey (fig. 1), or simply to delight in its manifold variety, as in the first films produced by the Cinématographe of the Lumière company, which revealed the magic of the ordinary, or the magic films of Georges Méliès, which revealed the apparent ordinariness of the impossible. But the danger lies in the fact that anything, as Shklovsky claimed, may become habitual and thereby fade from our consciousness. Art exists to make us rediscover the sensation of things—but sometimes an art form itself gets taken for granted. Then it is up to us to rediscover what has been neglected and forgotten. That is the task of art history and criticism.

When cinema first appeared at the end of the nineteenth century, it pursued the moving image. Before stories and stars, it was enough that a movie showed the multifaceted movement of daily life. Here is a description from Frank Norris's novel *McTeague* (1899) of a couple seeing a projected motion picture for the very first time:

> The kinetoscope fairly took their breaths away.
> "What will they do next?" observed Trina in amazement. "Ain't that wonderful, Mac?"
> McTeague was awe-struck.
> "Look at that horse move his head," he cried excitedly, quite carried away. "Look at the cable car coming—and the man going across the street. See, here comes a truck. Well, I never in all my life! What would Marcus say to this?"[4]

Lest we see this excited reaction simply as the stupefied gawking of a naïve couple, let's quote the Parisian Cubist painter Fernand Léger some twenty year later, just before he made one of the greatest films of the avant-garde, *Ballet Mécanique*:

> Here it is: 80% of the elements and objects that help us to live are only noticed by us in our everyday lives while 20% are *seen.* From this I deduce the cinematographic revolution is *to make us see everything that has been merely noticed.* Project these brand-new elements and you have your tragedies, your comedies, on a plane that is uniquely visual and cinematographic. The dog that goes by in the street is only noticed. Projected in the screen it is seen so much that the audience reacts as if it discovered the dog.[5]

Cinema does not simply present us with a technology that captures motion visually: it provides us with a sensory (that is, an aesthetic) tool that makes us see, that makes us *aware,* of movement, and that overcomes our habitual oblivion of taking movement for granted—unless, of course, we take cinema and the moving image for granted, which I fear we all too often do. The exhibition that this catalogue accompanies invites us to regain our wonder at visual movement, and therefore the wonder of the cinema itself.

### III. The Dialectic of Still and Moving Images

> The concept of the moving (time-consuming) image arises from the superimposition—or counterpoint—of two differing immobile images.
> —Sergei Eisenstein[6]

Cinema is the art of the visible—or, better phrased, following Léger, the art of making things visible. It is the art of movement, but more precisely of moving images, of pictures from delivered immobility, propelled into motion. This technically produced motion is not as simple as it may seem. The technology involves not just mechanical recording but also a process of perceptual transformation and discovery, through a dialectical interplay of the still and the moving and the nature of human perception.

Like Shklovsky and Léger, Walter Benjamin described how in our ordinary perception much of our daily lives remains invisible, due, however, less to habit than to the actual limits of our perception:

> Whereas it is a commonplace that, for example, we have some idea what is involved in the act of walking (if only in general terms), we have no idea at all what happens during the split second when a person actually takes a step. We are familiar with the movement of picking up a cigarette lighter or a spoon, but know almost nothing of what really goes on between hand and metal and still less how this varies with different moods.[7]

Our own everyday actions remain opaque, invisible, and paradoxically ungraspable to us owing to their unconscious, immediate, and automatic nature. It was the camera, Benjamin claimed, that penetrated into this "optical unconscious" of instinctive behavior, precisely by freezing the ongoing course of habit. Photography's ability to freeze motion, to capture and fix an instant, made the phases of motion, hitherto imperceptible, visible. When the first instantaneous photographs appeared around 1870, they revealed not only that in full gallop all four of a horse's hooves left the ground at the same moment, but also that strollers in the street displayed unexpected positions of heel and toe in the process of walking. Such instantaneous exposures (originally taken by amateurs more for amusement than enlightenment) opened a field of scientific investigation.

The unique control that instantaneous photography offered in capturing a brief slice of time allowed its transformation into "chronophotography"—a term that indicates the photography of time, but even more the recording of phases of motion through successive still images. Muybridge, and, even more systematically, the physiologist Marey, undertook a project of capturing images of humans, animals, and even inanimate objects as they moved through a quantifiable time.[8] What had been invisible to human vision was now captured by the rapid glance of the camera, placed in a temporally ordered sequence, and made available for future examination and analysis. The everyday motions of the body were now parsed out in a graph-like space into a concatenation of still images. For the scientist Marey, this method allowed observation of minutiae of physical stance and transformation that would yield the knowledge necessary for studying a modern body, subject to the rigors of warfare, industrial work, and athletic achievement (fig. 2). The body, with its unconscious movements now revealed, could also be disciplined in new rationally determined regimens of labor, marching, or acrobatics.

Still images of the phases of motion completed the first move of what I am calling the "dialectic of the moving image": chronophotography rendered motion visible by stilling action into a series of static images, braking the flow of movement into discreet pictures and lifting them out of the flow of time, while simultaneously rigorously recording their occurrence within a discreetly measured clock time. But did chronophotography capture motion or did such dissection represent its murder? At the end of the nineteenth century, science's phenomenal success in quantifying even those aspects of the physical world that had remained hidden for millennia was confronted by philosophies that proclaimed the value of lived experience over such abstraction. Thus philosopher Henri Bergson declared that the technological mastery of time and motion represented by chronophotography and even cinematography, rather than capturing motion, obscured our sense of it through quantification and segmentation.

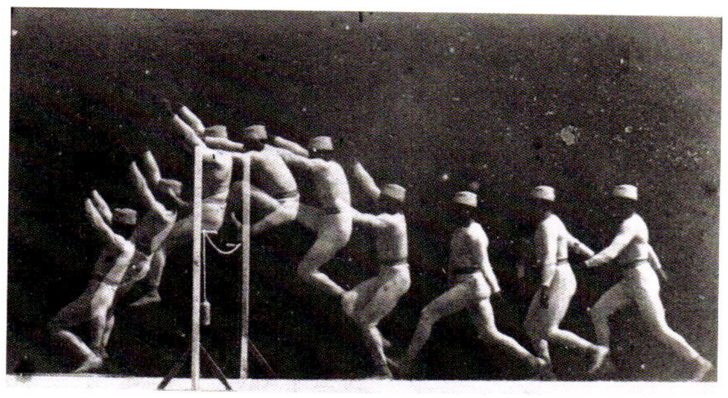

Fig. 2. Étienne-Jules Marey (1830–1904), Marey's chronophotographs of a man doing a high jump, 1892. National Media Museum, Bradford, United Kingdom

In his book *Creative Evolution* (1907) Bergson claimed that the mechanical production of motion pictures actually missed the experience of motion itself:

> Suppose we wish to portray on the screen a living picture such as the marching past of a regiment. . . . How could it, at its best, reproduce suppleness and variety of life? Now, there is another way of proceeding, more easy and at the same time more effective. It is to take a series of snapshots of the passing regiment and to throw these instantaneous views on the screen, so that they replace each other very rapidly. This is what the cinematograph does. With photographs, each of which represents the regiment in a fixed attitude, it reconstitutes the mobility of the regiment marching. It is true that if we had to do with photographs alone, however much we might look at them, we should never see them animated: with immobility set beside immobility, even endlessly, we could never make movement. In order that the pictures may be animated, there must be movement somewhere. The movement does indeed exist here; it is in the apparatus. It is because the film of the cinematograph unrolls, bringing in turn the different photographs of the scene to continue each other, that each actor of the scene recovers his mobility; he strings all his successive attitudes on the invisible movement of the film. The process then consists in extracting from all the movements peculiar to all the figures an impersonal movement abstract and simple, *movement in general*, so to speak: we put this into the apparatus, and we reconstruct the individuality of each particular movement by combining this nameless movement with the personal attitudes. Such is the contrivance of the cinematograph. Instead of attaching ourselves to the inner becoming of things we place ourselves outside them in order to recompose their becoming artificially.[9]

However amazing and useful this mechanical creation of moving images might be, Bergson claimed that such a portrayal of motion betrayed its essence as humans experienced it. The triumph of externality and measurement that the scientific method of observation sought obscures precisely the experience of motion that Bergson saw as essential to lived experience. This recorded motion is produced by adding still images to one another. But lived motion is not the accumulation of still images viewed from an objective external viewpoint of science. To quote Bergson further:

> In order to advance with the moving reality, you must replace yourself within it. Install yourself within change, and you will grasp at once both change itself and the successive states in which *it might* at any instant be immobilized. But with these successive states, perceived from without as real and no longer as potential immobilities, you will never reconstitute movement. . . . The movement slips through the interval, because every attempt to reconstitute change out of states implies the absurd proposition, that movement is made of immobilities.[10]

Does the dialectic of the moving image therefore break down into a pale simulacrum? Bergson would seem to claim the impossibility of a mechanically produced image of motion. From this eloquent description of the difference between the experience of motion and the analysis that breaks the motion into successive still frames, many theorists have claimed that Bergson denounced the cinema, and indeed this seems to be the claim of his description of the apparatus. However, Bergson appears to waver between descriptions of cinema and chronophotography here. If he describes the cinema, it is as the physical filmstrip with its successive frames that moves through the projector, rather than the projected image moving on the screen. Bergson seems to deny the step of the dialectic that moved from the *analysis* of motion achieved by Marey to the *synthesis* of motion that the Lumière Cinématograph offered. Marey felt that the synthesis of motion was of dubious scientific value, since it simply reproduced the ordinary experience of seeing motion, without correcting what Marey called the weakness of the human eye. Indeed, Marey broke quite bitterly with his assistant, Georges Demenÿ, who wished to exploit the moving image as a form of commercial amusement and entertainment, delighting viewers with the spectacle of athletes, dancers, and performers in motion.

We now come to the next threshold in this dialectic of the still and the moving: the production of the moving image. Cinema represents the second stage in this dialectic, as the visibility that chronophotography granted to each individual frame in its immobility disappears in a whirl of motion. The Lumière Cinématographe, the motion picture camera invented in 1895, depended on the breakdown of motion into discreet still images that had formed the basis of Marey's (and Muybridge's) photographic work. But the Cinématographe was also a device for *showing* motion pictures; it reversed the process of fixing the individual images and, through the motion of the projector, brought them to life again. No individual still images are seen on the screen, only the flow of motion. It was precisely this miracle that the Lumières offered as the essence of their spectacle in 1895 on the Boulevard des Capucines in Paris: the magical transformation of a still image into movement.

**IV. The Magic of Light and Transformation**

> The form and perfection of all bodies is light.
> —Robert Grosseteste[11]

An astute observer of the Lumière brothers' early film show, the magician Georges Méliès described the expectation he felt as one of the group invited to the preview of their new invention, which promised a major photographic novelty from France's largest photographic supply company. Suddenly, there appeared within the darkness an image, a projection of a photograph on a screen. This apparition provoked a heightened attention among the group, but also a murmur of disappointment. Méliès claimed he said to himself, "This is what they have gotten us here for? Lantern slides of photographs? We have seen those for decades. . . ." But he stopped in mid-sentence, as the image seemed to quiver, vibrate, or dissolve—and to *move.* The frozen image of a locomotive entering a station or a city street filled with traffic or a child eating breakfast suddenly exploded into motion (fig. 3). This motion seemed contagious, as the crowd itself began to stir and exclaim in wonder at this new device, the Lumière Cinématographe, that projected moving pictures. Delighted, Méliès, as an entrepreneur of magical optical illusions, exclaimed, "That's my métier!"[12] It was not the scientific precision that seized Méliès's imagination, but the effect of transformation, the astonishment of motion on the screen.

I would claim there was another frame of reception of the moving image at the end of the nineteenth century besides the scientific and the philosophical, one that stressed the amazement of the dialectical crossing from still to movement, allowing the individual frame to disappear in a flicker of motion. This frame of reception comes less from the quantifying sciences than from the realm of visual entertainment, of magical tricks and optical spectacles. I have claimed elsewhere that if the interrupted motions of Marey fell short of the experience of motion described by Bergson, he might have found his notion of the dependence of form on motion fulfilled at the Folies Bergère in the performance of the Chicago dancer Loïe Fuller.[13] The great avant-garde filmmaker Germaine Dulac said of Fuller in the 1920s: "Loïe Fuller created her harmonies with light at the very moment that the Lumières gave us the cinema."[14] Fuller could be considered an inventor of cinema, since she devised a spectacle of highly focused electrical light, color, and movement based in a transforming series of images and forms that premiered in Paris in 1893, just two years before the Lumières offered the first public exhibitions of the Cinématographe.

Fuller became one of the icons of turn-of-the-century art and entertainment, not only as a performer in her own right but through the plethora of images she inspired—the posters for her

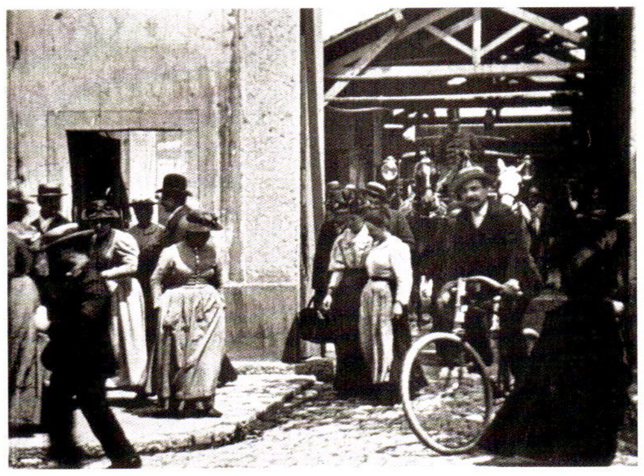

Fig. 3. "The workers going out of the Factory Lumière" from *Sortie d'usine* [I], 1895. Cat. Lumière No. 91.1. Camera operator: Louis Lumière; location: chemin Saint-Victor (now "rue du 1er film"), Monplaisir, Lyon, France

performances by Jules Chéret and Henri de Toulouse-Lautrec, of course, but also sculpture, jewelry, posters, and prints (figs. 4, 5). She offered a unique form of dance that I would claim belongs more strongly in the dialectic of the cinema than in the history of dance, conceived as the art of patterns of footwork and gesture. Fuller, as Stéphane Mallarmé, one of her devoted fans among the Parisian Symbolist artists, claimed, was less a dancer than a creator of images through the conjunction of her moving body and projected light. This description of an early performance, before she left New York for Paris, conveys her transformation from physical dancer to moving-light shaped image:

> Suddenly the stage is darkened, and Loïe Fuller appears in a white light which makes her radiant and a white robe which surrounds her like a cloud. She floats around the stage, her figure now revealed, now concealed by the exquisite drapery which takes forms of its own and seems instinct with her life. The surprised and delighted spectators do not know what to call her performance. It is not a skirt dance, although she dances and waves a skirt. It is unique, ethereal, delicious. As she vanishes, leaving only a flutter of her robe upon the stage, the theater resounds with thunders of applause. Again she emerges from the darkness, her airy evolutions now tinted blue and purple and crimson, and again the audience rise at her and insist on seeing her pretty, piquant face before they can believe that the lovely apparition is really a woman.[15]

Thus, Fuller's dance offered something to the new art of cinema not found in the many other dance numbers recorded by the new medium. Like other avant-garde visual forms that disarranged concepts of solidity and objectivity and conveyed the seeming insubstantiality of modern experience, Fuller's dance displayed motion as a matrix from which form is born, a possibility of continuous transformation. A new aesthetics, as embodied in Art Nouveau, embraced Fuller as the fulfillment of the ideal of an organic art form that saw motion as a force in itself, a plasmatic energy that created forms rather than simply moving them about. In this sense, it was strongly opposed to the classical conception of movement as a series of points along the trajectory of a self-sufficient object, a notion that Bergson had attacked as a confining illusion of the mind. In the films we have of Fuller's serpentine dances, her body seems swallowed by a flux and reflux of motion, less solid matter than a materialization of energy and movement itself.

In her attempt to both define and transcend binaries of man and woman, material and ideal, knowledge and mystery, Fuller literally embodies the modern dialectic of the representation of motion. But movement alone does not exhaust Fuller's direct relation to the cinema: As Dulac claimed, Fuller could be said to have created cinema before cinematography, by wedding movement to light. Fuller's art relied on light in several fundamental ways. Most importantly, projected light cloaked itself in colors, which supplied the most immaterial of covering for Fuller's form, staining her fabrics in a constant transit and transformation of hue. In their attempts to capture the spectrum of Fuller's effects, her publicity posters—and, even more so, the series of prints by Toulouse-Lautrec—clearly show the inspiration such a spectacle must have provided for a future abstract art of pure form and color endowed with an appearance of mutability. But more directly, Fuller's color symphonies provided the cinema with its first impulse toward color. Early films of serpentine dances demanded tinting of some sort. Both Edison and the Lumières handtinted their serpentine films with changing patterns of free-form color, making these first color films among the most satisfying instances of the art of motion in early cinema.

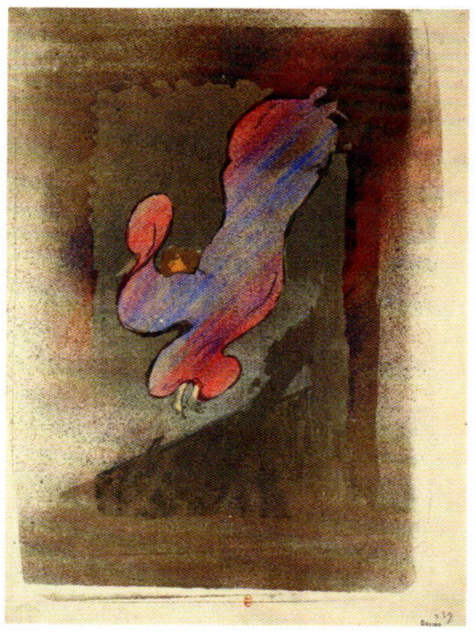

Fig. 4. Henri de Toulouse-Lautrec (1864–1901), *Miss Loïe Fuller*, 1893. Lithograph, image: 14 ½ x 10 9⁄16 in. (36.8 x 26.8 cm). Bibliotheque Nationale de France

Motion, as Bergson indicated, posed a challenge to the enduring habits of the mind, such as its tendency toward analysis into discreet and static images. It was the resolution of motion into

Fig. 5. Jules Chéret (1836–1932), *Loïe Fuller*, 1897. Lithograph (poster). Private collection

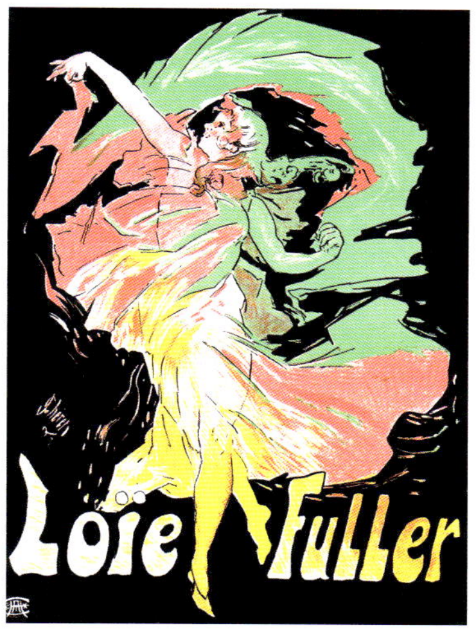


discreet images on both chronophotographs and the motion picture film that inspired Bergson to describe this distortion as "cinematographic." However, I believe that early films of motion such as those of serpentine dance, far from revealing the limitations of the cinema, conveyed this spectacle of the transformation of matter into motion. The contrasts between Marey and Fuller abound: scientist versus dancer; scorner of the popular spectacle in favor of the scientific laboratory versus the music-hall performer; producer of black-and-white still photographs (primarily of male nudes) revealing the action of muscles and joints versus the veiled, constantly transforming female performer bathed in variously colored light.

Fuller's spectacles of light and movement allow us to imagine a cinema unmoored by the material support of film, a moving image formed of light that provokes the imagination, dazzles the senses, and provides new pathways for both thought and vision. Perhaps this is the greatest ambition of the cinema, one that forbids any final answer to the question "What is cinema?" Because, as Bergson conceives it, motion is always invention, the appearance of something new, an experience beyond the petrification of ideas, and perhaps even evading the definitions of language. The works included in this exhibition not only explore the definitions of cinema, they also demonstrate that cinema is itself the experience of the protean, the shape-shifting, and the ever-constant renewal of time through the process of questioning what we see and, thereby, what we think.

NOTES

Part of this essay appeared in German in my essay "Kino Vital: Kinematografische Zeit zwischen Planze und Maschine" in *Gehen Blühen Flieschen: Naturvenhaltnisse in der Kunst*, ed. Ines Linder (Nurnberg : Verlag fur modern Kunst, 2014), pp. 186–202. The concluding section on Loie Fuller borrows some passages from my essay "Light, Motion, Cinema! The Heritage of Loïe Fuller and Germaine Dulac," *Framework* 46, no. 1 (Spring 2005), pp. 106–29.

1. Hollis Frampton, "For a Metahistory of Film: Commonplace Notes and Hypotheses," in *Circles of Confusion: Film Photography Video* (Rochester, NY: Visual Studies Workshop, 1983), p. 114.
2. Quoted in David Trotter, *Cinema and Modernism* (Oxford: Blackwell, 2007), p. 51.
3. Victor Shklovsky, "Art as Technique." *Russian Formalist Criticism: Four Essays*, ed. Lee T. Lemon and Marion J. Reiss (Lincoln: University of Nebraska Press, 1965), p. 12.
4. Frank Norris, *McTeague* (New York: Signet Classics, 1964), p. 85.
5. Fernand Léger, *The Function of Painting* (New York: Viking Press, 1965), p. 22.
6. Sergei Eisenstein, "A Dialectical Approach to Film Form," in *Film Form: Essays in Film Theory* (New York: Harcourt Brace and Company, 1949), p. 55.
7. Walter Benjamin, "The Work of Art in the Age of Its Mechanical Reproducibility," in *Walter Benjamin: Selected Writings*, vol. 4, *1938–1940*, ed. Howard Eiland and Michael W. Jennings (Cambridge, MA: Harvard University Press, 2006), p. 266.
8. See Marta Braun, *Picturing Time: The Work of Etienne-Jules Marey, 1830–1904* (Chicago: University of Chicago Press, 1992).
9. Henri Bergson, *Creative Evolution* (Lanham, MD: University Press of America, 1983), p. 305 (emphasis mine).
10. Ibid., p. 308.
11. Robert Grosseteste, *On Light (De Luce)*, trans. Clare C. Riedl (Milwaukee, WI: Marquette University Press, 1942), p. 10.
12. Méliès quoted in Anne-Marie Quévrain and Marie-George Charconnet-Méliès, "Méliès et Freud: un avenir pour les marchands d'illusions?" in *Méliès et la naissance du spectacle cinématographique* (Paris: Klincksieck, 1984), p. 235.
13. Tom Gunning, "Loïe Fuller and the Art of Motion," in *Camera Obscura, Camera Lucida: Essays in Honor of Annette Michelson*, ed. Richard Allen and Malcolm Turvey (Amsterdam: University of Amsterdam Press, 2003), pp. 75–90.
14. Germaine Dulac, *Écrits sur le Cinéma* (Paris: Éditions Paris Expérimental, 1994), p. 110.
15. Richard Nelson Current and Marcia Ewing Current, *Loïe Fuller: Goddess of Light* (Boston: Northeastern University Press, 1997), p. 35.

# Walt Disney: Experimental Animator

John Canemaker

The name Walt Disney is so identifiable with mainstream entertainment that it may seem absurd to call him an experimental animator. Yet during the 1920s and 1930s, arguably his most creative period, Disney (1901–1966) tenaciously pursued an experimental approach to commercial film animation. Even while learning the rudiments of his craft in Kansas City in the early 1920s, producing and directing silent shorts starring monodimensional characters and simple gags, Disney was dissatisfied with the limited narratives, aesthetics, and technologies of early animated films.

After arriving in Los Angeles in 1923, he sought ways to involve audiences emotionally with his cartoons. Just as Charlie Chaplin and Buster Keaton moved beyond simple slapstick comedy to create emotionally rich characters and stories, Disney wanted to break out of the rigid structure of the era's silent animated films: rubber-hose-and-circle character designs and stories in which, in the words of educator Donald W. Graham, the "emphasis was on the action, rather than on the character as an actor."[1]

Through the years, Disney drove himself and his artists to discover ways to engage viewers by offering them, in addition to comic situations and gags, moments in which they might actually empathize with these hand-drawn cartoons. Simultaneously, he continually pushed the envelope of possibilities in animated films by seizing upon technological advancements, such as combining live action and animation on screen, in the silent "Alice Comedies" (1923–27); synchronized sound, which Disney first used in 1928 in his Mickey Mouse shorts; three-strip Technicolor in 1932; and the Multiplane Camera in 1937. The latter two were first implemented in the music-based Silly Symphony shorts (1929–39) and served as a laboratory for his new ideas.

Technological and artistic progress quickened through the 1930s, eventually leading to breakthrough animated feature films that achieved Disney's goal of engaging audiences' hearts and minds. *Snow White and the Seven Dwarfs* (1937), *Pinocchio* (1940), and *Fantasia* (1940) altered the course of animation history through their exceptionally subtle and refined animation and unprecedented production values.

*Fantasia* is, in fact, one of the most experimental and radical long-form films ever produced by a Hollywood studio. It is a classical music "concert feature," with animated visuals that are as deliberately and consciously composed as the music, in representational, expressionistic, and abstract forms—a Silly Symphony writ large. Famed conductor Leopold Stokowski (1882–1977), himself a pioneer of high-fidelity sound recording, conducted the musical selections in an immersive multichannel process called "Fantasound," a first for commercial motion pictures.

A dozen years before *Fantasia*, Disney had seized upon sound as a way to bring his films *closer* to audiences. Mickey Mouse, in *Steamboat Willie* (released November 18, 1928), performed to an integrated soundtrack of music, effects, and voice. The then-scruffy rodent produced melodies by ruthlessly squeezing, poking, and kicking his "instruments" (barnyard animals). Tightly synchronized sounds appeared to come from the cartoon's actions, and audiences were delighted. Sound put Walt Disney on the map as a filmmaker of promise, and *Steamboat Willie* and Warner's *The Jazz Singer* (1927) are icons of movies' transition from silents to talkies.

Disney also instinctively sought "personality" in his cartoons because, he explained, "Comedy, to be appreciated, must have contact with the audience. There must be a familiar, subconscious association . . . a direct life connection."[2] In March 1927, for example, more than a year before Mickey's debut, Disney was in Hollywood producing/directing "Alice Comedies," a series in which a live-action little girl performs with cartoon animals in a cartoon world. In *Alice's Picnic* (released May 1927), he noticed a scene in which a mother cat bathes her kittens and dries them by running them

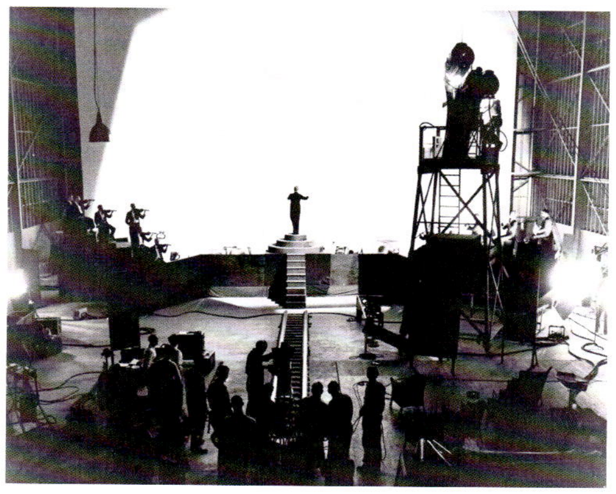

Shooting *Fantasia*'s live-action inserts with conductor Leopold Stokowski on the podium at The Walt Disney Studios, 1940

A parodic *pas de deux* in *Dance of the Hours*. Publicity still for *Fantasia*

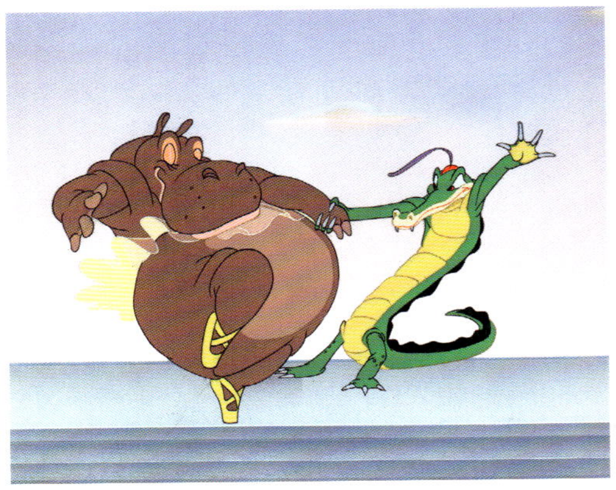

through a wringer. It was a typical broad gag of the period, capitalizing on animation's surreal possibilities to defy the laws of physics.

Disney called his small staff of animators together to point out something subtle within the scene. "That little kitten didn't just jump out of the water," he commented. "He climbed up and hung there and dropped down *like a little kid*. That's what I want to see in the pictures." Then, Disney put a fine point on his philosophy: "I want the characters to *be* somebody. I don't want them just to be a drawing!"[3] To be *somebody* in animation is to be "a contender," to quote Marlon Brando in *On the Waterfront* (1954). Personality animation made Walt Disney's characters—and Disney himself—contenders. He believed that when audiences can relate to a cartoon's behavior on the screen by comparing it to real life, they *empathize*; they believe in the characters and their actions, love or hate them, and sometimes even fear for their safety and weep for their sad "lives" and "deaths," as evidenced by *Snow White and the Seven Dwarfs*, *Pinocchio*, *Dumbo* (1941), and *Bambi* (1942). "Our study of the actual is . . . so that we may have a basis upon which to go into the fantastic, the unreal, the imaginative," Disney wrote in the mid-1930s, "and yet to let it have a foundation of fact, in order that it may more richly possess sincerity and contact with the public."[4]

Even in comedy situations, Disney espoused the importance of "a direct life connection" because "my experience has shown me that the most hilarious of comedies is always based on things actual, possible or probable."[5] Audiences watching *Fantasia*, for example, can identify some aspect of the human experience in the actions of a spunky mouse disobeying a stern parental sorcerer or a balletic hippo flirting with an amorous alligator or even a tiny dancing mushroom trying and failing to fit in.

To understand the extent of Disney's groundbreaking accomplishments in both short- and long-form films, we need to consider the roots of "personality" or "character" animation. Winsor McCay (1867–1934), the great comic strip and animation cartoonist, pioneered film characters who "think" before they act and whose individualism is expressed by how they move. McCay experimented with motion graphics in comic strips such as *Little Nemo in Slumberland*, begun in 1905 in the *New York Herald*, using cinematic layouts, flexible panels, and characters in dynamic, sequential storytelling poses. Inevitably, this led to his first animated film, in 1911, starring Nemo and friends, who moved wondrously on the screen but did not emote. Telling a story through an animated character's *personality* began tentatively in McCay's second film, *How a Mosquito Operates* (1912).

It was in *Gertie the Dinosaur* (1914), the third of his ten known films, that McCay's experiments in personality character animation came to dazzling fruition. One of the most famous and influential animated shorts of the silent era, *Gertie* stars a huge dinosaur, who behaves like a petulant little girl. The film points directly toward Disney's efforts twenty years later. McCay's superb draftsmanship and subtle animation predict Disney's mature work of the mid-1930s; the line drawings have weight, an illusion lending veracity to Gertie's movements.[6] "McCay's graphic art set a standard for later animators," notes film historian Donald Crafton: "[His] propensity for closed forms and trompe l'oeil illusionism . . . virtually defined the aesthetic

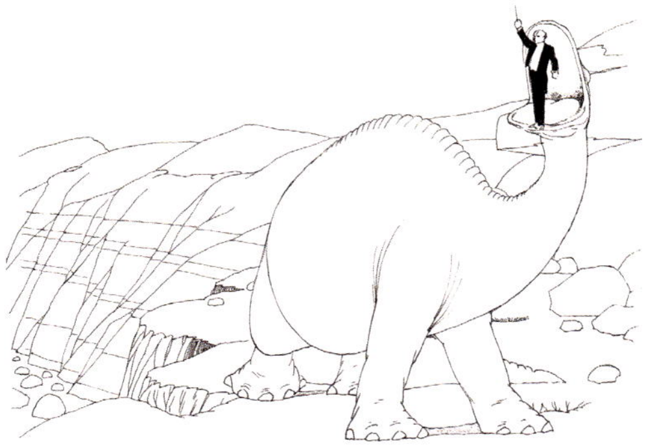

Gertie from Winsor McCay's 1914 pioneering masterwork of personality animation, *Gertie the Dinosaur*

ground rules for all later American animation . . . solidity, pragmatism, and pictorial realism."[7]

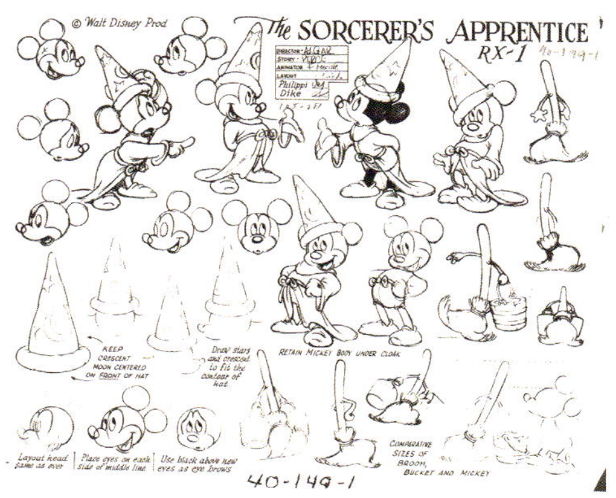


A 1938 model sheet suggesting expressions and acting attitudes for Mickey Mouse as the Sorcerer's Apprentice

McCay's timing of Gertie's actions and reactions was reality based because he performed with the cartoon onstage in his vaudeville act—an early example of multiplatform, immersive performance art. Standing alongside the movie screen, McCay cracked a whip and barked orders at his "trained dinosaur." The childish Diplodocus, in response, displayed a variety of attitudes and emotions. She dawdled, disobeyed, became distracted, literally ate and drank the scenery (tree, boulders, a lake), snapped at McCay in anger, and, most endearingly, wept giant tears when he admonished her. Audiences were enchanted by this realistic-looking, spunky, believably lovable creature.

Did Disney see McCay perform with *Gertie* live? Probably not, but during his teen years, the ambitious lad most likely viewed the widely distributed one-reel short of *Gertie the Dinosaur* containing a live-action prologue featuring the famed McCay.[8] Most certainly, Disney learned about McCay's live, multimedia performance in detail from his staff and associates who *had* witnessed it. Years later, Disney offered an homage to *Gertie* and Winsor McCay by re-creating McCay's vaudeville act on a *Disneyland* television program, *The Story of the Animated Drawing* (1955).[9] McCay never established a studio to develop the techniques he pioneered. "He was an incipient artist," writes Richard Eder. "His cartoons are primitive; not in the sense of crudeness but, like the Italian primitives, in the limited techniques they could command."[10]

Disney entered the burgeoning motion picture industry during a time of great technological change. By 1928, producer Pat Sullivan's "Felix the Cat" series was internationally popular. Felix was a "thinking character" who pondered problems before solving them, often by morphing his body parts into useful objects. His acting range was extremely limited, however, and Sullivan's penny-pinching refusal to invest in sound led to his cat's demise.[11] Disney, on the other hand, jumped at the opportunity to use sound technology *and* personality animation in new ways. He shared McCay's radical desire to make cartoons "real," but lacking McCay's brilliant draftsmanship, Disney instead built a vibrant studio of artists and artisans—more than 1,200 worked on *Fantasia*—and micromanaged every aspect of his films.

To improve his silent cartoons, Disney educated himself and his staff about live-action camera angles, effects, and editing and explored how to emulate them in cartoons. They studied Chaplin, Laurel and Hardy, Harold Lloyd, and Buster Keaton to learn how to base gags on empathetic personalities and *build* comic routines, rather than pile one gag atop another. They examined the shadow effects, montage, mise-en-scène, and action staging that stirred audiences' emotions in films starring Lon Chaney and Douglas Fairbanks.[12]

In 1929, Disney paid for his animators to attend night classes at Los Angeles's Chouinard Art Institute in figure drawing to improve their drafting skills, something no other cartoon producer did. In 1932, he opened a school on his studio lot and hired Chouinard teacher Donald W. Graham (1883–1976) to head it.[13] At the time, Disney was producing a bread-and-butter slate of popular Mickey Mouse and Silly Symphony shorts. But he was also planning his first cartoon feature, *Snow White and the Seven Dwarfs*. For this he hired a large staff consisting of veteran cartoonists from the silent era, who could animate but were not versatile draftsmen, and younger art school graduates, who could draw anything but had never animated. To conform the consistency of the two groups' drawing—a process Graham described as the "resolution of action into strong graphic statements that were exciting to view"[14]—Disney gave the instructor marching orders in a now-legendary 1935 eight-page studio memo of cogent curricular suggestions.

Among Disney's ideas:

- The first duty of the cartoon is not to picture or duplicate real action or things as they actually happen, but to give a caricature of life and action . . .
- I definitely feel that we cannot do the fantastic things, based on the real, unless we first know the real . . .
- I think a good study of music would be indispensable to the animator.[15]

Under Disney's leadership, Graham's classes scrutinized works of great masters of painting and analyzed live-action film performances. Basic principles of visual communication and motion emerged, forming new concepts and rules of drawing for animation, including:

- What is drawn must be legible: the cardinal rule of the animator.
- A volume or shape may be reasonable without in any way being factual.
- The location of a joint is more important than the joint itself.
- The audience must feel an intimacy with the picture on the screen.

"Put into simple terms," Graham concluded, "it amounted to this: a drawing principle is a drawing principle. If it works in a Rubens it must work in Donald Duck. If it works in the Duck, it must work in *Snow White*."[16] "From *Steamboat Willie* to *Fantasia*, every day was an excitement," recalled Marc Davis (1913–2000), one of Disney's master animators. "Whatever we were doing had never been done before. . . . There was excitement and there was competition. Everyone was young and everyone was doing something. We saw every ballet, we saw every film. If a film was good we would go and see it five times. It was a perfect time of many things coming together in one orbit. Walt was that lodestone."[17]

Fresh points of view on various subjects were contributed by guest speakers, including Frank Lloyd Wright, Alexander Woollcott, Jean Charlot, Rico Lebrun, Ballet Russes dancers, and experts on color and story structure. In *Snow White and the Seven Dwarfs* and *Pinocchio*, Disney created unprecedentedly rich character/personality animation that fully engaged audiences' emotions as few other animated films ever had. But it had not been easy. "Strong character animation had proved to be fiercely difficult to master at first in the shorts and then, especially, in *Snow White* and *Pinocchio*," wrote animation historian Michael Barrier. "Compared with the other two features, *Fantasia* must have looked to Disney like a vacation, free of gnarly challenges like those surrounding the animation of the dwarfs and Pinocchio."[18] But *Fantasia* was not any easier because of Disney's continuing, restless, expansionist ambitions for animated films. "This is not the cartoon medium," he announced in a 1938 story meeting on the "Ave Maria" section of the concert feature:

> It should not be limited to cartoons. We have worlds to conquer here. We're doing beautiful things with beautiful music. . . . It's an experimental thing, and I'm willing to experiment on it. We've got more in this medium than making people laugh. We love to make people laugh, but I think we can do both. . . . This stuff means more, it's richer. It's like a painting.[19]

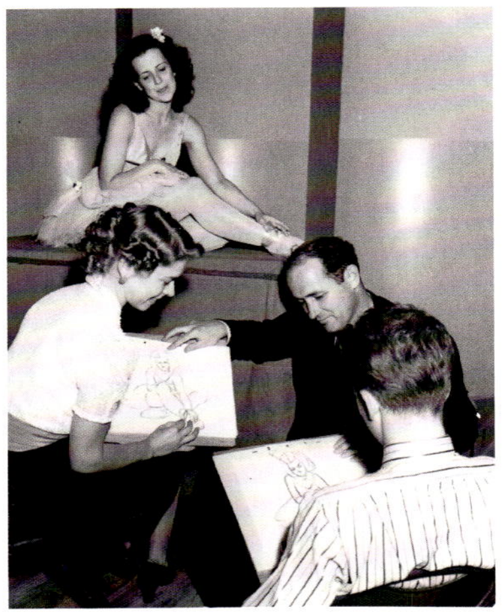

Donald W. Graham, The Walt Disney Studios' innovative art teacher, in a classroom, c. 1939

In a series of meetings in early September 1938, Disney, Stokowski, and composer and music critic Deems Taylor (1885–1966) began selecting the music for *Fantasia*. Igor Stravinsky's *Rite of Spring* was a daring choice for general audiences in 1938, barely three decades after the great modernist work's dissonance caused near riots at its Paris premiere. Equally unusual for a commercial feature was visualizing Bach's Toccata and Fugue in D Minor as abstract and semi-abstract moving designs. Disney had become interested in abstract films after seeing Len Lye's *Colour Box* (1935), which featured lively patterns painted directly onto film stock. After viewing German abstract filmmaker Oskar Fischinger's groundbreaking work, Disney hired him as an "effects" artist for the Bach section.[20]

*Fantasia* included a section featuring a visual interpretation of the film's abstract soundtrack, a still from which was used for this Italian theater lobby card from a reissue in the 1960s

At a meeting on September 14, 1938, fascinating modes of presentation were considered. Disney and his team became excited about the idea of wafting scents into the theater, including night-blooming cereus for a Debussy prelude, other flower perfumes for the *Nutcracker Suite*, incense for the "Ave Maria," and, for the magical incantations in *The Sorcerer's Apprentice*, Stokowski thought gunpowder "a very exciting smell."[21] Disney's lateral thinking also included viewing the sequence for Bach's Toccata through 3D glasses, as well as making the entire film in a wide-screen process.

He should have called the film *Synesthesia*. Like Aeschylus, Pythagoras, Alexander Scriabin, Athanasius Kircher, James Whitney, and numerous other visionaries, Disney wanted a fusion of art and technology to create what writer and philosopher K. F. E. Trahndorff and composer Richard Wagner called *Gesamtkunstwerk* ("total work of art"). *Time* magazine, in a 1940 cover story on *Fantasia*, saw Disney tripping "Mickey-like into an art form that immortals from Aeschylus to Richard Wagner have always dreamed of."[22]

Many of the techniques Disney considered had been attempted before in live-action movies, but not in animation. For example, Abel Gance's "Polyvision" in *Napoléon* (1927), and Fox Grandeur, a 1929 70mm film format, were early attempts to extend the visual plane. In February 1956, sixteen years after its premiere and during Walt Disney's lifetime, *Fantasia* was reissued in SuperScope. According to Scott MacQueen, head of preservation at the UCLA Film and Television Archive and former Walt Disney Company senior manager for film preservation, the process was "an ersatz in-the-lab anamorphic process . . . [in which] everything was just stretched in the east-west plane to fill that elongated letterbox frame. . . . Amazing and frightening to think that this was considered a viable option for *Fantasia II* reprises."[23] Also, several theater owners during film's earliest years attempted to add scents at screenings, but Disney was the first filmmaker to consider the idea.

Most of Disney's outré ideas were shot down by his pragmatic side. "Perfume might be expensive," he worried. And how would he get one scent out of the theater before introducing another? Nevertheless, the showman in him did regret losing "a great publicity angle." Disney's synesthetic dreams *were* realized, however, in *Fantasia*'s sound recording and reproduction. Stokowski devised and recorded the music on nine separate optical tracks, lending it the fidelity of a live concert hall performance. At the New York premiere and select theaters across America, speakers were installed behind the screen and throughout the orchestra and balcony, so that audiences were surrounded by the music. When a distant church bell vanquishes the devil on Bald Mountain, it sounded from the back of the theater; a celeste flitted from flower to flower with the *Nutcracker Suite*'s delicate Dewdrop Fairies; and *Rite of Spring* spectators were surprised by a tympanic

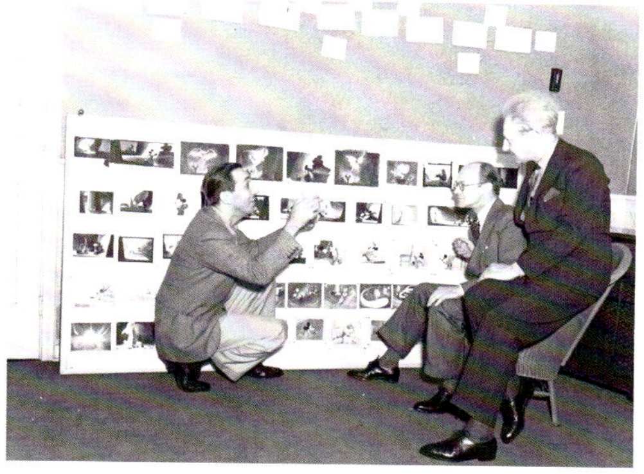

Walt Disney, Deems Taylor, and Leopold Stokowski in front of a storyboard of The Sorcerer's Apprentice, 1938

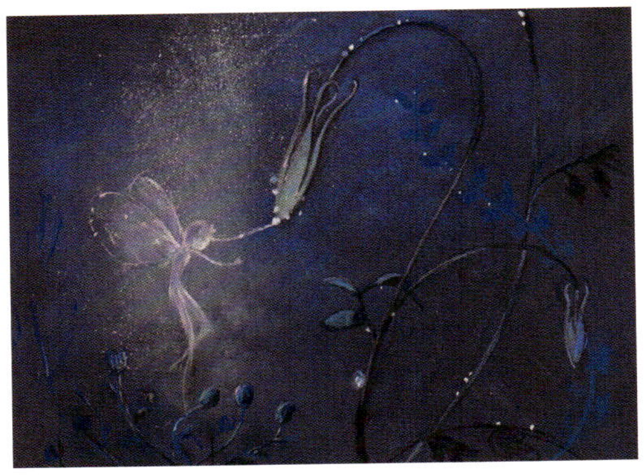

Evocation of Victorian fairy paintings come to life in the *Nutcracker Suite*

earthquake right under their seats! "The sound was extraordinary," Stokowski said in 1963, "the finest there ever had been."[24]

Visually, *Fantasia* is a fevered dream, a singular effort to move beyond conventional narratives and explore alternative storytelling possibilities in color, graphics, mood, motion, light, and sound. It represents the culmination of a decade of experimentation with animation, special effects, narrative, and wedding action to music.

Behind the scenes, predigital technologies reached new levels of ingenuity and achievement. In a series of illustrated notebooks discovered twenty-five years ago, Herman Schultheis (1900–1955), a photographic effects specialist at The Walt Disney Studios from 1938 to 1941, described in detail how dazzling handmade visual effects were created by mundane means. In order to create a mise-en-scène for fantastic dinosaurs, flowers, centaurs, and demons, as well as varied effects to animate water, snow, fire, and galaxies, teams of artisans built elaborate contraptions as needed. Schultheis explains how jury-rigged multiplane cameras shot oil paintings on several layers of glass, adding depth to backgrounds; mechanical and photochemical processes combined to make snowflake fairies fly through winter skies (using painted snowflakes pasted onto wooden spools moved frame-by-frame along Lionel toy train tracks); a mixture of mud, oatmeal, and coffee grounds created "lava," and white paint squirted through syringes into water tanks became "volcano smoke"; and a distorted reflection in a tin mirror of one long painting brought diaphanous ghosts back from the dead.[25]

Special effects dominate *Fantasia*, but personality animation holds its own with articulate pantomimic acting. Mickey Mouse as a sorcerer's wayward apprentice gives his greatest performance, as sensitive as Jean-Louis Barrault's mime in *Les Enfants du Paradis* (1944). There is perfect comic choreography in *Dance of the Hours*' anthropomorphic ballet; an enchanting evocation of Victorian fairy paintings come to life in the *Nutcracker Suite*; and, when a church bell tolls on Bald Mountain, the devil Chernobog's face and body rapidly express confusion, annoyance, anger, fear, and pain. And though Beethoven's *Pastoral Symphony* is awash in kitsch cupids and "centaurettes," when audiences soar alongside Pegasus over Mount Olympus, they experience mythology in exhilarating, graceful cinematography that no medium but animation could accomplish as well.

*Fantasia* was described by critic Franz Hoellering in 1940 as "a promising monstrosity." "In technical respects," he wrote, "the picture is of unsurpassed quality. . . . In spite of shortcomings partly due to the exploring character of the whole, partly to fundamental errors, [*Fantasia*] is a work of promise. One day, one feels, Walt Disney and his people may produce a film which will truly combine all the different branches of art."[26]

*Fantasia is* a sprawling *monstre sacré*, with lapses in taste and nerve, but also filled with triumphant creativity. It continues to inspire artists, and it has introduced generations of young people to classical and modern music, fine and abstract art, and animation. It has also engendered in many—including Stephen Jay Gould and Steven Spielberg—a love of science, evolution, and prehistoric life.[27] Otis Ferguson, reviewing *Fantasia* for the *New Republic* in 1940, summed it up best: "Dull as it is toward the end, ridiculous as it is in the bend of the knee before Art, and taking one thing with another, it is one of the strange and beautiful things to have happened in the world . . . something never thought of and not soon forgotten."[28]

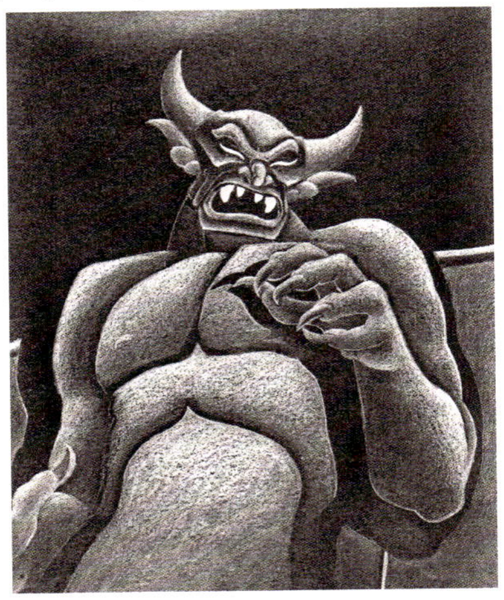

Chernobog hears a church bell toll during *Night on Bald Mountain*

NOTES

1. Donald W. Graham, "Building a Feature," unpublished manuscript, circa 1950s, p. 9, Walt Disney Archives, Burbank, CA.
2. Walt Disney, Inter-Office Communication memo, December 23, 1935, Walt Disney Archives.
3. Russell Merritt and J. B. Kaufman, *Walt in Wonderland: The Silent Films of Walt Disney* (Baltimore: John Hopkins University Press, 1993), p. 82.
4. Disney, Inter-Office Communication memo.
5. Ibid.
6. John Canemaker, *Winsor McCay: His Life and Art* (New York: Harry N. Abrams, 2005), pp. 156–99.
7. Donald Crafton, *Before Mickey: The Animated Film, 1898–1928* (Cambridge: MIT Press, 1982), pp. 134–35.
8. On June 20, 1915, *Gertie the Dinosaur*, with the live-action prologue, played "a special return engagement" in Kansas City, Missouri, when a teenaged Walt Disney lived there. See the Kansas City *Gazette Globe*, June 19, 1915. Donald Crafton, email to author, August 7, 2015.
9. Eyewitnesses to McCay's live performance with *Gertie* who later worked for The Walt Disney Studios include Vladimir Tytla, I. Klein, and Richard Huemer (who wrote the script for *The Story of the Animated Drawing* in consultation with Robert McCay, Winsor McCay's son), among others.
10. Richard Eder, "The Screen: A Program of Cartoons," *New York Times*, December 29, 1975.
11. John Canemaker, *Felix: The Twisted Tale of the World's Most Famous Cat* (New York: Pantheon, 1991).
12. Merritt and Kaufman, *Walt in Wonderland*, pp. 29–30.
13. Don Graham, "Animation: Art Acquires a New Dimension," *American Artist*, December 1940, p. 12; John Canemaker, "More Than a Drawing: Walt on Personality Animation." *Walt Disney Family Museum Members Newsletter*, vol. 1, no. 1 (2009), pp. 4–5. In 1961, Walt Disney and his brother, Roy O. Disney, coordinated and funded the merging of Chouinard Art Institute and the Los Angeles Conservatory of Music into the California Institute of the Arts.
14. Graham, "Building a Feature"; Graham, "Animation."
15. Disney, Inter-Office Communication memo.
16. Graham, "Truths of the Old Masters," in "Building a Feature," pp. 6–8.
17. "Two Disney Artists," *Crimmer's: The Harvard Journal of Pictorial Fiction*, Winter 1975, p. 40.
18. Michael Barrier, *Hollywood Cartoons: American Animation in Its Golden Age* (New York: Oxford University Press, 1999), p. 246–47.
19. *Fantasia* story conference notes, October 8, 1938, Walt Disney Archives.
20. William Moritz, *Optical Poetry: The Life and Work of Oskar Fischinger* (New Barnet, UK: John Libbey, 2004), pp. 83–87; John Canemaker, *Paper Dreams: The Art and Artists of Disney Storyboards* New York: Hyperion, 1999), pp. 187–96. The fiercely independent, uncompromising Fischinger disliked the studio's conference style and quit after nine months.
21. *Fantasia* story conference notes, September 14, 1938, Walt Disney Archives; Canemaker, *Paper Dreams,* p. 127; Neal Gabler, *Walt Disney: The Triumph of the American Imagination* (New York: Vintage, 2006), pp. 309–10.
22. *Time*, November 18, 1940, cover and pp. 52–55; John Canemaker, "The Fantasia That Never Was," *Print*, January/February 1988, pp. 76–87, 139–40.
23. Scott MacQueen, email to author, October 7, 2015.
24. John Molleson, "Disney's Glorious Flop," *New York Herald Tribune*, November 17, 1963.
25. John Canemaker, *The Lost Notebook: Herman Schultheis and the Secrets of Walt Disney's Movie Magic* (San Francisco: Walt Disney Family Foundation Press, 2014), pp. 112–275.
26. Franz Hoellering, "Films," *The Nation*, November 23, 1940, pp. 513–14.
27. *The Richness of Life: The Essential Stephen Jay Gould*, ed. Steven Rose (New York: W. W. Norton, 2006), p. 286; John Cawley, "The Land Before Time," in *The Animated Films of Don Bluth*, http://www.cataroo.com/DBland.html.
28. Otis Ferguson, "Both Fantasy and Fancy," *New Republic*, November 25, 1940, p. 724.

## The Screen as Object: Art and the Atmospheres of Projection

Giuliana Bruno

"We project our culture, our decipherment of things in the world, as if onto a screen. . . . Projection explains to me the birth of meaning, so in this way I see that the projection modifies the meaning of the object."
—Fabio Mauri[1]

“What is cinema?” asked the French film theorist and critic André Bazin.[2] “No more actors, no more story, no more sets,” he once replied, “which is to say that in the perfect aesthetic illusion of reality there is no more cinema.”[3] It is useful to introduce this notion of the spatial zero degree of cinema as a way of addressing the inception of the medium in history, and of considering the transformation and potential dissolution of its forms in contemporary times. In light of this, we might also ask, “Where is cinema?” Today, it has increasingly exited the theater and come to inhabit the art gallery and the museum. As we walk through exhibition sites, we often encounter moving-image installations that abandon strict narrative logic, movie stars, and sets and instead tend to expose the materiality of the film medium on their screens and in space. In their embrace of a zero degree of cinematic expression, many of the works featured in this catalogue and the exhibition it accompanies also defy traditional modes of narration and rather choose to “perform” their own capacity to create multiform spaces of light. In doing so, they evoke the luminous and hazy ways in which cinema exhibited itself at its very origin. The cinematic here is not a property of film per se but rather emerges through other art forms, such as painting, photography, and sculpture, and it is dispersed across various material terrains. It appears in the shape of canvas or as volume or space, acting as if these were screens, in ways that refashion the history of projection. Let us then take a look at this material loop that links pre-cinema to post-cinema and creates a convergence of old and new media, focusing on the screen and surveying its radiant, permeable “objecthood” as it has morphed in space and across time.

**The Emergence and Dissolution of the Screen**

In the beginning, there was light. And from here the screen surface was born, out of a desire to transform space through luminosity and shadow play. I propose that we think of this transformative history of light-space as the material zero degree of cinema, and that we further investigate how this fascination with the art of projection has migrated into contemporary art and architecture.[4] The interesting, evolving etymology of the word *screen* can begin to tell us about this “elemental” history of screening space.

It is important to note that the notion of the screen, and its luminous vision, greatly preceded the invention of cinema. The word *screen*, indeed, had long been used in relation to space before it was applied to the art of projection. It appeared during the Renaissance, evolving from an earlier Germanic root that also transferred to Latin languages. The term originally pointed to a variety of mediums, surfaces, and types of screening, mostly emerging from the world of architecture. As the media historian Erkki Huhtamo has shown, it designated in particular “a floor-standing piece of furniture, consisting of a sheet of lighter, often translucent material (paper, some kind of fabric, etc.) stretched on a wooden frame (or a series of connected, folding frames).”[5] By the nineteenth century its meaning had expanded to include a surface for projection. Transferred from architectural space to the realm of pre-cinematic media, the term came to define a new type of translucent membrane, and a new form of textural materiality: a light-reflecting fabric for the transmission of luminous images. It is significant to note that *The Century Dictionary and Cyclopedia,* published originally in 1899, defines the screen first architecturally, as “a covered framework, partition, or curtain . . . ; as, a fire-screen; a folding-screen; a window-screen,” but then includes in this form of spatial metamorphosis “a screen upon which images can be cast by a magic lantern.”[6]

The evolution of the term tells us that what we now call *screen* and understand to be a projective surface originated in the world of objects and material space. The screen was a “thing,” an object of furniture that inhabited domestic interiors. It served especially to negotiate inside and outside, and materially—even atmospherically—to transform space, acting in concert with light. When deployed to divide space in the home, a screen mediated between private and public zones of habitation, creating privacy and intimacy. Such is the spatial function that the screen most powerfully embodied when, at the end of the nineteenth century, it became a feature of the film theater, where spectators could experience the projection of exteriors into interiors in a social atmosphere of “public intimacy.”[7]

Born as a fabric that served as a translucent filter, the screen lives on in modern and contemporary visual art as such a piece of material culture and spatial function. In the hands of the artist Fabio Mauri, for example, it retains its genealogic character and architectural qualities. In the 1950s and 1960s Mauri made his first series of monochromatic Screens (fig. 1), delicate artworks made of translucent materials such as paper and fabric that resemble skins, which are stretched on frames. Reminiscent of the screens that decorate windows or act as passageways, such works remind us of how the filmic screen originated in architecture as a medium for the transpiration of light. Endowed with the textural quality of a curtain, partition, parchment, or filter, Mauri's objects, conjured as textile panels, reveal the actual fabric of the filmic screen. Often minimally inscribed with the phrase "THE END," these canvas screens even make direct reference to cinema, disclosing its zero degree of expression. They expose cinema's historical configuration and the material condition of its existence in a plastic dimension.

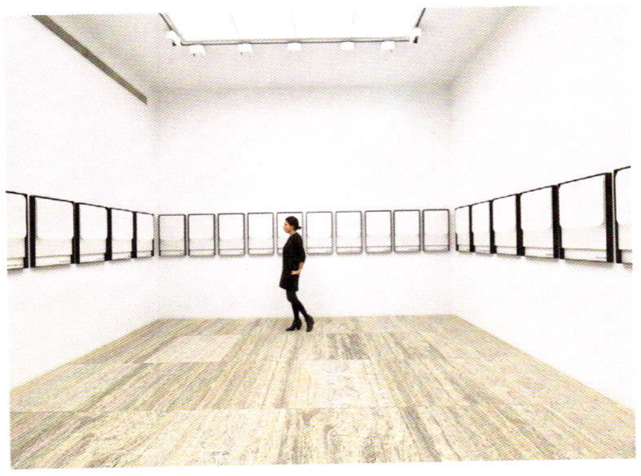

Fig. 1. Fabio Mauri (1926–2009), *Perché un pensiero intossica una stanza? (Why does a thought poison a room?)*, from the series *Schermi* [Screens], 1972. Iron, wood, and canvas with Letraset, thirty-six parts: 28 x 16 ⅞ in. each. Installation view, *Fabio Mauri. I was not new*, Hauser & Wirth, New York, March 5–May 2, 2015

The screen as an architectural configuration can act intimately on the materiality of light in the public space of the contemporary art gallery. Think, for instance, of how this object materializes in Josiah McElheny's *Three Screens for Looking at Abstraction* (2012; fig. 2), a work that also engages precisely with the question of what a screen is, physically, and how it emerged materially in history. Here, each screen is built as a sculptural presence, a volumetric object that occupies space and becomes an actual piece of architecture. Spatially configured, the screens create ambience and take on even more haptic qualities from the array of projective surfaces, both reflective and translucent, of which they are composed. As light is refracted on McElheny's dynamic screen surfaces, the viewer is given a tangible sense of how a material can transform a space. Fractured and recomposed with the projected abstract forms of classic experimental films, these mobilized screen fabrics create a sensory space that also reflects and incorporates the bodies of spectators, who cast their own shadows and reflections in phantasmagoric fashion onto the luminous surfaces.

Conceived as such a textured, plastic object of projection, the screen fully enters the realm of what the philosopher Jacques Rancière calls the "surface of design."[8] This surface of projection continues to design and transform our environment, both physically and imaginatively. For the French artist Philippe Parreno, a digital LED screen has both a sculptural dimension and a morphing surface that is at once electric and capable of electrifying the surrounding atmosphere—as envisaged, with flashing, animated drawings of fireflies, in his installation *With a Rhythmic Instinction to be able to Travel Beyond Existing Forces of Life (Green, Rule # 1)* (2014; pp. 98–99). The screen can also serve as a sensorial, mobile object, as in Trisha Baga's video installation *Flatlands* (2010), where it is variously configured in the shape of an airplane or a car window. Such a screen filters many planes of information. Viewers are asked to navigate through a layered screen surface, where a woman's interior, psychic space coalesces with a landscape of simulation. Rain further veils this multilayered window-screen, and a sign finally asks the viewer to "please clean the filter." Here we can sense how the screen, as it becomes relocated as an ever-present element in our digital culture, functions increasingly as a filter. As an object of daily life, the screen has become a major site for the

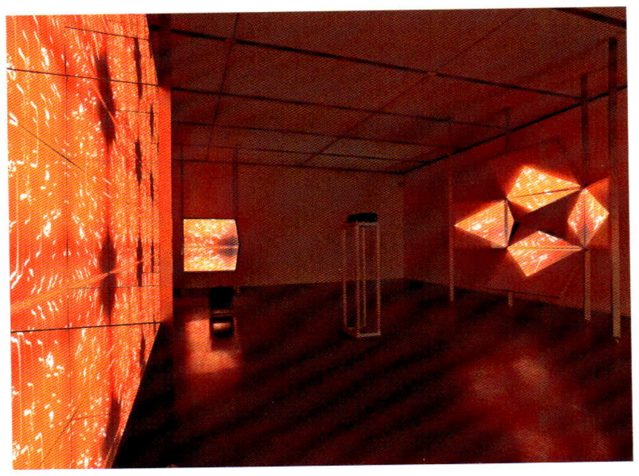

Fig. 2. Josiah McElheny (b.1966), *Three Screens for Looking at Abstraction*, 2012. Aluminum, low-iron mirror, projection cloth, film transferred to video, video projectors with stands, wood, and metal hardware, three parts: overall dimensions variable. Installation view, *Some Pictures of the Infinite*, Institute of Contemporary Art, Boston, June 22–September 23, 2012

mediation of planes, including the private and the public, and as such it constitutes the architecture of a sensory, social, and aesthetic transformation.

This sensory, experiential capacity of the screen to connect our perception of different spaces, including interior and exterior, as well as to move between art forms, was recognized at the very inception of the medium. In 1915 the poet and critic Vachel Lindsay articulated the zero degree of passage that is the filmic screen when he described this transitional, material surface as "sculpture-in-motion," "painting-in-motion," and "architecture-in-motion," and even considered it a form of "furniture-in-motion."[9] Lindsay touched on the materiality that the screen has now fully come to embody as both an object and a space of projection. How can we fail to think of these brilliant definitions when we consider the form of today's screens, as displayed in our homes and art galleries? We are indeed surrounded by screens that are pieces of "sculpture-in-motion"—haptic objects of transport, with a material configuration and a plastic quality. The portable digital screen is an "architecture-in-motion" that moves with us, and it functions as an actual piece of "furniture-in-motion" in our homes. And finally, moving-image installations offer us the sensory pleasure of the painterly brushstroke, materialized in movement within gallery and museum spaces.

**Luminous and Shaded Surfaces of Design**

The phenomena that we experience in the contemporary art gallery and in media culture resonate with the archaeology of the film medium itself, and they cannot be grasped fully without exploring the history of the screen and how it came to be articulated as a tensile architecture and luminous design surface. To further investigate this aspect of the screen, we should reconsider the pivotal decade of the 1920s, when the architecture of the screen developed as a surface for design.

The 1920s saw the rise of movie palaces: large, lavishly designed and richly ornamented public spaces of projection.[10] Here, as in the contemporary art gallery, the screen is part of a larger space—an element of an "installation"—and participates in the creation of the atmosphere of the site. This spatialization of the art of projection even took an environmental turn at this time, with the design of the "atmospheric theater." Modern-era movie palaces generally underscored the spectator's absorption in the surface of projection, and created surface space with simple ornamental lines, curves, and geometries.[11] But John Eberson, the master architect of atmospheric theaters, went further. He created film spaces that embodied the nineteenth-century notion of *Stimmung*—that is, affective atmospheres that instill a sentiment, state of mind, mood, or tonality.[12] In these theaters, built as if they were sets, spectators would experience inside and outside as fluid borders, for the surrounding interior décor was often an architectural reproduction of an exterior, and the textures of light and darkness were a featured part of the film show. In describing the Capitol Theatre he built in Chicago in 1925, Eberson emphasized the importance of artfully using "paint, brush, and electric light, tree ornament, furnishing, lights and shadows" in atmospheric theater design.[13] The Loew's Paradise Theatre he built in the Bronx in 1929 resembled Italian garden architecture and featured celestial ceiling lights that reproduced the full spectrum of the passage from day to night (fig. 3). This radiant atmosphere resonated with the luminous surface of the screen, conceived as one tiny element of the grand surface design of the immense, ornate theater environment.[14] These atmospheric theaters were truly immersive spaces that could surround and engage spectators sensorially, in ways that anticipated the digital immersion and sense of environmental geography experienced with current technologies, such as 3D, IMAX, and virtual reality.

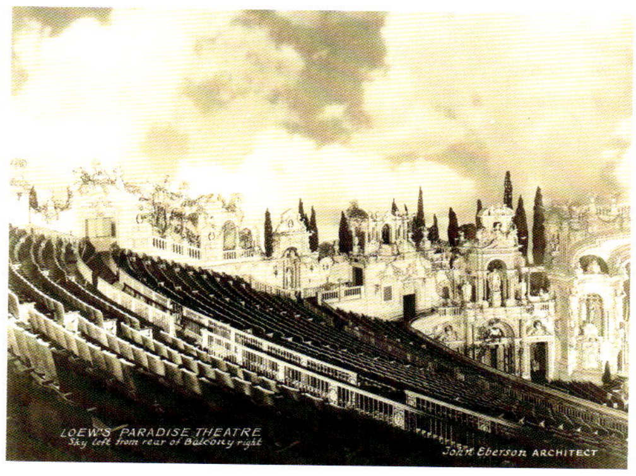


Fig. 3. Loew's Paradise Theatre, Bronx, New York, 1929, an "atmospheric movie palace." John Eberson, architect

A different kind of perceptual atmosphere was embodied in the Film Guild Cinema, designed in a Neoplastic modernist style by Frederick Kiesler.[15] For this cinema, built in New York in

1929, the vanguard architect conceived of a spectator ideally "projected" from the darkness of the theater into the light of a central screen, which resembled the diaphragm of a camera. With its lack of architectural decoration, ornament here was minimally created by the medium of light and the texture of sound waves. Mechanical panels enabled the screen to expand or contract, and the walls angled toward this flexible, kinetic screen, which Kiesler named a "screen-o-scope." His elastic screen design also called for an unrealized "project-o-scope" that would have extended the projection from the center screen onto the two side walls and ceiling to create multiple, continuous projections and a total, enveloping film environment. The way Kiesler projected light onto these wall-screens gave architectural form to the notion of cinema as surface space. In envisioning such a surface cinema, the architect stated that "the film is a play on surface, the theatre a play in space. . . . The ideal cinema is the house of silence. . . .The spectator must be able to lose himself in an imaginary, endless space.[16]

This perceptually absorbing model has been radically reincarnated in more recent times. In some respects, it informed Austrian filmmaker Peter Kubelka's design for the Invisible Cinema in New York (pp. 54–55).[17] Operating from 1970 to 1974, this theater was a modernist architectural expression of the Anthology Film Archives' mission to create a museum of film art, a temple especially devoted to avant-garde cinema.[18] The Invisible Cinema seated fewer than one hundred people but was visited by more than fourteen thousand spectators in its first year. In this "interior wholly sheathed in light-absorbing fabric," art and film theorist Annette Michelson found "the architecture of the Velvet Light Trap."[19] To ensure complete perceptual fusion in the environment of the cinema—a total black box—the velvet spectators' seats were outfitted with shell-like partitions that rose on each side and extended above. A screen in its own right, this divider encapsulated the spectator both atmospherically and aurally, with blinders that prevented peripheral vision or distraction from the side. The surroundings were "screened," and one was shielded as well as protected and sheltered. The spectator was thus clearly directed to face a "radiating" screen surface, as Kubelka put it, for "the screen and the film were the only visual points of reference" for the audience.[20] Silence and proper behavior were enforced in this "machine for viewing," though the designer emphasized a possible haptic connection among spectators.[21] "Only your eyes were shaded from your neighbor, approximately from the shoulders on," Kubelka explained, "but you could touch your neighbors, and since this was not a complete partition, you always felt that there was someone on your side."[22] He insisted that, in this way, "a sympathetic community was created," for "architecture has to provide a structure in which one is in a community that is not disturbing to others."[23]

In some ways, the architecture of the Invisible Cinema anticipated an aspect of our contemporary experience of visual space, especially as it concerns the screen. Looking at a photograph of Andy Warhol seated in the Invisible Cinema in 1970, or at other images of the audience in the space, one cannot help but reflect on the social isolation this cinematic situation effected. The individual spectator is totally absorbed in the lit screen in a way that seems to portend our current relation to our own portable screens. We, too, tend to sit alone while with others in public spaces, intently immersed in looking at our screens. And this digital isolation is as complex as the zero degree of cinema that was experienced in the Invisible Cinema, for privacy and publicness, intimacy and estrangement are involved at the same time. The experience of the screen has become individualized, as if a partition were built around us, as real as the ones in Kubelka's visionary design. To "screen" has come to imply a "screening out" both of other people and the surrounding environment. And yet, absorbed in the light of our individual, portable screens, we too become part of that community advocated by Kubelka. We create contact and communicate, getting "in touch" through our screens but always, of course, making sure not to disturb the others around us.

### Installing Cinema on Multiple Screens

The experimental, forward-looking filmic spaces created in the 1920s conveyed an inventive, sensory transformation of visual space that was experiential, and this transformation included the screen

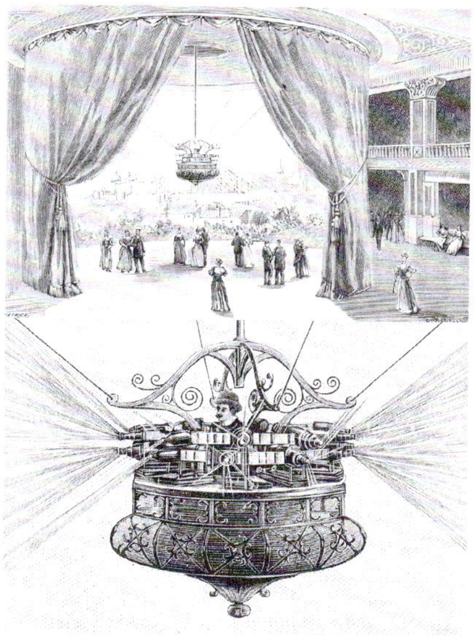

Fig. 4. View of cyclorama, in *La Nature*, no. 1180, January 11, 1896; Cyclorama, detail of projection device, in *La Nature*, no. 1180, January 11, 1896

becoming a tensile material of projection. The Café and Cinéma de L'Aubette, for example, designed in 1928 by the Dutch De Stijl artist Theo van Doesburg in Strasbourg, contributed to the extension of the screen's geometry. This multiuse space featured a screen surrounded by many other square and rectangular panels, in an orthogonal composition that created a montage of geometric frames. Here the screen became one "superficial" element of a decorative, spatial assemblage that extended from walls to ceiling.

At the onset of modernity in the nineteenth century, forms of panoramic viewing had already stretched our frame of vision to incorporate extended space.[24] A tensile filmic screen emerged from this modern movement of panoramic vision, which encompassed panorama paintings, dioramas, cycloramas, georamas, cosmoramas, and other spatial "–oramas," as well as ornamental surfaces such as panoramic wallpapers (fig. 4).[25] In the 1920s, these pre-cinematic forms of extended, magnified, multiplied, and portable screens, many of which have become part of contemporary art and culture, were further developed. The avant-garde experiments of this period resonate strongly with our contemporary experience of the screen, especially with respect to their rejection of its geometric fixity and singularity.

One such experiment surfaced in 1927, when the French director Abel Gance adapted pre-cinematic forms of panoramic exhibition to film and project a portion of his epic film *Napoléon* (fig. 5). Using a process called Polyvision, Gance cinematically reenacted the visual effect of a nineteenth-century "moving panorama": a gigantic visual display of images that scrolled horizontally, offering spectators the illusion of movement in space. The director experimented with using several projectors to simulate for the audience the sensation of being immersed in narrative space. Originally intended for six screens, *Napoléon* ended up using three to magnificent results. Adjacent screens ran sequences shot simultaneously by a three-camera system, as well as different scenes projected contiguously to give the actual sensation of a moving panorama. With *Napoléon*, Gance used the conjunction of the screens to mobilize the scene of the narrative and convey a flowing multiplicity, thus activating the diffracted mode of a continuously expansive, moving panorama.

Around the same time, the Bauhaus architect Walter Gropius advocated the use of multiple, surrounding projection. His "Totaltheater" project of 1927, an unrealized collaboration with the theater director Erwin Piscator, called for huge screens "stretched between the twelve columns of the auditorium" so that the audience could "find itself in the midst of a raging sea" of images.[26] Also within the realm of the Bauhaus, the transdisciplinary artist László Moholy-Nagy conceived an even more tensile screen.[27] In his 1925 book *Painting Photography Film*, he theorized luminosity as a connector of mediums and linked "Painting with Pigment" to "Light Displays Projected."[28] Treating the screen fabric as such a radiant, textured surface, the artist considered it a material in itself, an actual space to be architected creatively. In a chapter significantly titled "Simultaneous or Poly-Cinema," Moholy-Nagy suggested dynamic reconfigurations of the screen, including devices that would divide "the projection

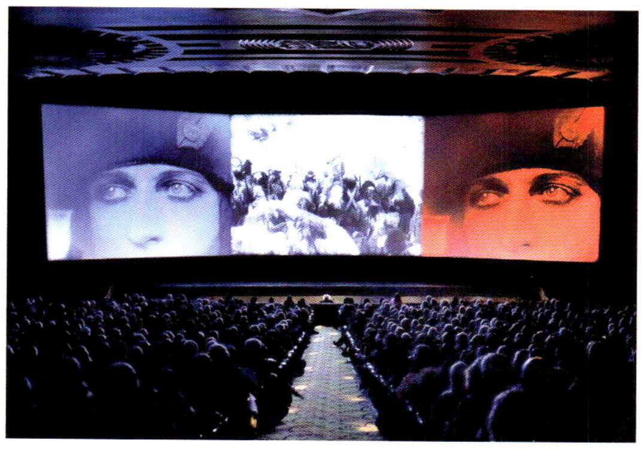

Fig. 5. Abel Gance (1889–1981), *Napoléon*, 1927. In 2012, the San Francisco Silent Film Festival presented a five-and-a-half-hour restoration of the film by Photoplay Productions and the British Film Institute at the Paramount Theatre, Oakland

plane" into different "cambers, like a landscape," and project "more than one film . . . on this projection screen" so that multiple "events" could "combine and present parallel and coinciding episodes."[29] In this imaginative experimentation, the screen, constructed as a "landscape," offers differing vistas and viewpoints. Its increased capacity "for simultaneous acoustical and optical activity" is moreover shared with the metropolis, which itself may be understood as a screen.[30]

This tonal landscape-screen was subjected to inventive planar mobilization not only with various shapes and split forms but also through multiple projections. Moholy-Nagy imagined screening "a sequence of pictures simultaneously" and "projecting extra prints of the running film-strip on to the screen through projectors standing next to one another."[31] The polyphonic multiple-screen space described by Moholy-Nagy was a modern landscape of communication, imagined well before multiple "windows" could be opened on a computer screen. Freed from static placements and from singular, fixed geometries, this tensile screen surface dreamt of an "expanded cinema" and of the portable digitality of the future in the way it enhanced simultaneity, parallelism, and the combination of heterogeneous situations onto a fluid, sensory, expansive screening space.

**Radiant Textures, Solid Light Space**

In the kind of experimentation Moholy-Nagy initiated, "the material pigment and the material light" are activated on a morphing landscape-screen in ways that create the experience of a zero degree of cinema.[32] There is an atmospheric quality to this material, a sensorial experience of light space that not only projects the future of film but reminds us of the very emergence of the medium. Luminous, textural materialities that surfaced at the inception of cinema can be seen returning today, at the time of the medium's dissolution.

Think of *Coney Island at Night*, made by Edwin S. Porter in 1905, part of an "electric" trend in early film that explored images made purely of light (pp. 2–3). An expression of the ornamental mode that the German theorist Siegfried Kracauer called "surface splendor," *Coney Island at Night* exemplifies how the dream of cinema materialized in the age of modernity.[33] As we glide across a glittering urban surface and are electrified by the twinkling and shimmering lights, we come to experience the sensory texture of the new media of modernity: the magic of magic lanterns and the shining projections of phantasmagoric shows.[34]

Here, the physical element of projection becomes evident. We are sensitized to the screen's phenomenological presence and material existence as a medium of passage. In *Coney Island at Night* we sense a pictorial surface that is porous. Porter's screen is figured as a cloth: a tissue that appears to have been perforated by luminous dots. Though superficially flat, this screen has volume, for the flickering light that activates it gives it depth, dimension, and plasticity. The dancing light particles, imprinted as if on a scrolling surface, show the character of the screen as a textured, moving plane, revealing its very fabric. As it comes alive in textile form, the screen-canvas here turns into a scrim on which the architecture of light can be reflectively sensed in surface tension.

As this screen becomes a scrim, it makes us reflect on the phenomenon of the "light," tensile screen textures that recur in the space of the contemporary art gallery, where the screen has come to dwell in a plastic condition and surface materiality. The pervasive return to a fascination with the art of projection in contemporary art creates a cinematic loop that links the turn of the last century with the beginning of the new millennium, as we return to the paradigmatic condition of projection and the superficial luminosity that characterized the history of early modernity, now reinvented in the museum.[35]

This contemporary return to modernity's phantasmagoric projections was pioneered by the artist Anthony McCall, who famously described his 1973 film installation *Line Describing a Cone* (pp. 52–53) as "a solid light film . . . [that] deals with one of the irreducible, necessary conditions of film: projected light."[36] This work projects—that is, envisions, casts, and transmits—a cone of light from a projector into a room, impelling the spectator to sense that zero degree of cinema of which we have spoken. Light here is experienced as a material entity as it is further filtered through smoke, which gives it a greater, more tangible density. Turned into a volume that has body, this luminous

Fig. 6. Anthony McCall (b. 1946), *Landscape for Fire II*, 1972. Gelatin silver print, 12 x 15 in. (30.5 x 38.1 cm). Performance, North Weald, UK

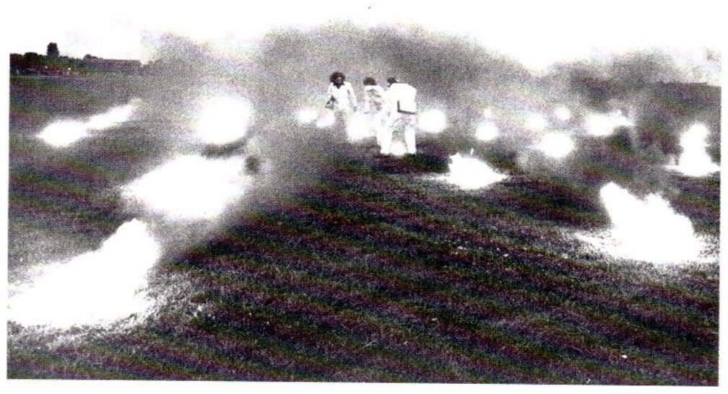

solid surface is sensed as a sculptural presence and becomes a situational site to engage with. Here, as in McCall's *Long Film for Four Projectors* (1974), the spectator is enticed to touch the cone of light, handle its surface, and drift around the projective environment-sculpture.

McCall's understanding of cinema has become ever more environmental in his recent return to "solid light" films, digitally produced since the early 2000s, where, again, we become absorbed in the luminous ambience of pure projections as we share in a public intimacy. In using digital technology to enhance material effects, this recent work renders the more atmospheric dimension of cinema, and, in this respect, refashions aspects of the artist's early environmental performances, such as *Landscape for Fire II* (1972; fig. 6). The "ambient experience" of cinema becomes the very surface materiality of McCall's installations.[37] The "air" of light is made tangible here, and we experience the depth inherent in surface space. While sensitized to the materiality of ether we become enveloped in a permeable, mutable atmospheric environment, in whose performance and permutation we are haptically invited to participate.

**Atmospheres: Immaterial Screen Density**

An understanding of the atmospheric dimension of projection also underlies, however differently, some of the experiences gathered under the umbrella term *expanded cinema*.[38] Notable in this expansive category are the sensorial intermedia environments created by the experimental filmmaker Stan VanDerBeek in his *Movie-Drome* (1963–66; pp. 44–45).[39] This hemispherical dome was an immersive environment, coated on its interior with the multifaceted surfaces of multiple still and moving-image projections. Atmosphere also became the key element of *Steam Screens*, an installation-performance that VanDerBeek created with the environmental artist Joan Brigham in 1979 in the sculpture garden of the Whitney Museum of American Art (fig. 7). Brigham had pioneered the use of steam in her work, and she undertook a series of collaborations with VanDerBeek in which they used steam as a screen onto which film images were projected. In the museum space, as Brigham put it, "moving steam waves" would "catch and refract the film images, forming and reforming them as the waves roll[ed] through the stream of projected light."[40]

Projected into steam, film could reach the ultimate stage of a zero degree of existence, coming into being in a state of dissolution. A material that is immaterial, steam even has the textural quality of a "film," in that it can filter and reflect luminosity and can make space and light tangible. With *Steam Screens*, the audience became enveloped in an experience of screening that was truly environmental, recalling Robert Morris's early work of Land art, *Steam*, from 1967.[41] VanDerBeek and Brigham designed a performative installation space, atmospherically clouded with particles of light, water, and air, in which the filmic surface became veiled and the ambience of projection shrouded. However, as Brigham noted, here the "clouds enhance vision, not obscure it" because the artists aimed in the work to act on "surfaces, distances, textures and volumes—the factors by which we orient ourselves in time and space," making the imagery "hover like apparitions in mid-air."[42] And thus, in these vapors of projection, the film image itself becomes a cloud.

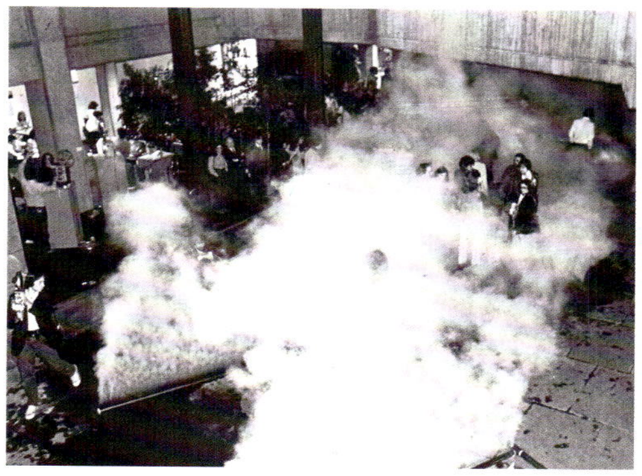

Fig. 7. Stan VanDerBeek (1927–1984) and Joan Brigham (b. 1935), *Steam Screens*, 1979. Installation and performance with steam and projected film. Installation view, Whitney Museum, New York, 1979

*Steam Screens* created a screen that was an atmospheric, almost electrical surface, for steam was used as a force of energy. As Brigham put it, "steam enters the working day and dreaming night like a dancer onstage, energizing the space with continuous movement."[43] This installation was not only performative but also interactive, because it placed the viewer in a position in which "the realities of each moment's perception are in flux; contradictory, insistent and elegant. As the steam changes the audience, the audience changes the steam."[44] This misty environment of projection became the site of a moving, participatory, material performance of public intimacy. Steam here was, ultimately, "a manifestation of the collective dream" of cinema, materialized in the dissolution of its forms.[45]

**Environments of Projection**

By engaging the materiality and atmospherics of projection, *Steam Screens* reminds us of how much the immaterial consistency proper to both light and air permeates the projective space, where the visible becomes "a quality pregnant with a texture."[46] The atmosphere of projection—whether in the theater or the gallery—is dense with moody, luminous particles that dance in space, imbued with an air of cloudy, permeable palpability. Projection was always a charged environment, and in the hands of contemporary artists it is becoming even more an atmosphere of vital energy. Screen space is a site haunted by the perturbations of surfaces.

To fully sense these vibrant, textural matters, think again of the material history of the screen and of the surface of design in history. After all, an ethereal consistency has always been the material base of the act of screening. As it emerged from the design of the fire screen and the window screen, and then turned into the exhibition space of the magic lantern and phantasmagoria, the idea of projection was born out of vibrant atmospheric surfaces, and this transformed into the *Stimmung* of "atmospheric theaters." The act of projection was designed to make images flare out and move, surfacing from the fabric of light and the density of air. Early forms of projection were furthermore a weathered kind of space, where the phantasmagoria of projection was imbued with such vaporous things as smoke and fog. Projection also was closely associated with elusive substances such as the hazy, misty quality of shades, silhouettes, and shadows, which were thought actually to materialize on-screen. It followed that Moholy-Nagy would dream of "light visions" even in "open spaces, and on unusual screens, such as fog, gas and clouds."[47] Similarly, Brigham would think of steam as a cinematic screen, for, "like other energy systems," it interacts "by transparent expansion in the surrounding environment," and "transmutes appearance to apparition."[48]

An electric, ethereal atmosphere can indeed provide a canvas for projection, as the artist Aldo Tambellini showed in his electronic intermedia experiments of the 1960s and 1970s (fig. 8). Tambellini created a phantasmagoric constellation of projections with his "electromedia" art. His film *Black Spiral (Split Screen)* (1969/2013) materialized the "airways" by capturing the emissions of television screens that had been manipulated by transforming the horizontal rasters into swirling storms of pixels, resulting in a "weathering" of the image surface. In this way, he gave texture to being "on the air" and turned this ether into black forms that evoked dark matter. With light and darkness, Tambellini created the sensorial experience of a moving cosmology, in which both old and new media atmospherically converge.

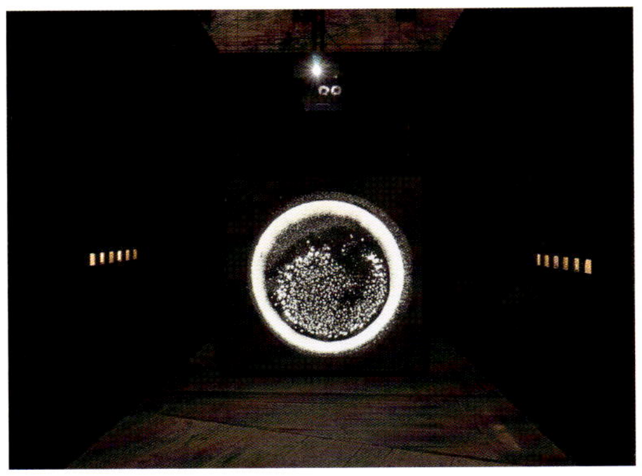

Fig. 8. Aldo Tambellini, *Study of Internal Shapes and Outward Manifestations*, 2015. Multiscreen high-definition video, color, sound; 10 min. Installation view, Italian Pavilion, Venice Biennale, 2015

Ether, steam, and sky continue to provide vibrant environments of projection. As if creating a new form of "sky art," Alex Israel's recent painting series *Sky Backdrop* (pp. 74–75), canvases produced with the Warner Bros. scenery department, depict a "screen" of light and create their own atmospheric zero degree of projection. The elemental, atmospheric, material conditions of projection further come to light in Jennifer West's *Flashlight Film Strip Projections* (2014; fig. 9), as light shines onto flat "screens" made

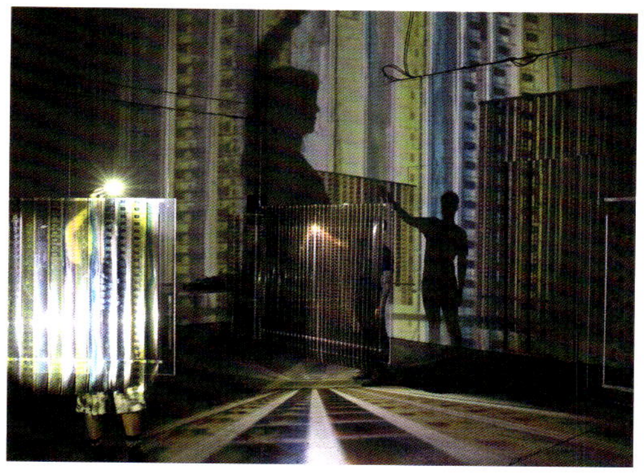

Fig. 9. Jennifer West (b. 1966), *Flashlight Filmstrip Projections*, 2014. Plexiglass, 35mm and 70mm filmstrips, inkjet prints, and flashlights, dimensions variable. Installation view, Portland Institute for Contemporary Art, Oregon, 2014

of strips of 35mm and 70mm celluloid film, hung like sculptures that function as translucent projective planes. In this installation, as the screens of filmstrips are filtered through light and reprojected onto the walls, the very texture of the filmic medium is ethereally conjured, and its physical materiality shines in a dim, atmospheric scene of projection. Finally, in Artie Vierkant's 2009 video *Exposure Adjustment on a Sunset* (pp. 110–11) we watch the slow unfolding of an ocean sunset, altered so that the sky remains bright while the image becomes digitally textured, bringing to life in digital form the experience of an environment-cinema. Images continue to create electric density and frequency when "moving through fiberglass cables," as Hito Steyerl says in her futuristic video *Factory of the Sun* (2015; pp. 102–105).[49] They do, indeed, as they travel into the ethereal digital space we have come to call "the cloud."

As current screen culture is reflected upon in these contemporary works, the atmospheric history of projection comes to be creatively, rather than nostalgically, reinvented and transformed. Far from being responsible for a dematerialization of forms, this fascination with projection in the art gallery strives to refashion the transformative, sensorial, communal architectures of materiality and public intimacy that originated in the cinema and its precursors. Surfaces of material resistance and permeability, integral to the very activity of screening, find their own digital substance in a new, vital atmosphere of projection, on yet other forms of screen-membrane. Atmospheres are here not simply represented on screens; they materialize *as* screens, in vibrant surface densities that, in Mauri's words, modify "the meaning of the object" and, ethereally, continue to "project our culture, our decipherment of things in the world."

NOTES

1. Fabio Mauri, *Alfabeta2*, no. 2 (September 2010), cited in Umberto Eco, "A Convinced Bewilderment," in *Fabio Mauri: Ideology and Memory*, ed. Studio Fabio Mauri (Turin: Bollati Boringhieri, 2012), p. xiv.
2. André Bazin, *What Is Cinema?*, ed. and trans. Hugh Gray, 2 vols. (Berkeley: University of California Press, 1967 and 1971). The essays were originally published between 1958 and 1965.
3. Ibid., vol. 2, p. 60. Out of this imaginary erasure of cinema, a radical view of the cinematic emerged that enhanced the spatial, material aspect of the medium, and this was concurrent with the start of a "new wave" of filmmaking.
4. For a further, extended treatment of the role of the screen in art, architecture, and film, see Giuliana Bruno, *Surface: Matters of Aesthetics, Materiality, and Media* (Chicago: University of Chicago Press, 2014).
5. Erkki Huhtamo, "Elements of Screenology: Toward an Archeology of the Screen," *ICONICS: International Studies of the Modern Image* 7 (2004), p. 35.
6. Cited in ibid., p. 31.
7. See Giuliana Bruno, *Public Intimacy: Architecture and the Visual Arts* (Cambridge, MA: MIT Press, 2007).
8. Jacques Rancière, *The Future of the Image,* trans. Gregory Elliott (London: Verso, 2007), chap. 4.
9. Vachel Lindsay, *The Art of the Moving Picture* (New York: Modern Library, 2000), chaps. 8–11.
10. See, among others, Maggie Valentine, *The Show Starts on the Sidewalk: An Architectural History of the Movie Theatre* (New Haven: Yale University Press, 1994).
11. See P. Morton Shand, *Modern Picture-Houses and Theaters* (Philadelphia: J. B. Lippincott, 1930).
12. Eberson built more than forty atmospheric movie palaces, the majority of which have been destroyed, and altogether about three hundred movie theaters, including streamlined, Art Deco versions. In the 1920s his wife and collaborator, Beatrice Lamb, directed the firm Michael Angelo Studios, which designed the theater interiors. For useful information on Eberson's atmospheric career, see Richard Stapleford, *Temples of Illusion: The Atmospheric Theaters of John Eberson*, exh. cat. (New York: Bertha and Karl Leubsdorf Art Gallery of Hunter College, 1988).
13. John Eberson, "A Description of the Capitol Theatre, Chicago (1925)," in *Moviegoing in America: A Sourcebook in the History of Film Exhibition*, ed. Gregory A. Waller (Oxford: Blackwell, 2002), p. 106.
14. The Loew's Paradise Theatre, located at 2403 Grand Concourse in Bronx, New York, was subdivided and stripped of features in the 1970s and then closed in 1994. It was renovated and reopened in 2005 as a live theater, and is now a church.

15. On Kiesler, see, among others, Stephen Phillips, *Elastic Architecture: Frederick Kiesler and Design Research in the First Age of Robotic Culture* (Zurich: Lars Müller, forthcoming); Laura M. McGuire, "A Movie House in Space and Time: Frederick Kiesler's Film Arts Guild Cinema, New York, 1929," *Studies in the Decorative Arts* 14, no. 2 (Spring–Summer 2007), pp. 45–78; *Frederick Kiesler, Artiste-architecte*, exh. cat. (Paris: Centre Georges Pompidou, 1996). Information on Kiesler's designs has also been drawn from the Kiesler Fund at the Harvard Theatre Collection, Houghton Library, Cambridge, MA.
16. Frederick Kiesler, "Building a Cinema Theater," *New York Evening Post*, February 2, 1929. The Film Guild Cinema, located at 52–54 West Eighth Street in New York, was short-lived. In 1930 it was renamed, and although it remained opened until 1992, it was stripped of Kiesler's screen-o-scope.
17. The Invisible Cinema was a part of Joseph Papp's Public Theater at 425 Lafayette Street in New York. For an oral history of this experimental theater, see Sky Sitney, "The Search for the Invisible Cinema," *Grey Room* 19 (Spring 2005), pp. 102–13.
18. See Kristen Alfaro, "Access and Experimental Film: New Technologies and Anthology Film Archives' Institutionalization of the Avant-Garde," *Moving Image* 12, no. 1 (Spring 2012), pp. 44–64.
19. Annette Michelson, "Gnosis and Iconoclasm: A Case Study of Cinephilia," *October*, no. 83 (Winter 1998), p. 5.
20. Peter Kubelka, "The Invisible Cinema," *Design Quarterly*, no. 93 (1974), pp. 32, 34.
21. Ibid., p. 36.
22. Ibid., p. 34.
23. Ibid.
24. See Stephan Oettermann, *The Panorama: History of a Mass Medium*, trans. Deborah Lucas Schneider (New York: Zone Books, 1997).
25. For a cultural archaeology of the film medium in relation to space, see, among others, Giuliana Bruno, *Atlas of Emotion: Journeys in Art, Architecture, and Film* (London: Verso, 2002).
26. Walter Gropius, "Theaterbau" (1934), cited in Siegfried Giedion, *Walter Gropius: Work and Teamwork* (New York: Reinhold, 1954), p. 64.
27. It is notable that Moholy-Nagy envisioned cinema as a *Light-Space Modulator* (1922–30), and in 1930 turned this kinetic sculpture, which looked like a film projector, into the film *A Light Play: Black, White, Gray*. On Moholy-Nagy's experiments with light in exhibition, see Noam M. Elcott, "Rooms of Our Time: László Moholy-Nagy and the Stillbirth of Multi-Media Museums," in *Screen/Space: The Projected Image in Contemporary Art*, ed. Tamara Trodd (Manchester: Manchester University Press, 2011), pp. 25–52.
28. László Moholy-Nagy, *Painting Photography Film*, trans. Janet Seligman (Cambridge, MA: MIT Press, 1969), p. 11.
29. Ibid., p. 41.
30. Ibid., p. 43.
31. Ibid.
32. Ibid., p. 12.
33. Siegfried Kracauer, *The Mass Ornament: Weimar Essays*, trans. and ed. Thomas Y. Levin (Cambridge, MA: Harvard University Press, 1995), p. 323.
34. *Coney Island at Night* bears witness to the phantasmagoria that—traveling all the way from the lanterns of Athanasius Kircher in the seventeenth century to the slides of Étienne-Gaspar Robertson in the late eighteenth and early nineteenth centuries—defined the invention of cinema as an art of projection. See, among others, Marina Warner, *Phantasmagoria: Spirit Visions, Metaphors, and Media into the Twenty-First Century* (Oxford: Oxford University Press, 2006); Wolfgang Schivelbusch, *Disenchanted Night: The Industrialization of Light in the Nineteenth Century* (Berkeley: University of California Press, 1995).
35. See Dominique Païni, "Should We Put an End to Projection?" *October*, no. 110 (Fall 2004), pp. 23–48; and, on elemental electric projections, *Electric Nights: Art and Pyrotechnics*, exh. cat. (Gijón, Spain: LABoral Centro de Arte y Creación Industrial; Paris: Centre Georges Pompidou, 2011), which accompanied an exhibition curated by Philippe-Alain Michaud.
36. Anthony McCall, "Two Statements," in *The Avant-garde Film: A Reader of Theory and Criticism*, ed. P. Adams Sitney (New York: New York University Press, 1978), p. 250. See also, among others, Christopher Eamon, ed., *Anthony McCall: The Solid Light Films and Related Works* (Evanston, IL: Northwestern University Press, 2005); George Baker, "Film beyond Its Limits," *Grey Room*, no. 25 (Fall 2006), pp. 92–125.
37. See McCall's own description of the ambient experience in "*Line Describing a Cone* and Related Films," in *Anthony McCall: Film Installations*, ed. Helen Legg, exh. cat. (Coventry, UK: Mead Gallery and University of Warwick, 2004), p. 44.
38. See, among others, Gene Youngblood, *Expanded Cinema* (London: Studio Vista, 1970); A. L. Rees et al., eds., *Expanded Cinema: Art, Performance, Film*, exh. cat. (London: Tate, 2011); Andrew V. Uroskie, *Between the Black Box and the White Cube: Expanded Cinema and Postwar Art* (Chicago: University of Chicago Press, 2014).
39. For an extensive treatment of this subject, see Gloria Sutton, *The Experience Machine: Stan VanDerBeek's Movie-Drome and Expanded Cinema* (Cambridge, MA: MIT Press, 2015).
40. Joan Brigham, statement accompanying the installation/performance of Stan VanDerBeek and Brigham's *Steam Screens* at the Whitney Museum of American Art, New York, November 27 and December 4, 1979, John G.

Hanhardt Film and Video Archive, Frances Mulhall Achilles Library, Whitney Museum of American Art, New York.

41. On this artist, see, among others, Julia Bryan-Wilson, ed., *OCTOBER Files: Robert Morris* (Cambridge, MA: MIT Press, 2013).

42. Joan Brigham, statement for the Whitney Museum.

43. Ibid.

44. Ibid.

45. Ibid.

46. See Maurice Merleau-Ponty, "The Intertwining—The Kiasm," in *The Visible and the Invisible*, trans. Alphonso Lingis (Evanston, IL: Northwestern University Press, 1968), p. 136.

47. Moholy-Nagy, cited in Erkki Huhtamo, "The Sky Is (Not) the Limit: Envisioning the Ultimate Public Media Display," *Journal of Visual Culture* 8, no. 3 (December 2009), p. 242.

48. Joan Brigham, "Steam," in *Centerbeam*, ed. Otto Piene and Elizabeth Goldring (Cambridge, MA: MIT Press, 1980), p. 69.

49. Hito Steyerl addresses digital space in her book *The Wretched of the Screen* (Berlin: Sternberg Press, 2013).

## Bodies in the Dark: Cinemas, Spectatorship, Discipline, Residue

Noam M. Elcott

## I. Wagnerian Darkness

> Please turn out the lights.
> As long as we're going to talk about films, we might as well do it in the dark.
> We have all been here before. By the time we are eighteen years old, say the statisticians, we have been here five hundred times.
> No, not in this room, but in this generic darkness. [ . . . ]
> We are, shall we say, comfortably seated. We may remove our shoes, if that will help us remove our bodies. [ . . . ]
> So we are suspended in a null space, bringing with us a certain habit of affections.
> —Hollis Frampton, 1968[1]

The suspension of bodies in a null space was a product of artificial, cinematic darkness. But cinematic darkness was not always generic. Indeed, at the turn of the century it was labeled "Wagnerian." Prior to the Wagnerian darkness revolution, the auditorium—contrary to its name—was a space to see and be seen, two aims that were often in conflict.[2] At Baroque court theaters, attention was generally divided between the spectacle on stage and the sovereign duke or king seated directly opposite or adjacent to it. Lighting was equally and—from a modern perspective—bizarrely balanced between stage and auditorium such that the stage was left too dark and the auditorium too bright. As explained in an 1823 text: "The incongruity stems from the fact that the court pays for the auditorium light, while the theater management pays for the stage lights."[3] Into the 1870s, preeminent architects such as Charles Garnier, who designed the Paris opera house that bears his name, voiced their dissatisfaction with darkened theaters and ensured that patrons—now primarily bourgeois—could encounter each other not only in elaborate promenades and foyers, but also in the auditorium itself. Darkness did not become the default condition of theatrical spectatorship until the final decades of the nineteenth century, with the success of Wagner's Festspielhaus (Festival Theater) in Bayreuth, Germany (fig. 1). It is "the revolutionary darkness of the *Festspielhaus*," Friedrich Kittler proclaims, "to which all the darknesses of our cinemas date back."[4]

After years of preparation and construction, Wagner's Festspielhaus was consecrated on August 13, 1876, for the exclusive presentation of his music-dramas. Otto Brückwald drew up the final plans, but the structure was deeply influenced by Wagner, the architect Gottfried Semper, and their failed collaboration on a Munich opera house, itself influenced by a range of mid-nineteenth-century sites of immersive illusion, from the panorama to the diorama (fig. 2). Decades before he broke ground in Bayreuth, Wagner left little doubt as to the intended effect of his future theater. In the fourth section of his essay "The Art-Work of the Future," the composer specified the goal of his theater design:

> In the arrangement of the space for the spectators [*Raum der Zuschauer*] the need for optical and acoustic understanding of the artwork will give the necessary law. . . . Thus the spectator transplants himself upon the stage, by means of all his visual and aural faculties; while the performer becomes an artist only by complete absorption into the public. . . . The public, that representative of daily life, disappears from the auditorium [*Zuschauerraum*] completely, and lives and breathes now only in the artwork which seems to it as Life itself, and on the stage which seems the wide expanse of the whole World.[5]

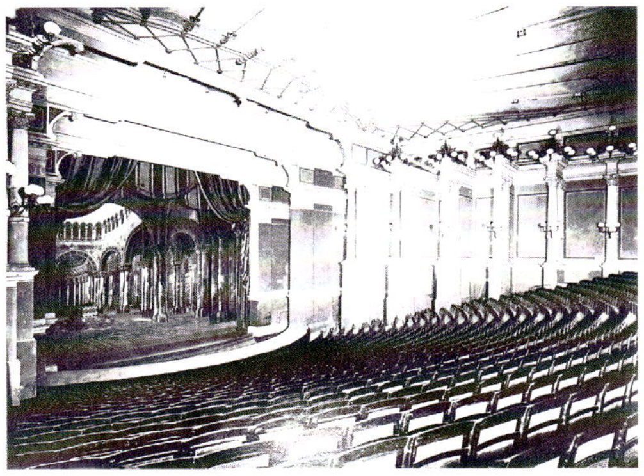

Fig. 1. Wagner's Festival Theater at Bayreuth, interior, undated photograph of the original *Parsifal* production from 1882

Wagner's turn-of-the-century English translator, William Ashton Ellis, could not equal the

Fig. 2. Detail of "Diorama et Wauxhall," in Alexis Donnet and Orgiazzi and continued by J. A. Kaufmann, *Architectonographie des théâtres de Paris, Lacroix et Baudry*, 1837, series 1, plate 23

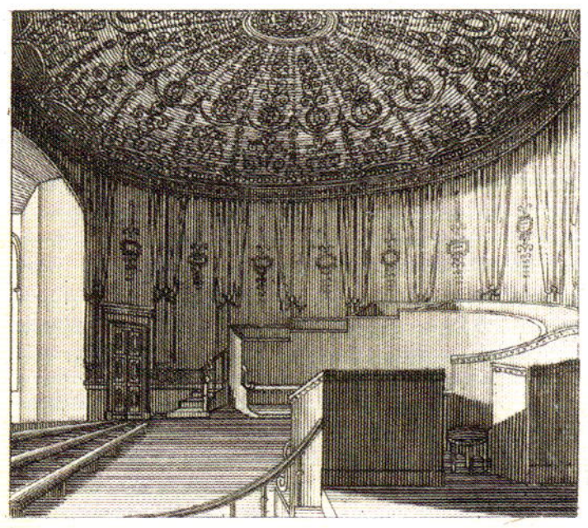

Vue intérieure de la Salle du Diorama

master's temerity and wrote that the public "forgets the confines of the auditorium," rather than "disappears" from the auditorium.[6] But viewed retrospectively from the rise of cinemas, disappearance is not too strong a word. As all moviegoers know, when the lights are extinguished, we do not remain in the dark, but rather forget the confines of our environment and project ourselves into the film. In the words of the Surrealist poet and cinephile Robert Desnos, "the hall and spectators disappear."[7] Architects soon took note of Wagnerian darkness and its artificial deprivation of distraction, but they did not like what they could not see.

**II. Spaceless Darkness**

The American film critic Seymour Stern appears to have recognized cinema's debt to Wagner, even as he vehemently denied his sources. Writing in the *National Board of Review Magazine* in 1927, Stern enumerated the features of the ideal film theater, namely, "a house constructed, architecturally and psychologically, for and by the proper unit, the screen."[8] The initial requisite was "Darkness: complete, solid, unbroken." Additionally, the orchestra was to be hidden, the seating steeply sloped, and the audience separated from the screen by a "chasm of darkness."[9] Stern hoped that the "film-house of the future," built on these principles, would attain the conditions of the liturgical drama of ancient Greek tragedy. A better approximation of the ambitions and conditions that prevailed in Wagner's Festspielhaus could hardly be envisioned. That Stern fervently toiled to differentiate his "chasm of darkness" from Wagner's celebrated "mystical abyss" made his plagiarism all the more preposterous. Indeed, by the 1920s, one could hardly construct a "chasm of darkness" without falling into a "mystical abyss."[10] As countless interwar cinema architects and theorists surmised, the film-house of the future was prefigured by Richard Wagner in 1849 as the artwork of the future.

The writer and architect Hans Schliepmann was among the first to address cinema architecture systematically.[11] In a 1914 anthology on Greater Berlin cinemas, Schliepmann reserved his highest praise for the Cines, a windowless, austere, stone movie theater on Nollendorfplatz (fig. 3). Designed by Oskar Kaufmann and completed in 1913, the Cines was enhanced with an extensive decorative program of glass painting and sculpture rife with film-related symbolism. Among the first major freestanding cinema structures built as such, it fulfilled nineteenth-century demands for monumental architecture and set the standard for a generation of film palaces. Lauded by critics as the finest practitioner of theater architecture, Kaufmann would go on to build some of the most important traditional theater structures in Berlin.

If Kaufmann and his monumental Cines exemplified all that was recognizably architectural in theater and cinema design, the designer Lucian Bernhard and his Prinzestheater on Kantstrasse exceeded the discipline of architecture altogether. By 1911, when he constructed the Prinzestheater cinema (fig. 4) as part of a larger commercial structure, Bernhard was already widely recognized as an initiator of the *Plakatstil* (poster style) and *Sachplakat* (object poster), which advanced simplified imagery, flat colors, and bold brand names. The interior of his Prinzestheater proved inassimilable into extant architectural discourse. According to Schliepmann:

> The hall's color scheme is reminiscent of the bizarre Bernhardian art principle of spatial negation. The dark violet walls, completely

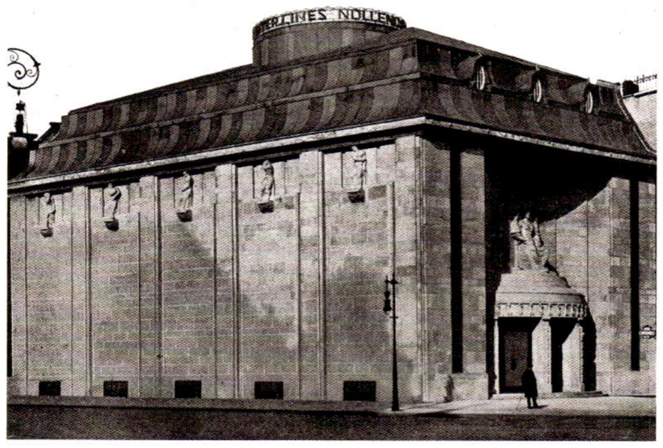

Fig. 3. Oskar Kaufmann, architect. "Cines" on Nollendorfplatz, Berlin, 1912–13. Exterior (top); interior (bottom)

Fig. 4. Lucian Bernhard, designer. Interior of Prinzestheater on Kantstrasse, Berlin, 1911

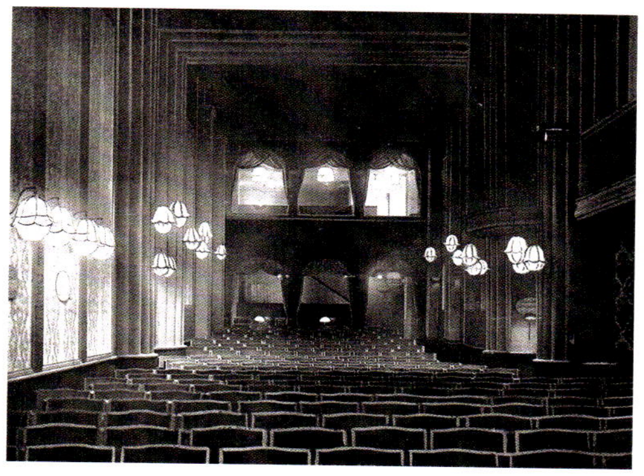

black in the rear, the deep dark gray ceiling, that, like the curtains of the loges, is decorated with bright splashes that provide color but no clear delineation of space. . . . All attention is directed solely at the image.[12]

The poster designer designed the cinema interior as a spaceless poster. But only an architecture critic could fail to recognize the importance of spatial negation and its lineage in the Wagner-type theater. For Schliepmann, the negation of space was nothing less than "the 'architecture of non-architecture.'"[13] The progressive architecture critic Adolf Behne was just as implacable, identifying in the Prinzestheater interior "a certain coarseness of space (which was hardly composed *architecture*)."[14] Unwilling or unable to recognize architecture in this new building type, Schliepmann and his cohort foreclosed the possibility of an animating architectural vision. "It is indicative that, for the solution to this task, not an architect, but rather a poster artist, was consulted."[15] The same could have been said about Wagner, the composer.

The reign of the projected image in artificial darkness was inaugurated with the sacrifice of the empirical spectator (the "public" that "disappears"), phenomenological space ("the art principle of spatial negation"), and the institution of architecture ("the architecture of non-architecture").

What was beyond the pale of architectural discourse at the start of World War I was constitutive for a nascent media theory in the 1920s. In his *Philosophy of Film* (1926), Rudolf Harms described—or, perhaps, idealized—the dominant features of interwar cinemas. For Harms, the "film-house of the future" had arrived. Like many critics, philosophers, and art historians, he advanced a modified Cartesian subject—all eye, no body—as the ideal subject of cinema. But unlike later film theorists who construed a transhistorical, transcendental subject from Plato's cave to modern cinemas, Harms understood that the radical abstraction of body and space required theaters that could "guarantee the highest degree of bodily detachedness and seek to alleviate the shortcomings of the individual's fixed and local bondedness."[16] Of necessity, his metaphysical reflections delved into operational details such as ventilation, comfortable seating, suitable background noise, and, above all, "spaceless darkness," the primary vehicle for bodily and spatial abstraction.[17] Only the darkness that presided over contemporary cinemas could secure the spectator's undivided attention to the image. What was unnamable for Wagner and inassimilable for Schliepmann was elementary for Harms. His inspired watchword—*raumlose Dunkelheit*—conjured a darkness calibrated to eradicate spectatorial space and bodies with enough technical precision and artistic pretensions to satisfy Wagner's idealist vision. Where architects saw nothing but negation—that is, nothing at all—Harms's opening salvo in his philosophy of film affirmed the medium "as its own art form, composed of moving light in spaceless darkness."[18]

### III. Contested Spacelessness

In a recent, sweeping survey of film spectatorship, Gabrielle Pedullà asserts that twentieth-century film theory failed to address the movie theater.[19] Film and film theory, he claims, were born of willful ignorance of actual cinemas. The statement is precisely half right. In fact, the movie theater was central to at least two moments of film theory: just before and just after the reign of classical cinema. The more famous moment arrived on the wings of the owl of Minerva during cinema's decline in the 1970s.[20] But the primary interest of this essay resides in the first groundswell of cinema theory, during the 1910s and 1920s, when cinemas had not yet consolidated their power over the movies. It was a moment when cinematic energies enchanted and disoriented, when cinematic darkness disciplined and liberated, when the conflicts and contradictions of the cinematic *dispositif* were already palpable, but not yet normalized. These new spectatorial conditions were recognized and contested throughout the first two decades of the twentieth century by filmmakers and theorists, cinema operators and lighting designers, critics and artists. To say that early theorists ignored the movie theater is simply a failure to see in the dark.

"The cinema? Three cheers for darkened rooms."[21] With two words—*salles obscures*—issued in his epoch-making *Surrealist Manifesto* (1924), André Breton identified the keystone in the Surrealist cinematic imagination.[22] "For us and us alone," the Surrealist poet Robert Desnos echoed, "the Lumière brothers invented the cinema. There we were at home. Its darkness was like that of our bedrooms before going to sleep."[23] The contested nature of this darkness was rarely addressed directly in the manifestos, reviews, and poems penned in the name of Surrealism. But its presence could be felt at the margins of avant-garde cinematic discourse; indeed, contested darkness was its condition of possibility.

The late 1910s and early 1920s marked a watershed in the history of film. The embourgeoisement of cinema retarded by World War I commenced with renewed vigor in its aftermath. As loosely regulated sites that gathered heterogeneous publics, cinemas became the objects of moral, technological, and medical scrutiny, and darkness—a central agent *and* impediment to the embourgeoisement of cinema—became the subject of endless debate. Where Breton cheered, others looked to discipline.

The first police ordinances directed at cinemas rarely discussed darkness. Their primary concerns were basic hygiene and the prevention of catastrophic fires. Lighting—more specifically, emergency lighting—was discussed only in the eventuality of power outages. But where police ordinances failed to intervene directly, a host of technicians, moralizers, corporations, doctors, cinema operators, and sociologists eagerly weighed in. As Frank Richardson noted in his *Motion Picture Handbook* (1916), "The amount of light to be used in the auditorium is a matter concerning which there has been a great deal of pretty hot debate."[24]

Two dominant positions emerged over the course of the 1910s: moral (sometimes couched as medical) and technical. The most frequent and high-pitched objections came from the self-appointed-cum-state-appointed guardians of morals. In the American heartland, the Reverend J. J. Phelan cited, with shared horror, a recent news story titled "Dark Movie Houses a Menace to Morals of Young, Court Officer Says":

> "Immorality among young boys and girls in Toledo can almost always be traced to the dark movie house. And it is getting worse," said Miss Sara Kaufmann, Juvenile Court Officer. . . . "Girls whose mothers pay no attention to their whereabouts go alone into the dark house. Boys go in and sit beside them in the darkness. They come out together."[25]

The impulse behind this anecdote was captured by the earlier sociological analysis of Emilie Altenloh, who as part of her dissertation at the University of Heidelberg, completed the most significant sociological study of German cinema audiences in the pre–World War I period. Based on a questionnaire and interview survey of some 2,400 filmgoers in Mannheim in 1912–13, Altenloh concluded that the primary draw for young workers was obvious:

> Eroticism is, of course, the reason many of them go to the cinema. . . . The movie theater that is "quiet and dark" and "where the most dramas are shown" is usually most popular. . . . For all lovers, the darkened cinemas are a popular place to spend time. "Come inside, our cinema is the darkest in town," is how one entrepreneur extols the virtues of his establishment.[26]

If the court officer's anecdotal account differed most obviously in tone from Altenloh's sociological analysis, we must remember that tone was everything. The British National Council of Public Morals, for example, established a Cinema Commission, whose 1917 report included a section ominously titled "The Moral Danger of Darkness."[27] Incendiary and unproven claims abounded:

"darkness may be used for evil purposes" and "darkness encourages indecency."[28] Almost a decade later, hysterical authors continued to cite Altenloh to link utterly reasonable claims—"In regard to the cinema as space, its darkening is the most interesting moment for a historical consideration of mores; for many spectators, [darkness] is the cinema's primary attraction"—to a series of ever-more alarmist pronouncements: Cinemas produce an erotic attraction even for strangers who meet there; thus, the presence of prostitutes. As a matter of course, homosexuals also try to profit from the darkness of the auditorium; thus, the presence of male prostitutes.[29] So-called light theaters promised to "eliminate the possibility of panic and the offensive conduct of degenerates who sometimes take advantage of the darkness."[30] Indeed, the entire moralizing assault was often a thinly veiled screed against the lower classes.

Class problems begot technical solutions, often couched in medical language, ostensibly to combat the eye strain and fatigue caused by excessive light-dark contrasts. But because high contrast creates a brighter, more powerful image, many cinema operators maintained maximum contrast or even plunged the house into darkness for several minutes before the show began so as to "make the picture appear brighter."[31] In theory, lighting engineers should have been torn between the demands of cinema exhibitors and spectators for maximum contrast and those of medical and moral professionals, who railed against it. But so great were their class bias and professional myopia that illumination engineers and architects often refused to comprehend the persistence of darkened cinemas. In an address to the Illuminating Engineering Society, E. L. Bragdon, technical editor of *Motion Picture News*, referenced the pitch-dark rooms of early storefront theaters and added: "This method of handling illumination of the auditorium should have disappeared early. But it did not."[32] The obvious retort to such "enlightened" incredulity was Upton Sinclair's famous jibe: "It is difficult to get a man to understand something, when his salary depends upon his not understanding it!" Lighting engineers were paid to engineer lighting. Darkness was a residue of the past.

Or rather, it was a residue of the disciplinary system imposed by 1910s cinemas. According to Michel Foucault, discipline is a "technique of power" by which the individual becomes the product of a specific disciplinary regime rather than the raw material from which that regime is constructed.[33] In other words, the student is produced by the school system, the soldier by the military, the prisoner by the penitentiary, the worker by the factory, and, most relevant here, the spectator by the cinema. As was widely recognized throughout the twentieth century—and hypostasized in the 1970s in "apparatus theory"—cinemas were veritable machines for the standardization of audiences into homogenous, disciplined crowds. "Discipline," Foucault argues further, "works in an empty, artificial space that is to be completely constructed."[34] Since Bayreuth, theaters have relied on darkness—"complete, solid, unbroken," in Stern's formula—to construct the ideal theater and individuated spectator. "Whatever lights are found legally necessary," instructed Stern, "should be properly diffused and softened [for they prove an impediment to] the spectatorial focus on the screen."[35] Despite the best efforts of moralizers and corporate monopolies, cinemas remained, of necessity, relatively or "absolutely" dark. The evils of darkness were not a condition that could be overcome, but a residue of a system that marshaled darkness in the name of discipline.

Disciplinary systems, according to Foucault, inevitably come up against those who defy classification, escape supervision, or refuse entrance into systems of distribution; they are "the stumbling block in the physics of disciplinary power. That is to say, disciplinary power has its margins."[36] No army without deserters; no schools without the feebleminded or mentally defective; no police or prisons without delinquents. No cinemas, we might add, without "degenerates who sometimes take advantage of the darkness." These "residues" first come into being in relation to the isotopy of discipline, its asymptotic approach toward homogeneity. Disciplinary regimes work tirelessly to recuperate the residues they produce: schools for the feebleminded and schools for those who fail the schools for the feebleminded, and so forth. Illumination was a core technology for the isotopic recuperation of darkness into the disciplinary regime of cinema.

Lighting engineers quickly understood, however, that only the screen required absolute darkness. Eventually, technicians developed screens that functioned under any lighting conditions. But illumination engineers were hardly content with indirect illumination. Rather, they perceived cinema exteriors and interiors as blank canvases, framed by natural and artificial darkness, on which to display their immaterial wares. Initially conceived as an ameliorative measure, lighting design soon became a fixture of cinema design. The dramatic change arrived in the early 1920s. James Cameron's standard work on film projection said nothing about "effect lighting" in the second edition (1921) but called it indispensable in the third edition, published just one year later: "Experience and popular approval has shown that *high class* lighting effects on the stage as well as in the auditorium are absolutely necessary."[37] By the end of the decade, the section on effect lighting covered more than twenty pages: starry ceilings, dramatically illuminated walls, abstract projections onto mist, and so forth.[38] Scores of technologies, attractions, and distractions were amassed in the auditorium to create what Siegfried Kracauer described, with Wagnerian flair, as the *Gesamtkunstwerk* (total work of art) of effects.[39] If, as the Austrian journalist Alfred Polgar quipped in 1911, cinema was "a world with a fourth but not a third dimension," the spatial dimension lost to the dreamlike events on screen was restored in the equally fantastic auditoriums of the 1920s.[40] As the *Gesamtkunstwerk* of effects aspired to the realm of art, lighting systems assumed the status of "visual music" or "light symphonies." These temples to petit bourgeois culture declared themselves "film palaces"; "to call them *movie theaters*," Kracauer lampooned, "would be disrespectful."[41]

**IV. Surrealists in the Cinema**

Despite the ideal of a perfectly passive spectator, bodies in darkened cinemas presented a bundle of contradictions. While the conditions of the theater tried to guarantee bodily detachedness, the threat of carnal contact remained. At times, the dark house was a morally compromised space—but just as often, it was no space at all. In the evocative, if contorted, words of the German author Konrad Haemmerling, "The real has become disembodied and it lives in space and yet not in space."[42] Disciplinary darkness, in other words, produced residues on both extremes of the embodiment-disembodiment spectrum: too much corporeality could lead to sexual liaisons, but too little encouraged an ecstasy of its own. Rather than choose between the sensual carnality of cinema and its dislocated disembodiment, a certain relation to darkness could paradoxically enhance both: Surrealists homed in on both residues of the disciplinary system. Desnos, the Surrealist most attentive to cinema, articulated the matter best: "Discipline, which indifferently defines army and prison, the strap and the ideal of the mediocre rhetoricians who defend tradition, should not be applied to this perfectly new form of cerebral pleasure."[43] Desnos considered cinema to be "the most powerful of all cerebral drugs . . . superior to opium."[44] Cerebral pleasures quickly led to carnal ones: "During the intermission we will seek out the man or woman who will sweep us along in an adventure equal to cinema's twilight dream."[45] The poet and novelist Louis Aragon similarly took note of the "discontented married women" and their implied availability: "You can see them in the cinema, quite unhinged in the darkness."[46] Breton, finally, recalled a naked woman wandering about the "Electric-Palace," a cinema famous less for its electric lights than its lascivious darkness and "the most commonplace sort of illicit sexual rendezvous."[47] The potential for real bodily contact, feared by moralizers worldwide, was the first residue of cinematic darkness.

Intoxicants, pleasures, carnality, corrosion, and the denunciation of discipline did not, however, necessitate the rejection of spaceless darkness or the return of the spectatorial bodies banished by Wagner and his (cinematic) followers. Quite the contrary, in fact: In the "perfect night of cinema," Desnos averred, "the room and the spectators disappear. The seated dreamer is transported to a new world compared to which reality is but a charmless fiction."[48] After World War II, Breton recalled his cinematic romps during the late 1910s:

> What we valued most in [cinema], to the point of taking no interest in anything else, was its *power to disorient* [*dépaysement*]. . . . The *marvel*, besides which the merits of a given film count for little, resides in the devolved faculty of the first-comer to abstract himself from his own life when he feels like it, at least in the large town, as soon as he passes through one of the muffled doors that give on to the blackness.[49]

Dislocating darkness and bodily abstraction—the twin pillars of cinematic discipline—were the *marvelous* cinematic operations most valued by Breton and his fellow Surrealists. It was in this spirit that Jean Goudal penned his seminal 1925 essay entitled "Surrealism and Cinema":

> Let's go into a cinema where the perforated celluloid is purring in the darkness. On entering, our gaze is guided by the luminous ray to the screen where for two hours it will remain fixed. . . . Our problems evaporate, our neighbors disappear. Our body itself submits to a sort of temporary depersonalization which takes away the feeling of its own existence. We are nothing but two eyes riveted to ten square meters of white canvas. . . . The darkness of the auditorium destroys the rivalry of real images that would contradict the ones on the screen.[50]

Goudal's Surrealist-inflected account echoes almost verbatim the claims made for cinema by its detractors and champions alike. Ecstatic disembodiment and dislocation—stripped of insipid narrative—marked the second residue of cinematic darkness. The genius of Surrealism was not to oppose disembodiment and dislocation to carnality and specific locales, but rather to unite them through cinematic darkness. Again, Desnos: "We go into the dark cinemas to find artificial dreams and perhaps the stimulus capable of peopling our empty nights."[51] Desnos's search for artificial dreams led him to the residues of artificial darkness.

NOTES

This essay is adapted from Noam M. Elcott, *Artificial Darkness: An Obscure History of Modern Art and Media* (Chicago: University of Chicago Press, 2016).

1. Hollis Frampton, *On the Camera Arts and Consecutive Matters: The Writings of Hollis Frampton*, ed. Bruce Jenkins (Cambridge, MA: MIT Press, 2009), p. 125.
2. The English word *theater* (from the Greek *theatron*) and the German *Zuschauerraum* (auditorium; literally "spectator-space") are among the many related terms that retain the primacy of vision.
3. August Klingemann, *Kunst und Natur* (1823), cited in Wolfgang Schivelbusch, *Disenchanted Night: The Industrialization of Light in the Nineteenth Century*, trans. Angela Davies (Berkeley: University of California Press, 1988), p. 204.
4. Friedrich Kittler, "World-Breath: On Wagner's Media Technology," in *Opera through Other Eyes*, ed. David J. Levin (Stanford: Stanford University Press, 1994), p. 216.
5. Richard Wagner, "The Art-Work of the Future" (1849), in *Richard Wagner's Prose Works*, trans. William Ashton Ellis (St. Clair Shores, MI: Scholarly Press, 1895; reprint, 1972), p. 185; *Das Kunstwerk der Zukunft* (Leipzig: Otto Wigand, 1850), pp. 188–89 (translation modified).
6. The original German reads: "aus dem Zuschauerraume aber verschwindet das Publikum, dieser Repräsant des öffentlichen Lebens, sich selbst."
7. Robert Desnos, *Cinéma*, ed. André Tchernia (Paris: Gallimard, 1966), p. 139.
8. Seymour Stern, "An Aesthetic of the Cinema House," *National Board of Review Magazine* (May 1927), p. 7.
9. Ibid., pp. 9, 19.
10. What Friedrich Nietzsche failed to detect (due not to his youthful enthusiasm, as Theodor Adorno maintained, nor even to his aged madness, but rather because of his physical blindness), namely, "the birth of film out of the spirit of music," was a commonplace of the interbellum. See Theodor W. Adorno, *In Search of Wagner* (1937–38), trans. Rodney Livingstone (London: Verso, 1991), p. 107.
11. Hans Schliepmann, *Lichtspieltheater: Eine Sammlung ausgeführter Kinohäuser in Gross-Berlin* (Berlin: Ernst Wasmuth, 1914).
12. Ibid., p. 28.
13. In German: "die 'Architektur der Nichtarchitektur.'" Ibid., p. 12.
14. Adolf Behne, "Kinoarchitekturen," *Bild und Film* 4, nos. 7–8 (1915), p. 138.
15. Schliepmann, *Lichtspieltheater*, p. 12.

16. Rudolf Harms, *Philosophie des Films* (Leipzig: Felix Meiner, 1926), p. 60.
17. Ibid., p. 58.
18. Ibid., p. iii.
19. Gabriele Pedullà, *In Broad Daylight: Movies and Spectators after the Cinema*, trans. Patricia Gaborik (London: Verso, 2012), p. 5 and passim.
20. Signal achievements included apparatus theory, in its French and Anglo-American variants; the Expanded Cinema movements that crisscrossed America, Europe, and the globe in the late 1960s and 1970s, nearly all of which attacked the institution and space of movie theaters; and art projects like Robert Smithson's 1971 quixotic plan to build a movie theater in a cave. See Roland Barthes's justly famous reflections in "Upon Leaving the Movie Theater" (1975), in *Apparatus*, ed. Theresa Hak Kyung Cha (New York: Tanam Press, 1980), p. 1.
21. André Breton, "Manifesto of Surrealism" (1924), in *Manifestoes of Surrealism*, trans. Richard Seaver and Helen R. Lane (Ann Arbor: University of Michigan Press, 1977), p. 46.
22. André Breton, Œuvres complètes, ed. Marguerite Bonnet, vol. 1 (Paris: Gallimard, 1988), p. 345.
23. Robert Desnos, "Fantômas, Les Vampires, Les Mystères de New York" (1927), in *French Film Theory and Criticism: 1907–1929*, ed. Richard Abel (Princeton: Princeton University Press, 1988), p. 398.
24. Frank Herbert Richardson, *Motion Picture Handbook* (New York: Moving Picture World, 1916), p. 635.
25. *News-Bee*, March 21, 1919. Cited in J. J. Phelan, *Motion Pictures as a Phase of Commercial Amusement in Toledo, Ohio* (Toledo: Little Book Press, 1919), p. 267.
26. Emilie Altenloh, "A Sociology of the Cinema: The Audience" (1914), reprinted in *Screen* 42, no. 3 (2001), pp. 266, 271.
27. National Council of Public Morals Cinema Commission of Inquiry, *The Cinema* (London: Williams and Norgate, 1917), pp. xxv–xxvi.
28. Ibid., pp. xxiii, xxv.
29. Curt Moreck [Konrad Haemmerling], *Sittengeschichte des Kinos* (Dresden: P. Aretz, 1926), pp. 209–10.
30. "Motion Picture Patents Company: Mayor McCellan Won Over," *Moving Picture World* 4, no. 17 (1909), p. 512.
31. Henry Charles Horstmann and Victor Hugo Tousley, *Motion Picture Operation* (Chicago: Frederick J. Drake, 1914), p. 110.
32. "The Artificial Illumination of Motion Picture Theatres, Parts I and II," *American Architect* 118, nos. 2343/2344 (1920), p. 646.
33. "Discipline is that technique of power by which the subject-function is exactly superimposed and fastened on the somatic singularity." Michel Foucault, *Psychiatric Power: Lectures at the College de France, 1973–1974*, trans. Graham Burchell (New York: Palgrave Macmillan, 2006), p. 55.
34. Michel Foucault, *Security, Territory, Population: Lectures at the Collège de France, 1977–1978*, ed. Michel Senellart and Arnold I. Davidson, trans. Graham Burchell (New York: Palgrave Macmillan, 2007), p. 19.
35. Stern, "An Aesthetic of the Cinema House," p. 9.
36. Foucault, *Psychiatric Power*, 53.
37. James R. Cameron, *Motion Picture Projection*, 3rd ed. (New York: Technical Book Company, 1922), p. 285 (emphasis added).
38. See Florian Nelle, *Künstliche Paradiese: Vom Barocktheater zum Filmpalast* (Würzburg: Königshausen und Neumann, 2005), p. 279.
39. Siegfried Kracauer, "Cult of Distraction" (1926), trans. Thomas Y. Levin, in *The Mass Ornament*, ed. Thomas Y. Levin (Cambridge, MA: MIT Press, 1995), p. 324.
40. Nelle, *Künstliche Paradiese*, pp. 256, 276.
41. Kracauer, "Cult of Distraction," p. 323.
42. Moreck, *Sittengeschichte des Kinos*, p. 74.
43. Robert Desnos, "Eroticism" (1923), in *The Shadow and Its Shadow*, ed. Paul Hammond (Edinburgh: Polygon, 1991), p. 196.
44. Ibid., p. 195.
45. Ibid., p. 196.
46. Louis Aragon, *Paris Peasant* (1926), trans. Simon Watson Taylor (Boston: Exact Change, 1994), p. 52.
47. André Breton, *Nadja* (1928), trans. Richard Howard (New York: Grove Press, 1994), p. 39.
48. Robert Desnos, *Cinéma*, ed. André Tchernia (Paris: Gallimard, 1966), p. 139.
49. André Breton, "As in a Wood" (1951), in *The Shadow and Its Shadow*, ed. Paul Hammond (San Francisco: City Lights Books, 2000), p. 73.
50. Jean Goudal, "Surrealism and Cinema" (1925), in Abel, ed., *French Film Theory and Criticism*, pp. 355–56 (translation slightly modified).
51. Robert Desnos, "Dream and Cinema" (1923), in Abel, ed., *French Film Theory and Criticism*, p. 283.

# After *2001*: The Dematerialization of the Film Object in the Twenty-First Century

J. Hoberman

Were we to choose a late twentieth-century motion picture that was at once exemplary and sui generis, popular and avant-garde, banal and cosmic, nonnarrative and epic, we could do worse than Stanley Kubrick's *2001: A Space Odyssey*, which, five years in the making (and with nearly two-thirds of its budget spent on special effects), opened in New York at the Loews Capitol Cinerama Theater on April 3, 1968.

Originally shown in 70mm, with full stereophonic sound, projected on a curved screen two stories tall, *2001* was a majestic, immersive film object, addressing the largest theme on the widest possible canvas. The movie began with "The Dawn of Man" and, blasting past Jupiter, went "Beyond the Infinite" to end on a note of religious triumphalism. A clean-cut corporate astronaut (Keir Dullea) drops out, literally, and passing through the "Star Gate Corridor" (a fifteen-minute psychedelic sequence using an automated slit-scan process elaborated from the work of filmmaker John Whitney by twenty-five-year-old special-effects artist Douglas Trumbull) becomes a Star Child . . . in outer space.

A movie of great technical virtuosity—precise sound design, detailed animation, elaborate models, computerized optical printing, an innovative deployment of front- and rear-screen projection—*2001* embodied cinema's state of the art and even its future. "If one considers the introduction of sound and then color as successive 'generations' in the history of cinema, it is possible to say that we've entered the fourth generation by marrying basic cinematic techniques to computer and video sciences," counterculture media journalist Gene Youngblood wrote.[1]

A history of the future that is today a relic, *2001* anticipated by several years the Hollywood blockbuster regime under which it could never be produced. At the same time, as what pioneering Soviet director Dziga Vertov called a "film object," *2001* can be seen as the successor to Oskar Fischinger's three-screen projection piece *Raumlichtkunst* (1926), a series of performances that included painted glass slides, 35mm film, and musical accompaniment (pp. 20, 21). *2001* prophesied and, in a sense, preempted the late twentieth-century white-cube cinema of movies made for galleries or museums. Audiences sometimes abandoned their seats and sprawled on the floor beneath the screen the better to enjoy the movie's perceptual vaudeville.

As originally projected at the Loew's Capitol, *2001* was an installation. Today, however, the technology has advanced to the point that it would be possible to stream *2001* digitally and watch it on a cell phone.

The dematerialization of the film object was well under way by the time the motion picture medium reached its centennial in the mid-1990s, let alone by 2001. The dematerialization of the cinematic apparatus—the initially hand-cranked but soon motorized exposure and projection of 35mm photographic film, more or less introduced by Auguste and Louis Lumière with their Cinématographe in December 1895—began even earlier.[2]

The first films, one-shot *actualités* (documentaries) made by the Lumières and others—notably the Edison cameraman Edwin S. Porter—might be termed modernist in that they often celebrated the medium itself. The urban scene and its modern amusements were popular subjects. In Porter's three-shot *Coney Island at Night* (1905; pp. 2–3), an elevated camera pans across or tilts down a landscape defined almost entirely by the illumination of various buildings, creating a "magical city of disembodied lights" that Lauren Rabinovitz called an example of "the electrified sublime."[3]

At the same time, *actualités* laid claim to a certain truth—an "integral realism," in the French critic and theorist André Bazin's phrase—predicated both on the camera's objective gaze and on the chemical reaction by which light left an authentic trace on photographic emulsion. A photograph (or, more precisely, a photographic negative) was a form of evidence. Because of this tangible or "indexical" connection between the photograph and that which was photographed, photographic motion pictures produced an image that, for Bazin, was "unburdened" by artistic interpretation.[4]

Interpretation came with contextualization or montage. By 1920, Soviet filmmakers such as Lev Kuleshov recognized that it was not necessary to have a camera and unexposed film stock to produce a movie; two years later, Esther Schub was reediting and transforming existing films;

soon after, Sergei Eisenstein made what might be considered the first fictional *actualité*, *Battleship Potemkin* (1925), a drama shot as though it were a newsreel. The found-footage film was successively reinvented by the American artists Joseph Cornell and Bruce Conner. That Cornell and Conner were also makers of sculptural assemblages and initially exhibited their films—*Rose Hobart* (1936; p. 23) and *A Movie* (1958), respectively—in art galleries reinforces the notion of a film object.

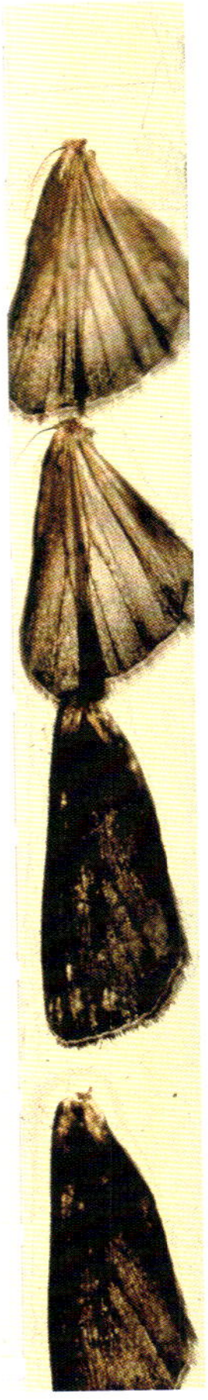

Fig. 1. Stan Brakhage (1933–2003), filmstrip from *Mothlight*, 1963. 16mm film, color, silent; 4 min. Whitney Museum of American Art, New York; purchase with funds from the Film and Video Committee 2000.264

As early as 1928, the New Zealand–born, British-based artist Len Lye did away with even repurposed photographic film and drew, scratched, or pasted directly on celluloid. The Austrian filmmaker Peter Kubelka alternated black and clear leader, as well as silence and static, in his *Arnulf Rainer* (1960). The most radical film object made without a camera or photographic film stock was Stan Brakhage's *Mothlight* (1963; fig. 1)—a film fashioned from dead moths, flowers, and leaves sandwiched between two layers of transparent 16mm Mylar editing tape that were then printed on film stock. *Mothlight* abolished photography altogether, and yet—more than any movie ever made—it is profoundly indexical. Animating the inanimate, *Mothlight* is pure cinema. Or at least it was: Thanks to its transfer to DVD, the movie is most often shown digitally and is thus a resurrection of itself—no longer an object that can be physically examined or projected frame by frame.

In 1964, Andy Warhol liquidated the entire cinematic apparatus, even as he asserted its existence, by making an epic *actualité* movie that one didn't have to see to "see." *Empire*, an eight-hour-plus, ten-reel 16mm film (fig. 2), is a fixed-camera contemplation of the Empire State Building that, as curator Callie Angell put it, "has thrived on a purely conceptual level since its creation."[5] Seven months after filmmaker Jonas Mekas suggested that *Empire* would become "the *Birth of a Nation* of the New Bag Cinema," Warhol's movie had its world premiere on March 6, 1965, at New York's City Hall Cinema, heralded by a brief excerpt from Beethoven's Fifth Symphony. Ten minutes into the projection, Mekas reported, "a crowd of thirty or forty people stormed out of the theatre into the lobby, surrounded the box office, Bob Brown, and myself, and threatened to beat us up and destroy the theatre unless their money was returned. 'This is not entertainment! This movie doesn't move,' shouted the mob."[6] A single screening was enough to secure *Empire*'s notoriety. Precisely because of its primary existence as a mental image, *Empire* dematerialized the screen. Thus, another element of the cinematic apparatus was dismantled.

A decade or so later, the American experimental filmmaker Stan VanDerBeek and the artist Joan Brigham were striving for "the ultimate point of dematerialization." In late 1979, using the Whitney Museum of American Art's sculpture garden, VanDerBeek and Brigham installed *Steam Screens* (p. 51), described in Brigham's program notes as "a system for suspending film images as light sculptures in open public spaces." Pressurized steam was sequenced through a series of pipes to create moving waves that, rolling through a stream of light from eight 16mm projectors, refracted images from the computer animation *Euclidean Illusions*, made by VanDerBeek in collaboration with Richard Weinberg. "The audience walks through or lingers inside the physical image, experiencing something close to a mirage or hallucination," Brigham wrote of the Whitney performance.[7] The motion picture is thus dispersed; the screen exists solely in the eye-brain of the beholder.

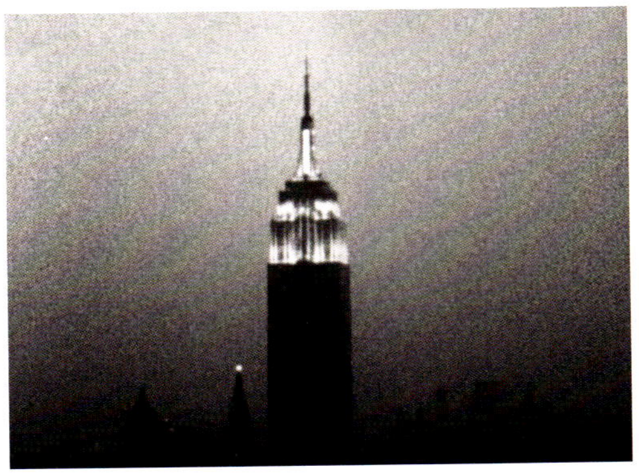

Fig. 2. Andy Warhol (1928–1987), still from *Empire*, 1965. 16mm film, black and white, silent; 8 hr. 5 min. at 16 fps

A more elaborate version of a dematerialized projection would be Chinese filmmaker Zhang Yimou's opening ceremony for the 2008 Beijing Olympics, the most-watched telecast in human history and a live broadcast that, because of its digital effects (and not unlike the Nuremberg rally that Leni Riefenstahl documented in *Triumph of the Will*) could not be seen in person but only on screen.

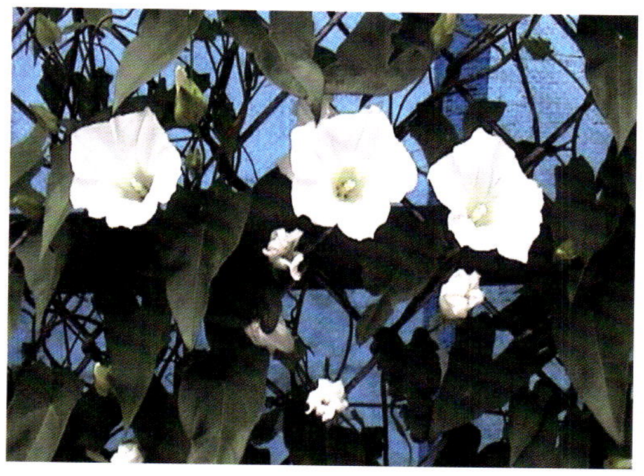

Fig. 3. Jonas Mekas (b. 1922), still from *Day 1, January 1, 2007* from *365 Day Project*, 2007. 365 videos, color, sound; approx. 38 hours total

Kindred, if disparate, forms of dispersal include Jonas Mekas's *365 Day Project* (2007; fig. 3), a series of diary-like short pieces exhibited through cyberspace on the artist's website, and the virtual career of the anime character Annlee, purchased by Pierre Huyghe and Philippe Parreno from a Japanese agency in 1999 and presented as the star subject of their own videos as well as those of other artists who employed her on loan (pp. 64–69).[8]

The accelerating use of digital technology, whether as a source of visual data or a delivery system, has introduced a radical impurity into the motion picture apparatus that was developed at the turn of the twentieth century and, save for the introduction of synchronous sound, remained markedly consistent for a hundred years.

In 1946, Bazin suggested a counternarrative to the notion that motion pictures developed in the spirit of scientific inquiry: Cinema was underwritten by an obsessive quest for the "recreation of the world in its own image," or what he called Total Cinema. In this view, each new technological development took cinema closer to its imagined essence, and once true cinema was achieved, the medium would, in effect, disappear into life. Bazin believed that this could happen by the year 2000, but in fact something else occurred: The development of digital computer-generated imagery (CGI) broke the special relationship that existed between photography and the world.

Thus, the photographic became a subset of the graphic and, as predicted by Cornell's *Rose Hobart* and its found-footage successors, the now highly malleable photograph superseded the world as raw material for image making. Whereas Bazin saw cinema as the objective "re-creation of the world," digital image making precludes the necessity of having the world, or even a really existing subject, before the camera—and even the need for the camera itself.

Digital technology displaced photography, but not the desire to produce images that moved. With the advent of CGI, the history of motion pictures was now, in effect, the history of animation—a word with powerful associations. To animate is to create or restore movement, to bring inert matter to life or back to life (as with Brakhage's *Mothlight* or, some sixty years earlier, the first time that a creative projectionist elected to run Edison's 1902 *Electrocuting an Elephant* in reverse).

Animation as a technique, predicated on single-frame or stop-motion photography, developed almost immediately after the invention of cinema in the trick films of the French stage magician Georges Méliès; it was further developed in those of his compatriot Émile Cohl, and produced its first flowering in the films of the Polish biologist Władysław Starewicz and the American newspaper cartoonist Winsor McCay.

McCay's animations extended the dreamlike control over time and space that characterized his comic strip *Little Nemo in Slumberland*. Movies like McCay's *Gertie the Dinosaur* (1914) were hand drawn, one sheet at a time, and thus required approximately sixteen drawings for each second of screen time. Equally labor-intensive, Starewicz's films, such as his 1912 *The Cameraman's Revenge*, were puppet animations populated by artfully reconstituted insects, and as such were precursors of movies like *The Lost World* (1925) and *King Kong* (1933), which were themselves proto-cyborg films in their juxtaposition of human actors and animated puppets.

Fig. 4. Still from *Jurassic Park*,1993

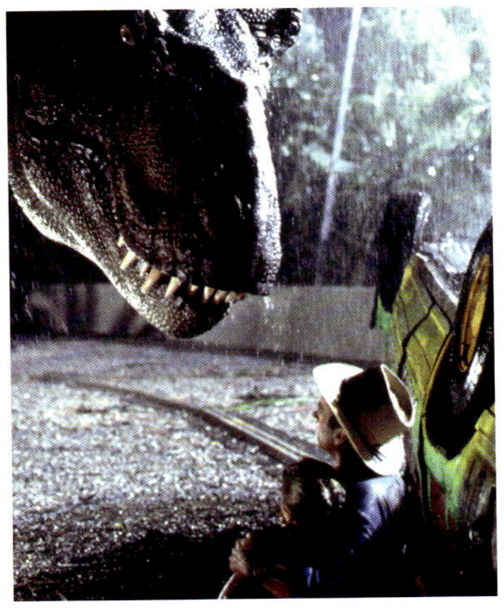

For over a century, animation maintained some degree of indexicality. The rotoscope, a device used to project and trace filmed images onto paper, first developed by Max and Dave Fleischer in the 1920s and taken to a more sophisticated level in the production of Walt Disney's *Snow White and the Seven Dwarfs* (1938), created another type of partially indexical animation. The break came in 1993 with Steven Spielberg's *Jurassic Park*, which seamlessly combined photographic and computer-generated imagery—actual people interacting on-screen with nonexistent creatures—to establish a new cyborg cinema that compromised the indexical relationship to reality that had long been the medium's claim to truth (fig. 4).[9] Like *Gertie the Dinosaur* and *The Lost World*, *Jurassic Park* reanimated prehistory and restored long-extinct creatures—and thus, since that was the subject of the movie, functioned as an allegory for itself.

Over the next decade, even the indexical presence of a drawing or painted cel would vanish. The computer animation *WALL-E* (2008), directed by Andrew Stanton, satirizes the technology it deploys (fig. 5). The protagonist of this unaccountably optimistic vision of human extinction is a solitary robot trash compactor single-mindedly organizing the endless detritus of an abandoned, implicitly analog world. *WALL-E* mourns the death of analog image making even as it consigns old-fashioned movies to the trash heap. While *2001* is parodied throughout, another 1968 Hollywood movie—the very epitome of elephantine, retrograde moviemaking—appears as *WALL-E*'s privileged artifact. An ancient VHS tape of *Hello Dolly* is the robot's most prized possession—a clip of actors cheerfully prancing on a long-lost Hollywood soundstage is embedded in the movie almost as an installation. Thus celebrating a doubly obsolete technology, *WALL-E* is the *2001* of 2008, a post-photographic film set in a post-human universe.

By facilitating instant, unobtrusive recording as well as inexpensive, elaborate special effects, digital technology has had the paradoxical effect of making movies both more naturalistic and more fantastic.

Thus, as digital image making (or animation) supplants photography as the basis for cinema, a venerable forefather reappears: Georges Méliès, less a filmmaker than a man of the theater who used motion pictures to automate stage magic, just as talkies would later render live musical accompaniment redundant. Replete with "impossible" digitally produced camera moves, Martin Scorsese's fictionalized Méliès biopic *Hugo* (2012) revives Méliès's primitive magic tricks by constructing an elaborate 3D frame for their projection.[10]

At the same time, digital technology enables works that make the motion picture medium more itself. In a brief essay on *Empire*, artist and critic Gregory Battcock declared that Warhol's unwatched and unwatchable movie demonstrated that the passing of time was "the most important single element that distinguishes film from the other visual art forms." The same point was made by Russian filmmaker Andrey Tarkovsky regarding Lumière *actualités*: "For the first time in the history of the arts, in the history of culture, man found the means to take an impression of time. Time, printed in its factual forms and manifestations: such is the supreme idea of cinema as an art."[11]

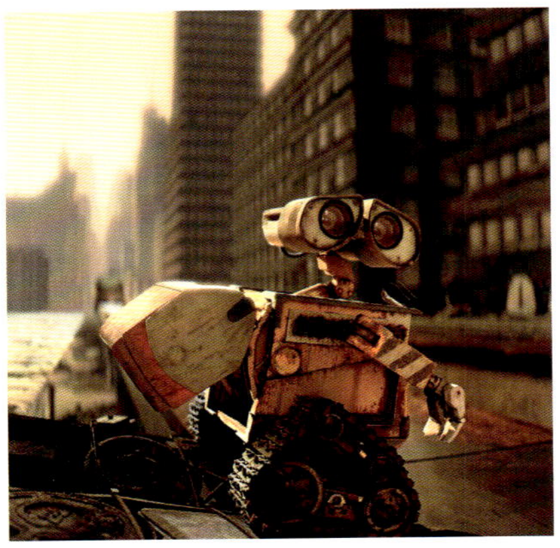

Fig. 5. Still from *WALL-E*, 2008

Aleksandr Sokurov's ninety-five-minute *Russian Ark* (2002), an eccentric guided tour of the Hermitage in

St. Petersburg, was distinguished by several historical achievements—as the first unedited single-screen, single-take full-length feature film, and as the first uncompressed high-definition movie recorded onto a portable hard disc. As *Russian Ark* creates a real-time contiguous cinematic space, so the visual artist and composer Christian Marclay's 2010 installation *The Clock*—a digitally projected assemblage of photographic motion pictures that, in its perfectly chronological, minute-to-minute temporal references, functions as a twenty-four-hour timekeeper—is a cinematic monument in time, providing a new sort of indexicality that is only possible as a form of digital image making.

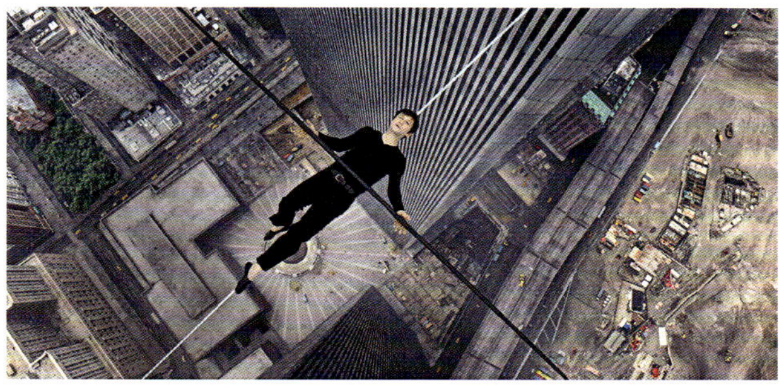

Fig. 6. Still from *The Walk*, 2015

Cinema makes time material and renders space imaginary—as in the production of stereoscopic 3D movies. The use of stereoscopy to create the illusion of depth is not new: the stereopticon was a popular nineteenth-century parlor toy, and American film pioneer Edwin Porter developed an early 3D system based on superimposed green and orange images. In his 1946 essay "The Myth of Total Cinema" and elsewhere, Bazin advanced the hypothesis that cinema was inspired by 3D photography: "It was not the discovery of photography but rather the stereoscope that opened the inventors' eyes. By capturing figures frozen in space, photographers realized that their images lacked the movement necessary to make their images of life a true copy of nature."[12]

What is new is the capacity to create the illusion of depth solely through digital means. The astronaut protagonists in Alfonso Cuarón's *Gravity* (2013) seem to swim (or drown) in an unlimited space where the mind knows that none actually exists. Robert Zemeckis's *The Walk* (2015) places the audience at eye-level or above the aerialist Philippe Petit, played with a bit of motion-capture by Joseph Gordon Levitt, on a high-wire suspended between the Twin Towers (fig. 6). (The movie, which digitally resurrects the World Trade Center, derives a measure of indexicality from reconstructing an actual event.) Like *2001*, these 3D spectacles, best seen as installations on the outsized IMAX screen, promote sensory disorientation—or better, reorientation.

At the same time, a number of artists, as recently noted by Erika Balsom, "engage with 3D in artisanal, low-tech ways." One of these is Trisha Baga, whose eighteen-minute projection *Flatlands* (2010; pp. 78, 79) uses a disco ball to defract and reflect light in a manner that mirrors three-dimensional rivulets on her camera's lens. Baga's video installations combine 3D illusion with 2D actuality (or vice versa) to create landscapes of simulated and real depth, as, in another way, do the films of Ken Jacobs, whom Balsom identifies as "the filmmaker who has done more than anyone to establish the place of 3D in experimental cinema."[13] Jacobs's seventy-three-minute digital film *The Guests* (2014) produces 3D illusion from a preexisting 2D film by applying a computer logarithm to mine the visual data in a thirty-second fragment from the 1897 Lumière Brothers *actualité* titled *Entrée d'une noce á l'église* (Entrance to a wedding at the church). As the virtual filmstrip advances, seemingly one frame at a time, elements of the original scene float out of the frame or recede into it.

Like a film reel unspooling through a projector, the history of motion pictures rolls on—if increasingly without the projector or the film, and sometime as a Möbius strip.

NOTES

1. Gene Youngblood, *Expanded Cinema* (New York: Dutton, 1970), p. 156. For Annette Michelson, *2001* was less a narrative movie than an exercise in spatial disorientation, which is to say something approaching pure cinema. Michelson, "Bodies in Space: Film as 'Carnal Knowledge'," *Artforum* 7, no. 6 (February 1969), pp. 54–64. Mainstream reviews of *2001* were often negative. Some, including those by the *New York Times*, the *New Yorker*, and the *Village Voice*, were hostile. And yet the movie—which would be advertised as "The Ultimate Trip"—was a remarkable commercial success, held over for months at Loews Capitol, and remaining in general release through 1972.

2. Stephen Heath, "The Cinematic Apparatus: Technology as Historical and Cultural Form," in *The Cinematic Apparatus*, ed. Teresa de Lauretis and Stephen Heath (New York: St. Martin's Press, 1980).
3. Lauren Rabinovitz, *Electrical Dreamland: Amusement Parks, Movies, and American Modernity* (New York: Columbia University Press, 2012), pp. 130–33.
4. André Bazin, "The Myth of Total Cinema," in *What Is Cinema?* (Berkeley: University of California Press, 1967), p. 21.
5. Callie Angell, *The Films of Andy Warhol: Part II* (New York: Whitney Museum of American Art, 1994), p. 15.
6. Jonas Mekas, *Movie Journal: The Rise of a New American Cinema, 1959–1971* (New York: Collier, 1972), pp. 150, 180–81.
7. The nine-minute film of fabricated geometric forms spinning in imaginary space may be the only tangible remnant of this evanescent performance. Existing photographs do not capture the projections and, Brigham's program notes aside, I have been unable to find any first-hand accounts of the Whitney event.
8. The Annlee project is exhaustively detailed in Huyghe and Parreno's exhibition catalogue *No Ghost Just a Shell* (Cologne: Buchhandlung Walther König, 2003), suggestively subtitled "Un film d'imaginaire." In a sense, the *2001* of 2001 was the events of September 11, which for many provided the ultimate movie experience that was more than a movie—spectacular destruction, broadcast live, and watched more or less simultaneously by an audience of billions.
9. *The Matrix* (1999) is a landmark cyborg film in its combination of live action with frame-by-frame digital manipulation. No previous animated film had so naturalistically represented the physical world.
10. Hyperaware of the motion picture apparatus, and repeatedly linking movies to clocks and railroad trains, *Hugo*'s trick is to provide the illusion that it can rewind and repair the broken machine of cinema even as cinema itself has long since ceased to be mechanical.
11. Gregory Battcock, "Notes on Empire: A Film by Andy Warhol," *Film Culture* 40 (Spring 1966), pp. 39–40; Andrey Tarkovsky, *Sculpting in Time* (New York: Alfred A. Knopf, 1987), pp. 62–63.
12. André Bazin, "A New Stage in the Process: Math Equations for 3D," in *André Bazin's New Media*, ed. Dudley Andrew (Oakland: University of California Press, 2014), p. 235.
13. Erika Balsom, "Parallax Plurality: 3-D Cinema beyond the Feature Film," *Artforum* 54, no. 1 (September 2015), pp. 355–61.

# Animation and Transformation

Esther Leslie

Animation is a more-or-less anarchic play of moving light broken into spectral colors or blacks, whites, and grays, which are coaxed into forms and figures that seem to possess life or liveliness. The kaleidoscopic experience that animated cinema affords was not invented along with projectors and film. Its immediate precursors can be found in animated optical delights such as the thaumatropes[1] of the 1820s onward.

Johann Wolfgang von Goethe seems to have anticipated such experiences in his *Theory of Colours*, published in 1810. Goethe undertook optical experiments, such as screwing up his eyes, twisting his head, staring at the sun, and diffracting the light, in order to make prismatic patterns play on the inside of his eyelids. His account of one such trial reads like a description of animation, as both process and product:

> If after breathing on a plate of glass, the breath is merely wiped away with the finger, and if we then again immediately breathe on the glass, we see very vivid colours gliding through each other; these, as the moisture evaporates, change their place, and at last vanish altogether. If this operation is repeated, the colours are more vivid and beautiful, and remain longer than they did the first time.[2]

Goethe here evokes the principles of animation: repetition, movement, color, transience, and transformation. There is a maker, who in this case literally breathes the life into the animation, and who roughens the surface of the glass with the wipe of a finger, intensifying the colors. But what occurs is also immanent to the materials: The colors slither, vaporize, transpose, and disappear. Goethe also observed this effect inside a carriage on a frosty day, when the breath misting the windows made a surface on which appeared "the most vivid play of colours."[3] The effect was all the more vibrant if the background was dark; as before, the colors changed in hue but withdrew as soon as the moisture became water droplets or ice.

Goethe saw animation in nature. The screens onto which he breathed were panes of glass. The pirouetting colors and shapes that appeared on them were fleeting and could not be captured. Such animation is a delicate coproduction of self and world, subject and object, whereby the viewer is also the author. In the decades that followed, a parade of optical technologies would automate the process, making animated figures and their exploits enduring and separating the creator from the viewer.

As cities grew and technologies proliferated, plays of color, light, and movement became routine experiences. Exposure to dancing lights and chromatic effects, to sudden reflections or vivid visions, might happen on any street corner—say, under the globular beacons of the electric street lamps that Guy de Maupassant describes in the story "The Night: A Nightmare" (1887) as "pale, shining moons, like lunar eggs fallen from the sky, like vibrant, monster pearls with their sea-shell clarity."[4] On that same corner, a few decades later, someone might have glimpsed a neon advertisement pulsing in the night sky of the sort that caused Walter Benjamin to ask:

> What, in the end, makes advertisements so superior to criticism? Not what the moving red neon sign says—but the fiery pool reflecting it in the asphalt.[5]

The "liquid fire"[6] leaps from the walls. The product's name and logo are less significant than the migration of the sign across space, its descent into the streets, the exorbitance that makes it leap outside itself so that it "hits us between the eyes." It "hurls things at us," notes Benjamin, transforming the blackness of the road into blazing swirls. Through this illuminated advertising, this profligate display of the commodity, Benjamin describes a type of vision that is animated in multiple ways. The sign travels across space. It is lively, and what it signifies is to be understood too as lively—a fetish-thing, an object or service whose vital powers will enter our lives and make them better or more dynamic. Such advertisements dazzled, just as cinematic culture came to saturate the world. Disney cast intense oranges and shining blues out into cinemas. They formed

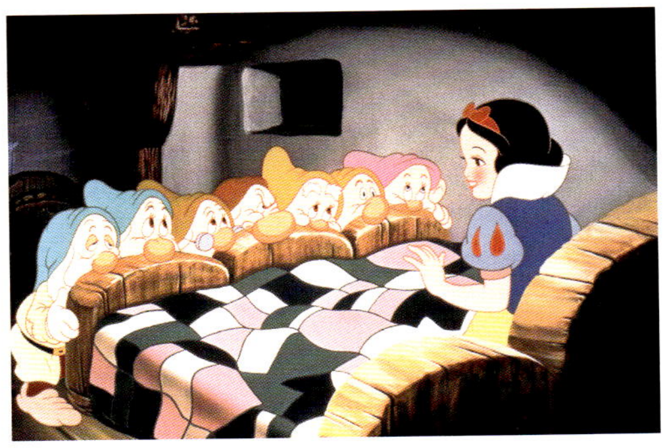

Fig. 1. Still from Walt Disney's *Snow White and the Seven Dwarfs*, 1937

a counterimage to what the Soviet film director and theorist Sergei Eisenstein called the gray squares and prisons of city blocks.[7] Eisenstein seized on the provisional quality of animation, which is thrown out, in utopian fashion, against the rigidities of the capitalist world. He affirmed animation's ability to range in any direction and embark on any exploit. Associating its shifting shapes with the protoplasmic forms of primordial matter, he saw in animation's ecstatic nature both the beginnings of time and the ends of things. The medium's most apt symbol was fire, which, observes Eisenstein, "is capable of most fully conveying the dream of a flowing diversity of forms."[8]

Animation mobilizes light and line and color, but it also mobilizes mobility itself through excessive and impossible movement, exaggerated gesture, and improbable physics. Its photographed sketches, sequential micro-gestures of clay maquettes, or digital characters depend on the external agency of the projector or computer for their mobility. Animation shatters the natural laws of everyday life in its wayward rearrangements of space, time, and matter, and so uses technology to concoct other worlds within our own. Animation condenses this shattering of nature in its various articulations (cel, stop-motion, CGI), as the objects and scenarios of its invented worlds are broken down into still frames or discontinuous gestures to be ushered into movement, set up as gags, or whirled into abstract plays of color and line. The movement is in the image—and it is in the action of morphing the real into the drawn, caricatured, reinterpreted, subjectified world. In Disney's *Snow White and the Seven Dwarfs* (1937), the dwarfs crowd at the foot of Snow White's bed, their noses drooped over the bedstead; each face is a little different from the others, but all are echoed in the surrounding features of the cottage (fig. 1). The differences among them are minute, and therein lies their significance. Such small differences, such tiny movements of form or type—which also involve other types of sameness in extended identifications across the animal, vegetable, and mineral kingdoms—are the very stuff of animation, just as much as the wild imaginings of unrecognizable worlds or the blazes of abstract light and sound.

Animation presents us with the illusion of movement, with a moving illusion, but there is another resonance to this. The movement of illusion proposes a dislocation of illusion—its moving off, its giving way as the animation concentrates the chimera to the point of dispelling it. That which is animated acts as if real, for it is moving and acting in the world of the animation. And yet the exaggerations and impossible gestures make plain that what occurs is of a different quality than what exists in the world outside the animation. We know it to be an illusion on two levels: first, that which is animated does not move itself; second, its world exists only for it and not for us. We are disillusioned. Animation questions the givens of nature not only in its altered physics, but also in its meshings of human and animal, its coalescences of machines and bodies. Nature is manipulated through its redrawing or remodeling, not in order to crush it, but rather—sometimes literally—to give voice to it. Animation deals in nature but reinvents it or sees it through different eyes. The illusion that is presented in animation comes back to itself as commentary and as critique of the world that is not depicted as such but lampooned. Animation cannot help but reflect on nature, or cause us to reflect on those worlds that we might inhabit, if only in dreams. The enchantedness of the motile image, which seems self-motivated, is dispersed in implausibilities—weird hybrids, overstretched

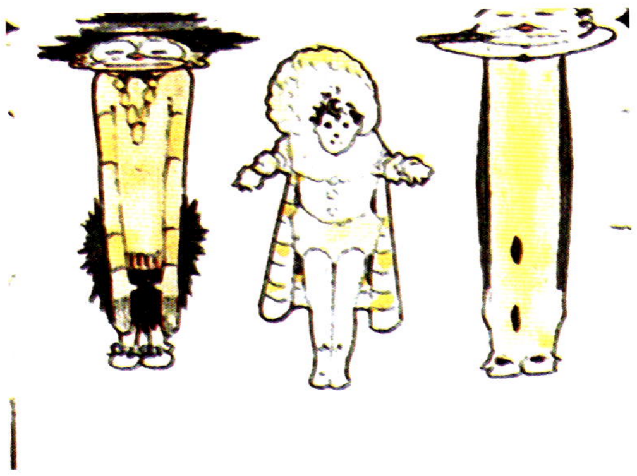

Fig. 2. Hand-tinted frame enlargement from Winsor McCay's *Little Nemo*, 1911

limbs, bouncy bodies, cats that rebound after being run over, pixie boys who fly. In this, animation distinguishes itself from other modes of mechanical visual culture, which aim at the illusion of nature, even as they spin out absurd story lines and ideological fictions. This is not to say that animation does not draw from the energies of the actual world as it exists. Perhaps it does so even more than some other forms of culture.

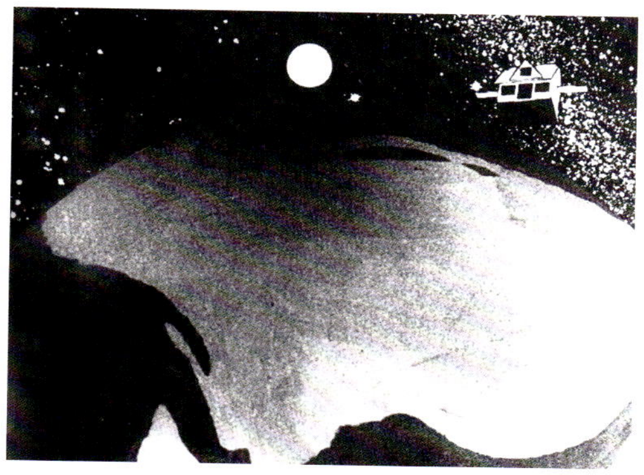

Fig. 3. Still from Winsor McCay's *The Flying House*, 1921

Modern metropolitan life—hurried, technological, fragmented, alienating, transient—gave birth to new cultural forms: illustrated magazines, radio, pulp fiction, movies, newspaper comic strips, and cartoons. Winsor McCay's comic strip *Little Nemo in Slumberland*, for example, envisions an unconscious modernity in formation. Beginning in 1905, the weekly dream escapades of Little Nemo drew newspaper readers into the unconscious of a snoozing boy working over the rhythms of urban life. The strips revel in the disquiets and utopian aspirations of an audience exposed to rapid change. Slumberland is a dream world, but it is also the world as it is experienced in all its intensity, transformation, choppy pace, adventurousness, and instability. Slumberland's cities are literally set in motion, with walking, growing, and shrinking buildings. From 1911 McCay was also an animator (fig. 2). His first animation depicted the translation of Little Nemo to the screen, as live-action footage shows animators conspiring to give flat shapes life and color, which they then accomplish through a series of bodily squeezings and stretchings. There is barely a plot; in fact, it displays nothing more than the key principles of cartooning: colorfulness, transformation, and motion.

In 1921, McCay made short animations titled *The Pet* and *The Flying House*, based on his *Dream of the Rarebit Fiend* comic strip, which ran from 1904 to the 1920s (fig. 3). That same year, Man Ray had announced to Tristan Tzara that all of New York was Dada and would not tolerate or notice a rival in the shape of the art movement Dada.[9] Animation, which thrived in the city in this period, could well lay claim to being a populist form of Dada. Like *Little Nemo*, McCay's films delimited the madness within a dream, but the elaborately detailed environments stalked by monster pets or whizzed over by a swooping house seemingly gave vent to everyday anxieties about out-of-control technologies, war, profiteering, impending apocalypse, and attack from vague but invincible threats.

Tapping into similar anxieties brought on by rapid technological change, Walt Disney's *Plane Crazy* (1928; fig. 4) opens with a scene of Taylorized labor.[10] The demands of labor under new conditions of industrial life apparently go so far as to insist that one of the workers coil himself inside the machine like an elastic band in order to make the plane fly. The apparatus starts, stops, and then goes out of control, becoming a vehicle of brutal interpersonal relations, as Mickey Mouse attempts to kiss an entrapped and unwilling Minnie Mouse. She attacks him and leaps from the plane, leading him to crash to the ground. The machine sends them to their doom. In the face of it, the characters lose control. The entire world—including a church spire—genuflects before this machine as it races through the sky.

As much as cartoons presented the impossible, they also reflected the rhythms and tensions of the modern world. Our modern viewing selves were shaped in the dots and lines and jerky, saccadic rhythms of cartoons, as well as in their seriality and their inhumaneness. For all the emphasis on animation's quest for liveliness, depth, and development, it remains movement mobilized by a machine; its vision of the actor in its world is as a mark, a point, a streak, both reduced and extended. And it is in this that animation articulates, in the animated overliveliness of everything—especially of that which is not human—the real illusion that is the secret of commodity fetishism: Things, or commodities, exert more effects on the world than people. The truth of who has agency, who has productive capacity, creativity, and value, is concealed in this mechanism of fetishism.

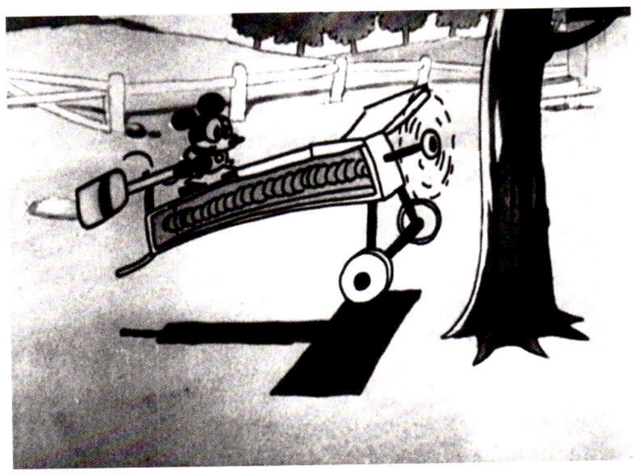

Fig. 4. Still from Walt Disney and Ub Iwerk's *Plane Crazy*, 1928

Animation is a lively and versatile form, continually adapting to new technologies and contexts. It migrated from parlors to cinemas and settled on TV. In 1928 the animated character Felix the Cat was one of the first test images broadcast to an electric kinescope receiver, thereby inaugurating the televisual age.[11] The thirteen-inch papier-mâché Felix, mounted to a turntable, warms up under the lights for broadcast. The viewers sit rapt before the box. In time, the TV fizzes with energy and life, and the humans sink into their sofas, rooted to the spot, as they watch Felix gyrate on the screen. The cartoon cat and the box in the corner become domesticated. Animation did not become a regular feature in this medium until the 1950s, but once it arrived, it remained. Today, animation is even more pervasive, on television, in the movies, on our computers, in our devices.

Contemporary touchscreen technologies—which rely on the merging of eye and hand—deliver synesthetic saturation through images, colors, sounds, and stimulations, returning our attention to the ways that color and light in motion engage with questions of life, labor, memory, self-formation, production, and sensuous experience. The touchscreen is the surface on which we work, shop, and learn—at all hours. It is the screen on which our photographs are displayed and through which we record our lives and the lives of others. It is the place of distraction, of idle games and shocking news. It is a sensitive surface that reflects all aspects of our existence. Goethe's finger sweeping across the image on a glass surface returns, though the mechanism of image production is now sealed below the screen. Every day we experience multicolored liquid crystals twirling at our fingertips before eyes that are seldom turned away. When an electrical charge shoots through them, these tiny animated forms rotate—as though they have bodies hit by Tasers and wracked with pain—to elicit hues that approximate those in nature.

Animation, especially in its liquid crystal forms, is pervasive. These days animation proposes modes of being. It fabricates second lives. It calculates our risks and conveys or mitigates violence. Animation distracts and entices. Always intimate with the commodity through advertising, animation now sells future lives, as developers use it to visualize the enclaves they plan to build. Animation has found in art not a rival but a home, as artists gravitate toward this seductive, endlessly reinventable, yet familiar form. Animation is part of our pasts, even as it models our futures. Animation is the patina that will coat these futures with projections of enlivened surfaces through Oculus Rift, Project Morpheus, Magic Leap, augmented and virtual-reality technologies that merge data with real-world environments, immersing the viewer-participant. These devices bejewel the landscapes of tomorrow (while also potentially weaponizing them). Animation becomes serious games with virtual worlds whose edges are remote, and which, as much as they lure us in and distract us, also provide new capacities for disruption. In the future, landscapes may be solely composed of physical materials and virtual data. At the interfaces between the two, havoc can be wrought, as in the animation project by Will Gowland, titled *HERE BE DRAGONS: The Unstable Landscapes of GPS* (fig. 5).[12] Digitally animated "protest icebergs" are calculated to interfere with the paths of oil tankers, which track their way through the seas by a reliance not on

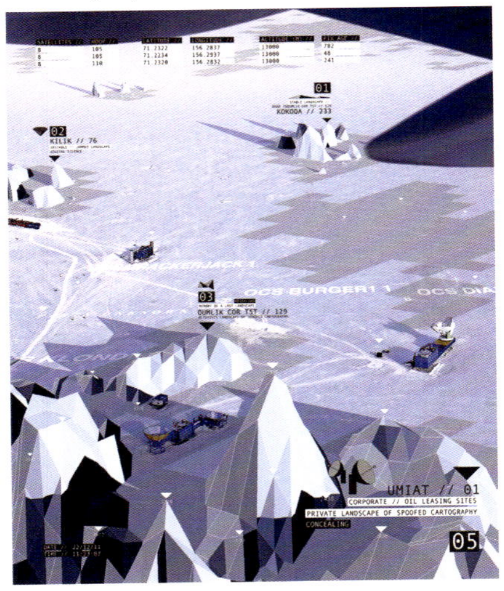

Fig. 5. Still from Will Gowland's *HERE BE DRAGONS: The Unstable Landscapes of GPS; Digital Mountains of the National Petroleum Reserve*, Barrow, Alaska, June 22, 2012

reading the tides and the environment but rather through the data provided by GPS.

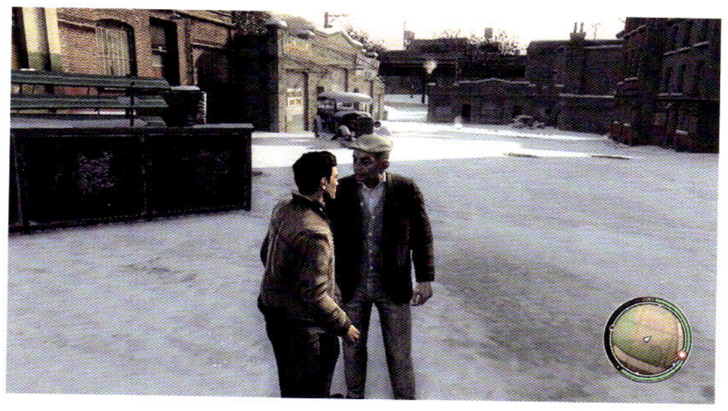

Fig. 6. Harun Farocki (1944–2014), still from *Parallel IV*, 2014. High-definition video, color, sound; 15:53 min.

In the animated afterworlds of the digital epoch, new rules emerge and new material for cinema arises, or at least the old falls away. With electronic money, will there be no bank heists? With Google cars, no car chases? With Tinder, no romcoms? Animation in some form or other might train us in these new landscapes of "second nature," these second lives, this new ontology of data that is mined, grown, and harvested. But the affect remains as it has always been for the viewer—a kind of mobility, a swinging over the scene that is sometimes impeded, as in the strange, ever-effortful figures of video games. Sometimes the viewer is swung along through the movement, not of a camera, but of something like one. And in each case the perspective is always ready again to swoop and be swooped over terrains, tracking, traveling, fluid, mobile, able to see things or nothingness, the end of things from the other side, beneath the water where there is nothing or where something is put. That was always the interest of animation—that it might reveal the impossible, which has yet a precise logic or a wishful truthfulness.

Any animation primer teaches about the reverberation of *anima*, or breath, in animation. Animation is a question of life impelled, brought into being illusionistically. But it is also—or has become, or was always—a question of life itself. What is animated has life, or at least the impression of it. Through a microscope, a hundred years ago or today, we can watch a chemical compound agitating, moving, developing, producing its own story as it forms and reforms in oil. Is it life? Is it synthetic life? Is it animation? And what new natures—inner ones, impossible ones, digital ones—might be revealed under and through and in front of the lens. Our nature is ever regenerating, ever drawing in and on states of matter, transforming the world through energetic deployments, circuiting back, reaching tipping points, once and again.

NOTES

1. A thaumatrope is paper disc with a picture on either side, which, when spun by attached strings, resolves two images into one through persistence of vision.

2. *Goethe's Theory of Colours*, trans. with notes by Charles Lock Eastlake (London: John Murray, 1840), para. 455, p. 189.

3. Ibid., para. 458, pp. 190–91.

4. Guy de Maupassant, *The Complete Works: Short Stories, Novels, Plays, Poetry, Memoirs and More* (e-artnow, 2015), n.p.

5. Walter Benjamin, "One-Way Street," in *Selected Writings*, vol. 1, *1913–1926*, ed. Marcus Paul Bullock and Michael W. Jennings (Cambridge, MA: Belknap Press of Harvard University Press, 1996), p. 476.

6. A colloquial name for neon.

7. S. M. Eisenstein, *Eisenstein on Disney*, ed. Jay Leyda (Calcutta: Seagull Books, 1986), p. 3.

8. Ibid., p. 24.

9. The letter is reproduced in Amelia Jones, *Irrational Modernism: A Neurasthenic History of New York Dada* (Cambridge, MA: MIT Press, 2004), p. 4.

10. Taylorism, or "scientific management," was a method of increasing industrial efficiency designed by Frederick Winslow Taylor at the turn of the twentieth century. One aspect of Taylorism involved breaking down the production process into small and standardized tasks performed by a series of workers.

11. *Felix Gets Broadcasted* is the title of a 1923 cartoon in which Felix is lured into electric wires and squeezed through them to Egypt. Five years later he would have a different broadcast experience.

12. See Will Gowland, *HERE BE DRAGONS* (2012), williamgowland.co.uk.

## Embodied Differences: Monsters, Cyborgs, and Cinema

Karen Archey

As a child, you pay little attention to your body until it starts to change, slowly at first, and then with bursts of blood and hormones coupled with paralyzing confusion and self-consciousness. These changes—the stuff that elevates puberty into a cultural narrative—feel both as impossible and as impending as the change of seasons. And then, without permission, our bodies break, age, or deform, losing synch with our minds—if they were ever connected to begin with.

There's something ineffable about the body, its processes, decisions, and otherness. As much as we feel at home in our own skin—or at least jailed in a familiar cell—we develop thoughts and prejudices against our bodies as they become unwittingly coded with societal ciphers. Sometimes we are surprised by what our bodies do, developing cancer or breeding infection. Those of us with monstrous, uncooperative, or diseased bodies have become accustomed to our social othering: the preconceived notions heaped upon us based on our appearance as signified by sex, class, racial, and other markers, no matter how our outward appearance might seem mismatched with our subjectivity.

It goes without saying that the Caucasian male is the neutral ideal while the female is rooted in otherness and peculiarity. Simone de Beauvoir writes in *The Second Sex* that men represent both the positive and the neuter so much that the word *hommes* also means "human beings," while "woman" represents negativity and "any determination is imputed to her as a limitation, without reciprocity."[1]

Our collective readings of the body are reinforced from a young age, silently passed down through generations. The archetypes relating to sexual difference evolve at a snail's pace, and it has taken us the better part of centuries to locate and dismantle them as social myths rather than scientific fact. De Beauvoir writes that the essentialisms attached to womanhood, Judaism, and blackness have faded since the time of Saint Thomas, when they were "defined with as much certainty as the sedative quality of a poppy." Instead, today we consider gender to be situational, a performance detached from a person's biological sex. De Beauvoir writes, "If there is no such thing today as femininity, it is because there never was."[2]

Though gender-based essentialisms have lost footing in science, related clichés have maintained a strong hold on Western culture, reappearing ad nauseam in literature, music, and cinema to the point of becoming instructive. Cinema, with its ability to reproduce embodied behaviors, is particularly suited to routinely confer and perpetuate notions of sexual difference and gender-coded behavior. In her essay "Visual Pleasure and Narrative Cinema," Laura Mulvey writes of the psychological experience of watching mainstream film and its soothing effect of recalling familiar archetypes. She states that the voyeuristic distance of the body from the screen begets a psychological separation between the ego and the screen's subject, which cultivates the ego's ideal version of the world in a private harmony.[3] In an industry where the overwhelming majority of films are directed by Caucasian males, this ideal worldview most often perpetuates the centrality of white male experience and casts women and people of color as auxiliary characters or sexual objects. Should one need any proof that the centrality of the white male is a crisis in mainstream filmmaking, look no further than the Oscars: in 2015 and 2016, not a single actor of color was nominated by the Academy. Further, nearly half of all movies made in 2014 didn't pass the Bechdel test, which simply requires that a film have at least two women in it who talk to each other about something other than a man.[4]

As women have historically been excluded from self-representation in all forms of culture, writing realistic portrayals of feminine (or differently gendered, nonmale) experiences is a political act. In *Laugh of the Medusa* (1976), Hélène Cixous writes that "Woman must write her self: must write about women and bring women to writing, from which they have been driven away as violently as from their bodies—for the same reasons, by the same law, with the same fatal goal. Woman must put herself into the text—as into the world and into history—by her own movement."[5] The imperative to write woman into existence by literature, song, or art has since become a feminist mandate. The artists discussed below—Valie Export, Lynn Hershman Leeson, Hito Steyerl, Andrea Crespo, Dora Budor, and Ivana Bašić—all consider the public display of embodied differences as a political act.

In 1969, the Austrian artist Valie Export walked into a Munich art-house cinema wearing pants with the crotch cut out, revealing her hairy vagina. A mostly male group of experimental

Fig. 1. Valie Export (b.1940), *Abrundung (Rounding Off)*, 1976. Gelatin silver print, 8 x 10 in. (20.3 x 25.4 cm)

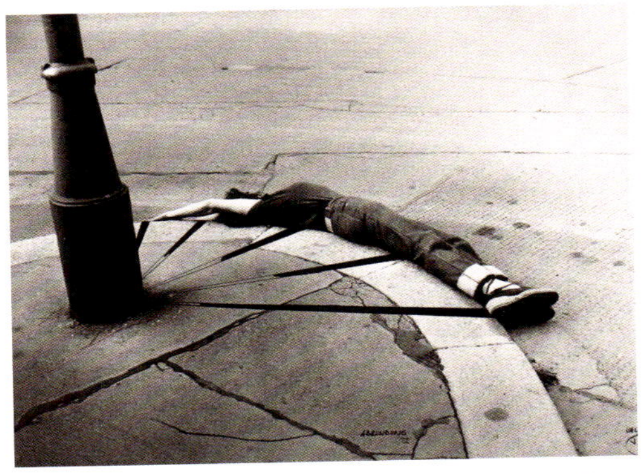

filmmakers was showing its work, and as the audience was seated it was confronted with the "reality" of Export's genitalia. Titled *Action Pants: Genital Panic*, this performance juxtaposed an actual vagina as a symbol of womanhood with the cinema as a public space that confers and perpetuates the idealization of the female body through the imagination of men. Similarly, in *Tap and Touch Cinema* (1968), a topless Export wore a cardboard box in Munich's Stachus public square, where she invited the public to touch her breasts. Like Export's revealing of her vagina in *Action Pants*, the tactile experience of the female body was meant to act as an antidote to the male voyeuristic fantasy in cinema.

In her *Körperkonfigurationen (Body Configurations)* of 1972–76, Export inserted herself into the skeleton of the city, rather than the cinema, lying on the ground, coiling her body around Munich's public architecture. In the photograph *Abrundung (Rounding Off)* (1976; fig. 1), Export lies on her side, arms outstretched, and curls herself around a curb. Drawn on the photograph are lines emanating from a nearby lamppost connecting to points from her fingertips to her toes, suggesting a dissolving of figure and architecture. Using her own body to flatten public and cinematic space, Export suggests that these are sites in which female self-identification is a charged, perhaps impossible, act. In the repressive climate of postwar Munich and Vienna, Export's feminist works examined the agency of women in the public sphere as well as the role of a largely misogynist cultural imagination in public and private life.

Export's works expand on cinema's relationship to male fantasy, voyeurism, and the popular representation of women and point to the reality of the body to deflate these projections. This was an important task for second-wave feminism, and one that set up the subsequent query: What if I don't want to identify as female at all? How can I emancipate myself from the so-called "natural" origins and limitations of my body? From the 1960s onward, the cyborg has become a central cultural allegory through which to understand the body in a society increasingly marked by advancements in info- and biotechnology.

The term *cyborg* was coined in 1960 by scientists Manfred E. Clynes and Nathan S. Kline as space exploration was becoming a reality. They proposed the term to describe "the exogenously extended organizational complex functioning as an integrated homeostatic system unconsciously."[6] In 1983, Donna Haraway published her essay "Cyborg Manifesto," in which she writes, "Our best machines are made of sunshine; they are all light and clean because they are nothing but signals, electromagnetic waves, a section of a spectrum, and these machines are eminently portable, mobile—a matter of immense human pain in Detroit and Singapore. People are nowhere near so fluid, being both material and opaque. Cyborgs are ether, quintessence."[7] In Haraway's conceptualization, the body is not immaterial or dematerialized, but actually fully materialized in the form of lines and fiber optics.

New media art pioneer Lynn Hershman Leeson was already thinking about cyborgs and the burgeoning biotechnology industry in the mid-1960s, a few years after the term was coined. In the early part of the decade, Leeson was experiencing breathing difficulties due to a heart ailment, and she looked to the cyborg as an evolutionary potentiality. She was living in Los Angeles, where smog was an ever-present issue, and she "focused on breathing because that was all I could do."[8] In 1963, Leeson was photocopying an image of a woman when the paper caught in the Xerox machine's internal mechanisms and the woman's image spat out as a "crumpled smear of technology." This prompted her series of cyborg drawings that envision women as invincible creatures cobbled together from flesh and technological bits. *Smog Protector* (1970) combines a drawing of a woman in a bathing suit and cap with diagrams relating to various cyborgian air-filtration systems—she bears a heat-resistant adhesive shield and filters air via pores.

In *Breathing Machine II* (1968; fig. 2), a wax face donning a wig is encased in a motion-sensitive vitrine, which emanates breathing sounds as viewers pass by. Butterflies and feathers adorn the mummified face as if in a funeral rite for a barely alive organism. The animals in this work are meant to reference the transmutation of species—an evolutionary theory predating Charles Darwin's natural selection that supposed one species could transform into another. Eighteenth-century evolutionary theory did much to suggest that Caucasian men are quantifiably superior to others, with women, people of color, and the disabled being evolutionally closest to animals. Writes Rosi Braidotti, "Linnaeus, in his classification system of all living beings, assumes a hierarchical relationship between the races, which was to become central to the European world-view. Thus, in the tenth edition of his *Systema naturae* (1759), Linnaeus postulates a race called *homo monstrous*, which is one of the branches of *homo sapiens*, living in remote regions of the earth."[9] Against this backdrop, Leeson's *Breathing Machines* act as mutant beings that breathe themselves into existence as a radical act.

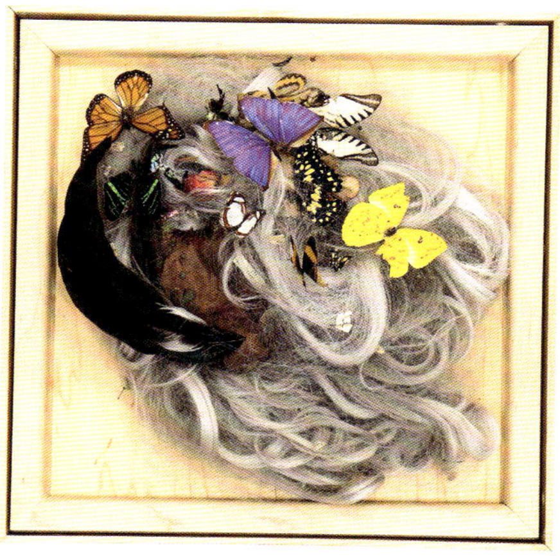

Fig. 2. Lynn Hershman Leeson (b. 1941), *Breathing Machine II*, 1968. Wax face, wig, paint, butterflies, feathers, sensors, sound, wood base, and acrylic hood, 13 x 16 ½ x 16 ½ in. (33 x 41.9 x 41.9 cm)

Hito Steyerl's 2015 *Factory of the Sun* updates cyborg theory to address more contemporary concerns—namely, omnipresent surveillance and the debt economy. The video features protagonist Yulia, a video game designer, and her brother, the Internet dance sensation TSC, or "takesomecrime," in a game-ified, half-CGI world haunted by high-frequency trading algorithms (fig. 3). The title is a direct reference to a line in Haraway's "Cyborg Manifesto," "Our best machines are made of sunshine." *Factory of the Sun* begins with Steyerl's voice repeating the mantra-like statement, "Our machines are made of pure sunlight . . . sunshine is our factory . . . all photos are created equal." The video cuts to Yulia, who is wearing a gold catsuit and says, "Hello, my name is Yulia. I am coding a game called Factory of the Sun. But you will not be able to play this game. It will play you."

The video focuses primarily on Yulia and TSC's biography growing up as orphans after their other family members are murdered at the Soviet-Chinese border as enemies of Stalinism. From early childhood, Yulia and TSC are raised in an orphanage called "Orphans of the Enemy," later moving to Israel and then Canada. And yet, true to Steyerl's maverick video practice, *Factory of the Sun* positions Yulia and TSC's exceedingly specific background into a universally relatable story through the blending of various leitmotifs and filmmaking genres. Steyerl weaves together interviews, science-fiction fantasy game animation, and a metadocumentary of the filmmaking process to create a nonlinear narrative about these two remarkable siblings, who in adulthood now live in an environment marked by the debt economy. The real-life, high-frequency, liquidity-seeking trading algorithms Sniper (Credit Suisse) and Stealth SuperX Plus (Deutsche Bank) pop up in Steyerl's video in a game environment as disembodied Stalin heads that attempt to shoot you. The ideas of death and transformation through trauma are major threads in Steyerl's work, and are usually portrayed as a joyful process. Haraway writes, "By the late twentieth century, our time, a mythic time, we are all chimeras, theorized and fabricated hybrids of machine and organism. In short, we are cyborgs."[10]

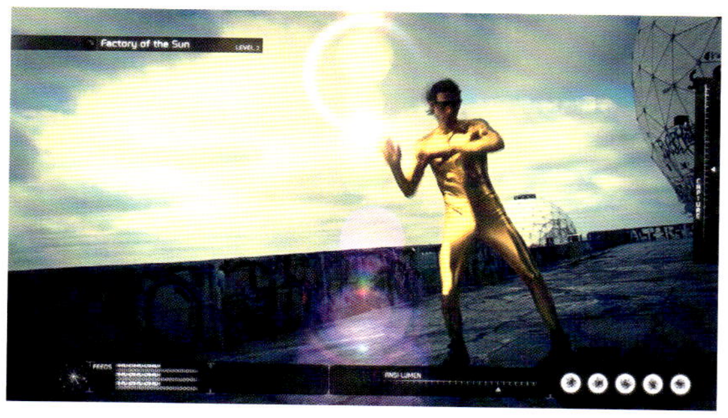


Fig. 3. Hito Steyerl (b. 1966), still from *Factory of the Sun*, 2015. Video, color, sound; 22:56 min., looped; with environment

In recent years, Steyerl's videos have taken form as installations that span entire rooms, often with custom seating and architectural components. For the German Pavilion at the 2015 Venice Biennale, *Factory of the Sun* was installed as an environment marked by a luminescent grid recalling an early vector-monitor/CGI-surface grid dotted with beach chairs (pp. 102–105). In this constellation, the viewer's body is fully immersed in the installation; Steyerl's dystopic world ruled by chimeric algorithms extends from the screen to meet the viewer. It imbricates us in associations that are in one sense fantastical, and in another, all too real.

For artists born in the 1980s and 1990s, the cyborg is a legendary cultural allegory pioneered by mid-to-late-twentieth-century second-wave feminists. The historical contributions of these women artists are both lauded and seen as deeply flawed: too much heed was paid to the white, cisgendered, conventionally attractive and able female body. We now understand that the exclusive visibility of these "normative" bodies alienates others, and even serves patriarchal ends. Artists and other creative producers can still resuscitate the cultural image of the cyborg, with its concomitant associations, to include an element of twentieth-century nostalgia in their work. In a younger generation, however, we can detect a collective interest in bodies that are traditionally othered: transgendered, nonwhite, fat, ugly, needy, deformed, and monstrous bodies.

Deformed bodies, in particular, provoke unbridled curiosity in most people. Braidotti writes that the fascination and disdain with which teratological deformities (those formed in the womb) have been met stem from an intense desire to understand their causes lest such things happen to one's own kin. This epistemophilia (love of knowing) arises from a historical and deep-seated mistrust in women's ability to procreate, as the mother is often blamed for prenatal deformities. Thus, the idea of the monstrous body is particularly tied to womanhood because "the child's entire morphological destiny is played out during conception and the period of gestation."[11]

While the cyborg bears more recent and specific emancipatory cultural associations, the monstrous body is a much older negative archetype that recurs in freak shows and in film, particularly anime and science fiction, and has only recently been considered an empowering allegory. Andrea Crespo's *parabiosis* videos focus on communities that congregate on user-generated art websites such as DeviantArt to draw characters that are conjoined or have multiple appendages. DeviantArt largely hosts amateur anime drawings, a genre that is fascinated with teratological and biological transformations—usually into something monstrous or abject. Crespo centers her attention on this community because it represents a seldom-understood subjectivity: many of the artists who create twinned or conjoined characters on DeviantArt are either physically disabled or have mental health disorders such as autism or dissociative personality disorder, or simply feel disenfranchised. Members' fascination sometimes goes beyond drawing and into a morbid obsession with the idea of becoming a conjoined twin, or with fetishizing actual conjoined twins. Others develop a pornographic interest in amputees or those with teratological bodies. Some become so obsessed with achieving physical deformity that they maim or blind themselves—a condition known as disintegrity disorder. For others, the fascination with deformed bodies has a more spiritual motivation separate from disintegrity disorder.

Crespo's video *parabiosis: neurolibidinal induction complex 2.2* (2015; fig. 4 and pp. 94–95) opens with a black background punctuated by lines of light. A scanner bar slowly pulls across the screen, as if marking one's entrance to a portal, while an ambient soundtrack squeaks and drones. Paced by the hypnotic, luminescent scanner bar, the monochromatic video bears both a clinical and science-fiction feel. A puzzle piece breaks off from its set as the scanner bar again wipes the scene clear and starts anew, as if denoting a hypnotic, ritualistic entrance into DeviantArt. Graphs representing cellular processes and psychological disorders fade in and out, interspersed with tracings of manga drawings of conjoined

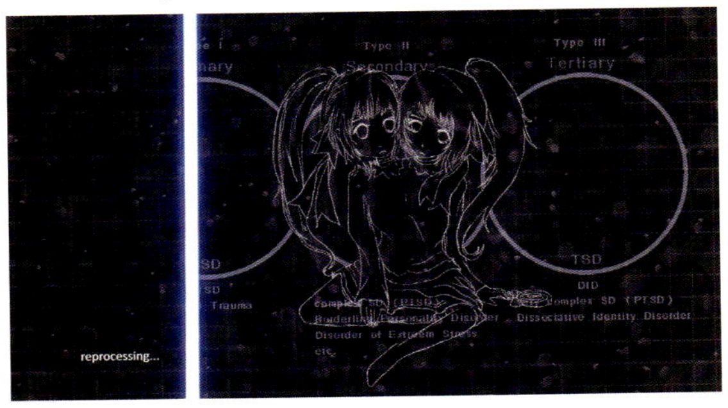


Fig. 4. Andrea Crespo (b. 1993), still from *parabiosis: neurolibidinal induction complex 2.2*, 2015. Video, color, sound; 11:12 min.

twins as well as a series of words that appear on the screen: "Wandering . . . mirroring . . . dissolving . . . breathing . . . encoding . . . you are flowing . . . return . . . you are emanating . . . softly emanating . . . you are never alone . . . you are a signal." The idea of being a signal is one that harkens again to Haraway's "Cyborg Manifesto." In an understated narrative arc, the video's subject—or perhaps multiple subjects—finds itself newly at home in itself, segmented. "Wandering . . . you are splitting . . . forgetting . . . replicating . . . duplicating . . . you are a signal . . . never alone . . . always together."

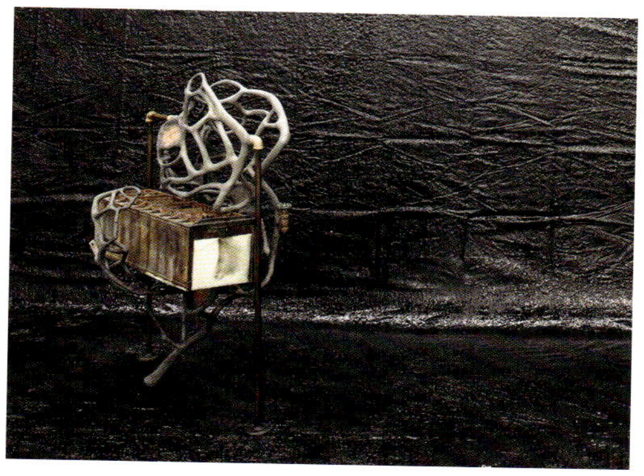

Fig. 5. Dora Budor (b.1984), *What Kind of a Person Does This*, 2015. Screen-used miniature living container from *Johnny Mnemonic* (1995), steel armature, epoxy clay, infected silicone prosthetics, acrylic polymer with pigment suspension, SFX paint, weathering paint, and assorted metal hardware, 45 ⅝ x 37 ¾ x 21 ¼ in. (116 x 96 x 54 cm)

The work of both Crespo and Haraway contains a clear call for a sort of ethereal solidarity. For Haraway, the cyborg emancipates the body from its natural origins—it is a death knell to sex-positive "goddess feminism" and suggests, not a worshiping of traits traditionally considered female, but rather a total reconsideration of the body, its definition and peripheries. For Crespo, the massive population that inhabits online communities such as DeviantArt proves that the preexisting modes for expressing alternative, teratological subjectivity are insufficient. Given that teratological bodies are still the subject of such disdain, one could argue that it took the Internet to provide a meeting place for those who identify with inhabiting such bodies.

Artist Dora Budor examines fantastical disembodied teratology—black ooze, warty skin, disintegrating bodies—as ideological connotations at play in the aesthetics and production of popular science fiction, particularly as a responsive anxiety to the earth's rapidly changing climate. Rather than working through film, Budor takes real props from popular science-fiction movies, often found on collectibles websites, and melds them into sculpture for the striking bodily reaction these images beget.

*Spring*, her 2015 exhibition at Swiss Institute in New York, was installed in the basement boiler room—the metaphorical circulatory system or spine of the building. Budor designed metal-pipe structures that look like hybrids of heating units and biological circulatory systems to engulf props that are architectural miniatures from movies of the 1990s (fig. 5). These included a garage into which Bruce Willis drove a flying car in *The Fifth Element* (1997), a Gotham City rooftop from *Batman Returns* (1992), and two living containers from *Johnny Mnemonic* (1995). That these props are all pre-Y2K mean that the vision of the future imbued in them—our present—involves widespread environmental ruin and decay, some of which has come true. They are instilled with a fake age—the futuristic era they are meant to inhabit—but also with a real age, meaning when they were fabricated. Miniatures have lost favor with special effects artists as CGI has become increasingly less expensive and more realistic, so that these objects have a vintage quality to contemporary viewers. Due to their miniature scale, viewers can also easily imagine themselves inside these scenes.

Covering the walls and floor of the Swiss Institute was a black varnish goo, which Budor envisioned as an engulfing, infectious life-form—a rogue version out of which humans grew in the primordial earth. The menacing black goo is a well-worn cinematic trope—see *Prometheus* (2012) or *Under the Skin* (2013)—that has now become a reality; due to virulent bacteria growth catalyzed by global warming, ancient Chilean mummies are now decomposing into black goo, blending cinematic fiction with reality.

Budor's installation *Kata Doksa* (2014, pp.100–101) functions as a bioreactive organism that responds, via fluctuations in light, to human movement. Its ceiling features frogs from Paul Thomas Anderson's 1999 movie *Magnolia* that are cast in resin in such a way that it appears that they are falling into the beds of a fluorescent light fixture. The frog as cultural allegory is both biblical, as in the story of the plagues of Egypt in the book of Exodus, and contemporary, as it has become a widespread symbol of ecological frailty. Underlying the visions of the future in the films from

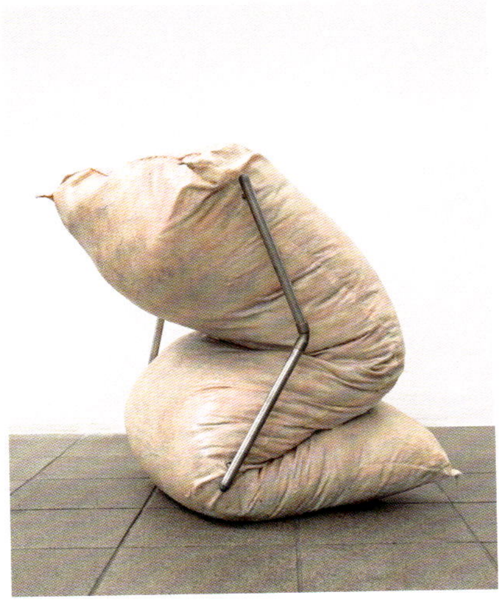

Fig. 6. Ivana Bašić (b. 1986), *Fantasy vanishes in flesh III*, 2015. Feathers, cotton, stainless steel, and silicone, 16 ⅞ x 19 ⅝ x 19 ⅝ in. (43 x 50 x 50 cm)

which Budor borrows is a paranoia that should we not curtail our prodigal consumption, we are doomed to an ecological dystopia. Budor takes the ontological shock we experience from fantastical teratology—humans turning into giant flies and the like—and removes it from the realm of social rejection, repurposing it as a parable for the increasingly disfigured earth.

Looking back to the body proper, the work of Ivana Bašić envisions the body as a monstrous, ineffable container at odds with the mind. Skin is sloughed off in sheets of blushing silicone, draped around makeshift bones, stuffed with feathers or pierced and propped up on titanium stilts. Bašić's work draws from her experiences as a child growing up in war-torn former Yugoslavia, where death was an imminent reality, and perhaps distinct from a specifically feminist mission, speaks to the universality of feeling entombed in one's own flesh. She depicts the body in a state of pain or dying, yet with no blood except for contusions inflicted from the inside. All suffering is internalized, kept in the inescapable hermetic space delineated by our skin. Though the forms invoked by Bašić are at times otherworldly, her work responds to the fallacy of the singular, whole body, and its consequent otherness.

Bašić often creates metal armatures to act as crutches for her works, though they wound as much as they support. In *World is all of one skin* (2014), satin pillows printed with images of the artist's skin are pinned against a wall by titanium-coated stainless steel rods. The pillows are both impaled and supported by the titanium rods, which reference sterile medical bone implants. *Fantasy vanishes in flesh* (2015; fig. 6) consists of three silicone-coated body pillows hand-painted in trompe l'oeil to appear as contused, varicose skin. The body pillows are arranged to describe a death scene, as one is curled into fetal position, while the others look on in mourning. Bašić psychically animates her works, speaking as if they were sentient entities that she brings to life and nurtures. "In all of my work I create these armatures to prop up these sick, dying bodies," she said in a recent studio visit. These works manifest a pathetic body, one in which pain and suffering are not hidden but foregrounded.

*SOMA*, an ongoing digital work begun in 2013, is an exhaustive, state-of-the-art 3D model of the artist's entire body using high-definition images (pp. 86, 87). The model, sold through an online store, is film- and animation-ready and could even be used in 3D pornography, should the purchaser desire. Bašić saw creating an exact, realistic replica of herself as a way of being freed from her own body, appearance, and mortality, as well as a way toward anonymity and multiplicity. The idea that there is a oneness between the mind and body is a fallacy to Bašić. Rather than fearing a technology-driven collapse of privacy, Bašić chose the opposite—to become a multiple, fully embedded in public space. If traditional film and cinema have historically chained female and othered bodies to their limiting, conventional representations, the Internet has given back some control to individuals seeking self-representation.

While repressive scientific notions such as eugenics and Linneaus's *homo monstrous* have become a thing of the past, their societal effects live on. Across decades and cultural and technological conditions, the artists presented here highlight embodied differences as a political act in solidarity with other monstrous bodies—disabled bodies, nonsexual women's bodies, black bodies, and transgender bodies—all of which are still marginalized by popular culture. Perhaps through writing them into existence, as a form of cultural exposure therapy, they will become not monstrous, but just bodies.

NOTES

1. Simone de Beauvoir, *The Second Sex*, trans. Constance Borde and Sheila Malovany-Chevallier (New York: Vintage, 2011), p. 5.
2. Ibid., pp. 3–4.
3. Laura Mulvey, "Visual Pleasure and Narrative Cinema," *Screen* 16, no. 3 (Fall 1975), pp. 6–18.
4. Andrew Pulver, "Films That Pass the Bechdel Test Plummet in 2014," *The Guardian*, March 24, 2015. The test is named after the American cartoonist and graphic novelist Alison Bechdel, who first proposed it in 1985 in her comic strip *Dykes to Watch Out For*.
5. Hélène Cixous, "Laugh of the Medusa," *Signs* 1, no. 4 (Summer 1976), p. 875.
6. Manfred E. Clynes and Nathan S. Kline, "Cyborgs and Space," *Astronautics* (September 1960), p. 27.
7. Donna Haraway, "A Cyborg Manifesto: Science, Technology, and Socialist-Feminism in the Late Twentieth Century," in *The Cybercultures Reader*, ed. David Bell and Barbara M. Kennedy (New York; Routledge, 2000), p. 294.
8. Lynn Hershman Leeson, interview with the author, December 14, 2015.
9. Rosi Braidotti, "Signs of Wonder and Traces of Doubt: On Teratology and Embodied Differences," in *Feminist Theory and the Body: A Reader*, ed. Janet Price and Margrit Shildrick (Edinburgh: Edinburgh University Press, 1999), p. 295
10. Haraway, "A Cyborg Manifesto," p. 292.
11. Braidotti, "Signs of Wonder and Traces of Doubt," p. 297.

## On the Logically Paradoxical Task of New Beginning

David Lewis

*Initium ergo ut esset, creatus est homo*
[That there be a beginning, man was created]
—Augustine, *The City of God*[1]

A dramatic shift has occurred in cinema away from a lens-, apparatus-, and theory-based set of practices and toward a model that instead emphasizes an intensity of aesthetic effects. This dominance of what might be called the sensorium leads to a different apprehension of space and, most crucially, a logically paradoxical revision of our idea of time. This essay will flesh out some of these patterns and possibilities, citing examples in chronological order and in ascending order of intensity.

Edwin S. Porter's *Coney Island at Night* (1905, pp. 2–3) serves as a good introduction, conceptually and chronologically, to the line of practice that we here seek to delineate. A dreamlike, nocturnal image of the Dreamland of Coney Island, Porter's film is dismissible, perhaps, as mere phantasmagoria. Its primary achievement is not epistemological, but rather technological (the display of the new medium of film) and aesthetic, meaning that it concerns the senses and perception. This shift from epistemology to aesthetics can also be described as a shift from the Enlightenment project of *knowledge* (and, with that, rational self-mastery) to one of *sensation*.

Of course, a shift from knowledge to sensation is itself a form of meaning or knowledge, however fleeting, paradoxical, or phantasmagorical. And this form of meaning is historical. The late stages of dying civilizations produce a pure and powerful form of *beginning*—of the power to begin. But this form of efficacy and practice is necessarily obscured by the spell cast by a more celebrated, better understood, and dominant form of decadence and meta-knowledge that also typifies late civilizations. So it will be necessary to briefly explore the entwined origins of these decadent forms.

The dominant, clearly visible decadent form of late civilizations is, roughly speaking, Mannerist or Hellenistic. In our own late-capitalist era this form finds a very clear father in the figure of Édouard Manet, to whom Baudelaire famously wrote: "You are only the *first* in the decrepitude of your art."[2] Manet was the dandified master of superior position that allows for the development of an extraordinary *meta-language* of art; an art of great power and truly—like that of Bronzino and Fiorentino—illimitable elegance and sophistication; an allegorical and ironic art. In his *Jesus Mocked by the Soldiers* (1865; fig. 1), for example, the Savior is clearly a model in a studio; the dream of paradise and salvation is reduced by the artist to theater, to sophisticated intellectual sport. The iconographic errors (Christ's wound is on the wrong side), the radical shift in facture and technique from section to section of the painting, build and simultaneously undermine empathy (or escape), rewarding an astute viewer with the pleasure of knowing oneself to be in a hall of intellectual mirrors—and knowing, haughtily, paradoxically, that that is all that remains to be known. Such an awareness of false consciousness is, according to many of the greatest modernist critics, the highest achievement of modern art. As Theodor Adorno put it: "All the paradoxes of art in high capitalism—and its very existence is a paradox—culminate in the single paradox that it speaks of the human by virtue of its reification, and that it is only through the perfection of its character as illusion that it partakes of truth."[3]

This model is beautiful and efficacious and almost classical now. It is present in contemporary art mostly by way of Martin Kippenberger and his Cologne circles and epigones and the sophisticated aesthetic grammar that has been expanded and developed for the past decade or more, demanding the attention of many of the most astute, ambitious artists and audiences in New York. This Kippenbergian form of dandified theatricality and self-knowing (the performance of meta-knowledge) is best described by way of David Joselit's 2009 essay "Painting Beside Itself."[4] A sophisticated painter in the past decade, Joselit argues, could not help but attempt to demonstrate his or her awareness of painting as an aspect of a networked system, and in doing so to provide—as did Manet—an articulation of art as theatrical meta-knowledge,

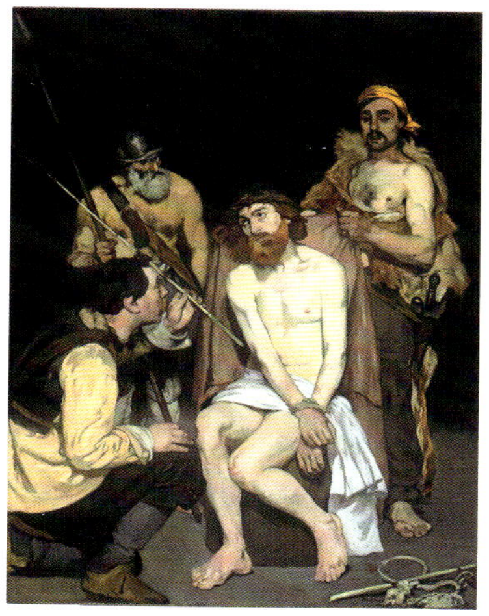

Fig. 1. Édouard Manet (1832–1883), *Jesus Mocked by the Soldiers*, 1865. Oil on canvas, 74 ⅞ x 58 ⅜ in. (188.8 x 147.7 cm) The Art Institute of Chicago; gift of James Deering 1925.703

a performance of theater about art's own parameters, limits, possibilities, dreams, belonging. Call this the masculine (dandified) form of decadence, or perhaps the solar form: the sun.

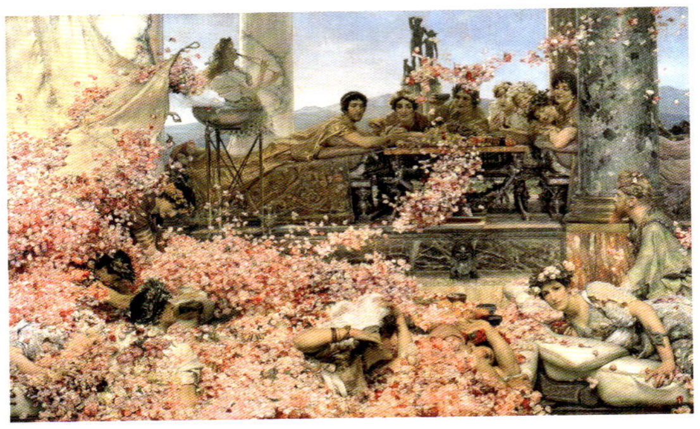

Fig. 2. Lawrence Alma-Tadema (1836–1912), *The Roses of Heliogabalus*, 1888. Oil on canvas, 52 3/16 x 84 3/8 in. (132.3 x 213.7) Perez Simon Collection

Imagine, though, in place of Manet, Lawrence Alma-Tadema's *The Roses of Heliogabalus* (1888; fig. 2). Instead of a hall of mirrors and the attendant sophistication thus far described, *The Roses of Heliogabalus* articulates both the power of technology (in this case, as archeological accuracy: What did antiquity actually look like?) and a reward that is primarily sensorial, not epistemological. This creates a paradox: Alma-Tadema's meticulous research leads to sensory abandon, while Manet's denial of that research creates meta-knowledge. But is Alma-Tadema's paradoxical form of intensity and abundance a matter of *mere* sensation, *mere* decadence? What additional, hidden power and possibilities might such a practice—this crystal, clasped at the neck of an invisible queen, this Mallarméan (because hidden) star—allow, or bring to light?

Let's call *Coney Island at Night*, *The Roses of Heliogabalus*, and related symbolist-modernist forms of decadence and synesthesia *preparatory*: They emphasize sensation rather than epistemology; they deploy research and technology in the service of *imagination*, and articulate a dream of sensory superabundance; they are only incidentally ironic. The limits of this preparatory system are demonstrated in the 1940 Disney film *Fantasia* (whose first sequence is a form of color music, the definitional modernist example of the preparatory system). There is no irony in *Fantasia*, nor any overt demonstration of meta-knowledge of dandified reflexivity. Instead, technical achievement (and the film was, for its time, technically extraordinary) and aesthetic intensity are at the service of *imagination*, and description. The aesthetic questions are not dialectical but rather imaginative: What would a prelapsarian fantasy world, set to the music of Beethoven, look and feel like? What would the death of the dinosaurs look and feel like?

Imagination can also be described as a dream of *life* (in the symbolic and vitalist sense of Friedrich Nietzsche's second "Untimely Meditation"), a task of bringing, by way of the technological possibilities of sensation, a dream (or reality) to life. The most famous sequence in this most famous of animated films, featuring Mickey Mouse and set to Paul Dukas's *L'apprenti sorcier* [The Sorcerer's Apprentice, 1896–97], is an allegory of magic as technology, with the goal as a form of literal animation —the transmutation of aesthetic material into a form of imaginative life. Mickey loses control of the magic/technology, however, and has to be rescued by the sorcerer Yen Sid. This can serve as an allegory of the *conventional* limits of this practice. *Fantasia* takes us to the threshold but does not know how to cross it. The film uses technology, sensation, and imagination but does not explicitly attempt to make good on the temporal promise of the line of practice we are here examining.

Stanley Kubrick's *2001: A Space Odyssey* (1968) charts the human journey from the dawn of civilization to its end in space (and beyond). The monolith, which marks the stages of this journey, can be seen as a film screen, making *2001* a cinematic odyssey, and therefore a film about film. In the film's penultimate sequence, the end of the "Jupiter and Beyond the Infinite" segment, an aged David Bowman (Keir Dullea) beholds the monolith at the final stage of civilization in a puzzling rococo (and rococo always signifies decadence) interior. This is followed by the celebrated image of beginning: the space-baby, called the Star Child (fig. 3). One could not ask for a clearer illustration of our thesis that the last moments of civilization produce a mute, pure, potent form of beginning, of birth.

It could be tempting to read this story as a circle, or, as per Yeats, as a spiral: civilization begins with the appearance of technology (the monolith), develops to its zenith, then dies and is born again. That is not, however, what we are proposing here. What we are searching for is not a grand historical circle but rather a form of *practice* that appears most clearly in the late stages of civilization, like a star rising above the horizon after sunset.

The word *apocalypse*, which we tend to use as marking a spectacular form of ending, in its origins refers to nothing of the sort. Rather, it means to *uncover*, to reveal (*apo- + kalyptein*)—that is, to allow something new to be revealed, or revealed again. Not accidentally, we find in the last book of the New Testament the appearance, or revelation, of the divine expressed precisely in terms of the temporal efficacy we have been discussing: "And he that sat upon the throne said: Behold, I make all things new" (Revelations 21:5).

It would be shortsighted, as well as too literal, to imagine that the Star Child symbolizes the start of a new historical epoch. The point is rather that the Star Child is the emblem of a form of practice or insight. Such an image does not attest to a divine or superhuman or transcendent moment, or to the arrival of a god. On the contrary, it is, as Hannah Arendt wrote, "an affirmation of the divinity of birth as such, that the world's potential salvation lies in the very fact that the human species regenerates itself constantly and forever." It is worth quoting from *On Revolution* at length:

> I have dwelt upon Virgil's poem at some length because it seems to me as though the poet of the first century B.C. developed in his way what the Christian philosopher Augustine in the fifth century A.D. was to articulate in conceptual and Christianized language: *Initium ergo ut esset, creatus est homo*—"That there be a beginning, man was created," and what finally must have become apparent in the very course of the revolutions of the modern age. What matters in our context is less the profoundly Roman notion that all foundations are re-establishments and reconstructions than the somehow connected but different idea that men are equipped for the logically paradoxical task of making a beginning because they themselves are new beginnings and hence beginners, that the very capacity for beginning is rooted in natality, in the fact that human beings appear in the word by virtue of birth.[5]

To draw out the consequences of this particular power, or possibility, of beginning, let us examine *The Fast and the Furious: Tokyo Drift* (2006), the third installment in a franchise that as of this writing includes seven films. It is apparent that *Tokyo Drift,* with its sensuality and excess, its anthropomorphic (or rather superhero-pheropomorphic) custom cars, and its twisting, jagged races, is more like *The Roses of Heliogabalus* or *Fantasia*—that is, an imaginative machine of exotic sensory intensity—than like Manet or Adorno. Moreover, the coda of the film enacts an incredible temporal readjustment that rewrites the meaning and history of the previous and subsequent films in an act of perpetually self-renewing aesthetic re-creation. The hero of *Tokyo Drift* is Sean Boswell (played by Lucas Black). A key character is Han Seoul-Oh (Sun Kang), Sean's patron and an addict of the eternal present—"Life is simple: you make choices and don't look back." Han is killed late in the film in a car chase. In the film's extraordinary coda, however, Sean, now Tokyo's drift king, is challenged out of nowhere to a race—and everything suddenly changes and becomes new again. The challenger, Dominic Toretto (Vin Diesel), the hero of the whole franchise, who has not appeared or even been mentioned in *Tokyo Drift*, suddenly claims to have been a close friend of the deceased Han.

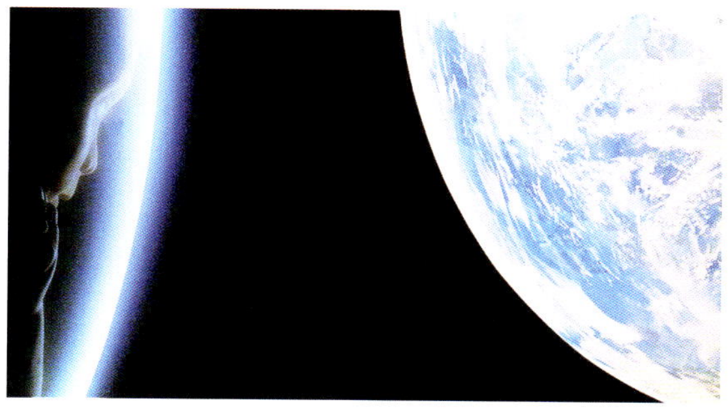

Fig. 3. Still from *2001: A Space Odyssey*, 1968

By having suddenly known Han, Dominic resurrects him: The next three movies in the franchise will take place before *Tokyo Drift*, and Han will therefore be brought to life to appear in them. But the fourth, fifth, and sixth films are emphatically not prequels: time has simply become malleable, looping toward the strange coda of *Tokyo Drift*, and to the ever-changing meaning of Han's murder. Han's crash is replayed in the coda to *Fast and Furious 6* (2013), but with the paradoxical addition of a new character, the brother of the film's defeated villain, now named as the murderer. This new interpretation motivates the conflict of *Furious 7* (2015). In another temporal loop, the coda of *Tokyo Drift* is reinserted as a key plot point in the present of *Furious 7*, with its meaning further adumbrated.

This reorganizing of temporality is a good example of the practice whose allegorical emblem is the Star Child of *2001*. Time is shown by *Tokyo Drift* to be a glittering, malleable mosaic, in which certain meanings are ever-modified and renewed; the present is merely a nodal mountain range of possible *presence*, around which the meaning of the past (and therefore the possibilities for the future) crashes, ever-changing, like waves.

*Initium ergo ut esset, creatus est homo.* Put differently: "The beginningless begins forever. In the same way, I give eternally because I have nothing. To be nothing, to have nothing, to keep nothing for oneself is the greatest gift, the highest generosity."[6] Or, as Dominic says: "I got nothing but time."

And so we arrive at the meaning of the model: If (1) classical practices imagine that time is the truth of being, that we are therefore *in* time, and if they consequently strive for teleological verity, narrative mastery, heroism, and coherence, and if (2) the Manet model counters this claim by ironizing and deconstructing it, thereby constructing a dark and pulsing meta-knowledge, a hall of intellectual mirrors, our (3) bejeweled space-baby instead knows—and seeks to make known—that being is the truth of time. And so she or he wears temporality like a cape. Time trails serpent-like behind the permanent power of beginning, to which we are all, as beginners, entitled, forever.

NOTES

1. Augustine of Hippo, cited in Hannah Arendt, *The Origins of Totalitarianism* (New York: Harcourt Brace, 1979), p. 479.

2. "Vous n'êtes que le premier dans la décrépitude de votre art." Charles Baudelaire to Édouard Manet, May 11, 1865, cited in Michael Fried, "Three American Painters: Kenneth Noland, Jules Olitski, Frank Stella," in *Art and Objecthood: Essays and Reviews* (Chicago: University of Chicago Press, 1988), p. 213.

3. Theodor Adorno, *In Search of Wagner*, trans. Rodney Livingstone (New York: Shocken Books, 1981), p. 73.

4. "Simply to hang a painting on the wall and say that it's art is dreadful. The whole network is important! Even spaghettini. . . . When you say art, then everything possible belongs to it. In a gallery that is also the floor, the architecture, the color of the walls."
Martin Kippenberger, cited in David Joselit, "Painting Beside Itself," *October*, no. 130 (Fall 2009), pp. 125–34.

5. Hannah Arendt, *On Revolution* (New York: Viking, 1968), p. 211. A further link from Arendt between the late phases of civilizations and the possibility of ontological renewal in mannerist art: "It was not the spreading of alien cults—the Isis cult or the Christian sects—in the declining empire which prompted the Romans to accept the cult of the 'child' more readily than they accepted almost anything else from the strange cultures of a conquered world; it was rather the other way round: because Roman politics and civilization had this unequaled, intimate connection with the integrity of a beginning in the foundation of their city, the Asiatic religions which centered around the birth of a child-saviour attracted them so strongly, not their strangeness as such but the affinity of birth and foundation." Ibid., pp. 212–13.

6. Sri Nisargadatta Maharaj, *I Am That*, 3rd ed. (Durham, NC: Acorn Press, 2012), p. 92.

# The Cinema of Feels

Brian Droitcour

Ninety minutes is too long. A feature-length story can easily be interrupted by distractions—from another browser tab, if the movie is watched on a laptop, or from another screen, like the one on a phone or a computer, if watched at home on TV. Diffuse attention endangers the focus and closure of a singular, sustained narrative.

Ninety minutes is too short. Only a storyteller with special gifts can tell an engaging tale in such a brief span of time without relying on archetype, cliché, and other props of genre. Ninety minutes is usually not enough to populate a fictional world with characters of lifelike richness and emotional depth.

In the twentieth century, film drew comparisons to the novel as the culture's main vehicle for popular narrative. But in the twenty-first century, the film—the film of auteurs, of gifted storytellers—looks more like the short story, the narrative of evocative detail and lyrical precision. Now the "large, loose, baggy monsters" are on TV, where the engrossing realist sagas of our time unfold in ten or twenty episodes a season.

This shift happened slowly, but it turned out to be a drastic switch. TV time used to be curt and looped. Sitcoms, courtroom procedurals, and murder mysteries would stage and resolve the same conflicts week after week, rearranging the elements of character and plot without continuity or growth. (Rare developments were reserved for season finales and other special episodes.) But on-demand TV and streaming made continuity mandatory—or, to be more exact, they allowed for binge-watching that made the conventions of weekly episodes feel repetitive and quaint. (Even reality TV—the most formulaic programming today—demonstrates the personal growth of the contestants over the course of a season.)

Meanwhile, movies have become more episodic than ever. Hollywood funds superhero films and other genre franchises. Their tall tales refer to vast worlds, the details of which are catalogued and discussed by fandoms as they are continuously rearranged in sequels, prequels, and reboots. They elicit strong emotional reactions in their audiences, but through fan identification and the layering and repetition of clichés. Popular cinema now is less a vehicle for storytelling than a machine of feeling. Its repertoire of effects and impacts matters more than techniques of narrative. As the shifting media landscape has revealed, narrative is not an inherent trait of cinema—it is simply one tool that cinema has assimilated, and it's not as important to the medium's workings as a twentieth-century media diet led us to believe.

Ninety seconds is too long. As a launching pad for microfame, YouTube, with its attention spans of a minute or two, has been eclipsed by Vine, a social media app that lets users make and post six-second looping videos on their phones—not enough time to develop a story, but great for pranks, pratfalls, crude jokes, and funny juxtapositions. Vine also has the advantage of sound, which is missing from another, briefer and more popular format for looped moving images: the animated GIF.

A GIF can be a still image, but the file format's advantage over JPEG, TIFF, and others that can hold more information (and accommodate better image resolution) is that it can loop a series of frames, producing an animation that requires less memory than a video and loads more quickly on a webpage, without needing to be started or stopped, which made it especially popular in web design in the 1990s.

Theorists have compared the animated GIF to early cinema, drawing on Tom Gunning's description of the cinema of attractions—the short films shown at carnivals around the turn of the twentieth century, before producers invested in narrative film and the construction of movie theaters that disposed an audience toward sustained attention—as "less as a way of telling stories than as a way of presenting a series of views to an audience."[1] Lisa Nakamura, for example, has compared GIFs to early films in terms of their low cultural respectability, as well as the relative privacy in which they are viewed, from peep-show booths at nineteenth-century fairgrounds to the individual user at a computer.[2] Nakamura's argument relies not only on the GIF's status as a moving image, but also on a spatial conception of the Internet as a site for semipublic, shared experiences.

Cinema is a medium. A cinema is a place—the theater you go to take in a movie. Victor Hugo, ventriloquizing through the archdeacon in *Notre Dame de Paris*, pitched the cathedral as an information technology, a medium for the distribution of ideas and stories where communication was enfolded in place and set in habit. The fairground where early films were screened was like this, too: a place visited by habit on holidays, a heterogeneous field of sights and experiences where cultural imagination was shared through images, architecture, signs, sounds, and speech. The cinema, as a place, is hard to compare with the cathedral or the fair because of its singular unity of medium and form: the hushed darkness suppressing all stimuli outside the glowing screen. But cinema as a medium is flexible: it could be encountered on the fairground, as it was in its infancy, and it can be seen in cathedrals now. It's also found online, where movies can be torrented or streamed, and reviews of them can be read on IMDb or posted to Facebook, in which case responses and discussions are implicitly solicited from friends. More than the cinema, social media feeds are like those older gathering places, stimulating with heterogeneous messages.

But the space of social media is encased in a screen, and interactions in it occur without bodily proximity. As ordinary as the communication that happens there may be, the physical cues of gesture and mimicry that accompany any face-to-face social encounter are missing. This lack can be compensated by punctuation—think of the exclamation points that accrue in professional correspondence to indicate a chipper, upbeat voice. Forms of expressive punctuation have been invented, too, from the simple colon-and-parenthesis smiley face to the cartoon faces and digital stickers that Facebook and Gmail have made available for their chat apps. The nonlinguistic aspects of face-to-face communications have been transformed into on-screen approximations.

Perhaps the most elaborate form of emotive punctuation is the "reaction GIF": an animated GIF with a short clip of a close-up, sometimes with captions of what the face is saying as it moves and emotes. The faces of reaction GIFs grimace and grin, array their features in grotesque concentrations of disgusted surprise or selfless elation. Eyebrows leap, nostrils flare, jaws drop. The sources of these GIFs vary as much as the tastes of the users who send them—the faces can come from Disney movies, Japanese anime, audience shots at awards shows, talk shows, cutaway interviews on reality TV, popular or obscure movies—but the basic form can always be recognized: a close-up of a face in the process of expression.

Users proficient with the software can make reaction GIFs in Photoshop. But there are many sites and apps that make it easy to rip video footage and save a selection as a GIF. Most of the users who send reaction GIFs, however, don't make them. They see someone else using them on social media or in forums, or look them up in user-generated databases,[3] and save them to a folder on their computer desktop, or in a photo album on their phone. They're not neatly organized by file name, but rather cluttered like a hoarder's closet—a mess where everything is more or less handy to the person familiar with it.

Reaction GIFs were first used on the discussion forums of Reddit and 4chan, where users initiate a conversation with a post, and responses accrue in a thread below as boxes of text. Users got in the habit of embedding a reaction GIF in the response field to express an intensity difficult to put in words, or when they had nothing to say but wanted to convey their disdain (more often than not, reaction GIFs express negative reactions, especially mockery and dismissal). When Twitter allowed for images (including animated gifs) in its feed in October 2013, the use of reaction GIFs spread beyond the relatively limited social contexts of forums, which can be cliquish and surly. Black Twitter, a loosely associated network of user communities that regularly makes news for raising awareness about police violence and other manifestations of systemic racism, made extensive use of reaction GIFs and helped bring them to the mainstream of social media. Reaction GIFs are also commonly used in texting or in messaging apps like Gchat, as responses in private conversations.

These habits of using moving images to convey the emotional experiences accompanying online communication amount to a user-generated cinema threaded throughout the networked spaces

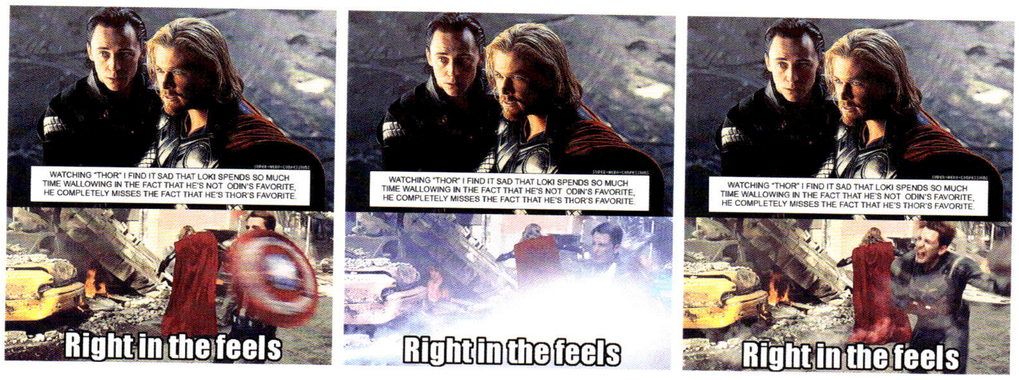


Fig. 1. "Right in the feels" GIF

of digital media. It's an ad hoc, spontaneous cinema that entertains, provokes, and delights, but its main purpose is to communicate the affect of users who are just like those who view it. It's not a cinema of attractions, designed by a filmmaker to produce reactions in an audience. It uses cinema's effects in social encounters to express reactions. It is a cinema of feels.

"Feels" is short for "feelings," a bit of Internet slang popularized through catchphrases like "I know that feel, bro" (an expression of empathy) or "right in the feels" (a description of an intense emotional reaction). The clipped form sounds tougher than "feelings," or at least like a jokey admission of vulnerability, which could explain its popularity on the male-dominated message boards of Reddit and 4chan. But the removal of the gerund ending also makes feeling sound like less of an action and more of a thing, a tangible, embodied object that grounds the reality of emotional responses to online communication.

The French philosopher Gilles Deleuze defined affect as "a sort of motor tendency on a sensitive nerve, that is a motor effort on an immobilized receptive plane." Facial expressivity contrasts moving features—eyebrows, lips, and so on—to an unmoving skeletal framework, to the planes of skin; the screen, as another unmoving plane that conveys expression by receiving movement, is thus a technological double of the face. In his writing on cinema, Deleuze described the close-up as an "affection-image," a reduction of the face to its essence as an expression of affect.[4] The reaction GIF isolates the close-up in order to reuse it in other contexts as a sign of expressivity. This is distinct from other means of representing and producing affect in cinema, music hall, or theater, which need to impact audiences at a distance. Soviet filmmaker and theorist Sergei Eisenstein, writing about the theater, used the term "attraction" to describe elements such as the kinetic relations of bodies and objects on the stage as elements of expressivity. Attractions, he noted, "can be verified and mathematically calculated to produce certain emotional shocks in a proper order within the totality."[5]

The manipulation of mise-en-scène and movement in space to elicit audience reactions thrives in Hollywood special effects, where directors "mathematically calculate" the gut-wrenching reactions of awe. Elaborate scenes of combat and explosions are valuable as attractions, but they're alien to everyday communication—that's what makes those effects so special. GIFs can be made from the most spectacular scenes of action adventure movies, but the small files diminish and degrade the attractions. They're of little or no use in conversation because they don't approximate any nonlinguistic elements of ordinary speech. They don't belong to the cinema that matters most in telecommunications, the cinema of feels.[6]

A GIF that popularized the catchphrase "right in the feels" had it superimposed on a clip of Captain America and Thor during the climactic battle scene from *The Avengers* (2012) (fig. 1). It doesn't show the inhuman scale of the alien invaders attacking the heroes, or the swarming, screaming crowd around them. It just shows two men—or rather, a deity and a chemically enhanced super-body, but here they look like men. Vulnerable, Captain America doubles over and his mouth soundlessly groans as a ray of bluish ray strikes his gut—where the feels are.

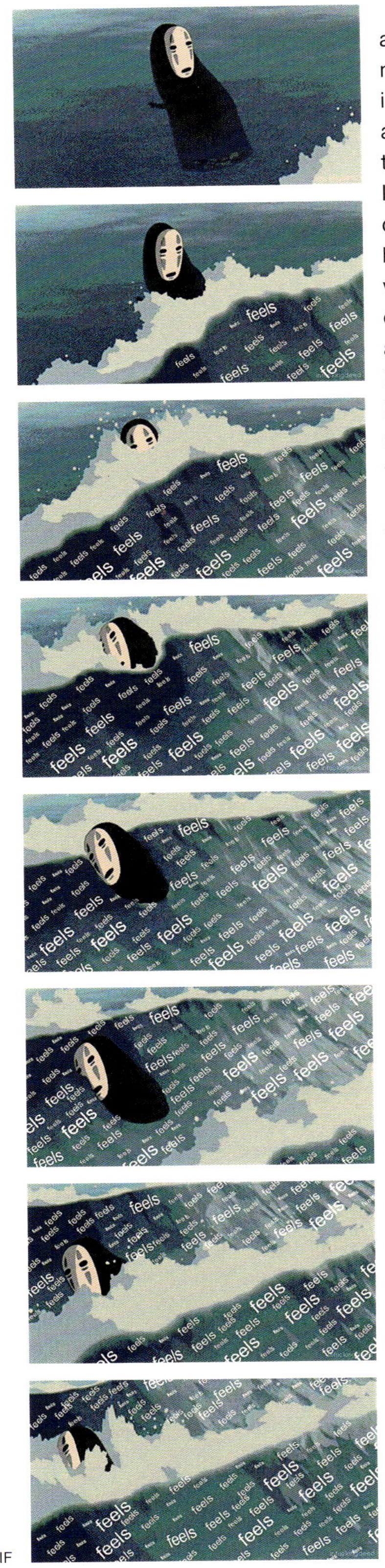

Fig. 2. "Feels Wave" GIF

Another popular GIF is based on a clip from the Japanese animated film *Spirited Away* (2001) (fig. 2). It shows a ghostly masked figure (called No-Face in the movie) standing upright in the sea for a brief moment before being knocked down by an onslaught of crashing waves. The maker of the GIF printed the word "feels" all over the waves.[7] The popularity of this GIF, I would say, comes from its inversion of the reaction GIF's conventions. It is usually the face that matters, but here we have No-Face. The text is in Arial or Helvetica, a faceless font with nothing expressive about it, not even a serif. The feels are external to the body (insofar as No-Face can be said to have a body, and not just be a shapeless mass shrouded in black). No-Face is faceless because it lacks expressive features like brows and lips—Deleuze's "immobile receptive plane" without a sensitive nerve—and the mask remains motionless as the body is carried away by an external movement of feels.

Through the comedy of its negation, the GIF derived from *Spirited Away* shows what matters about expressivity. Ordinary reaction GIFs are interesting because they are instances of users putting those cinematic tools to personal use. Eisenstein obsessively theorized the processes by which cinema impacts its viewers, but their reactions were ephemeral, invisible; the reaction GIF, however, puts it in writing. Interestingly, users deploy reaction GIFs outside the context of a conversation in order to define a situation rather than respond to one. TFW, MFW, and MRW are abbreviations—for "that feel when," "my feel when," and "my reaction when," respectively—that introduce a reaction image when there's no thread to react to. Usually found at the start of tweets, these GIFs entertain with the ingenuity of the user in combining fresh news with a familiar image, or a familiar situation with an unexpected picture. "As cinema *spectators* we have to understand space, but as computer *users* we both have to understand and *act* within digital space," writes film theorist Per Persson,[8] in a neat summary of the constant dual role of users as producers and consumers, authors and audience.

For both reactions and the decontextualized, TFW presentation of them, still images (in the form of JPEGs) are used as well as GIFs. Without a moving image, the montage of text and caption matters more. Viewed as a frame in Facebook or Twitter, where the feed is a reel activated by scrolling, the juxtaposition of still image and caption is minimal montage, a montage without duration. Duration—ninety minutes, ninety seconds, or no time at all—becomes inconsequential in the diffuse attention fostered by computer use, where the screen splits into smaller surfaces of simultaneity, with notifications and incoming messages interrupting any fixed concentration. Cinema becomes a prosthesis for gesture and mimicry in commonplace communication. Duration is replaced by the constant accessibility and intertextuality of anytime, all the time, a cinema of whenever.

NOTES

At the time of printing, the "Right in the feels" GIF could be accessed at http://gph.is/YBCA1q and the "Feels Wave" GIF at http://gph.is/1Qdgluo.

1. Tom Gunning, "The Cinema of Attractions: Early Films, Its Spectators, and the Avant-Garde," in *Early Cinema*, ed. Thomas Elsaesser (London: BFI, 1990), p. 57.

2. Lisa Nakamura, *Digitizing Race: Visual Cultures of the Internet* (Minneapolis: University of Minnesota Press, 2007), pp. 63–66. Essays about the connection of GIFs to cinema include Kelli Marshall's post to the *JSTOR Daily* blog, "Animated Gifs: A Throwback to Cinema's Beginnings," February 24, 2015, http://daily.jstor.org/animated-gifs-a-throwback-to-cinemas-beginnings/; and A. D. Jameson's post for Indiewire's *Press Play* blog, "Are Animated Gifs a Type of Cinema?" April 17, 2013, http://blogs.indiewire.com/pressplay/are-animated-gifs-a-type-of-cinema#.UXV5sP41j6s.twitter. While these authors discuss the connection of GIFs to cinema primarily through their mutual status as movement and entertainment, I am more interested in understanding cinema as a set of social effects and functions, which GIFs fulfill through their use in particular contexts.

3. Such databases include a collection of reaction GIFs on Imgur, a hosting site used by posters to Reddit and other forums, that indexes popular GIFs by categories such as "No/Nope," "STFU/Shut Up," "Mind Blown," "Not Giving A Fuck," "Deal with it," and "Erections/Fapping." There is also a Tumblr called "Fuck Yeah Reactions" that aggregates and tags reaction GIFs to make them easy for other users to find. "Lets say you're searching for a smile reaction," writes the Tumblr's keeper. "All you need to do is type in http://fuckyeahreactions.tumblr.com/tagged/smile, Simple as that." A note in the "About" column on the Tumblr's front page reads: "This blog is a public service."

4. Gilles Deleuze, *Cinema 1: The Movement-Image*, trans. Hugh Tomlinson and Barbara Habberjam (Minneapolis: University of Minnesota Press, 1986), p. 87.

5. Sergei Eisenstein, "Montage of Attractions," in *The Film Sense*, trans. and ed. Jay Leyda (New York: Harcourt Brace, 1947), pp. 230–31. It should also be noted that Gunning, in applying Eisenstein's terminology of attractions to early cinema, was talking about films that never used close-ups, that depicted bodies at a distance familiar from theater as well as photographic portraiture.

6. There are meme incubators, notably Failblog, that specialize in collecting GIFs and videos of accidental gags and embarrassing moments. These are about entertainment rather than communication—a cinema of fails.

7. Details about the origins of the *Avengers* and *Spirited Away* GIFs analyzed here can be found in the "Feels" entry of Know Your Meme, a web resource that catalogues the history of Internet culture: knowyourmeme.com/memes/feels.

8. Per Persson, "Cinema and Computers," in *Technospaces: The New Media*, ed. Sally R. Munt, Critical Research in Material Culture (New York: Bloomsbury Academic, 2001), p. 52.

# Illustrated Plate List

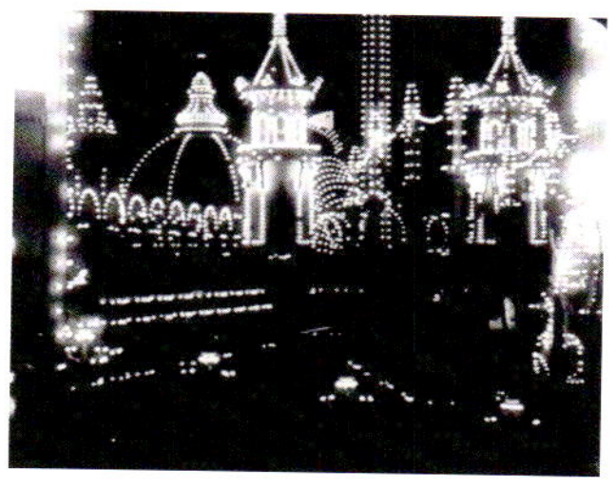

Pages 2–3
Edwin S. Porter (1870–1941)
Edison Manufacturing Company
Frame enlargement from *Coney Island at Night*, 1905
16mm film, black-and-white, silent; 2 min.

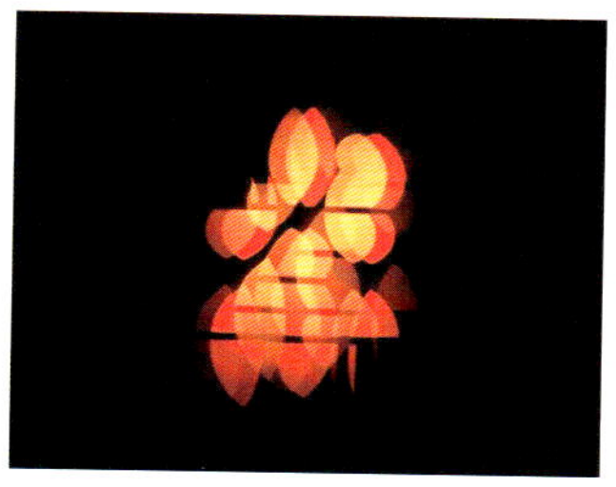

Page 4
Kurt Schwerdtfeger (1897–1966)
Still from *Reflektorische Farblichtspiele* [Reflecting Light Games], 1922/1968
16mm film transferred to video, color, sound; 17:53 min.
Direction, camera, and production by Rudolf Jüdes

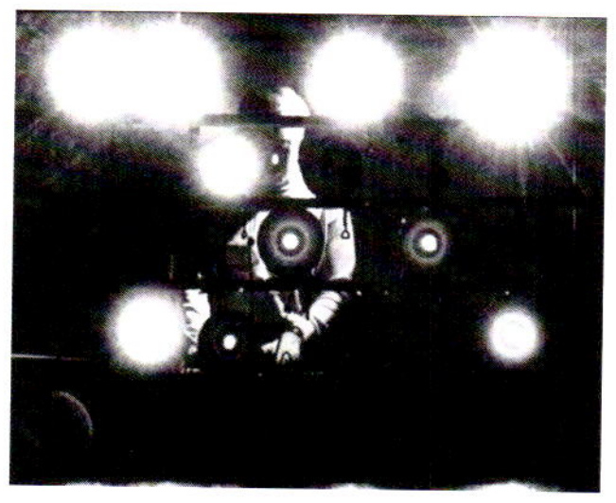

Page 5
Still from *Making Reflektorische Farblictspiele*, 1968
16mm film transfered to video, black-and-white, sound; 4:46 min.
Direction, camera, and production by Rudolf Jüdes

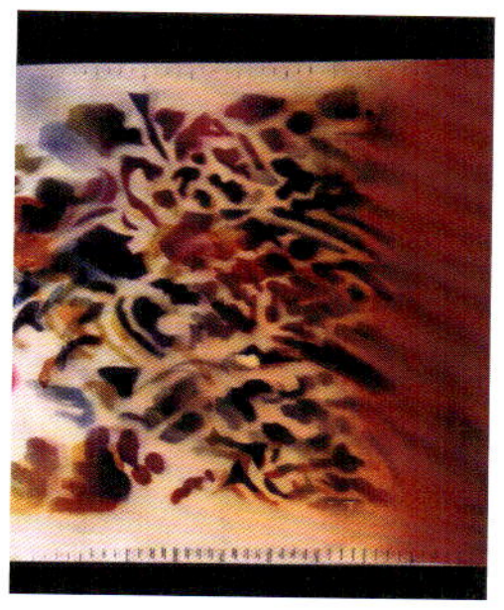

Page 6
Mary Elizabeth Hallock Greenewalt (1871–1950)
Color roll 1 for "Color Play" Phonograph, 1920
Hand-painted acetate
Mary Elizabeth Hallock Greenewalt Papers (Collection 867), Historical Society of Pennsylvania, Philadelphia

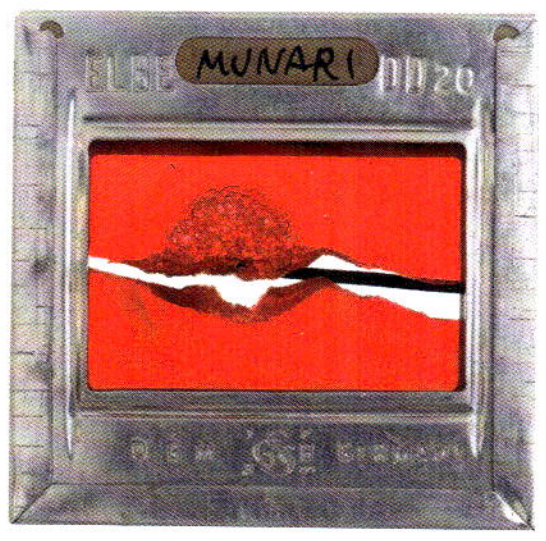


Page 7
Bruno Munari (1907–1998)
Slide from *Direct Projections*, 1951
Cellulose acetate in slide mount, 2 x 2 in. (5 x 5 cm)
Vodoz-Danese Foundation, Milan

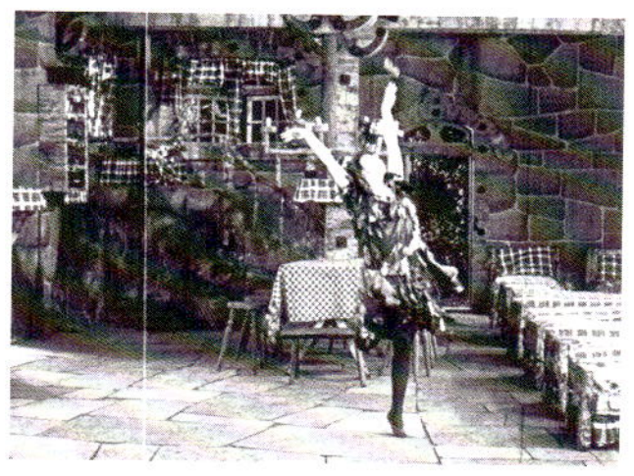

Pages 8, 9
J. Searle Dawley (1877–1949)
Frame enlargements from *Snow White*, 1916
35mm film, black-and-white (tinted and non-tinted), silent; 63 min.

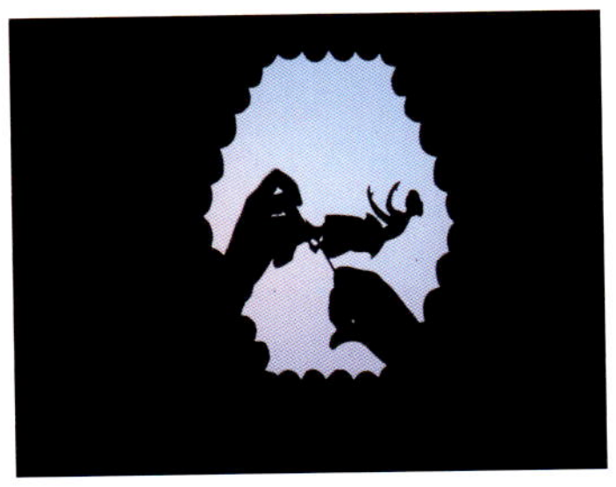

Pages 10, 11
Lotte Reiniger (1899–1981)
Stills from *Aschenputtel* [Cinderella], 1922
35mm film transferred to video, black-and-white (tinted), silent; 11 min.

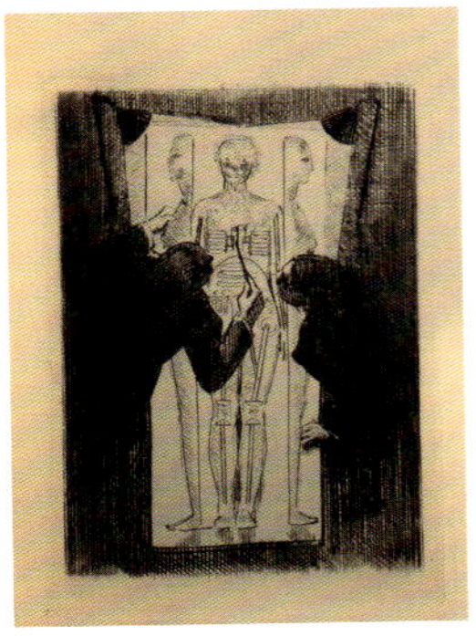

Page 12
Raphaël Drouart (1894–1972)
Engraving from *Villiers de l'Isle-Adam, L'Ève future* (Paris: Henri Jonquieres, 1925)
Sheet, 7 ⅞ x 5 ½ in. (20 x 14 cm); plate, 6 x 4 ½ in. (15.2 x 11.4 cm)

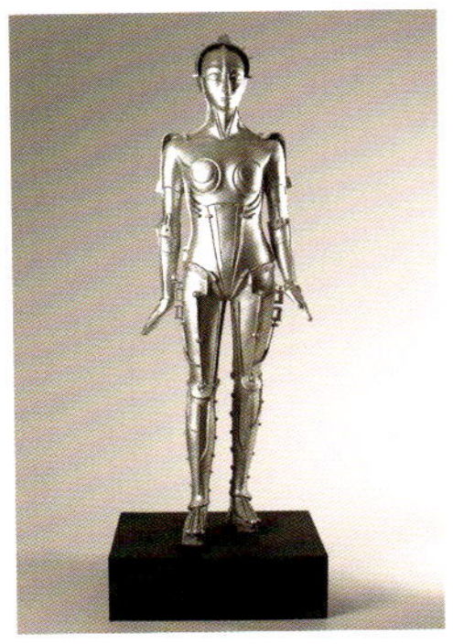

Page 13
After Walter Schulze-Mittendorff (1893–1976)
Replica of "Maria Robot" from *Metropolis* (c. 1927), 1994
Painted resin, 71 ¼ x 23 ⅝ x 11 ¾ in. (181 x 60 x 30 cm) with wooden pedestal, 3 ½ x 29 ⅛ x 23 ¼ in. (9 x 74 x 59 cm)
La Cinémathèque française, Paris

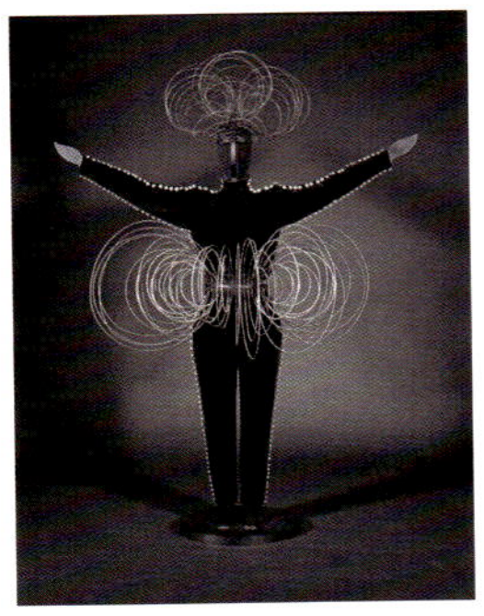

Page 14
Oskar Schlemmer (1888–1943)
*Wire Figure*, 1922
Nickel wire and metal, 80 ¾ x 61 x 47 ¼ in. (205 x 155 x 120 cm)
Staatsgalerie Stuttgart, on loan from the Friends of the Staatsgalerie
GVLP 127

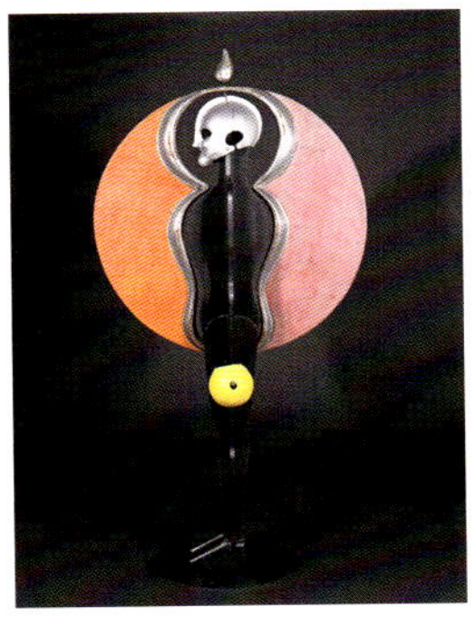

Page 15
Oskar Schlemmer (1888–1943)
*Disk Dancer*, 1922
Painted papier-maché and wood, 76 ⅜ x 24 ⅜ x 39 ⅜ in. (194 x 62 x 100 cm)
Staatsgalerie Stuttgart, on loan from the Friends of the Staatsgalerie
GVLP 126

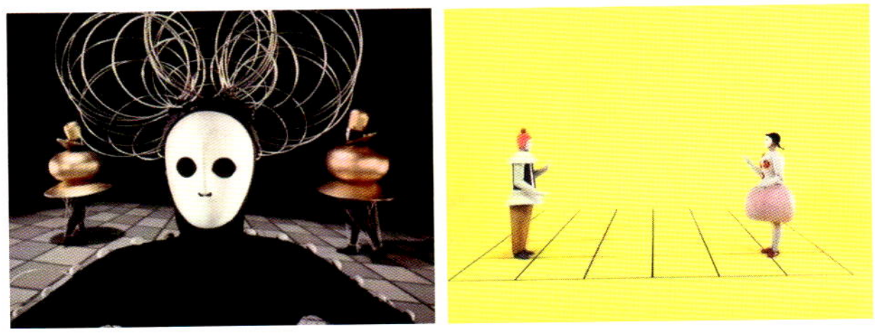

Pages 16, 17
After Oskar Schlemmer (1888–1943)
Stills from *Das Triadische Ballett* [Triadic Ballet], 1970
35mm film transferred to video, color, sound; 29 min.
Direction by Helmut Amann

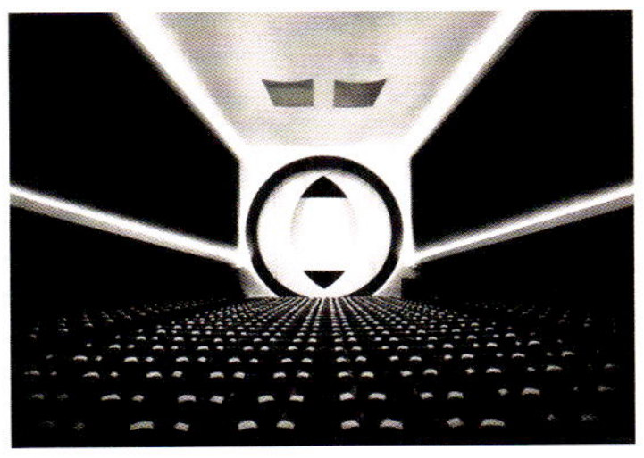

Pages 18–19
Ruth Bernhard (1905–2006)
*8th Street Theater*, 1946 [Architect Frederick Kiesler (1890–1965), auditorium at the Film Arts Guild Cinema (1929) with the "screen-o-scope" partially opened]
Gelatin silver print, 9 ½ x 13 ⅜ in. (24 x 34 cm)
Princeton University Art Museum, New Jersey; bequest of Ruth Bernhard (2008-578)

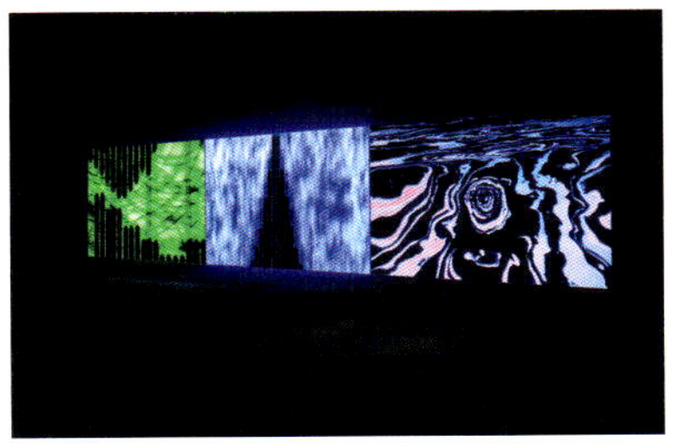

Pages 20, 21
Oskar Fischinger (1900–1967)
*Raumlichtkunst* [Space Light Art], 1926/2012
Three-screen projection: three 35mm films transferred to high-definition video, black-and-white and color, sound; 10 min. each, looped
Center for Visual Music, Los Angeles
Restored and reconstructed in 2012 by the Center for Visual Music
Installation views, Whitney Museum, 2012

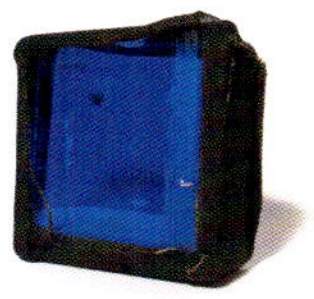

Page 22
Blue glass used as filter for projecting Joseph Cornell's *Rose Hobart*, c. 1936
Glass, 1 ¾ x 1 ¾ x ½ in. (4.5 x 4.5 x 1.3 cm)
Anthology Film Archives, New York

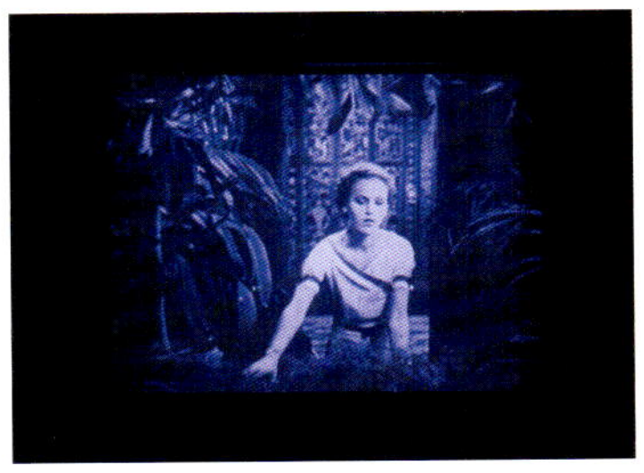

Page 23
Joseph Cornell (1903–1972)
*Rose Hobart*, 1936
16mm film transferred to video, black-and-white, silent; 20 min., with blue glass filter, 78 rpm records, and record player
Installation view, Château Shatto, Los Angeles, 2015

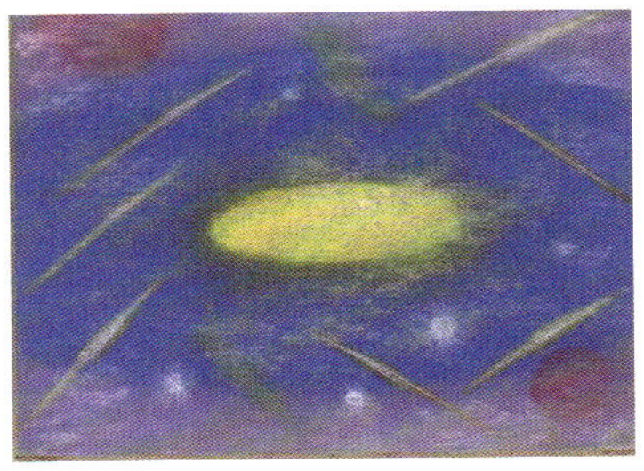

Page 24
Oskar Fischinger (1900–1967)
Preliminary concept drawing for *Fantasia*, c. 1938
Pastel on paper, 5 ½ x 7 ½ in. (14 x 19 cm)
Center for Visual Music, Los Angeles; gift of The Fischinger Trust

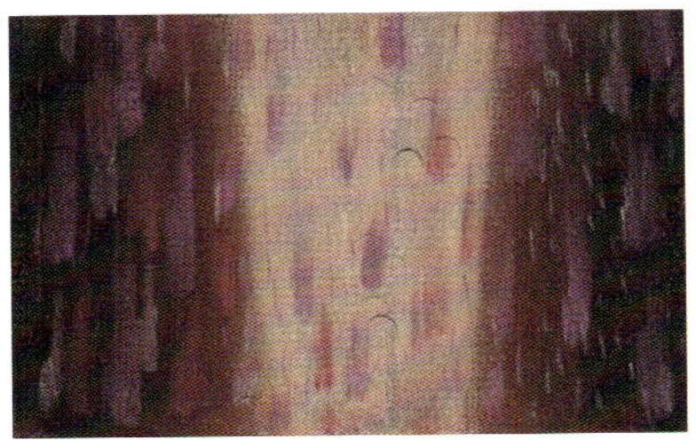

Page 24
Oskar Fischinger (1900–1967)
Preliminary concept drawing for *Fantasia*, c. 1938
Pastel on paper, 2 ¾ x 4 ¼ in. (7 x 10.8 cm)
Center for Visual Music, Los Angeles; gift of The Fischinger Trust

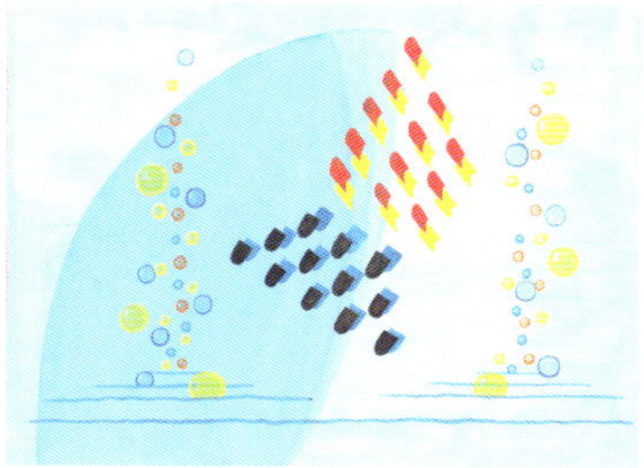

Page 25
Oskar Fischinger (1900–1967)
Concept drawing for *Fantasia*, c. 1938
Tempera on paper, 5 ¼ x 7 in. (13.3 x 17.8 cm)
Center for Visual Music, Los Angeles; gift of The Fischinger Trust

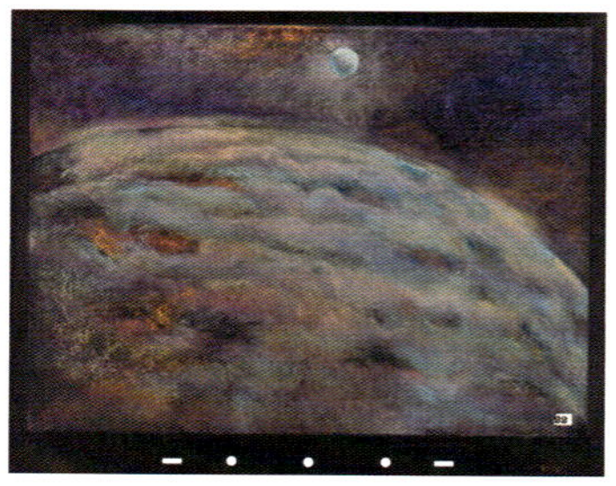

Page 26
Disney Studio Artist
Story sketch for *Fantasia*, 1940
Pastel and opaque watercolor on paper, 12 ½ x 15 ½ in. (31.8 x 39.4 cm)
Walt Disney Animation Research Library, Glendale, California

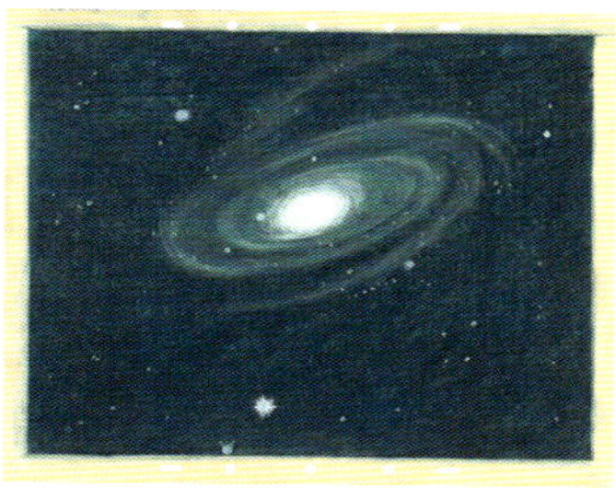

Page 26
Disney Studio Artist
Story sketch for *Fantasia*, 1940
Pastel and opaque watercolor on paper, 12 ½ x 15 ½ in. (31.8 x 39.4 cm)
Walt Disney Animation Research Library, Glendale, California

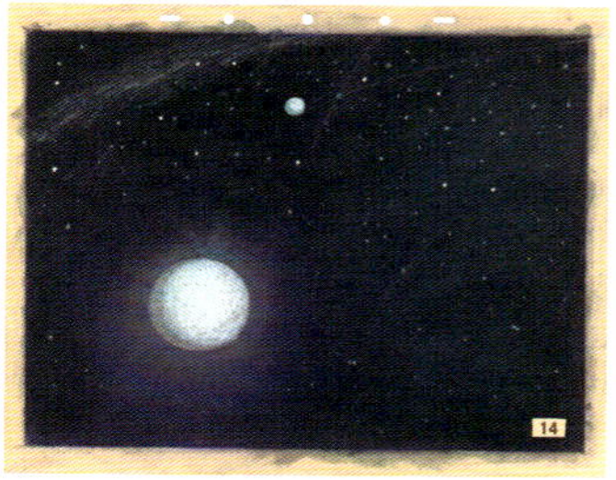

Page 26
Disney Studio Artist
Story sketch for *Fantasia*, 1940
Pastel and opaque watercolor on paper, 12 ½ x 15 ½ in. (31.8 x 39.4 cm)
Walt Disney Animation Research Library, Glendale, California

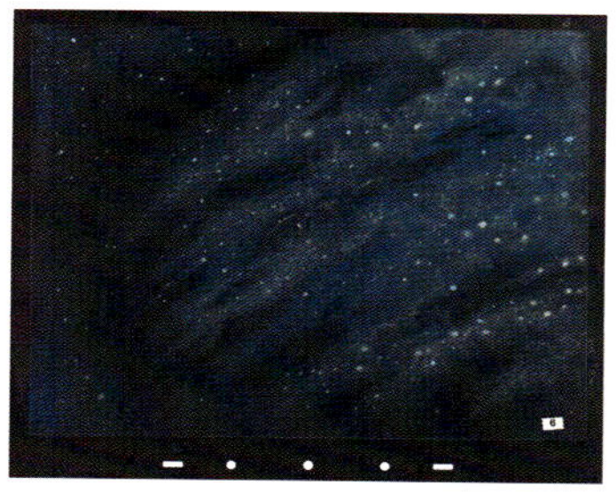

Page 26
Disney Studio Artist
Story sketch for *Fantasia*, 1940
Pastel and opaque watercolor on paper, 12 ½ x 15 ½ in. (31.8 x 39.4 cm)
Walt Disney Animation Research Library, Glendale, California

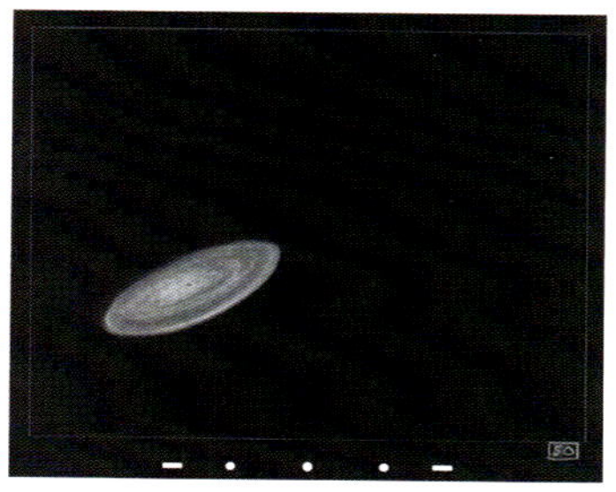

Page 26
Disney Studio Artist
Story sketch for *Fantasia*, 1940
Pastel and opaque watercolor on paper, 12 ½ x 15 ½ in. (31.8 x 39.4 cm)
Walt Disney Animation Research Library, Glendale, California

Page 26
Disney Studio Artist
Story sketch for *Fantasia*, 1940
Pastel and opaque watercolor on paper, 12 ½ x 15 ½ in. (31.8 x 39.4 cm)
Walt Disney Animation Research Library, Glendale, California

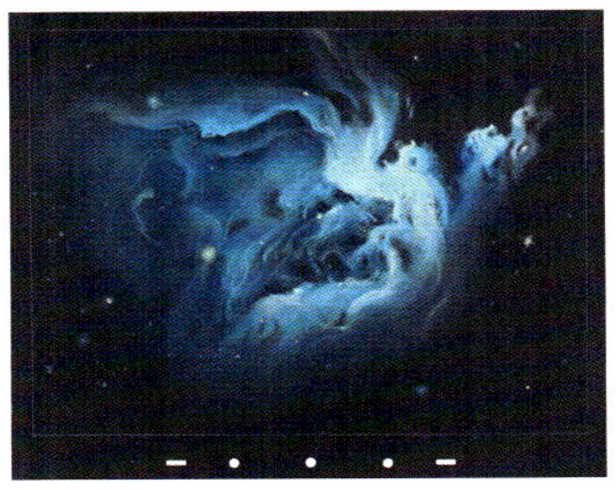

Page 27
Disney Studio Artist
Story sketch for *Fantasia*, 1940
Pastel and opaque watercolor on paper, 12 ½ x 15 ½ in. (31.8 x 39.4 cm)
Walt Disney Animation Research Library, Glendale, California

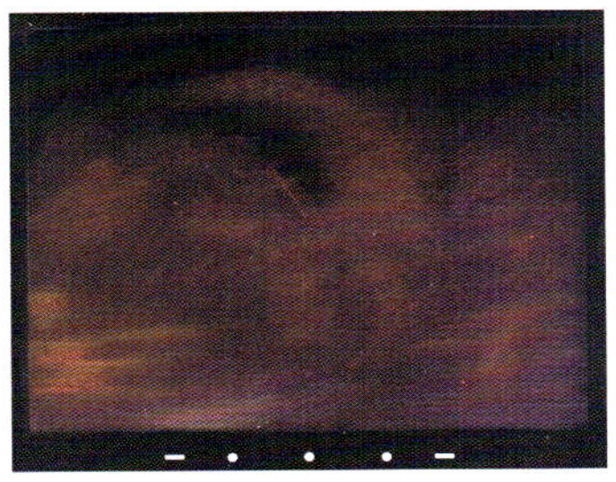

Page 27
Disney Studio Artist
Story sketch for *Fantasia*, 1940
Pastel and opaque watercolor on paper, 12 ½ x 15 ½ in. (31.8 x 39.4 cm)
Walt Disney Animation Research Library, Glendale, California

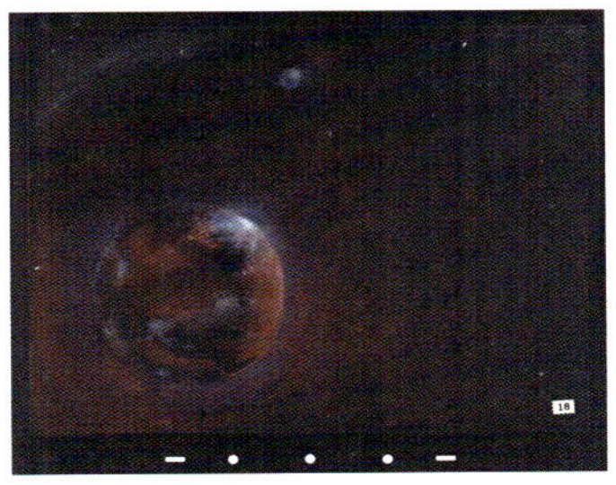

Page 27
Disney Studio Artist
Story sketch for *Fantasia*, 1940
Pastel and opaque watercolor on paper, 12 ½ x 15 ½ in. (31.8 x 39.4 cm)
Walt Disney Animation Research Library, Glendale, California

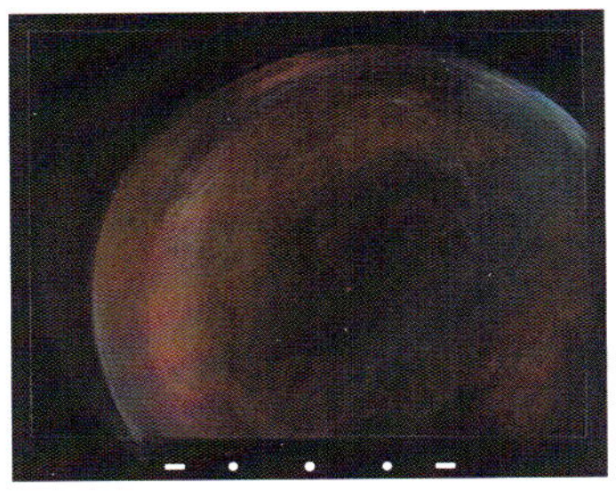

Page 27
Disney Studio Artist
Story sketch for *Fantasia*, 1940
Pastel and opaque watercolor on paper, 12 ½ x 15 ½ in. (31.8 x 39.4 cm)
Walt Disney Animation Research Library, Glendale, California

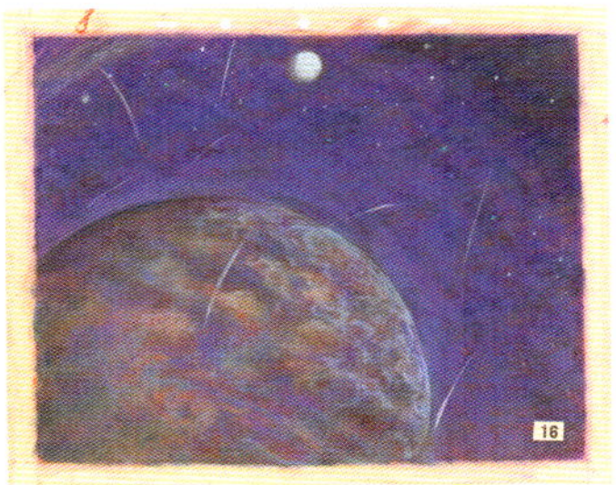

Page 27
Disney Studio Artist
Story sketch for *Fantasia*, 1940
Pastel and opaque watercolor on paper, 12 ½ x 15 ½ in. (31.8 x 39.4 cm)
Walt Disney Animation Research Library, Glendale, California

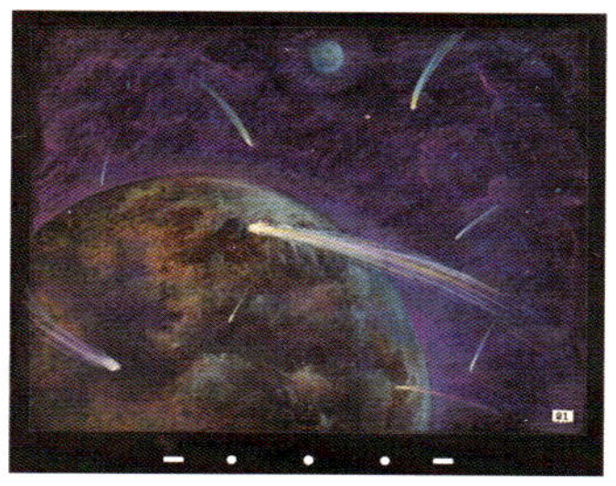

Page 27
Disney Studio Artist
Story sketch for *Fantasia*, 1940
Pastel and opaque watercolor on paper, 12 ½ x 15 ½ in. (31.8 x 39.4 cm)
Walt Disney Animation Research Library, Glendale, California

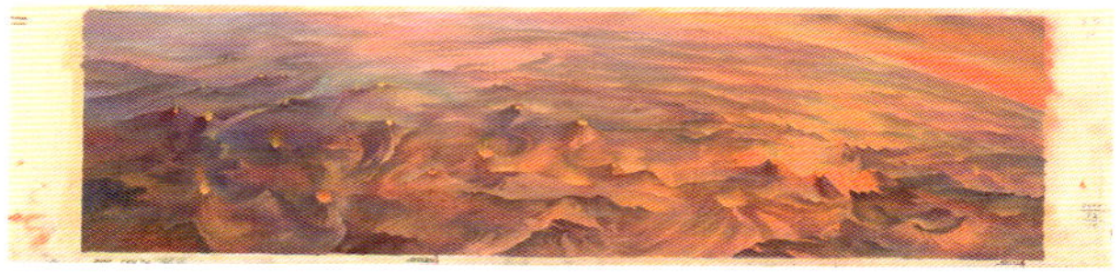

Pages 28–29
Disney Studio Artist
Background for *Fantasia*, 1940
Opaque watercolor on paper, 12 x 50 in. (30.5 x 127 cm)
Walt Disney Animation Research Library, Glendale, California

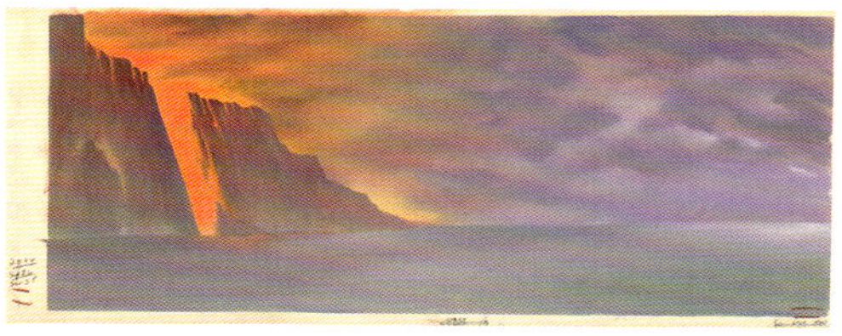

Pages 28–29
Disney Studio Artist
Background for *Fantasia*, 1940
Opaque watercolor on paper, 12 x 30 ¼ in. (30.5 x 78.1 cm)
Walt Disney Animation Research Library, Glendale, California

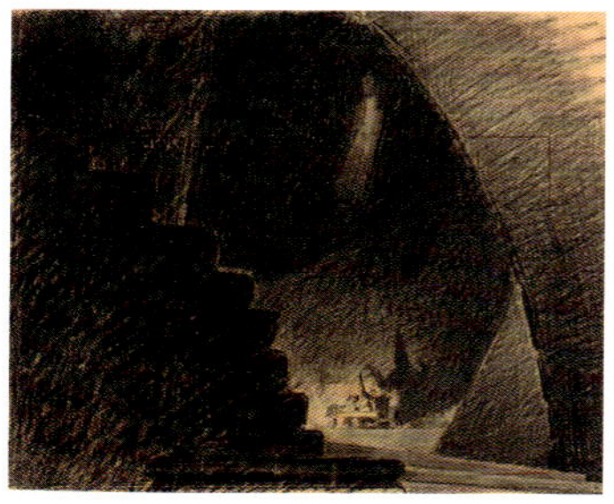

Page 30
Disney Studio Artist
Story sketch for *Fantasia*, 1940
Graphite and colored pencil on paper: image, 11 ¼ x 13 ½ in. (28.6 x 34.3 cm)
Walt Disney Animation Research Library, Glendale, California

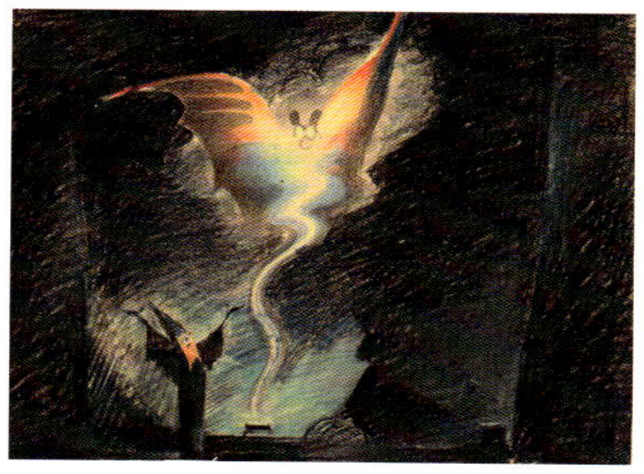

Page 30
Disney Studio Artist
Story sketch for *Fantasia*, 1940
Colored pencil on paper: image, 7 ½ x 9 ¾ in. (14 x 17.1 cm)
Walt Disney Animation Research Library, Glendale, California

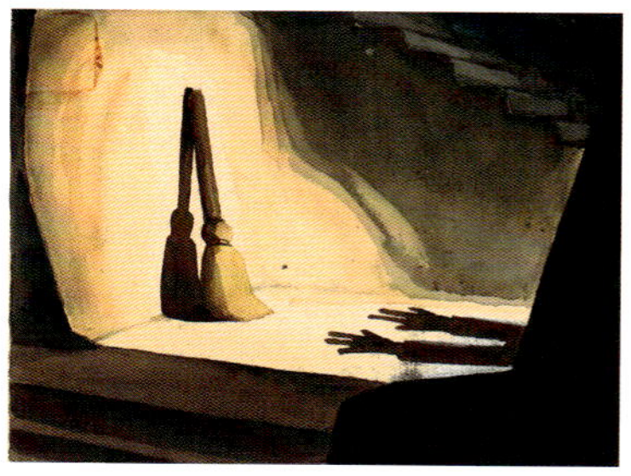

Page 30
Disney Studio Artist
Story sketch for *Fantasia*, 1940
Opaque watercolor on paper: image, 5 ½ x 6 ¾ in. (19 x 24.8 cm)
Walt Disney Animation Research Library, Glendale, California

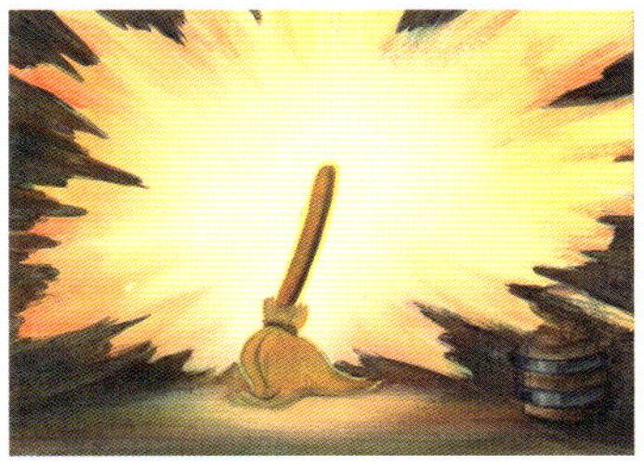

Page 30
Disney Studio Artist
Story sketch for *Fantasia*, 1940
Opaque watercolor on paper: image, 7 x 8 ½ in. (17.8 x 21.6 cm)
Walt Disney Animation Research Library, Glendale, California

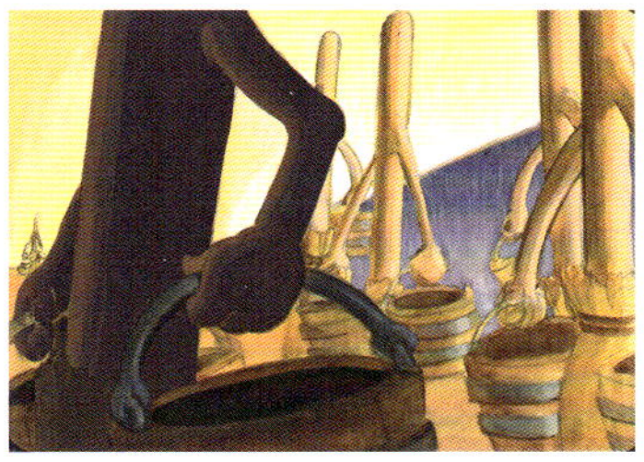

Page 30
Disney Studio Artist
Story sketch for *Fantasia*, 1940
Opaque watercolor on paper: image, 7 x 8 ¼ in. (17.8 x 21 cm)
Walt Disney Animation Research Library, Glendale, California

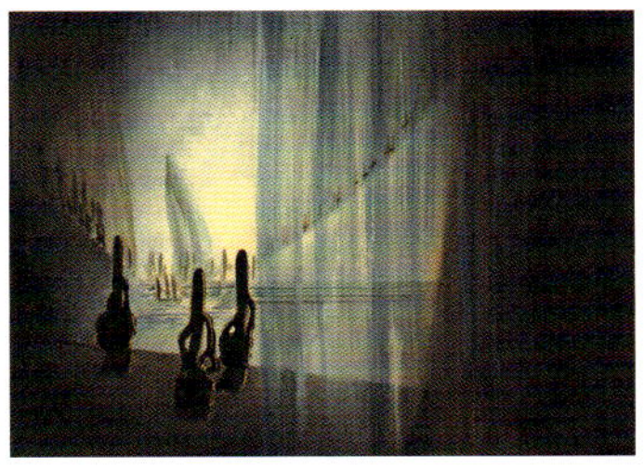

Page 31
Disney Studio Artist
Story sketch for *Fantasia*, 1940
Opaque watercolor on paper: image, 6 ¾ x 8 ¼ in. (17.1 x 21 cm)
Walt Disney Animation Research Library, Glendale, California

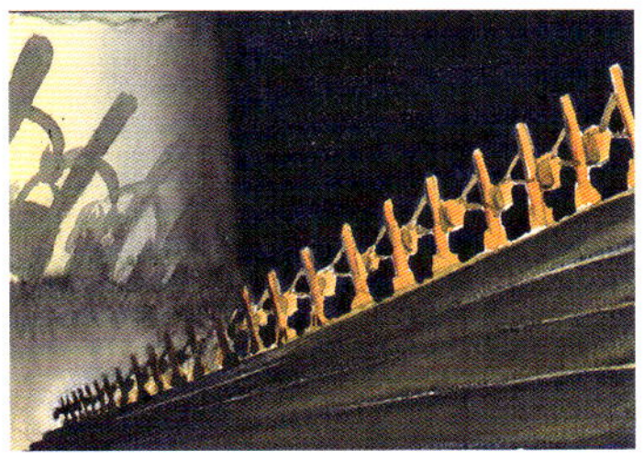

Page 31
Disney Studio Artist
Story sketch for *Fantasia*, 1940
Opaque watercolor on paper: image, 3 ½ x 4 ½ in. (8.9 x 11.4 cm)
Walt Disney Animation Research Library, Glendale, California

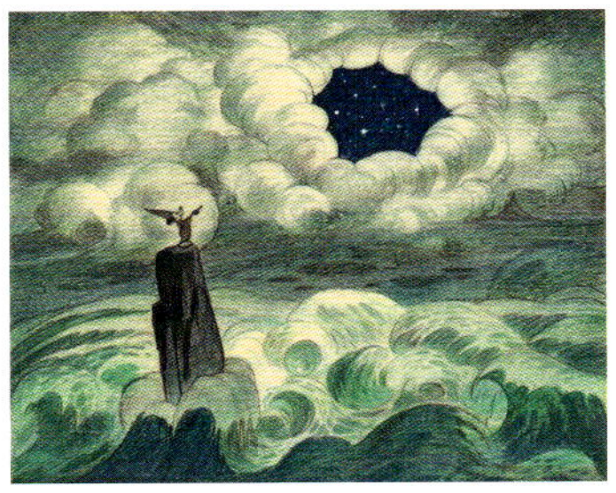

Page 31
Disney Studio Artist
Story sketch for *Fantasia*, 1940
Graphite and colored pencil on paper: image, 7 x 8 ½ in. (17.8 x 21.6 cm)
Walt Disney Animation Research Library, Glendale, California

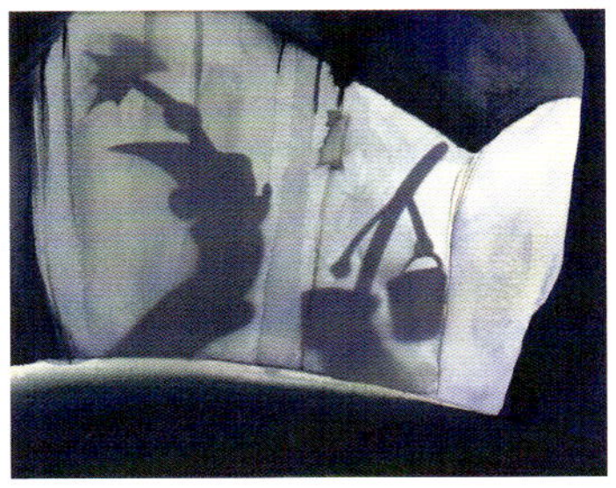

Page 31
Disney Studio Artist
Story sketch for *Fantasia*, 1940
Watercolor on paper and gum-based cel paint on cellulose acetate:
image, 6 ¾ x 8 ¾ in. (17.1 x 22.2 cm)
Walt Disney Animation Research Library, Glendale, California

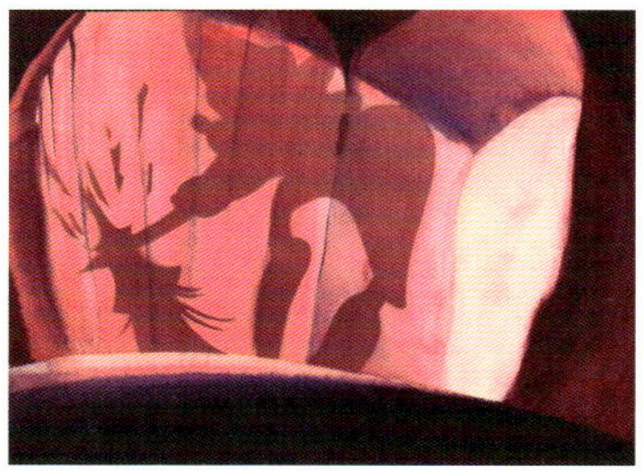

Page 31
Disney Studio Artist
Story sketch for *Fantasia*, 1940
Watercolor on paper and gum-based cel paint on cellulose acetate: image, 8 x 10 in. (20.3 x 25.4 cm)
Walt Disney Animation Research Library, Glendale, California

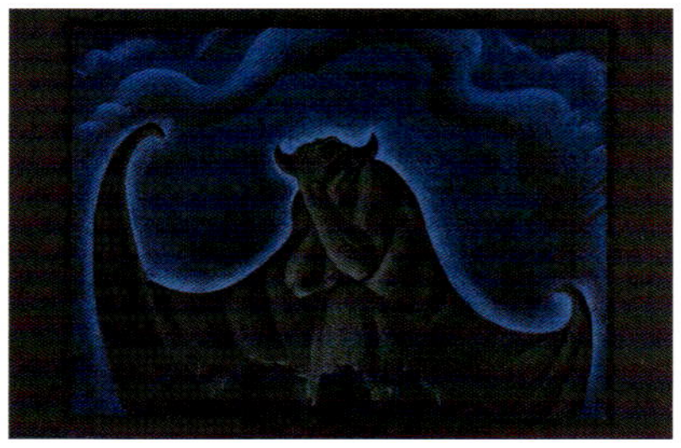

Pages 32–33
Disney Studio Artist
Story sketch for *Fantasia*, 1940
Pastel on paper, 12 ½ x 15 ½ in. (31.8 x 39.4 cm)
Walt Disney Animation Research Library, Glendale, California

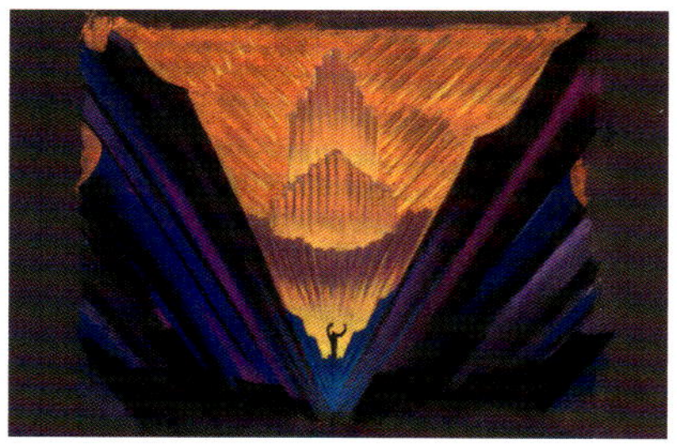

Page 34–35
Disney Studio Artist
Story sketch for *Fantasia*, 1940
Pastel on paper, 6 ¾ x 8 ¼ in. (17.1 x 21 cm)
Walt Disney Animation Research Library, Glendale, California

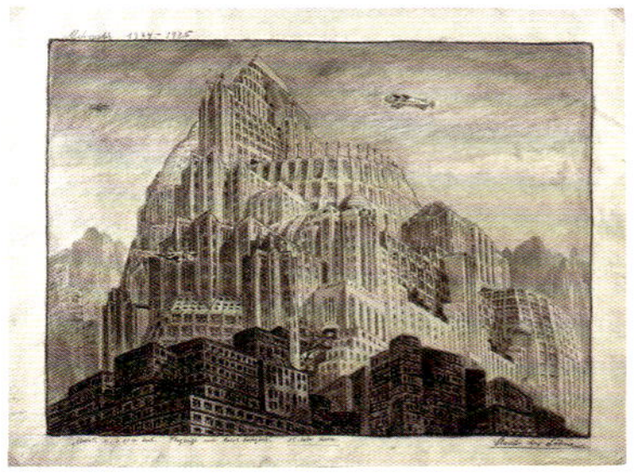

Page 36
Erich Kettelhut (1893–1979)
*City of Sons*, 1924–25
Production drawing for *Metropolis* (1927), 1924–25
Colored pencil and ink wash on paper, white heightened, 17 ¾ x 23 ¾ in. (45.3 x 60.4 cm)
Stiftung Deutsche Kinemathek, Berlin; Collection Erich Kettelhut

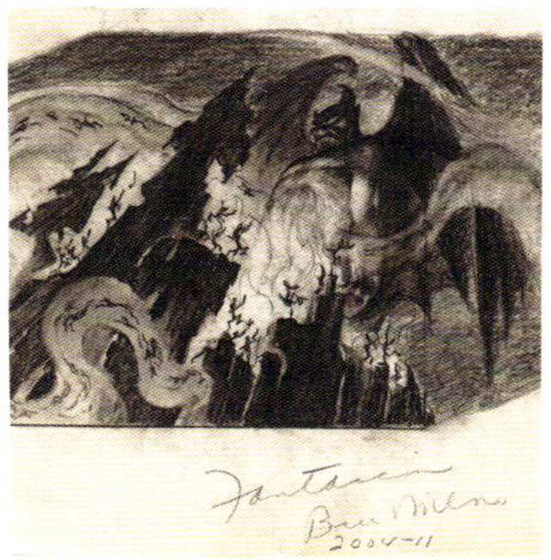

Page 36
Disney Studio Artist
Story sketch for *Fantasia*, 1940
Charcoal on paper, 8 ¾ x 8 in. (22.2 x 20.3 cm)
Walt Disney Animation Research Library, Glendale, California

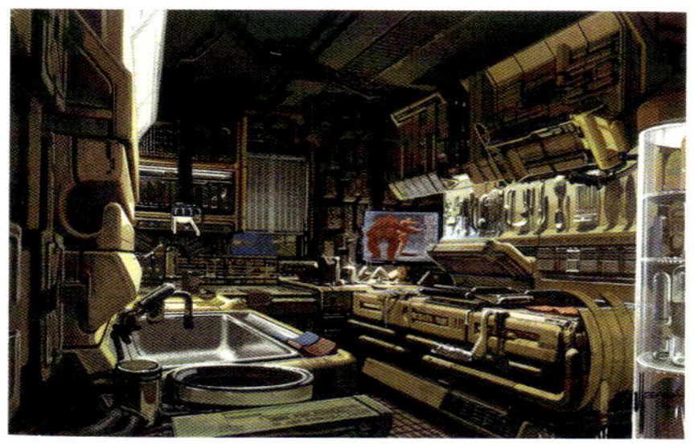

Page 37
Syd Mead (b. 1933)
Concept design painting for *Blade Runner*, 1982
Opaque watercolor on illustration board, 10 x 15 in. (25.4 x 38.1 cm)
Collection of the artist

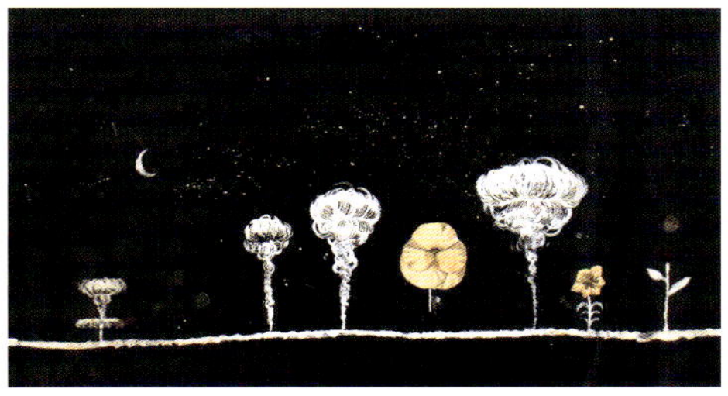

Page 38
Stan VanDerBeek (1927–1984)
Animation frame from *Breathdeath*, 1963
Collage and paint on paper, 12 ½ x 23 in. (31.8 x 58.4 cm)
Private collection

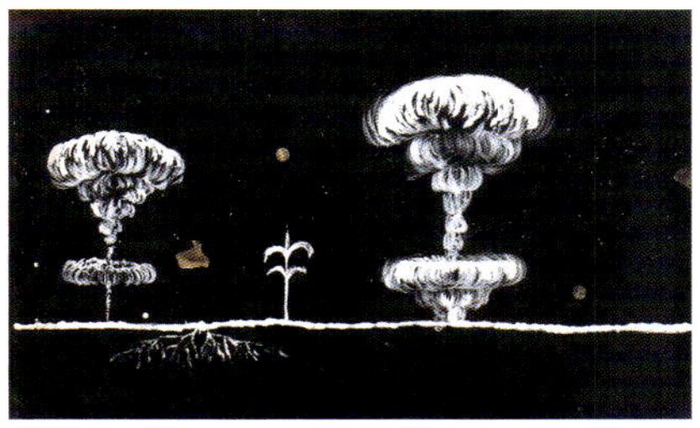

Page 39
Stan VanDerBeek (1927–1984)
Animation frame from *Breathdeath*, 1963
Collage and paint on paper, 15 ½ x 21 ¾ in. (39.4 x 55.3 cm)
Private collection

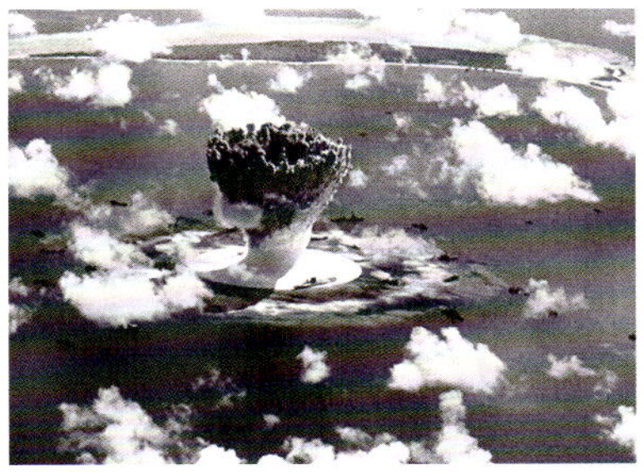

Pages 40, 41
Bruce Conner (1933–2008)
Frame enlargements from CROSSROADS, 1976
35mm film, black-and-white, sound; 37 min.

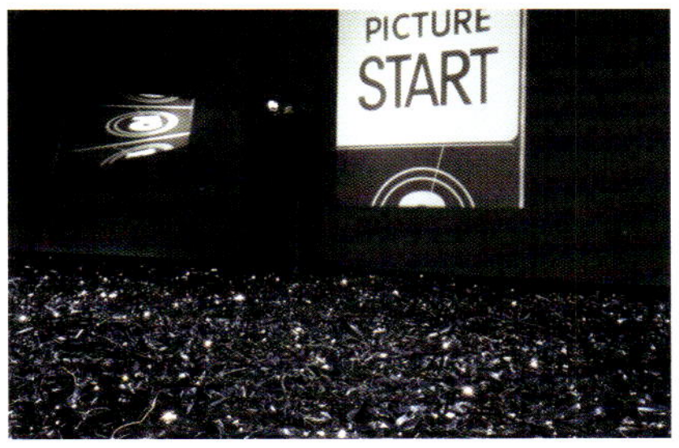


Pages 42–43
Jud Yalkut (1938–2013)
*Destruct Film*, 1967
16mm film, color, silent; 16mm film projector; film looper; two 35mm color slides; two slide projectors; two motorized beam-splitter mirrors; and loose film prints
Whitney Museum of American Art, New York; purchase with funds from the Film and Video Committee 2002.92
Installation view, Whitney Museum, New York, 2000

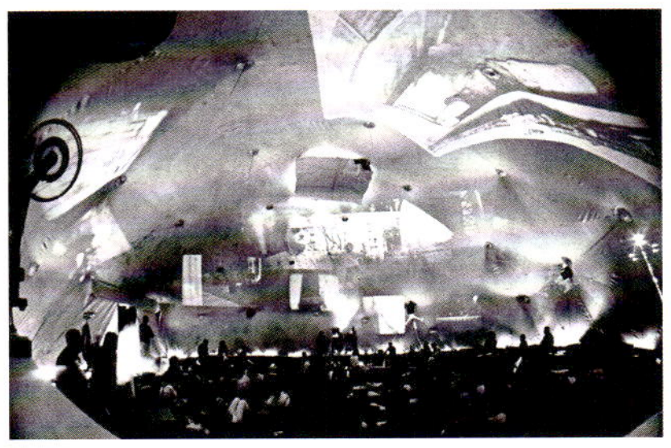

Pages 44–45
Stan VanDerBeek (1927–1984)
*Movie-Drome*, 1963–65
Moving and still images, color and black-and-white, with sound projected simultaneously inside dome structure
Installation view, Design-In, Central Park, New York, 1967

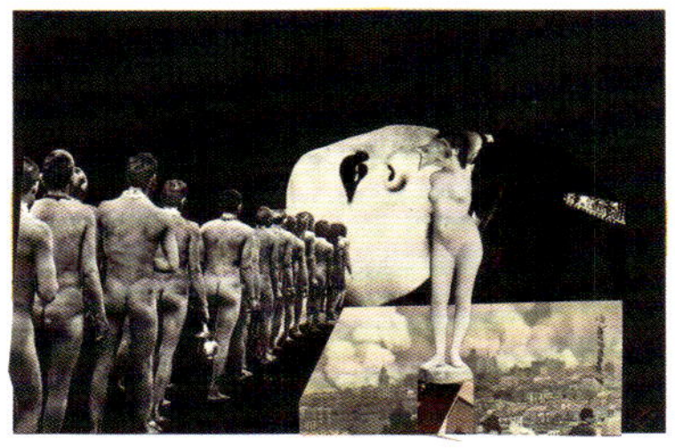

Pages 46–47
Stan VanDerBeek (1927–1984)
*Photomontage of stills from "Facescapes"*, 1965
Collaged gelatin silver prints and magazine pages, mounted on paper and cardboard, 11 ⅝ x 17 ½ in. (29.5 x 44.5 cm)
Whitney Museum of American Art, New York; purchase with funds from the Drawing Committee; the Film, Video, and New Media Committee; the Photography Committee; Gregg G. Seibert; and Craig F. Starr 2015.70

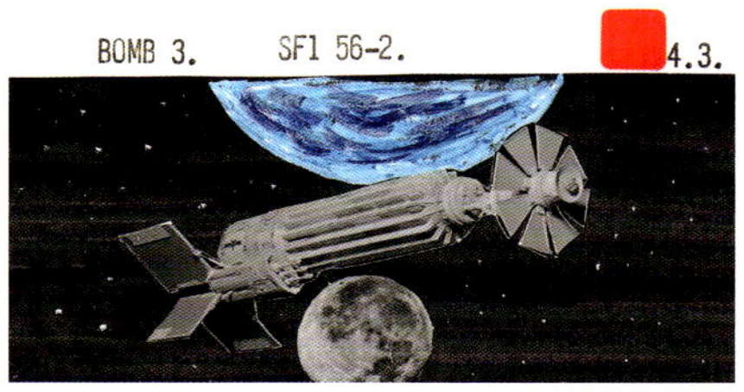


Pages 48, 49
Stanley Kubrick (1928–1999)
Sasco cards for *2001: A Space Odyssey*, 1963–68
Paint and felt-tip pen on card, 29 ½ x 49 ¼ in. (75 x 125 cm) each
Stanley Kubrick Archive, University of the Arts London

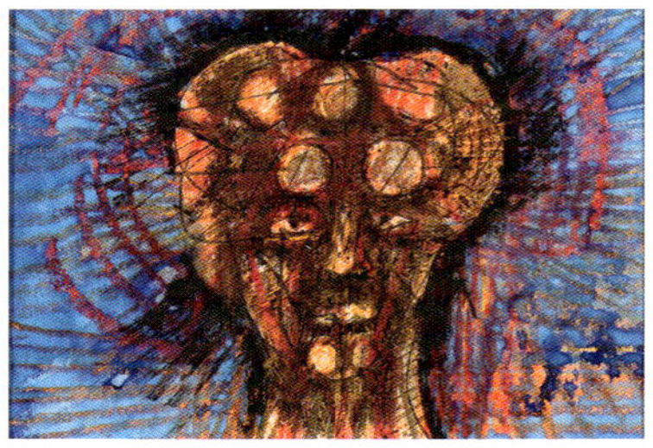

Page 50
Stan VanDerBeek (1927–1984)
*Untitled*, n.d.
Opaque watercolor and pastel on vellum, 5 13⁄16 x 6 13⁄16 in. (14.8 x 17.3 cm)
Whitney Museum of American Art, New York; purchase with funds from the Drawing Committee; the Film, Video, and New Committee; the Photography Committee; Gregg G. Seibert, and Craig F. Starr 2015.62

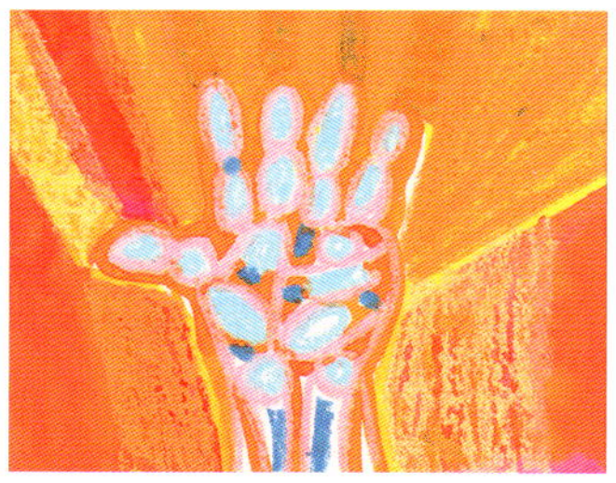

Page 50
Stan VanDerBeek (1927–1984)
*Untitled*, n.d.
Opaque watercolor and pastel on vellum, 5 ⅜ x 6 ¾ in. (13.7 x 17.1 cm)
Whitney Museum of American Art, New York; purchase with funds from the Drawing Committee; the Film, Video, and New Committee; the Photography Committee; Gregg G. Seibert; and Craig F. Starr 2015.68

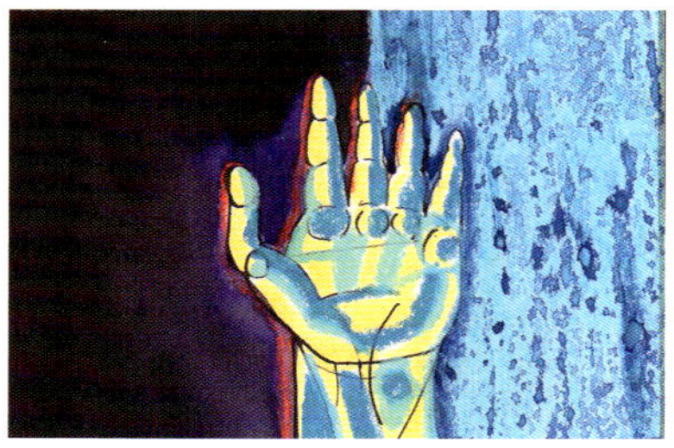

Page 50
Stan VanDerBeek (1927–1984)
*Untitled*, n.d.
Opaque watercolor, pastel, and ink on vellum, 4 15⁄16 x 6 13⁄16 in. (12.5 x 17.3 cm)
Whitney Museum of American Art, New York; purchase with funds from the Drawing Committee; the Film, Video, and New Committee; the Photography Committee; Gregg G. Seibert; and Craig F. Starr 2015.64

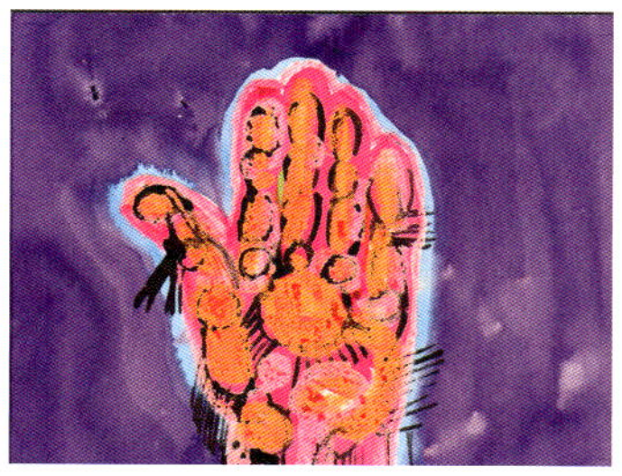

Page 50
Stan VanDerBeek (1927–1984)
*Untitled*, n.d.
Opaque watercolor and pastel on vellum, 5 7⁄16 x 6 ⅞ in. (13.8 x 17.5 cm)
Whitney Museum of American Art, New York; purchase with funds from the Drawing Committee; the Film, Video, and New Committee; the Photography Committee; Gregg G. Seibert; and Craig F. Starr 2015.66

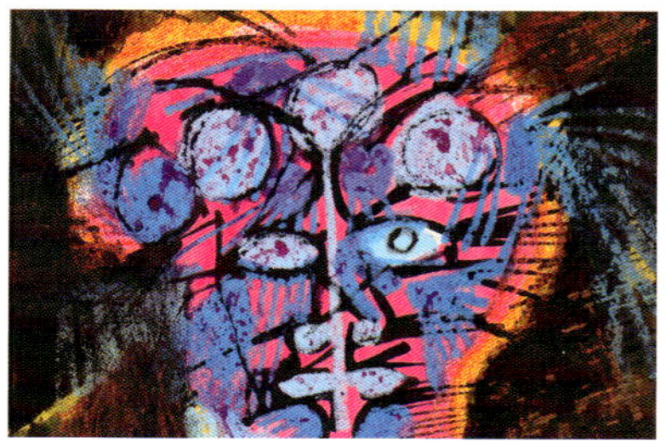

Page 50
Stan VanDerBeek (1927–1984)
*Untitled*, n.d.
Opaque watercolor and pastel on vellum, 5 15⁄16 x 6 15⁄16 in. (15.1 x 17.6 cm)
Whitney Museum of American Art, New York; purchase with funds from the Drawing Committee, the Film, Video, and New Committee, the Photography Committee, Gregg G. Seibert, and Craig F. Starr 2015.61

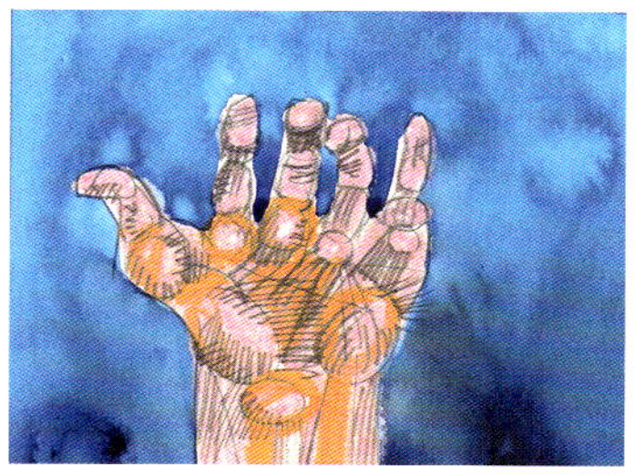

Page 50
Stan VanDerBeek (1927–1984)
*Untitled*, n.d.
Opaque watercolor and graphite pencil on vellum, 4 ⅞ x 6 ¹³⁄₁₆ in. (12.4 x 17.3 cm)
Whitney Museum of American Art, New York; purchase with funds from the Drawing Committee; the Film, Video, and New Committee; the Photography Committee; Gregg G. Seibert; and Craig F. Starr 2015.65

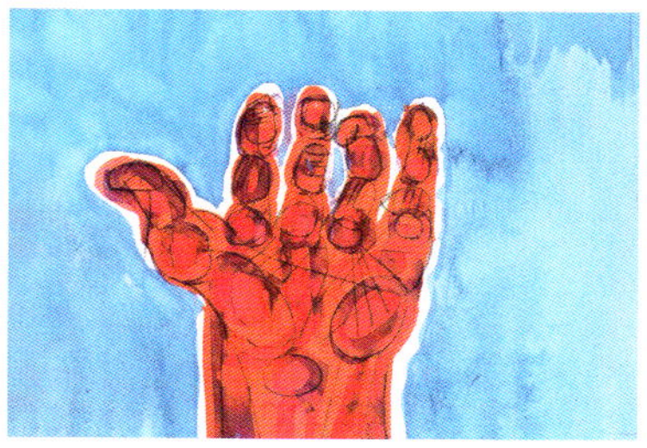

Page 50
Stan VanDerBeek (1927–1984)
*Untitled*, n.d.
Opaque watercolor and pastel on vellum, 4 ⅞ x 6 ¹³⁄₁₆ in. (12.4 x 17.3 cm)
Whitney Museum of American Art, New York; purchase with funds from the Drawing Committee; the Film, Video, and New Committee; the Photography Committee; Gregg G. Seibert; and Craig F. Starr 2015.67

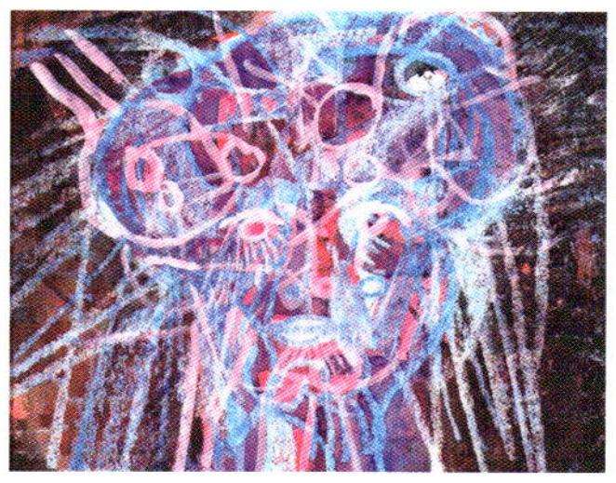

Page 50
Stan VanDerBeek (1927–1984)
*Untitled*, n.d.
Opaque watercolor and pastel on vellum, 5 ⅞ x 6 ⅞ in. (14.9 x 17.5 cm)
Whitney Museum of American Art, New York; purchase with funds from the Drawing Committee; the Film, Video, and New Committee; the Photography Committee; Gregg G. Seibert; and Craig F. Starr 2015.63

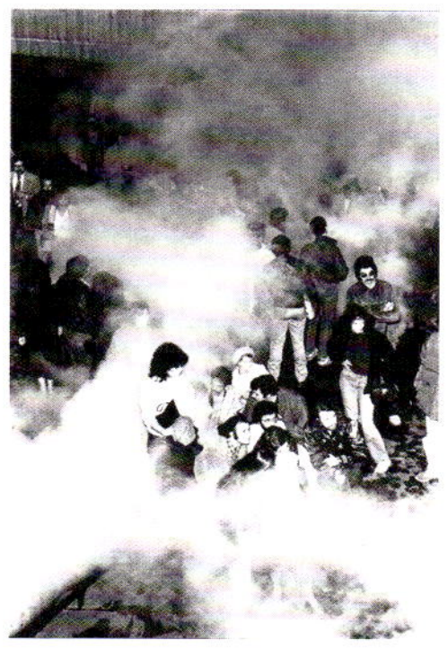

Page 51
Stan VanDerBeek (1927–1984) and Joan Brigham (b. 1935)
*Steam Screens*, 1979
Installation and performance with steam and projected film
Installation view, Whitney Museum, New York, 1979

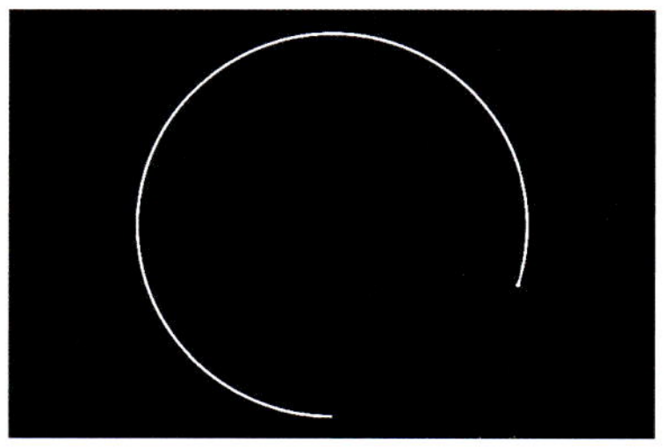

Page 52
Anthony McCall (b. 1946)
Frame from the 24th minute of *Line Describing a Cone*, 1973
16mm film, black-and-white, silent; 30 min.
Whitney Museum of American Art, New York; purchase with funds from the Film and Video Committee 2001.248

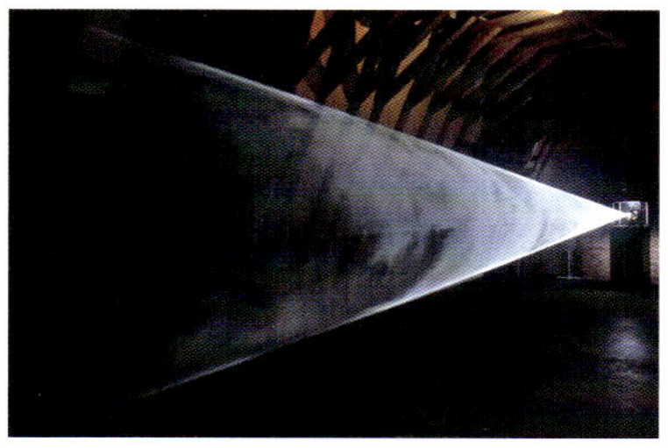

Page 52
Anthony McCall (b. 1946)
*Line Describing a Cone*, 1973
Installation view depicting the 24th minute, Musée Départemental d'Art Contemporain de Rochechouart, 2007

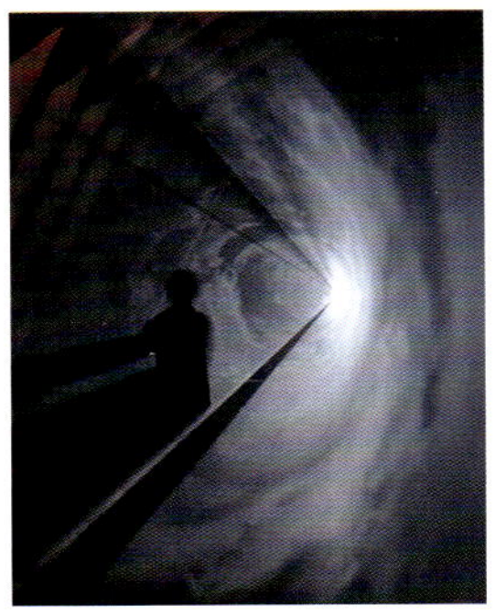

Page 53
Anthony McCall (b. 1946)
*Line Describing a Cone*, 1973
Installation view depicting the 24th minute, Musée Départemental d'Art Contemporain de Rochechouart, 2007

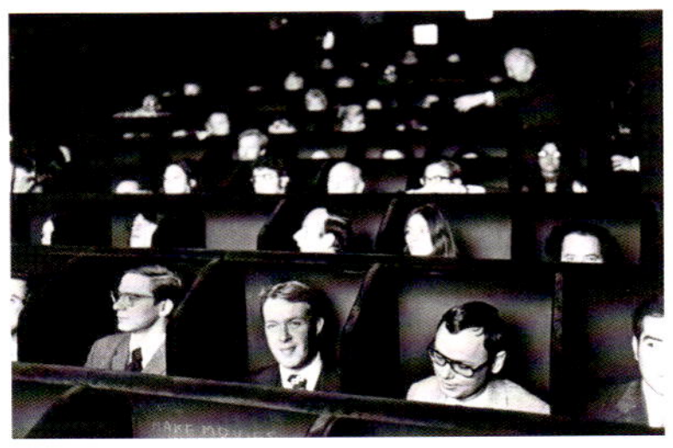

Pages 54–55
Peter Kubelka (b. 1934) and Jonas Mekas (b. 1922)
Invisible Cinema, Anthology Film Archives, New York, 1970

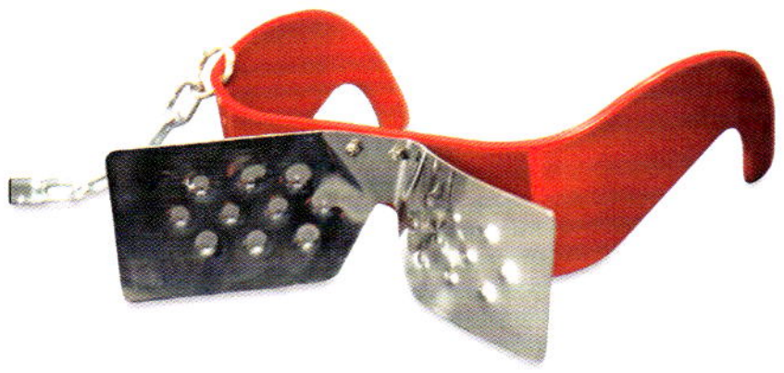

Page 56
Julio Le Parc (b. 1928)
*Lunettes pour une autre vision*, 1965
Plastic and steel, approx. 2 x 6 x 8 in. (5 x 15.3 x 20.3 cm)
Collection of the artist

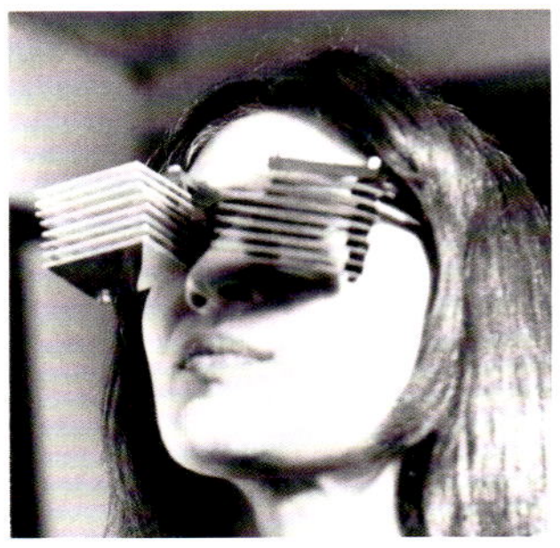

Page 56
Martha Le Parc wearing *Lunettes pour une autre vision*, 1965

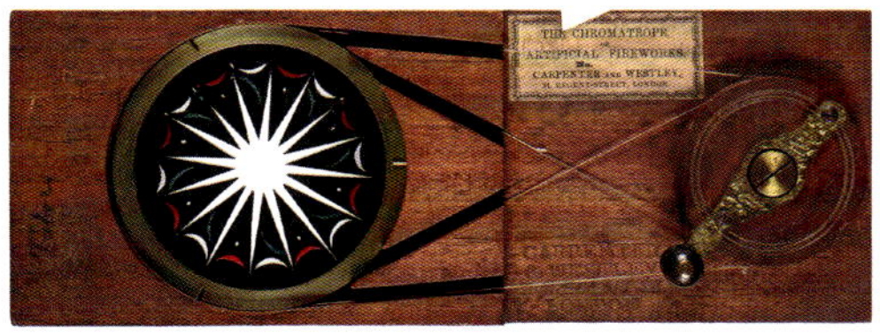

Page 56
Carpenter and Westley (1808–1914)
The chromatrope or artificial fireworks, c. 1880
Wood, glass, and metal, 3 ¾ x 9 ⅞ x 1 ¾ in. (9.5 x 25 x 4.5 cm)
Getty Research Institute, Los Angeles (97.R.57)

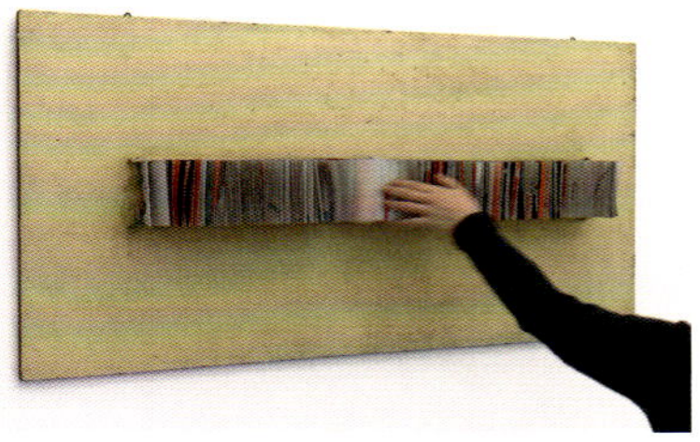

Page 57
Robert Breer (1926–2011)
*Mural Flip Book*, 1964
Wood, metal, and paper, 22 x 46 x 5 in. (55.9 x 116.8 x 12.7 cm)
Coleção Teixeira de Freitas

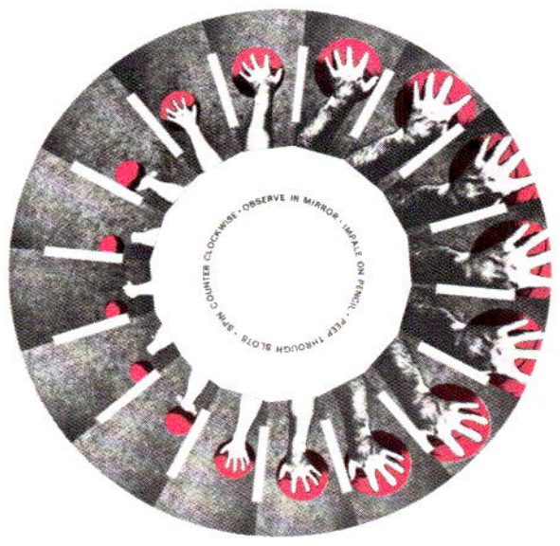

Page 57
Hollis Frampton (1936–1984)
*Penakisticope*, 1968 (recto and verso), from the portfolio *S.M.S. #4*
Ink on paper, 7 in. (17.8 cm) diameter
Frances Mulhall Achilles Library, Whitney Museum of American Art, New York

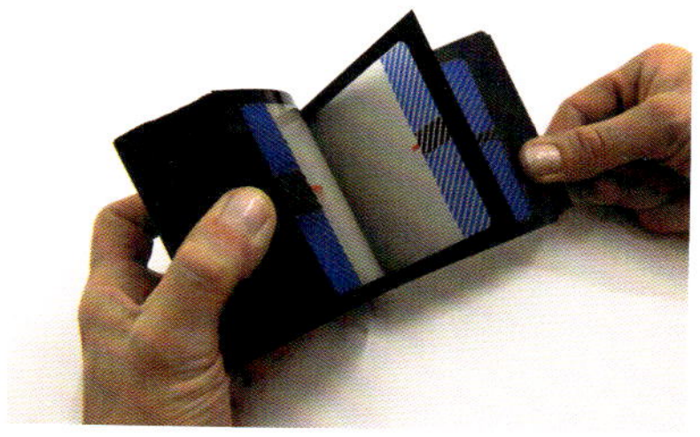

Page 57
Robert Breer (1926–2011)
*Flip book*, 1950
Slidecraft and screws, 4 x 3 ¼ x 1 ⅛ in. (10.1 x 8.2 x 3 cm)
Collection of Kate Flax

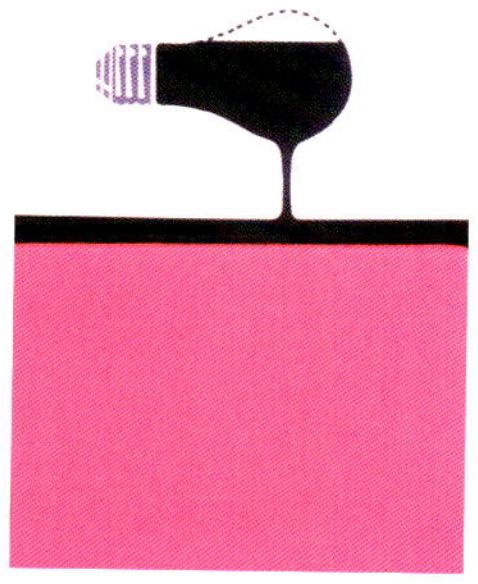

Page 58
Paul Sharits (1943–1993)
Frame enlargement from *N.O.T.H.I.N.G.*, 1968
16mm film, color, sound; 36 min.

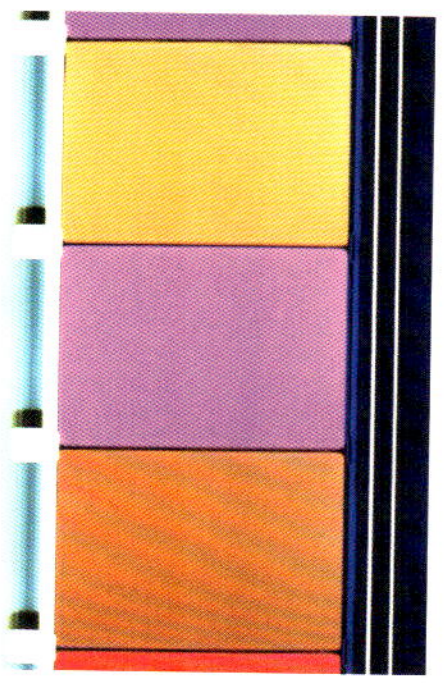

Page 59
Paul Sharits (1943–1993)
Film strip from *N.O.T.H.I.N.G.*, 1968
16mm film, color, sound; 36 min.

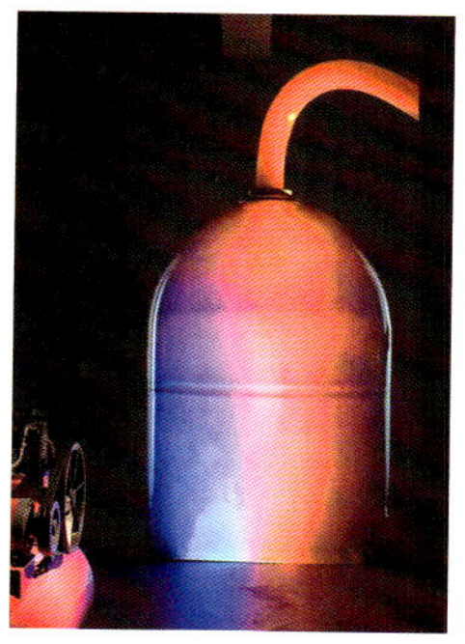

Page 60
Mike Kelley (1954–2012)
*Bottle 4*, 2007
Video, color, sound; 18:25 min.

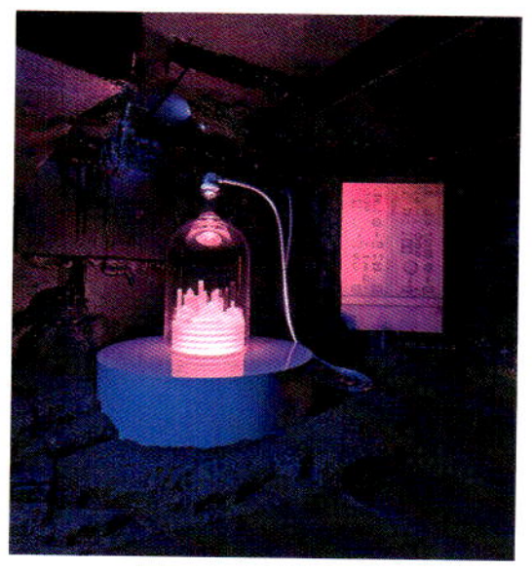

Page 61
Mike Kelley (1954–2012)
*Kandor 10B (Exploded Fortress of Solitude)*, 2011
Mixed-media installation, 9 ½ x 50 x 75 ft. (2.9 x 15.2 x 22.9 m)

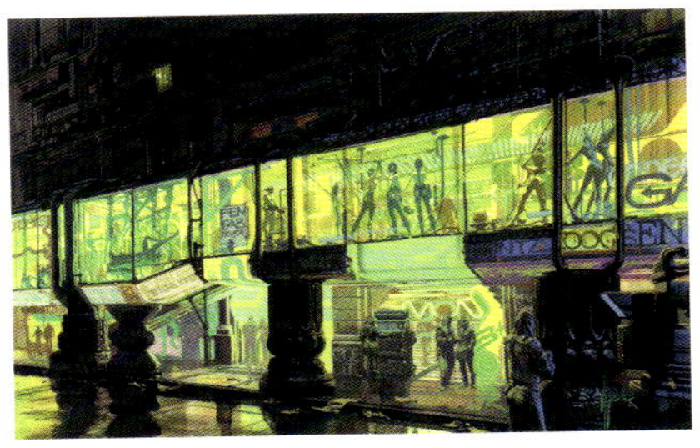

Page 62
Syd Mead (b. 1933)
Concept design painting for *Blade Runner*, 1982
Opaque watercolor on illustration board, 10 x 15 in. (25.4 x 38.1 cm)
Collection of the artist

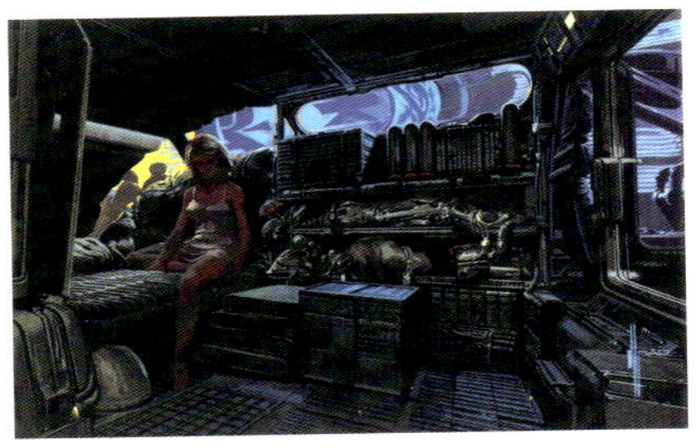

Page 63
Syd Mead (b. 1933)
Concept design painting for *Blade Runner*, 1982
Opaque watercolor on illustration board, 10 x 15 in. (25.4 x 38.1 cm)
Collection of the artist

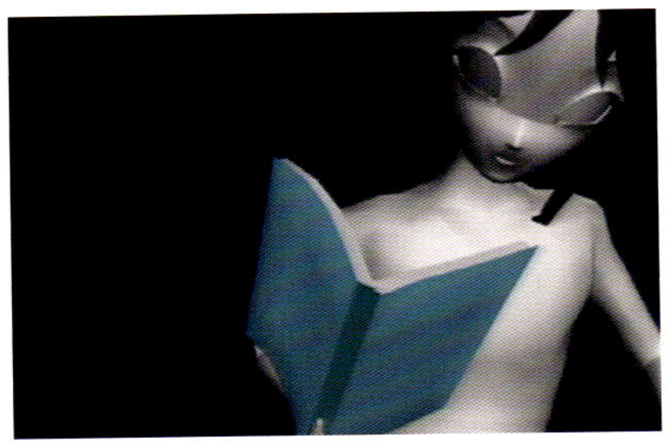

Page 64
Rirkrit Tiravanija (b. 1961)
Stills from *(Ghost Reader C.H.)*, 2002
Video, color, sound; 510 min.

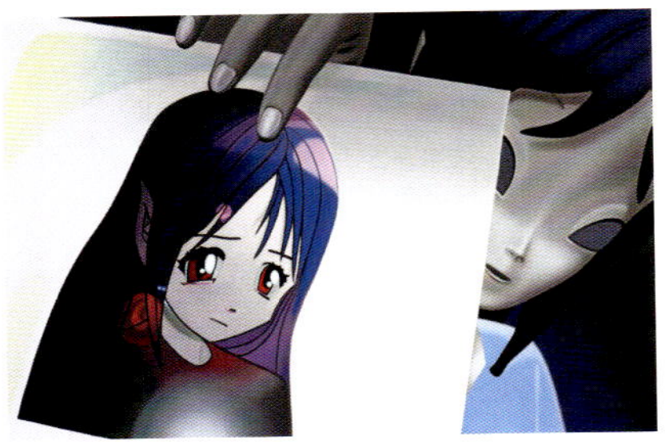

Page 65
Philippe Parreno (b. 1964)
Still from *Anywhere Out of the World*, 2000
Video, color, sound; 4 min.

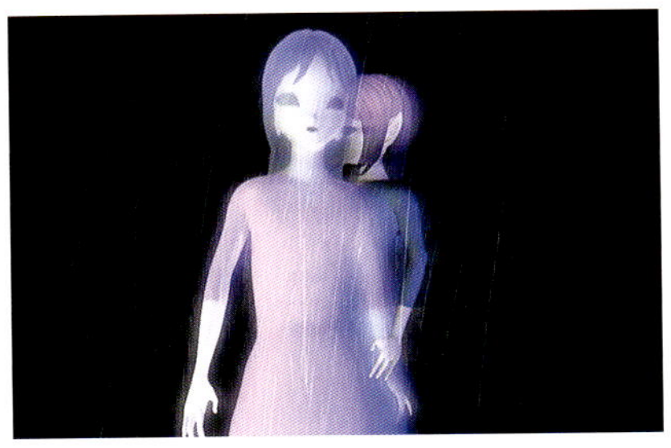

Page 66
Dominique Gonzalez-Foerster (b. 1965)
Still from *Ann Lee in Anzen Zone*, 2000
Video, color, sound; 3:25 min.

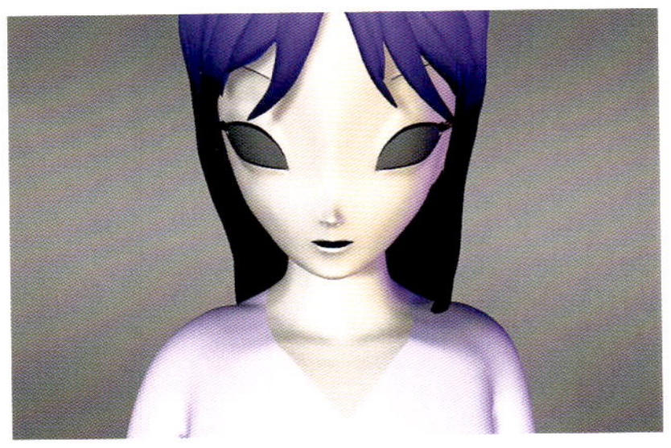

Page 67
Pierre Huyghe (b. 1962)
Still from *Two Minutes Out of Time*, 2000
Video, color, sound; 4 min.

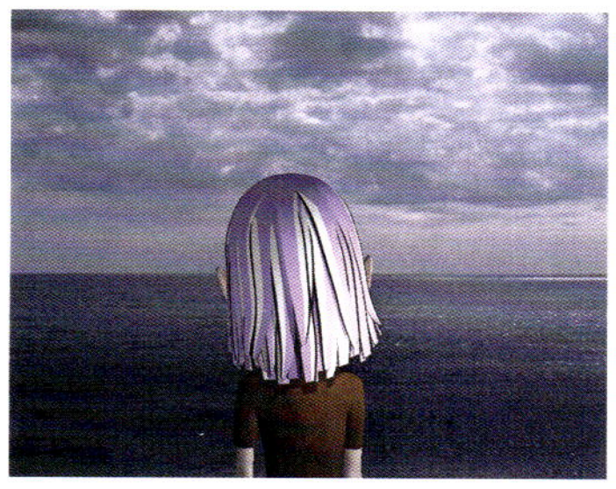

Page 68
François Curlet (b. 1967)
Still from *Witness Screen*, 2002
Video, color, sound; 5:31 min.

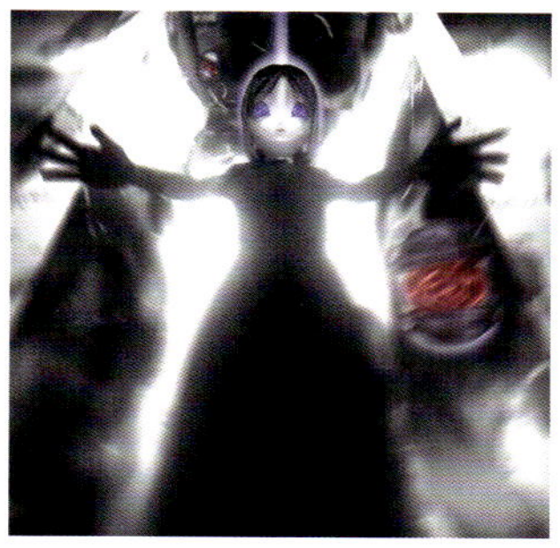

Page 68
Liam Gillick (b. 1964)
Still from *Annlee You Proposes*, 2001
Three-channel video, color, sound; 2:58 min., with furniture and lighting

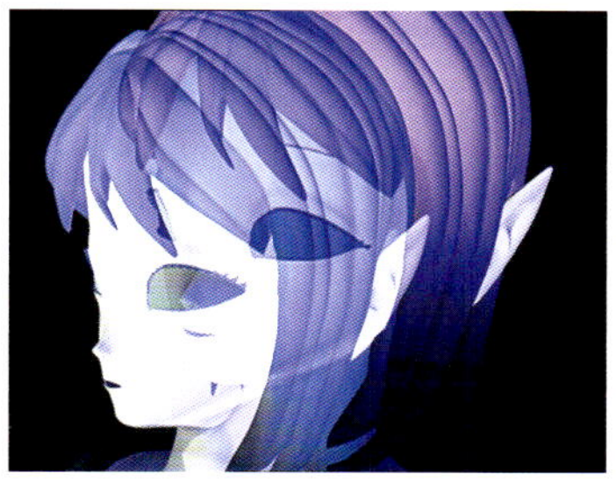

Page 68
Dominique Gonzalez-Foerster (b. 1965)
Still from *Ann Lee in Anzen Zone*, 2000
Video, color, sound; 3:25 min.

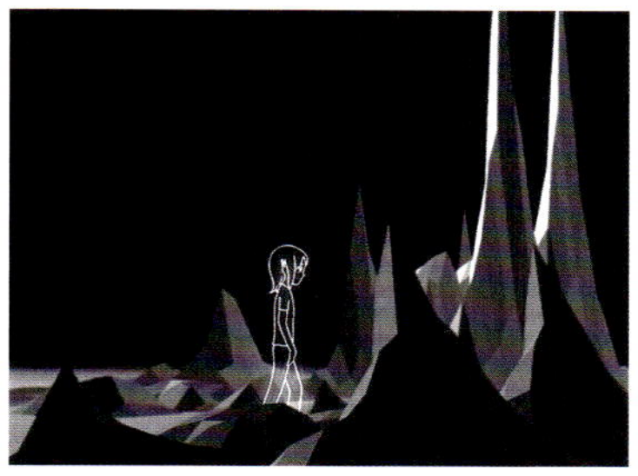

Page 69
Pierre Huyghe (b. 1962)
Still from *One Million Kingdoms*, 2000
Video, color, sound; 4 min.

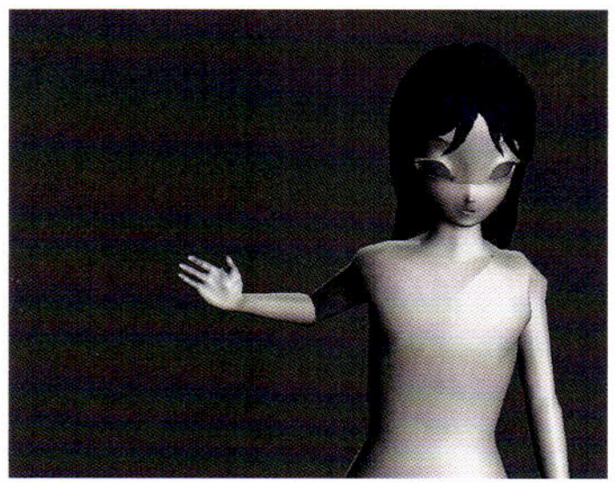

Page 69
Pierre Joseph (b. 1965) with Mehdi Belhaj Kacem (b. 1973)
Still from *Trickster Theory*, 2002
Video, color, sound; 34:59 min.

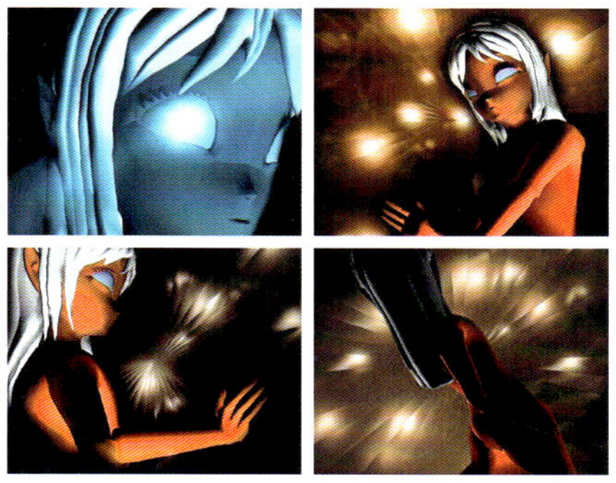

Page 69
Melik Ohanian (b. 1969)
Stills from *Ann Lee, I'm dreaming about a reality*, 2002
Video, color, sound; 4:07 min.
Music by Varou Jan

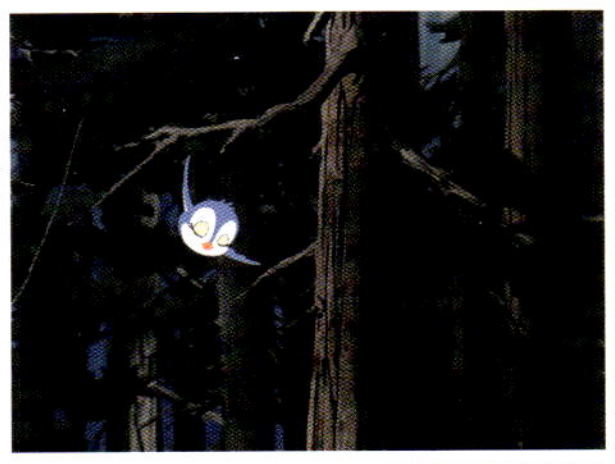

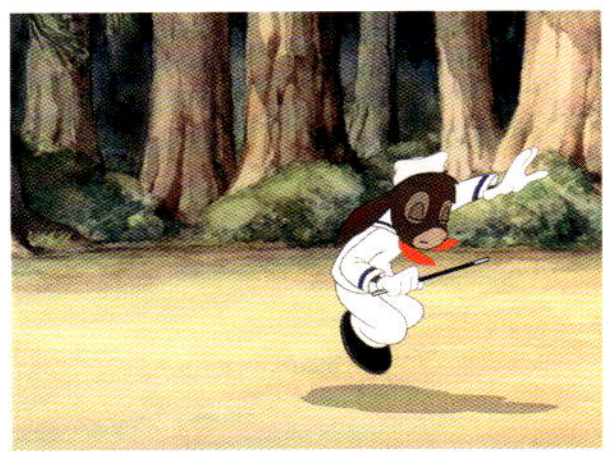

Pages 70–73
Mathias Poledna (b. 1965)
Frame enlargements from *Imitation of Life*, 2013
35mm film, color, sound; 3 min.

Pages 74–75
Alex Israel (b. 1982)
*Sky Backdrop*, 2012
Acrylic on canvas, 9 x 16 ft. (2.7 x 4.9 m)
Private collection

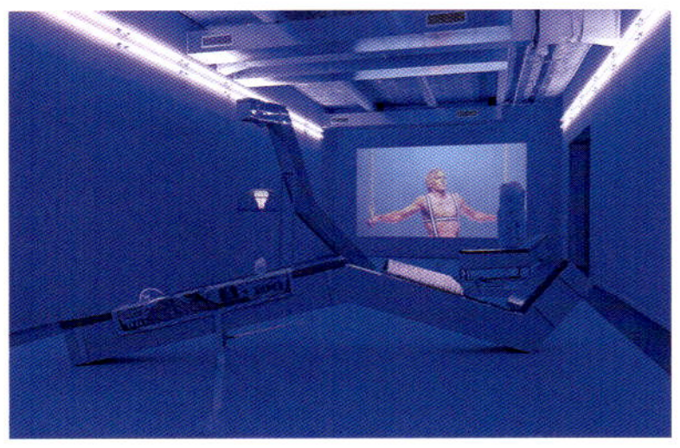

Pages 76–77
Alex Da Corte (b. 1980)
*Taut Eye Tau*, 2015
Projector, high-definition digital video, speakers, carpet, laminate, wood, plexiglass, spray paint, mirror, powder-coated steel, hardware, vinyl, foam, nylon webbing, plastic buckles, neon, IKEA bags, sand, dog leash, *Disney Animation: The Illusion of Life* by Frank Thomas and Ollie Johnston, spatula, blue tape, funnel, rubber banana, wood stain, Christmas ornament, Sharpie marker, hand-dyed One Hundred Dollar Bill beach towel, plastic dome, Finger Wet Money Casher, Smurf figurine, carpet tape, car windshield sun shade, wigs, thread, wicker lamp shade, pear light, Arduino board, LEDs, lamp hardware, broom, broom handle, paper towel holder, IKEA LILLABO train tracks, candles, Sony Playstation controller, Avon perfume bottle, Babe the Blue Ox porcelain figurine, Bud Light stash can, candlestick holder, Velcro, crystal paperweight, paint roller, Selsun Blue shampoo bottle, scissors, toy car, CD case, chain, macramé plant holder, hair ties, and Cool Water by Davidoff, dimensions variable
Musee d'art contemporain de Lyon, France
Installation view, La Sucrière, 13th Biennale de Lyon, 2015–16

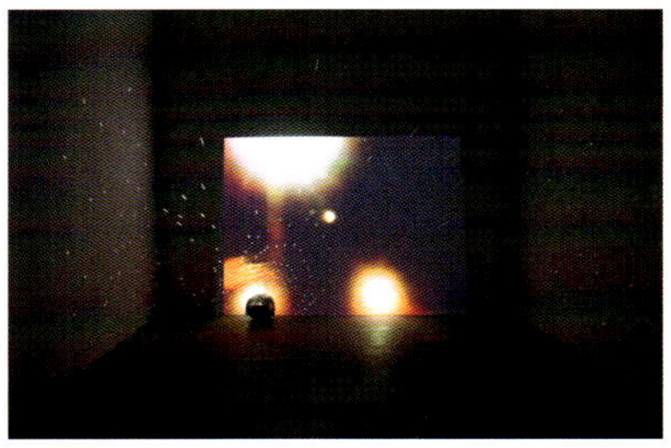

Pages 78, 79
Trisha Baga (b. 1985)
*Flatlands*, 2010
Video, color, sound; 18 min., with disco ball, and 3D glasses
Collection of the artist; courtesy Greene Naftali Gallery, New York
Installation views, Greene Naftali Gallery, New York, 2011

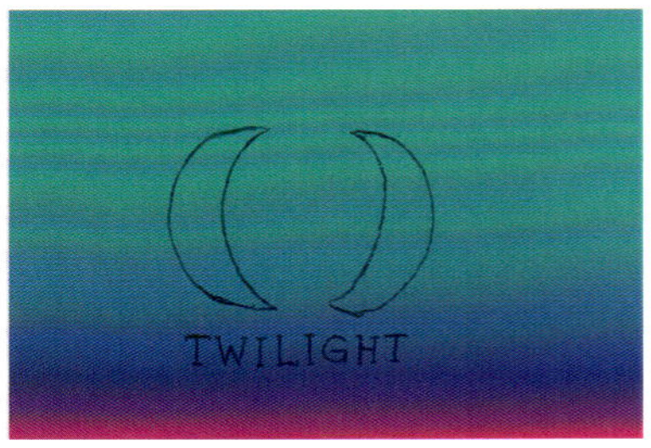


Pages 80, 81
Jenny Perlin (b. 1970)
Frame enlargements from *Twilight Arc*, 2016
Desmet-tinted black-and-white 16mm film printed on color 16mm film, silent; 12:10 min.
Collection of the artist; courtesy Simon Preston Gallery, New York; and Galerie M+R Fricke, Berlin

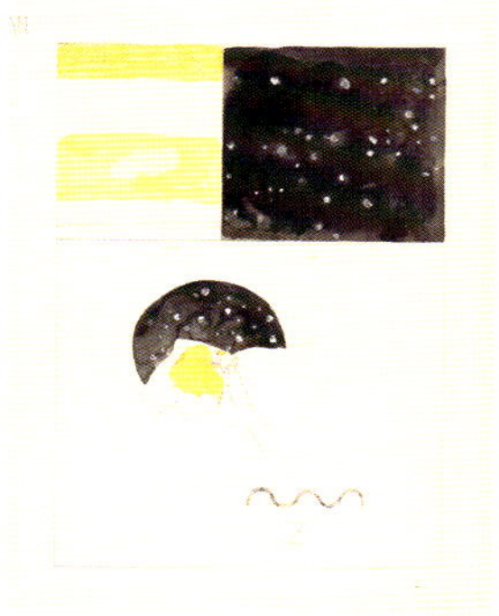

Page 82
Aidan Koch (b. 1988)
*Untitled* (drawings for pages from *The Blonde Woman*), 2012
Graphite, colored pencil, opaque watercolor, and ink, 11 x 8 ½ in. (27.9 cm x 21.6 cm) each
Collection of the artist
*The Blonde Woman*, 2012. Offset-printed softcover book, 48 pages, 9 x 6 ½ in. (22.9 x 16.5 cm), edition of 500, published by the artist

Page 83
Aidan Koch (b. 1988)
*Untitled* (page eight from *Impressions*), 2014
Opaque watercolor and pencil, 11 x 7 in. (27.9 x 17.8 cm)
*Impressions*, 2014. Offset-printed softcover book, 72 pages, edition of 1000, published by Peradam

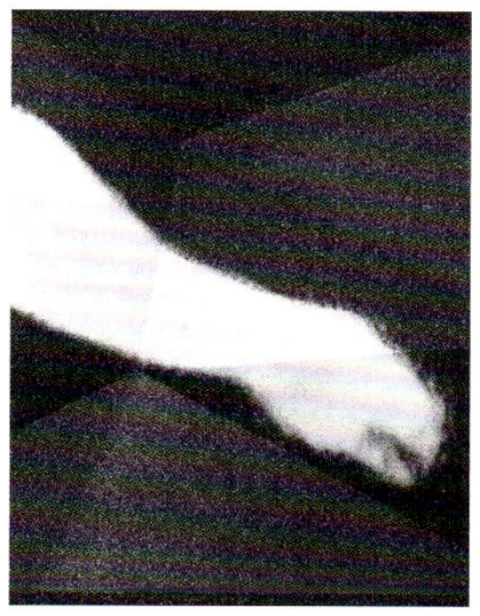

Page 84
Josiah McElheny (b. 1966)
Detail of *Projection Painting II*, 2015

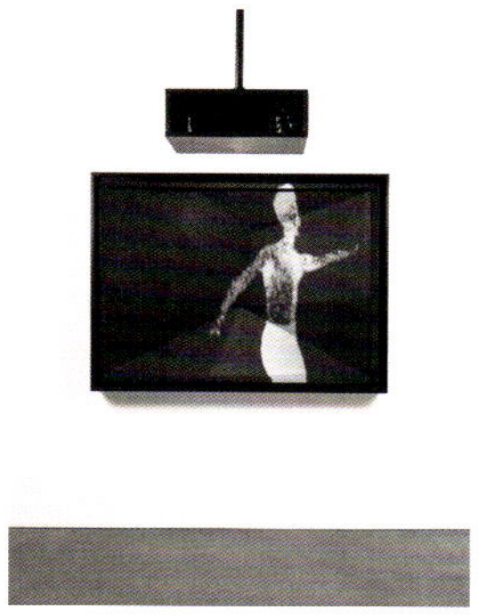

Page 85
Josiah McElheny (b. 1966)
*Projection Painting II*, 2015
Projection paint, anti-reflective glass, wood, ink, projector, hardware, and looped film footage transferred to video, black-and-white, silent, dimensions variable
Collection of the artist; courtesy Andrea Rosen Gallery, New York

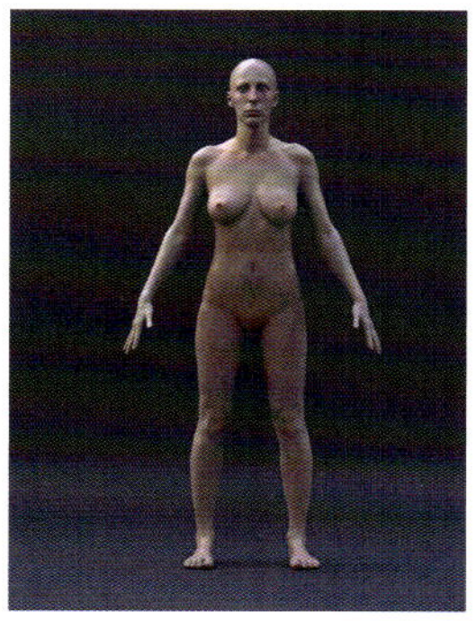

Pages 86, 87
Ivana Bašić (b. 1986)
*SOMA*, 2013–
Digital 3D model
3D modeling and rendering by Mohammad Modarres

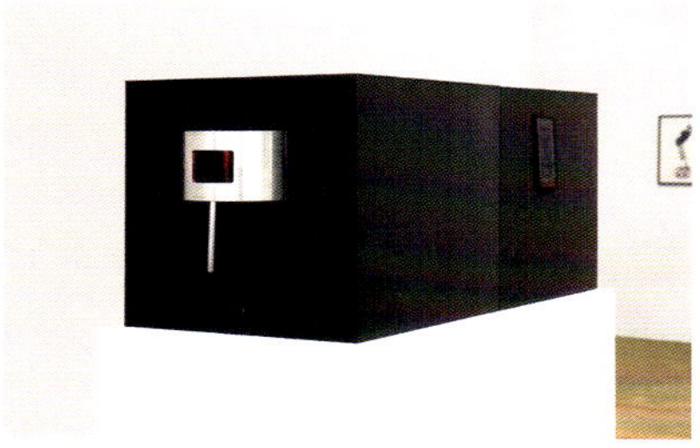

Pages 88, 89
Lynn Hershman Leeson (b. 1941)
*Room of One's Own*, 1990–93
Steel and acrylic with closed-circuit camera; video, color, sound; LEDs; and miniature furniture, 15 x 16 x 35 in. (38.1 x 40.6 x 88.9 cm)
Collection of the artist; courtesy Bridget Donahue Gallery, New York
Installation view (left) and details (right), Bridget Donahue Gallery, New York, 2015

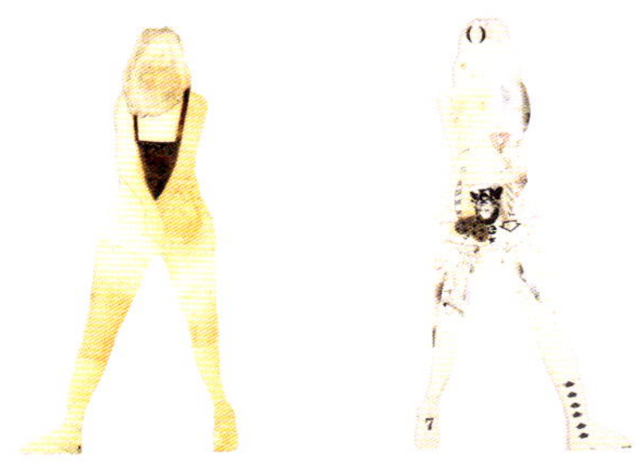

Pages 90, 91
Lynn Hershman Leeson (b. 1941)
*Double Drawing*, 1966 (verso, recto)
Ink, colored pencil, transfer type, watercolor, collaged gelatin silver prints, and plastic on paper, 8 x 4 in. (20.3 x 10.2 cm)
Collection of the artist; courtesy Bridget Donahue Gallery, New York

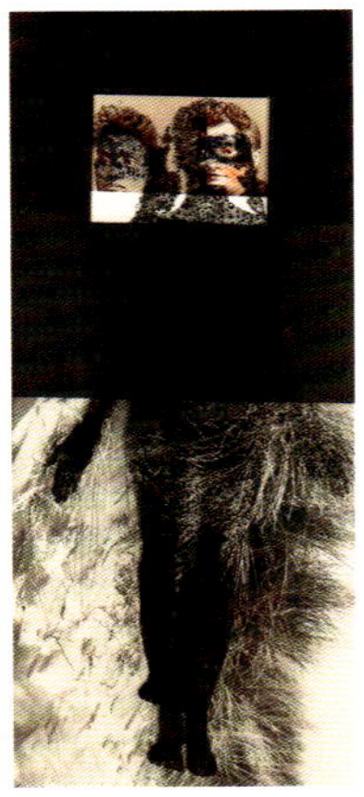

Page 92
Lynn Hershman Leeson (b. 1941)
*Water Woman 5*, 1978
Collaged photographs with acrylic, watercolor, pen on paper, and acetate, 10 x 4 in. (25.4 x 10.2 cm)
Private collection

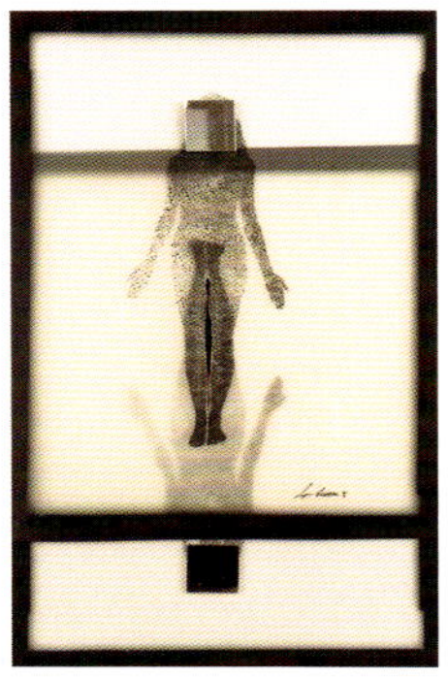

Page 93
Lynn Hershman Leeson (b. 1941)
*Water Woman 7*, 1978
Collaged photographs with mirrors on vellum, 13 ½ x 8 in. (34.3 x 20.3 cm)
Collection of the artist; courtesy Bridget Donahue Gallery, New York

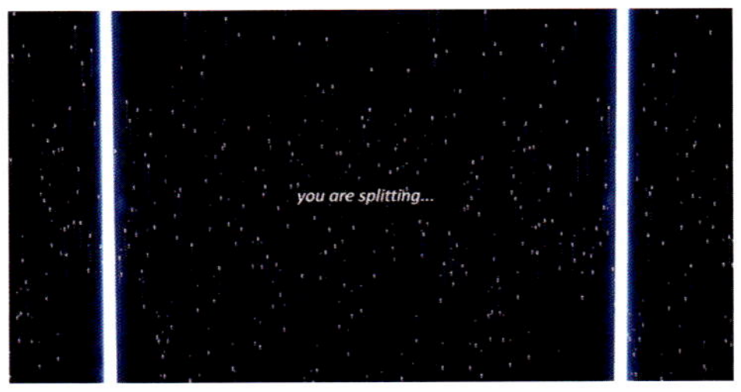


Pages 94, 95
Andrea Crespo (b. 1993)
Stills from *parabiosis: neurolibidinal induction complex 2.2*, 2015
Video, color, sound; 11:12 min.
Whitney Museum of American Art, New York, purchase with funds from the Film, VIdeo, and New Media 2016.3

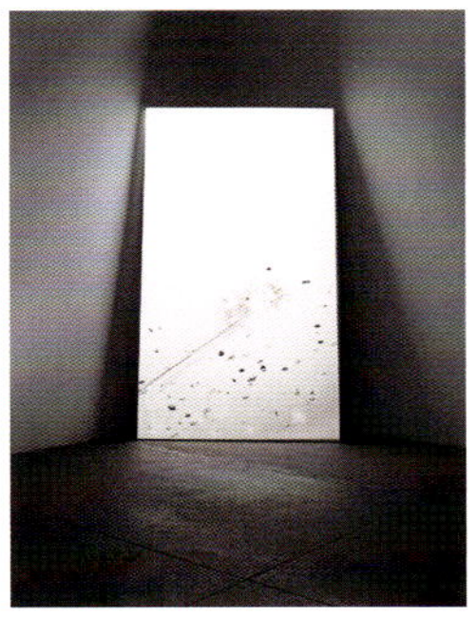

Pages 96, 97
Ian Cheng (b. 1984)
*Baby feat. Ikaria*, 2013
Video, color, sound; infinite duration, with live simulation and artificial intelligence services
Whitney Museum of American Art, New York; gift of Candy and Michael Barasch 2015.197

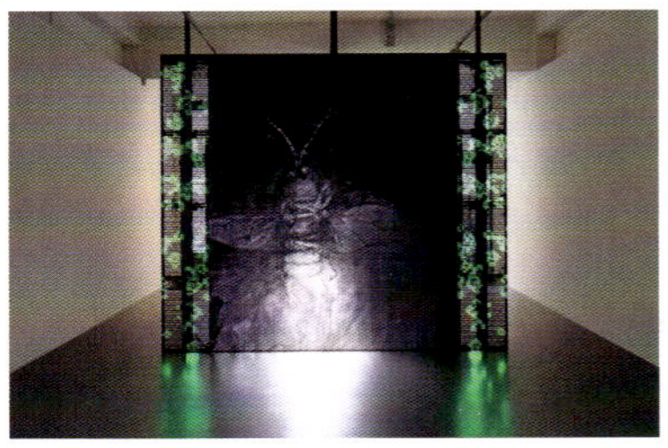

Pages 98–99
Philippe Parreno (b. 1964)
*With a Rhythmic Instinction to be Able to Travel Beyond Existing Forces of Life (Green, Rule #1)*, 2014
Eight Martin Professional EC-20 LED panels, ten Martin Professional EC-10 LED panels, Mac mini, speakers, and amplifiers, dimensions variable
Maja Hoffmann/LUMA Foundation
Installation view, Pilar Corrias, London, 2014

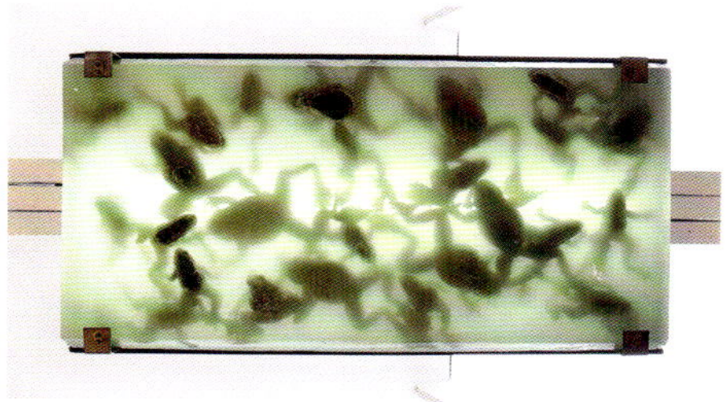

Pages 100–101
Dora Budor (b. 1984)
*Kata Doksa*, 2014
Resin, dye, frog props used in the film *Magnolia* (1999), parabolic lamp fixture, fluorescent lamp, and metal hardware, 26 x 50 x 8 in. (66 x 127 x 20.3 cm)
Collection of the artist; courtesy New Galerie, Paris

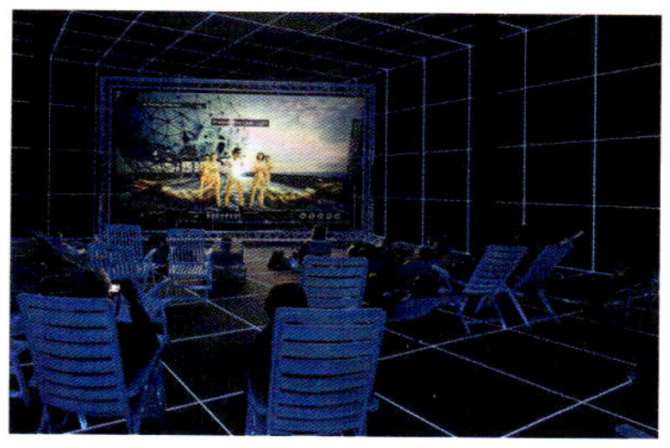

Pages 102–103
Hito Steyerl (b. 1966)
*Factory of the Sun*, 2015
Video, color, sound; 22:56 min., with environment, dimensions variable
Installation view, German Pavilion, 56th Venice Biennale, 2015

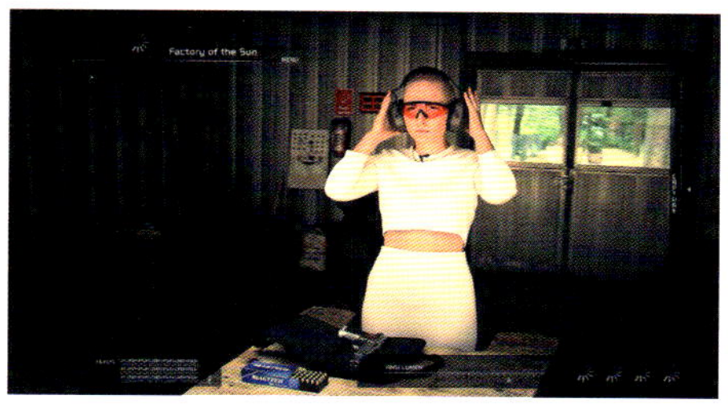

Pages 104, 105
Hito Steyerl (b. 1966)
Stills from *Factory of the Sun*, 2015

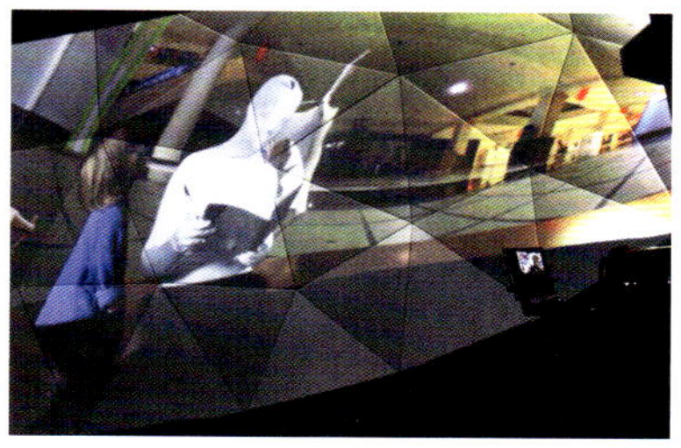

Pages 106–107
Ben Coonley (b. 1976)
*Trading Futures*, 2016
360-degree 3D video (color, sound; 11 min.) projected onto a spherical mirror in a geodesic cardboard dome, with Oculus Rift headsets, dimensions variable
Collection of the artist; courtesy Microscope Gallery, Brooklyn
Installation view, Microscope Gallery, Brooklyn, 2016

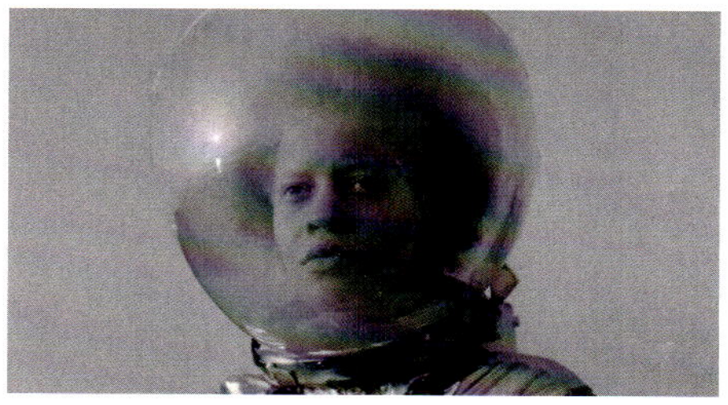

Pages 108, 109
Frances Bodomo (b. 1988)
Stills from *Afronauts*, 2014
Video, black-and-white, sound; 13 min.

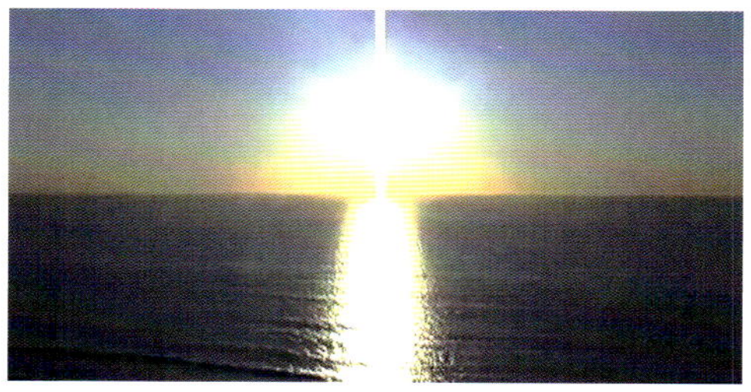

Pages 110–111
Artie Vierkant (b. 1986)
Still from *Exposure Adjustment on a Sunset*, 2009
Video, color, silent; 39 min.

## Checklist of the Exhibition

As of June 1, 2016

Works are organized alphabetically by artist. For all entries, height precedes width precedes depth. These works will be complemented by an extensive film and video screening program, whose details were not available at the time of printing.

**Trisha Baga (b. 1985)**

*Flatlands*, 2010
Video, color, sound; 18 min., looped; with disco ball and 3D glasses
Collection of the artist; courtesy Greene Naftali Gallery, New York

**Ivana Bašić (b. 1986)**

*SOMA*, 2013–
Digital 3D model
3D modeling and rendering: Mohammad Modarres
Software: Autodesk Maya, Arnold Renderer, The Foundry Mari, and Pixologic XBrush

**Frances Bodomo (b. 1988)**

*Afronauts*, 2014
Video, black-and-white, sound; 13 min.
Collection of the artist

**Dora Budor (b. 1984)**

Not yet titled, 2016
Mixed-media installation, 10 x 20 x 12 ft. (3 x 6.1 x 3.7 m)
Collection of the artist; courtesy New Galerie, Paris

**Ian Cheng (b. 1984)**

*Baby feat. Ikaria*, 2013
Video, color, sound; infinite duration, with live simulation and artificial intelligence services, dimensions variable
Whitney Museum of American Art, New York; gift of Candy and Michael Barasch 2015.197

**Bruce Conner (1933–2008)**

CROSSROADS, 1976
35mm film transferred to video, black-and-white, sound; 37 min.
Courtesy Conner Family Trust and Kohn Gallery, Los Angeles

**Ben Coonley (b. 1976)**

*Trading Futures*, 2016
360-degree 3D video, color, sound; 11 min.; with spherical mirror, cardboard geodesic dome, and Oculus Rift headsets
Collection of the artist; courtesy Microscope Gallery, Brooklyn

**Joseph Cornell (1903–1972)**

*Rose Hobart*, 1936
16mm film transferred to video, black-and-white, silent; 20 min., projected through a blue filter
Anthology Film Archives, New York

Blue glass used in early screenings of *Rose Hobart*, c. 1936
Glass, 1 ¾ x 1 ¾ x ½ in. (4.5 x 4.5 x 1.3 cm)
Anthology Film Archives, New York

**Andrea Crespo (b. 1993)**

*parabiosis: neurolibidinal induction complex 2.2*, 2015
Video, color, sound; 11:12 min.
Whitney Museum of American Art, New York; purchase with funds from the Film, Video, and New Media Committee 2016.3

**François Curlet (b. 1967)**

*Witness Screen*, 2002
Video, color, sound; 5:31 min.
Tate: Presented by the Tate Americas Foundation and the Institute of Contemporary Art, Miami, courtesy of Carlos and Rosa de la Cruz 2013

**Alex Da Corte (b. 1980) and Jayson Musson (b. 1977)**

*Easternsports*, 2014
Four-channel video, color, sound; 152 min., with four screens, neon, carpet, VCT tiles, metal folding chairs, artificial oranges, orange scent, and diffusers
Score by Devonté Hynes
Collection of the artists; courtesy David Risley Gallery, Copenhagen; Maccarone, New York and Los Angeles; and Salon 94, New York

**Disney Studio Artists**

Background for *Fantasia*, 1940
Opaque watercolor on paper, 12 x 50 in. (30.5 x 127 cm)
Walt Disney Animation Research Library, Glendale, California

Background for *Fantasia*, 1940
Opaque watercolor on paper, 12 x 30 ¼ in. (30.5 x 78.1 cm)
Walt Disney Animation Research Library, Glendale, California

Story sketch for *Fantasia*, 1940
Pastel on paper, 12 ½ x 15 ½ in. (31.8 x 39.4 cm)
Walt Disney Animation Research Library, Glendale, California

Story sketch for *Fantasia*, 1940
Opaque watercolor on paper: sheet, 12 ½ x 15 ½ in. (31.8 x 39.4 cm); image, 5 ½ x 6 ¾ in. (14 x 17.1 cm)
Walt Disney Animation Research Library, Glendale, California

Story sketch for *Fantasia*, 1940
Graphite and colored pencil on paper: sheet, 12 ½ x 15 ½ in. (31.8 x 39.4 cm); image, 11 ¼ x 13 ½ in. (28.6 x 34.3 cm)
Walt Disney Animation Research Library, Glendale, California

Story sketch for *Fantasia*, 1940
Opaque watercolor on paper: sheet, 10 x 12 in. (25.4 x 30.5 cm); image, 6 ¾ x 8 ¼ in. (17.1 x 21 cm)
Walt Disney Animation Research Library, Glendale, California

Story sketch for *Fantasia*, 1940
Opaque watercolor on paper: sheet, 9 x 12 in. (22.9 x 30.5 cm); image, 3 ½ x 4 ½ in. (8.9 x 11.4 cm)
Walt Disney Animation Research Library, Glendale, California

Story sketch for *Fantasia*, 1940
Watercolor on board and gum-based cel paint on cellulose acetate, 6 ¾ x 8 ¾ in. (17.1 x 22.2 cm)
Walt Disney Animation Research Library, Glendale, California

Story sketch for *Fantasia*, 1940
Watercolor on paper and gum based cel paint on cellulose acetate: sheet, 9 ½ x 11 ½ in. (24.1 x 29.2 cm); image, 8 x 10 in. (20.3 x 25.4 cm)
Walt Disney Animation Research Library, Glendale, California

Story sketch for *Fantasia*, 1940
Pastel on paper: sheet, 15 ½ x 12 ½ in. (39.4 x 31.8 cm); image, 6 ½ x 8 ¼ in. (16.5 x 21 cm)
Walt Disney Animation Research Library, Glendale, California

Story sketch for *Fantasia*, 1940
Charcoal on paper, 8 ¾ x 8 in. (22.2 x 31.8 cm)
Walt Disney Animation Research Library, Glendale, California

Story sketch for *Fantasia*, 1940
Colored pencil on paper: sheet, 15 ½ x 12 ½ in. (39.4 x 31.8 cm); image, 7 ½ x 9 ¾ in. (19.1 x 31.8 cm)
Walt Disney Animation Research Library, Glendale, California

Story sketch for *Fantasia*, 1940
Graphite and colored pencil on paper: sheet, 15 ½ x 12 ½ in. (39.4 x 31.8 cm); image, 7 x 8 ½ in. (17.8 x 21.6 cm)
Walt Disney Animation Research Library, Glendale, California

Story sketch for *Fantasia*, 1940
Pastel on paper, 6 ¾ x 8 ¼ in. (17.1 x 21 cm)
Walt Disney Animation Research Library, Glendale, California

**Oskar Fischinger (1900–1967)**

*Raumlichtkunst* [Space Light Art], 1926 / 2012
Three-screen projection: three 35mm films transferred to high-definition video, black-and-white and color, sound; approx. 10 min. each, looped
Center for Visual Music, Los Angeles
Restored and reconstructed in 2012 by the Center for Visual Music

Concept drawing for *Fantasia*, c. 1938
Pastel on paper, 2 ¾ x 4 ¼ in. (7 x 10.8 cm)
Center for Visual Music, Los Angeles; gift of The Fischinger Trust

Concept drawing for *Fantasia*, c. 1938
Colored pencil on storyboard animation paper, 8 ¾ x 8 ¼ in. (22.2 x 21 cm)
Center for Visual Music, Los Angeles; gift of The Fischinger Trust

Concept drawing for *Fantasia*, c. 1938
Tempera on paper, 5 ¼ x 7 in. (13.3 x 17.8 cm)
Center for Visual Music, Los Angeles; gift of The Fischinger Trust

Preliminary concept drawing for *Fantasia*, c. 1938
Pastel on paper, 5 ½ x 7 ½ in. (14 x 19.1 cm)
Center for Visual Music, Los Angeles; gift of The Fischinger Trust

Preliminary concept drawing for *Fantasia*, c. 1938
Pastel on paper, 5 ½ x 7 ½ in. (14 x 19.1 cm)
Center for Visual Music, Los Angeles; gift of The Fischinger Trust

Sketch for *Fantasia*, c. 1938
Pastel on paper, 8 ½ x 8 in. (21.6 x 20.3 cm)
Center for Visual Music, Los Angeles; gift of The Fischinger Trust

**Liam Gillick (b. 1964)**

*Annlee You Proposes*, 2001
Three-channel video, color, sound; 2:58 min., with furniture and lighting
Tate: Presented by the Tate Americas Foundation and the Institute of Contemporary Art, Miami, courtesy of Carlos and Rosa de la Cruz 2013

**Dominique Gonzalez-Foerster (b. 1965)**

*Ann Lee in Anzen Zone*, 2000
Video, color, sound; 3:25 min.
Tate: Presented by the Tate Americas Foundation and the Institute of Contemporary Art, Miami, courtesy of Carlos and Rosa de la Cruz 2013

**Pierre Huyghe (b. 1962)**

*Two Minutes Out of Time*, 2000
Video, color, sound; 4 min.
Tate: Presented by the Tate Americas Foundation and the Institute of Contemporary Art, Miami, courtesy of Carlos and Rosa de la Cruz 2013

*One Million Kingdoms*, 2001
Video, color, sound; 6 min.
Tate: Presented by the Tate Americas Foundation and the Institute of Contemporary Art, Miami, courtesy of Carlos and Rosa de la Cruz 2013

**Alex Israel (b. 1982)**

*Sky Backdrop*, 2016
Acrylic on canvas, 10 x 30 ft. (3 x 9.1 m)
Collection of the artist; courtesy Reena Spaulings Fine Art, New York

**Pierre Joseph (b. 1965) and Mehdi Belhaj Kacem (b. 1973)**

*Trickster Theory*, 2002
Video, color, sound; 34:59 min.
Tate: Presented by the Tate Americas Foundation and the Institute of Contemporary Art, Miami, courtesy of Carlos and Rosa de la Cruz 2013

**Aidan Koch (b. 1988)**

*Untitled* (page 3 from *Little Angels*), 2015
Graphite pencil and opaque watercolor on paper, 11 x 7 in. (17.8 x 25.4 cm)
Collection of the artist

*Untitled* (page 4 from *Little Angels*), 2015
Graphite pencil and opaque watercolor on paper, 11 x 7 in. (17.8 x 25.4 cm)
Collection of the artist

*Untitled* (page 5 from *Little Angels*), 2015
Graphite pencil and opaque watercolor on paper, 11 x 7 in. (17.8 x 25.4 cm)
Collection of the artist

*Untitled* (page 6 from *Little Angels*), 2015
Graphite pencil and opaque watercolor on paper, 11 x 7 in. (17.8 x 25.4 cm)
Collection of the artist

*Untitled* (page 7 from *Little Angels*), 2015
Graphite pencil and opaque watercolor on paper, 11 x 7 in. (17.8 x 25.4 cm)
Collection of the artist

*Untitled* (page 8 from *Little Angels*), 2015
Graphite pencil and opaque watercolor on paper, 11 x 7 in. (17.8 x 25.4 cm)
Collection of the artist

*Untitled* (page 9 from *Little Angels*), 2015
Graphite pencil and opaque watercolor on paper, 11 x 7 in. (17.8 x 25.4 cm)
Collection of the artist

*Untitled* (page 10 from *Little Angels*), 2015
Graphite pencil and opaque watercolor on paper, 11 x 7 in. (17.8 x 25.4 cm)
Collection of the artist

Not yet titled, 2016
Video, silent; duration to be determined
Collection of the artist

**Lynn Hershman Leeson (b. 1941)**

*X-Ray Woman*, 1963
Acrylic, graphite, and ink on canvas, 36 ⅝ x 19 ¼ in. (93 x 48.8 cm)
Collection of the artist; courtesy Bridget Donahue Gallery, New York

*Double Drawing*, 1966
Ink, colored pencil, transfer type, watercolor, collaged gelatin silver prints, and plastic on paper, 8 x 4 in. (20.3 x 10.2 cm)
Collection of the artist; courtesy Bridget Donahue Gallery, New York

*Untitled (Cyborg)*, 1970
Acrylic, ink, plastic, and metal on board, 18 x 12 in. (45.7 x 30.5 cm)
Private collection

*Water Woman 7*, 1978
Collaged photographs with mirrors on vellum, 13 ½ x 8 in. (34.3 x 20.3 cm)
Collection of the artist; courtesy Bridget Donahue Gallery, New York

*Room of One's Own*, 1990–93
Steel and acrylic, with closed-circuit camera; video, color, sound; LEDs; and miniature furniture, 15 x 16 x 35 in. (38.1 x 40.6 x 88.9 cm) overall
Collection of the artist; courtesy Bridget Donahue Gallery, New York

*Water Twins*, 1994
Inkjet print, 40 x 30 in. (101.6 x 76.2 cm)
Collection of the artist; courtesy Bridget Donahue Gallery, New York

*DiNA*, 2000–6
Custom software, voice recognition, voice synthesis, sensors, sound, and one-way mirror
Collection of the artist; courtesy Bridget Donahue Gallery, New York

*Blue Crown*, 2001
Chromogenic print, 60 x 26 in. (152.4 x 66 cm)
Collection of the artist; courtesy Bridget Donahue Gallery, New York

*Water Woman Evaporating x 3*, 2003
Vellum, mirror, ink, celluloid, and plastic, 13 ½ x 17 ½ in. (34.3 x 44.5 cm)
Collection of the artist; courtesy Bridget Donahue Gallery, New York

*Double Water Woman*, 2010
Inkjet print on plastic, 17 x 14 in. (43.2 x 35.6 cm)
Collection of the artist; courtesy Bridget Donahue Gallery, New York

**Anthony McCall (b. 1946)**

*Line Describing a Cone*, 1973
16mm film, black-and-white, silent; 30 min.
Whitney Museum of American Art, New York; purchase with funds from the Film and Video Committee 2001.248

**Josiah McElheny (b. 1966)**

*Projection Painting II*, 2015
Projection paint, anti-reflective glass, wood, ink, projector, hardware, and looped film footage transferred to video, black-and-white, silent, dimensions variable
Collection of the artist; courtesy Andrea Rosen Gallery, New York

**Syd Mead (b. 1933)**

Concept design paintings for *Blade Runner*, 1982
Opaque watercolor on illustration board, 10 x 15 in. (25.4 x 38.1 cm) each
Collection of the artist

**Lorna Mills (b. 1958)**

*Ways of Something*, 2014–15
Video, color, sound; 117:24 min.
Courtesy TRANSFER, Brooklyn

*Episode 1*
with one-minute contributions by Daniel Temkin; Rollin Leonard; Sara Ludy; Rhett Jones; Jaakko Pallasvuo; Dafna Ganani-Tomares; Jennifer Chan; Rea McNamara; Theodore Darst; Matthew Williamson; Hector Llanquin; Christina Entcheva; V5MT; Marisa Olson; Joe McKay; Carla Gannis; Nicholas O'Brien; Eva Papamargariti; Rosa Menkman; Kristin Lucas; Jeremy Bailey and Kristen D. Schaffer; Giselle Zatonyl; Paul Wong; Alfredo Salazar-Caro; Sally McKay; RM Vaughan, Keith Cole, and Jared Mitchell; Andrew Benson; Christian Petersen; Faith Holland; and Jennifer McMackon
Video, color, sound; 31:02 min.

*Episode 2*
with one-minute contributions by Kevin Heckart; Geraldine Juárez; Gaby Cepeda; Angela Washko; Emilie Gervais; LaTurbo Avedon; Lyla Rye; Mattie Hillock; Antonio Roberts; Georges Jacotey; Daniel Rourke; Sandra Rechico and Annie Onyi Cheung; Yoshi Sodeoka; Alma Alloro; LoVid; Andrea Crespo; Adriana Minolti; Arjun Ram Srivatsa; Carrie Gates; Isabella Streffen; Esteban Ottaso; ZIL & ZOY (Silke Kuhar and Zoy Winterstein); Hyo Myoung Kim; Jesse Darling; Tristan Stevens; Erica Lapadat-Janzen; Claudia Hart; and Anthony Antonellis
Video, color, sound; 29 min.

*Episode 3*
with one-minute contributions by Carine Santi-Weil; Nicolas Sassoon; Tom Sherman; Kim Asendorf and Ole Fach; Rafaela Kino; Alex McLeod; Kate Wilson and Lynne Slater; Aleksandra Domanović; Systaime (Michaël Borras); Erik Zepka; Adam Ferriss; Rodell Warner and Arnaldo James; Debora Delmar; Brenna Murphy; Nick Briz; Carlos Sáez; Jenn E Norton; Juliette Bonneviot; Luis Nava; Vince McKelvie; Claudia Maté; Evan Roth; Shana Moulton; Sabrina Ratté; Jordan Tannahill; Vasily Zaitsev feat. MON3Y.us; and Ann Hirsch
Video, color, sound; 27:56 min.

*Episode 4*
with one-minute contributions by Mert Keskin a.k.a. Haydiroket; Bill Miller; Alix Desaubiaux; Krystal South; Rachel Archibald; Will Pappenheimer; Dave Greber; Chiara Passa; John Boyle-Singfield; Gunilla Josephson; Melanie Clemmons; Curt Cloninger; Terrell Davis; Morehshin Allahyari; Amy Lockhart; John Marriott; Lilly Handley; Emily Vey Duke; Kate Armstrong; Myfanwy Ashmore; Luke Painter; Aram Bartholl; Elena Garnelo; Lorna Mills; Ellectra Radikal; Nicole Killian; Jacob Ciocci; and Rick Silva
Video, color, sound; 29:26 min.

**Melik Ohanian (b. 1969)**

*Ann Lee, I'm dreaming about a reality*, 2002
Video, color, sound; 4:07 min.
Music by Varou Jan
Tate: Presented by the Tate Americas Foundation and the Institute of Contemporary Art, Miami, courtesy of Carlos and Rosa de la Cruz 2013

**Philippe Parreno (b. 1964)**

*Anywhere Out of the World*, 2000
Video, color, sound; 4 min., with carpet
Tate: Presented by the Tate Americas Foundation and the Institute of Contemporary Art, Miami, courtesy of Carlos and Rosa de la Cruz 2013

*With a Rhythmic Instinction to be Able to Travel Beyond Existing Forces of Life*, 2014
LED screen with automated computer system, sound; 98 ¼ x 59 x 19 ¾ in. (250 x 150 x 50 cm)
Gladstone Gallery, New York and Brussels

**Jenny Perlin (b. 1970)**

*Twilight Arc*, 2016
Desmet-tinted black-and-white 16mm film printed on color 16mm film, silent; 12:10 min.
Collection of the artist; Simon Preston Gallery, New York, and Galerie M+R Fricke, Berlin

*Canopy*, 2016
Sound installation, 12 hrs.
Collection of the artist; Simon Preston Gallery, New York, and Galerie M+R Fricke, Berlin

**Mathias Poledna (b. 1965)**

*Imitation of Life*, 2013
35mm film, color, sound; 3 min.
Courtesy the artist; Galerie Buchholz, Cologne/Berlin/New York; Galerie Meyer Kainer, Vienna; and Richard Telles Fine Art, Los Angeles

**Edwin S. Porter (1870–1941)**
**Edison Manufacturing Company**

*Coney Island at Night*, 1905
35mm film transferred to video, black-and-white, silent; approx. 2 min.

**Oskar Schlemmer (1888–1943)**

Archival footage of Oskar Schlemmer, Lis Beyer, and Joost Schmidt dancing in costumes from *Das Triadische Ballett* [Triadic Ballet], 1926
35mm film transferred to video, black-and-white, silent; 1 min.
Original film housed in the Film Department, Bundesarchiv, Berlin, Inventory Number M 1484/K 40179
Courtesy Noam M. Elcott

*Das Triadische Ballett* [Triadic Ballet], 1970
35mm film transferred to video, color, sound; 29 min.
Courtesy Global Screen, Munich
Produced by Bavaria Atelier for the Südfunk, Stuttgart, in collaboration with Inter Nationes and RTB (Belgian Television)
Director: Helmut Amann
Choreography and costume designs: Oskar Schlemmer, 1922
Artistic advisors: Ludwig Grote, Xanti Schwinsky, and Tut Schlemmer

**Hito Steyerl (b. 1966)**

*Factory of the Sun*, 2015
Video, color, sound; 21 min., looped; with environment, dimensions variable
Collection of the artist; courtesy Andrew Kreps Gallery, New York

**Rirkrit Tiravanija (b. 1961)**

*(Ghost Reader C.H.)*, 2002
Video, color, sound; 510 min.
Tate: Presented by the Tate Americas Foundation and the Institute of Contemporary Art, Miami, courtesy of Carlos and Rosa de la Cruz 2013

**Stan VanDerBeek (1927–1984)**

*Movie Mural*, 1968
Multiple 35 and 16mm films transferred to video, black-and-white and color, sound and silent; durations vary; with black-and-white and color slide projections
Estate of Stan VanDerBeek

**Artie Vierkant (b. 1986)**

*Exposure Adjustment on a Sunset*, 2009
Video, color, silent; 39 min.
Collection of the artist

**Jud Yalkut (1938–2013)**

*Destruct Film*, 1967
16mm film, color, silent; 3:10 min., looped; with 16mm film projector, two slide projectors, eight 35mm color slides, two motorized beam-splitter mirrors, and loose film prints
Whitney Museum of American Art, New York; purchase with funds from the Film and Video Committee 2002.92

## Acknowledgments

First and foremost, my profound thanks go to all the artists in *Dreamlands*. This exhibition is a testament to their extraordinary work and its enduring power. Many people have worked over the course of several years to realize this ambitious project. I am deeply grateful to Adam D. Weinberg, the Whitney's Alice Pratt Brown Director, for understanding the importance of presenting this exhibition at a key moment in the history of both the Museum and the moving image, and for his unwavering enthusiasm for the project. His steadfast support of such an ambitious undertaking both underlines the Whitney's ongoing commitment to artists and demonstrates the Museum's strong belief that film, video, and new media should be thoroughly integrated into its programming at all levels. Scott Rothkopf, deputy director for programs and Nancy and Steve Crown Family Chief Curator, provided continuous encouragement and a guiding hand throughout the process of realizing this challenging exhibition. His keen eye and astute judgment have been key to its success. Donna De Salvo, deputy director for international initiatives and senior curator, supported this project from its earliest days and her insight over the course of its development was invaluable. The curatorial department's program team—De Salvo and Rothkopf along with Jay Sanders and Elisabeth Sussman—provided important feedback. I would also like to acknowledge my fellow Whitney curators: Carter Foster, Jennie Goldstein, Barbara Haskell, Claire Henry, David Kiehl, Christopher Lew, Dana Miller, Jane Panetta, Christiane Paul, Laura Phipps, Elisabeth Sherman, and Carrie Springer.

An exhibition of such complexity requires top-notch coordination. I am indebted to my curatorial assistant Mary Potter for her tireless work on the project. Her eye for detail, precision, intelligence, and wry good humor are the backbone of this exhibition and its accompanying catalogue, and I am extremely thankful for her meticulous work. I could not have wished for a better second-in-command. I would also like to commend Lauren DiLoreto for her extraordinary work as exhibitions manager. She provided wise and calm counsel throughout the organization of the exhibition. Emily Russell, director of curatorial affairs, provided staunch guidance and unflagging support that ensured the exhibition in all its nuanced complexity was realized. Special thanks are due as well to my intern John Crowther, for his important research for the exhibition. Additional research was conducted by interns Carmen Corbera, Caroline Partamian, Emily Sussman, and Catherine Wang.

It was critical to me that a scholarly book accompany the exhibition, and I am most appreciative of Beth Turk, who has worked assiduously to produce a book of the highest-quality design and scholarship, navigating the complexities of this ambitious publication with great skill. Joseph Logan and Rachel Hudson of Joseph Logan Design realized my vision for a book that would be the material counterpart to this immersive exhibition so beautifully. I owe tremendous thanks to the authors of the essays: Karen Archey, Giuliana Bruno, John Canemaker, Brian Droitcour, Noam Elcott, Tom Gunning, J. Hoberman, Esther Leslie, and David Lewis. Their scholarship collectively articulates the seismic shift that has occurred in optical vision and immersive viewing. David Updike provided skillful copyediting of the entire manuscript and Diana Kamin managed the complex image-rights clearances with aplomb. Thanks also to Beth Huseman, director of publications; Nerissa Dominguez Vales and Sue Medlicott of the Production Department; Anita Duquette, manager of rights and reproductions; and Patricia Fidler, publisher of art and architecture at Yale University Press, our distributor.

All exhibitions at the Whitney depend upon the hard work and commitment of its talented staff, and this exhibition challenged the Museum in every way. I gratefully acknowledge Mark Steigelman, exhibition design and construction manager, working with Anna Martin, exhibition design and construction associate designer, for his elegant design and endless patience through the many iterations of the floorplan. Tremendous thanks are also due to Reid Farrington, our audio visual manager, who expertly coordinated the technical needs of this complex exhibition, and to his predecessor in the position, Jeffrey Bergstrom; senior technician Richard Bloes, whose long experience with film and video at the Whitney was key to the successful presentation of a moving-image exhibition of this scale; Jehad Abu-Hamda, whose far-reaching technical skill ensured the impeccable installation of the works; and senior technician Peter Berson. I also wish to recognize Christy Putnam, associate director for exhibitions and collections management; Emilie Sullivan, the exhibition's registrar; Zoe Tippl, exhibitions assistant; Barbi Spieler, head registrar, permanent collection; and Maura Heffner, assistant director, exhibitions management. Special thanks must go as well to curatorial project assistant Clemence White, for her support during installation, and the art-handling team, especially Joshua Rosenblatt, Graham Miles, and Matthew Moon.

Our advancement team—and in particular Stephanie Adams, Marilou Aquino, Karen Huang, Eunice Lee, Erin Malone, Gina Rogak, Michele Snyder, and Hillary Strong—under the leadership of deputy director Alexandra Wheeler has worked tirelessly to raise funds for the exhibition, and it deserves kudos. I. D. Aruede, chief financial officer; Adrian Hardwicke, director of visitor experience; Nicholas S. Holmes, general counsel; Jen Leventhal, chief of staff; Amy Roth, chief planning officer; John Stanley, chief operating officer; and Farris Wahbeh, Benjamin and Irma Weiss Director of Research Resources, provided advice at various stages of the project. Kathryn Potts, associate director, Helena Rubinstein Chair of Education, along with Megan Heuer, director of public programs and public engagement, and Lily Foster, manager of public programs, organized vibrant education programs around the exhibition. I thank Danielle Linzer, director of access and community programs, and Anne Byrd, director of interpretation and research, as well. I also wish to acknowledge Carol Mancusi-Ungaro, Melva Bucksbaum Associate Director for Conservation and Research, and her team, particularly conservation coordinator Heather Cox and assistant conservator Clara Rojas-Sebesta; the marketing and communications team, especially chief marketing and communications officer Jeff Levine, director of communications Stephen Soba, and director of marketing Zoe Jackson; Jennifer Heslin, director of retail, and Lauri Freedman, retail product development manager; Hilary Greenbaum, director of graphic design; and our digital media team—Sofie Andersen, director of digital media; Alison Abreu-Garcia, senior manager, digital technology; and Elyse Mallouk, senior manager, digital content—for extending the show into the virtual realm.

This exhibition began in 2012 with a question—What is cinema?—that seemed especially urgent at a moment when the Internet, digital technology, virtual reality, 360-degree cameras, global tracking, and Oculus Rift were radically transforming the conditions of spectatorship and the very nature of what constitutes a moving image. As my research for the exhibition developed, it soon became evident that the issue was not the state of cinema, but rather the implications of this new optical and spatial reality. At the beginning of the project, as I looked at the prismatic terrain of the cinematic, I realized that, in order to understand what the exhibition was going to be, I had to confront each facet in turn and interrogate it. I am indebted to Noam Elcott, associate professor of art history at Columbia University, for the generosity of spirit with which he shared his scholarship. The core of this exhibition was shaped by our conversations. Early on in the research process, it felt important to bring together a group of colleagues in the field for a roundtable discussion. Its participants—Basel Abbas, Ruanne Abou-Rahme, Elle Burchill, Tacita Dean, Thomas Demand, Elcott, Bradley Eros, Ed Halter, Branden Joseph, Josiah McElheny, Jonas Mekas, Antonio Monda, Marina Sagona, Artie Vierkant, and Jonathan Walley—provided invaluable insights that have enriched the exhibition tremendously. I thank Glenn Phillips and Derek Quezeda at the Getty Research Institute, Los Angeles; and Mary Walsh, managing director, Kristen McCormick, art exhibitions and conservation manager, and Fox Carney, manager of research, at the Walt Disney Animation Research Library, Glendale, California, for so generously sharing their expertise and time. I also wish to acknowledge David Schwartz, chief curator, for his advice, as well as Jannette Pinson, collections manager, and Barbara Miller, curator of the collection and exhibitions, at the Museum of the Moving Image here in New York for enabling me to examine the blueprints for the set designs for *Blade Runner*. Douglas Trumbull, film director, special-effects supervisor, and inventor, provided important insights into the history of cinema and special effects; Cindy Keefer, director of the Center for Visual Music, Los Angeles, shared her scholarship on Oskar Fischinger; and Barbara Fischinger so generously allowed me to view Fischinger's paintings and works on paper. I am also thankful for my many discussions with artists, including an ongoing dialogue with Dora Budor, whose thoughts on cinema, science fiction, and the cyborgian body deepened my research in important ways.

For their generous assistance in the preparation of the exhibition and the catalogue, I am also grateful to: Cara Yarmolowicz and John Riggi, Alex Da Corte Studio; Andrea Rosen and Andrea Cashman, Andrea Rosen Gallery, New York; Andrew Kreps, Alex Fitzgerald, and Alice Conconi, Andrew Kreps Gallery, New York; John Mhiripiri and John Klacsmann, Anthology Film Archives, New York; Nicole Wittenberg, Anthony McCall Studio; James Rondeau and Nora Riccio, Art Institute of Chicago; Reinhard Bek and Christine Frohnert; Marilyn Brakhage; Bridget Donahue, Bridget Donahue Gallery, New York; Tom Eccles and Marcia Acita, Center for Curatorial Studies, Bard College, Annandale-on-Hudson, New York; Liv Barrett, Château Shatto, Los Angeles; Philip Martin, Cherry and Martin, Los Angeles; La Cinémathèque Française, Paris; Balázs Nyeri and János Pilenyi, Cineric Inc.; Michelle Silva, Conner Family Trust; David Risley, David Risley Gallery, Copenhagen; MM Serra and Joel Schlemowitz, Film-makers' Cooperative, New York; Gavin Brown, Lucy Chadwick, and Thor Shannon, Gavin Brown's enterprise, New York; Barbara Gladstone and Allyson Spellacy, Gladstone Gallery, New York and Brussels; Ellen Alderman, Graham Foundation; Carol Greene and Vera Alemani, Greene Naftali Gallery, New York; Alex Ross, Hester, New York; Dev Hynes; Michael Kohn, Kohn Gallery, Los Angeles; Ian Alteveer, associate curator, Department of Modern and Contemporary Art, Metropolitan Museum of Art, New York; Annette Michelson; Elle Burchill and Andrea Monti, Microscope Gallery, Brooklyn; Anne Morra and Kitty Cleary, Film Department, Museum of Modern Art, New York; Marion Dana and Corentin Hamel, New Galerie, Paris; Emmanuelle and Jérôme de Noirmont, Noirmontartproduction, Paris; Pilar Corrias, Pilar Corrias Gallery, London; Jeanne Greenberg, Salon 94, New York; Sean Kelly and Lauren Kelly, Sean Kelly Gallery, New York; Jasper Sharp; Simon Preston, Simon Preston Gallery, New York; Sara VanDerBeek and Chelsea Spengemann, Stan VanDerBeek Estate; Syd Mead, visual futurist, and Roger Servick, manager of business affairs, Syd Mead Inc.; Sherry Dobbin, Times Square Alliance and Times Square Arts; and Kelani Nichole, Transfer Gallery, Brooklyn.

I would like to express my special gratitude to Anne and Joel Ehrenkranz, whose generosity is exemplified by their endowment of my position, and to the Whitney's Film, Video and New Media Committee. Their support of the Whitney's collection—and of my vision for the show—is a great honor, and has enabled it to become a reality.

Finally, I would like to thank José Castillo-Pazos for his unwavering support throughout the making of this exhibition; it would not have been what it is without him, and I am deeply grateful. I dedicate it to him.

—Chrissie Iles, Anne and Joel Ehrenkranz Curator

**Whitney Museum of American Art Board of Trustees**

**Chairman Emeritus**
Leonard A. Lauder

**Honorary Chairman**
Flora Miller Biddle

**Co-Chairmen**
Neil G. Bluhm
Laurie M. Tisch

**President**
Richard M. DeMartini

**Chairman of the Executive Committee**
Robert J. Hurst

**Vice Chairmen**
Susan K. Hess
Warren B. Kanders
Scott Resnick
Thomas E. Tuft

**Vice Presidents**
Nancy Carrington Crown
Pamella G. DeVos
Beth Rudin DeWoody
Paul C. Schorr, IV
Anne-Cecilie Engell Speyer
Fern Kaye Tessler

**Secretary**
Nancy Poses

**Treasurer**
Miyoung Lee

**Alice Pratt Brown Director**
Adam D. Weinberg, *ex officio*

**Trustees**
J. Darius Bikoff
David Carey
Joanne Leonhardt Cassullo
Henry Cornell
Frederic Cumenal
Fiona Irving Donovan
Fairfax N. Dorn
Lise Evans
Victor F. Ganzi
Henry Louis Gates, Jr.
Philip H. Geier, Jr.
Robert Gersh, *ex officio*
Robert B. Goergen
Sondra Gilman Gonzalez-Falla
James A. Gordon
Anne Dias Griffin
Kenneth C. Griffin
Gaurav K. Kapadia
George S. Kaufman
Raymond J. Learsy
Jonathan O. Lee
Paul S. Levy
Raymond J. McGuire
Brooke Garber Neidich
John C. Phelan
Donna Perret Rosen
Richard D. Segal
Jonathan S. Sobel
Fred Wilson
David W. Zalaznick

**Honorary Trustees**
Joel S. Ehrenkranz
Emily Fisher Landau
Thomas H. Lee
Gilbert C. Maurer
Peter Norton

*In Memoriam*
Melva Bucksbaum
B. H. Friedman
Brendan Gill
Susan Morse Hilles
Michael H. Irving
Roy R. Neuberger
Robert W. Wilson

**Founder**
Gertrude Vanderbilt Whitney

*As of March 25, 2016*

**Whitney Museum of American Art Staff**

Brook Abrams
Alison Abreu-Garcia
Jay Abu-Hamda
Stephanie Adams
Adrienne Alston
Martha Alvarez-LaRose
Casey Amspacher
Marilou Aquino
Morgan Arenson
Kristina Arike
David Armacost
I. D. Aruede
Ahmed Attia
Wendy Barbee-Lowell
Caroline Barnett
Matthew Barnett
Marvada Barthelemy
James Bartolacci
Courtney Bassett
Caroline Beasley
Bernadette Beauchamp
Teo Beauchamp
Harry Benjamin
Caitlin Bermingham
Danielle Bias
Stephanie Birmingham
Eliza Blackman
Ivy Blackman
Hillary Blass
Richard Bloes
Alexandra Bono
Algernon Brown
Hollister Brown
Christa Brunks
Douglas Burnham
Thomas Burns
Ron Burrell
Garfield Burton
Anne Byrd
Pablo Caines
Margaret Cannie
Jane Carey
Amanda Carrasco
Dennis Castillo-Perez
Maritza Castro
Christina Cataldo
Inde Cheong
Claire Cheyney-Henry
Virginia Chow
Ramon Cintron
Randy Clark
Ron Clark
Errol Coore
Brenna Cothran
Heather Cox
Kenneth Cronan
Monica Crozier
Mia Curran
Regine David
Amanda Davis
Monserrate DeLeon
Margo Delidow
Donna De Salvo
Lauren DiLoreto
Michelle Donnelly
John Donovan
Kelly Donovan
Marisa Donovan
Lisa Dowd
Anita Duquette
Kasim Earl
Erica Eaton
Bradley Eberts
Cesar Espinoza
Alvin Eubanks
Reid Farrington
Katherine Flores
Seth Fogelman
Carter Foster
Lily Foster
Caroline Fox
Shaniece Frank
Samuel Franks
Murlin Frederick
Lauri Freedman
Kyle Freeman
Annie French
Donald Garlington
Anthony Gennari
Ronnie George
Claudia Gerbracht
Sarah Giovanniello
Jennie Goldstein
Alex Goodship
Hilary Greenbaum
Peter Guss
Stewart Hacker
Rita Hall
Adrian Hardwicke
Julie Hare
Tara Hart
Greta Hartenstein
Barbara Haskell
Maura Heffner
Dina Helal
Peter Henderson
Jennifer Heslin
Megan Heuer
Ann Holcomb
Nicholas S. Holmes
Abigail Hoover
Jacob Horn
Ayyub Howard
Sarah Humphreville
Beth Huseman
Chrissie Iles
Gina Im
Carlos Jacobo
Zoe Jackson
Patricia James
Jesse Jenkins
Bailey Johnson
Dolores Joseph
Vinnie Kanhai
Tracy Keenan
Chris Ketchie
Farrah Khatibi
David Kiehl
Thomas Killie
Elizabeth Kobert
Kathleen Koehler
Irene Koo
Tom Kraft
Melinda Lang
Eunice Lee
Sang Soo Lee

Danielle Lencioni
Monica Leon
Rachel Lesser
Jen Leventhal
Jeffrey Levine
Christopher Lew
Danielle Linzer
Ruth Lizardi
Kelley Loftus
Robert Lomblad
Doug Madill
Trista Mallory
Elyse Mallouk
Claire Malloy
Erin Malone
Jessica Man
Carol Mancusi-Ungaro
Louis Manners
Joseph Marode
Anna Martin
Heather Maxson
Meredith McDevitt
Patricia McGeean
Caitlin McKee
Michael McQuilkin
Sandra Meadows
Nicole Melanson
Sarah Meller
Bridget Mendoza
Conor Messinger
Graham Miles
Dana Miller
David Miller
Lana Mione
Christie Mitchell
Matthew Moon
Lorryn Moore
Sara Mora
Michael Moriah
Victor Moscoso
Lara Moynagh
Maggie Mugharbel
Sung Mun
Angela Munoz
Eleonora Nagy
Anthony Naimoli
Daniel Nascimento
Ruben Negron
Randy Nelson
Tracey Newsome
Katy Newton
Carlos Noboa
Pauline Noyes
Jaison O'Blenis
Brianna O'Brien Lowndes
Kimie O'Neill
Rose O'Neill-Suspitsyna
Suzanna Okie
Nelson Ortiz
Ahmed Osman
Nicky Ozir
Luis Padilla
Jane Panetta
Christiane Paul
Mary Paul
Jessica Pepe
Natasha Pereira
Jason Phillips
Laura Phipps
Angelo Pikoulas
Elizabeth Plahn
Mary Potter
Kathryn Potts
Eric Preiss
Rachel Pridgen
Linda Priest
Eliza Proctor
Stephen Ptacek
Eric Pullet
Vincent Punch
Christy Putnam
Shama Rahman
Julie Rega
James Reyes
Gregory Reynolds
Emanuel Riley
Felix Rivera
Richard Robinson
Manuel Rodriguez
Gina Rogak
Clara Rojas-Sebesta
Mariah Rollins
Justin Romeo
Joshua Rosenblatt
Jamie Rosenfeld
Amy Roth
Scott Rothkopf
Sara Rubenson
Emily Russell
Isaiah Russell
Angelina Salerno
Leo Sanchez
Jay Sanders
Galina Sapozhnikova
Lynn Schatz
Meryl Schwartz
Peter Scott
Michelle Sealey
David Selimoski
Jason Senquiz
Leslie Sheridan
Elisabeth Sherman
Dyeemah Simmons
Justin Singleton
Matt Skopek
Kristin Smallwood
Adrienne Smith
Joel Snyder
Michele Snyder
Stephen Soba
Laura Solomon
Barbi Spieler
Carrie Springer
John Stanley
Mark Steigelman
Minerva Stella
Jennifer MacNair Stitt
Betty Stolpen
Hillary Strong
Paul Suarez
Emily Sufrin
Emilie Sullivan
Denis Suspitsyn
Elisabeth Sussman
M'kina Tapscott
Ellen Tepfer
Ashley Thimm
Latasha Thomas
Zoe Tippl
Ana Torres
Stacey Traunfeld
Betsy Tsai
Beth Turk
Lauren Turner
Lucas Underwood
Matthew Vega
Ray Vega
Eric Vermilion
Emily Villano
Billie Rae Vinson
Farris Wahbeh
Rebecca Walsh
Jenyu Wang
Anteneque Webb
Adam D. Weinberg
Alexandra Wheeler
Andrew Wojtek
Sasha Wortzel
Sefkia Zekiroski
Kayla Zemsky
Lily Zhou
Nicolette Zorn

*As of April 21, 2016*

Index

Note: Page numbers in *italic* type indicate illustrations.

**Photograph and Reproduction Credits**

Unless otherwise indicated, all images are copyright © the artist and appear courtesy the artist, estate, and/or owner. The following applies to images for which additional acknowledgment is due.

**Boldface** indicates page numbers.

**2–3** Images courtesy The New American Cinema Group Inc./The Film-Makers' Cooperative and The Circulating Film & Video Library, The Museum of Modern Art, New York. **7** © Roberto Marossi; image courtesy Fondazione Jacqueline Vodoz e Bruno Danese. **8, 9** Images courtesy George Eastman Museum, Rochester, NY. **10, 11** Images courtesy British Film Institute. **13** © Walter Schulze-Mittendorff. **14, 15** Photographs © Staatsgalerie Stuttgart. **16, 17** ©1970 Bavaria Atelier for SWR in collaboration with Inter Nationes and RTB. **18–19** Image © 2016 Austrian Frederick and Lillian Kiesler Private Foundation, Vienna; reproduced with permission of the Ruth Bernhard Archive, Princeton University. © Trustees of Princeton University. **20, 21** © Fischinger Trust; images courtesy the Whitney Museum of American Art, New York, and Center for Visual Music, Los Angeles. **22** © Anthology Film Archives. Image courtesy Anthology Film Archives, New York. **23** © 1995 The Museum of Modern Art, New York; courtesy the Museum of Modern Art. Photograph courtesy Château Shatto, Los Angeles. **24, 25** © Disney; images courtesy Center for Visual Music, Los Angeles. **26–35** © Disney. **36** © Stiftung Deutsche Kinemathek; Collection Erich Kettelhut. **36** (bottom): © Disney. **37** © Oblagon Inc. **40, 41** © Conner Family Trust. **42–43** Photograph by David Allison. **44–45** Photograph by Bob Hanson. **48–49** Licensed by: Warner Bros. Entertainment Inc. All rights reserved; image courtesy the SK Film Archives LLC, Warner Bros., and University of the Arts London. **50** Digital images © Whitney Museum of American Art, New York. **51** Photograph by Francene Keery. Courtesy Whitney Museum of American Art, Frances Mulhall Achilles Library, John Hanhardt Film and Video Image Files, VanDerBeek, Stan. **52 (bottom), 53** Photograph by Freddy Le Saux. **54–55** Photograph by Michael Chikiris. Image courtesy Anthology Film Archives, New York. **56 (top)** Photograph by Atelier Le Parc. **57 (top)** Photograph by Marc Domage. Image courtesy gb agency, Paris. **57 (bottom)** Photograph by Eric Boutin. Image courtesy gb agency, Paris. **58, 59** Images courtesy the Estate of Paul Sharits and Anthology Film Archives, New York. **60, 61** Art © Mike Kelley Foundation for the Arts. All Rights Reserved/Licensed by VAGA, New York. Photographs by Fredrik Nilsen. **62, 63** © Oblagon Inc. **64** Images courtesy the artist and Gavin Brown's enterprise, New York/Rome. **65** Courtesy the artist and Pilar Corrias Gallery, London. **66** © Dominique Gonzalez-Foerster; courtesy 303 Gallery, New York. **67** Image courtesy the artist and Marian Goodman Gallery. **68 (top)** Image courtesy Air de Paris, Paris; **(center)** Image courtesy the artist; **(bottom)** © Dominique Gonzalez-Foerster; courtesy 303 Gallery, New York. **69 (top)** Image courtesy the artist and Marian Goodman Gallery; **(center)** Image courtesy Air de Paris, Paris; **(bottom)** © Melik Ohanian/ADAGP, Paris. Images courtesy the artist and Galerie Chantal Crousel, Paris. **70–73** Images courtesy the artist; Galerie Buchholz, Cologne/Berlin/New York; Galerie Meyer Kainer, Vienna; and Richard Telles Fine Art, Los Angeles. **76–77** © MAClyon; photograph by Blaise Adilon. **78, 79** © the artist and Greene Naftali Gallery, New York. **80, 81** Courtesy the artist; Simon Preston Gallery, New York; and Galerie M + R Fricke, Berlin **84, 85** © Josiah McElheny. Photographs by EPW Studio/Maris Hutchinson. Images courtesy Andrea Rosen Gallery, New York. **88–93** © Lynn Hershman Leeson. Photographs by Marc Brems Tatti. Images courtesy Bridget Donahue Gallery, New York. **96, 97** © Ian Cheng. **98–99** Courtesy Maja Hoffmann/LUMA Foundation. **100–101** © Dora Budor; courtesy the artist and New Galerie, Paris. **102–103** Photograph by Manuel Reinartz. Image courtesy the artist and Andrew Kreps Gallery, New York. **104, 105** Creative Commons 4.0 Hito Steyerl. Images courtesy the artist and Andrew Kreps Gallery, New York. **106–107** © 2016 Microscope Gallery. Image courtesy the artist and Microscope Gallery, New York. **117** Digital images © Whitney Museum of American Art, New York. **121** Photograph by Markus Gradwohl. **123** © Barbara Moore/Licensed by VAGA, New York, NY; courtesy Paula Cooper Gallery, New York. **124** © Lynn Hershman Leeson. Photograph by Marc Brems Tatti. Image courtesy Bridget Donahue Gallery, New York. **125 (top)** © Walter Schulze-Mittendorf and Horst von Harbou

– Deutsche Kinemathek; image courtesy Deutsche Kinemathek; **(bottom)** Image courtesy the artist; David Zwirner, New York; and Sadie Coles HQ, London. **128** Photograph by Marcus Leith and Andrew Dunkley. Image courtesy the artist; Frith Street Gallery, London; and Marian Goodman Gallery. **132** Photograph by Casey Kelbaugh. **134** © Horst von Harbou – Deutsche Kinemathek. Image courtesy Deutsche Kinemathek. **136** © 2014 Trumbull Ventures LLC. **141** Digital image © The Museum of Modern Art/Licensed by SCALA/Art Resource, NY. **143** SSPL/National Media Museum/Art Resource, NY. **145** © Institut Lumière. **146** Erich Lessing/Art Resource, NY. **147**: HIP/Art Resource, NY. **149** © Disney. **150 (top)** © 1940 Disney. **151–54** © Disney. **158 (top)** Photograph by Genevieve Hanson. Image courtesy the Estate of Fabio Mauri and Hauser & Wirth. **158 (bottom)** © Josiah McElheny. Image courtesy Andrea Rosen Gallery, New York. **159** Image courtesy Athenaeum of Philadelphia. **161 (bottom)** Photograph © Pamela Gentile. Image courtesy the photographer and San Francisco Silent Film Festival. **163 (top)** Photograph by Carolee Schneemann; **(bottom)** Photograph by Francene Keery; courtesy Whitney Museum of American Art, Frances Mulhall Achilles Library, John Hanhardt Film and Video Image Files, VanDerBeek, Stan. **164** Image courtesy Atelier Impopulaire. **165** Photograph by Evan La Londe. Image courtesy the artist and Marc Foxx, Los Angeles. **180 (top)** Image courtesy the Estate of Stan Brakhage and Fred Camper (www.fredcamper.com). **180 (bottom)** © 2015 The Andy Warhol Museum, Pittsburgh, PA, a museum of the Carnegie Institute. All rights reserved. **182 (top)** © Universal Pictures; image courtesy Universal/Photofest; **(bottom)** © 2008 Disney•Pixar. **183** © Sony Pictures Releasing; image courtesy Sony Pictures Releasing/Photofest. **188 (top)** © 1937 Disney; **(bottom)** © General Film Company; image courtesy General Film Company/Photofest. **189** © Lumivision; image courtesy Lumivision/Photofest. **190 (top)** © 1928 Disney; **(bottom)** © Will Gowland (www.willgowland.co.uk). **191** Image © the artist, courtesy Video Data Bank (www.vdb.org). **194** Photograph by and © Valie Export. **195 (top)** © Lynn Hershman Leeson. Photograph by Marc Brems Tatti. Image courtesy Bridget Donahue Gallery, New York; **(bottom)** Creative Commons 4.0 Hito Steyerl. Image courtesy the artist and Andrew Kreps Gallery, New York. **197** Photograph by Daniel Perez. Image courtesy the artist; New Galerie, Paris; and Swiss Institute, New York. **202** © Whitford Fine Art, London, UK/Bridgeman Images. **203** © MGM; image courtesy MGM/Photofest.

This catalogue was published on the occasion of the exhibition *Dreamlands: Immersive Cinema and Art, 1905–2016*, organized by Chrissie Iles, Anne and Joel Ehrenkranz Curator, Whitney Museum of American Art, New York.

Whitney Museum of American Art, New York
October 28, 2016–February 5, 2017

*Dreamlands: Immersive Cinema and Art, 1905–2016* is sponsored by Audi.

Major support is provided by the Dalio Foundation, The Robert Rosenkranz Foundation, and the National Committee of the Whitney Museum of American Art.

Significant support is provided by The Horace W. Goldsmith Foundation.

Generous support is provided by Alexandre and Lori Chemla, George and Mariana Kaufman, the Orentreich Family Foundation, and public funds from the New York City Department of Cultural Affairs in partnership with the City Council.

Additional support is provided by Susan and Matthew Blank, Colby Jordan, and Melissa Schiff Soros.

Copyright © 2016 by the Whitney Museum of American Art, New York

"The Screen as Object: Art and the Atmospheres of Projection" copyright © Giuliana Bruno

All rights reserved. This book may not be reproduced, in whole or in part, including illustrations, in any form (beyond that copying permitted by Sections 107 and 108 of the U.S. Copyright Law and except by reviewers for the public press), without written permission from the publishers.

Whitney Museum of American Art
99 Gansevoort Street
New York, NY 10014
whitney.org

Distributed by
Yale University Press
302 Temple Street
P.O. Box 209040
New Haven, CT 06520
yalebooks.com/art

Library of Congress Cataloging-in-Publication Data

Names: Iles, Chrissie, author. | Whitney Museum of American Art, host institution, issuing body.
Title: Dreamlands : immersive cinema and art, 1905–2016 / Chrissie Iles.
Description: New York : Whitney Museum of American Art, [2016] | Catalog of an exhibition held at the Whitney Museum of American Art, New York, October 28, 2016–February 5, 2017.
Identifiers: LCCN 2016019553 | ISBN 9780300221879 (hardcover)
Subjects: LCSH: Motion pictures—United States—Themes, motives—Exhibitions. | Art and motion pictures—United States—Exhibitions. | Motion picture industry—Technological innovations—Exhibitions. | Shared virtual environments—Exhibitions.
Classification: LCC PN1993.5.U6 I45 2016 | DDC 791.430973/0747471—dc23
LC record available at https://lccn.loc.gov/2016019553

This catalogue was produced by the publications department at the Whitney Museum of American Art, New York: Beth A. Huseman, director of publications; Jennifer MacNair Stitt, editor; Beth Turk, editor; Anita Duquette, manager, rights and reproductions; and Jacob Horn, editorial assistant.

Project manager: Beth Turk
Editor: David Updike
Designers: Joseph Logan and Rachel Hudson
Curatorial assistant: Mary Potter
Image coordinator: Diana Kamin
Production: The Production Department
Proofreader: Chesley Hicks
Indexer: David Luljak
Separations: Altaimage
Printing and binding: Artron Art (Group) Co., Ltd., Shenzhen, China

Typeset in Helvetica
Printed on 157gsm Stora Enso SPCO matte

Printed and bound in China
10 9 8 7 6 5 4 3 2 1

ISBN 978-0-300-22187-9